THE CONCEPTION OF GOD

IN THE PHILOSOPHY OF

AQUINAS

by

ROBERT LEET PATTERSON

Ph.D., M.A., B.D.

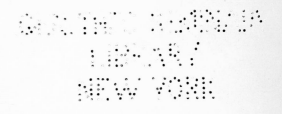

LONDON

GEORGE ALLEN & UNWIN LTD

MUSEUM STREET

FIRST PUBLISHED IN 1933

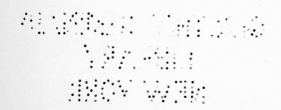

TO
MY MOTHER

PREFACE

THE substance of what is contained in this book was submitted as a thesis for the degree of Doctor of Philosophy in the University of London. In it I have endeavoured to give both a detailed and an accurate account of what St. Thomas Aquinas believed about God. The Latin quotations of the text of St. Thomas have been taken, when possible, from the Leonine edition. In the case of such works as are not yet available in that edition,[1] I have made use of the Vivès.[2] The Greek quotations are likewise drawn from the same source so far as possible. In the case of the Metaphysics I have been fortunate in being able to avail myself of Ross's edition. In translating passages from St. Thomas into English, I have found the Dominican Fathers' translations of the *Summa Theologica* and the *Summa contra Gentiles* very helpful, although I have by no means slavishly followed their rendering.

The pleasantest task which an author can perform in writing his preface is to acknowledge his obligations. In the first place, then, I desire to thank Professor G. Dawes Hicks of the University of London for his very helpful advice, his encouragement, and his kindness, graciously extended over a period of years. I wish also to record my obligations to Professor W. G. De Burgh of the University of Reading for certain fruitful suggestions, and for the kindness with which they were offered; and to my friend, Dr. S. V. Keeling of the University of London, both for practical advice and for invaluable assistance in putting this book into its final form, I owe more than I can well express.

[1] In quoting from the *De Ente et Essentia* I have availed myself of M. Roland-Gosselin's recent edition.
[2] For the sake of uniformity in spelling I have substituted the letter i for j in quotations drawn from the Vivès.

ABSTRACT

In this essay I have undertaken to examine the nature and extent of such knowledge of God as St. Thomas Aquinas believed it possible for the human reason to attain without the aid of revelation. In so doing I have generally followed the order in which his thought is presented to us in the *Summa contra Gentiles*, which, of all his works, most nearly resembles a purely philosophical treatise, at the same time endeavouring to co-ordinate it with parallel statements in the *Summa Theologica* and the *Compendium Theologiae*. I have also consulted such relevant passages as I have been able to find in his other works, especially the *Quaestiones Disputatae*, the *Opuscula*, and the commentaries on Aristotle's *Physics, Metaphysics, De Caelo et Mundo,* and *De Generatione et Corruptione*. I have made no attempt to criticize the Aristotelian foundations of his system, but have confined myself solely to Thomas himself.

The chief points of criticism which I have made are as follows. I have maintained that the first three proofs of the existence of God are not genuinely distinct, and that the first and second proofs presuppose and contribute nothing to the third, which depends upon the principle of sufficient reason. I have also argued that the fourth and fifth proofs are special applications of the same principle. I have discussed the contention of modern Neoscholastics that the Kantian critique has not destroyed St. Thomas's proofs, and I have admitted that it is sound. I do not believe, that is, that his method can be condemned *a priori*, but that it must be judged by its results. I have further pointed out that, if the term *God* be understood to connote, not *Ultimate Reality*, but the Deity of Theism and Religion, M. Sertillanges is right in his assertion that "the proof of God is the task of the entire theodicy"—in other words that the ground covered in the first three parts of this essay forms one long, complicated argument for the existence of God.

I have also argued that Aquinas's distinction between the knowledge *that* God is and *what* God is—*quia est* and *quod est*—is illegitimate. And I have contended that his doctrine of degrees of being, which I feel requires far more critical treat-

*

ment than he has given it, infects the entire universe of finite beings with some degree of unreality. The most crucial point of all will be found in the last three chapters of the third part, where I maintain that his attempt to harmonize the Aristotelian and the Christian conceptions of God breaks down owing to the impossibility of reconciling the multiplicity of objects known and willed by the Deity with the simplicity of the divine essence.

In connection with Aquinas's doctrine of creation I have urged that his distinction between "real relations" and "relations of reason" is indefensible; and I have also contended that his insistence that finite entities are not in time for God carries with it the corollary that time is—to some degree at least—illusory. This implication, and also the consequences of the doctrine of degrees of being, are, I believe, slurred over by the average Neoscholastic of to-day. In conclusion I have discussed Aquinas's view of the possibility and extent of mystical knowledge of God, and have called attention to the unmistakable inclination—strange in so devout a philosopher as St. Thomas—to discount the claims of mysticism to metaphysical importance.

CONTENTS

CONTENTS

PART FOUR

GOD AND THE WORLD

ABBREVIATIONS

THE following abbreviations will be frequently used throughout this book in referring to the works of St. Thomas:

Sum. Theol.	*Summa Theologica*
Con. Gen.	*Summa contra Gentiles*
Com. Theol.	*Compendium Theologiae*
De Pot.	*De Potentia*
De Verit.	*De Veritate*
Quodlib.	*Quodlibetum*
Nic. Eth.	*Nicomachean Ethics*
Dist.	*Distinctio*
q.	quaestio
a.	articulus
c.	corpus
sol.	solutio
ob.	obiectum

The word *corpus* is used in referring to the body of an article in the *Summa Theologica* or the *Contra Gentiles*. In the case of the *Commentary* on Peter Lombard's *Sentences* the term *solutio* is used in its stead. In references to the latter work the number of the book is given first, then follows the distinction and its number, next the question and its number, and lastly the article and its number. Thus 2 Dist. 3. q. i.: a. 5. signifies the fifth article of the first question of the third distinction of the second book. In referring to a reply to an objection in any of the various works the word *ad* is used. Thus, *ad* 2^m signifies the reply to the second objection.

PART ONE

THE EXISTENCE OF GOD

CHAPTER I

THE DEMONSTRABILITY OF THE DIVINE EXISTENCE

BEFORE proceeding to deal with Aquinas's evaluation of the various arguments for the existence of God, we must first notice briefly the position of those who deny that the divine existence is susceptible of demonstration and insist that it must be accepted by faith alone. Their position is obviously a self-refuting one, since faith, in the very act of accepting any revelation, of necessity presupposes the existence of the God who reveals himself therein, and consequently cannot draw its assurance thereof from that revelation itself. Nevertheless there were those who maintained it in Aquinas's day, as there are those who do so in ours; and therefore he felt the same need as does the modern metaphysician to establish a satisfactory refutation of this theory before entering upon what would otherwise be debatable territory. Many people, he remarks, are led to take up this attitude by the weakness of some of the arguments which are often used to prove the divine existence; an observation which the subsequent history of philosophy has amply justified.

The arguments advanced by his opponents are five:—

1. They urge that since in God essence and existence are one (a proposition the truth of which Aquinas would not only admit but himself later undertakes to prove), and since the human intellect cannot attain to the knowledge of the divine essence (a fundamental principle of Thomas's Aristotelianism), it follows that it is not able to attain to the knowledge of the divine existence. This argument is practically the antithesis of the ontological argument of Anselm which we shall later consider. The latter, beginning with the assumption that we possess a certain amount of knowledge of the essence of God, labours to show that in this knowledge the concrete and objective existence of that essence is involved; the former, beginning with the Aristotelian view of the transcendent nature of the essence so far as the human understanding is con-

cerned, argues from that to the indemonstrability of its existence.[1]

2. In the second place it is asserted that the existence of God is an article of faith and for that reason indemonstrable, for while demonstration yields scientific knowledge faith attaches itself to the invisible.[2]

3. The third argument points out that the process of demonstration, as expounded by Aristotle, requires us to take for our middle term the essence or signification of the thing the existence of which is to be proved, and that in the present instance this requirement cannot be fulfilled, since we lack knowledge of the essence of God.[3]

4. The fourth argument advances the objection that since, according to Aristotle,[4] it is only through the senses that we are able to become aware of the principles of demonstration, we cannot use these principles to prove the existence of super-sensible realities. There is a decidedly Kantian ring about this argument with its emphasis upon the unlawfulness of attempting to extend the application of the logical forms of human thought beyond the boundaries of the phenomenal universe. Yet there is this difference between the earlier and the later ways of thinking, that the disputants to whom Thomas referred did not conceive the human understanding as itself contributing a subjective element to the content of knowledge. On the contrary, they regarded it as incapable of rising to the cognition of purely spiritual realities merely because it was embodied, and because its capacities, as they believed, were formed and limited by, and valid only in relation to, the world of sense-experience.[5]

5. The fifth argument closely resembled the fourth. Basing itself upon the Aristotelian principles that what is super-sensible cannot be known *a priori*, and that the divine existence, if demonstrable at all, must be proved from its effects, it raises the objection that no cause can be demonstrated by an effect not proportional to it, and urges that no proportion can exist between cause and effect when the effect is finite and the cause is the infinite.[6]

---

[1] *Con. Gen.* lib. I. cap. 12. [2] *Sum. Theol.* I.a. q. 2: a. 2. ob. 1.
[3] *Sum. Theol.* I.a. q. 2: a. 2. ob. 2; *Con. Gen.* lib. I. cap. 12.
[4] *Posterior Analytics*, lib. I. cap. xviii.
[5] *Con. Gen.* lib. I, cap. 12. [6] *Sum. Theol.* I.a. q. 2: a. 2. ob. 3.

Thomas replies to the first of these arguments in much the same strain as he afterwards replies to the ontological argument. Essence and existence are, he agrees, identical in God; but he adds the qualification that it is impossible for the human mind to comprehend this identity since the divine essence, being super-sensible, cannot be known as it is in itself. Our minds, however, can comprehend the meaning of the statement, God exists; and it is possible to demonstrate the fact of his existence *a posteriori*.

To the second argument Thomas returns the answer that the existence of God is not an article of faith but one of the preambles to the articles, and that faith presupposes natural knowledge as grace presupposes nature, and perfection something which may be perfected. He observes, however, that a truth capable of demonstration may yet be accepted on faith by a man who himself lacks the ability to follow and comprehend the process of proof.

To the third argument Thomas replies that the correct procedure in proving the existence of a cause is to introduce the effect into the middle term of the syllogism in lieu of the definition of the essence of the cause, and that this holds good more especially in the present case since all our names and ideas of God are derived from the divine effects.

To the fourth argument Thomas returns the brief reply that while God is not an object perceptible by the senses yet those of his effects which furnish us with the proofs of his existence are sensible objects, and that thus our knowledge even of super-sensible existence has its origin in sense.

In answer to the fifth argument Aquinas admits that perfect knowledge of a cause cannot be obtained from effects which are not proportionate to it; but he points out that, since every effect must have a cause, the existence of an effect is sufficient to demonstrate the existence of its cause. Therefore, he urges, the existence of God can be demonstrated from his effects, although since these effects are not proportional to him they cannot yield us knowledge of what he is essentially and in himself.

Brief as it is, the preceding discussion is of interest to us, for it shows that Aquinas consciously faced the same difficulties as those which confront the thinker of to-day, and that he was

compelled to deal with opponents whose position was practically identical with the Phenomenalism of modern philosophy. The question at issue between them as to whether the
logical laws which govern the process of demonstration, and
the law of cause and effect upon which Aquinas based all his
arguments for the existence of God, are principles universally
valid in themselves and applicable throughout the entire
domain of existence, or are, on the contrary, merely observed
modes of behaviour on the part of the physical world and
possessed of no inner necessity which renders their inapplica-
bility unthinkable in other spheres, is one which has been
continually recurring in the history of philosophy. It is noteworthy that there is no difference of opinion between Thomas
and his adversaries as to the manner in which our knowledge
of these principles is acquired. They are agreed that such
knowledge arises empirically and out of contact with the
objects of sense. Aquinas has no more desire than have they to
posit innate ideas independent of experience and coeval with
the mind itself. But he is concerned to emphasize his view that
when we do become aware of these truths we recognize their
necessity and universality, and he is equally earnest in repudiating the notion that they are nothing more than generaliza-
tions descriptive of the way in which nature acts.

In simply stating clearly his own position and then dismissing the subject Thomas is in full accord with his master
Aristotle; for it is explicitly taught by the latter that universals,
though they are apprehended empirically by a process of
sense-perception and comparison of natural objects, are nevertheless, when once perceived, intuitively recognized as necessary and self-evident. Their truth is independent of and not
susceptible to argument.[1] Consequently, when the issue has
once been clearly stated, further discussion is vain. But for him
who perceives the universals in their self-evident completeness
the way is now open into the province of metaphysics.

[1] Cf. *Posterior Analytics*, lib. II, cap. xv. lect. 20; also W. D. Ross's *Aristotle*,
ch. vii. p. 217.

CHAPTER II

PROOFS OF THE EXISTENCE OF GOD REJECTED BY AQUINAS

AQUINAS's proofs of the existence of God are to be found in the opening pages of his two greatest works, the *Summa Theologica* and the *Summa contra Gentiles*. In each instance, however, he thinks it necessary to preface the discussion by a refutation of those who hold "that the existence of God cannot be demonstrated because it is *per se notum*." The importance which he attached to this step is evident from the fact that a section of his earlier work, the *Commentary on Peter Lombard's Sentences*,[1] is devoted to the same topic, while yet a fourth treatment of the question—the most extensive of all—is to be found in the *De Veritate*.[2] The arguments which are criticized and refuted in these various works are of very unequal importance. It will be convenient, however, to assemble them at this point, together with their respective refutations, although the majority of them will require neither elucidation nor comment.

1. Those things are *per se nota* which are known as soon as their terms are known. Thus, when we know what is meant by the words "whole" and "part," we know at once that the whole is greater than its part. So it is with the word "God." By it we mean "something than which nothing greater can be conceived" ("*aliquid quo maius cogitari non potest*"). As soon as the name God is heard and understood, God exists in the intellect at least. But God cannot exist in the intellect alone; for a being which existed in the intellect and in fact (*in re*) would be greater than a being which existed only in the intellect. God must, therefore, exist in fact.[3]

2. It is possible to conceive that something exists which cannot be conceived not to exist, and this is evidently greater than that which can be conceived not to exist. Consequently, something could be conceived greater than God, were it possible to conceive of him as not existing. But this is contrary

[1] 1 *Dist.* 3. q. 1: a. 2. [2] q. 10: a. 12.
[3] *Con. Gen.* lib. I. cap. 10; *Sum. Theol.* I.a. q. 2: a. 1. ob. 2.

to the meaning of the name *God*; hence it must be conceded that God's existence is *per se notum*.[1]

3. Those propositions are *per se nota* in which the same thing is predicated of itself as, *Homo est homo*; or in which the predicates are included in the definition of the subject as *Homo est animal*. But God's essence is the same as his existence, so that an identical answer must be given to the question what he is and to the question whether he is. Accordingly when it is said God is, the predicate is the same as the subject, or is included in the definition of the subject. Hence God's existence is *per se notum*.[2]

4. Those propositions which are known naturally are known *per se*, since we do not attain to the cognition of them by study. So God is naturally known, for man's desire tends naturally to God as to its last end.[3] Consequently, the existence of God is *per se notum*.[4]

5. That through which all other things are known must be known *per se*. But God is that through which all other things are known, for as the light of the sun is the principle of all visual perception so the divine light is the principle of all intelligible cognition. Hence the existence of God must be *per se notum*.[5]

6. The being of truth is known *per se*; for, if truth have not being, then it is true that truth has not being. But if any proposition be true, truth must have being. And God is truth itself.[6] Hence the existence of God is *per se notum*.[7]

7. The primal truth surpasses all created truth. But any created truth is evident in so far as it cannot be conceived not to have being—such truth, for instance, as inheres in the proposition that affirmation and negation are never true simultaneously. Much less, then, is it possible to conceive that the uncreated truth has no being. But the uncreated truth is God.[8]

8. It is truer that God exists than that the human soul

[1] *Con. Gen.* lib. I. cap. 10; I *Dist.* 3. q. 1 : a. 2. ob. 4; *De Verit.* q. 10 : a. 12. ob. 2.
[2] *Con. Gen.* lib. I. cap. 10; I *Dist.* 3. q. 1 : a. 2. ob. 4; *De Verit.* q. 10 : a. 12. ob. 4.
[3] This proposition Aquinas labours to make good elsewhere—*Con. Gen.* lib. III. cap. 25.
[4] *Con. Gen.* lib. I. cap. 10; *De Verit.* q. 10 : a. 12. ob. 5.
[5] *Con. Gen.* lib. I. cap. 10; I *Dist.* 3. q. 1 : a. 2. ob. 2; *Comment. on Boethius's De Trinitate*, q. 1 : a. 3. ob. 1.   [6] John xiv. 6.
[7] *Sum. Theol.* I.a. q. 2 : a. 1. ob. 3 : *De Verit.* q. 10 : a. 12. ob. 3.
[8] *De Verit.* q. 10 : a. 12. ob. 6.

exists. But the soul cannot believe that it does not exist. Even less, therefore, is it able to think that God does not exist.[1]

9. Everything which is was true while it was yet future.[2] But truth is. Accordingly it also was true while yet future. Yet it could not have been true, had truth not had being. It is impossible, therefore, to think that truth did not always have being. And God is truth. Hence it is impossible to think that God does not have being, and has not always had being.[3]

10. Everything which is true *secundum quid* can be reduced to that which is true *simpliciter*, even as the imperfect can be reduced to the perfect. If, therefore, the being of future truth be *secundum quid*, something must nevertheless be true *simpliciter*, and so it will be true *simpliciter* to say that truth has being.[4]

11. The name proper to God is, He who is.[5] But it is not possible to think that being has no being.[6] Hence it is impossible to think that God has no being.[7]

12. Those things are said to be *per se nota* the knowledge of which is naturally implanted in us. Such is the case with regard to the proposition that the whole is greater than the part. And such also is the case with regard to the existence of God, according to St. John of Damascus.[8] Hence the existence of God is *per se notum*.[9]

13. Every act of cognition involves the union of the knower and the known. But God is himself within the soul, more so even than the soul is within itself. Hence God is able to be known in himself, *per seipsum*.[10]

What is most striking in the formulation of these arguments is the use of the phrase *per se notum*. It appears to be strictly equivalent to "self-evident." But if the proposition that God exists be self-evidently true, no arguments are needed in its support, nor would the multiplication of them be of any avail; for the very meaning of self-evidence is knowledge so ultimate and direct, so basic and fundamental, that analysis can go no

[1] *De Verit.* q. 10: a 12. ob. 7.
[2] "Omne quod est, prius fuit verum esse futurum."
[3] *De Verit.* q. 10: a. 12. ob. 8.   [4] *De Verit.* q. 10. a. 12. ob. 9.
[5] Exod. iii.   [6] "Sed non potest cogitari ens non esse."
[7] *De Verit.* q. 10: a. 12. ob. 10.   [8] *De Fide Orth.* lib. I. cap. i.
[9] I *Dist.* 3. q. 1: a. 2. ob. 1; *Sum. Theol.* I.a. q. 2: a. 1. ob. 1; *De Verit.* q. 10: a. 12. ob. 1; *Comment. on Boethius's De Trinitate*, q. 1: a. 3. ob. 6 and ad 6m.   [10] I *Dist.* 3. q. 1: a. 2. ob. 3.

further. It is that simple apprehension of truth which is one of the irreducible factors in human consciousness. Upon it, as upon an immovable foundation, all argument is built up. It sustains the logical structure which the understanding rears upon it, but itself receives no support in return, remaining, as it does, for ever self-sufficing. To attempt, therefore, to show by argument that the truth of the proposition that God exists is self-evident is suicidal. Such, however, is the course which Aquinas appears to conceive his opponents to be taking.

As a matter of fact, the first of the thirteen arguments quoted above is none other than Anselm's famous ontological argument, and the second is but another form of the same, derived from the third and fourth chapters of the *Proslogium*. Each involves a chain of reasoning. Anselm, indeed, does say that no one who understands the meaning of the word "God" can conceive of God as not existing any more than a man who understands what is meant by the word "fire" can conceive fire to be water. Yet he makes this remark only after he has proved to his own satisfaction that the idea of God involves that of necessary existence; and this conclusion is reached by a process of argumentation. Similarly, when we have followed step by step the demonstration of the proposition that the square of the hypotenuse of a right-angled triangle is equal to the sum of the squares of the other two sides, we are unable to conceive of a right-angled triangle concerning which this proposition would not hold good. Yet it is not a self-evident proposition since it rests upon a process of logical reasoning, which in turn rests upon a basis supplied by geometrical axioms. To these alone does self-evidence appertain.

It is tempting to suggest that by the phrase *per se notum* St. Thomas means to designate what modern neo-scholastic writers term the *a priori* as opposed to *a posteriori* method. Thus in the *Manual of Modern Scholastic Philosophy*, edited by Cardinal Mercier,[1] we read that "an *a priori* proof is one that proceeds from cause to effect, from reason to consequent" in contradistinction to the *a posteriori* proof which proceeds "from an effect to a cause or principle."[2] In the sense in which the term

[1] Tr. by T. L. Parker and S. A. Parker.
[2] Vol. II. p. 29. Cf. also Garrigou-Lagrange, *Dieu, son existence et sa nature*, pp. 69–70, and G. H. Joyce's *Principles of Natural Theology*, p. 199.

is generally used to-day, the proofs of God's existence which St. Thomas esteems valid are—with the possible exception of the teleological—thoroughly *a priori*, since, although founded upon some aspect of the universe known to us empirically—such as the fact of motion, the existence of contingent being, etc.—they proceed upon the assumption that the logical principles which they employ are self-evidently valid, and profess to yield absolute demonstration without any admixture of probability, and avoid any appeal to the principle of induction. None the less, it is true that the ontological argument does profess to deduce the notion of existence from the bare idea of God, without any reference whatsoever to data empirically known. Is it possible that it was this distinction which St. Thomas intended to specify?

Various considerations render this suggestion highly improbable. In the first place the twelfth and thirteenth arguments are unmistakably intended to refer to a knowledge of God which is in no sense dependent upon deductive logic, but is direct and immediate. In the second place, the opponents of St. Thomas maintain that "the existence of God cannot be demonstrated,"[1] a position obviously inconsistent with any sort of argumentation, whether *a priori* or *a posteriori*. In the third place, St. Thomas's definition of the phrase *per se notum*,[2] appears equally to exclude any attempt at proof. And in the fourth place, Aquinas's own words leave no doubt that the error with which he meant expressly to charge his adversaries was precisely that of attempting to prove a proposition which, if true, was self-evident. "No one," he observes, "can think the opposite of that which is *per se notum*." Hence their position is faulty upon two counts: (*a*) they have tried to prove a proposition which they claim to be self-evident, and (*b*) the proposition is not self-evident for, "it is possible to think the opposite of the proposition that God exists, according to the fifty-second Psalm, 'The fool hath said in his heart, there is no God.' Hence the existence of God is not self-evident."[3]

---

[1] "Deum esse demonstrari non potest" (*Con. Gen.* lib. I. cap. 10).

[2] "Those things are said to be *per se nota* which are known as soon as the terms are known." "Illa enim per se nota dicuntur quae statim notis terminis cognoscuntur."

[3] *Sum. Theol.* I.a. q. 2: a. 1. sed contra; 1 *Dist.* 3. q. 1: a. 2. contra et sol.

We are accustomed from childhood, Aquinas reminds us, to hearing and invoking the name of God, and habit causes us to hold no less firmly beliefs so acquired than those which are *naturaliter et per se nota*. Moreover, we must distinguish between propositions which are self-evident in themselves (*per se simpliciter*) and those which are self-evident to us (*quoad nos*). A proposition is *per se notum*, the predicate of which is included in the notion of the subject: it is known, therefore, by all who understand the meaning of its terms. Thus certain truths, such as the relation of part to whole, are plainly seen by all men; others, such as the truth that the incorporeal is not in space, are evident only to the wise; while yet others are beyond the grasp of human reason. Now, since in God essence and existence are one, the proposition that God exists must be self-evident in itself,[1] inasmuch as the predicate is the same as the subject; but it is not so to us, for it is impossible for man's intellect to conceive what God is. His existence must, therefore, "be demonstrated by means of those things which are more evident to us though less so in themselves (*naturaliter*), that is by its effects."[2]

The possibility must be reckoned with, however, that arguments which fail to accomplish the impossible task of proving that the existence of God is self-evident may none the less be valid proofs that God exists. Consequently, each proof must be individually examined and, if faulty, refuted. Accordingly, to each of the thirteen proofs given above St. Thomas framed a reply, and these replies we shall now review in order.

1. The first proof is, as we have seen, St. Anselm's own formulation. Aquinas's initial objection is that Anselm's definition of God is not what is always meant even by those who admit that God exists; for, he remarks, some of the ancients have held that this world is God,[3] and others have believed God to be a body. Moreover, none of the interpretations of the word given by St. John of Damascus answers to this definition.[4]

---

[1] "Quantum in se est, per se nota est." *Sum. Theol.* I.a. q. 2: a. 1. c.

[2] *Sum. Theol.* I.a. q. 2: a. 1. c; cf. *Con. Gen.* lib. I. cap. 11; 1 *Dist.* 3. q. 1: a. 2. sol; *De Verit.* q. 10: a. 12. c.

[3] "Cum multi antiquorum mundum istum dixerint Deum esse." *Con. Gen.* lib. I. cap. 11.

[4] *Con. Gen.* lib. I. cap. 10; *Sum. Theol.* Ia. q. 2: a. 1. ad 2m.

As an objection levelled against St. Anselm these arguments must be pronounced irrelevant, but they are none the less interesting. They are irrelevant because the ontological argument is not in the least concerned with what, in point of fact, men have believed about God. It is an attempt to establish the existence of God *a priori*, and with this purpose in view it advances its own definition of God which, it assumes, will be accepted by its opponent. So far it is an *argumentum ad hominem*. In truth, St. Anselm explicitly tells us that he adopted this particular definition rather than another because it lent itself more easily to such a process of demonstration.[1] It was useless for Aquinas to urge that it had never been universally accepted. Of this St. Anselm was quite aware; but it is wholly beside the point. The only germane question is, does St. Thomas himself refuse to accept it? If so, well and good; he may then consistently reject the entire argument without more ado. But is it not plain that he cannot refuse? The irresistible logic of the situation compels him to accept it; as St. Anselm shrewdly foresaw, a medieval Catholic, sharing his own presuppositions, could do naught else.

A thousand years before, when Christian theology was forming and while its dogmas were not yet crystallized, there was room within the fold of faith for difference of opinion and comparative freedom of thought. Then various and conflicting views of the nature of God obtained among believers. But behind thinkers of the thirteenth century there lay wellnigh a thousand years during which Christian monotheism had been cast in the mould of a Neoplatonic philosophy. The dominant influence of St. Augustine lay like a shadow over medieval Christendom. Theologians no longer seriously disputed as to whether the Deity had a body, or was in space. The word *God* had been given that stereotyped and conventional significance which it was to retain for five hundred years, down to and through the period of the Deistic controversy and practically until the beginning of the nineteenth century. Incorporeality, aseity, omniscience, immutability, eternity, were attributes included as a matter of course in the conception of divinity.

Moreover, the fact that St. Anselm's definition is not universally received is, as has been said, irrelevant. The onto-

---

[1] *Contra Insipientem*, cap. 5.

logical argument, if valid at all, was just as much so before St. Anselm discovered it as afterward. To the man who accepts the definition it offers of the word *God*, the fact that others reject it can have no weight. He is committed to following the argument to the end, and to judging it by the accuracy or faultiness of its own inherent logic.

As a matter of fact, the objection which we have been considering was raised by St. Thomas in a more or less incidental manner, and is clearly subordinate to the main issue. His main reason for refusing to accept the ontological argument is the same that has influenced all philosophers who have rejected it from Gaunilo to Kant—the abysmal nature of the gap that separates the world of existence from that of thought. In his view there is no aerial pathway by which this gap may be traversed. It is as impassable as that which sunders Dives from Lazarus. No idea contains in itself the guarantee of the existence of its object.

"Granting that the name *God* is understood by all men to mean something than which nothing greater can be thought, it is not necessary that there should be something than which nothing greater can be thought in the actual world. For we must take a thing and the meaning of a name in the same way. From the fact that the mind conceives what is proffered to it under the name *God* it does not follow that God exists, except in the intellect. Hence it is not necessary that something than which nothing greater can be thought exist, except in the intellect; and from this it does not follow that there is anything in the actual world than which nothing greater can be thought. And so no difficulty has appeared for those who hold that God does not exist. For it is not a difficulty that, something being given either in fact or in the intellect, something greater should be able to be conceived—except to him who concedes that there is in the actual world, something than which nothing greater can be conceived."[1]

[1] "Dato quod ab omnibus per hoc nomen *Deus* intellegatur aliquid quo maius cogitari non possit, non necesse erit aliquid esse quo maius cogitari non potest in rerum natura. Eodem enim modo necesse est poni rem, et nominis rationem. Ex hoc autem quod mente concipitur quod profertur hoc nomine *Deus*, non sequitur Deum esse nisi in intellectu. Unde nec oportebit id quo maius cogitari non potest esse nisi in intellectu. Et ex hoc non sequiter quod sit aliquid in rerum natura quo maius cogitari non

A significant admission is, indeed, made by Aquinas. Could we comprehend the essence of God, then we should perceive that it is identical with the divine existence, and the truth that God does exist would so become self-evident to us. But to comprehend the divine essence is beyond the power of our embodied minds; and no logical process can ever make up to us for the lack of that immediate and intuitive vision.

It is worth while to dwell upon this last point. The being of all created things is, according to Aquinas, contingent. It depends upon the unfettered will of God. The essence of any material thing or of any finite spirit—the sum, that is to say, of all the qualities which enter into its definition—does not involve its existence. The essence, for example, of a man involves the possession of a body; but it does not involve the existence of any particular or individual man, or indeed of any men at all. The essence of man is an abstract and universal idea forever comprehended by the mind of God; but the number of concrete instances in which it finds expression is not in any way logically dependent on or derivative from itself; that number is determined solely by the arbitrary fiat of the Deity.

When we turn to consider the essence of God, however, we find all this changed. There is no abstract Platonic Form of godhead to which God must, as it were, correspond. He is not the concrete instance of a universal; nor is there any mind in which that universal could subsist. He is not one of a species; he is the One alone, and there is none beside him. Hence his existence cannot be dependent on anything external: it is necessary, following from his own nature; it is he and he is it. To know God in the sense of conceiving him is, therefore, as Aquinas truly says, to know not only what he is but that he is, and to know that the whatness and the thatness are the same. It is to attain that complete union of thought with existence which human reason is driven to postulate as its goal. Such attainment constitutes salvation. It is the Beatific Vision which is the portion of the saints *in patria*. In such transparency of

possit. Et sic nihil inconveniens accidit ponentibus Deum non esse: non enim inconveniens est quolibet dato vel in re vel in intellectu aliquid maius cogitari posse, nisi ei qui concedit esse aliquid quo maius cogitari non possit in rerum natura" (*Con. Gen.* lib. I. cap. 11).

intuition the perfect and absolute idea of God is seen to contain its objective existence within itself. To us, however, who are still *in via*, this soaring flight of knowledge is impossible. We are, indeed, able to know that God is; but to comprehend what he is lies far beyond our present capacity. No argument is valid which takes as its point of departure the nature of God, for of that nature we are ignorant.

"If the human intellect comprehend the substance of anything, as, for instance, that of a stone or of a triangle, none of the intelligible attributes of that thing lies beyond the range of the faculty of human reason. But it is not so in regard to God. For to the conception of his substance the human intellect is not able to attain by its natural power, since, according to the mode of this life, its cognition begins from sense. And, therefore, those things which do not fall under sense cannot be grasped by the human intellect, except in so far as the knowledge of them is collected from sensible things. Moreover, sensible things cannot lead our intellect so far that in them may be seen what the divine substance is, since they are effects unequal to the power of the cause. Yet our intellect is led from sensible things into divine knowledge so far as to know concerning God that he is, and other things of this nature, which it is necessary to attribute to the first principle. There are, therefore, some intelligible attributes of divinity which are pervious to human reason; but others, in truth, there are which lie altogether beyond the power of human reason."[1]

Since this is the case, the only sound method of proving the existence of God is the reverse of Anselm's. It is to begin with

[1] "Si intellectus humanus alicuius rei substantiam comprehendit, puta lapidis vel trianguli, nullum intelligibilium illius rei facultatem humanae rationis excedet. Quod quidem nobis circa Deum non accidit. Nam ad substantiam ipsius capiendam intellectus humanus naturali virtute pertingere non potest: cum intellectus nostri, secondum modum praesentis vitae, cognitio a sensu incipiat; et ideo ea quae in sensu non cadunt, non possunt humano intellectu capi, nisi quatenus ex sensibilibus earum cognitio colligitur. Sensibilia autem ad hoc ducere intellectum nostrum non possunt ut in eis divina substantia videatur quid sit: cum sint effectus causae virtutem non aequantes. Ducitur tamen ex sensibilibus intellectus noster in divinam cognitionem ut cognoscat de Deo quia est, et alia huiusmodi quae oportet attribui primo principio. Sunt igitur quaedam intelligibilium divinorum quae humanae rationi sunt pervia; quaedam vero quae omnino vim humanae rationis excedunt" (*Con. Gen.* lib. I. cap. 3).

the empirical and contingent and, arguing from thence, to establish the truth which Anselm sought to reach by a single leap. Indeed, the ontological argument offers us a spurious satisfaction. It attempts to gain by use of the discursive reason results which, from the nature of things, can be achieved only by the direct perception of mystical vision. It detaches reason from its proper task of arguing from observed effects to their conjectural causes, and sets it the hopeless problem of trying to prove what, if apprehended at all, must be apprehended as self-evident.

It has been urged by a contemporary writer,[1] that the ontological argument represents the intuitive interest, while the cosmological and teleological arguments represent the scientific and the anthropomorphic. In the light of our preceding discussion this verdict appears quite unjustified. As we have seen, the ontological argument is very much in the nature of an opiate thrown to the religious instinct unsatisfied in its yearning for the mystical vision. It is knowledge of God made easy; a short road to religious certainty. Does not its author guarantee success for all but the fool?

Far other than this is the intuition of the mystic. That comes as the reward of long and patient training, as the crown of a holy life. Indeed, according to a somewhat radical view of St. Thomas, direct apprehension of the divine essence can be attained in this life only by a miracle. In thus postponing to the future life the vision of God, he does in truth run counter to the opinion of many mystics. Nevertheless, in asserting the impossibility of the human intellect, as such, obtaining any real conceptual knowledge of God's essence, *secundum modum praesentis vitae*, he is but repeating the declarations of that great multitude of mystics of all ages and countries who have sought to ascend to God by the *via negativa*, whereof we must speak in due course.

2. As this proof is derived from the preceding, so Aquinas's reply is based upon the same view of the relation of God's essence to his existence and of our knowledge of that essence which determined his rejoinder in that case. His refutation is as follows: It is possible, as a matter of fact, for us to conceive that God does not exist, but we can do so only because of the

[1] H. Wildon Carr, *A Theory of Monads*, p. 101 ff.

weakness of our understanding which is not able to know God
as he is in himself, but merely to know him from his effects.
Could we in reality know what the divine essence is, we should
be unable to think of it as non-existent. In other words, essence
and existence in God are identical; but we, who have an
inferential knowledge of God's existence, have none at all of
his essence, and therefore cannot comprehend that identity.
To us the necessity of the existence of the divine essence is no
more obvious than the necessity of the existence of man's
essence. Since, however, this is due to our weakness, it is no
derogation from God's greatness, nor does it compel us to
conceive of a being greater than he.[1]

A moment's reflection will make the cogency of this reply
perfectly evident. Let us take the idea of a dragon. Almost
inevitably at the word we call to our aid the wonderful and
constructive power of imagination. We visualize our dragon,
and he stands before us in all his grotesque completeness. To
imagine him, then, is to picture him as existing. What comes
before the eye of fantasy is, so far, real. We cannot picture our
dragon as non-existent any more than we can see the invisible.
But to imagine a dragon is not the same thing as to conceive
of him, though, as we have seen, it is a powerful assistance. To
conceive of a dragon is to posit as attributes of one subject all
the qualities of dragonhood. This is to know the essence of a
dragon. It is possible, however, to do this without in the least
supposing that such an object actually exists. Most people, in
fact, know perfectly well what is meant by *dragon*, and, it is safe
to say, none of them has the remotest notion that a concrete
instance of it could be found anywhere in the universe.

Yet it is also possible to conceive of an existent dragon. This
means that we can perceive the possibility of predicating
existence of the essence which we have conceived without any
resulting contradiction or incompatibility. Similarly, we are
able to predicate non-existence of it, that is we can perceive
the fact that there is nothing in the essence *dragon* which
implies the existence of a concrete individual dragon. So also
we can predicate existence or non-existence of any finite being,
since, as we have seen, none of them exists of necessity but all

[1] *Con. Gen.* lib. I. cap. 11; I *Dist.* 3. q. 1: a. 2. ad 4[m]; *De Verit.* q. 10:
a. 12. ad 2[m].

are contingent upon the will of God. He, however, does exist of necessity. Yet, since the identity of the divine essence and existence is not immediately known to us, our understanding can perceive no more contradiction or incompatibility in predicating non-existence of God than of anything' else, though that contradiction and incompatibility are actual facts. In conclusion we may remark that not even the rational demonstration of the identity of the divine essence and existence could serve as the basis of an argument for God's existence, since the latter must be proved first, it being a necessary premise for the demonstration of the former proposition.

3. The same consideration which availed for the overthrow of the two foregoing arguments is also sufficient for the demolition of this. For just as it is self-evident to us that the whole is greater than its part, so to those who behold the divine essence itself (i.e. the angels and the saints *in patria*) it is most self-evident that God exists, since his essence is his existence. But inasmuch as we are not able to behold his essence, we arrive at the knowledge of his existence, not through himself, but through his effects.[1]

4. This proof is practically identical with the twelfth. Yet in the *De Veritate*[2] each is given a separate place in the list of *obiecta*; for which reason it seems advisable to include them here as separate arguments. But to anyone who will read the replies to the twelfth proof which are to be found in the *Commentary on Peter Lombard's Sentences*[3] and in the *Summa Theologica*[4] and compare them with the reply to the fourth, which is contained in the *Contra Gentiles*,[5] it will be obvious that it is one and the same argument which is being refuted.

The claim, in each instance, is that God is known directly. The fourth argument endeavours to press home this assertion in the only way in which it is possible to substantiate the authority of a self-evident truth, that is indirectly, by pointing

---

[1] "Nam sicut nobis per se notum est quod totum sua parte sit maius, sic videntibus ipsam divinam essentiam per se notissimum est Deum esse, ex hoc quod sua essentia est suum esse. Sed quia eius essentiam videre non possumus, ad eius esse cognoscendum non per seipsum, sed per eius effectus pervenimus" (*Con. Gen.* lib. I. cap. 11; cf. 1 *Dist.* 3. q. 1: a. 2. ad 4^m; *De Verit.* q. 10: a. 12. ad 4^m).

[2] q. 10: a. 12. ob. 1. 5.   [3] 1 *Dist.* 3. q. 1: a. 2. ad 1^m.

[4] I.a. q. 2: a. 1. ad 1^m.   [5] Lib. I. cap. 11.

out that the contrary assumption would be inconsistent with other known truths, or with the possibility of any knowledge whatever. Hence it urges that the fact that all men desire the *summum bonum* involves direct awareness on their part of God who is the *summum bonum*. It is clear, however, from his replies to the twelfth argument that Aquinas conceives that the same contention is implicitly contained in it also. He points out in answer that, while it is true that all men do desire the *summum bonum*, it is not true that they are all aware of what the *summum bonum* is. They naturally desire happiness, and what they naturally desire must be naturally known by them; but from this it does not follow that they have absolute knowledge of God's existence, any more than the knowledge that someone comes involves the knowledge that it is Peter. What is naturally implanted in man is not a direct and intuitive knowledge of God, but the ability to arrive at the knowledge of God's existence by the use of his reason.

5. This argument has indeed a familiar sound. It harks back, on the one hand, to the Aristotelian conception of νοῦς as an eternal and immaterial faculty, above and apart from man's animal nature, and to the universal soul of certain Mohammedan philosophers; while, on the other hand, it suggests to us moderns in no uncertain accents the language of some of the eminent Hegelians of the nineteenth century. The belief that no knowledge is possible without participation in a universal principle of knowing, that the simplest affirmation involves an appeal to an absolute standard of truth which is the consciousness of an infinite mind, is a well-worn idea in philosophy. But St. Thomas will not accept it in any form which entails the consequence that our knowledge of God is immediate, and prior to our knowledge of other things. The simile is a false one. "Our sight is proportionate to the seeing of corporeal light in itself, but our intellect is not proportionate to the knowledge by natural cognition of anything, except through the senses; wherefore it is not able to arrive at pure intelligibles otherwise than by argumentation."[1]

---

[1] "Visus noster est proportionatus ad videndum lucem corporalem per seipsam; sed intellectus noster non est proportionatus ad cognoscendum naturali cognitione aliquid nisi per sensibilia; et ideo in intelligibilia pura devenire non potest nisi argumentando" (1 *Dist.* 3. q. 1: a. 2. ad 2m).

To say that in God all things are known does not mean that God must first be known in himself as *principia per se nota* must be known in themselves before that which follows from them can be known, but that the divine influence is the cause of every cognition which occurs in the human mind.[1] Since knowledge of the divine essence constitutes beatitude, it is clear that, if it were true that God must be known before aught else is known, all men would be in a beatific state. Moreover, inasmuch as all the attributes which can be predicated of the Deity are actually identical with one another in the divine essence, it would follow that no one could ever be in error in regard to the qualities which can legitimately be ascribed to God. Experience, however, teaches us that, in this life, men are not in a beatific state, and that they can err in what they assert concerning God. Again, the intellect is most certain of those entities which are first known by it, and of this certainty it can assure itself by attempting to doubt that they exist. But the Deity is not one of these entities, for it is written, "No man can see me and live."[2] Accordingly some have urged that when we say that God is first known by us, the statement must be understood to mean that what is first known is not the divine essence itself but the outflowing of the divine light. This, however, is not the case, for the first light that flows from God into our minds is a natural light. Nor is it this light that is first known by us, either as regards *what* it is—for it is only after much inquiry that we arrive at a knowledge of what the intellect is—or as regards whether it is—for it is only through perceiving the activities of our own minds that we perceive that we have minds.

Furthermore there are two senses in which we can speak of something being first known by man—according to the order of divers powers—or according to the order in which objects are subsumed under one power. On the one hand, since all our knowledge is derived from the senses, we may say that sense-knowledge is prior to intellectual knowledge. On the other hand, since the *intellectus agens* provides the *intellectus possibilis* with its objects by abstracting forms from *phantasmata*, those things are known first which are first grasped by the abstracting intellect. Accordingly that which is more uni-

[1] *Con. Gen.* lib. I. cap. 11.   [2] Exod. xxxiii. 20.

versal, and can be known without any activity of composition on the part of the intellect, is first known. And, similarly, as regards sensation, the more common particulars are the first known—*this body* rather than *this animal*.[1] From all this it is apparent that God, and other "separate substances" (*substantiae separatae*), so far from being first known by the intellect, can only be known indirectly according as their existence is inferred from that of other substances.[2]

It will be observed that Aquinas's position in this matter is seemingly at the opposite pole from that of St. Augustine. Nevertheless, he makes an earnest effort to persuade his readers that this is not the case, being doubtless moved to do so by his own reverence for his great predecessor as well as by a desire to escape the violent opposition which a frank and open attack upon his teaching would be sure to arouse. It had been maintained, he tells us,[3] that St. Augustine taught that it is by the primal truth that we judge of all things. But this, he insists, is not to be understood to mean that the uncreated truth is the proximate principle whereby we know and judge. On the contrary we know and judge by the light imparted to our own minds, which is the image of the primal light and which derives from it all its own efficacy; even as in the process of demonstration the secondary principles are conclusive only by virtue of the primary. Nor is it necessary that this light be known by us directly, for the medium of cognition is known only in so far as it makes all things known; even as light is not seen by the eye except as it illumines colour.[4]

6. This argument, which is apt to strike the reader at first as purely verbal, involves a reference to Aquinas's theory of truth. Into this, however, we need not enter now, as we shall have occasion to deal with it later, since upon his theory of truth one of the arguments for God's existence which he believes to be valid (i.e. the fourth) is founded. The plea before us St. Thomas dismissed with a single sentence. "That truth in

[1] An extraordinary statement, since it attributes to the senses a power of discrimination and selection practically equivalent to that of abstraction.
[2] *Comment. on Boethius's De Trinitate*, q. 1 : a. 3. c.
[3] *Comment. on Boethius's De Trinitate*, q. 1 : a. 1. ob. 1.
[4] *Comment. on Boethius's De Trinitate*, q. 1 : a. 3. ad 1ᵐ.

general has being is self-evident, but that there is a primal
truth is not self-evident to us."[1]

7. In a manner consistent with what we have seen to be his
general position, Aquinas rejected this proof with the observation that, while it is true that uncreated truth surpasses all
created truth, this is not inconsistent with the fact that created
truth is better known to us.[2]

8. To this argument Aquinas replied that there is no difficulty at all in a man contemplating his own non-existence,
just as there is no difficulty in his contemplating the fact that
he did not always exist. Such non-existence is, however, a
merely abstract possibility. He cannot assent to the proposition that he actually is non-existent, for in the very act of so
thinking he perceives himself to be—an interesting anticipation
of Descartes' *Cogito*.[3] The underlying thought is not further
developed, but the idea seems to be that it is no more difficult
for a man to contemplate the possibility that God does not
exist than to contemplate the possibility that he himself might
not exist, and that, while he has an awareness of his own
existence certain enough to render any denial of it a contradiction in fact, he has no such awareness of the existence of
God.

9. The preliminary assumption of this proof is true, according to Aquinas, only on the supposition that *something* had
being at the time that the truth referred to was yet future. We
may, however, assume *per impossibile*, that nothing had being.
In that case nothing would have been true except *materialiter*,
for the matter of truth is not only being but non-being, since
truth can be spoken of both. And so it does not follow that
truth had being except *materialiter* and *secundum quid*.[4]

10. The tenth argument is obviously a rebuttal of the refutation of the ninth. Aquinas's refutation consists of the brief
statement that the assertion that what is true *secundum quid* can
be reduced to that which is true *simpliciter* holds good only on
the supposition that there is any truth at all, not otherwise. As

---

[1] "Quod veritatem esse in communi, est per se notum: sed primam
veritatem esse, hoc non est per se notum quoad nos" (*Sum. Theol.* I.a.
q. 2: a. 1. ad 3m). For a somewhat more elaborate refutation cf. *De Verit.*
q. 10: a. 12. ad 3m).   [2] *De Verit.* q. 10: a. 12. ad 6m.
[3] *De Verit.* q. 10: a. 12. ad 7m.   [4] *De Verit.* q. 10: a. 12. ad 8m.

his reply to the preceding argument apparently conceded the being of truth *secundum quid*, the point of this answer is not obvious.[1]

11. This proof is to all intents and purposes identical with the third. However, since it is treated as a separate argument in the *De Veritate*, I have accorded it a place of its own. St. Thomas dismisses it with the remark that although the name of God is, *He who is*, yet this is not self-evident to us. Hence the conclusion does not follow from the premises.[2]

12. This proof has already been dealt with in connection with the fourth.

13. The idea underlying this argument is the same as that which inspired the fourth and the twelfth. Yet in the *Commentary on Peter Lombard's Sentences* it is distinguished from the twelfth, while its phraseology suggests a slightly different point of view from that of the fourth. It is based upon the Aristotelian notion that "where the objects are immaterial that which thinks and that which is thought are identical."[3]

Aquinas's answer is that "although God is within the soul by essence, presence, and power, yet he is not within it as an object for intellect, which is requisite for cognition. Moreover, while the soul is present to itself, yet in self-knowledge there is the greatest difficulty, so that the soul attains it only by reasoning from actual objects and from potential acts."[4]

Having now reviewed in order Aquinas's refutations of the thirteen proofs, it will be well, before we take leave of the topic, to allow our attention to dwell upon one outstanding feature of his method of treating it, and that is the very cavalier manner in which he rejects the claim of the religious consciousness to possess immediate knowledge of God. This tendency on the part of St. Thomas to discount the metaphysical importance of mysticism is very pronounced, and must be constantly kept in mind throughout all our study of his thought. It was a characteristic which he shared with his friend and teacher, Albertus Magnus, and which sharply distinguished both of them from the generality of scholastics.[5]

---

[1] *De Verit.* q. 10: a. 12. ad 9$^\mathrm{m}$.   [2] *De Verit.* q. 10: a. 12. ad 10$^\mathrm{m}$.
[3] *De Anima*, lib. III. cap. iv. 12. tr. by R. D. Hicks.
[4] 1 *Dist.* 3. q. 1: a. 2. ad 3$^\mathrm{m}$.
[5] Cf. Wicksteed, *Reactions between Dogma and Philosophy*, p. 390.

In addition we may note that in the present connection he considers only the degree of religious consciousness possessed by all men. A modern philosopher might well try to argue from the highly developed awareness of God attained by saints and mystics to the existence of an Object which those saints and mystics know, and to the existence of a more or less dormant capacity in all men to rise to similar knowledge. It is an arresting fact that, although Aquinas himself makes use of a very similar argument to justify the acceptance of the authority of Revelation,[1] here, where he is dealing with the basic problem of his entire philosophy, he neither defends nor attacks the validity of such a train of reasoning, but abstains from all discussion of it. Perhaps we should be right in surmising that while he regarded such considerations as valuable aids to faith—which is essentially an act of will—he nevertheless despaired of founding upon them an argument for the divine existence which would yield a sufficiently high degree of probability to be of use in philosophy.

[1] *Con. Gen.* lib. I. cap. 6.

CHAPTER III

PROOFS OF THE EXISTENCE OF GOD ACCEPTED BY AQUINAS

I

THE proof of the existence of God which Aquinas regarded as "most manifest" was the Aristotelian argument from motion. He briefly stated it as follows: "Everything that is moved is moved by something else. Moreover, it is evident to our senses that there are objects in motion, as for instance the sun. Therefore such an object is moved by something else. That which moves it is itself also either moved or not moved. If it be not moved we have reached a point where it is necessary to posit an unmoved mover, and this we call God. If, however, it be moved, then its movement must be caused by something else which moves it. Consequently we must either proceed to infinity or posit an unmoved mover; but we cannot proceed to infinity, therefore we must posit a primal unmoved mover."[1]

This argument as it stands depends upon the truth of two propositions which themselves require demonstration, namely that every moving thing is moved by another and that it is not possible to proceed to infinity. Both of them had already been dealt with by Aristotle, and Thomas was content to repeat Aristotle's arguments.[2]

(a) Three proofs are advanced in support of the first proposition:

1. If anything move itself, it must have the principle of movement in itself; otherwise it would evidently be moved by something else. Furthermore, it must be moved primarily;

---

[1] "Omne quod movetur ab alio movetur. Patet autem sensu aliquid moveri, utpota solem. Ergo alio movente movetur.—Aut ergo illud movens movetur, aut non. Si non movetur, ergo habemus propositum, quod necesse est ponere aliquod movens immobile. Et hoc dicimus Deum.—Si autem movetur, ergo ab alio movente movetur. Aut ergo est procedere in infinitum: aut est devenire ad aliquod movens immobile. Sed non est procedere in infinitum. Ergo necesse est ponere aliquod primum movens immobile" (*Contra Gentiles*, lib. I. cap. 13; cf. *Sum. Theol.* I.a. q. 2: a. 3. c.; *Com. Theol.* Pars Prima, cap. ii). [2] See *Con. Gen.* loc. cit.

that is it must be moved by reason of itself and not by reason
of its parts, as an animal is moved by the motion of its foot.
For, were that the case, the whole would not be moved by
itself but by a part, and one part would be moved by another.
Nor can it escape having parts, since everything that moves is
divisible. Moreover, as it is moved primarily, the quiescence of
the whole follows upon the quiescence of a part; for, if one
part were in motion when another was quiescent, then not
the whole but that one part alone would be moved primarily.
But nothing which is quiescent because of the quiescence of
some other thing is moved by itself, for since its quiescence
follows upon the quiescence of the other so does its movement
upon the movement of the other. The assumption that it is
self-moved is consequently false, and we are compelled to
assume that it is moved by something else.[1]

For a proof of the statement that whatever moves is divisible
we must turn to Aristotle's *Physics*, and to Aquinas's commentary thereon.[2] The movement of anything from one space
into a contiguous space involves its transference from being
wholly in the one space to being wholly in the other. This
can be accomplished only by its passing through the inter-
vening state of being both in the first space and in the second.
But this requires that part of it be in the first space and part
in the second, since it cannot be wholly in both at once. Therefore it must be divisible and have parts.[3]

In regard to the main argument Aquinas further observes
that it is of no avail to object that, in a thing which is self-
moved, it is impossible for a part to be quiescent; or to assert
that a part can be quiescent or be in movement only *per
accidens*. For the whole point of the argument lies in this, that,
if anything be moved primarily and *per se* and not by movement
of its parts, it cannot be dependent for its movement upon
anything else; and that the movement, like the being, of a
divisible thing depends on its parts, and that, therefore, it is
not possible for it to move itself primarily and *per se*. Nor is it
essential that we assume that the quiescence of a part is an

[1] *Phys.* lib. VII. cap. i. lect. 1 and lect. 2.
[2] *Phys.* lib. VI. cap. iv. lect. 5.
[3] It should be added that Thomas points out that this argument is concerned only with continuous local motion.

actual fact; all that is requisite for the validity of the proof is the admission of the truth of the proposition that if a part be quiescent the whole is quiescent.

2. Thomas's second proof is, to use his own phraseology, "by induction," *per inductionem*. Everything which is moved *per accidens* is not moved by itself, for its movement depends on another. And, likewise, nothing is self-moved which is moved by force; nor are those things which are moved by nature and of themselves (*ex se*), as animals are known to be moved by their own souls; nor yet again those things which are moved by nature inasmuch as they are heavy or light, and are susceptible to movement by a generating cause and through the removal of hindrances. Since, then, everything that is moved is moved either *per accidens* or *per se*, and since those things that are moved *per se* are moved either through force or through motion proceeding from themselves—as animals are —or through motion that does not proceed from themselves, we must conclude that whatever is moved is moved by something else.

3. The third proof is based upon the proposition that nothing can be both actual and in potentiality in the same respect and at the same time. But everything that is moved is, just in so far, in potentiality; for motion is the act of something existing in potentiality as such. Moreover, everything that moves is, just in so far, actual. Therefore nothing is both moving and moved in the same respect, and consequently nothing moves itself.

(*b*) The principle that it is impossible to proceed to infinity in a series of things moving and moved is likewise demonstrated by proofs drawn from the *Physics*. The first of these is as follows:[1]

1. In an infinite series there will, of course, be an infinite number of bodies, for whatever is moved is divisible and, therefore, corporeal.[2] Furthermore, each body that moves is at the same time moved. Hence the series will be moved in the same time that it takes to move one of its members. Each member, however, is finite, and is moved in a finite

[1] Cf. *Phys.* lib. VII. cap. i. lect. 2.
[2] It is clear that Aquinas here also refers to local motion. See *Phys.* lib. VI. cap. iv. lect. 5.

time. Also, the mover and the body moved must be together,[1] and to be together bodies must be in continuity or contiguity, and thereby form one mobile whole. This infinite whole will then be moved in a finite time, which is impossible.[2]

2. The second argument[3] starts from the premise that if a series of things which move and are moved take its beginning from a prime mover, and if that prime mover be taken away or cease from motion, then none of the other things will either move or be moved, since the prime mover is the cause of the motion of all the others. We are next asked to conceive of an infinite series. In this there is no prime mover, but every member is a mover mediate. Such a notion is clearly inadmissible. None of the members of the series can possibly be moved, and thus, as Thomas observes, "nothing will be moved in the whole world."

3. The third argument[4] is practically the same as the second, although couched in different words. Thomas remarks that, as the second proof begins with the series of moved and moving things and ascends thereby to the prime mover, so the third proof begins conversely with the prime mover and descends the series. Whatever moves instrumentally cannot move unless there be something which moves principally (*principaliter*). But in an infinite series of things, each of which both moves and is moved, there will be no principal mover, since each member depends for its movement upon something else. Consequently nothing will be moved.

4. Another argument for the existence of a prime mover is drawn from the same chapter in the *Physics* to which we have just had occasion to refer. The proposition that every mover is moved, if true, is true either *per se* or *per accidens*; that is to say, the predicate is either included in the notion of the subject or else it is not. If the proposition be true *per accidens* it is not necessary. In that case it is possible that no mover is moved, and hence that no mover can initiate movement. Therefore it is possible that nothing is moved. Aristotle, however, held that the non-existence of motion at any time is an impossibility,[5]

[1] *Phys.* lib. VII. cap. i. lect. 2 ; cap. ii. lect. 3.
[2] *Phys.* lib. VI. cap. vii. lect. 9.   [3] *Phys.* lib. VIII. cap. v. lect. 9.
[4] *Phys.* lib. VIII. cap. v. lect. 9.   [5] *Phys.* lib. VIII. cap. i. lect. 2.

for motion requires a subject which logically is prior to it; consequently, if that subject be ever completely at rest, it cannot thereafter pass into a state of motion without suffering change. But motion includes all forms of change. Therefore, to exist at all, motion must have existed before it began to exist, which is impossible.

Furthermore, if two qualities be found accidentally united in a certain subject, and if one of these qualities be elsewhere found without the other, it is probable that the other can also be found without the first. Thus, if in Socrates we find the qualities white and musical, and in Plato white but not musical, it is probable that in some other subject we shall find musical but not white. Accordingly, if we find the quality of being a mover and the quality of being moved joined accidentally in one subject, and if we find in another subject the latter without the former, it is probable that in a third subject we shall find the former without the latter. Nor does it avail to urge against this conclusion the instance of two things the first of which depends upon the second while the second is independent of the first, as accident and substance; for these are united *per se* and not *per accidens*.

Let us now assume that the proposition is true *per se*. Clearly the mover is moved either by a motion similar to that which it causes or by one dissimilar to it. The first supposition involves the assumption that one and the same thing can, at the same time and in the same respect, be both actual and in potentiality, an assumption which implies that a healer must be healed at the same time that he heals, and that a teacher must be taught at the same time that he teaches. This, however, is inadmissible. If we take the alternative and suppose that the motion is dissimilar, we may then conjecture that what causes alteration will itself be moved in space, that what causes movement in space will itself be augmented, and so on in like manner. But since the genera and species of motion are finite in number, we cannot proceed to infinity, but must come to a prime mover which is not moved by anything.

The objection may be raised that it is possible that, the genera and species of motion having been exhausted, a return may be made to the beginning of the process and the whole gone through again. Thus, we may suppose, what causes movement in space is itself altered, what causes alteration is itself augmented, and what causes augmentation is itself moved in space. But then the same difficulty which arose before would confront us a second time, for once more we should be supposing a thing to be moved by the same species of motion as that which it itself originates, only in this case mediately and not immediately. As a result we are again driven to the hypothesis of a prime mover.[1]

It has now been made clear that the prime mover is not moved from without. Is it, however, completely immovable, or does it move itself? The latter conjecture appears the more probable because what is of itself (*per se*) is always prior to what is of another (*per aliud*). Hence it seems reasonable that the prime mover should be moved by itself and not by another.[2] But it cannot move itself as a whole, for then it would be actual and in potentiality in the same respect and at the same time. Consequently one part of it must be moved by another. But this leads us once more to the hypothesis of an immovable prime mover. For it is impossible that each part should move the other, or that one part should move itself and move the other, or that the whole should move the part, or the part the whole, all these suggestions being inconceivable since they again involve us in the contradiction just referred to.[3] It remains for us, then, to suppose that one part moves and the other part is moved.

As far as our experience goes, in the case of those things that move themselves—such as animals—the moving part, i.e. the soul, is immovable in itself but is moved *per accidens*. In the case of the prime mover, on the contrary, as Aristotle has shown,[4] the part which gives rise to motion is moved neither of itself nor *per accidens*. For these self-moving things are corruptible, and therefore must be reducible to a prime self-mover which is everlasting. Hence that which moves itself must have some mover which is moved neither *per se* nor *per accidens*. It must also be everlasting. For if we admit Aristotle's contention that movement is everlasting, the generation of

---

[1] *Phys.* lib. VIII. cap. v. lect. 9.
[2] Cf. *Com. Theol.* Pars Prima, cap. iii.
[3] Cf. *Com. Theol.* loc. cit.; also 1 *Dist.* 8. q. 3: a. 1. ad 3^m.
[4] *Phys.* lib. VIII. cap. vi. lect. 12.

these self-moving and corruptible things must be perpetual. Yet none of them can be the cause of this perpetuity, since it is not itself perpetual; nor can all of them together be the cause, for their number would be infinite, and moreover they would not all exist at once. Accordingly there must be a perpetual self-mover which is the cause of the generation of all these inferior self-moving things.[1]

Furthermore, we see that some of these self-movers are moved *de novo* by some external motion, as when an animal is excited by digestion or change of air, in which case that self-mover is moved *per accidens*. From this we may conclude that no self-mover, of which the mover is moved either *per se* or *per accidens*, is always in motion. But the prime mover must always be in motion, otherwise motion would not be ever-lasting; therefore the prime mover must itself be moved by a mover which is not moved either in itself or *per accidens*. To the objection, quaint enough as it seems to us but natural to the medieval mind, that the movers of the lower spheres cause an everlasting motion and yet are moved *per accidens*, Aquinas answers that these are said to be moved *per accidens* not by reason of themselves but by reason of the spheres which they move, each of which follows the movement of a superior sphere.

Since God, however, is not part of a self-mover, Thomas at

---

[1] *Phys.* loc. cit.

In the *Compendium Theologiae* the same idea is also set forth. "Every motion," we are told, "is seen to proceed from some immobile source which is not moved according to the same species of motion. So we see that the instances of alteration, generation, and corruption in inferior subjects are to be referred to a prime mover in a heavenly body, which is not moved according to this species of motion, since it is ungenerated and incorruptible and unalterable. Hence that which is the first principle of a motion must be incorruptible." "Omnis enim motus videtur ab aliquo immobili procedere, quod scilicet non movetur secundum illam speciem motus; sicut videmus quod alterationes, et generationes, et corruptiones quae sunt in istis inferioribus, reducuntur sicut in primum movens in corpus coeleste, quod secundum hanc speciem motus non movetur, cum sit ingenerabile et incorruptibile et inalterabile. Illud ergo quod est primum principium omnis motus, oportet esse immobile" (loc. cit.).

In the *Commentary on Peter Lombard's Sentences* (1 *Dist*. 8. q. 3: a. 1. sol.) the immutability of God is deduced from the absence of potentiality in him, a point which has not yet been established in the *Contra Gentiles*.

this point turns to Aristotle [1] for the proof that, separate from the mover which is part of a self-mover, there is another mover which we call God. Every self-mover is moved by its appetite, and for this reason the mover which is part of the self-mover must move for the sake of something appetizing, for it is a moved mover, and the object of its appetite is a mover not moved at all. And this prime mover, separate and wholly immovable, is God.

Aquinas alludes next to two objections which might be levelled against the above arguments. The first is that they proceed from the supposition that motion is eternal, which is inconsistent with orthodoxy. To this he returns the reply that the most effective way to prove the existence of God is to build one's demonstration upon those very assumptions which, if true, would render his existence less manifest. If we assume that the world and motion had a beginning, our task is the easier; since, if they have come into existence *de novo*, they clearly have had an origin in some agent (*ab aliquo innovatore*), for nothing can bring itself out of potentiality into actuality.

The second objection is that these arguments assume that the first thing moved, which is a heavenly body, is moved of itself, which means that it is animated, a supposition that many will repudiate. Aquinas rejoins that, if the prime mover be not self-moved, it must be moved immediately by something immovable. He notices that Aristotle [2] has pointed out that it is necessary either to arrive straightway at an unmoved prime mover or else to posit something which moves itself, and that the latter hypothesis at once drives us back to the former.

In conclusion we should note that Aquinas seeks to show, in connection with this argument, that there is no real disagreement between Aristotle and Plato. The former, he tells us, meant by motion the act of that which exists in potentiality as such,[3] a conception which applies only to bodies which occupy space and are divisible.[4] Thus, in his commentary on the

---

[1] *Metaphys.* lib. XII. cap. vii. lect. 5.

[2] *Phys.* lib. VIII. cap. v. lect. 11, cap. vi. lect. 12.

[3] "Aristoteles enim proprie accepit motum, secundum quod est actus existentis in potentia secundum quod huiusmodi" (*Con. Gen.* lib. I. cap. 13).

[4] *Phys.* lib. VI. cap. iv. lect. 5.

Physics,[1] he observes that Aristotle speaks of the prime mover as being unmoved *ab omni exterius mutatione*.[2] He does this, says St. Thomas, "not intending to exclude the type of motion termed operation, which is immanent in the operator; even as intellection is called motion, and the appetite is said to be moved by the appetible. Motion of this sort is not excluded from the prime mover of which he treats."[3]

On the other hand, Plato, we are told, used the term *motion* to signify any operation,[4] so that mental activities, such as knowing and opining, would rank as forms of motion. Aquinas adds that Aristotle himself has referred to this difference of usage in the *De Anima*.[5] It appears, then, that Aristotle's unmoved prime mover is identical with Plato's self-moving prime mover.[6]

II

The second of Aquinas's arguments for the existence of God is the argument from an efficient cause. Like its predecessor, it is derived from Aristotle.[7] Its point of departure is the series of efficient causes which we observe in the world of sense-perception. In this series no member can be its own efficient cause, for to be so it would have to be prior to itself, which is impossible. It is likewise impossible to proceed to infinity in a series of efficient causes, because in such a series the first member is the cause of the intermediate, and the mediate of the last; and this is as true if there be many intermediate

---

[1] Lib. VIII. cap. vi. lect. 12.

[2] The Greek text is as follows: Ὅτι δ' ἀναγκαῖον εἶναί τι τὸ ἀκίνητον μὲν αὐτὸ πάσης τῆς ἐκτὸς μεταβολῆς, καὶ ἁπλῶς καὶ κατὰ συμβεβηκός, κινητικὸν δ' ἑτέρου, δῆλον ὧδε σκοποῦσιν.

[3] "Dicit autem *ab omni exterius mutatione*, non intendens excludere motum, idest operationem, quae est in operante, prout intelligere dicitur motus, et prout appetitus movetur ab appetibili. Huiusmodi enim motus non excluditur a primo movente de quo intendit."

[4] "Accipiebat enim motum pro qualibet operatione, ita quod intelligere et opinari sit quoddam moveri; quem etiam modum loquendi Aristoteles tangit in III *De Anima*" (*Con. Gen.* loc. cit.).

[5] Lib. III. cap. vii. lect. 12.

[6] *Con. Gen.* loc. cit. Cf. 1 *Dist.* 8. q. 3: a. 1. ad 2[m], where Aquinas argues that it is also identical with St. Augustine's.

[7] *Metaph.* lib. II. cap. ii. lect. 3.

members as if there be but one. Moreover, if a cause be removed, its effect is removed with it; hence, if the first cause be removed, no intermediate members and no last member of the series will be left. If, however, we proceed to infinity, there will be no first cause at all, and therefore no last member and no intermediate efficient causes. But such a result is evidently false. Therefore we must suppose that there is a primal efficient cause, and this we name God.[1]

Commenting upon the passage just referred to in the *Metaphysics*, Aquinas wrote: "In the first place he (i.e. Aristotle) puts forward a proposition which is, that in the case of all those entities which are intermediate between two extremes, of which extremes one is the last and the other the first, that which is first must be the cause of all those posterior to it, whether intermediate or last. And this proposition he demonstrates by division; because, if we have to say that one of three entities, primal, intermediate, and last, is the cause, we say of necessity that that one is the cause which is first. For we cannot say that the one which is last is the cause of all, for it is the cause of none; otherwise it would not be the last, for the effect is posterior to the cause. Nor yet can we say that the intermediate is the cause of all, for it is the cause of one alone, that is of the last. And lest someone should think that the intermediate is never followed by more than one, namely the last—which is the case only when there is but one intermediate term between the two extremes—he concludes, in order to exclude this view, that it makes no difference whether there be one intermediate term or many; since an entire plurality of intermediate terms will stand in place of one, inasmuch as they are all included under the concept of intermediate. And likewise it makes no difference whether the intermediate terms are finite or infinite, since, provided that the concept of *intermediate* is applicable to them, they are each incapable of being the primal moving cause. For, inasmuch as every secondary moving cause must be preceded by a primal moving cause, every intermediate cause must be preceded by a primal cause, which is in no way intermediary, as though there were any other cause before itself. But, if moving causes be assumed to proceed to infinity in the mode aforesaid, it follows that all

[1] *Sum. Theol.* I.a. q. 2: a. 3, and *Con. Gen.* lib. I. cap. 13.

causes are intermediate. And so it must be said universally of any infinite, whether in the order of causes or the order of magnitudes, that all its parts are intermediate; for, if there were some part that was not intermediate, it must be either the first or the last, and each is incompatible with the concept of the infinite which excludes every term and beginning and end. Moreover, another consequence can be deduced, which is that if there be many intermediate parts in any finite series, they cannot all be conceived as intermediate in a like sense. For some will be nearer to the first term and others to the last. But in the infinite, which does not have a first or last term, no part can be nearer either to the beginning or the end. And, therefore, everywhere, as regards whatever part you may signify, all parts will be similarly intermediate. And so, if moving causes proceed to infinity, there will be no first cause, but the first cause is the cause of all the others; hence it will follow that all causes will be wholly removed; for if the cause be removed, all those things are also removed, of which it is the cause." [1]

[1] "Primo proponit quamdam propositionem: scilicet, quod in omnibus his, quae sunt media inter duo extrema, quorum unum est ultimum, et aliud primum, necesse est quod illud quod est primum, sit causa posteriorum, scilicit medii et ultimi. Et hanc propositionem manifestat per divisionem: quia, si oporteat nos dicere quid sit causa inter aliqua tria, quae sunt primum, medium, et ultimum, ex necessitate dicemus causam esse id quod est primum. Non enim possumus dicere id quod est ultimum, esse causam omnium, quia nullius est causa; alioquin non est ultimum, cum effectus sit posterior causa. Sed nec possumus dicere quod medium sit causa omnium; quia nec est causa nisi unius tantum, scilicet ultimi. Et ne aliquis intelligat, quod medium nunquam habeat post se nisi unum, quod est ultimum, quod tunc solum contingit, quando inter duo extrema est unum medium tantum, ideo ad hoc excludendum concludit quod nihil ad propositum differt, utrum sit unum tantum medium, vel plura: quia omnes plura media accipiunt loco unius, inquantum conveniunt in ratione medii. Et similiter non differt utrum sint media finita vel infinita; quia dummodo habeant rationem medii, non possunt esse prima causa movens. Et quia ante omnem secundam causam moventem requiritur prima causa movens, requiritur, quod ante omnem causam mediam sit causa prima, quae nullo modo sit media, quasi habens aliam causam ante se. Sed, si praedicto modo ponantur causae moventes procedere in infinitum, sequitur quod omnes causae sunt mediae. Et sic universaliter oportet dicere, quod cuiuslibet infiniti, sive in ordine causae, sive in ordine magnitudinis, omnes partes sint mediae: si enim esset aliqua pars quae non esset media, oporteret, quod vel esset prima vel ultima: et utrumque repugnat rationi

III

The third argument is found in the *Summa Theologica*,[1] and appears to have been derived through Maimonides from Avicenna.[2] It is called the argument from possibility and necessity, and is, in effect, as follows: We find that among sensible things some can either be or not be, since they are generated and suffer corruption. It is impossible that such things should always exist, because whatever can be non-existent, at some time must be non-existent. If, then, all things could be non-existent, nothing would exist. Were this true, however, nothing would exist now, since what is not does not begin to be except through something which is. So, had no being existed, nothing could have begun to exist, and so there would be no existent world, which is evidently false. From this it follows that all beings are not possible, but that something must exist which is necessary. Furthermore, everything which is necessary has the cause of its necessity either in another or in itself. But it is no more possible to proceed to infinity in a series of necessary beings, the necessity of each of which exists in its predecessor, than it is possible to do so in a series of efficient causes. Therefore we must posit something which is necessary in itself, something which, so far from having the cause of its necessity in another, is itself the cause of the necessity of others; and this something all call God.[3]

infiniti, quod excludit omnem terminum et principium et finem. Est autem et ad aliud attendendum: quod, si alicuius finiti sunt plures partes mediae, non omnes partes simili ratione sunt mediae. Nam quaedam magis appropinquant primo, quaedam magis appropinquant ultimo. Sed in infinito quod non habet primum et ultimum, nulla pars potest magis appropinquare vel minus principio aut ultimo. Et ideo usque ad quamcumque partem, quam modo signaveris, omnes partes similiter sunt mediae. Sic igitur, si causae moventes procedant in infinitum, nulla erit causa prima: sed causa prima erat causa omnium: ergo sequeretur quod totaliter omnes causae tollerentur: sublata enim causa tolluntur ea quorum est causa."

[1] I.a. q. 2 : a. 3.

[2] Cf. Gilson's *The Philosophy of St. Thomas Aquinas*, tr. by Edward Bullough, ch. v. pp. 63–64.

[3] In the *Compendium Theologiae*, where the only proof of God's existence offered is the argument from motion, the *necessity* of his existence is deduced from his immobility. Since everything which can either exist or not exist

IV

' The fourth argument is that from degrees of truth and being. It is stated both in the *Contra Gentiles*,[1] and also in a longer and rather different form in the *Summa Theologica*.[2] In the *Contra Gentiles* it runs as follows: Aristotle has shown that that which is in the highest degree true is also the highest degree of being.[3] And he has also shown that there is a highest truth,[4] inasmuch as we say that of two propositions one is more false than the other, whence it follows that one is also truer than the other. And it is truer in so far as it approximates to that which is

is mutable, and since God is immutable, it follows that it is impossible that God should not exist (*Pars Prima*, cap. v). Furthermore, in the same chapter a second proof is advanced in support of the same conclusion, which is substantially identical with the third proof of the divine existence given in the *Summa Theologica*. It proceeds as follows: Everything which can either exist or not exist—in other words, every contingent being— owes its existence to something prior to itself, inasmuch as in itself it is indifferent with respect both to existence and non-existence. The existence of certain entities is, indeed, derivatively necessary, since each of them depends upon an entity ontologically prior to itself which is the cause of its necessity. (The notion of a necessary existence which is yet dependent upon a cause is due to Avicenna. See his *Metaphysices Compendium*, libri primi, quarta pars, tractatus, II. cap. i.) But nothing is prior to God; the divine existence is, therefore, necessary, and its necessity is not dependent upon anything other than itself.

[1] Lib. I. cap. 13.   [2] I.a. q. 2: a. 3. c.

[3] "Ostendit quod ea quae sunt maxime vera, sunt et maxime entia." The passage of the *Metaphysics* here referred to reads: "Οὐκ ἴσμεν δὲ τὸ ἀληθὲς ἄνευ τῆς αἰτίας· ἕκαστον δὲ μάλιστα αὐτὸ τῶν ἄλλων καθ᾽ ὃ καὶ τοῖς ἄλλοις ὑπάρχει τὸ συνώνυμον (οἷον τὸ πῦρ θερμότατον· καὶ γὰρ τοῖς ἄλλοις τὸ αἴτιον τοῦτο τῆς θερμότητος), ὥστε καὶ ἀληθέστατον τὸ τοῖς ὑστέροις αἴτιον τοῦ ἀληθέσιν εἶναι. διὸ τὰς τῶν ἀεὶ ὄντων ἀρχὰς ἀναγκαῖον ἀεὶ εἶναι ἀληθεστάτας (οὐ γάρ ποτε ἀληθεῖς, οὐδ᾽ ἐκείναις αἴτιόν τί ἐστι τοῦ εἶναι, ἀλλ᾽ ἐκεῖναι τοῖς ἄλλοις), ὥσθ᾽ ἕκαστον ὡς ἔχει τοῦ εἶναι, οὕτω καὶ τῆς ἀληθείας." (*Metaph*. lib. II. cap. i; cf. Aquinas, *Comment*. lect. 2.)

[4] "Maxime verum." I give the relevant passage in the *Metaphysics*: "Ἔτι εἰ ὅτι μάλιστα πάντα οὕτως ἔχει καὶ οὐχ οὕτως, ἀλλὰ τό γε μᾶλλον καὶ ἧττον ἔνεστιν ἐν τῇ φύσει τῶν ὄντων· οὐ γὰρ ἂν ὁμοίως φήσαιμεν εἶναι τὰ δύο ἄρτια καὶ τὰ τρία, οὐδ᾽ ὁμοίως διέψευσται ὁ τὰ τέτταρα πέντε οἰόμενος καὶ ὁ χίλια. εἰ οὖν μὴ ὁμοίως, δῆλον ὅτι ἅτερος ἧττον, ὥστε μᾶλλον ἀληθεύει. εἰ οὖν τὸ μᾶλλον ἐγγύτερον, εἴη γε ἄν τι ἀληθὲς οὗ ἐγγύτερον τὸ μᾶλλον ἀληθές. κἂν εἰ μὴ ἔστιν, ἀλλ᾽ ἤδη γέ τι ἔστι βεβαιότερον καὶ ἀληθινώτερον, καὶ τοῦ λόγου ἀπηλλαγμένοι ἂν εἴημεν τοῦ ἀκράτου καὶ κωλύοντός τι τῇ διανοίᾳ ὁρίσαι." (*Metaph*. lib. IV. cap. iv; cf. Aquinas's *Comment*. lect. 3.)

simply and in the highest degree true (*simpliciter et maxime verum*). Accordingly, since there is a *maxime verum* there must also be a *maxime ens*, and this we call God.

In the *Summa Theologica* the argument is stated thus. Among sensible things we find that some are less good, true, and noble than others; and so is it likewise with regard to other qualities. But "more" and "less" are predicated of different things according to their degrees of approximation to something which is the maximum, as a thing is hotter, for instance, in so far as it more nearly approaches the maximum heat. There exists, consequently, something which is truest, best, and noblest, and therefore possesses being in the highest degree; for those things which are truest do possess the highest degree of being.[1] Moreover, what possesses the highest degree of being in any genus is the cause of all things which are of that genus; as fire, which is in the highest degree hot, is the cause of all hot things. Therefore there is something which is, in all beings, the cause of being and of goodness, and of every perfection, and this something we call God.

V

The fifth and last argument is likewise found in the *Contra Gentiles*[2] and in the *Summa Theologica*.[3] It is derived, so Thomas informs us, from St. John of Damascus,[4] although he is careful to add that indications of it are to be found in Aristotle as well.[5] This proof is none other than the famous argument from design, or, as Aquinas phrases it, *ex gubernatione rerum*. As stated in the *Contra Gentiles*, it runs as follows: It is impossible that contrary and dissonant things should accord always or often in order except through the governance of something which so directs them, one and all, that they tend to a certain end. But in our own experience of the actual world we do see that things of the most diverse natures do so accord with one another, and that not rarely and by chance, but always, or in a majority of instances. Hence there must necessarily be

---

[1] *Metaph*. lib. II. cap. ii. lect. 2. [2] Lib. I. cap. 13.
[3] I.a. q. 2: a. 3. [4] *De Fide Orth*. 1 : 3.
[5] *Phys*. lib. II. cap. viii. lect. 12, lect. 13, lect. 14.

something by the providence of which the world is governed, and this we call God.

In the *Summa Theologica* the proof is formulated in much the same manner, except that stress is laid upon the presence of cognition and intelligence in the ordering power. We see, Thomas observes, that certain things which are destitute of cognition, such as natural bodies (*corpora naturalia*), operate toward an end; as appears from the fact that always or frequently they operate in the same mode, and that they adopt the mode that is best. From this it is evident that not by chance but by intention do they arrive at that end. Moreover, those that do not possess intelligence do not tend to an end unless directed by some conscious and intelligent power, as an arrow is directed by an archer. Therefore there is an intelligence by which all natural things are ordered to an end, and this intelligence we call God.

CHAPTER IV

CRITICISM OF THE PROOFS OF GOD'S EXISTENCE

AQUINAS's proofs of the existence of God are now before us in detail. If we compare them one with another it will become evident to us that of these five arguments the first three and the fifth depend for their validity upon the principle of causality. In the case of the fourth the situation is much less clear, and modern neo-scholastic writers have hotly debated the pros and cons of the question. To this topic we shall shortly return. Provisionally, however, we may conclude that the fourth argument is also an application of the concept of cause.

In the second place we may notice that these arguments—with the possible exception of the fifth—are all *a priori*. It is true that Scholastic and Neoscholastic writers are in the habit of using a different phraseology. The ontological argument, they are wont to say, is *a priori*; the proofs of St. Thomas, on the other hand, are *a posteriori*, inasmuch as they attempt to demonstrate the existence of God by reasoning from the effects of which God is the cause. But it is clear that this statement holds good only of the conclusions of the respective arguments, not of the arguments themselves. Thus, if the ontological argument be valid, its conclusion, embodied in the proposition "God exists," is *a priori*, since the existence of God is logically involved in the idea of God. If, however, the ontological argument be invalid, as St. Thomas maintained, then the existence of God is not immediately implied in the idea of God, and consequently the above proposition is in no way self-evident, and can be established only as the result of further reasoning.

Turning now to the proofs themselves, we see at once that the first four, although certainly empirical in the sense that they rest upon an appeal to experienced facts, are in no degree dependent upon induction, and involve no element of probability. The principle of causality, which itself reposes upon that of sufficient reason, is an *a priori* principle; and upon it, as upon a common foundation, these four arguments are built If valid, they yield not probability but certainty. Thus the

first proof takes its departure from the fact that motion—
that is change—is present in the universe. The amount of
change is of no importance. If the reasoning be valid, the argument holds if there be any change at all. Similarly the second
argument depends upon the existence of a causal sequence in
the universe. The number of actual causes and effects is
irrelevant. The existence of one genuine cause and one genuine
effect—in other words of one genuine case of causation—
suffices as well as would an infinite number of such instances.
The third argument, again, demands only the presence of
contingency in the universe. The existence of a single contingent
being is all that is required. As regards the fourth argument
the situation is somewhat different. This proof depends upon
the notion of degrees of truth and of being, a theory which we
shall examine at length in the course of a few pages. It appears
that in this case no single true proposition, no single existent
entity, no single instance of goodness will provide an adequate
foundation. The conception of degree introduces also the
notions of plurality and of comparison. None the less, it is
evident that we have not here to do with an argument which
is the outcome of induction in the modern sense of the term.
No enumeration of instances is implied by it. The idea which
inspired it was that of *participation*. The possession of such
"perfections"—as St. Thomas styled them—as truth or goodness was conceived by him to involve dependence upon an
ultimate source in which these perfections and qualities
existed in their purity, dissociated from all limitation and
imperfection. We seem here to be confronted by a particular
application of the principle of causality. Clearly, then, we are
still in the realm of the *a priori*.

When we pass to the fifth proof, however, we seem at first
sight to have left this realm behind us. The teleological argument appears to rest firmly upon the principle of induction.
The greater the number of instances wherein purpose and
intelligence can plausibly be conjectured to be present, the
more cogent the proof—or so we are wont to think. The
claim has nevertheless been made that the principle of finality
is "necessary and self-evident" and in no sense dependent
upon induction.[1]

---

[1] P. Fr. R. Garrigou-Lagrange, *Dieu, son existence et sa nature*, sec. 40, p. 338.

Let us now examine the five proofs one by one, beginning with the argument from motion. We must realize, in the first place, that by motion Aquinas almost certainly meant change of any sort, not merely the passage of physical bodies through space. It is important that we should grasp this fact at the outset, that we may not fall into the error of devoting ourselves to an elaborate analysis of physical motion under the impression that this is the main point at issue, whereas in reality it is merely one of the forms of change which St. Thomas had in mind. Qualitative alterations come equally under the head of motion.[1] So also does intellectual activity.[2] This last statement appears at first sight inconsistent with the position taken by Aquinas in his attempt to reconcile the teaching of Aristotle with that of Plato in regard to the prime mover. It will be recalled that the latter philosopher is stated to gave equated motion with "any operation,"[3] while Aristotle, on the contrary, is said to have "taken motion in its strict sense according to which it is the act of something existing in potentiality as such."[4] Accordingly Plato was justified, Aquinas urges, in referring to God as a self-mover, since for him movement did not involve corporeality; and Aristotle, on the other hand, was equally justified in affirming that God is an unmoved mover, since for him movement did involve both divisibility and corporeality.[5] So far there is no inconsistency. But when we find St. Thomas elsewhere referring to intellectual activity as itself a form of movement, and directly linking it to the argument from motion, a discrepancy seems to arise. To make this evident beyond doubt it is sufficient to translate the first of the references given above.[6] "Since Nature operates with

---

[1] "Motus qui est in qualitate, vocatur alteratio" (*Phys.* lib. V. cap. ii. lect. 4. Cf. *Phys.* lib. VII. cap. ii. lect. 4).

[2] Cf. *Sum. Theol.* I. a. q. 2 : a. 3. ad 2ᵐ, I.a. q. 79 : a. 4. c., I.a.–II.ae. q. 9 : a. 4. c. Cf. also *Dieu, son existence et sa nature*, sec. 34, p. 228.

[3] "Accipiebat enim motum pro qualibet operatione" (*Con. Gen.* lib. I. cap. 13).

[4] "Aristoteles enim proprie accepit motum, secundum quod est actus existentis in potentia secundum quod huiusmodi" (*Con. Gen.* lib. I. cap. 13).

[5] Cf. *Phys.* lib. VI. cap. iv.

[6] "Cum Natura propter determinatum fidem operetur ex directione alicuius superioris agentis, necesse est ea quae a natura fiunt, etiam in Deum reducere, sicut in primam causam. Similiter etiam quae ex proposito fiunt, oportet reducere in aliquam altiorem causam, quae not sit ratio et

reference to a definite end and under the direction of a superior agent, of necessity those things accomplished by nature must be referred to God, as their first cause. Similarly those things which are done purposively must be referred to some higher cause which is not human reason or will, because these are mutable and subject to passing away, and all things mutable and subject to passing away must be referred to some first principle immovable and necessary in itself, as has been shown." The concluding words, "*ut ostensum est*," have reference to the body of the article to which this passage is subjoined, and which contains the statement of the argument from motion.

The discrepancy, however, is a verbal one. Aquinas's contention is that, while in their precise and original sense the terms *potentiality* and *motion* have significance only in regard to physical bodies in space, yet by a legitimate and natural extension they may be applied to immaterial and non-spatial entities such as the human mind.[1] Thus in the *Summa Theologica* we read: "To be a subject and to be changed pertain to matter because it is in potentiality. Accordingly just as the potentiality of intellect is other than the potentiality of primary matter, so also the reason for being a subject and for undergoing change is different in the one case from what it is in the other. For the intellect is subject to knowledge, and is changed from ignorance into knowledge because it is in potentiality with respect to the intelligible species."[2] Similarly, in the preceding objection in the same article, we read: "The receptive potentiality in the intellectual soul is other than the receptive potentiality of primary matter, as is apparent from the diversity

voluntas humana: quia haec mutabilia sunt et defectibilia; oportet autem omnia mobilia et deficere possibilia reduci in aliquod primum principium immobili et per se necessarium, sicut ostensum est" (*Sum. Theol.* I.a. q. 2: a. 3. ad 2^m).

[1] Cf. *De Anima*, lib. III. lect. 6; also *Con. Gen.* lib. I. cap. 15, where we read: "Omne quod incipit esse vel desinit, per motum aut mutationem hoc patitur."

[2] "Quod subiici et transmutari convenit materiae secundum quod est in potentia. Sicut ergo est alia potentia intellectus, et alia potentia materiae primae, ita est alia ratio subiiciendi et transmutandi. Secundum hoc enim intellectus subiicitur scientiae, et transmutatur de ignorantia ad scientiam, secundum quod est in potentia ad species intelligibiles" (I.a. q. 75: a. 5. ad 2^m).

of that which is received. For primary matter receives individual forms, while the intellect, on the other hand, receives absolute forms."[1]

These extracts make it clear that for St. Thomas the concepts of potentiality and motion, taken in their widest sense, were applicable to mind, inasmuch as it is subject to change; and that consequently he was justified in regarding mental activity as one of the presuppositions of the argument from motion, since the latter is based upon these concepts.[2] We are now free to argue from the fact of its occurrence to the existence of a permanent and unchangeable cause, and at the same time to conceive of that permanent and unchangeable cause as itself a mind.

Having now cleared away the initial difficulties, let us examine the argument more closely. Its fundamental contention is that the potential—which *per se* is non-existent as yet—cannot of itself pass into actuality, for this would involve that the non-existent can be the cause of the existent. In other words, were the potential capable of becoming actual of itself, it would be its own cause, which is to say that it existed before it began to exist. But such a statement is absurd. Consequently we are forced to posit the existence of some other entity which, itself wholly actual, is capable of fulfilling the function of a cause, and through its agency the passage from potentiality to actuality is accomplished. This entity, however, must either be eternal and changeless, or is itself likewise in motion. On the first supposition our argument has reached its goal, for this eternal and changeless being is what we mean by God. On the second supposition we are compelled to posit a third entity which in its turn may act as a cause. And so the process may continue indefinitely. But at each stage the same alternative

---

[1] "Est autem alia potentia receptiva in anima intellectiva, a potentia receptiva materiae primae, ut patet ex diversitate receptorum: nam materia prima recipit formas indivuales, intellectus autem recipit formas absolutas" (cf. *Quodlib.* III. q. 8: a. 20. c.).

[2] Cf. Garrigou-Lagrange, *Dieu, son existence et sa nature,* p. 259: "Le principe '*Quidquid movetur ab alio movetur,*' loin de reposer sur une image spaciale, repose sur la nature même du devenir, rendu intelligible en fonction, non pas de l'être corporel, mais de *l'être,* objet formel de l'intelligence. Aussi cette notion et ce principe peuvent-ils s'appliquer à un devenir qui n'a rien de spacial, comme celui de volonté."

confronts us. Either we must go on to infinity or else we must arrive at a being which, while itself the cause of motion and change, remains, nevertheless, unmoved and changeless.

An infinite regress, however, is impossible. This is an extremely important point, and it is essential for our understanding of his argument to realize at the outset that it was not a temporal regress which Aquinas had in mind. The priority of the unmoved mover is a logical priority. This is brought before us with unmistakable clearness in the *Commentary on Peter Lombard's Sentences* in the discussion of the question whether or not the world is eternal. "If the world existed from eternity, then from eternity there was generation both of men and animals. But all generation implies both a generator and that which is generated, moreover the generator is the efficient cause of the generated; and so we should be compelled to proceed to infinity in efficient causes which is impossible, as is proved in the second book of the *Metaphysics*. Therefore it is impossible that generation and the world should always have been."[1] Aquinas's reply is as follows: "That an infinite number of causes which are causes *per se* and essentially should precede the same effect is impossible, but accidentally it is possible; that is to say that it is impossible that there should be an effect the concept of which involved that it should proceed from an infinite number of causes, but as to those causes the multiplication of which makes no difference as regards the effect, it may happen that they should be infinite in number. For example, for the existence of a knife certain moving causes *per se* are required, such as a smith and an instrument; and that these should be infinite is impossible, for this would involve that an infinity of instruments should exist actually at one time. But that the knife should be made by an old smith who had many times renewed his instruments, and that it should thus succeed a multitude of successive instruments, this is possible *per accidens*;

[1] "Si mundus fuit ab aeterno, ergo et generatio fuit ab aeterno tam hominum quam animalium. Sed omnis generatio habet generans et generatum; generans autem est causa efficiens generati; et sic in causis efficientibus est procedere in infinitum, quod est impossibile, ut probatur in II *Metaphys.*, text 5. Ergo impossibile est generationem semper fuisse et mundum" (2 *Dist.* 1. q. 1 : a. 5. sed contra ob. 5).

and nothing forbids that an infinite number of instruments should have preceded this knife if the smith existed from eternity. And the same thing is true in regard to the generation of an animal, for the seed of the father is the moving cause instrumentally with respect to the power of the sun. And because instruments of this sort, which are secondary causes, are generated and corrupted, it may happen that they are infinite in number. In the same way it may be that an infinite number of days have preceded this day, because the substance of the sun from eternity is in accordance with them and any circulation is finite."[1]

//The meaning of this passage is obvious. There is nothing contradictory in the conception of an infinite number of secondary causes succeeding each other in time; consequently the existence of such a series is perfectly possible and cannot be denied upon philosophic grounds. Aquinas did not believe in the actual existence of a series of this kind because to do so would be to depart from the Catholic faith which teaches that the world was created, but he did emphatically deny that the truth of the doctrine of creation could be demonstrated philosophically.[2] His attitude in this matter was original and daring, and to it was due the first widespread interest in his teaching. Hence it is beyond question that he held it to be entirely illegitimate to argue to the existence of God from the

---

[1] "Quod eundem effectum praecedere causas infinitas per se, vel essentialiter, est impossibile; sed accidentaliter est possibile hoc est dictu, aliquem effectum de cuius ratione sit quod procedat a causis infinitis, esse impossibilem; sed causas illas quarum multiplicatio nihil interest ad effectum, accidit effectui esse infinitas. Verbi gratia, ad esse cultelli exiguntur per se aliquae causae moventes, sicut faber et instrumentum; et haec esse infinita est impossibile, quia ex hoc sequeretur infinita esse simul actu; sed quod cultellus factus a quodam fabro sene, qui multoties instrumenta sua renovavit, sequitur multitudinem successivam instrumentorum, hoc est per accidens; et nihil prohibet esse infinita instrumenta praecedentia istum cultellum, si faber fuisset ab aeterno. Et similiter est in generatione animalis; quia semen patris est causa movens instrumentaliter respectu virtutis solis. Et quia huiusmodi instrumenta, quae sunt causae secundae, generantur et corrumpuntur, accidit quod sunt infinitae: et per istum etiam modum accidit quod dies infiniti praecesserint etiam istum diem: quia substantia solis ab aeterno est secundum eos, et circulatio eius quaelibet finita" (2 *Dist.* 1. q. 1: a. 5. sed contra ad 5^m). [2] Cf. the *De Aeternitate Mundi.*

supposed necessity of a *prius* to the temporal series. On the contrary, his contention was that any and every causal series, whether temporally finite or infinite, is inherently contradictory unless regarded as depending upon an ultimate cause which is not in time at all. In any such series each member is moved by its predecessor, and this in turn by the member previous to it, and though we proceed in this manner to infinity we are no nearer reaching an ultimate and self-explanatory source of motion.[1]

In the *Summa Theologica*[2] the same point is worked out in greater detail in reply to the same argument that if the world were eternal the process of generation would also be eternal, and so there would be an infinite series of efficient causes, since a father is the efficient cause of his son. "In efficient causes it is impossible to proceed to infinity *per se*; that is to multiply to infinity causes *per se* which are required for an effect, as would be the case if a stone were moved by a stick, the stick by the hand, and so on to infinity. But to proceed to infinity *per accidens* in causal agents is not impossible, that is if all the causes which are multiplied to infinity occupy a position equivalent to that of one cause only, and then multiplication is *per accidens*, as would be the case if an artisan were to use many hammers *per accidens*, because one hammer after the other was broken. It is accidental to each hammer that it acted after the action of another hammer; and similarly it is accidental to this man, inasmuch as he generates, that he is generated by another man, for he generates inasmuch as he is a man, not inasmuch as he is the son of another man. So all men generating occupy one position in the series of efficient causes—that of a particular generator. Hence it is not impossible that man should be generated by man *ad infinitum*, but it would be impossible if the generation of *this* man depended upon *this* man, and upon an elementary body, and the sun—and so on to infinity." [3]

[1] Cf. *Phys*. lib. VIII. lect. 8.   [2] I.a. q. 46: a. 2. ad 7ᵐ.

[3] "In causis efficientibus impossibile est procedere in infinitum *per se*; ut puta si causae quae per se requiruntur ad aliquem effectum, multiplicarentur in infinitum; sicut si lapis moveretur a baculo, et baculus a manu, et hoc in infinitum. Sed per accidens in infinitum procedere in causis agentibus non reputatur impossibile; ut puta si omnes causae quae in infinitum multiplicantur, non teneant ordinem nisi unius causae, sed

The situation which now confronts us with respect to the series of efficient causes is analogous, St. Thomas urges, to that in which we find ourselves when we consider the question of material causes.[1] We cannot say that water is made from fire and earth from water, and so on indefinitely. In the end we "must posit a primal principle as the foundation and basis of the others." [2]

The passages just quoted make it clear beyond question that the infinite series which Aquinas had in mind and which he considered vicious was a series involving not temporal but logical priority. His contention was that a succession of dependent entities, each member of which refers us to the one before it, can be rendered intelligible only by positing as its terminus an independent entity which is its own *raison d'être*, that the notion of a series of this sort without such an ultimate ground is unintelligible and self-contradictory, and that the contradiction cannot be removed by supposing the series to extend to infinity. The dependent implies the independent, the relative implies the absolute. As Professor Taylor has well said: "The dependence meant in the argument has nothing to do with the succession in time. What is really meant is that our knowledge of any event in nature is not complete until we know the full reason for the event. So long as you know only that A is so because B is so, but cannot tell why B is so, your knowledge is incomplete. It only becomes complete when you are in a position to say that A is so because Z is so, Z being something which is its own *raison d'être*, and therefore such that it would be useless to ask why Z is so. This at once leads to the conclusion that since we always have the

earum multiplicatio sit per accidens; sicut artifex agit multis martellis per accidens, quia unus post unum frangitur. Accidit ergo huic martello quod agat post actionem alterius martelli. Et similiter accidit huic homini, inquantum generat, quod sit generatus ab alio: generat enim inquantum homo, et non inquantum est filius alterius hominis; omnes enim homines generantes habent gradum unum in causis efficientibus, scilicet gradum particularis generantis. Unde non est impossibile quod homo generatur ab homine in infinitum. Esset autem impossibile, si generatio huius hominis dependeret ab hoc homine, et a corpore elementari, et a sole, et sic in infinitum" (cf. *Con. Gen.* lib. II. cap. 38).

[1] Cf. *Metaph.* lib. II. lects. 2 and 3.
[2] "Supponitur unum primum, quod sit fundamentum et basis aliorum."

right to ask about any event in Nature why that event is so, what are its conditions, the Z which is its own *raison d'être* cannot itself belong to Nature. The point of the reasoning is precisely that it is an argument from the fact that there is a 'Nature' to the reality of a 'Supernature,' and this point is unaffected by the question whether there ever was a beginning of time, or a time when there were no events." [1]

St. Thomas's argument is founded upon his conceptions of actuality and potentiality, and of the relation of one to the other. The potential is that which does not yet exist, but which is capable of existing as the result of the action of an efficient cause. Thus in the *De Potentia* we read that "actuality strictly speaking is prior to potentiality both in Nature and in time; although in a particular instance of the passage from potentiality to actuality the potential may be prior in time, yet since it is necessary that it should be brought into actuality through some being which is already actual, it is also necessary that, strictly speaking, the actual should be prior to the potential even in time. Hence, since every body is in potentiality, as its motion makes evident, of necessity there must be an immobile eternal substance prior to all bodies." [2]

We are here dealing with one of the foundation-stones of St. Thomas's philosophy. The division of being into the actual and the potential is vital for his system. "Potentiality and actuality," he wrote, "divide being and every genus of being." [3]

In this connection M. Sertillanges has remarked: "We shall see how decidedly, with respect to matter, St. Thomas establishes himself at this point of view, refusing to discuss with those who do not admit the reality of movement, of becoming of every kind, of substantial generation. Being given these

---

[1] "The Vindication of Religion" in *Essays Catholic and Critical*, p. 50.
[2] "Actus est prius potentia, et natura et tempore simpliciter loquendo; quamvis in uno aliquo quod de potentia exit in actum potentia tempore praecedat: sed quia oportet quod in actum reducatur per aliquod ens actu, oportet quod actus sit simpliciter prior potentia etiam tempore. Unde cum omne corpus sit in potentia, quod ipsius mobilitas ostendit, oportet ante omnia corpora esse substantiam immobilem sempiternam" (q. 6: a. 6. c. Cf. *Sum. Theol.* I.a. q. 82: a. 3. ad 2m).
[3] "Cum potentia et actus dividant ens et quodlibet genus entis" (Cf. *Sum. Theol.* I.a. q. 77: a. 1. c.).

postulates, being given also his invincible confidence in the
validity of our conceptions of being and of the *necessary*, he
will no longer permit anyone to touch the governing theory of
his system. He will not spend time in demonstrating it, content
to apply it, considering that the success of these applications,
and their universal character, bring to the preliminary analyses
the unique confirmation required. A theory beyond which one
cannot pass, and which, admitted, illumines all—is not this
better than proved? No proof can equal such a test, and
usefulness, raised to this level, cannot be called anything
but truth. Such seems to have been the state of mind of St.
Thomas, as it was also that of Aristotle." [1]

It is, indeed, true that what we most miss in the writings
of St. Thomas is a criticism of such concepts as potentiality,
change, and time. Yet it would not be fair to say that either
Aquinas or Aristotle made no attempt to show that the concept of potentiality is a legitimate one. We have only to turn
to the eighth chapter of the ninth book of the *Metaphysics*, and
to St. Thomas's commentary upon this chapter, to see what
their arguments are. They both point out—for St. Thomas
repeats the arguments of Aristotle—that the very conception
of the potential is derived from our experience of the actual,
and that as a matter of fact we observe in the generation of
the members of a species that the potential is the result of a
prior actuality. The boy who is a potential man is himself
generated by an actual man. Furthermore, they urge that the
potential, inasmuch as it is contingent and therefore capable

---

[1] "Nous verrons à quel point, à propos de la matière, saint Thomas
s'établit dans ce point de vue, refusant de discuter avec qui n'admet pas
la réalité du mouvement, du devenir dans tous les genres, de la génération
substantielle. Étant donné ces postulats, étant donné aussi sa confiance
invincible en la validité de nos conceptions de l'être et du *nécessaire*, il ne
permettra plus qu'on touche à la maîtresse théorie de son système. Il ne
s'attardera pas à la démontrer, content de *l'appliquer*, estimant que le
bonheur des applications, leur caractère universel, apportent aux analyses
du début l'unique confirmation requise. Une théorie dont on ne peut
point se passer et qui, admise, éclaire tout, n'est-elle pas mieux que
prouvée? Nulle preuve ne peut valoir une telle épreuve, et la commodité,
portée à ce niveau, ne peut que s'appeler vérité. Tel semble avoir été
l'état d'esprit de saint Thomas, après avoir été celui d'Aristote" (*S. Thomas
d'Aquin*, tome I. pp. 73–74).

both of existence and non-existence, implies in its very conception that which exists by itself and of necessity. To pursue this line of reflection further would lead us to the consideration of the third argument of which the argument from motion is really only a special instance. Moreover, since for Aquinas motion is equivalent to change, the assertion that the actual is prior to the potential is equivalent to the proposition "whatever is moved is moved by another," and we have already noticed the arguments advanced in defence of this proposition in the elaborate statement of the argument from motion in chapter thirteen of the *Contra Gentiles*.[1] The equivalence for St. Thomas of motion to change, to which we have just referred, suggests, however, another interesting question. Why, in his statement of the first proof in the above chapter, does he lay such stress upon local motion? The answer is that in the first place local motion is the cause of quantitative and qualitative change in physical things,[2] and in the second place that local motion is, of all forms of motion, the most obvious to the senses. Furthermore, it has already become clear that if mental operations are included in the definition of motion, the first argument is practically identical with the third, as the same principle is involved in both. In order to keep them at all distinct it is necessary to lay stress upon physical motion.

Attention should also be called to the fact that in certain passages Aquinas emphasizes the difference between mental operations and physical changes. Thus in the *Commentary on Peter Lombard's Sentences*[3] he remarks that, "strictly speaking motion is always the act of that which is potentially existent, but sometimes the operation itself of a thing, such as knowledge and sensation, is improperly called motion; and then motion is the act of the perfect."[4] In defence of this statement we are referred to the *De Anima* of Aristotle,[5] where the operation of the mind is contrasted with the changes of physical

---

[1] Cf. *Phys*. lib. VII. cap. i. lect. i. and lib. VIII. cap. iv. lect. 7.
[2] 1 *Dist*. 8. q. 3: a. 3. ad 3ᵐ.   [3] 1 *Dist*. 37. q. 4: a. i. ad 1ᵐ.
[4] "Motus, proprie sumendo, semper est existentis in potentia; sed aliquando improprie ipsa operatio rei dicitur motus eius, ut intelligere et sentire; et tunc motus est actus perfecti" (cf. *Phys*. lib. VII. cap. i. lect. i).
[5] Lib. III. cap. vii.

bodies.[1] ("And manifestly the sensible object simply brings the faculty of sense which was potential into active exercise: in this transition, in fact, the sense is not acted upon or qualitatively changed. Consequently this must be a different species of motion. For motion is, as we saw, an activity of that which is imperfect; but activity in the absolute sense, that is activity of that which has reached perfection, is quite distinct."— R. D. Hicks's translation.)

Commenting on this passage Aquinas wrote: "since motion, which occurs in corporeal things, and of which an examination is made in the *Physics*, is from contrary to contrary, it is evident that sensation, if it be called motion, is another species of motion from that which is examined in the *Physics*: for motion is the act of that which exists potentially, since it is clear that, when it has withdrawn from one contrary, during the interval when it is in motion it has not attained the other contrary which is the term of its motion, but is *in potentia*. And since everything which is in potentiality is in so far imperfect, that motion is the act of the imperfect. But this motion is the act of the perfect, for it is the operation of sense which is already made actual by its species. For sensation does not occur in the sense unless the latter is already existent; that motion, therefore, is, strictly speaking, other than physical motion, and motion of this sort, sensation, knowledge, and volition, is properly called operation. And according to this operation the soul moves itself, according to Plato, inasmuch as it knows itself and loves itself." [2]

[1] " Φαίνεται δὲ τὸ μὲν αἰσθητὸν ἐκ δυνάμει ὄντος τοῦ αἰσθητικοῦ ἐνεργείᾳ ποιοῦν· οὐ γὰρ πάσχει οὐδ' ἀλλοιοῦνται. διὸ ἄλλο εἶδος τοῦτο κινήσεως· ἡ γὰρ κίνησις τοῦ ἀτελοῦς ἐνέργεια ἦν, ἡ δ' ἁπλῶς ἐνέργεια ἑτέρα ἡ τοῦ τετελεσμένου."

[2] "Quia motus, qui est in rebus corporalibus, de quo determinatum est in libro *Physicorum*, est de contrario in contrarium, manifestum est quod sentire, si dicatur motus, et alia species motus ab ea de qua determinatum est in libro *Physicorum*: ille enim motus est actus existentis in potentia: quia videlicet recedens ab uno contrario, quamdiu movetur non attingit alterum contrarium, quod est terminus motus, sed est in potentia. Et quia omne, quod est in potentia, inquantum huiusmodi, est imperfectum, ideo ille motus est actus imperfecti. Sed iste motus est actus perfecti: est enim operatio sensus iam facti in actu, per suam speciem. Non enim sentire convenit sensui nisi in actu existenti; et ideo iste motus simpliciter est alter a motu physico. Et huiusmodi motus dicitur proprie operatio, ut

Why, we may ask, did Aquinas qualify his own assertion in this way? Why did he expressly equate motion with change, and yet in the very act of doing so affirm that such an equation is, strictly speaking, improper? The answer is that Aristotle had used the same term in both the wider and narrower sense. It is clear that the same principle is involved, whether the point of departure be change in general, or a particular variety of change, such as physical motion. The principle is that of sufficient reason. But this is the principle which inspires the other three arguments also, as we shall see. Is there then only one argument as some have contended? The answer is that the same underlying principle is involved in all. Each has, however, a different starting-point.

The Neoscholastic writer, P. R. Garrigou-Lagrange, who has himself repeatedly emphasized the fact of the equivalence for St. Thomas of motion and change,[1] is also concerned to vindicate the right of the argument from motion to be regarded as a separate proof.[2] He calls attention to the fact that at the Catholic Congress at Brussels in 1894 one of the members proposed that, instead of motion itself, the passage from quiescence to motion should be taken as the point of departure for this proof; to which the reply was made that it would then be no longer the argument from motion, but would have become the argument from contingency. The reason for this proposal was that many had come to feel that the Aristotelian concept of motion no longer corresponded to the actual facts. The notion that particles of matter, once put in motion, were capable of continuing to move for an indefinite period until they were brought to rest by the action of other material bodies seemed to them to destroy the validity of the proof. For the medieval schoolmen a moving body required a cause not only for its passage from quiescence to motion, but for each stage of its motion until it came once more to rest. Garrigou-Lagrange argues that the more ancient conception is still the true one. "Que le mouvement une fois donné à un corps se

sentire et intelligere et velle. Et secundum hunc motum anima movet seipsam secundum Platonem, inquantum cognoscit et amat seipsam" (*De Anima*, lib. III. lect. 12).

[1] Cf. *Dieu, son existence et sa nature*, pp. 228 and 765.
[2] Cf. *Dieu, son existence et sa nature*, pp. 250–252.

continue indéfiniment, c'est là une fiction *commode* peut-être pour *représenter* certaines relations mathématiques ou mécaniques en astronomie, mais philosophiquement très contestable." [1] He urges that "one cannot speak of a *state of movement*; movement, being essentially change, is the contrary of a state, which implies stability. There is no less change in the passage from this position to that other in the course of movement, than in the passage from quiescence to movement itself; if then this first change demands another cause, the following changes demand it with the same right." [2]

This may be true. But it does not alter the fact that the concept of motion either includes mental operations or else it does not. If it be taken as including them, then the argument from motion must be based upon some characteristic common to all forms of motion. What is the characteristic? Aquinas himself, in the very passage in his *Commentary on the De Anima* which we have just examined, has sharply contrasted physical movement with the operations of a mind. The former, he has told us, is "the act of an imperfect being," "of that which exists potentially," while the latter is "the act of the perfect," "of that which is already existent." Were we to take this statement literally we might well conclude that for Aquinas there was no potentiality in mind at all. But it is clear from other passages [3] that he did conceive of the mind as possessing potentiality, but that its potentiality is of another sort than that of matter. "As the potentiality of the intellect, therefore, is other than the potentiality of primary matter, so the reason why it is a subject and undergoes transmutation is different also. For the intellect is made the subject of knowledge and is transmuted from ignorance into knowledge, inasmuch as it is in potentiality with regard to the intelligible forms." [4]

---

[1] Cf. *Dieu, son existence et sa nature*, p. 253 n.

[2] "On ne peut pas parler *d'état de mouvement*: le mouvement, étant essentiellement un changement, est le contraire d'un état, qui implique la stabilité. Il n'y a pas moins de changement dans le passage de telle position à telle autre au cours de mouvement, que dans le passage du repos au mouvement lui-même; si donc ce premier changement demande une autre cause, les suivants en demandent une au même titre" (*Dieu, son existence et sa nature*, pp. 251–252).

[3] *Sum. Theol.* I.a. q. 75: a. 5. ad 1 and ad 2ᵐ; also I.a. q. 79: a. 2. c.

[4] "Sicut ergo est alia potentia intellectus, et alia potentia materiae primae, ita est alia ratio subiiciendi et transmutandi. Secundum hoc enim intel-

The mind, then, possesses potentiality, but a different sort of potentiality from that possessed by matter. It is also capable of movement, as we have seen,[1] but in a different sense from that in which a body moves. What is there in common between these two very disparate forms of motion? Only this, surely, that each involves a passage from potentiality to actuality. Upon this fact alone, then, can argument which takes both of them together as its starting-point be based. But this is the point of departure of the third proof. Moreover, as has been said, the principle underlying the first and third proofs is the same—that of sufficient reason. Where is there the difference between them? The answer is, there is none. Even if the field of the first argument be limited to the consideration of physical motion, its individuality is still in peril. For, whereas the third argument reasons from contingency in general to a necessary being which is its cause, the first argument reasons from a particular form or aspect of contingency to the same necessary being. It is difficult to see how it can be contended that we have here two genuinely different proofs.

Before dismissing the argument from motion, we may ask one more question. It will be remembered that St. Thomas in his endeavour to reconcile Aristotle and Plato conceded to the latter that, in the sense in which it is permissible to speak of thought and volition as movement, it is also permissible to speak of God as a self-mover. But does not this contradict his claim to have demonstrated the existence of an unmoved mover? Or is it possible that he was not concerned to show that God is immobile in this sense, and was satisfied to have shown that the first mover does not move as a material being moves?

The answer is that the mental activity or *operatio* of God is an unvarying activity, a perpetual fullness of actuality, which, as it neither waxes nor wanes nor undergoes any sort of transmutation, cannot properly be spoken of as either changing or temporal. This is a doctrine to which we shall have later to return, as it is an important feature of the thought of Aquinas.[2]

lectus subiicitur scientiae, et transmutatur de ignorantia ad scientiam, secundum quod est in potentia ad species intelligibiles" (*Sum. Theol.* I.a. q. 75: a. 5. ad 2^m).   [1] Cf. also *Sum. Theol.* I.a. q. 105: a. 3. c. and a. 4. c.   [2] Cf. *Sum. Theol.* I.a. q. 9.

The existence of the second proof complicates the situation which confronts us. Difficult as it is to find any valid reason for discriminating between the first and third arguments, it is even more difficult to distinguish the second argument from the other two. It is based upon the actual existence of causal connections in nature. "We find in sensible things," says St. Thomas, "an order of efficient causes." [1] But does not this statement merely frame in different words the very propositions which constitute the point of departure of the argument from motion? For did we not see reason to identify motion and change? And was it not shown that nothing moves or changes except as the result of a prior movement or change? And is not this exactly what we mean when we speak of causal connection? Even if we grant that we were in error in identifying motion and change, and concede that the former term is to be restricted to physical change only, the problem is in no way simplified. For it is beyond question that quantitative and qualitative changes are included in the Aristotelian and Thomist conception of motion no less explicitly than movement in space. Our concession, therefore, will have accomplished nothing beyond excluding mental operations from our consideration. In so doing we may, indeed, plead that Aquinas himself laid special stress upon the argument from motion because he considered this approach the "more manifest way" (*manifestior via*), inasmuch as physical changes are directly observed by the senses. But this plea will not avail us, for, as we have just noticed, Aquinas has stated that the order of efficient causes is likewise discovered in "sensible things." Consequently, as regards the point of departure, it is difficult to distinguish the second argument from the first. Garrigou-Lagrange is forced to confess: "Les deux principes qui permettent de s'élever de ce fait à une cause première sont à peu près les mêmes que ceux qui conduisent au premier moteur : 1° 'Tout ce qui est causé est causé par un autre, rien ne peut être causé de soi, car pour causer il faut être.' 2° 'On ne peut remonter à l'infini dans la série des causes essentiellement et actuellement subordonnées.' " [2]

[1] "Invenimus enim in istis sensibilibus esse ordinem causarum efficientium" (*Sum. Theol.* I.a. q. 2: a. 3. c.).
[2] *Dieu, son existence et sa nature*, pp. 267–268.

In this connection Professor Gilson has written: "It is well to notice the close relation between the second Thomistic proof of the existence of God and the first; in both cases, the necessity of a first cause rests on the impossibility of an infinite regress in an ordered series of causes and effects. Nowhere is one more strongly tempted to admit the thesis, recently put forward, that there are not five proofs but one single proof of the existence of God divided into five parts. But if by this is meant that the five demonstrations of St. Thomas condition each other—and one critic has gone so far as to assert that the proof from the first Mover is merely the preparation of the proof—this contention is inacceptable. Each proof is self-contained and self-sufficient, and this is eminently true of the proof from the first Mover: *prima et manifestior via.* Yet it is true to say that the five proofs of St. Thomas have the same structure, and even that they mutually complete each other; for, though each of them is sufficient to establish that God exists, yet each starts from a different order of effects and consequently throws light on a different aspect of divine causality. Whereas the first proof shows us God as the cause of cosmic movement and of all movements dependent on it, the second presents him as the cause of the very existence of things. We have found that God is a moving Cause; now we know that he is the efficient Cause. In a system of knowledge which in respect of the Divine essence subordinates the determination of the *quid est* to that of the *an est* the multiplicity of convergent proofs could not be a matter of indifference." [1]

Our quarrel with this passage is based, not upon the objection that it is illegitimate to apply the principles of causality or of sufficient reason to different orders of effects, but upon the contention that, so far as the first three proofs are concerned, there is only one order of effects. If motion and change be identical, the series of movers and things moved is likewise identical with the chain of cause and effect, and this in turn is one with the realm of contingency which forms the basis of the third argument.

The objection may, of course, be raised that, inasmuch as it is founded upon the observed facts of generation and corrup-

[1] *The Philosophy of St. Thomas Aquinas,* pp. 61–62, Bullough's translation.

tion, and since generation and corruption are concepts which, in the strict sense, are applicable only to substances,[1] the third argument is in no wise concerned with the processes of accidental change. Accordingly it may be urged that this proof is reared upon a narrower base than that upon which the first and second proofs are built.

The reply, however, could be made that although the concepts of generation and corruption, strictly speaking, apply only to substances, nevertheless the same terms are used in a wider sense with respect to accidents also.[2] But even were the usage otherwise, it is obvious that the accidents of a substance are at least as contingent as the substance in which they inhere. And it is upon the fact that there is contingent being in the universe that the third argument is founded. So it would seem that the basis of this proof is the same as that of the second.

We must note, nevertheless, that there is a special reason why St. Thomas should wish to lay emphasis upon the generation and corruption of substances. Were there only accidental changes in the universe it might be contended that in existing substances there was present an adequate ground and a sufficient explanation of these changes, and therefore that there was no need to pass beyond the material world in quest of some more ultimate principle. The fact that substances come into being and pass away drives us on beyond Nature to what Professor Taylor has called "Supernature." At the same time we must also remark that these considerations were not touched on by St. Thomas in his presentation of this proof. He did not assert that the necessary being is supernatural or immaterial. Nor, as we shall see, did he attempt to infer the spiritual nature of God directly from the fact of his existence, but arrived at it indirectly by a chain of arguments.

Have we found, then, in the emphasis upon substantial generation and decay a feature peculiar to the third argument? Many contemporary writers upon scholastic philosophy would contend that we had not, for the reason that they find that this feature characterizes the second argument also. Thus, in the

[1] Cf. *Phys.* lib. V. cap. i. lect. 2, 6 and 7.
[2] Cf. also *De Verit.* q. 21 : a. 5. c.; *Sum. Theol.* I.a.–II.ae. q. 110: a. 2. ad 3ᵐ.

passage just quoted, Professor Gilson asserts that, "whereas the first proof shows us God as the cause of cosmic movement, and of all movements dependent on it, the second presents him as the cause of the very existence of things." In a similar strain Garrigou-Lagrange observes: "Cette preuve prend pour point de départ, non plus le *devenir*, mais *l'être* qui est au terme du devenir et demeure après lui"; and again: "Il ne s'agit plus ici des mouvements ou changements qui se produisent dans le monde, mais des causes efficientes dont dépendent des êtres permanents, comme les plantes, les animaux, les hommes. En d'autres termes, cette preuve ne part pas précisément du mouvement ou de *devenir*, mais de *l'être* qui est le terme du devenir; et elle nous conduit à admettre l'existence d'une première cause efficiente, nécessaire non seulement à la production de toutes choses, mais à leur con-servation dans l'existence." [1]

The second argument then, according to these writers, is concerned not with becoming but with being. The ground for this assertion lies in the distinction drawn by Aquinas between the *causa secundum fieri* and the *causa secundum esse.* "Every effect depends upon its cause, according as it is its cause. But it is to be remarked that there is an agent which is the cause of its effect only as regards its becoming, and not directly as regards its being, as indeed happens in the case both of artificial and of natural things. So the builder of a house is the cause of the house as regards its becoming, but not directly as regards its being. For it is manifest that the being of a house depends upon its form; the form, moreover, is composition and order, and itself depends upon the natural virtue of certain things. So the cook cooks food by using a certain natural virtue, that of fire; and so the builder builds a house by using cement, stones, and wood which are sus-ceptible to and conservative of such composition and order. Hence, the being of the house depends upon the natures of these things, as its becoming depends upon the action of its builder. And the same is true in the case of natural objects, since, if a certain agent is not the cause of a form as such, it will not be the cause *per se* of being which depends upon that

[1] *Dieu, son existence et sa nature*, pp. 266 and 766–767. Cf. also G. H. Joyce, S.J., in *Principles of Natural Theology*, p. 60.

form, but it will be the cause of the effect as regards its becoming alone."[1]

The contention of the writers just quoted is that the second argument is founded upon the concept of causation *secundum esse*. Is this contention sound? At first sight it may well seem that the reverse is the case. Nature appears to present us with countless instances of causes *secundum fieri*, and Joyce himself has argued forcefully for the metaphysical significance thereof. "The sensationalist," he writes, "appeals to his chosen illustration of the two billiard balls. What we see here, he says, is succession, and succession alone: the impact of one ball is *followed* by the motion of the other. And he claims that, so far as experience is concerned, our knowledge is limited to this: that the notion of causation is a gratuitous addition of our own." In reply Joyce urges: "When I watch a potter mould the yielding clay with his hand, do I not see the clay actually *receive its determination* from his fingers? Here surely there is much more than succession. Indeed, succession does not enter into the case, for no interval of time separates the pressure of the fingers from the shape newly taken by the clay. No one, we believe, will maintain that when we affirm that we see the hand communicate its shape to the clay, we are introducing a new notion in no way gathered from experience. I could not, if I would, leave this notion out."[2]

Very well then, why should we not make the most of this

---

[1] "Omnis enim effectus dependet a sua causa, secundum quod est causa eius. Sed considerandum est quod aliquod agens est causa sui effectus secundum fieri tantum, et non directe secundum esse eius. Quod quidem convenit et in artificialibus, et in rebus naturalibus. Aedificator enim est causa domus quantum ad eius fieri, non autem directe quantum ad esse eius. Manifestum est enim quod esse domus consequitur formam eius: forma autem domus est compositio et ordo, quae quidem forma consequitur naturalem virtutem quarundam rerum. Sicut enim coquus coquit cibum adhibendo aliquam virtutem naturalem activam, scilicet ignis; ita aedificator facit domum adhibendo caementum, lapides et ligna, quae sunt susceptiva et conservativa talis compositiones et ordinis. Unde esse domus dependet ex naturis harum rerum, sicut fieri domus dependet ex actione aedificatoris.—Et simile ratione est considerandum in rebus naturalibus. Quia si aliquod agens non est causa formae inquantum huiusmodi, non erit per se causa esse quod consequitur ad talem formam, sed erit causa effectus secundum fieri tantum" (*Sum. Theol.* I.a. q. 104: a. 1. c.).

[2] *Principles of Natural Theology*, pp. 28–29.

concept? To perceive concrete instances of it we have but to turn to the processes of Nature. Friction kindles fire; water wears away the stone. But all these causes are causes only of becoming, not of being. Joyce, however, points to certain instances of the sort in question. There are, he informs us, "certain effects which require the continued action of the same thing which first produced them. In this case we have a cause which is at one and the same time a cause *in fieri* and *in esse*. Thus not only does a candle produce light in a room in the first instance, but its continued presence is necessary if the illumination is to continue. If it is removed, the light forthwith ceases. Again, a liquid receives its shape from the vessel in which it is contained; but were the pressure of the containing sides withdrawn, it would not retain its form for an instant. Similarly, a certain measure of heat was needed that the ice cap, which once covered Northern Europe, should melt and the soil become capable of supporting vegetation. But the same cause must remain in operation if the effect is to continue. If ever the temperature of these regions should sink to its former level, Europe would again become ice-bound. In all these cases we have causes *in fieri et in esse*."[1]

Convincing though these instances appear to be, it must be remembered that Aquinas has himself laid it down that "this is the difference between a divine agent and a natural agent, that the natural agent is the cause only of motion, while the divine agent is the cause of being."[2] In other words, it would seem that St. Thomas did not conceive that the processes of Nature ever reveal to us the actual and absolute impartation of existence by one finite substance to another. The agencies which we see at work in the external world are secondary causes, acting by virtue of their dependence upon the ultimate and primal cause. This primal cause is not perceived by us, otherwise the fact that it existed would be self-evident. And the fact that God exists is not self-evident, but is arrived at by inference.

[1] *Principles of Natural Theology*, p. 59.
[2] "Haec est differentia inter agens divinum et agens naturale, quod agens naturale est tantum causa motus, et agens divinum est causa esse" (1 *Dist.* 37. q. 1: a. 1. sol.; cf. *Con. Gen.* lib. III. cap. 65; also *De Potentia*, q. 5: a. 1. c.).

To these statements Garrigou-Lagrange and Joyce would doubtless agree. But they would urge that we do perceive secondary causes which nevertheless, so far as they are causes at all, are causes *secundum esse*, and that consequently, since an infinite regress in the series of such causes has been shown to be impossible, we are compelled to posit an ultimate cause *secundum esse* upon which they all depend. Furthermore, in support of their position they could invoke the words of Aquinas himself. "The action of a corporeal agent," we read, "does not extend beyond the limits of motion, and therefore it is the instrument of the primal agent in the educing of forms from the potentiality of matter, which is accomplished through motion; but they are not its agents in the conservation of these things, except in so far as, owing to a certain motion, dispositions are retained in matter which render it susceptible to a particular form; so, indeed, through the motion of the heavenly bodies inferior bodies are kept in being."[1]

Again in the *Summa Theologica* we read: "It is clear that, in the case of two things of the same species, one cannot be the cause of the other's form as such, for then it would also be the cause of its own form, inasmuch as each form is of the same character; but it is possible for it to be the cause of that other form in so far as it is in matter—which is to say that it may cause *this* matter to acquire *this* form. Such a cause is a cause of becoming, as when man generates man and fire fire. And so when a natural agent is disposed to receive the impression of a form in the same mode in which the form exists in the agent, then the becoming of the effect depends upon the agent, but not the being of it. But sometimes an effect is not disposed to receive the impression of an agent in the same mode in which it exists in the agent, as appears in the case of all agents which do not cause an effect of the same species as themselves. Thus heavenly bodies are the cause of the generation of inferior bodies unlike them in species. Such an agent can be

---

[1] "Actio corporalis agentis non se extendit ultra motum, et ideo est instrumentum primi agentis in eductione formarum de potentia in actum, quae est per motum; non autem in conservatione earum, nisi quatenus ex aliqua motu dispositiones in materia retinentur, quibus materia fit propria formae: sic enim per motum corporum caelestium inferiora conservantur in esse" (*De Pot.* q. 5: a. 1. ad 7^{m}).

the cause of form as such, and not merely the cause of the form being received by *this* matter; and so it is the cause, not only of becoming, but also of being."[1]

It is beyond doubt, then, that Aquinas did hold that in the case of the heavenly bodies we have an actual instance of a *causa secundum esse in rerum natura*. And as a single instance suffices to settle the question we need carry our investigation no further.[2] Nor does the fact that the astronomy and physics of his time are obsolete to-day have any bearing upon the matter. It must be admitted that Garrigou-Lagrange and Joyce are right in their contention that Aquinas did recognize the existence in Nature of causality *secundum esse*. But does this fact alone give to the second argument a character peculiarly its own? It would seem that it does not. For it must be remembered that any cause *secundum esse* which is to be found in Nature is, after all, a secondary cause. The primal impartation of being comes from God alone. And the causal activity of God is not directly apprehended by us. We infer it. How do we infer it? We do so by employing the principle of sufficient reason. In this we are certainly acting in accordance with Aquinas's teaching; but we are equally justified if we apply the same principle to the order of causes *secundum fieri*. We have already seen reason to identify this order with the series of things which move and are moved upon which the

[1] "Manifestum est autem quod, si aliqua duo sunt eiusdem speciei, unum non potest esse per se causa formae alterius, inquantum est talis forma: quia sic esset causa formae propriae, cum sit eadem ratio utriusque. Sed potest esse causa huiusmodi formae secundum quod est in materia, idest quod haec materia acquirat hanc formam. Et hoc est esse causa secundum fieri; sicut cum homo generat hominem, et ignis ignem. Et ideo quando-cumque naturalis effectus est natus impressionem agentis recipere secundum eamdem rationem secundum quam est in agente, tunc fieri effectus dependet ab agente, non autem esse ipsius.—Sed aliquando effectus non est natus recipere impressionem agentis secundum quam eandem rationem secundum quam est in agente: sicut patet in omnibus agentibus quae non agunt simile secundum speciem; sicut caelestia corpora sunt causa generationis inferiorum corporum dissimilium secundum speciem. Et tale agens potest esse causa formae secundum rationem talis formae, et non solum secundum quod acquiritur in hac materia: et ideo est causa non solum fiendi, sed essendi" (I.a. q. 104: a. 1. c.).

[2] Cf., however, *Principles of Natural Theology*, p. 58, where it is stated that the substance of an iron horseshoe is the *causa in esse* of its shape, and that the materials composing a house are the *causa in esse* of its permanence.

first argument is founded, to which the principle of sufficient reason gave the breath of life. Once again we may point out that it is not the impossibility of an infinite regress in time, but in ontological priority which compels us to posit an ultimate source of all change and becoming. If the argument from motion be valid, the argument from the order of efficient causes *secundum fieri* is valid also, and it is valid because it is the same argument. Consequently Joyce's contention that the argument from efficient causes *secundum fieri* is invalid because it involves us in an infinite temporal regress appears to be unfounded.[1] On the other hand, we must grant that to admit its validity is to identify it with the argument from motion.

It might, of course, be maintained that the argument from motion is founded upon the occurrence of *accidental* changes in substances physical and spiritual, whereas the notion of efficient cause applies also to cases of substantial transformation in generation and corruption. Such, however, is not the view of Garrigou-Lagrange and Joyce. "Le point de départ," writes the former in regard to the first proof, "est l'existence du mouvement ou de la mutation, sans préciser mutation substantielle ou accidentelle, mouvement spirituel ou sensible, mouvement local, qualitatif, ou d'accroissement,"[2] and once more, "*Il est certain expérimentalement qu'il y a du mouvement dans le monde*; et non seulement du mouvement local, mais aussi des mutations substantielles, des mouvements qualitatifs selon l'intensité croissante ou décroissante d'une qualité, et même des mouvements spirituels, ceux de notre intelligence et de notre volonté."[3] And Joyce, in a similar strain, remarks: "By motion (κίνησις) is signified the process by which a potency is realized. It may be defined as the energetic and therefore incomplete actualization of a potency belonging to some form of being. The end towards which the process tends may be a new quality: or an increased quantity: or, again, a specific nature as is the case in the development of a seed or an embryo."[4] It appears, then, that the attempt to distinguish the first proof from the second in this way would be unsatis-

---

[1] Cf. *Principles of Natural Theology*, pp. 72–75.
[2] *Dieu, son existence et sa nature*, p. 241.
[3] *Dieu, son existence et sa nature*, p. 765.
[4] *Principles of Natural Theology*, p. 86.

factory to these writers. Moreover, the distinction is a purely arbitrary one, for which reason it is not likely to be satisfactory to anyone else.

Let us then take the other alternative, as we have been exhorted to do, and assume the second argument to deal only with causes *secundum esse*. Is its individuality thereby preserved? The answer is, No. For how does the cause of being, the ultimate *causa secundum esse*, differ from the necessary and permanent being which the third argument requires us to admit as the sufficient reason for the contingent and the transitory? Clearly it differs in no wise. It is one and the same entity. And how does the impartation of being differ from the process of generation to which the second argument refers, or the withdrawal of that being differ from the process of corruption? Again, they are unmistakably the same. The second argument, viewed from this angle, has transformed itself into the third argument.

Evidently, then, we must confess that the second argument has no genuine individuality of its own. For how is one argument to be distinguished from another except by difference of principle and method, or diversity of starting-point? But we have not found the second argument to possess either.

Yet we may ask ourselves one more question. Have we at last discovered a real difference between the first and the third arguments? It will be remembered that at any earlier point in our examination of them we suggested that the first argument might properly be regarded as concerned with change *per se*, accidental as well as substantial, while the third argument might be considered to deal only with substantial change, with the process of generation and corruption. It will also be remembered that we saw reason to reject the suggestion. Our subsequent investigations have given us no reason to revise our opinion. The difference between the two proofs is one of presentation and language, not of reasoning or of method. The third argument is based upon the contrast between necessary and contingent being, and the implied relation between them. The accidents of contingent substances are themselves contingent, and so fall within the same province. The principles upon which the argument is based are those of sufficient reason and of the ontological priority of the actual to the potential. These also are the concepts employed in the first proof. Neither in point of departure nor in method, then, do these proofs differ.

We have now examined the first three proofs of the existence of God, and we have found that at the bottom they form but one. This is not a popular view, but it is the one which the facts seem to support. Which of the three formulations of it, we then inquire, expresses most clearly the fundamental idea? The answer is, the third. For in it we have no suggestion of extraneous considerations, of motion or of temporal succession. M. Sertillanges has well said: "The third proof is built upon permanent being, and therefore can be regarded, so far at least as its foundation is concerned, as the centre of the others."[1]

The fourth argument has become the battle-ground of rival interpretations. The critics who see in it another application of the causal principle are assailed by other critics who vigorously deny that this is the case.[2] The difficulty which confronts the latter is to show how, if the causal interpretation be incorrect, this proof is to be distinguished from the ontological argument of St. Anselm. A detailed discussion of this question is to be found in an article by Professor Charles Lemaitre, S.J., of Namur, entitled, *La preuve de l'existence de Dieu par les degrés des êtres.*[3]

The solution which he offers is along the lines suggested by Descartes. We are empirically aware, he urges, of varying degrees of goodness and truth, even as Aquinas has stated. This initial reference to experience is designed to save us from the predicament in which St. Anselm became involved when, having begun with a pure concept, he endeavoured to bridge the gap between it and the realm of existence. Our feet, on the contrary, are firmly planted at the outset upon facts which we actually experience. When, however, we come to reflect upon that experience and to ask ourselves how it is

---

[1] "La troisième preuve s'appuie sur l'être constitué, et par là elle peut être regardée, quant à son fondement tout au moins, comme le centre des autres" (*S. Thomas d'Aquin*, tome I, pp. 152–153).

[2] For a moderate statement of the conflicting views see Gilson's *The Philosophy of St. Thomas Aquinas*, pp. 66–72.

[3] *Nouvelle Revue Théologique*, tome 54me, Nos. 5 and 6.

that we can make judgments in regard to degrees of being, of goodness, and of truth, it becomes evident to us that these judgments have reference to a *maxime ens*, to absolute being, absolute goodness, absolute truth, and that without this reference they would have no meaning. "Thus each time that an affirmation falls upon a given reality, it posits this reality as a degree of being, a measure of being, *of* Being, that is to say as evoking an *ultra* which is not given."[1] Since this is the case, it follows that absolute being, goodness, and truth must actually exist. "If at the heart of every judgment directly provoked by experience there is a reference which is the condition of the validity of that judgment, it is impossible that the term of this reference should be an incoherent chimera. As the principle of intelligibility, this reference cannot itself lack intelligibility, as would be the case if the term did not possess objectivity. To affirm a thing as a degree or measure of that which has no objectivity would be to nullify that affirmation."[2]

Ingenious as this argument may be, it is difficult to regard it as identical with that of St. Thomas. In the first place, as we have had occasion to observe, the first three proofs and the fifth proof depend upon the principles of causality. It would seem unlikely, therefore, that Aquinas would insert into their very midst a proof of an entirely different nature, and so disturb the orderly sequence of his reasoning and mar the symmetry of its presentation. Too much stress, doubtless, should not be placed upon such a minor consideration, but it is none the less permissible to point out that this procedure would be the reverse of what might be expected. Professor Lemaitre, indeed, replies[3] that we have no right to interpret

[1] "Ainsi chaque fois que l'affirmation tombe sur une réalité donnée, elle pose celle-ci comme degré d'être, mesure d'être, *de* l'être, c'est-à-dire comme évoquant un *ultra* qui n'est pas donné" (*Nouvelle Revue Théologique*, tome 54me, No. 6, pp. 445–446).

[2] "Si au cœur de tout jugement directement provoqué par une expérience se trouve une référence qui est condition de la valeur de connaissance de ce jugement, il est impossible que le terme de cette référence soit une incohérente chimère. Principe d'intelligibilité, cette référence ne peut manquer elle-même d'intelligibilité: ce qui serait, si l'idée du terme n'avait pas d'objectivité. Affirmer une chose comme degré ou mesure de ce qui n'a aucune objectivité, c'est un néant de l'affirmation" (*Nouvelle Revue Théologique*, tome 54me, No. 6, p. 447).

[3] *Nouvelle Revue Théologique*, tome 54me, No. 5, p. 335.

the fourth argument in the light of the principle of causality, inasmuch as that principle is not explicitly appealed to in the text. But the same objection might be raised against Professor Lemaitre's right to advance his own interpretation. No critic endeavours to add anything of his own to St. Thomas's actual meaning. But that meaning has been disputed, and it can scarcely be supposed that St. Thomas intentionally left it obscure. We have every right, therefore, to inquire as to what his actual statements assume or imply. Now Aquinas himself has explicitly referred us, for the source of his proof, to the second book of the *Metaphysics*,[1] where it is distinctly affirmed that all derivative beings and derivative truths depend upon the eternal principles of being and of truth as their *causes*.[2] How then can it be contended that the notion of causality has been illegitimately introduced into the interpretation of this argument? Moreover, we have but to turn to Aquinas's commentary upon the passage just quoted to see that he himself fully accepted and endorsed the teaching of Aristotle.

"He (Aristotle) concludes that the principles of those things which always exist—such as a heavenly body—of necessity are the most true, and this for two reasons. In the first place they are not sometimes true and sometimes not true, and in this respect they surpass in truth generated and corruptible things which sometimes exist and sometimes do not exist. In the second place nothing is their cause, whereas they themselves are the causes of the existence of other things. And in this respect they surpass in truth and in being the heavenly bodies which, although they are incorruptible, yet have a cause not only of their motion, as some have believed, but also of their existence, as the Philosopher here expressly says. And this is necessary, inasmuch as it is necessary that all those things which are composite and which participate in some essence should be referred for their causes to essences which exist *per se*. Now all corporeal things are actual entities, since they participate in some forms; whence it is necessary that there be a separate substance which is essentially form and

---

[1] Cap. i.

[2] "Διὸ τὰς τῶν ἀεὶ ὄντων ἀρχὰς ἀναγκαῖον ἀεὶ εἶναι ἀληθεστάτας (οὐ γάρ ποτε ἀληθεῖς, οὐδ᾽ ἐκείναις αἴτιόν τί ἐστι τοῦ εἶναι, ἀλλ᾽ ἐκεῖναι τοῖς ἄλλοις) ὥσθ᾽ ἕκαστον ὡς ἔχει τοῦ εἶναι, οὕτω καὶ τῆς ἀληθείας."

which is the principle of corporeal substance. If, therefore, to this deduction we add the consideration that the first philosophy deals with first causes, it follows that by its very nature it deals first with those things which are in the highest degree true. Accordingly, it is itself in the highest degree the knowledge of truth."[1]

The same conception is developed more fully in the *De Potentia*. After giving a brief historical sketch of the manner in which the Greek philosophers, beginning with the conception of matter as the cause of all things, gradually approached the idea of universal being, Aquinas concludes: "The later philosophers, indeed, such as Plato and Aristotle and their successors, arrived at the consideration of universal being itself; and, accordingly, they posited a universal cause of things, by which all things come into being, as was made clear by St. Augustine. With this opinion the Catholic faith is in agreement, and this may be demonstrated along three lines of reasoning, the first of which is as follows. If some one quality be possessed in common by many things, it must needs be produced in them by some one cause: for that which is common to each thing cannot be the product of that thing, since each thing according as it exists in itself is distinguished from any other, and a diversity of causes produces diverse effects. Consequently, inasmuch as there is a mode of being common to all these things which in themselves are distinct from one another, it

[1] "Concludit quod principia eorum, quae sunt semper, scilicet corporum coelestium, necesse est esse verisima. Et hoc duplici ratione. Primo quidem, quia non sunt 'quandoque vera et quandoque non,' et per hoc transcendunt in veritate generabilia et corruptibilia, quae quandoque sunt et quandoque non sunt. Secundo, quia nihil est eis causa, sed ipsa sunt causa essendi aliis. Et per hoc transcendunt in veritate et entitate corpora coelestia: quae etsi sint incorruptibilia, tamen habent causam non solum quantum ad suum moveri, ut quidam opinati sunt, sed etiam quantum ad suum esse, ut hic Philosophus expresse dicit. Et hoc est necessarium: quia necesse est ut omnia composita et participantia, reducantur in ea, quae sunt per essentiam, sicut in causas. Omnia autem corporalia sunt entia in actu, inquantum participant aliquas formas. Unde necesse est substantiam separatam, quae est forma per suam essentiam, corporalis substantiae principium esse. Si ergo huic deductioni adiungamus quod philosophia prima considerat primas causas, sequetur ut prius habitum est quod ipsa considerat ea, quae sunt maxime vera. Unde ipsa est maxime scientia veritatis" (*Metaph.* lib. II. lect. 2).

must be attributed not to the things themselves but to some other single cause. And this seems to have been the reasoning of Plato, who wished to posit before all multiplicity a certain unity, not only in numbers, but also in the natures of things. The second reason is that, since it is found that the same quality is participated in by many things and in diverse modes, of necessity it is ascribed to those things in which it is found less perfectly because of that thing in which it is found more perfectly. For those things which are said to be positively 'more' or 'less' are so graded by their nearness to or distance from that one; for did each of these entities occupy its own grade of itself, there would be no reason why the quality in which they all participate should be found more perfectly in one than another; whereas we see that fire, which is in the highest degree hot, is the principle of heat in all hot things. Accordingly, we posit one being, which is a being most perfect and most true: which is proved from this, that there is a mover wholly immobile and most perfect, as was proved by the philosophers. It is necessary, therefore, that all less perfect things receive their being from it. And this is the proof of the Philosopher, in II *Metaph*. text. comm. iv. The third reason is this. That which exists through something other than itself can be referred for its cause to that which exists of itself. Consequently, if there were one colour which existed of itself it must needs be the cause of all colours, which would then possess colour by participation. And this is equivalent to positing some being which is its own existence: which is proved from this consideration that there must be some primal being which is pure actuality, in which there is no composition. Hence it is necessary that from that one being all things should receive their existence inasmuch as they are not their own existence, but have existence by participation. This is the reasoning of Avicenna, lib. VIII. *Metaph*. cap. viii et lib. IX. cap. iv. So, therefore, it is demonstrated by reason and held by faith that all things are from God."[1]

---

[1] "Posteriores vero philosophi, ut Plato, Aristoteles et eorum sequaces, pervenerunt ad considerationem ipsius esse universalis; et ideo ipsi soli possuerunt aliquam universalem causam rerum, a qua omnia alia in esse prodirent, ut patet per Augustinum. Cui quidem sententiae etiam catholica fides consentit. Et hoc triplici ratione demonstrari potest: quarum prima

Notice the constant appeals in this passage to the principle of causality. It will be observed that the second of the three arguments here presented very closely resembles the fourth argument for the existence of God as stated in the *Summa Theologica*. Opponents of the causal interpretation of the latter argument have urged that the concluding reference to fire as the cause of heat in all hot things is in no sense part of the proof proper, but, on the contrary, in the nature of an illustration introduced almost as an after-thought.[1]

But it is of the very essence of an illustration that between itself and its subject there should be a certain similarity, and it is just this similarity and nothing else which gives it point, est haec. Oportet enim, si aliquid unum communiter in pluribus invenitur, quod ab aliqua una causa in illis causetur; non enim potest esse quod illud commune utrique ex seipso conveniat, cum utrumque, secundum quod ipsum est, ab altero distinguatur, et diversitas causarum diversos effectus producit. Cum ergo esse inveniatur omnibus rebus commune, quae secundum illud quod sunt, ad invicem distinctae sunt, oportet quod de necessitate eis non ex seipsis, sed ab aliqua una causa esse attribuatur. Et ista videtur ratio Platonis, qui voluit, quod ante omnem multitudinem esset aliqua unitas, non solum in numeris, sed etiam in rerum naturis. Secunda ratio est, quia, cum aliquid invenitur a pluribus diversimode participatum, oportet quod ab eo in quo perfectissime invenitur, attribuatur omnibus illis in quibus imperfectius invenitur. Nam ea quae positive secundum magis et minus dicuntur, hoc habent ex accessu remotiori vel propinquiori ad aliquid unum; si enim unicuique eorum ex seipso illud conveniret, non esset ratio cur perfectius in uno quam in alio inveniretur; sicut videmus quod ignis, qui est in fine caliditatis, est caloris principium in omnibus calidis. Est autem ponere unum ens, quod est perfectissimum et verissimum ens: quod ex hoc probatur, quia est aliquid movens omnino immobile et perfectissimum, ut a philosophis est probatum. Oportet ergo quod omnia alia minus perfecta ab ipso esse recipiant. Et haec est probatio Philosophi, in II. *Metaph.*, text. com iv. Tertia ratio est, quia illud quod est per alterum, reducitur sicut in causam ad illud quod est per se. Unde is esset unus calor per se existens, oporteret ipsum esse causam omnium calidorum, quae per modum participationis calorem habent. Est autem ponere aliquod ens quod est ipsum suum esse: quod ex hoc probatur, quia oportet esse aliquod primum ens quod sit actus purus, in quo nulla sit compositio. Unde oportet quod ab uno illo ente omnia alia sint, quaecumque non sunt suum esse, sed habent esse per modum participationis. Haec est ratio Avicennae, lib. VIII. *Metaph.* cap. vii, et lib. IX. cap. iv. Sic ergo ratione demonstratur et fide tenetur quod omnia sunt a Deo" (q. 3: a. 5. c.).

[1] Cf. Lemaitre, *Nouvelle Revue Théologique*, tome 54me, No. 5, p. 335, and No. 6, pp. 436–444; also Gilson, *The Philosophy of St. Thomas Aquinas*, p. 70.

which makes it in fact an illustration. It seems strange that an instance of causal connection should be introduced to illustrate the nature of a non-causal argument. Moreover the same illustration is used a third time in the *Summa Theologica*, and here its significance is clear beyond a doubt.[1]

To clinch our contention let us turn to Aquinas's earlier work, his *Commentary on Peter Lombard's Sentences*. There, under the heading *Utrum sint plura prima principia*, we find practically the same argument stated as follows: "The nature of being is found in all things, in some more nobly, in others less so; yet the natures of these things are not identical with the being which they have, otherwise their being could be known from the very conception of their quiddities, which is false, since the quiddity of anything can be known without it being known whether the thing exists. It is necessary, therefore, that they should have their being from something else the nature of which is identical with its being, otherwise we should have to proceed to infinity. This entity gives being to all things, and cannot itself be other than one, since the nature of being must be conceived similarly in all things according to analogy; for unity of the caused requires unity in that which is cause *per se*, and this is the way of Avicenna, VIII Metaphysics."[2]

---

[1] "It is necessary, therefore, that all things which are diversified according to a diverse participation in being, so that they are more perfect or less perfect, should be caused by one primal being which is most perfect. Whence Plato said that it is necessary to posit unity before multiplicity; and Aristotle says in 11 Metaphys. that that which is in the highest degree being and in the highest degree true is the cause of all being and of all truth, as that which is in the highest degree hot is the cause of all heat." ("Necesse est igitur omnia quae diversificantur secundum diversam participationem essendi, ut sint perfectius vel minus perfecte, causari ab uno primo ente, quod perfectissime est.—Unde et Plato dixit quod necesse est ante omnem multitudinem ponere unitatem. Et Aristoteles dicit in 11 Metaphys., quod id quod est maxime ens et maxime verum, est causa omnis entis et omis veri: sicut id quod maxime calidum est, est causa omnis calidi") (I.a. q. 44: a. 1. c.).

[2] "Invenitur enim in omnibus rebus natura entitatis, in quibusdam magis nobilis, et in quibusdam minus; ita tamen quod ipsarum rerum naturae non sunt hoc ipsum esse quod habent: alias esse esset de intellectu cuiuslibet quidditatis, quod falsum est, cum quidditas cuiuslibet rei possit intelligi etiam non intelligendo de ea an sit. Ergo oportet quod ab aliquo esse habeant, et oportet devenire ad aliquid cuius natura sit ipsum suum esse; alias in infinitum procederetur, et hoc est quod dat esse omnibus,

The causal nature of this argument can scarcely be contested. But not less obvious is its identity with the proof which we have been considering. Moreover, if we accept this apparently unescapable conclusion, Aquinas's illustration from contemporary physics becomes at once significant. Fire, he tells us, is the cause of heat in all hot things. This is but a particular instance of his general principle that what is the maximum in any genus is the cause of all other members of that genus. The varying degrees of heat approaching ever nearer and nearer to the intensity of fire are evidently introduced to illustrate how the varying degrees of being, of unity, of truth, and of goodness depend upon and are caused by the absolute Being which is at once absolute unity and truth and goodness.

To understand St. Thomas's argument we must realize that for him being was not a genus under which the different orders of existence could be ranked after the manner of species. The concept of being was not univocal but analogical. As M. Sertillanges has written: "What is univocal is, in effect, that which is participated in by many entities according to one identical *concept: secundum eamdem rationem.* What is *equivocal* is that which is participated in according to *concepts* entirely diverse, the word alone being common to all. The *analogical* is intermediate and expresses a notion really common, creating true relations between the terms which it connects, yet without involving that they participate in it in the same manner. The unity of being is of this kind."[1]

What is true of being is true of the other "transcendentals," as they are called, among which are included unity, truth, and goodness. The unity of a spiritual being is other than the unity of a material being. It is also unity of a higher order.

nec potest esse nisi unum, cum natura entitatis sit unius rationis in omnibus secundum analogiam; unitas enim causati requirit unitatem in causa per se; et haec est via Avicennae, VIII Metaphysicorum" (2 *Dist.* I. q. I : a. I. sol.).

[1] "Ce qui est univoque, en effet, c'est ce qui est participé par plusieurs selon une *raison* identique : *secundum eamdem rationem.* Ce qui est *équivoque,* c'est ce qui est participé selon des raisons entièrement diverses, le mot seul restant commun. *L'analogue* est intermédiaire et se dit d'une notion réellement commune, créant des rapports vrais entre les termes qu'elle relie, sans que d'ailleurs ils la participent de la même manière. L'unité de l'être est de ce dernier genre" (*S. Thomas d'Aquin,* tome I. pp. 27–28).

The concept is applicable to both entities but applicable only analogously. Similarly the notion of goodness can be shown to admit of degrees. But at first sight it might well appear that truth does not admit of more or less. Aquinas, however, maintained the contrary no less earnestly than Mr. Bradley has done in our own day. "The same is the disposition of things in being and in truth; whence those things which possess being in a greater degree are more true; wherefore in demonstrations the first principles are more to be believed than the conclusions."[1]

It is also to be observed that in the illustration drawn from contemporary physics the degrees of more and less are strictly limited by the concept of the genus. There may be varying degrees of heat, but there is only one kind of heat. The doctrine of analogy does not enter here. But there are many kinds of being, of unity, of goodness, and of truth. The transcendentals are not limited after the manner of a genus. Moreover, the concept of a transcendental does not imply imperfection. There is nothing contradictory, or so at least Aquinas would assert, in the conception of infinite being, infinite goodness, etc.

Such are the presuppositions of the fourth argument. Like its fellows, it depends upon the principle of sufficient reason. It affirms that an entity which *participates* in being must depend upon some other entity which does not participate in being but which *is* being, that an entity which *has* unity and goodness and truth is not self-explanatory but refers us to that which *is* unity, and goodness and truth. In the ultimate being, existence and essence are identical, as was affirmed in the passage which we have quoted from the *Commentary on Peter Lombard's Sentences*.[2] Consequently, such a being is its own *raison d'être*, and in it is found the sufficient reason for the being of all finite entities.

Unlike the first three arguments, the fourth argument is not based upon characteristics which can be predicated univocally of all existents. We have seen that the first three are in reality

---

[1] "Eadem est dispositio rerum in esse et in veritate; unde quae sunt magis entia, sunt magis vera; et propter hoc in scientiis demonstravis magis creduntur principia quam conclusiones" (*Quaestiones Disputatae, De Caritate*, q. 1: a. 9. ad 1 m; cf. Garrigou-Lagrange, *Dieu, son existence et sa nature*, p. 281).   [2] 2 *Dist.* 1. q. 1: a. 1. sol.

one, and that this one proof is based upon the contingent character of all finite beings. The fourth argument, on the other hand, takes as its point of departure the doctrine of degrees of reality—to use our modern and convenient term. Consequently it is genuinely a distinct proof in itself; for, although employing the same causal principle as the other proofs, it does so with reference to a unique class of facts upon which its predecessors do not touch.

It might, indeed, be contended that it is a perilous step to argue from degrees of goodness to a supremely good Being, on the ground that in a similar manner one may reason from degrees of evil to an absolutely evil being. Such an objection, even if valid, could scarcely be said to invalidate the argument, although it would have very embarrassing consequences for Aquinas. To admit the existence of an absolutely evil being is not equivalent to denying the existence of an absolutely good being. An ultimate incompatibility there may be, but it is not self-evident. Nevertheless, such an admission would ruin the whole system of St. Thomas's philosophy, and would also involve him in the dreaded heresy of the Manichaeans. It is, however, an admission which he would never have dreamed of making. For him evil was in its very nature negative. It was a lack, a deficiency, not a positive element *per se*. The existence of an absolutely evil being would involve a contradiction, for existence is itself a good. Accordingly the causal series leads us only upward.

The fifth argument is often thought to be purely inductive, and if this be the case it can, of course, yield us only probability. Furthermore, there is the additional disadvantage that, just as it is possible to argue from the instances of apparent design for a benevolent purpose to a benevolent designer, so also one may argue from the instances of apparent design for a malevolent purpose to a malevolent designer. Nor can such an argument be dismissed on the ground that it would lead to the assertion of the existence of an absolutely evil being, for it is not necessary that a malevolent designer should be wholly evil in order that he should be more evil than good.

It has been maintained, however, by Garrigou-Lagrange[1] that the fifth argument is not based upon induction, but that

---

[1] *Dieu, son existence et sa nature*, pp. 185–192, 314–338 and 769–771.

it is, on the contrary, deductive, and that consequently its conclusion is absolutely valid. He contends, in the first place, that chance is not something ultimate. It does not manifest the fundamental principle of the universe. It is, by its very nature, derivative, it implies necessity and can exist only within the realm of necessity. "The fortuitous effect is an *accidental* effect and happens as if the action that produced it had been determined so as to produce it. One breaks open a tomb —it is an effect which has been willed—and one finds accidentally a treasure. But precisely because this is something *accidental*, chance could not have been the cause of the *natural* order of each agent in relation to its proper effect. It cannot be pretended that all the effects in Nature are accidental, *for the accidental necessarily presupposes the essential*; one finds a treasure in breaking open a tomb, but it is with intention that one breaks the tomb, and it was previously with intention that the treasure was hidden in the earth. Chance is only the encounter between two acts which themselves are not accidental, but intentional."[1]

The regular and determinate order of the nature which the accidental presupposes is not, however, something which has its *raison d'être* in itself. The laws of nature are not necessary in the sense in which the propositions of logic and mathematics are necessary. They are not transparently self-evident. On the contrary, it is perfectly possible to conceive that nature might have been ordered otherwise. Consequently these laws require a cause.

Garrigou-Lagrange's next step is to affirm that the order of nature must be the product of an intelligent cause, in which alone its sufficient reason can be found. "Un moyen ne peut

---

[1] "L'effet fortuit est un effet *accidentel* qui arrive comme si l'action qui le produit avait été ordonnée à le produire. On creuse une tombe c'est là l'effet voulu, et l'on trouve accidentellement un trésor. Mais précisément parce qu'il est chose *accidentelle*, le hasard ne peut être cause de l'ordre *naturel* de chaque agent à son effet propre. On ne peut prétendre que tous les effets produits dans la nature sont accidentels, car *l'accident suppose nécessairement l'essentiel*; on trouve un trésor en creusant une tombe, mais c'est avec intention que l'on creuse la tombe, et auparavant c'est avec intention que ce trésor a été caché dans la terre. Le hasard n'est que la rencontre de deux actions qui, elles, ne sont pas accidentelles, mais inten-tionnelles" (*Dieu, son existence et sa nature*, p. 321).

en effet être ordonné à une fin que par une intelligence, car seule une intelligence peut saisir ce rapport, cette raison *d'être* (*objectum intellectus est ens*), et ramener le moyen et la fin à l'unité d'une même conception."[1]

Furthermore, the end in relation to which the means are determined is itself a future event. Such determination implies prevision, and can be the work of intelligence alone, for naught but intelligence is able to grasp the reasons of things.[2]

It is this second step of Garrigou-Lagrange's which is most likely to awaken dissent in the minds of his readers. That the order which we find in Nature is not the outcome of chance would seem to be a necessary assumption unless we are willing to posit a primal chaos, but the proposition that the presence of system and order involves the activity of a mind which is the source of that system and order is one which will not only be accepted by many but will also be denied by many. If there be a universe at all, the entities which compose it must possess certain characteristics, otherwise they would not be distinguishable one from another, nor would being differ in any respect from non-being. Accordingly these different and variously characterized entities must stand to one another in various relations, and there must also be relations which hold between quality and quality. So much seems implied in the very conception of an existent universe, and are not these implications sufficient to give us an ordered world without invoking the assistance of a supra-mundane intelligence?

This suggestion is one which must be subjected to a close scrutiny before it can be accepted. One has but to turn to Dr. McTaggart's *Nature of Existence* or Professor Lossky's *World as an Organic Whole* to see that there are philosophers who are ready both to defend and to attack it. The question must, however, be raised and answered. We have no right to proceed upon assumptions in such a matter. The whole teleological argument falls to the ground unless we can reply to it in the negative.

---

[1] "A means can be ordered to an end only by an intelligence, for only an intelligence is able to seize this *rapport*, this sufficient reason (the object of the intellect is being) and to include means and end in the unity of a single conception" (*Dieu, son existence et sa nature*, p. 190).

[2] Cf. *Dieu, son existence et sa nature*, pp. 334–335.

Moreover, the same problem which confronted us when we were regarding the teleological argument from the standpoint of those who hold it to be inductive, will arise once more in connection with the present theory. For, once again, we may ask why, on the supposition that an intelligence is required to explain the order in nature, must we also suppose that it is a good intelligence? In reply it might be urged that an evil intelligence could never be the cause of order, that evil is inherently chaotic, and consequently can enjoy no more than a parasitic existence within the ordered system of the universe. "The parts of the universe," wrote Aquinas, "stand in orderly relations to one another according as one acts upon another, or is the end and exemplar of another. Moreover, as has been said, this cannot be the case as regards evil, unless by reason of its being joined to some good. Hence evil does not pertain to the perfection of the universe, nor is it included in the order of the universe, unless accidentally, that is by reason of being joined to some good."[1] And again we read, "Evil has not a cause *per se*, but only *per accidens*."[2]

The opinion has been very widely held among philosophers that the various arguments for the existence of God have been for ever shattered by the critique of Kant. It is contended, however, by Neoscholastic writers that this opinion is a mere prejudice which has no warrant in actual fact, and that a candid examination of the Thomist proofs shows that they are as cogent to-day as they were deemed to be before Kant put pen to paper. The point is one of far too great importance to be passed by without examination. Accordingly we shall devote the concluding paragraphs of this chapter to the consideration of it.

At the outset, however, it is to be observed that it is a matter of the greatest importance whether or not we approach the problem from the point of view of Kant himself, sharing his

[1] "Partes universi habent ordinem ad invicem, secundum quod una agit in alteram, et est finis alterius et exemplar. Haec autem, ut dictum est, non posunt convenire malo, nisi ratione boni adiuncti. Unde malum neque ad perfectionem universi pertinet, neque sub ordine universi concluditur, nisi per accidens, idest ratione boni adiuncti" (*Sum. Theol.* I.a. q. 48: a. 1. ad 5^m).

[2] "Malum non habet causam per se, sed per accidens tantum" (*Sum. Theol.* I.a. q. 49: a. 1. ad 4^m).

epistemological presuppositions. If we regard the categories, particularly those of substance and causality, as forms imposed by the mind upon the raw material of experience in the effort to reduce it to order, and as having no counterparts in the world of unknown and unknowable things in themselves, it is scarcely possible that we should avoid arriving at the same conclusions as those stated in the *Critique*. If, on the contrary, we set out from a more realistic position, it is possible that we may reach a very different goal.

Needless to say, in our present inquiry we must leave on one side all discussion of the fundamental tenets of Kant's philosophy, and confine ourselves to noticing the objections which he raised to individual arguments. Unfortunately for our purpose the proofs which Kant regarded as worthy of refutation were only three in number—the ontological, the cosmological, and the physico-theological. The first of these Aquinas has already rejected. The cosmological proof is that termed by Leibniz the *argumentum a contingentia mundi*, and is identical with the third proof of St. Thomas. The physico-theological argument is none other than the teleological, and is, therefore, identical with the fifth. The first, second, and fourth of St. Thomas's arguments are not represented at all. We have already reached the conclusion that the first and second arguments are, in principle, identical with the third. If this conclusion be justified we need not lament the fact that they were not referred to. Only the fourth argument has really escaped all mention.

What the Thomist must consider, however, to be a genuine misfortune is the fact that Kant criticized these arguments, not as they were framed by Aquinas himself, but as they were formulated by later writers. Nevertheless, inasmuch as his criticisms have been believed by many to be fatal to every formulation of these proofs, we must endeavour to determine whether they do in fact apply to them as they were stated by St. Thomas.

We shall begin with the cosmological argument, that is the argument from the possible and the necessary. This proof, which reveals in its clearest form the application of the principle of sufficient reason, is the very soul of the Thomist system. Kant's objection is that, while pretending to take as its point of departure actual experience, it does as a matter of fact presuppose the ontological argument and is consequently invalid. Is this true? Let us ask again, what is the fallacy of the ontological argument? The answer is that the ontological argument is invalid because, beginning in the world of abstract concepts, it passes by an illegitimate transition to the realm of existence. The argument of Aquinas, on the other hand, begins with existence. Now the proposition, Something exists, is not known *a priori*. The contrary proposition, Nothing exists, is not self-contradictory. But a contradiction does arise the moment anyone affirms this proposition, for then the affirmation exists. More than one philosopher has made this his point of departure, Descartes, for instance, and Dr. McTaggart, and—if McTaggart rightly interprets him—Hegel. But Aquinas's path is not the same as that of any of these, though not without some resemblances to that of Descartes. He does not begin simply with the assertion, Something exists, but with the affirmation of contingent existence, with the assertion, Something exists through another. His contention is that this proposition implies a second proposition, Something exists of itself. Here we have arrived at a necessary being which he calls God. In all this there is no assumption that the ontological argument is valid.

But here the voice of Kant makes itself heard. We can go no further, he tells us. We have no right to equate this necessary being with the *ens realissimum*, and to do so is to presuppose the validity of the ontological argument. But the terms "necessary being" and "*ens realissimum*" are not unambiguous, and it is important to realize just what they are intended to signify.

The principle of sufficient reason asserts that whatever exists has a sufficient reason for its existence. This reason may be either in itself or in another being. In the latter case, the first being is dependent for its existence upon a second; in other words, it is a possible, or as we should say a contingent, being. In the former case we have a being which does not depend for its existence upon any other, and which is therefore a necessary being.

The phrase *ens realissimum*, "most real being," implies the recognition of degrees of reality. The fourth argument, as we know, is founded upon this concept, and from the existence of degrees of being and reality has inferred the existence of a supreme cause which is also supreme being, *maxime ens*. But by the phrase *ens realissimum* Kant evidently meant the God of the ontological argument whose existence was logically included in the very concept of his essence. Now, had Aquinas committed the error of simply equating *necessary being* in the sense we just defined, with *ens realissimum* in the sense which Kant had in mind, he would have been guilty of the same fault which Kant condemned. But this would have been a very strange mistake on the part of one who had already rejected the ontological argument as sternly as he had, and as a matter of fact Aquinas did nothing of the sort. What he did do was to take the concept of necessary being, and to bring out one by one the characteristics which are logically implied therein, as we shall see in the following chapters. His method, in other words, is simply the ordinary *a priori* method of logical implication. As Professor Gilson has observed, "All the proofs assume simultaneously two things: the use of rational principles transcending sense-experience, and a solid foundation, supplied by the sense-objects themselves on which the principles which are to lead towards God can rest."[1]

It may be urged, nevertheless, that Aquinas did lay himself open to the Kantian criticism after all, inasmuch as he claimed to prove, at a later stage of his argument, that in God essence and existence are identical. Is not this the God of St. Anselm, the *ens realissimum* of Kant? Has he not thereby formulated the fatal equation, and is he not then compelled, as Kant pointed out, to allow to us to convert it and to affirm "Every *ens realissimum* is a necessary being,"[2] and what is this but to fall back upon the ontological argument?

In reply to this objection we may first observe that Aquinas has not simply drawn the equation, *necessary being = ens realissimum*. On the contrary he has reached his conclusion as to the identity of the divine essence and existence by a complicated chain of arguments, each point therein being logically deduced from its predecessors. For our present purpose we may anticipate the detailed examination which will follow later and briefly summarize his argument as follows: A neces-

---

[1] *The Philosophy of St. Thomas Aquinas*, p. 72.
[2] Cf. the *Critique of Pure Reason*, Norman Kemp Smith's translation, p. 510.

sary being must be a changeless being. In a changeless being there can be no potentiality. Where there is no potentiality there can be no composition; a necessary being, therefore, is absolutely simple. Consequently there can be no distinction of essence from existence in such a being, for such a distinction would involve composition, and hence potentiality and change.

Whatever errors may possibly have been incidentally committed in the course of this argument, it is clear that the method employed is, as I have remarked, none other than that of *a priori* deduction generally employed in speculative philosophy. The conclusion to which it leads us does indeed imply that the ontological argument is valid in itself. If essence and existence be identical in God, it follows that a being capable of cognizing the divine essence would, *ipso facto*, perceive this identity. But, as we are already aware, Aquinas has expressly asserted that the ontological argument is valid *per se*, and would be perceived to be valid by such a being. He has rejected it on the ground that it is not valid for us, *quoad nos*, by reason of the fact that we are incapable of cognizing the divine essence, and consequently are incapable of making the *a priori* deduction essential to the validity of the ontological argument. Our position is analogous to that of a man ignorant of geometry who, by the use of ruler, pencil, and paper, has succeeded in measuring the hypotenuse and the other two sides of a right-angled triangle, and also the dimensions of their squares. Such a man would be aware of the truth of the proposition of Pythagoras, and he would also be aware that a mathematician would be able to demonstrate its truth by geometry. But he could not so demonstrate it himself because of his ignorance of Euclid.

Such in substance is the position of Aquinas. We cannot, he asserts, begin with the divine essence and proceed to demonstrate that it exists, because we are ignorant of what the divine essence is. But we can begin with what we perceive to exist, namely, contingent being, and, arguing from thence, we can demonstrate the existence of a necessary being, immutable and simple, and therefore a being in whom essence and existence are one. It does not appear that in so arguing Aquinas has been guilty of the error which Kant denounced. Nor can it be well maintained that in admitting the ontological argument to be valid *per se* he incurred this danger, for the Kantian critique is explicitly concerned with human reason alone.[1]

We turn now to the teleological proof. The objection here advanced is that, even if we admit the validity of the inference from the alleged evidences of design in Nature to an architect of the universe, we are unable to go further. The argument fails us at this point. It yields us no justification for identifying such an architect with the creator of the universe, nor does it enable us to show that this creator possesses absolute power and wisdom. If the teleological be considered in abstraction from all other arguments, Kant's criticism is undoubtedly just. By itself it is inadequate, and can lead us only to a super-human intelligence. But Aquinas did not intend it to be taken by itself, nor, if his other proofs be valid, is there any reason why it should be so taken. Its function is to furnish additional support to the central structure of his argument, or, in other words, to the third proof. Kant's observation that the physico-theological proof is based upon the cosmological is an over-statement. It is based upon the same principle as the cosmo-logical, namely, upon that of sufficient reason, but it involves a special application of that principle to a unique set of facts and furnishes an additional confirmation. Without too great a stretch of fancy we might liken it to a buttress leaning against the base of a tower, the sole function of which is to give increased security to the foundations.

[1] Cf. the *Critique of Pure Reason*, Transcendental Aesthetic, pp. 89–90. For a defence of the principle of sufficient reason and of first principles in general, cf. Garrigou-Lagrange, *Dieu, son existence et sa nature*, Ire Partie, chapitre ii.

PART TWO

NEGATIVE KNOWLEDGE OF GOD

CHAPTER V

THE *VIA REMOTIONIS*

WE have already seen that, on Thomas's theory, we can know only that God is, not what he is. It might, therefore, not unnaturally be supposed by anyone unfamiliar with the general outlines of his thought that, the existence of God being proved, nothing further remained to be investigated with respect to the divine nature. Such, however, is far from being the case. Though Thomas does indeed hold that no positive propositions concerning God can be affirmed *simpliciter*, nevertheless he also teaches that a genuine knowledge of God can be obtained through negation, through the determination of what he is not. This process, technically known as the *Via Negativa*, had already played a prominent part in the history of metaphysical speculation before Thomas's day, and has continued from his time to our own to commend itself to certain minds among philosophers and theologians. In particular it has become the approved and conventional method among thinkers of the Roman Catholic Church, and this popularity it undoubtedly owes very largely to the fact that it secured the approval of Aquinas.

The *Via Negativa* represents a mode of thought congenial to mystics of a certain type in all ages and all lands. Centuries before Thomas was born it had been carried to a high degree of development by the metaphysicians of India. In the West it had appeared in philosophy coincidently with the rise of Neoplatonism; in truth it may be said to have provided the most characteristic expression of that union of speculative daring and mystical devotion which was the very soul of this great movement. Thence, with so much else, it passed into Christian theology. As early as the second century we find Clement of Alexandria stating it with uncompromising thoroughness:

"We may follow the way of purgation with confession, and the way of the higher mysteries by analysis, proceeding through analysis to the primal knowledge. We may begin with those things that are subject to analysis, removing from body its natural characteristics, stripping it of the dimension of depth,

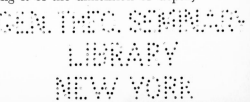

next that of breadth, and after these that of length. What is left is a mere point, that is to say unity having position. If from this we strip off position, unity is now understood in itself. So, having removed all things that belong to corporeal bodies, and then those that are said to belong to incorporeal existents, we may cast ourselves upon the greatness of Christ; and thence we may proceed with holiness into the abyss, and so arrive in some way at the knowledge of the Almighty, discovering not what he is but what he is not. Form and motion, rest, a throne, place, a right hand, and a left hand—all these are not to be thought of with regard to the Father of all nor yet to be written of him."[1]

The classic statement of the *Via Negativa* is to be found, however, in the writings of Pseudo-Dionysius the Areopagite, where it is worked out with considerable thoroughness and detail. The prestige enjoyed by this author because of his supposed relationship to St. Paul rendered his works far more influential than would otherwise have been the case. They were looked upon as embodying the most spiritual type of primitive Christian thought, the wisdom spoken "among them that are perfect" (1 Cor. ii. 6). In this guise they were well known to all medieval theologians and philosophers, and to none better than to Aquinas, one of whose standard authorities they are, and who himself wrote a commentary upon the *Divine Names*.

For Dionysius the *Via Negativa* forms not the first but the second stage in the knowledge of God. The first stage is rather the *Via Affirmativa*, as it has been called, which corresponds to what Aquinas terms knowledge by analogy. We should not be

---

[1] "Λάθοιμεν δ᾿ ἂν τὸν μὲν καθαρτικὸν τρόπον, ὁμολογίᾳ, τὸν δὲ ἐποπτικὸν ἀναλύσει, ἐπὶ τὴν πρώτην νόησιν προχωροῦντες δι᾿ ἀναλύσεως, ἐκ τῶν ὑποκειμένων αὐτῷ τὴν ἀρχὴν ποιούμενοι, ἀφελόντες μὲν τοῦ σώματος τὰς φυσικὰς ποιότητας, περιελόντες δὲ τὴν εἰς τὸ βάθος διάστασιν· εἶτα, τὴν εἰς τὸ πλάτος· καὶ ἐπὶ τούτοις τὴν εἰς τὸ μῆκος. Τὸ γὰρ ὑπολειφθέν ἐστι σημεῖον μονὰς, ὡς εἰπεῖν, θέσιν ἔχουσα· ἧς ἐὰν περιέλωμεν τὴν θέσιν, νοεῖται μονάς. Εἰ τοίνυν, ἀφελόντες πάντα ὅσα πρόσεστι τοῖς σώμασι, καὶ τοῖς λεγομένοις ἀσωμάτοις, ἀπορρίψωμεν ἑαυτοὺς εἰς τὸ μέγεθος τοῦ Χριστοῦ· κἀκεῖθεν εἰς τὸ ἀχανὲς ἁγιότητι προϊοιμεν, τῇ νοήσει τοῦ παντοκράτορος ἀμηγέπη προσάγοιμεν, οὐχ ὅ ἐστιν, ὁ δὲ μὴ ἔστι γνωρίσαντες, σχῆμα δὲ καὶ κίνησιν, ἢ στάσιν, ἢ θρόνον, ἢ τόπον, ἢ δεξιὰ, ἢ ἀριστερὰ, τοῦ τῶν ὅλων Πατρὸς οὐδ᾿ ὅλως ἐννοητέον, καίτοι καὶ ταῦτα γέγραπται" (*Strom.* V. 11. 67–72).

far wrong if we styled it, in modern phraseology, the way of anthropomorphism. It is set forth by Dionysius in his *Divine Names*, the second stage being dealt with in his *Mystical Theology*. Yet the validity of this second mode of knowledge and of the principles that underlie it is assumed from the beginning, for Dionysius warns his readers in the opening paragraphs of the *Divine Names* that neither he nor they may dare to speak or to form any conception of the Super-Essential Godhead beyond what has been revealed in the Scriptures.[1] The finite cannot comprehend the Infinite. To this bald assertion an immediate qualification is, however, subjoined. It is the native weakness of the human intellect, the limitations which constitute its finitude, not an inherent unintelligibility or irrationality in the Godhead itself, that renders comprehension thereof for us impossible. Partial knowledge, according to the measure of the receptive capacity of the knowing subject, is not only possible; it is of the very nature of the Deity so to reveal itself.[2] Therefore the truth of such conceptions as we are able to form is not absolute; on the contrary, it is of necessity relative to the degree of intelligence possessed by him who forms them. Consequently, while none of them will be adequate to its infinite object, one will be more so than another. Accordingly, it will be possible to arrange them in a hierarchy of ascending degrees of adequacy, or, if we like to phrase it so, of truth and reality. It is, indeed, of interest to observe how closely the position here outlined approaches that of our twentieth century philosopher, Mr. Bradley.

It is from this notion of degrees of truth that both the positive and the negative roads take their departure. The former begins with the most abstract and highly intellectualized conceptions which the human mind can form and descends gradually toward the concrete and particular, each successive affirmation, as it becomes more adequate to a lower level of intelligence, becoming also more metaphorical and less adequate to express the fullness of Reality. The negative method proceeds in a wholly contrary manner. Beginning with the crudest and most figurative statements which possess any semblance of truth, it denies that they are able fully to embody or set forth that truth. Ascending to loftier and more

[1] *Div. Nom.* cap. i. [2] *Div. Nom.* cap. i. 2.

spiritual conceptions, it reiterates its denial, though with a lessened vehemence. The element of negation diminishes at each step of our upward progress, but never wholly vanishes. In the highest flights of metaphysical speculation we never comprehend the Deity.

It is evident that all philosophical doctrines as to the nature of God belong to the lower and affirmative stage of knowledge. None of them can contain more than an admixture of truth. One can claim precedence of another only upon the ground of a closer approximation to a standard supreme yet unattainable. And each may serve a useful purpose in so far as it presents to some groping intelligence the highest degree of truth which it is capable of apprehending. Of such a teaching it may be said, even as Bradley remarked in regard to his own position, that it is compatible with a very great deal of what is called Pragmatism. But where the method of metaphorical suggestion and analogy ends, there the *Via Negativa* begins. It insists relentlessly that God is not bound by the limitations of human thought. The confidence of the theologian who is certain that his doctrine embodies absolute truth is foreign to the tolerant atmosphere of mystical philosophy; how foreign let the following quotation from one who was a student both of Dionysius and Aquinas testify. "If I say God is good, it is not true: I am good, God is not good. I say more: I am better than God is, for what is good can be better and what is better can be best. But God is not good, therefore he cannot be better; and since he cannot be better, therefore he cannot be best. These three: good, better, best, are remote from God who is above all. And if, again, I say that God is wise, it is not true: I am wiser than he. Or if I say, God is a being, it is not true: he is a transcendental essence, a super-essential nothing. St. Augustine says, 'The finest thing a man can say of God is that he is silent from consciousness of interior fullness.' Wherefore hold thy peace and prate not about God, for prating of him thou dost lie, committing sin. If thou wouldst be free from sin and perfect, babble not of God. Neither know anything of God, for God is beyond knowing."[1]

The most striking characteristic of this type of thought is the very practical motive that inspires it. It is intended primarily

[1] Eckhart's sermon on *Renewal in the Spirit*, No. 99, Pfeiffer Collection.

as an aid to devotion. The intellect is stimulated up to the point where such stimulation kindles love and urges the soul onward toward its encounter with the Eternal, but so soon as the tendency toward purely speculative and theoretical reflection begins to show itself, such a tendency is sharply repressed. The stimulus is furnished by the *Via Affirmativa* which assures us that, while no affirmation about the Godhead is absolutely true, yet the noblest conceptions that we can form of it and the loftiest predicates that we can apply to it are in error only in so far as they are inadequate to the divine Reality, in so far as they attempt to limit its infinite fullness or fail to image its infinite grandeur; and which by its insistence on the symbolic and metaphorical nature of such affirmations denies their right to fetter the aspirations of the soul.

The value of such a stimulus for religion is obvious. A feeling however exalted, an experience however impressive, comes to its own only when it is appreciated aright. To this end the support of the intellect must be enlisted. On the other hand, it is no less true, from the same standpoint, that speculation, unless coupled with devotion, is worthless. This would hold good even were knowledge of the Deity, knowledge absolute and valid, attainable. Of what avail were it to know the truth about God, yet not to know God? He must be known as a friend is known, by contact and communion.

Here we enter upon the *Via Negativa*. We are now assured that all our previous affirmations are not to be taken as literally true. They are analogies, metaphors, pictures: not scientific statements, the product of an adequate intellectual analysis. In other words the mystical theology of Dionysius and his disciples belongs in the realm of poetry rather than of philosophy; for (as Wordsworth and Tennyson have shown in our own day) poetry at its highest aims at suggesting a loftier truth than it is able to embody, and so to spur the mind to pass beyond the sphere of abstract generalization into that of concrete Reality. The *Via Negativa* continues to stimulate the same spirit of religious aspiration as the preceding affirmative way. Now, however, we are beyond the stage where we need the milk that is given to babes, now we are prepared to face the stark verities of Eternity and to plunge into the homeless waste of the Absolute.

Our present concern is, nevertheless, not with the practical value for religion of such a mode of thought, but rather with its philosophical significance. Is it consistent with itself? In the first place, then, we may note that Dionysius denies existence to the Godhead.[1] But what is meant by this? Certainly Dionysius does not mean to declare himself an atheist. In fact, he expressly denies also that non-existence can be predicated of God.[2] Nor can we imagine him to be indicating the distinction drawn by certain modern philosophers between the subsistence of an essence known only to thought and the existence of a concrete individual. The situation becomes clearer when we realize that for Dionysius being implies a temporal, though not necessarily also a spatial, existence. As Boethius points out, it involves the union of substance and quality. Whatever is must exist as something, as this or that. But the Godhead is neither this nor that. It is neither substance nor qualities. It is above all distinction and differentiation. "Homo non integre ipsum homo est . . . quod enim est, aliis debet quae non sunt homo." "Man is not wholly man in himself . . . for what he is he owes to other realities which are not man." But, "Deus uero ipsum deus est." "God is God in himself," for, "homo alter, alter iustus, deus uero idem ipsum est quod est iustum," "man is one thing and justice is another, but God is the same thing as justice."[3] In other words, the Godhead is so perfectly and fully what it is and all that it is that we cannot speak of its existence as though that were something separable from its essence, as is the case with finite beings. The divine unity is so perfect that the differentiation between substance and quality, between particular and universal, is therein completely transcended. To say that God is just and to say that he exists is to make a single affirmation, for in him justice and existence are one.

This explanation, however, is not sufficient to disarm criticism. To one who objects that such a being is inconceivable to us, and that the idea of it is merely an impossible association of incompatible notions, it may indeed be replied, in the same spirit in which Bradley responds to his critics,[4] that what transcends reason is not necessarily irrational, and thought can, without inconsistency, contemplate the possi-

[1] *Mys. Theol.* cap. v; cf. *Div. Nom.* cap. v: 4.   [2] *Mys. Theol.* cap. v.
[3] *De Trinitate*, cap. iv.   [4] *Appearance and Reality*, ch. xv.

bility of losing itself in something higher. But there is another objection which cannot be met in this manner. If the Godhead be of such a nature that all the categories of human thought are inapplicable to it, if neither existence on the one hand nor non-existence on the other can be predicated of it, must not its reality of necessity be utterly beyond demonstration? For we cannot think of it at all except as this or that. Pure being, as Hegel contended, is practically identical with nothingness. If, then, we are not permitted to apply the categories; if, to use Eckhart's vigorous phraseology, in making any affirmation in regard to it "we lie," we appear to be faced with a hopeless *impasse*. The intellect, forbidden alike either to affirm or to deny, knows not whither to turn. And we may safely conclude that it is to just such a state that Dionysius desires that we should be brought. As his unknown English disciple of the fourteenth century assures us, "Of all other creatures and their works, yea, and of the works of God's self, may a man through grace have fulhead of knowing, and well can he think of them: but of God Himself can no man think. And therefore I would leave all that thing that I can think, and choose to my love that thing that I cannot think. For why; He may well be loved, but not thought. By love may He be gotten and holden; but by thought never."[1]

In fact we may go further and ask whether, were we to carry out the implications of such a position to their logical conclusions, we should not be led to the following paradox, that the very impossibility of establishing by intellectual demonstration the existence of God is itself the strongest proof of that existence; or, to put the same thought in other words, that any proof of the existence of God would be a disproof of the existence of such a deity as Dionysius believes in. For no demonstration, however subtle, can apprise us of the being of a substance totally devoid of attributes, of a subject which possesses no predicates whatever. Any proof, be its nature what it may, must reveal God to us under some category, as Providence, as Cause, as the supreme Good—in a word, as this or that. Consequently, he would not be the nameless divinity of the *Mystical Theology*. Direct experience of the Godhead would appear to be not only independent of but incom-

[1] *The Cloud of Unknowing*, ch. vi.

patible with an intellectual knowledge thereof attained by logical argument.

From such a conclusion Dionysius himself might well have shrunk, for it would totally invalidate the mode of thought which he himself saw fit to pursue in the *Via Affirmativa*, which must now appear a tissue of falsehoods rather than an ascending series of less and less inadequate approximations to absolute truth. It is one thing to insist upon the limitations of all conceptions which the human mind is capable of forming, and another thing to deny that these conceptions embody any truth whatever. Yet to this denial we have been led by following undeviatingly a single line of reflection.

Having now viewed the predicament into which the *Via Negativa* lured its most thorough and systematic advocate among ancient philosophers, we are in a position to consider the same difficulty as we find it in the thought of Aquinas, upon whom indeed it presses with far greater force. The barrier that he seeks to establish between our knowledge of the existence of God, which he believes himself to have demonstrated, and knowledge of the essence of God, which he asserts to exceed the power of the human intellect, appears at first sight to involve him in a hopeless contradiction. For all the arguments in proof of the former which he has himself advanced agree in predicating qualities of God, and only through such predication have they any significance. Each of them leads up to him as Cause; moreover, each, beginning as it does by considering his effects from a unique standpoint, ends by attaching to him some further predication. According to the first God is the end which attracts the universe toward itself and so initiates movement and change; according to the second he is the originator of the temporal series of cause and effect; according to the third he is the permanent and abiding reality which underlies the world of change and becoming, the necessary and self-existent One upon which depends the realm of contingency and generation; according to the fourth he is the source of truth, goodness, and every value; and according to the fifth he is an intelligent and all-directing providence. But if it be illegitimate to attribute any qualities to God, how are these arguments to stand? We seem to be confronted by an absolute contradiction.

Yet Aquinas explicitly asserts that the divine essence is beyond human comprehension.[1] "The divine substance surpasses every form to which our intellect extends, and so we are not able to apprehend it in such a way as to know what it is."

Two ways of escape from this dilemma are considered by Thomas only to be rejected. The first suggestion is that all affirmations in regard to God are really inverted negations intended to signify degrees of *removal (aliquid removendum de Deo)*. Thus the statement that God lives would mean merely that God is not inanimate. This teaching Aquinas finds in the writings of Maimonides.[2] The Jewish philosopher does indeed severely denounce those who say that existence, life, power, knowledge, and will can be predicated of God in the same sense that they are of us, except that it will of course be understood that the existence of God is more stable than ours, his life more lasting, his power greater, his knowledge more perfect, and his will of wider scope. In reply Maimonides affirms that attributes ascribed to God and those predicated of men have nothing in common but their names. Identity of meaning there is none.[3]

The other alternative is to take the position that we are justified in applying qualities to God only to express his relation to created things, not to denote what he is in himself. This theory would reduce us to much the same state of ignorance as that in which we are left by Kant, with this difference, that, according to it, our inability to know what God is springs, not from a subjective element in our knowledge contributed by the understanding itself, but merely from the human intellect's incapacity for cognizing super-sensible realities.

Neither of these doctrines commends itself to Aquinas. In the first place, as he observes,[4] neither of them offers any reason why some names should be more applicable to God than others. God is the cause of bodies just as he is the cause of good things. If, then, the statement that God is good mean no

---

[1] "Divina substantia omnem formam quam intellectus noster attingit, sua immensitate excedit: et sic ipsam apprehendere non possumus cognoscendo quid est" (*Con. Gen.* lib. I. cap. 14).
[2] *Le Guide des Egares,* tr. into French by S. Munk, Première Partie, chs. l–lx.
[3] *Le Guide des Egares,* tr. into French by S. Munk, Première Partie, ch. lvi.
[4] *Sum. Theol.* I.a. q. 13: a. 2. c.

more than that he is the cause of good things, it follows that it is equally legitimate to call God a body, since he is the cause of bodies, and since to assert that he is a body implies he is not merely being in potentiality like *materia prima*.

In the second place, according to either of these theories all predicates would apply to God only in a secondary sense, as, for example, a medicine that makes the body healthy is itself called healthy. But this is not what men mean when they speak of God, for when they say that God is living they do not mean only that he is the cause of our life or that he differs from inanimate bodies.[1]

Names of this sort, Thomas concludes, do really signify the divine substance and are predicated of God substantially.[2] They fail, however, to represent him adequately, because our intellect knows God only from creatures and only in so far as they represent him. This, of course, they can do only in so far as they possess perfections; they cannot, however, represent him as one being can represent another of the same species or genus as itself, but rather as the principle whose effects they are and whose form they are unable to reproduce. So the true meaning of the statement that God is good is this, that whatever good we predicate of creatures pre-exists in God, in some higher mode.

Aquinas has escaped from his dilemma, but at the price of minimizing much of what the *Via Remotionis* at first appeared to involve. We are once more at the standpoint which we occupied when considering the *Via Affirmativa*. Predication is, after all, permissible with respect to God, so long as we do not conceive it to embody ultimate truth. Our affirmations are but approximations thereto, but they are truly approximations. As Dionysius says, God is more truly life or goodness than he is air or stone.[3] Thus the position of Aquinas is as far as possible removed from that of Spinoza, who assures us that if intellect and will are indeed attributes of the divine essence, they cannot be thought to bear more resemblance to intellect and will as

[1] *Sum. Theol.* I.a. q. 13 : a. 2. c.
[2] "Huiusmodi quidem nomina significant substantiam divinam, et praedicantur de Deo substantialiter."
[3] "'Η οὐχὶ μᾶλλον ἐστι ζωὴ καὶ ἀγαθότης ἢ ἀὴρ καὶ λίθος;" (*Mys. Theol.* cap. iii).

existing in men than the constellation called the Dog bears to the dog that barks.[1]

To this topic we shall later return when we come to consider the knowledge of God which Thomas believes that we can obtain by the method of analogy. In the first place, however, we must proceed to examine the knowledge which he professes to gain by the method of negation.

[1] *Ethics*, bk. I. prop. xvii. Schol.

CHAPTER VI

THE NEGATIVE QUALITIES OF GOD

WE shall now proceed to follow Aquinas in his process of determining what God is not. By means of a complicated chain of arguments he has deduced a large number of propositions, each of which his method requires us to understand in a purely negative sense. We have already seen reason to regard such a divorce between the positive and the negative as inadmissible, since every negation implies an antithetical affirmation. A preliminary glance over the various predicates which Aquinas actually does attribute to God as the result of his use of the *Via Remotionis* will hardly incline us to modify our previous contention. Among those predicates we find such qualities, for example, as goodness and perfection which, to modern ears at least, bear a very positive significance. We shall, however, have abundant occasion to emphasize this objection when considering the various steps of the argument in detail.

In the *Summa Theologica*, in the *Contra Gentiles*, and in the *Compendium Theologiae*, we find three separate lines of argument set forth. Each begins by adopting the negative method, and each, after making extensive use of it, enters upon a general discussion of the capacity of the human mind to attain to knowledge of God, particular attention being devoted to the method of analogy with which we shall concern ourselves later. Each, thereafter, takes up once more the consideration of the divine nature and proceeds to ascribe yet more attributes to God. At first sight this appears to indicate that a hard and fast distinction has been drawn between two mutually independent principles, and likewise between their respective applications. The negative way, it would seem, is followed until it ceases to yield further knowledge, and thereupon a different method is resorted to. It might then, naturally enough, be conjectured that, while the results of each process are capable of being harmoniously united with those of the other in a coherent system of knowledge, each method requires, nevertheless, to be applied by itself and in isolation from the other.

As a matter of fact, it must be admitted that Aquinas has provided us with considerable justification for taking precisely this point of view. In the opening sentences of the third question in the first part of the *Summa Theologica* we read:[1] "But since we cannot know what God is but only what he is not, we are not able to consider concerning God in what manner he is, but rather in what manner he is not. First, therefore, we must consider in what manner he is not; secondly, how he is known by us; thirdly, how he is named.

"Moreover, it is possible to show in what manner God is not by removing from him those qualities which cannot fitly be attributed to him, such as composition, motion, and others of this sort. First, therefore, we must inquire concerning his simplicity, through which composition is removed from him. And because whatever corporeal things are simple are also imperfect and are parts of other things, we must inquire, secondly, concerning his perfection; thirdly, concerning his infinity; fourthly, concerning his immutability; and fifthly, concerning his unity."

And in turning to the beginning of the twelfth question which follows the discussion of the divine unity, we find that it opens with the words:[2] "Since in the preceding questions we have considered God as he is in himself, it remains for us to consider him as he is in our knowledge; in other words, consider how he is known by creatures."

On turning to the first book of the *Contra Gentiles* we find that the fourteenth chapter, which sets forth the principle of the *Via Remotionis*, is followed by fourteen other chapters dealing with those attributes of God which are discoverable by means

[1] "Sed quia de Deo scire non possumus quid sit, sed quid non sit, non possumus considerare de Deo quomodo sit, sed potius quomodo non sit. Primo ergo considerandum est quomodo non sit; secundo, quomodo a nobis cognoscatur; tertio, quomodo nominetur.

"Potest autem ostendi de Deo quomodo non sit, removendo ab eo ea quae ei non conveniunt, utpote compositionem, motum, et alia huiusmodi. Primo ergo inquiratur de simplicitate ipsius, per quam removetur ab eo compositio. Et quia simplicia in rebus corporalibus sunt imperfecta et partes, secundo inquiretur de perfectione ipsius; tertio, de infinitate eius; quarto de immutabilitate; quinto, de unitate."

[2] "Quia in superioribus consideravimus qualiter Deus sit secundum seipsum, restat considerandum qualiter sit in cognitione nostra, id est quomodo cognoscatur a creaturis."

of it. Then follow several chapters dealing with man's ability to know God, with the likeness which God bears to creatures, and of the sense in which qualities may be ascribed to him. And these are in turn succeeded by others which are again occupied with the determination of the divine attributes. A similar course is pursued by the *Compendium Theologiae*. Its opening chapters are concerned with the process of negation. The thirteenth, fourteenth, fifteenth, and sixteenth chapters discuss the topic of human knowledge of the divine in much the same spirit as the corresponding sections of the *Contra Gentiles*. And they are in like manner followed by a process of further predication.

It appears then that all three books are so far constructed upon the same general plan. It requires no great subtlety to suspect that this scheme of division was inspired by the arrangement adopted by the Pseudo-Dionysius. The *Via Remotionis* obviously corresponds to the negative way which that author expounded in his *Mystical Theology*, and the method of analogy, as we shall see in due course, stands in a similar relationship to the affirmative way which he elaborated in his *Divine Names*.

None the less, were we to adopt the suggestion that has just been made as to the mutually exclusive spheres of application of the two methods, we should at once be faced with an awkward problem. We have just seen that Aquinas has stated explicitly in the *Summa Theologica* that the *Via Remotionis* involves the consideration of the divine simplicity, and that this in turn involves the consideration of God's perfection, infinity, immutability, and unity. Perfection, infinity, immutability, and unity are, therefore, according to this express statement, qualities determinable by the process of negation. If now we examine in detail the treatment which these qualities receive individually, we shall discover that perfection is distinctly said to involve goodness,[1] and infinity to involve ubiquity and omnipresence.[2] Accordingly, it would appear that all these attributes are deducible by the negative method alone. On consulting the *Contra Gentiles*, we discover, however, that goodness, infinity, and unity are relegated to the second division, which, at first sight, we were inclined to regard as the exclusive province of analogy; while, as for ubiquity and

[1] I.a. q. 4.   [2] I.a. q. 7.

omnipresence, demonstration is given of them only in the sixty-eighth chapter of the third book.

It is evident, therefore, that either Aquinas has been guilty of flagrant inconsistency, or, that the division is of another sort than we have provisionally conjectured. Which of these alternative explanations is the true one? If we accept the first, we are confronted at once with a serious difficulty. Is it possible that a thinker of the profundity of Aquinas could have failed to be aware of so obvious and glaring a contradiction? It is hard, indeed, to suppose that he was. Is the discrepancy the result of a change of view on his part? It is difficult to believe that so honest and thorough a thinker would have changed his view on so vital a topic without laying all the pros and cons of the matter before us. But is the inconsistency, after all, more than apparent? With some plausibility we might argue that it is not. The two methods, we might urge, are distinct but not incompatible. On the contrary, they supplement each other and proceed *pari passu*. The negative is logically the prior of the two and provides the material which is utilized by the second; but since the whole of Aquinas's argument endeavours to show that they gradually blend one into the other, we might assume that the distinction which he has drawn between them is to a certain extent arbitrary and intended to be no more than approximate. Further discussion on this point may be deferred until we deal with Aquinas's theory of analogy.

I shall follow, in the detailed examination of the negative process of determining the divine attributes, the course of argument set forth in the *Contra Gentiles*, which takes as its point of departure the argument from motion which Thomas regarded as the "most manifest of the proofs of God's existence,"[1] availing myself, at the same time, of the *Summa Theologica* and the *Compendium Theologiae* for purposes of comparison and supplementation.[2] We shall, accordingly, consider the claims of the following concepts to be applicable to God.

---

[1] Cf. Gilson's *Philosophy of St. Thomas Aquinas*, p. 78.

[2] In the *Summa Theologica* (I.a. q. 9: a. 1.) three arguments are advanced to prove that God is immutable: (1) God is *actus purus*, and therefore without potentiality, whereas change implies potentiality. (2) God is without composition, whereas that which is the subject of motion remains in

(a) ETERNITY

1. We have seen that the conclusion to which the argument just referred to leads is that of the existence of an unmoved mover, which is called God. Furthermore, it will be recalled that, for Aquinas, movement includes every form of change, all passage from potentiality to actuality and *vice versa*.[1] Since, then, God is without movement, he is also without change, and so without beginning or end. Consequently he is eternal.[2]

2. The same conclusion can be reached from the conception of time, which Aristotle defined as the measure of movement.[3] Since there is no movement in God, God is not in time. In God, therefore, there is no before and after, no passage from non-being into being or from being into non-being, no succession of any sort.[4] Accordingly, God is without beginning or end, possessing at once the entire fullness of being. And this is to be eternal, for eternity is no other than "interminabilis vitae tota simul et perfecta possessio."[5] [6]

part and passes away in part. Thus a substance which is changed from white to black still remains as a substance. (3) God is infinite. But that which is changed acquires that which it did not possess before; and is therefore finite.

In the following article it is argued that God alone is wholly immutable. We are informed that a thing can be mutable either through some power in itself, or through some power external to itself. But all creatures are mutable in the latter sense of the word, since they are produced and conserved in being by God. (This statement is inconsistent with the doctrine which, as we shall find later, was held by St. Thomas, that creation is neither movement nor change and does not involve succession.) Every creature is also mutable in the former sense of the word, since it possesses potentiality with respect either to substantial change, local change, change in regard to its being ordered with respect to some end, and to the application of its powers to divers ends.

[1] "Omne quod incipit esse vel desinet, per motum vel mutationem hoc patitur" (*Con. Gen.* lib. I. cap. 15).

[2] Cf. *Sum. Theol.* q. 10: a. 2. c.; *Com. Theol.* Pars Prima, cap. iv.

[3] *Phys.* lib. IV. cap. xi.

[4] Cf. *Com. Theol.* Pars Prima, c. vii.

[5] Boethius, *Consolatio Philosophiae*, book V. prosa vi.

[6] Cf. the *Compendium Theologiae*, Pars Prima, cap. vii, where two arguments are given to prove the absence of succession in God: (1) Succession is found only in entities which are subjects of motion. But God is immovable. Hence there is no succession in God. (2) In any entity the being of which

3. The eternity of God can also be demonstrated if we take as our starting-point the second argument in proof of the divine existence—that from causality. If at any time God did not exist, and if he thereafter came into being, he must have done so as the result of an already existing cause, for the actual must precede the potential, and that which is not cannot be the cause of its own coming into being. But the argument from causality has already shown that God himself is the First Cause. Hence he cannot have come into being, neither is it possible for him to pass out of being. Therefore he is eternal.

4. On turning to the third proof, we find that no supplementary argumentation is at all necessary, since it itself proceeds to demonstrate God's existence by the attribute of eternity which we are now discussing. God is the necessary being, the ground of all possibility and change, the permanent Reality which underlies all becoming and passing away.

5. Reverting once more to the idea of motion, Aquinas observes that Aristotle had pointed out[1] that if time is everlasting, motion must be everlasting also, and likewise the substance which is the cause of motion. Therefore, since God is the first substance, he must be everlasting. Here we have evidently an *argumentum ad hominem* directed against those who were not prepared to admit the doctrine of creation. For Aquinas himself there is, of course, no question of the eternity of movement or time. But, as we know, he does not believe that the falseness of this theory can be shown by philosophical arguments. Consequently, as in the case of the first proof of the divine existence, he boldly meets an opponent on his own ground. The moving world, if it be without beginning or end, requires nevertheless a cause which is itself without beginning or end, to the reality of which that world is an everlasting witness. For the Christian, the case is even simpler. If movement had a beginning, it must have had a cause which was itself without beginning—which was, in a word, eternal.

This last argument must be pronounced insufficient. As

is not a *totum simul*, something must pass away and something else come into being. But this involves transition, which is impossible in God, because he is immovable. The second proof is quite clearly nothing but a re-statement of the first, since the point made in each is precisely the same.

[1] *Phys.* lib. VIII. cap. i. lect. 2.

perpetual change would be impossible unless grounded in the changeless and permanent, so perpetual motion would indeed be impossible without the persistence of elements which were able to move and be moved, without the persistence of a motive power which did not cease to act. So much everyone but the most ardent Bergsonian would admit. But for Aquinas's purpose this is not sufficient. The motive power present in the universe, he would insist, is not to be thought of as an agent which picks up an object here and sets it down there. The God of St. Thomas is far removed from the deity of primitive monotheism in whom one volition is followed by another, in whom thought succeeds thought and act succeeds act. He is utterly beyond and above the temporal series in transcendent aloofness. Consequently, it must be shown that he is not only the abiding source of all movement and change, but is himself unmoved and changeless. And this is what the argument from the existence of motion to the unmoved mover has already done The proof which we are now considering must, therefore, be pronounced not only insufficient but unnecessary, and its inadequacy can be remedied only by appealing to another argument which has already been given.

The first three arguments—those from motion, causality, and possibility and necessity—are clearly just as valid in the present instance as they were when previously employed to prove the divine existence. The fact is, it is evident that we are not really dealing with another problem at all. As Aquinas has well said, God "is his own eternity."[1] We have discovered that of these three arguments the last is the expression of the central principle of which the other two are but special instances. It is the argument from possibility to necessity that is fundamental in the system of Aquinas.[2]

It is important to notice, however, that Aquinas did not conceive of the necessary or the permanent as that which *does*

[1] *Sum. Theol.* I.a. q. 10: a. 2. c.; cf. 1 *Dist.* 19. q. 2: a. 1.

[2] In the *Commentary on the Sentences* it is pointed out that God alone can be said to possess eternity in its perfection, inasmuch as the divine eternity is underived and is identical with the divine being. It is, indeed, the case that the being of spiritual and immobile creatures is also a *totum simul*, yet since their being and eternity is communicated to them by God, they cannot be said to possess eternity in its perfection (1 *Dist.* 8. q. 2: aa. 1 and 2).

change, which endures through all transmutation, which manifests itself in the transient and finite objects of the world of becoming, but rather as a Reality beyond this world, separate from it, not immanent but transcendent, unaffected by and without participation in the processes of generation and conception. God does not persist through change; God is changeless. And we can appreciate now Aquinas's reason for emphasizing the fact that his argument is from possibility to necessity rather than from the changing to the permanent. Change is rooted immediately in its ground, and, if that ground be God, pantheism in some form or other would result as the natural outcome of our thinking. Possibility and contingency obviously have reference to a cause or agent rather than a ground, and lend themselves more easily than the latter to a theistic argument.

Two serious difficulties at once confront us, however, as the result of this reasoning. The first we need merely notice at present since it did not escape the observation of Aquinas himself, who, as we shall see, made a strenuous attempt to surmount it. We may frame our question as follows: if God be changeless, how can he be capable of life and thought and love and volition? Or, granting that we can, without contradiction, conceive of a changeless life, a changeless thought, a changeless love, and a changeless volition, how can God, who is the cause of the everchanging world, enter into relations with that world, unless he responds to its multitudinous changes by corresponding changes on his part? In fact, does not the very act of creation itself imply a change in the Creator? We shall consider hereafter Aquinas's reply to this fundamental question. It is evident, however, that unless such a reply is successful, the changing and the permanent can no longer be held apart, and we shall be faced with the alternative of denying the reality of change or else of admitting it into the realm of ultimate Reality. The acceptance of this latter alternative would not mean the denial of the reality of permanence, of that which persists through change. But it would mean that the life and thought of God must be conceived as analogous to the life of man, as ever one yet ever manifold.

The second difficulty concerns the reality of the finite world of change and becoming. What is it that changes and becomes,

that is generated and that undergoes decay? In seeking the
ground of this world in a transcendent realm, Aquinas would
seem to have divested it of any ground whatsoever. Had he
been content to dismiss it as appearance, the difficulty would
not have arisen, at least not in this form. Appearances must be
appearances of something, and what we apprehend as a spatial
and temporal world might have been regarded as a series of
inadequate perceptions of a changeless Reality. But if it be a
real world, how are we to conceive of it? As pure flux, or as
absolute change? The very attempt to frame such a conception involves us in self-contradiction. What remains of
change if the element of permanence be banished? In human
experience we know becoming only as an aspect or manifestation of being; we know change only as the expression of
something which abides. For us change is, as Kant put it,
change of the permanent. *How* the two are linked together is
doubtless a problem, but that they *are* linked together seems to
be a matter of everyday knowledge. If, however, the permanent be removed to a transcendent world, we are left with
that anomalous thing—a change of the changing. The realm
of becoming, destitute of continuity, seems to dissolve into a
phantom world. Such is the problem which here confronts us,
and which I shall return to in due course when I come to deal
with Aquinas's doctrine of creation.

Meanwhile it will be worth while to observe that we are
now in a position to appreciate the danger that lurked in the
doctrine of primary matter. It is conceived as a relatively
permanent substance underlying all the changing phenomena
of nature. To it, as to God, no predicates can be applied. The
identification of the two by some daring thinker can scarcely
be looked upon as an extraordinary event in the history of
speculation, and, as a matter of fact, we know that such an
identification was made by David of Dinant. St. Thomas,
moved perhaps by the unfortunate consequences drawn in the
realm of morals from his theory by some of David's disciples,
permitted himself to stigmatize the teachings of that philosopher as *insania*.[1] Without attempting to pronounce upon the
justice of this condemnation, it may be pointed out that the
identification itself may well have appealed to persons of a

[1] *Con. Gen.* lib. I. cap. 17.

monistic temperament, as a plausible way of escape from the difficulties involved in the doctrine of creation.

In regard to Aquinas's own view of the eternity of God, we must remember that it is not the God of religion, the living and conscious being whom the human heart adores, whose eternity has so far been demonstrated. The other aspects of deity remain still to be determined. He is, if we may so express it, a "transcendent ground" of the Universe, the changeless cause of temporal becoming, the motionless sustainer of all motion, the necessary source of the possible and the contingent, the origin of all that is.[1]

---

[1] In the *Compendium Theologiae* a special chapter (Pars Prima, cap. vi) is devoted to proving that God always exists—*quod Deus semper est*—regardless of the fact that it has already been argued in the same work that God is eternal. Such procedure is, indeed, extraordinary. It is inconceivable that Aquinas should have meant to affirm that God exists in time, for such an assertion would have been utterly incompatible with his conception of eternity as a *totum simul*. Yet the only other interpretation which can be put upon his statement is that at any moment of time the proposition, God exists, is true. Upon Aquinas's theory such is, of course, the case; but this is only another way of saying that God is eternal. If his thoughts appear confused at this point, the arguments which he brings forward to make good his assertion are scarcely less so. In the first place, he argues that God must always exist because his existence is necessary. In the second place, he argues that God must always exist because he is immutable. Inasmuch as the necessity of the divine existence has already been deduced from the divine immutability, it would be necessary to contest the validity of the former of these two arguments, were it not for the fact that the necessity of the divine existence has also been demonstrated by the argument from possibility and necessity. In the third place, St. Thomas argues that what does not always exist must be brought into existence by some prior actuality, and that, since nothing is prior to God, God must always exist. And lastly, he contends that that which does not accrue to some entity through an extrinsic cause belongs to it *per se*, and that it is impossible that God should owe his existence to an extrinsic cause, for such a cause would be prior to God. Hence, God's existence pertains to him *per se*. But that which exists *per se* exists of necessity. Obviously, these last two arguments do no more than state the same thought in different words—the thought, namely, that, since God does not owe his existence to any cause external to himself, God must always exist.

(*b*) POTENTIALITY

Aquinas's next step is to show that in God there can be no potentiality.[1] This follows directly from the establishment of God's eternity.

1. Potentiality involves the possibility of non-existence. That which a thing is potentially, it has not yet become. But since God possesses the fullness of existence all at once, he is wholly actual and totally removed from all non-being. Therefore he possesses no potentiality of becoming anything other than he really is.

2. Moreover, although from the point of view of time, potentiality is prior to actuality, yet ultimately (*simpliciter*) actuality is prior to potentiality; because that which is in potentiality cannot bring itself into actuality, but is dependent for such transformation upon some cause which is already actual. But God, who is the first being and the first cause, is dependent upon nothing prior to himself; consequently there can be no potentiality in God.[2]

3. Furthermore, it is inconceivable that that which exists of necessity should exist as a possibility,[3] for that which is necessary has no cause, while the possible has causes. The existence of God is, however, necessary in itself; hence God is devoid of potentiality.

4. Again, everything acts in the degree in which it is already actual. That which is not wholly actual does not act as a whole but by some part of itself. But that which does not act as a whole is not the first agent; it acts merely through participation in another and not by its own essence. Therefore the first agent, God, has no admixture of potentiality but is pure actuality.

5. Yet another argument in support of this contention is to be found in the Aristotelian definition of motion as the act of that which is in potentiality.[4] It is natural for a thing to act in so far as it is actual and to be acted upon in so far as it is in potentiality. But God is immutable and impassible, and hence without potentiality.

---

[1] *Con. Gen.* lib. I. cap. 16.   [2] Cf. *De Pot.* q. 7: a. 1. c.
[3] "Illud quod est per se necesse esse, nullo modo est possibile esse" (*Con. Gen.* lib. I. cap. 16).   [4] *Phys.* lib. III. cap. i. lect. 2.

6. The impossibility of an infinite regress is once more invoked to provide the final argument. We observe in our own experience that the passage from potentiality to actuality does sometimes take place. Now, since that which is not cannot act, the potential, which is not yet, cannot bring itself into actuality. It requires, therefore, a cause. If this cause have in like manner made a similar passage from potentiality, it must also have had a cause in its turn. Since, however, we cannot go on to infinity in a regress of this sort, we are compelled to posit the existence of that which is wholly actual and in no degree potential.

This last argument is evidently merely a more elaborate statement of the second. The passing of the potential into the actual is, of course, the common element in the first three proofs of the existence of God. The question as to whether it has been validly employed has been discussed already, and it is unnecessary to repeat here what has been said elsewhere. This applies also to the third of the arguments just summarized, which is nothing more than the same contention turned the other way round, and stated from the point of view of the eternal and the actual rather than from that of the transient and the potential. What all these arguments alike seek to demonstrate is that the changing implies the permanent, and that this permanent, just because it is permanent, does not change but remains for ever the same. The dualism is identical with that which we have noticed in connection with Aquinas's conception of eternity. Change and permanence seem to fall apart, and a metaphysical chasm suddenly yawns at our feet. A change is not a change of the permanent; it is, apparently, a change of the changing. The same difficulties which faced us before here recur again.

If, however, we are prepared to grant the legitimacy of such a division, we can see that the conclusion which Aquinas has drawn from it is entirely justified. If God be identified with the changeless, it must follow that he is exempt from all potentiality, for the changeless cannot become other than it is. Again, as the first argument emphasizes, the same conclusion is deducible from the conception of God's eternity. That which possesses the whole fullness of its being at once, and which is incapable of passing into non-being, can in no respect be potential; for potentiality implies the possibility of non-

existence, and in whatever degree or in whatever aspect anything is potential, to that degree and in that aspect it is possible
for it not to be.

The fourth argument is more complicated. The potential,
being as such non-existent, cannot act. Accordingly an
existent being, whatever potentialities of further existence it
may possess, is able to act only in so far as it is already existent.
In other words, it does not act by its essence, but by a part of
itself,[1] and by participation in what is other than itself. That
which acts essentially, however, must be itself wholly existent,
that is, wholly actual and in no respect potential.

This argument introduces no new factor into the discussion
except a difficulty. Clearly it rests upon the same contention of
the priority of the actual to the potential, as do the others, and
to this it returns in its conclusion. It is, in fact, an argument in
a circle. If the potential need not depend upon an already
existent actuality, then our hypothetical entity which exists in
part will be able to act on its own initiative, to finish the process for itself, and to bridge the gap completely between
potentiality and actuality, unaided by any primal agent. If,
on the other hand, this priority be granted, then all that the
argument aims at proving is granted already. The introduction
of the concepts of agent and activity serves only to confuse the
issue, for the first cause has heretofore been represented as a
timeless, motionless Reality. How can the changeless act or
the timeless enter into time? To discuss these questions would
be at this stage premature, for we have not yet had opportunity
to consider how Aquinas was prepared to deal with them. But
to introduce them into an argument is also premature, and
can be vindicated only if the justification, when it is given, is
shown to be in no way dependent upon the conclusion which
the present argument is meant to prove.

It remains for us to examine the fifth proof which is based
upon the same principle as the others. The underlying idea
seems to be that since the potential can be transformed into
the actual only if the subject in which it is inherent be acted
upon by another being, and since God cannot be acted upon
by any being, it follows that God has no potentialities. But, we
may ask, does this really follow? A heap of dry straw is in itself

[1] "Non toto se agit, sed aliquo sui" (*Con. Gen.* lib. I. cap. 16).

combustible; but if owing to external conditions—such as being buried by an avalanche in a cavern—no fire can be put to it, it is impossible that a conflagration should take place. This rough illustration will serve to reveal our difficulty. Are impassivity and absence of potentiality quite the same thing? Would action upon God involve change in him? Is the assertion that no finite being possesses the potential ability of acting upon God equivalent to saying that God is free from potentiality in himself?

Aquinas apparently would answer all these questions in the affirmative. He has given us no other proof of the divine impassibility than the proof of the divine eternity—that is God's changelessness. It would seem that he regarded this as sufficient. But the questions that we have asked involve certain others to which as yet no answers have been given. How far do the relations of one being to other beings constitute that being itself? Do changes in one being involve changes in all other beings or in some other beings? How far is the being of God analogous in these respects to that of finite entities, and how far does it possess characteristics peculiarly its own? To these questions we must seek for answers as we continue our investigation.

We have now dealt with the various arguments offered by Aquinas for the absence of all potentiality in God, and we have seen that while the first of these is based upon the theory that God is eternal and therefore changeless, the other five depend upon the priority of the actual to the potential, a proposition that is admirably stated and defended in the sixth. We pass to the consideration of Aquinas's proof of the immateriality of God.

(c) MATERIALITY

1. This follows directly from the preceding argument. "From this, moreover, it appears that God is not matter: because matter, such as it is, is in potentiality."[1] Here the doctrine of primary matter, to which we have had occasion already to refer as a possible source of danger to the theistic realism of

[1] "Apparet etiam ex hoc Deum non esse materiam. Quia materia id quod est, in potentia est" (*Con. Gen.* lib. I. cap. 17; cf. *Sum. Theol.* I.a. q. 3: a. 2. c.).

Aquinas, shows itself to be capable also of lending active assistance as well. The argument is undoubtedly valid if both its premises be granted. If it be granted that God is wholly actual and that matter is mere potentiality, then certainly God cannot be in any sense material. But if we examine the second of these statements a little more closely, a curious difficulty will be seen to arise.

From Aristotle our author had derived the conception of primary matter as the utterly passive recipient of form. Destitute of all qualities and incapable even of existing in isolation, it was nevertheless believed to supply the common element in all physical objects, the *suppositum* or basis of each thing, the principle in which its positive characteristics were able to take root and make up a unified whole. Matter was thought to be actually found only in such conjunction and as receptive of formal determinations. Viewed from this point of view, it was termed secondary matter. Primary matter, since it had no existence of its own, could never be known as a concrete object, and was capable of being thought only by an act of logical abstraction. A mere plastic potentiality of becoming all things through transmutation, it was in itself devoid of all characteristics by which it might be distinguished and defined.

Obviously, such a purely negative entity could have nothing in common with God who is wholly actual. Consequently, Aquinas felt justified in dismissing the contention of David of Dinant, that God and primary matter are identical. David's view was undoubtedly the outcome of a more or less adequate appreciation of the principle afterwards rendered famous by Leibniz under the title of the Identity of Indiscernibles. Were God and primary matter not the same, he insisted, they must differ by certain differences; and it was impossible, therefore, that they should be simple, for they could differ only by possessing diverse qualities and thereby revealing a composite character. Aquinas rejoined that God and primary matter were not different but diverse. Things which are different differ in respect to some quality, but things which are diverse are absolutely other.[1] "A man and a horse differ by differences of rationality and irrationality, which differences, however, do

---

[1] *Con. Gen.* lib. I. cap. 17.

not differ from each other by other differences."[1] Could we point to any differences between God and matter, it would follow that they had something in common. But pure actuality and pure potentiality have nothing in common.

However effective such a reply may have seemed to the contemporaries of Aquinas, it cannot be said to solve the difficulty inherent in his position. It will be recalled that the third proof of the existence of God requires us to conceive of God as the ground of the changing universe, and that, while Aquinas had endeavoured to give a transcendental turn to the argument by laying stress rather upon possibility and contingency and their dependence upon an external cause, and had forbidden us in the name of his *Via Remotionis* to speculate as to what that cause might be in itself, his treatment of the question appeared to be neither consistent nor adequate. Furthermore, we shall find, when we come to treat of his doctrine of analogy, that, in spite of the *Via Remotionis*, Aquinas did believe that, "All perfections which are in things are originally and eminently in God."[2] Similarly, he says[3] that "effects that are less than their causes do not agree with them in name and definition. Yet it is necessary that there be some likeness between them, for it is of the nature of action that an acting thing should produce something like itself, for everything acts according as it is actual."

This last passage clearly shows that its author was not thinking of cause in the sense of temporal antecedent, but in the sense of ground or sufficient reason; and that he held that there must be some community of nature between that which produces and that which is produced. Moreover, as we shall see, Aquinas conceived of God as pure being, as possessing in himself all the fullness of existence in contradistinction to finite entities, the being of which is distinct from their essences and

[1] "Homo enim et equus differunt rationali et irrationali differentiis: quae quidem differentiae non differunt amplius ab invicem aliis differentiis" (*Sum. Theol.* I.a. q. 3: a. 8. ad 3m).

[2] "Omnes perfectiones quae sunt in rebus originalter et eminenter sunt in Deo" (*Com. Theol.* Pars Prima, cap. xx).

[3] "Effectus enim a suis causis deficientes non conveniunt cum eis in nomine et ratione, necesse est tamen aliquam inter ea similitudinem inveniri: de natura enim actionis est ut agens sibi simile agat, cum unumquodque agat secundum quod actu est" (*Con. Gen.* lib. I. cap. 29).

is imparted to them by the first cause. But if God be the ground of the universe, he must be the ground of the material entities in it. And if there be always some likeness between cause and effect, or ground and consequence, then there must be some likeness between God and primary matter. And if God possess in himself fullness of being and if matter be a mode of being, how are we to avoid the conclusion that God must be in some sense material?

Here, once more, we seem to be confronted by a complete contradiction. One way of escape would be to deny the reality of matter; and, if we accept the definition of it as pure potentiality, what could be more plausible? For is not such a conception, as Lotze concluded,[1] itself contradictory? Nothing can sustain anything, or allow anything to attach to or depend on itself, which does not by its own form and powers afford this other points of contact and support. And even if we waive this vital point, how are we to conceive of God as the source and cause of matter if he be, as Aquinas has asserted, wholly diverse from and unlike it? To do so, we must relinquish the theory that there must be a certain community of nature between cause and effect; and that theory is, as we shall find, the core of Aquinas's doctrine of analogy. Could we, however, regard primary matter not as an existing element in concrete things, but as a mere abstraction, a "logical construct," a theoretical terminus assigned by the intellect to the descending series of degrees of being, the contradiction which faces us would perchance disappear.

Tempting as such an effort at harmonization may be, it can be accomplished only by flying in the face of Aquinas's own utterances on the subject.[2] "In all corruption, when the actual has been removed, the potential remains; for a thing is not corrupted into complete non-being just as a thing is not generated out of complete non-being."

The dilemma appears to be insoluble. The difficulty which confronts us is similar to that which we found involved in Aquinas's treatment of change and permanence. It is another

[1] *Metaphysics*, bk. I. secs. 29–30.
[2] "In omni corruptione, remoto actu, manet potentia: non enim corrumpitur aliquid in omnino non ens, sicut nec generatur aliquid ex omnino non ente" (*Con. Gen.* lib. II. cap. 55). For a full exposition of Aquinas's view see *Phys.* lib. I. cap. ix. lect. 15.

instance of that tendency to over-abstraction which is characteristic of Scholastic thought. A hard and fast distinction is drawn which is found to lead to an intellectual *cul de sac* which must in some manner be evaded. In our experience we never encounter pure potentiality or pure being. Every finite entity is in a state of reciprocal interaction with other finite entities, subject both to generation and corruption. It is an inhabitant of the world of becoming, and consequently, as Aquinas has himself told us,[1] "equally related both to being and non-being." Pure potentiality is obviously an abstraction from that world, and, as we have seen reason to think, an illegitimate abstraction. To conceive it, we must conceive of non-being as a subsistent reality. Being in the sense of absolute and complete Existence is, on the other hand, an abstraction at the opposite end of the scale. Every reality we know is not only possessed of positive qualities but subject by this very possession to corresponding limitations. To have those qualities which make it what it is, it must be devoid of all the qualities which would make it what it is not. But Being, or God, is to be conceived as without limitation, as possessing in perfect harmony the fullness of Reality. As such God would transcend our experience as completely as primary matter or as pure potentiality sinks below it.

We have not yet to inquire whether such a conception is consistent with itself or can even be said to have any meaning. We are concerned for the moment only with an aspect of the larger problem. Aquinas has asserted that primary matter—that is, pure potentiality—cannot be conceived of as an element in the nature of God—who is pure being. Certainly it is true that if the intellect has once abstracted pure being and pure potentiality from the world of becoming with which it is acquainted in sense-experience, it cannot conceive them as in any way united or as participating in each other's nature, except by retraversing the road it has taken and returning once more to the actual objective world which it knows empirically. For the process of abstraction is nothing else than the consideration of a thing or characteristic by itself, *in vacuo* as it were, and apart from the rest of reality. If, however, we regard these abstractions as actual existents, there is no way of escape

[1] *Con. Gen.* lib. I. cap. 15.

left to us. In sense-experience, on the contrary, we are aware of actual objects endowed with positive qualities, yet through that very endowment subject to limitations no less real. Why assume that in ultimate Reality both elements are not present? The question leads us back to Aquinas's fundamental conception of God as the perfect and changeless being, separate from and not participating in the world of finite and changing things. The difficulties which met us in connection with the doctrine of the eternity of God pursue us here also.

2. A second argument for the immateriality of God is based upon the conception of God as efficient cause. Matter is not the principle of activity, and therefore efficient and material causes are not identical. "Matter is certainly not the same in species or number as the other causes; because matter as such is being in potentiality, while the agent is certainly being in actuality as such, and either the formal or the final cause is actuality or perfection."[1] Since God is the primal efficient cause of all things, God is therefore immaterial.[2]

This argument adds nothing to the preceding. Since matter had already been defined as pure potentiality, the principle of activity cannot exist within it. But matter, on the scholastic theory, can and does exist in conjunction with form, and, as Aquinas explicitly teaches,[3] formal and efficient causes at times coincide. How, then, if in God, the efficient cause, a formal and active principle be united with matter? There appears to be nothing in the above argument to render such a combination contradictory. To show that it is, we must fall back on the first argument which is based upon the absence of potentiality in God. The argument appears, therefore, to be valueless.

It is interesting, however, to inquire why Aquinas introduced at this point the concept of activity. His thought appears to revert back to the argument from motion. But the two cases are not analogous. If matter be pure potentiality it is, of course, inactive. And if, as a matter of fact, we observe it in conjunc-

---

[1] "Materia vero non est nec idem specie nec idem numero cum aliis causis; quia materia inquantum huiusmodi est ens in potentia, agens vero est ens in actu inquantum huiusmodi, forma vero vel finis est actus vel perfectio" (*Phys.* lib. II. cap. vii. lect. 11).

[2] Cf. *Sum. Theol.* I.a. q. 3: a. 2. c.   [3] Cf. *Sum. Theol.* I.a. q. 3: a. 2. c.

tion with form, and in movement, we are certainly justified in arguing that its motion has been imparted to it from without, and so the source of that motion we may call God. Yet how are we to know that such a source is itself wholly devoid of matter? If God be the ground of the forms of finite things as well as of their matter, it seems natural to infer that God's own nature includes not only form but matter also. To prove that the source of motion is immaterial it would be necessary to fall back upon the argument for the existence of an unmoved mover, to which recourse has already been had in proving the absence of potentiality in God.[1] Consequently this entire argument appears to be useless repetition of what has been said elsewhere.

3. The third argument is founded upon the reasoning of Aristotle in the *Physics*,[2] in which he refutes the theory that there is no purpose in nature and that everything is the product of chance. Such a theory, Aquinas observes, is bound to be held by those who regard matter as the first cause of all things. If, then, we say that God, who is the first cause, is material, this theory must be held by us also. Since, however, Aristotle has shown it to be inadmissible, we cannot hold it. Therefore God, the first cause, is immaterial.

This argument is evidently a special application of the teleological argument for the existence of God. We have already discussed the validity of this proof, and here it remains to consider its cogency when applied to this particular problem. That in nature abundant instances are found in the phenomena of plant and animal life of adaption to ends is a matter of common knowledge. Let us grant for the moment that we are justified in inferring from that, that these are the product of design, and that therefore there must exist a conscious and intelligent designer. What then? Does this prove that such an intelligence is wholly separated from the material universe which it controls? In everyday human experience we are aware of design only as it is found in conscious minds incarnated in material bodies. What if, like the Stoics, we conceive the teleological principle of the universe to be a Logos or world-soul which is united to the physical world in a manner analogous to that in which the mind of a man is united to his

[1] *Con. Gen.* lib. I. cap. 16.   [2] Lib. II. cc. viii and ix.

body? It would appear that such a union would form a single individual much as the union of body and soul form a single human being, and that the former unity could be called God as truly as the latter can be called man. Yet the cause of the teleological phenomena of nature, the source of the design which brought them into being, would be referred to the mind and not the body of God as inevitably as a human design is referred to the mind and not to the body of a man.

Has Aquinas taken such a theory into account? We know that he was acquainted with it,[1] but it cannot be said that he has so far refuted it. The absolute dualism which he has affirmed to exist between the eternal and the temporal realms probably rendered such a view preposterous in his eyes.[2] We have seen reason, however, to regard this dualistic conception as unsatisfactory. The presence of matter and consequently of potentiality in the eternal world was doubtless felt by St. Thomas to imply the possibility of change—for what else can be meant by potentiality?—and so to involve a contradiction. Such a consideration brings us back, however, once more to the first proof of the immateriality of God. Neither the second nor the third arguments can be said to have added anything to it.

4. The fourth argument is stated as follows: "Matter does not become the cause of anything actual except in so far as it is altered or changed. If, therefore, God be immovable, as has been proved, he cannot in any way be the material cause of things."[3] At first sight this proof seems merely to be repeating the same consideration that was urged in the second. Nevertheless, on further scrutiny we see that there is a difference. The second argument proceeded from the utter passivity of matter to the existence of an efficient and immaterial cause. The fourth argument begins with the susceptibility of matter to change, and then urges that, since God is changeless, God cannot be the material cause of finite entities. In other words, it insists that the physical universe is distinct from God, and has a being of its own. It was clearly against pantheism that

---

[1] *Con. Gen.* lib. I. cap. 11.   [2] *Com. Theol.* Pars Prima, cap. viii.
[3] "Materia non fit causa alicuius in actu nisi secundum quod alteratur et mutatur. Si igitur Deus est immobilis, ut probatum est, nullo modo potest esse rerum causa per modum materiae" (*Con. Gen.* lib. I. cap. 17).

this reasoning was directed. And, granting the dualism of which we have just spoken, it is certainly valid. The changeless cannot itself be the changing. The only question is, how are they related to one another? For Aquinas, God is the changeless; the changing world is called into existence by him "non de sua substantia sed de nihilo."[1]

5. The fifth argument is found in the *Summa Theologica*.[2] Everything which is composed of matter and form attains its perfection and goodness through its form; in other words, it possesses them by participation, according as its matter participates in its form. But God does not possess his perfection and goodness by participation but by his essence, for essential good is prior to participated good. Therefore, God is not composed of matter and form.

We may grant that essential good is logically prior to participated good, but is it always temporally prior? This is really the question at issue. Let us admit that material beings that come into and pass out of existence possess such goodness as they have by participation. How do we know even then that matter may not form an integral part of the essence or nature of God? In that case, the matter in God would derive its goodness and perfection from participation in him. But God himself, as a single individual composed of matter and form, would owe his perfection to no being external to himself.[3]

---

[1] *Con. Gen.* lib. I. cap. 17.   [2] I.a. q. 3: a. 2. c.

[3] In the *Commentary on the Sentences* (1 *Dist.* 19. q. 3: a. 1.) St. Thomas maintained that, although there is no matter in God, yet it is permissible to ascribe magnitude to him. He admitted that in respect of its genus —i.e. quantity—magnitude is a "condition of matter" (*conditio materiae*), and that in this sense it cannot be predicated of the Deity; yet he insisted that in respect of its differentia it is subsumed under the concept of completion—for we say that from being little a thing is made great when it attains its complete quantity—and accordingly that magnitude in the sense of completion can be attributed to God. To the objection that magnitude is continuous quantity, and that there can be no continuity in God who is simple and indivisible, Aquinas replied that continuity is, indeed, involved in dimensional magnitude but not in magnitude of *virtus*, a term which can, perhaps, best be translated virtue, and which differs from *potentia* (power) in that it can be attributed to God not only with respect to operation but also in other modes. Virtue is a perfection; and in every mode in which a subject attains to the ultimate it possesses virtue. This can happen in three ways: first, in

(d) COMPOSITION

The next point which we have to consider is the absence of all composition in God.

1. The first proof in support of this proposition, as was also the case with the first proof advanced in support of its predecessor, is based upon the absence of potentiality in God. In every composite thing where many things become one, there must be both actuality and potentiality; for actual things are united only in collections and groups, and such composite things are not one simply (*simpliciter*) but only potentially in respect to the union of their elements. Since these are actually united, they must have had potential capacity for such union (*fuerunt in potentia unibiles*). But there is no potentiality in God; hence there can be no composition in him.[1]

2. The second proof points to the fact that every composite thing is formed out of pre-existing parts. God, however, is the first being (*primum ens*). Hence there can be no composition in God.[2]

3. Furthermore, it follows from the very meaning of composition that every composite thing is potentially dissoluble, although actually in some composite entities there is an element repugnant to dissolution. But whatever is dissoluble is potentially non-existent. God, on the contrary, necessarily exists. Therefore, God is free from composition.[3]

4. All composition requires a compounding cause because things, many in themselves, cannot become one unless united by such a cause. Accordingly, if God be composite he must

respect of operation in which there are grades of perfection; hence, when a subject attains to its complete operation, it has virtue; secondly, in respect of existence, and so an entity may have the virtue of existing always; thirdly, with respect to fullness of perfection of existence, according as a thing attains the ultimate capacity of its nature. In the first sense the divine virtue is a virtue of operative power, in the second its virtue will be its eternity, in the third its magnitude. Thus by virtue of his omnipotence God is the source of all operative powers and operates in them; by virtue of his eternity he establishes and sustains every duration; and by virtue of his magnitude he fills and contains all things.

[1] *Con. Gen.* lib. I. cap. 18. Cf. *Sum. Theol.* I.a. q. 3: a. 7. c.; *De Pot.* q. 7: a. 1. c.; *Com. Theol.* Pars Prima, cap. viii.

[2] *Con. Gen.* loc. cit. Cf. *Sum. Theol.* I.a. q. 3: a. 7. c. and *Com. Theol.* Pars Prima, cap. viii; *De Pot.* q. 7: a. 1. c.   [3] *Con. Gen.* loc. cit.

have a cause, since nothing is the cause of itself. And this compounding cause will of course be an efficient cause. Therefore God will have an efficient cause, and will not himself be the first cause, which is impossible.[1]

5. In any genus the more excellent a thing is the simpler it is, as fire in the genus hot has in itself no mixture of cold. Accordingly, the most excellent of all beings is also the most simple. And this most excellent of all beings we call God, inasmuch as God is the first cause, for certainly the cause is more excellent than the effect. Therefore, there is no composition in God.[2]

6. Of every composite being it is true that its goodness and perfection belong to the whole and not to this or that part; for the parts are imperfect in respect to the whole, as the parts of a man are not a man, nor have the parts of the number six the perfection of that number, nor do the parts of a line possess the perfection of that measure which inheres in the whole line. So, if God be composite, his perfection and goodness will belong to him as a whole and not to any one of his parts. But then the goodness which belongs to God will not be purely in him, and he will not be the first and highest good.[3]

The underlying idea in this argument is expressed more fully and clearly in a corresponding passage in the *Summa Theologica*. "Every composite thing is something which does not pertain to any of its parts. This is indeed evident in wholes of dissimilar parts; for no part of a man is a man, nor is any part of a foot a foot. In wholes of similar parts, though it is possible that what is predicated of the whole can be predicated also of a part, as a part of air is air and a part of water is water, yet something can also be predicated of the whole which does not pertain to any of its parts, as if the entire quantity of water be two cubits, the part is not two cubits. So, therefore, in every composite thing there is something which is not it itself. It is possible, however, that it should be said of that which has a form that it has something which is not it itself, as in white there is something which does not pertain to the conception of whiteness; yet in the form itself there is nothing

[1] *Con. Gen.* loc. cit. Cf. *Sum. Theol.* I.a. q. 3: a. 7. c.; *De Pot.* q. 7: a. 1.; *Com. Theol.* Pars Prima, cap. viii.
[2] *Con. Gen.* loc. cit. Cf. *Com. Theol.* Pars Prima, cap. viii; *De Pot.* q. 7: a. 1. c,   [3] *Con. Gen.* loc. cit. *Sum. Theol.* I.a. q. 3: a. 7. c.

other than itself. Whence, since God is Form itself, or rather Being itself, in no way is it possible for him to be composite."[1] Here the fundamental idea evidently is that God is pure and simple Being, identical with his own essence and his own existence, without differentiation into subject and predicates or substance and attributes.

7. Before multiplicity there must always be found unity. But in every composite thing there is multiplicity. Therefore God, who is before all things, must be devoid of composition.[2]

The point to be noticed first in connection with these seven arguments is that the first, second, third, and fourth require us to understand by composition the amalgamation of pre-existing entities in a new entity. For if by composition were meant merely complexity or multiplicity, then not one of these four arguments would achieve the desired end. On the other hand, if this meaning be accepted, it is difficult to see how the sixth argument differs from the second or the fourth. When we turn to the corresponding section in the *Summa Theologica*,[3] we find that it follows upon articles which deal not only with the question of whether God is composed of matter or form, but with these problems also; whether God is a body, whether God is the same as his essence or nature, whether in God essence and existence are the same, whether God is in any genus and whether there are any accidents in God. All these questions have been answered in the negative. Consequently, before discussing whether God is wholly simple, practically all theories involving plurality or multiplicity in God have been dismissed; the word *compositio* can, therefore, be used in the widest sense conceivable, without affecting the validity of the

---

[1] "Omne compositum est aliquid quod non convenit alicui suarum partium. Et quidem in totis dissimilium partium, manifestum est: nulla enim partium hominis est homo, neque aliqua partium pedis est pes. In totis vero similium partium, licet aliquid quod dicitur de toto, dicatur de parte, sicut pars aeris est aer, et aquae aqua; aliquid tamen dicitur de toto, quod non convenit alicui partium: non enim si tota aqua est bicubita, et pars eius. Sic igitur in omni composito est aliquid quod non est ipsum. Hoc autem etsi possit dici de habente forman, quod scilicet habeat aliquid quod non est ipsum (puta in albo est aliquid quod non pertinet ad rationem albi): tamen in ipsa forma nihil est alienum. Unde, cum Deus sit ipsa forma, vel potius ipsum esse, nullo modo compositus esse potest" (*Sum. Theol.* I.a. q. 3: a. 7. c.).

[2] *Con. Gen.* loc. cit.   [3] I.a. q. 3: a. 7.

argument. And in the opening sentences of the corpus of *article* 7 it is used to include all the relations just mentioned. "Since in God there is no composition, either of quantitative parts, since he is neither a body nor a composition of form and matter; nor in him is there any otherness of nature and *suppositum*; nor any otherness of essence and being; nor in him is there any composition of genus and difference nor of subject and accident; it is manifest that God is in no way composite but is wholly simple."[1]

In the *Contra Gentiles*, however, none of the problems just mentioned—with the exception of the immateriality of God— have so far been discussed. Since, therefore, we cannot take for granted that such forms of composition and plurality as are involved in the relations of nature and *suppositum*, of essence and being, of genus and difference, and of subject and accident are non-existent in God, these must remain for us possibilities until their impossibility has been demonstrated.

Now it is clear that in the first four arguments no such demonstration is given. The utmost that they can be said to prove is that God is not a compound in some such sense as water is a compound, that God is not something which can be put together out of pre-existing elements and which has the potentiality of once more being dissolved into those same elements. They cannot possibly show, for instance, that God is not a subject possessing accidents. To reach such a conclusion it must first be proved that every subject possessing accidents is dependent for its origin upon something else or is potentially dissoluble. No such proof has so far been advanced.

Taking the first four arguments together, we can see that, if we grant their premises, they do succeed in proving that God is not a compound in any artificial or physical sense. The first is based upon the principle with which we are now so familiar, that there is no potentiality in God. It is also clear that the various entities or elements which are united in one compound

---

[1] "Cum enim in Deo non sit compositio, neque quantitativarum partium, quia corpus non est; neque compositio formae et materiae: neque in eo sit aliud natura et suppositum; neque aliud essentia et esse: neque in eo sit compositio generis et differentiae; neque subiecti et accidentis: manifestum est quod Deus nullo modo compositus est, sed est omnino simplex" (*Sum. Theol.* loc. cit.).

must before their union possess the potentiality of forming such a compound, otherwise their union could never take place. If, then, there be no potentiality in God, it is impossible that God should be a composite being of this sort. The question naturally arises: did anyone ever suppose that he was? Such a position at first sight seems scarcely worthy of a refutation. A consideration such as this has, of course, nothing to do with the validity of the argument, which depends upon the cogency of its logic and not upon the importance of its conclusion. But to ask the question is to realize that the conclusion is not so unimportant as it may have seemed. A pantheism which identified God with matter, and consequently involved him in the process of physical change, becoming, and dissolution, was probably what Aquinas had in mind in making this point. Such a pantheism was, as we know, current at the time, and had not only found philosophical defenders but had inspired the teaching of certain popular but heretical sects. Metaphysically contemptible though it seemed in the eyes of St. Thomas, it was for that reason no less important that it should be refuted.

The same considerations apply to the second argument. Here the phrase, "Every composite thing is posterior to its components,"[1] makes it clear that Aquinas was thinking in this connection of an amalgamation after the analogy of a physical compound; and his assertion that such a compound must have a cause is certainly valid for all who are not prepared to admit the possibility of uncaused change. From this it follows that God, who is the first cause, cannot be such a compound.

The third argument rests, like the first, upon the absence of potentiality in God. If God be not potential in any sense whatever, it is certain that he cannot be potentially dissoluble. And since whatever dissolves must be dissoluble potentially before it is so actually, it is evident that God cannot be a composite of this kind.

Are all composites, however, potentially dissoluble? When writing these words was Aquinas taking account of the relations of genus and difference, of subject and accident, which as we

[1] "Omne compositum posterius est suis componentibus" (*Con. Gen.* lib. I. cap. 18).

have seen elsewhere,[1] he included under this term? This is a question which we cannot answer until we have examined his treatment of these relations.

The fourth argument differs from the second only by making explicit the invocation of causality which is implicit in the former.

The fifth and sixth arguments, unlike their predecessors, involve logical and not temporal priority. Neither of them, however, can be regarded as having proved its conclusion. The first sentence of the statement of the fifth argument involves us at once in difficulty. "In any genus the more excellent a thing is the simpler it is."[2] But is God in a genus? If we glance at the chapter in which this question is discussed by Aquinas,[3] we shall find that God is not so to be conceived. How, then, can inference of any kind be made from the simplicity of the most excellent members of each genus to the simplicity of him who is above all things and who is in no genus? The legitimacy of such a step certainly requires a defence.

Furthermore, is it true that, in any genus, the more excellent a thing is the more simple it is? Aquinas has chosen the example of fire in the genus hot. But let us take another example. Let us take man in the genus animal. Aquinas would certainly not deny that man is the most excellent member of that genus; but is he the simplest?

Again, granting that the statement which we have called in question is true, and granting also that it is permissible to argue from the greater simplicity of the more excellent members of any genus to the simplicity of God who is no genus, even then are we justified in asserting the *absolute* simplicity of God, the utter absence of any mode of composition in him— even such composition as is involved in the relation of subject to attribute? From the premises upon which the argument is built, it certainly does not appear that we are. And it is to be remembered that such simplicity must be reconciled with the assertion that "all the perfections which are in things are originally and eminently in God.[4]

[1] See p. 137; cf. *Sum. Theol.* I.a. q. 3: a. 7. c.
[2] "In quolibit genere tanto quid est nobilius quanto simplicius" (*Con. Gen.* lib. I. cap. 18).
[3] Cap. 25.   [4] *Com. Theol.* Pars Prima, cap. xx.

The sixth argument is based upon the assumed contradiction of the existence in the perfect whole or totality of God of parts which, because they are parts,[1] are imperfect in relation to that whole. In the *Summa Theologica*, as has been pointed out, this contradiction is said to arise when God is conceived as Form itself and Being itself.[2] Such an addition is certainly necessary, but it changes the import of the argument. The original contention was that perfection in God is incompatible with his possession of parts. The new contention is that there can be no parts in pure Form or pure Being. This latter contention may be true, but we are at present concerned with the former. And the degree of cogency which it possesses we may try to bring to light by asking ourselves a test question. Is it inconceivable that a perfect world-soul should be united with the physical universe so as to form a single individual being? Such a conception may be inconsistent with itself or inadmissible on other grounds, but it cannot be said that the present argument has shown it to be so.

We turn now to the seventh proof which may be dismissed in a few words. Either it involves temporal priority or it does not. In the first instance it adds nothing to the first three arguments, in the second it adds nothing to the fifth.

We have now examined all the proofs offered by Aquinas in support of his contention that there is no composition in God. So far as composition is understood to mean the amalgamation of pre-existing entities we have found that—if the validity of his premises be granted—Aquinas has demonstrated that God is not a composite being. On the other hand, we have also seen that, if composition be taken in the wider sense in which he seemed to understand it elsewhere, then its absence from the nature of God has not been satisfactorily proved, and that the arguments, if valid at all, require the support of certain other propositions the truth of which has not yet been demonstrated.

---

[1] Cf. *Con. Gen.* lib. I. cap. 18.

[2] "Ipsa forma, vel potius ipsum esse" (I.a. q. 3: a. 7. c.).

(e) VIOLENCE

Aquinas's next step was to attempt to show that in God there can be nothing "forced or against nature."[1] The phraseology is strange. The very suggestion that the ultimate and primal being is not at harmony with itself seems bizarre and absurd. Yet the fact that Aquinas did not think it a waste of time to devote a chapter to the establishment of a point which most people would consider an unimportant corollary is itself significant. It shows the vast care and ungrudging pains which St. Thomas lavished upon his work. It should make us chary of rejecting off-hand any argument which Aquinas advances and which does not appear at first sight to be con-clusive. We have been examining arguments which we were unable to accept because they involved the admission of the truth of certain assumptions which themselves required to be demonstrated. But this does not necessarily mean that these arguments are invalid. Our verdict is merely that of "not proven." Aquinas was quite capable of looking ahead and invoking in advance a principle which he intended to substan-tiate in the future. The order of his thought as presented in the two *Summae* shows this very clearly. We have noticed that certain steps in the discussion—proofs of various negations which can be made in regard to God—are arranged in the *Summa Theologica* in reverse order to that which they occupy in the *Contra Gentiles*. Accordingly, we must reserve our final judgment until we have completed our examination of the Negative Way when it will be our task to gather up the threads and attempt a general estimate of the cohesion and cogency of the argument as a whole.

The arguments advanced in the present instance are four in number. Anything forced or against nature involves the entrance into an entity of something not itself, since "what is of the substance of a thing cannot be forced or against nature."[2] Now in God this is impossible, for:

1. No simple thing as such can have anything added to its nature, for such addition would render it a composite. God,

---

[1] "Violentum nihilque praeter naturam" (*Con. Gen.* lib. I. cap. 19).
[2] "Quod est de substantia rei non potest esse violentum nec praeter naturam" (*Con. Gen.* lib. I. cap. 19).

however, is not composite but simple. Therefore there is nothing added to God's nature, and consequently there is in God nothing forced or against nature.[1]

2. A necessity that is constrained is imposed from without by another. But in God there is no necessity imposed from without, since God's own being is necessary and is itself the cause of necessity in others. Therefore, in God there is no constraint.[2]

3. Neither can there be any constraint within God which is not imposed from without, for wherever there is violence there is something beyond that which pertains to a thing *per se*; since violence is contrary to that which is according to nature. But since God's being is necessary, there can be nothing unnatural in God.[3]

4. Everything in which there is any violence or anything unnatural is subject to being moved by another. For violence is the act of something the principle of which is without and which acts without co-operation on the part of the patient.[4] But God is wholly immovable, therefore in God there can be nothing forced or unnatural.[5]

It is clear that these four proofs spring from a common root. The first rests upon the simplicity of God. This in turn has been deduced from the absence of potentiality in God, and this again from his eternity. The second and third, in like manner, rest upon the necessary character of God's being—that is upon his eternity.[6] And the fourth rests upon the immobility of God, that is upon his changeless or eternal being.[7] That is to say, they all stand or fall with Aquinas's doctrine of the eternity of God.

(f) CORPOREALITY

We turn now to the consideration of a point to which Aquinas devoted great attention: the establishment of the incorporeality of God. The arguments are as follows:

---

[1] *Con. Gen.* lib. I. cap. 19. 　　　[2] *Con. Gen.* loc. cit.
[3] *Con. Gen.* loc. cit.
[4] "Violentum est *cuius principium est extra nil conferente vim passo*"; cf. *Nic. Eth.* lib. III. cap. i.
[5] *Con. Gen.* loc. cit.
[6] *Con. Gen.* lib. I. cap. 15. 　　　[7] *Con. Gen.* lib. I. cap. 15.

1. Every body, inasmuch as it is continuous, is composite and has parts. But God is not composite. Therefore God is not a body.[1]

2. Whatever possesses quantity is in some mode in potentiality, for that which is continuous is potentially divisible to infinity; and since every body has quantity, every body is potentially divisible to infinity. But God is without potentiality, consequently he is not a body.[2]

3. If God be a body he must be a natural (i.e. a physical) body, for a mathematical body does not exist *per se*,[3] since dimensions are accidents.[4] But every natural body is movable, while God is immovable, therefore God is not a body.[5]

The assertion that a mathematical body cannot exist apart from a physical body, inasmuch as its dimensions can exist only as accidents of a physical body, is supported by reference to Aristotle.[6]

4. Every body whether it be square or rectilinear is finite. But we are able by intellect and imagination to transcend any finite body. If God be a body, our intellect and imagination

---

[1] *Con. Gen.* lib. I. cap. 20.

[2] *Con. Gen.* loc. cit.; cf. *Sum. Theol.* I.a. q. 3: a. 1. c.

[3] The reference here is to the *Metaphysics*, lib. III. cap. v. lect. 13.

[4] "Si Deus est corpus, oportet quod sit aliquid corpus naturale: nam corpus mathematicum non est per se existens, ut Philosophus probat, eo quod dimensiones accidentia sunt."

[5] Cf. *Sum. Theol.* I.a. q. 3: a. 1. c.

[6] Cf. *Metaph.* lib. III. cap. v, the entire chapter, especially the sentences: "'Ἀλλὰ μὴν εἰ τοῦτο μὲν ὁμολογεῖται, ὅτι μᾶλλον οὐσία τὰ μήκη τῶν σωμάτων καὶ αἱ στιγμαί, ταῦτα δὲ μὴ ὁρῶμεν ποίων ἂν εἶεν σωμάτων (ἐν γὰρ τοῖς αἰσθητοῖς ἀδύνατον εἶναι), οὐκ ἂν εἴη οὐσία οὐδεμία. ἔτι δὲ φαίνεται ταῦτα πάντα διαιρέσεις ὄντα τοῦ σώματος, τὸ μὲν εἰς πλάτος τὸ δ' εἰς βάθος τὸ δ' εἰς μῆκος."

"But if this be admitted, that lines and points are substances more than bodies, but we do not see to what sort of bodies these could belong (for they cannot be in perceptible bodies), there can be no substance. Further, these are all evidently divisions of the body,—one a division in breadth, another in depth, another in length" (Smith's and Ross's translation). Cf. also Aquinas's *Commentary on the Metaph.*, especially the sentence: "Puncta autem et linae et superficies quandoque quidem sunt, quandoque vero non sunt, et tamen non generantur nec corrumpuntur; ergo nec sunt substantiae." "Moreover, points and lines and surfaces sometimes are and sometimes are not, yet they are not generated, neither are they corrupted; therefore they are not substances."

would therefore be able to know something greater than God; and thus God would not be greater than our intellect. But God is greater than the human intellect, which is unable to attain to the knowledge of the Divine essence. Therefore God is not a body.[1]

For the proof that every body, whether circular or rectilinear, is finite we are referred to the elaborate arguments set forth by Aristotle in the *De Caelo et Mundo*.[2] Aquinas's own brief statement of the matter we find in the *Summa Theologica*.[3]

"It is manifest that no natural body can be actually infinite. For every natural body has some determinate substantial form. Since, therefore, accidents follow upon substantial form, of necessity determinate accidents follow upon determinate form, among which is quantity. Hence every natural body has a determinate quantity, be it larger or smaller. Hence it is

---

[1] *Con. Gen.* loc. cit.
[2] Cap. v; cf. *Phys.* lib. III. cap. v. lect. 8 and lect. 9.
[3] I.a. q. 7: a. 3. c.

"Et de corpore quidem naturale, quod non possit esse infinitum in actu, manifestum est. Nam omne corpus naturale aliquam formam substantialem habet determinatam: cum igitur ad formam substantialem consequantur accidentia, necesse est quod ad determinatam formam consequantur determinata accidentia; inter quae est quantitas. Unde omne corpus naturale habet determinatam quantitatem et in maius et in minus. Unde impossibile est aliquod corpus naturale infinitum esse.—Hoc etiam ex motu patet. Quia omne corpus naturale habet aliquem motum naturalem. Corpus autem infinitum non posset habere aliquem motum naturalem: nec rectum, quia nihil movetur naturaliter motu recto, nisi cum sit extra suum locum, quod corpori infinito accidere non possit; occuparet enim omnia loca, et sic indifferenter quilibet locus esset locus eius. Et similiter etiam neque secundum motum circularem. Quia in motu circulari oportet quod una pars corporis transferatur ad locum in quo fuit alia pars; quod in corpore circulari, si ponatur infinitum, esse non posset: quia duae lineae protractae a centro, quanto longius protrahuntur a centro, tanto longius distant ab invicem; si ergo corpus esset infinitum, in infinitum lineae distarent ab invicem, et sic una nunquam posset pervenire ad locum alterius.

"De corpore etiam mathematico eadem ratio est. Quia si imaginemur corpus mathematicum existens actu, oportet quod imaginemur ipsum sub aliqua forma: quia nihil est actu nisi per suam formam. Unde, cum forma quanti, inquantum huiusmodi, sit figura, oportebit quod habeat aliquam figuram. Et sic erit finitum: est enim figura, quae termino vel terminis comprehenditur."

impossible that any natural body should be infinite. This, indeed, appears from motion, for every natural body has some natural motion. An infinite body, on the other hand, cannot have any natural movement; neither direct, because nothing is moved naturally by a direct motion except when it is out of its place, a thing that could not happen to an infinite body which would occupy all places so that indifferently every place would be its place—nor yet circular, because in circular motion it is necessary that one part of the body be transferred to a place where another part was before, which could not happen in a circular body, if we suppose it to be infinite. For, if two lines be extended from the centre, the farther they are extended, the farther will they be distant from each other. If the body were infinite, the lines would therefore be infinitely distant from each other, and thus one would never occupy the place of the other.

"The same reasoning holds good with regard to mathematical bodies. For if we imagine a mathematical body actually to exist, we must imagine it under some form; for nothing is actual except by its form. Hence, since the form of quantity as such is figure, the body will have a figure, and so will be finite; for that is figure which is comprehended by some bound or bounds."

5. Intellectual cognition is more certain than sensible cognition. But sensible cognition has always its object in the external world; the same must, therefore, be the case with intellectual cognition. Moreover, the faculties of the human mind are ranked according to the order of their objects. Hence, intellectual cognition must have an external object which is above all sensible things. But every body is a sensible object. There must, therefore, exist an entity which is above all bodies. Accordingly, if God were a body, he would not be the first and the supreme being (*primum et maximum ens*). Therefore, God is not a body.[1]

This argument is of interest in connection with Aquinas's theory of knowledge, the characteristic features of which are here excellently illustrated. All knowledge arises from sense-perception—so far Aquinas and Aristotle would agree with the modern empiricist. But knowledge, in their opinion, is not

[1] *Con. Gen.* loc. cit.

confined to sense-perception. Starting from sensible experience, it finds involved therein ideas and conceptions which have valid application in a super-sensible and intelligible world where the intellect is at home. This theory of knowledge forms the basis of the present argument and is thoroughly consistent with it.

Here, however, a difficulty presents itself. Can God be an object to the intellect? We have seen that the intellect is unable to cognize the divine essence; indeed, this principle has just been made use of in the argument immediately preceding. The existence of God can, indeed, be inferred from his effects, but a being whose existence is demonstrated only by a detailed process of inference, and of whom nothing can be known beyond the bare fact that he exists, seems scarcely to fulfil the function of an intellectual object.

Yet a way of escape lies open. The existence of any intellectual object whatever is sufficient to vindicate Aquinas's argument. Every substance of which we may become aware fills such a rôle, for though its physical qualities—if it have any—are objects for our senses, it itself is known only to the intellect which penetrates behind the phenomena and becomes aware of the substratum in which they inhere. In the same degree, then, as the intellect is nobler than the senses, to that degree is the object which it knows more excellent than that which is perceived through the senses. Accordingly, were God a body, he would be on a level with the meanest substance in the universe. But, since he is the supreme Reality, he must excel all other beings, and therefore all intellectual objects. Hence, it is impossible that he should be a body.

6. A living thing is nobler than a body without life. Furthermore, the life of a living body is nobler than the body itself, since it is because of its life that it is nobler than other bodies. Therefore, that than which nothing is nobler is not a body. Consequently, God is not a body.[1]

A cogent objection was brought against this argument by Francis Sylvester. While it proves that God has not a lifeless body, it does not, so he urged, prove that he has not a living body. For, if we regard a living body as a whole, a compound of soul and body (*compositum ex anima et corpore*), then since the

[1] *Con. Gen.* loc. cit.; cf. *Sum. Theol.* I.a. q. 3: a. 1. c.

part is not nobler than the whole, we cannot regard the soul as nobler than the animated body.

Furthermore, it is not always true that an animate body is nobler than an inanimate one. The nobility of a body is derived from its form, but it is possible that a form, nobler in itself, should become more ignoble by union with a particular sort of body. An intellectual soul is in itself nobler than an inanimate body, but it is not nobler when united to its own body, since the body of the heaven is incorruptible while the animated human body is corruptible.[1] (Both Aquinas and Francis Sylvester are careful to state that they are assuming for the moment that the heaven is inanimate.) In support of this last statement, he was able, with some plausibility, to cite Aquinas's own words.[2]

How Aquinas would have replied to this objection we can only conjecture. The whole strength of his argument lies, however, in the conviction, so inevitable for the human mind, that life is something unique and *sui generis*, and that it not only exists in its own right but possesses also a value of its own, an inherent worth such as is not to be found in the realm of matter. It was this appeal to an experience which is familiar in every century and every country, and which forms part of the common heritage of humanity, that gives a dignity and interest to the thought of Aquinas which modern eyes cannot fail to discern through its unfamiliar dress. But his proof, as formally stated, lies open to the objection just raised. His contention is that, since an animate body is "nobler" than an inanimate body, it is so because it possesses life. Life, then, is nobler than body. The Supreme Being, in whom there is the highest degree of nobility, must, therefore, be bodiless. The justification of this last step, it may be observed, appears to be doubtful; for, unless God be perfect—which has not yet been proved—his supremacy need not involve absolute nobility or excellence, and such nobility as he possesses might not be incompatible with bodily existence. Dismissing this considera-

---

[1] "Sic dicimus muscam esse simpliciter nobiliorem caelo, secundum quid autem caelum nobilius esse musca." "So we say that a fly, considered absolutely, is nobler than the heaven, but as qualified the heaven is nobler than the fly."

[2] *Sum. Theol.* I.a. q. 70: a. 3. ad 2m; *De Pot.* q. 6: a. 6. ad 13m.

tion, however, we can see that, even if it be admitted that this argument has proved that a disembodied soul is nobler than an inanimate body, it has not proved that it is nobler than an animate body. A Platonist might, indeed, fearlessly urge that it is. He would be able, without inconsistency, to stigmatize the body as the prison-house of the soul, as an impediment to the spirit, and to contend that death is an escape from bondage and a return of the soul to its native condition. But it was impossible for Aquinas to take that line, for consistency would then have compelled him to deny the doctrine of the resurrection of the dead. Were the state of disembodiment more excellent than that of union with a body, the resurrection, so far from being a necessary preliminary to the state of final perfection, would be an actual retrogression. To press this consideration upon Aquinas would be obviously an *argumentum ad hominem*. It would have no efficacy against an opponent who was prepared to deny the doctrine in question. Yet it seems clear that, against one who did accept it, the objection would be perfectly valid.

The remaining arguments for the incorporeality of God are derived from Aristotle,[1] and are based, as was the first argument for the existence of God, upon the assumption that motion is eternal.

7. In connection with the argument from motion to which we have just referred it was shown that in all everlasting motion the prime mover cannot be moved either *per se* or *per accidens*. Now the body of the heaven is moved with an everlasting circular motion; therefore, its prime mover is moved neither *per se* nor *per accidens*. Consequently, the prime mover cannot be a body. For a body that causes local motion must itself be moved, since in local motion mover and moved are simultaneous. Nor can it be any power in a body, because no power in a body causes movement without itself being moved *per accidens*. Accordingly, the prime mover of the heaven is neither a body nor a power in a body. But it has already been proved that the prime mover of the heaven is God. Therefore, God is incorporeal.[2]

---

[1] Cf. the Seventh and Eighth Books of the *Physics*.
[2] *Con. Gen.* loc. cit.; cf. *Sum. Theol.* I.a. q. 3: a. 1. c.; *Com. Theol.* Pars Prima, cap. xv.

8. No infinite power is a power resident in any magnitude. But the power of the prime mover is an infinite power. Therefore, it cannot be contained in any magnitude. Hence, God, the prime mover, can be neither a corporeal body nor possess a bodily power.[1]

The validity of this proof depends upon the validity of its two premises which also require to be proved. The proposition that no infinite power is resident in any magnitude[2] is demonstrated as follows:[3]

If any magnitude be possessed of infinite power, that magnitude must either be finite or infinite. But there cannot be any such thing as an infinite magnitude.[4] Nor can a finite magnitude possess infinite power. For a greater power in a lesser time will produce an effect equal to that produced by a lesser power in a greater time; and this whether the effect be one of alteration, or of local change, or of motion of any kind. Now an infinite power is greater than any finite power. It must, therefore, produce its effect more quickly by causing a more rapid movement than any finite power. Yet it is not possible that this greater quickness should be quickness of time. (*Ergo oportet quod in minori perficiat effectum, velocius movendo, quam potentia quaecumque finita. Nec potest esse quod in minori quod sit tempus.*) Accordingly, the moving, the being moved, and the motion will be instantaneous. This, however, is contrary to the demonstration given by Aristotle in the sixth book of the *Physics*.[5]

---

[1] *Con. Gen.* loc. cit.

[2] "Nulla potentia infinita est potentia in magnitudine."

[3] Cf. *Phys.* lib. VIII. cap. x. lect. 21.

[4] Cf. the fourth argument, and the references to Aristotle there given.

[5] " "Ὅτι δ' οὐδὲν ἐν τῷ νῦν κινεῖται, ἐκ τῶνδε φανερόν· εἰ γὰρ ἐστιν, ἐνδέχεται καὶ θᾶττον κινεῖσθαι ἐν αὐτῷ καὶ βραδύτερον. Ἔστω δὴ τὸ νῦν, ἐφ' ᾧ Ν, κεκινήσθω δ' ἐν αὐτῷ τὸ θᾶττον τὴν Α Β. Οὐκοῦν τὸ βραδύτερον· ἐν τῷ αὐτῷ ἐλάττω τῆς Α Β κινηθήσεται, οἷον τὴν Α Γ. Ἐπεὶ δὲ τὸ βραδύτερον ἐν ὅλῳ τῷ νῦν κεκίνηται τὴν Α Γ, τὸ θᾶττον ἐν ἐλάττονι τούτου κινηθήσεται. Ὥστε διαιρεθήσεται τὸ νῦν. Ἀλλ' ἦν ἀδιαίρετον. Οὐκ ἄρα ἔστι κινεῖσθαι ἐν τῷ νῦν." (*Phys.* lib. VI. cap. iii).

Upon this passage Aquinas made the following comment: "Dicit ergo primo, manifestum esse ex iis quae sequuntur, quod in nunc nihil possit moveri: quia si aliquid potest moveri in nunc, continget in nunc moveri duo mobilia, quorum unum sit velocius, et aliud tardius. Sit ergo ipsum nunc N, et aliquod corpus velocius moveatur in N per AB magnitudinem. Sed tardius in aequali minus movetur: ergo tardius in hoc instanti movetur

It is not at first sight clear what is meant by the statement that an infinite power produces its effect more quickly than any other finite power, but that this quickness is not quickness of time. Aquinas's thought, however, appears to be somewhat as follows. We can conceive of an indefinite series of finite powers, each superior to the one preceding it, and each consequently producing its effect in a shorter period of time than the one before it. As we prolong this series indefinitely towards infinity, the moments of time continuously diminish and approach the vanishing point. (Furthermore, motion includes not only local change but alteration, and some forms of alteration, like the illumination of a room or the rise of flush to the cheek, are practically instantaneous.) Now, since an infinite body infinitely excels any body we can conceive, it must produce its effect infinitely more quickly. But this means that it does not take place in time at all. Yet we know that God produces local change. Hence, if God possess an infinite body, he will produce instantaneously local change, which, as has been said, is impossible.

This argument was reinforced by another which was designed to prove that an infinite power of finite magnitude could not cause motion in time. Let A be the infinite, and let AB be a part of it. AB will then take a longer time to move than will A. Of necessity, however, there will be some proportion between the time taken by AB and that taken by A, since the motion caused by each of them will occupy a finite time. Accordingly, let us assume that the time taken by A is one-tenth of that taken by AB. Now, as we increase the power of AB, we must make proportionate subtraction from the amount of time which it takes to cause motion. Let us, then, increase the power of AB tenfold and reduce the time occupied to one-tenth of its previous duration. The result will be that AB will still remain a finite power, but the time in which it causes motion will be exactly equal to that taken by the infinite

per minorem magnitudinem quae est AG. Sed velocius idem spatium pertransit in minori quam tardius. Quia ergo corpus tardius movebatur per AG magnitudinem in toto ipso nunc, sequitur quod velocius moveatur per eandem magnitudinem in minori quam nunc: ergo nunc dividitur. Sed ostensum est quod nunc est individibile: ergo non potest aliquid moveri in nunc" (lect. 5).

power A. Therefore, no infinite power of finite magnitude could cause motion in time.

That the power of the prime mover is infinite is proved as follows. No finite power can cause motion in an infinite time. But the power of the prime mover does cause motion in an infinite time, inasmuch as the primal motion is everlasting. Therefore, the power of the prime mover must be infinite.

Here once more the first proposition requires to be proved, namely, that no finite power can cause motion in an infinite time,[1] or in other words, that the time occupied by any finite power in causing motion must itself be finite. If any finite power of any body cause motion in an infinite time, a part of that body, possessing a portion of that power, will cause motion in less time.[2] The reason is that the greater the power the longer the motion caused by it continues. (This statement appears at first sight to be a contradiction of the assertion made a few paragraphs previously that a greater power produces in less time an effect equal to that produced by a lesser power in a longer time, but it is not really so; for there reference was made to an isolated act aimed at the production of a particular, definite, and concrete result, while here we are concerned with the length of time during which a force can exert continuous activity productive of local change.) Thus the part of which we have spoken will cause motion for a finite time, and a greater part will cause motion for a longer time. In other words, as the power of the mover is increased the time during which it will be able to cause motion will increase proportionately. But to whatever degree such increase be carried we are still dealing with a finite power and a finite time. Therefore, in order to find a mover capable of causing motion for an infinite time, it is clear that we must posit an infinite power.

To this train of reasoning the objection may be raised that it presupposes the prime mover to be divisible, while it is possible to regard it as indivisible, like a heavenly body. Such

[1] "Nulla potentia finita potest movere tempore infinito."
[2] "Si aliqua potentia finita alicuius corporis movet tempore infinito, pars illius corporis, habens partem potentiae, movebit in tempore minori"—that is to say, the motion caused by a finite power cannot persist for ever, but must terminate within a finite period of time.

was actually the criticism passed upon Aristotle by Avicenna.[1] Aquinas replied that a conditional clause may be true even if its antecedent be false. Thus, his own argument does not assert that the prime mover is actually divisible, or that it is actually possible to measure the capacity of finite powers by comparison between the periods during which they cause motion.[2]

A second objection which Thomas deemed worthy of consideration was that it is possible that the power resident in a divisible body may itself be indivisible, even as the rational soul is not divided by the division of the body. To this Aquinas replied that his argument was not intended to prove that God is not related to a body in the same way that a soul is related to its body. The hypothesis that God is the soul of the world was not what he intended to refute. All that he aimed at proving was that God cannot be a material power resident in a body and divisible as it is divisible.[3]

The introduction at this point of the conception of a material power is of interest. Heretofore we have been led to think of matter as a wholly inert substratum, the passive recipient of form; and the argument from motion implied that all activity on the part of material bodies is due to their being acted upon, directly or indirectly, by some intelligence. What may be meant here, however, is the qualities, such as heat, cold, which while they are not divisible *per se* in their character of universals, nevertheless, as concrete elements in a material substance are divisible as that substance is.[4]

The third objection referred to by Aquinas is one that has for us merely an antiquarian interest, the objection, namely, that if the power of every body be finite, and if because of the finitude of its power no body can produce an effect which will persist through infinite time, it follows that no body can endure through infinite time, and consequently that even a heavenly body is necessarily corruptible. Aquinas's answer is based on the assertion that the very conception of movement involves quantity and extension—whence it follows that the

---

[1] *Phys.* lib. VIII. cap. x. lect. 21.   [2] *Con. Gen.* loc. cit.
[3] "Quod non est virtus in corpore sicut virtus materialis, quae dividitur ad divisionem corporis" (*Con. Gen.* loc. cit.).
[4] Cf. *Comment.* of Francis Sylvester.

infinite duration of movement requires that the moving power be infinite—while being, on the contrary, does not involve extension. Hence the duration of a finite body may be infinite without its power being infinite. This is true of the heaven which is an invariable being and only affected by time *per accidens*; consequently, there is no difference between causing it to exist for an instant and for ever.[1]

A fourth objection is that the proposition that whatever causes movement for an infinite time must have infinite power does not hold good of those movers which in causing movement do not themselves suffer change or alteration; for, since the movement that they cause does not involve the expenditure of any energy on their part, their ability to continue to cause it does not decrease. The example given is that of the sun, which is able to continue causing movement indefinitely with undiminished vigour.

Aquinas's rejoinder is that, since no body moves unless it be moved, such movement is contingent. It is possible for every body that is moved not to be moved, and for every body that is not moved to be moved. Consequently, whatever is able not to be moved is not liable of itself to be moved perpetually, nor yet perpetually to cause movement. He further urged that his demonstration was based on the finite power of a finite body which is not able of itself to cause perpetual movement. He was prepared to admit it to be quite possible that such a body might acquire perpetual movement from an extrinsic source, but he insisted that such a source must be incorporeal.[2]

A fifth and last objection remained to be considered, and that a cogent one. It might be urged that there is no more reason why an infinite power should not exist in a magnitude than apart from a magnitude, since it would follow that in either case it must move instantaneously and not in time.

A possible reply is to assert that a material and an immaterial infinite are not comparable. We have the authority of Aristotle to support the contention that in magnitude, time, and motion finite and infinite are found in a univocal sense,[3] but it is open to argument that in immaterial entities finite and infinite are to be found only in an equivocal sense. Such

[1] *Con. Gen.* loc. cit.   [2] *Con. Gen.* loc. cit.
[3] *Phys.* lib. III. cap. iv. and lib. VI. cap. ii.

a reply was not, however, countenanced by Aquinas.[1] Doubt-less he was influenced by the considerations mentioned by Francis Sylvester,[2] namely, that the "infinity of power is com-parable to the infinity of time by the proportion of cause and effect," and that "the action of a power is to be measured not by the greatness of extension but of its perfection; just as more warmth is produced by intense heat in an object of small extension than by mild heat in one of greater extension."

A second possible answer would be to affirm that the heaven has two movers, one of which is its proximate mover, a being of finite power which imparts to the heaven its motion of finite velocity; while the other, its ultimate mover, is of in-finite power, whence it derives its capacity of maintaining a perpetual motion. Such was the theory of Averroes.[3] (The per-petuity of the heaven's motion is not directly asserted, since it is contrary to the doctrine of creation and to the Catholic Faith; but it is to be remembered that Aquinas regarded the eternity of the world as perfectly tenable from a philosophical point of view, and that he embraced the doctrine of creation as a truth imparted by Revelation.) Upon this theory the infinite power moves the heaven through the mediation of a finite mover. By such a device we escape the difficulty involved in assuming that an infinite power, if it act upon matter, must act in no time. It would imply, however, as an inevitable corollary the impossibility of any direct contact between God and the material world. In fact, the transcendence of God would be thereby so enhanced that it would seem to be almost meaningless to refer to him as in any sense the ground of the world, which would appear to derive its being from an inter-mediate power. Such a view was thoroughly familiar to Neoplatonic thought. Aquinas was, however, loath to commit himself to it, and accordingly we find that he preferred yet another possible reply. A power which is not in a magnitude must be an intellect, and it will cause motion by its will; more-over, the exercise of its will will be dependent, not upon its own power, but upon the state of the thing which is to be moved. A natural force, on the other hand, which is resident in a magnitude acts only by the necessity of its nature and in

[1] *Phys.* lib. VIII. lect. 21.   [2] Cf. *Comment.*   [3] *Metaph.* xii. t. c. 41.

proportion to its quantity, so that if it move it moves in an instant.[1]

Having thus disposed of those objections which he thought relevant, Aquinas proceeded to advance two other arguments.

9. No motion which proceeds from a moving body can be continuous and regular, since in local change a corporeal mover moves by attraction and repulsion, and that which is attracted or repelled is not in precisely the same relation to the source of motion from the beginning to the end of the movement, for now it is nearer to it and now farther away. But the motion of the prime mover is continuous and regular. Therefore, the prime mover is not a body.

The statement that all movement is by attraction and repulsion has been made the subject of an interesting comment by Francis Sylvester. It is not true on Aristotelian principles, he argued, that all movement is by attraction or repulsion, since an object may also be dragged or propelled. Consequently, he conjectured that Aquinas has here in mind the prime mover who, being himself immovable, does not change his place, a conjecture which removes from the argument the difficulty he had raised.

10. No movement can be perpetual which is directed toward an end which is passing from potentiality to actuality, for when it has become wholly actual the movement ceases. Accordingly, the end of a perpetual movement must be wholly actual. Now, such an end cannot be a body, nor a power resident in a body, for as such it would be movable *per se* or *per accidens*. But the end of the primal movement is the prime mover which moves as the object of desire, and which is God. Therefore, God is neither a body nor a power resident in a body.

We have followed one by one the various proofs by which Aquinas sought to establish the incorporeality of God. It was a doctrine to which he attached considerable importance. By establishing it he would refute not only what he conceived to be the ancient errors of Tertullian and other anthropomorphic theorists as well as the early Greek materialists who admitted only material causes, but also the contemporary theology of the Manichaeans who held that God existed as a body of light extending through limitless space.

[1] *Con. Gen.* loc. cit.

Glancing back now over the arguments as a group we can see that they are the logical development of what has gone before. They are faithful to the general spirit and tenor of the thought of Aquinas and carry forward the development of the *Via Remotionis*. As in the case of the existence of God, the proof upon which Aquinas laid the most stress was the argument from motion. Little that is new can be said about it here. We have followed its application through details which possess for us little but historic interest as well as through others which embody matters of permanent significance. The underlying idea, of course, is that the source of movement must itself be immaterial.

It did not escape the penetrating intellect of Francis Sylvester[1] that Aquinas's presentation of this argument requires the establishment of the identity of infinite power in the sense of energy or force with infinite power in the sense of perpetual activity and unceasing duration, of *potentia infinita secundum vigorem* with *potentia infinita secundum durationem*. It cannot be said that the legitimacy of this identification has been defended with as much fullness or clearness as could be desired; nevertheless, the lines upon which it is reached are sufficiently obvious. It is evident that Aquinas was prepared to admit that while perpetual movement might be imparted to a finite body, this perpetuity was not really inherent in that body at all, but was rather participated in by it, and was to be regarded as the property of a Reality whose power equalled the boundlessness of its manifestation. Perpetual duration and unlimited outgoing energy may be looked upon as the characteristics of a single infinite identity.

(g) ESSENCE

The necessity next arises of proving that God is identical with his essence. Before examining the various arguments in detail it will be well to make clear if we can what meaning the term "essence" conveyed to the mind of Aquinas himself; and for this purpose we may conveniently refer to his own treatise upon the subject which is entitled *De Ente et Essentia*. We find

[1] Cf. *Comment.*

there in the opening sentences the following definition.[1] "Essence connotes that which is common to all natures, through which diverse beings are ordered in diverse genera and species: just as humanity is the essence of man, and so in regard to other things."

This brief definition is elaborated in the remainder of the paragraph.[2] "And since that through which a thing is constituted a member of its own genus or species is what we connote when we form a definition indicating what the thing is; the term *essence* has been changed by philosophers into the term *quiddity*, and this is what the philosopher (Aristotle) in VII Metaphysics frequently calls essence (τὸ τί ἦν εἶναι), which is to say that through which something has a definite being. Also it is called form, by which is connoted the perfection or definite character of any thing, as Avicenna says in II *Metaphysics*. The other term *nature* is to be understood in the first of the four meanings which Boetius assigns it in his book *Concerning the Two Natures*; according to which nature is said to be that which can in any mode be comprehended by the intellect. For a thing is not intelligible except through its definition or essence; and so the Philosopher says in V *Metaphysics* that all substance is nature. The term *nature* in this sense is seen to

---

[1] "Oportet quod essentia significet aliquid commune omnibus naturis per quas diuersa entia in diuersis generibus et speciebus collocantur, sicut humanitas est essentia hominis, et sic de aliis" (*De Ente et Essentia*, cap. i).

[2] "Et quia id per quod res constituitur in proprio genere vel specie est hoc quod significatur per diffinitionem indicantem quid est res, inde est quod nomen essentie a philosophis in nomen quiditatis mutatur; et hoc est quod Philosophus frequenter nominat quod quid erat esse, id est hoc per quod aliquid habet esse quid. Dicitur autem forma secundum quod per formam significatur certitudo uniuscuiusque rei, ut dicit Auicenna in tercio *Methaphysice* sue. Hoc alio nomine natura dicitur, accipiendo naturam secundum primum modum illorum quatuor modorum quos Boecius in libro *De duabus naturis* assignat, scilicet secundum quod natura dicitur omne illud quod intellectu quocumque modo capi potest; non enim est res intelligibilis nisi per diffinitionem et essentiam suam. Et sic eciam Philosophus dicit in quarto *Methaphysice* quod omnis substantia est natura. Tamen nature nomen hoc modo sumpte uidetur significare essentiam rei secundum quod habet ordinem ad propriam operationem rei, cum nulla res propria operatione destituatur; quiditas uero nomen sumitur ex hoc quod diffinitionem significat; set essentia dicitur secundum quod per eam et in ea ens habet esse" (*De Ente et Essentia*, cap. i).

connote the essence of a thing from the point of view of its own operative activity, for nothing is destitute of such activity. The term *quiddity* is applied to that which is connoted by the definition; but essence connotes that through which and in which the thing has its being."

Clearly these various terms are used to signify one and the same thing regarded from differing points of view. Thus Aquinas points out (cap. ii) that since the definition of a physical object specifies a being compounded of matter and form, it follows that the essence of the object is also compounded of matter and form. The matter included in the essence is not, however, *materia signata*, which is the principle of individuation. "In the definition of man *this* bone and *this* flesh are not posited, but bone and flesh absolutely, which are the non-signate matter of man." "*Non enim in definitione hominis ponitur hoc os et haec caro, sed os et caro absolute quae sunt materia hominis non signata.*"[1]

As the result of what is thus said we may accept as a succinct and adequate definition of essence that which is offered us in the second chapter of the same work, "*essentia est id quod per definitionem rei significatur,*" "the essence is that which is connoted by the definition of a thing."[2]

1. The first argument is extremely simple. If a thing be not identical with its essence it must include something beside its essence. In that case it is composite. But in God there is no composition. Therefore in God there is nothing beside his essence.[3]

2. The definition of a thing signifies what the thing is, and, as we have seen, is identical with its essence. Accordingly, whatever is in anything beside its essence does not enter into its definition. This rôle can be filled only by the accidents of the thing. But in God, as will hereafter appear, there are no accidents. Consequently, there is nothing in God beside his essence.[4]

---

[1] *De Ente et Essentia*, cap. ii.

[2] Cf. *Com. Theol.* Pars Prima, cap. ix. "Essentia enim unuiscuiusque rei est illud quod significat definitio eius." "The essence of any thing is that which is connoted by its definition."

[3] *Con. Gen.* lib. I. cap. 21.

[4] *Con. Gen.* loc. cit.

3. The third argument is found both in the *Contra Gentiles*[1] and also in the *Summa Theologica*.[2] Forms which are not predicated of subsistent things either universally or singly (i.e. either of the individual Socrates or of the species humanity) do not themselves subsist as individuals. We do not say that Socrates, or that man, is whiteness; because whiteness does not exist singly in itself (*singulanter per se*), but only when individualized by a subsistent subject. Similarly, the essences of genera or species, although they include matter and form, are, nevertheless, individualized by the *materia signata* of this or that individual thing; they do not subsist in themselves, and for this reason we do not say that Socrates, or that man in general, *is* humanity. Thus, in things composed of matter and form, the essence or nature differs from the *suppositum*. "Individual matter, with all the accidents which individuate it, does not fall under the definition of a species."[3]

There are, however, subsistent entities which are not composed of matter and form. Consequently, their individuation is not due to their connection with matter; on the contrary, their forms are themselves subsistent individuals. Accordingly, in such subsistents there is no distinction of *suppositum* from nature.[4]

[1] Loc. cit.

[2] I.a. q. 3: a. 3. c.

[3] "Materia individualis, cum accidentibus omnibus individuantibus ipsam, non cadit in definitione speciei" (*Sum. Theol.* I.a. q. 3: a. 3. c.).

[4] Aquinas's attitude in regard to the question of the identity of essence and *suppositum* in spiritual beings other than God was not consistent. In the article of the *Summa Theologica* just cited, he affirms it emphatically. "In his igitur quae non sunt composita ex materia et forma, in quibus individuatio non est per materiam individualem, idest per hanc materiam, sed ipsae formae per se individuantur, oportet quod ipsae formae sint supposita subsistentia. Unde in eis non differt suppositum et natura." In the *Quodlibeta*, however (II. q. 2: a. 4), he upholds the contrary view. "Restat ergo considerandum, cum suppositum vel individuum naturale sit compositum ex materia et forma, utrum sit idem essentiae vel naturae: et hanc quaestionem movet Philosophus in VII *Metaph.* text com. xxi; ubi inquirit utrum sit idem unumquodque, et quod quid est eius: et determinat, quod in his quae dicuntur per se, idem est res et quod quid est rei; in his autem quae dicuntur per accidens, non est idem. Homo enim nihil est aliud quam quod quid est hominis: nihil enim aliud significat homo quam animal gressibile bipes: sed res alba non est idem omnino ei quod quid est album, quod scilicet significatur nomine albi: nam album

God is, of course, a being of this character, since he is not composed of matter and form. There is, therefore, in God no distinction of *suppositum* from nature or essence; or, in other words, God and his essence are identical.

4. The essence of a thing is either identical with it or is related to it as its cause, inasmuch as the species of a thing is determined by its essence. God, however, is the primal Being, and has no cause. Therefore, God is his essence.[1]

5. In any thing which is not identical with its essence there is a relation of potentiality to actuality, since a thing is actual through its essence and without it would relapse into non-entity. But since in God there is no potentiality, there can be in him no distinction of essence from existence; consequently, God is his own essence.[2]

The first argument depends upon the truth of the assertion that there is no composition in God. We have examined Aquinas's proof of this proposition and have seen reason to regard it as unsatisfactory. The kinds of composition which it did not show to be absent from the being of God were those of nature and *suppositum*, of essence and being, of genus and difference, of substance and accidents; and it is precisely with these that we are now concerned. The argument appears to be circular, and if we are not to dismiss it as such, it is essential that it be proved upon other grounds that these forms of composition are absent from the divine nature.

nihil significat nisi qualitatem, ut dicitur in praedicamentis : res autem alba est substantia habens qualitatem.

"Secundum hoc ergo cuicumque potest aliquid accidere quod non sit de ratione suae naturae, in eo differt res et quod quid est, sive suppositum et natura. Nam in significatione naturae includitur solum id quod est de ratione speciei : suppositum autem non solum habet haec quae ad rationem speciei pertinent, sed etiam alia quae ei accidunt; et ideo suppositum significatur per totum, natura autem, sive quidditas, ut pars formalis. In solo autem Deus non invenitur aliquod accidens praeter eius essentiam, quia suum esse est sua essentia, ut dictum est; et ideo in Deo est omnino idem suppositum et natura. In Angelo autem non est omnino idem : quia aliquid accidit ei praeter id quod est de ratione suae speciae; quia et ipsum esse Angeli est praeter eius essentiam seu naturam; et alia quaedam ei accidunt quae omnino pertinent ad suppositum, non autem ad naturam."

[1] *Con. Gen.* loc. cit.
[2] *Con. Gen.* loc. cit.; cf. *Com. Theol.* Pars Prima, cap. ix.

The second argument rests upon the proposition that there are no accidents in God. The proof of this is to be given later,[1] and we need discuss it no further at present.

The third proof is founded upon the Aristotelian theory that the essences of things are not in themselves existent entities apart from the substances with which they are united. Deity in the abstract is not an existent; it is a conception of the intellect. Deity in the concrete is an existent. It is not, however, susceptible of union with matter. If it were there might be many gods; because, in that case, matter would be the principle of individuation, and a material individual is capable of indefinite reproduction. But, since such union is impossible, the essence of deity must contain its principle of individuation within itself. It is, in its very nature, singular and incapable of reproduction. Deity is, therefore, neither an abstract quality predicable of many substances, nor is it a form which enjoys its existence as an individual through union with matter—it is a form or essence which possesses concrete existence in itself. Hence, there enters into it no other element—it is form pure and simple without admixture of aught else.[2]

There is one consideration which militates very strongly against the acceptance of this argument—namely, that it appears to be inconsistent with Aquinas's theory of the nature of angels. Here we touch upon one of those questions which at the present time we are accustomed to think of as purely theological, but which were nevertheless approached by Aquinas in a thoroughly philosophic spirit, and which—when examined in the light of the treatment which they received at his hands—are seen to involve issues vitally related to the scope of his general inquiry, and the solution of which was essential to the harmony of his system. For our purpose it is sufficient to point out that for Aquinas there existed, beside God, other spiritual substances which were not embodied in matter. So far as the argument which we are now considering has succeeded in proving anything, its conclusions would seem to apply to all these substances as fully as they do to God, since matter is equally absent from them all. Accordingly, if God be his own essence, it appears that an angel must be its own essence also.

[1] Con. Gen. lib. I. cap. 21.   [2] Cf. Sum. Theol. I.a. q. 3: a. 2. c.

We happen to know, however, that Aquinas vigorously dissented from such reasoning. It is quite true that he held that the essence of an angel, since it is not united to matter, must possess its principle of individuation within itself; and that he drew from this the corollary that there can be no more than one angel in a species.[1] "Since the essence of a simple substance is not received into matter, it is impossible that the being of such entities should be capable of multiplication: and therefore of necessity there could not be more than one individual in each species of these substances: so that the number of individuals equals the number of species as Avicenna expressly says." It is none the less true, however, that he insisted that, in an angel, being is distinct from essence.[2] "Being is other than essence or quiddity, unless there be something whose quiddity is its being; and this could not be other than the unique and primal being."

We are therefore involved in the following contradiction. Aquinas's argument was that God is identical with his essence because he is a concrete subsistent entity not united to matter, and having his principle of individuation within himself. But the same is true of an angel; the angel must, therefore, also be identical with its essence. This, however, is contrary to the teaching of Aquinas who held that the being of an angel is other than its essence and is related to it as the actual to the potential.[3] Consequently, if the argument do not hold true of the angel, it does not hold true of God. It requires, for its completion, to be supplemented by the fifth argument which is based upon the absence of potentiality in God. But the fifth argument, if valid, is sufficient in itself. We may therefore dismiss the third argument as unavailing.

Before passing on to the next, however, we shall do well to notice another apparent contradiction in Aquinas's thought which is revealed by this argument. We have already found his

---

[1] "Cum essentia simplicis non sit recepta in materia non potest ibi esse talis multiplicatio. Et ideo oportet ut non inueniantur in illis substantiis plura indiuidua, eiusdem speciei, set quotquot sunt ibi indiuidua tot sunt species, ut Auicenna expresse dicit" (*De Ente et Essentia*, cap. iv.).

[2] "Esse est aliud ab essentia uel quiditate. Nisi forte sit aliqua res cuius quiditas sit ipsum suum esse. Et hec res non potest esse nisi una et prima" (*De Ente et Essentia*, cap. iv; *Quodlib.* ii. q. 2: a. 3.).

[3] *Sum. Theol.* I.a. q. 50: a. 2. ad. 3^m.

conception of matter as pure potentiality to be unsatisfactory. But in the present discussion we have just had occasion to refer to his theory of the nature of angels, and we have discovered that in his view the essence of an angel stands to its being as the potential to the actual. If matter, however, be equivalent to potentiality, it follows that an angel is a material being. But nothing is more certain than that St. Thomas believed an angel to be nothing of the kind, and that he regarded it as purely immaterial and spiritual entity. But, if this be the case, then the definition of matter as pure potentiality is inadmissible. It must possess some characteristic which distinguishes it from potentiality in general.

That Aquinas did regard the being of an angel as other than its essence there is no doubt whatever. It is true that in his statement of the argument which we have just been considering he asserted that, "in those things, accordingly, which are not composed of matter and form, and the individuation of which is not by means of individual matter—that is, through *this* matter—but which are themselves individuated *per se*— the forms are of necessity identical with the subsisting *supposita*. Hence, in them *suppositum* does not differ from nature."[1] But in the same article he also affirms that "in created things the *suppositum* is not identical with its nature."[2]

The meaning seems to be that while the essence of an angel does not require for its individuation to be connected with matter, it nevertheless does require that its being or existence be imparted to it from without. In other words, the existence of the essence is a logical existence, and in crossing the gap between logical and actual existence we are dependent upon the fiat of God. As a mere logical entity it is only potentially existent. Yet matter has been described as pure potentiality. Are we to regard a logical entity as material?

Aquinas himself realized that there was a difficulty here. He explicitly stated that "in a spiritual substance there is

[1] "In his igitur quae non sunt composita ex materia et forma, in quibus individuatio non est per materiam individualem, id est per hanc materiam, sed ipsae formae per se individuantur, oportet quod ipsae formae sint supposita subsistentia. Unde in eis non differt suppositum et natura" (*Sum. Theol.* I.a. q. 3: a. 3. c.).

[2] "In rebus creatis non est idem suppositum quod sua natura" (*Sum. Theol.* I.a. q. 3: a. 3. ob. 2.; cf. *Quodlib.* ii. q. 2.).

composition of potentiality and actuality, and consequently of matter and form—that is, if all potentiality is to be called form. But this is not correctly worded according to the common use of names."[1] He added further that "according as a thing is more actual so is it more perfect, and according as it is more potential so is it more imperfect. Moreover, the imperfect things are referred for their origin to the perfect but not conversely. Hence it is not necessary that everything which is in some mode in potentiality should thereby be involved in pure potentiality, which is matter. And in this Avicebron (Solomon ibn Gabirol) is seen to have been deceived in his book *Fons Vitae*, for he believed that everything which is in potentiality or which is a subject (of accidents) is in a certain measure involved in primary matter."[2]

Aquinas solved the problem in this way. He pointed out that in composite things there is a twofold potentiality and a twofold actuality.[3] First, there is the potentiality of matter in relation to form. Both matter and form are, however, included in the essence of a composite thing, since the essence is the definition of the thing.[4] Accordingly there is, in the second place, the potentiality of this essence or form in relation to its existence through participation in which it becomes through its union with *materia signata* a concrete object in the world of nature. In the essence of a simple substance, however, there is no matter. Essence and form, therefore, are here identical. Consequently in a simple substance there is but a single potentiality—namely, the potentiality of essence in relation to being.

---

[1] "In substantia spirituali est compositio potentiae et actus, et per consequens formae et materiae; si tamen omnis potentia nominetur forma. Sed tamen hoc non est proprie dictum secundum communem usum nominum" (*De Spiritualis Creaturis*, q. 1 : a. 1. c.).

[2] "Quanto aliquid est plus in actu, tanto perfectius est; quanto autem aliquid est plus in potentia, tanto est imperfectius. Imperfecta autem a perfectis sumunt originem, et non e converso. Unde non oportet quod omne quod quocumque modo est in potentia, hoc habeat a pura potentia quae est materia. Et in hoc videtur fuisse deceptus Avicebron in libro *Fontis Vitae*, dum crededit quod omne illud quod est in potentia vel subiectum, quodammodo hoc habeat ex prima materia" (*De Spirit. Creat.* q. 1 : a. 1. ad 25^m).

[3] *De Spirit. Creat.* q. 1 : a. 1. c.; cf. *Con. Gen.* lib. II. cap. 54.

[4] Cf. *De Ente et Essentia*, cap. ii.

In this manner the immateriality of angels is, indeed, vindicated, but only at the price of admitting that there is a distinction between potentiality and matter. We return, then, to the original question suggested by this argument. What is the peculiar characteristic of matter, which distinguishes it from potentiality in general, and how, if it possess such a characteristic, can it be identical with pure potentiality?

The question is one which we need not pursue further at present,[1] and we may now return from this digression, which has been necessary to make clear the precise nature of the difficulty and the inconsistency in which the argument had become involved, to the consideration of the fourth proof of the identity of God with his essence.

This proof, like its predecessor, is dependent upon the Aristotelian theory of essences or forms. The argument is a causal one. But we must remember that, for Aquinas as for Aristotle, there were four kinds of causes. In the first place there was the material cause of an object—that is, the matter out of which it was composed. Secondly, there was the formal cause—in other words, the form or essence which was impressed upon the

---

[1] For a more elaborate refutation of Avicebron, see the fifth, sixth, and seventh chapters of the *De Angelorum Natura*. (Cf. also *Sum. Theol.* I.a. q. 50: a. 2. and *De Ente et Essentia*, cap. iv.) In the sixth chapter we find the following exposition of Aquinas's own view: "Accordingly it is evident wherein the potentiality which is in spiritual substances differs from the potentiality which is in matter. For the potentiality of a spiritual substance is in respect only to its relation to existence; but the potentiality of matter is in respect to its relation both to form and to existence. If anyone, however, say that each is matter, it is clear that he uses the term matter equivocally." ("Patet igitur in quo differt potentia quae est in substantiis spiritualibus, a potentia quae est in materia. Nam potentia substantiae spiritualis attenditur solum secundum ordinem ipsius ad esse; potentia vero materiae secundum ordinem et ad formam et ad esse. Si quis autem utrumque materiam esse dicat, manifestum est quod aequivoce materiam nominabit.") In other words, Aquinas's use of the term *matter* is quite different from that of Aristotle. It is intimately connected with the concept of corporeality—not that primary matter is itself extended, yet it is conceived as the metaphysical support, as it were, not only of extension, but of all the other qualities which we find in signate matter. Whatever were the reasons which induced St. Thomas to take up such a position, they must have seemed to him very cogent, for in so doing he was flying in the face of contemporary opinion. See Roland-Gosselin's introduction to his edition of the *De Ente et Essentia*.

matter and which imparted to it its characteristic nature, its array of qualities. Thirdly, there was the efficient cause; in an artificial object, its human designer, in a natural object, God. And, lastly, there was the final cause, the end or purpose for which an object was called into being. In purely spiritual entities, such as angels, the material cause was absent but the other three were present.

It is evident, of course, that God, the primal Being, can have neither efficient nor final cause. Nor, if Aquinas's proof of God's immateriality be accepted, can he have a material cause. Furthermore, it is clear that in God there can be no union of form and being imposed from without as in the case of an angel, since such union would of course require an efficient cause. In this sense, at least, there can be no potentiality in God. His being is not derived from another but is inherent in, and an integral part of, his nature. Consequently he must be pure self-existent form.

The weak point in this argument would seem to be that the immateriality of God has not yet been demonstrated in convincing fashion. How do we know that in the primal Being there may not be a union of form and matter eternally subsistent? This objection cannot be pressed at the moment, however, because we have not yet examined Aquinas's refutation of the various possible theories of the nature of such a union. And apart from that, if the fundamental distinction of matter and form be once admitted, the argument appears to be perfectly sound.

The fifth proof is the direct corollary of the proposition that there is no potentiality in God. If essence stands to existence as potentiality to actuality, there can be no such distinction in a being in whom potentiality does not subsist. Consequently this argument can be refuted only by disproving the premise on which it is based.

There is, however, one question which arises in connection with it. Aquinas was accustomed to speak of essence as standing to existence as the potential to the actual. In this instance the statement is reversed. His words are these:[1] "That which is not its own essence is, as regards some portion of itself, related

---

[1] "Quod non est sua essentia, se habet secundum aliquid sui ad ipsam ut potentia ad actum."

to that essence as potentiality to actuality." In the commentary on the *Contra Gentiles* written by Francis Sylvester of Ferrara we find the following explanation:[1] "It is said that matter is limited by form and form also by matter: for they are reciprocal causes as is said in II. *Phys.* Whence it pertains to form to limit and determine potentiality, and to matter to limit and determine actuality. For signate matter—which is the principle of individuation—and those accidents which individuation adds to it in addition to the essence—since they are related to matter as impressions made upon it—do not limit the essence in the manner in which actuality limits and bounds potentiality, but in the manner in which matter limits and bounds the amplitude of form."

The citation from the *Physics* seems to refer to a passage in that section of the *Commentary* of Aquinas[2] which deals with the third chapter of the second book. In discussing the relation of efficient and final causes to one another, Aristotle had remarked that they might be *ad invicem causae* (ἀλλήλων ἄιτια). Upon this Aquinas commented as follows:[3] "Some causes are reciprocal according to diversity of species; as labour is the efficient cause of a good state and a good state is also the final cause of labour. For nothing prevents one thing from being both prior and posterior to another according to different points of view, for the end is prior in conception but posterior in existence, while with the agent the reverse is the case. And

---

[1] "Dicitur quod et materia per formam, et forma per materiam limitatur: sunt enim *sibi invicem causae*, ut dicitur II *Phys.* Unde formae est potentiam limitare et determinare, materiae autem est determinare et limitare actum. Materia ergo signata, quae est principium individuationis, et ipsa accidentia quae addit individuum supra essentiam, cum se teneant ex parte materiae tanquam ipsam signantia, non limitant essentiam per modum quo actus potentiam limitat et contrahit, sed modo quo materia limitat et contrahitque formae amplitudinem."

[2] Lect. 5, 7.

[3] "Quaedam sibi invicem sunt causae secundum diversam speciem causae; sicut laborare est causa efficiens bonae habitudinis, bona autem habitudo est causa finalis laboris. Nihil enim prohibet aliquid esse prius et posterius altero secundum diversas rationes: finis enim est prius secundum rationem, sed posterius in esse; agens autem e converso. Et similiter forma est prior quam materia secundum rationem complementi; materia autem est prius quam forma generatione et tempore in omni eo quod movetur de potentia in actum."

similarly form is prior to matter in a complementary conception, while matter is prior to form in generation and time and in everything which is moved from potentiality into actuality."

The explanation of Sylvester does, indeed, offer a way of escape from our predicament. Certainly it is as difficult to conceive of existence without essence as of essence without existence. So far as they are distinct from one another they undoubtedly appear to stand in a relation of mutual dependence and reciprocity. We may admit, then, that if from one point of view essence be potential and existence its actuality, from another existence is merely potential and that union with essence gives it actuality. But the problem why Aquinas should have chosen this manner of expressing himself just at this point remains a mystery.

(h) EXISTENCE

The next question to be considered is almost identical with that which we have just been discussing. Indeed, at first sight, it is not at all obvious why Aquinas should have distinguished between them. Nevertheless, in point of fact he did so distinguish, and the problem with which we are now to deal is whether in God essence and existence are identical. Before doing so, however, it will be well to inquire into the grounds upon which this distinction is based. That it was an important one to the mind of St. Thomas appears from the fact that it is to be found in all his works which bear upon the general topic of the nature of God.[1] Yet each statement is so thoroughly involved in the other that it is rather puzzling that the distinction should have been drawn.

To say that God is identical with his essence—that is, with his definition—implies that there are in him no accidents. It also implies that in him there is no composition of essence and existence, for, were he so composed, God would consist of essence plus existence, and accordingly he would not be identical with his essence alone. Similarly, to say that in God essence and existence are identical is to affirm that nothing can exist in God beside his essence. The two statements, like

[1] *De Ente et Essentia,* cap. v; *De Pot.* q. 7: a. 2; *Con. Gen.* lib. I. cap. 22; *Sum. Theol.* I.a. q. 3: a. 4; *Com. Theol.* Pars Prima, cap. x.

opposite sides of the same shield, directly imply one another; and neither can be true if the other be false.

Why, then, did Aquinas devote a separate section to each? There is probably little risk of error in conjecturing that he did so in order to lay emphasis upon what was, for him, a most important truth. That God exists of necessity—or, in other words, that God's existence is not, so to speak, a mere brute fact, but is logically involved in the very conception and definition of his nature, so that to postulate God's non-existence would be to be guilty of a self-destroying contradiction—this is a conviction which lies at the heart of the Thomist system. In this matter Aquinas was in complete agreement with Anselm, as has been pointed out already. The objection of Aquinas to the ontological argument was that the human intellect is unable to attain to the perception of immaterial essences. If we cannot perceive the essence of God we cannot know *how* the necessity of his existence is involved in it. We can only know the *fact* that it is so involved by going through a process of *a posteriori* reasoning[1] by first demonstrating the existence of God, by arguing from his effects, and then, by the application of the negative method, making it clear that in him essence cannot be distinct from or other than existence. It was, therefore, desirable to devote special attention to this point, and to elucidate it as fully as possible. The arguments advanced by Aquinas in support of his contention are six in number.

1. In the discussion of the eternity of God it has been shown that God exists of necessity, and that there is in him no contingency or potentiality. Now, if necessary existence appertain to any essence which is not identical with that existence, it must either be inconsistent with and repugnant to that essence, as *per se* existence is to the abstract quality of whiteness, or consistent with and kindred to it, as accidental existence in a substance is to whiteness. The former relation is obviously an impossible one, since, apart from its occurrence as a quality in concrete and particular objects, whiteness does not exist at all. If, however, necessary existence can enter into a consistent relationship with an essence not itself, it must do so in one of three ways. Either the existence depends upon the essence, or

---

[1] *A posteriori* in Aquinas's sense.

both essence and existence depend upon something other than themselves, or else the essence depends upon the existence. Now, the first two hypotheses are contrary to the conception of necessary existence which can depend on nothing but itself. On the third hypothesis the essence must inhere in the existence, since that which follows upon the existence of a thing is accidental to it.[1] But that which inheres accidentally is not of the essence. Consequently, since each of these attempts to distinguish essence from necessary existence has led to absurdity we must admit that the two are identical.[2]

Aquinas next considers the objection that it is possible that the existence does not depend wholly upon the essence, so that without the latter the former would cease to be; but that the existence, while necessary *per se*, is united to the essence in a conjunction which is not necessary. To this he replies that if an existence could be understood without its essence, then the essence must stand in no more than an accidental relation to the existence. But that which is related accidentally to a necessary existence cannot be the essence of that existence. If, on the other hand, the existence cannot be understood without the essence, then it depends absolutely upon that which determines the conjunction with the essence. But then, as has been pointed out, it is not a necessary existence.

2. Everything exists by its own existence. Whatever is not its own existence does not, therefore, exist necessarily *per se*. But God does exist necessarily *per se*. Therefore, God is his own existence.[3]

3. If the existence of God be not identical with his essence it cannot be a part of it, for the divine essence is simple and without composition. God's existence must, therefore, be something beside his essence. Moreover, whatever is not of the essence of a thing and yet pertains to that thing must pertain to it through some cause; for things which are not one *per se* are united only by some cause. Existence pertains, therefore, to the divine essence through some cause. This cause may be part of the essence, or it may be the essence itself, or again, it may be something other than the essence. On the first two suppositions the essence would be the cause of its own exist-

---

[1] Cf. *De Ente et Essentia*, cap. vi.
[2] *Con. Gen.* lib. I. cap. 22.
[3] *Con. Gen.* loc. cit.

ence. This is impossible, for the intellect regards a cause as existing before its effect—unless it be granted that a being may be the cause of its accidental existence. This last suggestion is not impossible, "for we may find an accidental being caused by the principles of its subject before the subject itself is understood to exist."[1] But this consideration does not apply to the case of substantial being. There remains, then, the third hypothesis, that the existence of God is imparted to him by a cause existing outside his essence. But this also is impossible, since God is the first cause of all things. Therefore God's existence must be identical with his essence.[2]

4. The term "existence" is applied to something that is actual; for a thing is said to exist not because it is potential but because it is actual. Thus everything to which actuality pertains but which is distinct from its existence is related to its existence as potentiality to actuality, for potentiality and actuality are correlative terms. So, if the divine essence be other than its existence, it is related to that existence as potentiality to actuality. But in God there is no potentiality. Therefore, there is no distinction in God between essence and existence.[3]

In the *Compendium Theologiae* this argument is stated somewhat differently. "God is pure actuality without any admixture of potentiality. His essence must, therefore, be the ultimate actuality; for anything actual beside the ultimate actuality is in potentiality with respect to it. Moreover, the ultimate actuality is its existence. For since all motion is a going forth from potentiality into actuality, that toward which all motion is directed must be the ultimate actuality; and since natural motion is directed toward what is naturally desired, that must be the ultimate actuality which all things desire. That which they desire is existence. Therefore, the divine essence which is pure and ultimate actuality must be existence."[4]

---

[1] "Invenitur enim aliquod ens accidentale causatum ex principiis sui subiecti, ante quod esse intelligitur esse substantiale subiecti."
[2] *Con. Gen.* loc. cit.; cf. *Sum. Theol.* I.a. q. 3: a. 4. c.; *De Ente et Essentia*, cap. iv.
[3] *Con. Gen.* loc. cit.; cf. *Sum. Theol.* I.a. q. 3: a. 4. c.
[4] "Deus est actus purus absque alicuius potentialitatis permixtione. Oportet igitur quod eius essentia sit ultimus actus: nam omnis actus qui est circa ultimum, est in potentia ad ultimum actum. Ultimus autem

5. Everything which cannot exist except through the union of a plurality of things is composite. But nothing in which essence and existence are distinct can exist except through a plurality of things—namely, of essence and existence. Everything in which essence and existence are distinct is, therefore, composite. But it has been shown that God is not composite. Therefore in God essence and existence are not distinct.[1]

6. Everything exists because it has the quality of existence. (*Omnis res est per hoc quod habet esse.*) Nothing of which the essence is distinct from its existence exists, therefore, through its essence. On the contrary, it exists through its participation in something else—namely in existence. Now, nothing which exists through participation in something else can be the first cause, for that through participation in which a thing exists must be prior to it. But nothing is prior to God. Consequently, God's essence is his existence.[2]

The same argument is to be found in the *De Potentia*,[3] although again stated somewhat differently. Since causes productive of diverse effects are sometimes found to have one effect in common, it follows that their common effect must be produced by them by virtue of some superior cause of which it is the proper effect, for an effect is produced by a cause according to its own proper nature and form, so that diverse causes, having diverse natures and forms, must produce diverse effects. Consequently, a common effect cannot be the proper effect of any one of them, but must be referred to a superior cause in virtue of which they act. However, all causes agree in one effect which is existence. Thus fire causes fire and a builder causes a house, but both cause something to exist. Thus, there must be some cause superior to all others in virtue of which they all cause existence, and of which existence is the proper effect. This supreme cause is, of course, God. But the proper effect of every cause bears a likeness to its nature. Therefore,

actus est ipsum esse. Cum enim omnis motus sit exitus de potentia in actum, oportet illud esse ultimum actum in quod tendit omnis motus: et cum motus naturalis in hoc tendat quod est naturalitur desideratum, oportet hoc esse ultimum actum quod omnia desiderant. Hoc autem est esse. Oportet igitur quod essentia divina, quae est actus purus et ultimus, sit ipsum esse" (*Com. Theol.* Pars Prima, cap. x).

[1] *Con. Gen.* loc. cit.; cf. *Com. Theol.* Pars Prima, cap. x.
[2] *Con. Gen.* loc. cit.; *Sum. Theol.* I.a. q. 3: a. 4. c.   [3] q. 7: a. 2. c.

existence must be the very nature and substance of God.

The first of these arguments appears to be needlessly involved. It is obvious that, if an existence be necessary in itself, it cannot be dependent upon something other than itself. Consequently, it is clear that it cannot be dependent upon its essence. Furthermore, Aquinas was doubtless thoroughly in accordance with his own principles in arguing that, if whatever depends upon the existence of anything is accidental to it, the essence of something necessarily existent cannot be dependent upon that existence; since if it were so dependent, it would no longer be its essence, but would have become an accident.

The validity of the argument as a whole rests, however, upon the correct use of Aquinas's general theory of essence and existence, of substance and accidents. Is there any meaning in predicating necessity of the sum-total of existence? Are the real and the rational so inextricably interwoven in the ultimate nature of things that the notion of non-existence when applied to the ultimate Being involves a self-contradiction? Or is existence at bottom a mere arbitrary and non-rational fact, a surd before which all reasoning must stop short? Is Aquinas's conception of substance tenable? Is his distinction between essential and accidental existence a valid one? Such are the vital questions upon the answers to which the cogency of this argument depends.

The phraseology of the second argument is interesting. "Everything exists by its own existence. Whatever is not its own existence does not, therefore, exist necessarily *per se*."[1] The meaning appears to be that where essence and existence are distinct, contingency enters in, and that only where they are identical is necessary existence to be found. This seems sufficiently obvious. The idea is the same as that which underlies the preceding argument, but here it is stated in a much briefer and more compact form.

The third argument depends, in the first place, upon the previously discussed proofs of the absence of composition in God. Assuming these to be valid it asserts that, since God's essence is simple, his existence cannot be a part of it, and that consequently it must either be identical with the essence, or

---

[1] "Unumquodque est per suum esse. Quod igitur non est suum esse non est per se necesse esse" (*Con. Gen.* lib. I. cap. 22).

else wholly distinct from and outside it. Especially does it retraverse the ground already covered by the fourth of these proofs, when it urges that, if the divine existence be wholly distinct from the essence, the fact that they are nevertheless in conjunction must be due to the agency of some cause. At this point it appeals to the principle of causality. Nothing can be the cause of its own existence. Hence the cause of the conjunction of essence and existence cannot be identical with the essence nor can it be included within it. It must, therefore, be without the essence. But previous arguments from causality have already shown that God is the primal cause. Hence God can owe his existence to nothing outside himself. Thus the attempt to regard the divine essence as other than the divine existence ends in a contradiction. The only solution is, then, to identify them.

This argument is completely in harmony with all that has gone before. Its appeal to the principle of causality links it firmly with the causal arguments for the existence of God. Its initial reference to the doctrine that in God there is no composition makes fully evident its connection with the general train of reasoning based upon those proofs.

The fourth argument is practically the same as the fifth proof of the identity of God and his essence. The two conclusions are completely involved and mutually implied by one another. And the two proofs depend alike upon the previous contention that the divine nature is devoid of potentiality.

The fifth argument may be dismissed with similar brevity. It is a direct corollary to the proposition which St. Thomas believed himself to have already established, that in God there is no composition. It is clear that his view of the relation between essence and existence in finite beings could be fairly described as composition. In fact, it is just this feature of his theory that it is most difficult for the modern mind to appreciate. Essence and existence are spoken of as being conjoined and united in language similar to that in which we should speak of the combination of two already existent entities. It is apt to impress one as a hopelessly mechanical and artificial theory, as hopelessly abstract and unreal. But these features of it are assets in the present discussion. Granting that the relation is one of composition, and granting also that there is no composi-

tion in God, we see at once that in God there can be no distinction between essence and existence. Thus, once more, the
only solution is to identify them.

The sixth argument refers us back to the fourth proof of the
existence of God, which, like itself, is built upon the notion of
participation. This conception, as is made clear not only in the
statement of the fourth proof as given in the *Summa Theologica*,
but also in the form in which the present argument is set forth
in the *De Potentia*, involves the principle of causality. Moreover,
emphasis is laid upon the inherent and necessary connection
between cause and effect, upon the innate tendency of a cause
to act in a uniform manner in obedience to an inner constraint
which proceeds from its own peculiar nature and giving to it
an individual character of its own, forces it to endeavour to
reproduce its own likeness. This, as we already know, is a
fundamental characteristic of the principle of causality as
Aquinas understood it. The identity between the divine
essence and existence is arrived at in a manner which reminds
us of Anselm's *Monologium*.[1] All beings have one characteristic
in common, namely, existence. But this characteristic must be
the effect of a cause similar to itself—a cause which is simply
and purely existence. This cause is, of course, God.

To the modern mind the conception of God as simple
existence appears indeed extraordinary. We are at once
reminded of Hegel's dictum that Being and Non-Being are
one and the same. Existence with no positive content seems
but a bare and meaningless abstraction. Were Aquinas alive
to answer such a criticism he might reply that it is an abstraction only because we have abstracted it, and that it was not
with such an abstraction that he was concerned. And from his
point of view such a reply would be thoroughly justified, for
to him God was the most concrete and individual of beings.

We must remember that according to Aquinas's theory
every finite entity is composed of essence and existence. It is,
in fact, a compound of two separable elements. The Kantian
contention that existence is not a predicate is here to some extent
anticipated.[2] "Existence is not an actuality which is part of

---

[1] cc. 1–5.
[2] " 'Esse' non est actus qui sit pars essentiae, sicut forma" (*Quodlib*. ix.
q. 4: a. 6. c.).

the essence, as is form." Existence is not, therefore, one of the qualities of a substance. It is not *that which* an essence is, but *that by which* it is.[1] It adds to it nothing new, but it brings it out of the realm of potentiality into that of actuality.

This conception is, indeed, a noteworthy one. Existence appears to be an indescribable something, without form, quality, or characteristic, capable of being added to any essence. It enters into combination with essence much as one physical element enters into combination with another, yet that with which it combines is, before that combination, non-existent. The wave of a magician's wand, which gives body and shape to the content of a dream, is no more mysterious than this elusive something, this pure actuality, which adds nothing to anything yet makes all things real.

It is evident that we are here dealing with an intellectual abstraction, with a separation of the *that* from the *what* such as we never actually encounter in experience. Had it been existence in this sense that Aquinas identified with God, we might well have looked upon such an identification as a *reductio ad absurdum* of his entire philosophical system. But such is by no means the case. The whole burden of the arguments which we have just examined is this, that in God no such separation of existence from essence is possible. God is not existence reduced to its lowest terms; he is existence in its fullness, he embraces within himself every aspect of reality. All finite entities exist only in so far as they *participate* in that being which he *is*. A created thing is perfect only in that it has being, that it is actual; its being because of its very finitude is partial and limited, it has *this* quality and not *that*. God, on the contrary, *has* no qualities; he *is* all that is real.[2]

Clearly we are here dealing with a conception which, whether or not it can be consistently worked out, undoubtedly contains elements of considerable metaphysical depth and

[1] Cf. *Com. Theol*. Pars Prima, cap. x.

[2] "Esse enim rei quamvis sit aliud ab eius essentia, non tamen est intelligendum quod sit aliquod superadditum ad modum accidentis, sed quasi constituitur per principia essentiae" (*Metaph*. lib. IV. lect. 1). "Esse non dicitur accidens quod sit in genere accidentis, si loquamur de esse substantiae (est enim actus essentiae), sed per quamdam similitudinem, quia non est pars essentiae, sicut nec accidens" (*De Pot*. q. 5: a. 4, ad 3ᵐ). Cf. Boethius's *De Trinitate*, cap. iv.

which will always rank among the great achievements of the human intellect. Before attempting to examine it, we must, however, proceed to consider the further developments which the theory underwent in the hands of Aquinas. We are thus brought to the next stage in the discussion, in which the attempt is made to demonstrate that in God there are no accidents.

(i) ACCIDENT

1. The first argument, as stated in the *Contra Gentiles*, has the superficial appearance of being in direct contradiction to what has just been said. Existence, Aquinas argued, cannot participate in anything except its essence, although it is possible for an existent thing to participate in something other than its essence. The reason for this is that "nothing is more formal or simple than existence."[1] Existence cannot, therefore, participate in anything else. And since the divine substance is its existence, there can pertain to it nothing beyond its substance; consequently, it is not possible that any accidents should inhere in it.

The conception of existence which here confronts us is identical with the Hegelian conception of pure being. In other words, it seems as abstract, bare, and empty an idea as it is possible for the mind to form. It is with interest, then, that we return to the passage in the *Summa Theologica* where the same argument is presented in different words.[2]

A concrete existent thing (*id quod est*) may, Aquinas tells us, have something else added to itself; but existence itself (*ipsum esse*) can have nothing added to itself.[3] Just so it is possible that a hot thing (*calidum*) should possess some other property than heat, such as whiteness; but in heat itself (*ipse calor*) there can be nothing else than heat. So also in God, who is his own existence, it is impossible that any accident should inhere.

Here once more we seem to be faced with the same conception of existence as something separable from essence which characterized Aquinas's attitude toward finite entities, but which we have seen reason to believe had no place in his idea of God. Is there inconsistency here? I think it is possible to

---

[1] "Nihil enim est formalius aut simplicius quam esse."
[2] I.a. q. 3: a. 6. c.   [3] See Boethius, *De Hebdomadibus*, cap. ii.

answer definitely that there is not. It is not because existence—
in the case of God—is a mere bare and featureless somewhat
that nothing can be added to it. On the contrary, it is because
there is in God no distinction between, and no composition of
existence and essence, that nothing can be added to God's
existence.[1] How conceivably could God participate in something other than himself when God contains within himself
the whole fullness of being, in which there is no potentiality
because he is complete and utter actuality? Were the divine
essence susceptible to the addition of accidents it would
follow that God is not in himself the primal and wholly real
Being, that he is only one among other reals, a constituent in
the universe, not its ground and source.

The correctness of this interpretation of Aquinas's meaning
is borne out by a passage in *De Potentia*[2] dealing with the same
topic. "To no nature or essence or form," we are told, "is
anything extraneous added."[3] Thus humanity does not receive
into itself anything which is not contained in the conception
of humanity. But the concrete individual human being who
participates in the essence of humanity may possess numerous
qualities which, while not involved in that essence, are nevertheless not inconsistent with it. He may be white or he may be
black. He may be tall or he may be short. Moreover, as we
have already learned, in a compound substance such as man
there is a two-fold composition, that of *suppositum* and form,
and that of essence and existence. "Man is neither humanity
nor is he his own existence; whence in man it is possible for
some accident to inhere, but not in humanity, nor in his
existence."[4] In simple substances there is nevertheless the
composition of essence and existence. An angel "is not his own
essence; his quiddity, therefore, itself subsists in his existence.
Whence in substances of this kind it is possible to find some
intelligible accident, though not a material accident."[5] In

---

[1] Cf. *Sum. Theol.* I.a. q. 3: a. 4. ad 1ᵐ; 1 *Dist.* 8. q. 4: a. 3. sol.

[2] q. 7: a. 4. c.

[3] "Nulli naturae vel essentiae vel formae aliquid extraneum adiungitur."

[4] "Homo enim nec est humanitas nec esse suum; unde homini potest
inesse aliquod accidens, non autem ipsi humanitati vel eius esse."

[5] "Non est autem suum esse; unde ipsa quidditas est in suo esse subsistens.
Unde in huiusmodi substantiis potest inveniri aliquod accidens intelligibile,
non autem materiale."

God, however, there is no difference or composition, there is nothing which participates and nothing which is participated in, there is no union of *suppositum* and form or of essence and existence. Consequently in God there are no accidents.

2. The second argument points out that, since an accident is something not essential to a subject, it must inhere in a subject as the result of the action of some cause. This cause must be either the divine substance itself or something exterior to it. If the cause be exterior, it must act upon the divine substance in order that the accident may inhere in it. "Nothing," says Aquinas, "introduces any form, either substantial or accidental, into any recipient except by acting upon it in some mode; for to act is nothing other than to make something actual, which it is by form."[1] If this be the case, however, then God must be in the position of patient, and must be acted upon and moved by some agent. But there is no potentiality in God, as has already been proved. Consequently the hypothesis that the cause is external to the divine substance is inadmissible.

The second hypothesis is equally inadmissible. If we grant that the divine substance is itself the cause of an accident inhering within it, we must nevertheless see that it is clearly impossible for it to be the cause in the same respect as it is the recipient, because, in that case, the same thing in the same respect would cause itself to be actual. This, however, is impossible. Accordingly the divine substance must be cause in one respect and recipient in another. But, were this true, it would follow that there is composition in God. The contrary of this supposition has, however, already been proved. Consequently it is impossible that there should be any accident in God.[2]

It is clear that this argument really divides into two others, one of which rests upon the absence of potentiality in God, and the other[3] upon the absence of composition in

---

[1] "Nihil enim inducit aliquam formam, vel substantialem vel accidentalem, in aliquo recipiente, nisi aliquo modo agendo in ipsum; eo quod agere nihil aliud est quam facere aliquid actu, quod quidem est per formam" (*Con. Gen.* lib. I. cap. 23).

[2] Cf. *De Pot.* q. 7: a. 1. c.; also q. 7: a. 4. c.

[3] Cf. *Com. Theol.* Pars Prima, cap. xxii.

him.[1] The third argument in the *Contra Gentiles*, however, is also based—and that explicitly—upon the absence of potentiality in God.

3. It is worded as follows:[2] "Every subject of an accident is to be compared to it as potentiality to actuality: because an accident is a kind of form which produces an existence which is both actual and accidental. But in God there is no potentiality, as has been shown. Therefore in him there can be no accident."

How does this argument, we may ask, differ from the other? The answer seems to be that it does not differ at all. In the former case it is introduced to support the contention previously made that no external agent can cause an accident to exist in the substance of God. Here it is introduced as an argument conclusive in itself. This leads us to the following considerations: If it be conclusive in itself, the argument must apply equally to the hypothesis that the divine substance is the cause of its own accidents. And it seems quite clear that it does so. To quote the words of the *Commentary* of Francis Sylvester, "*in omnibus quae causant aliquid in seipsis, oportet esse diversitatem actus et potentiae.*" And similarly we may inquire whether the argument from the absence of composition in God does not in its turn apply equally to the hypothesis of an external agent. Once again the answer is in the affirmative.[3] In the *Compendium Theologiae*[4] the present argument is reduced to the simple observation that the relation of accident to subject involves composition, without any suggestion that this statement does not hold true if the accident be introduced through the activity of an external agent. Moreover, it is obvious that if an accident be the result of activity from without, composition is certainly present in as great a degree as if the accident were produced from within. Consequently, it is evident that the second argument in the *Contra Gentiles*—which we may call

[1] Cf. 1. *Dist.* 8. q. 4: a. 3. sol.
[2] "Omne subiectum accidentis comparatur ad ipsum ut potentia ad actum: eo quod accidens quaedam forma est faciens esse actu secundum esse accidentale. Sed in Deo nulla est potentialitas, ut supra ostensum est. In eo igitur nullum accidens esse potest" (*Con. Gen.* loc. cit.). Cf. *Sum. Theol.* I.a. q. 3: a. 6. c.; *Com. Theol.* Pars Prima, cap. xxii; also *De Pot.* q. 7: a. 1. c.; also q. 7: a. 4. c.
[3] Cf. *De Pot.* q. 7: a. 1. c.   [4] Pars Prima, cap. xxii.

the argument from causality, since it rests upon the assumption that every accident inheres in its subject as the result of some cause—depends upon two other arguments for its vindication, each of which is fully adequate and conclusive in itself—that from the absence of potentiality in God, and that from the absence of composition in him. Accordingly the argument from causality may be dismissed as useless, without further discussion.

4. Whatever possesses accidents is in some mode susceptible to change, for it is of the nature of an accident that it may inhere or may not inhere in a subject. But there is no change or movement in God who is eternal. Therefore he cannot possess any accidents.[1]

5. Everything in which there is an accident *is* not whatever it *has* within itself (*non est quidquid habet in se*), since an accident is not of the essence of its subject. God is, however, whatever he has in himself. There is therefore no accident in him. The middle proposition of this argument itself requires proof which is as follows: Everything is found in a higher degree (*nobilius*) in the cause than in the effect. God is, moreover, the cause of all things. Whatever, therefore, is found in him is found in the highest degree. What accords most perfectly with anything is, however, it itself, for it is more perfectly a unity than something which is united with another as form with matter, which union is in its turn more perfect than the union of accident with subject. Therefore it follows that God *is* whatever he *has* (*quod Deus sit quidquid habet*).[2]

Practically the same argument, although somewhat differently expressed and conceived, is to be found in the twenty-second chapter of the first part of the *Compendium Theologiae*. It begins with the statement that it is impossible to add to infinite perfection any perfection at all; an assertion the denial of which is self-contradictory. From this it follows that, if any perfection be an accident, the essence in which it inheres

---

[1] *Con. Gen.* loc. cit.
[2] *Con. Gen.* loc. cit. This argument presupposes the identity of God and the divine essence. But the second argument in support of the latter doctrine presupposed the absence in God of any accidents. Since in each instance a number of other proofs are advanced, this circularity is merely useless, and not fatal.

cannot be itself infinitely perfect. But God is infinitely perfect. Therefore there are no accidents in him.

The statement that God is infinitely perfect is justified in the *Compendium Theologiae* by the fact that proof of it has already been advanced in the preceding chapters (xvii–xxi). In the *Contra Gentiles*, however, the perfection of God has not as yet been discussed. Consequently, it is necessary to demonstrate it at this point in order to prove the middle proposition of the argument. Accordingly, when later we find Aquinas devoting a whole chapter to the subject of the divine perfection, the proof of it has already been presupposed here.

6. Substance is not dependent upon accident, although accident is dependent upon substance. Moreover, if one of two entities be not dependent upon the other, it may sometimes be found without that other. It is possible, therefore, that some substance should be found which possesses no accident. This would seem especially appropriate in the case of the simplest substance, such as the divine substance. Therefore in the divine substance there is no accident whatever.[1]

7. Another argument is to be found, briefly expressed in *Compendium Theologiae*,[2] and stated more fully in the *Summa Theologica*.[3] Whatever is *per se* is prior to what is *per accidens*. Whence, since God is absolutely primal, there can be in him nothing accidental. Nor are there in him essential accidents (*accidentia per se*), even as laughter is an essential accident in man, because accidents of this sort are caused by the principles of the subject.[4] For in God nothing can be caused, since he is the primal cause. Hence God is without accidents.

8. Yet another argument is advanced in the *Compendium Theologiae*.[5] Like the variation of the fifth argument set forth there, it also depends upon the previously demonstrated perfection of God. In God all perfections are one.[6] To perfection, however, belong existence, power, activity, and everything of this nature (*esse, posse, agere, et omnia huiusmodi*). In him all these must, therefore, be the same as his essence. (This statement depends for its validity upon the identity of existence and essence in God. In the *Compendium*, as in the

---

[1] *Con. Gen.* loc. cit.
[2] Pars Prima, cap. xxii.
[3] I.a. q. 3: a. 6. c.
[4] Cf. *Posterior Analytics*, lib. I. cap. iv.
[5] Cf. *Posterior Analytics*, lib. I. cap. iv.
[6] Cf. Pars. Prima, cap. xxi.

Contra Gentiles, proof of this identity has already been given.) Therefore none of these is an accident in God.

The last statement presupposes that existence, power, activity, and other qualities of the same kind—such as knowledge, for instance—are the only sort of accidents which God might conceivably possess. We may naturally inquire why this should be presupposed. We may be willing to grant that God can possess none of the qualities of material bodies. But are there not in God qualities or accidents resulting from his relation to the material world, and to the created universe in general? This is a question which we shall be able to raise later when we pass to consider the problem of creation.

In the *De Potentia*[1] the seventh argument is so stated as to connect it with the argument from the absence of composition in God. God is the most perfect of beings, and consequently the best. The best is that in which there is nothing that lacks goodness, just as that is most white in which there is no admixture of black. In the best there can therefore be no composition. For the goodness that results from the composition of parts through which the whole is good, is not itself in any one of the parts. Accordingly the parts are not good through that goodness which is the property of the whole. Therefore it is necessary that what is best should be the simplest, and should lack all composition.

So much, then, for the various arguments which Aquinas advanced. It is clear that he was quite right in saying that the first proof follows at once upon the identity of the divine essence and existence, which he believed himself to have already established. The demonstration of this identity we have already discussed. If we are prepared to accept it, we cannot refuse to admit the validity of the argument now under consideration, which is merely its logical development. If essence and existence be one, it is evident that the multiplicity which we associate with essence must somehow or other be reconciled with the simplicity and unity characteristic of existence. In other words, we have here a tacit admission that the conception of substance and accidents, which Aristotle and the Scholastics who followed him found applicable to the universe of finite beings, is inapplicable to God, its origin, and ground. There is

[1] q. 7: a. 1. c.

nothing astonishing in this. It is only the natural result of the negative method we have been pursuing. Here, indeed, our concern is with accidents; but accidents and substance cannot be separated, and in the pages which follow we shall see that it is equally impossible to apply the term *substance* to God in the same sense in which it is applied to finite objects. The transcendant Reality is beyond conception and beyond words.

Viewed from this standpoint there is a strong resemblance between the God of Aquinas and the Absolute of so modern a thinker as Bradley. For each of these philosophers the ultimate Being occupies a level of existence and of reality wholly above that in which the terms which we have just used have any meaning. Substance and accident, and such relations as we commonly conceive as subsisting between a substance and its accidents, have no place in that perfect and eternal unity. Such a passage as the following from Bradley's *Appearance and Reality*,[1] will make clear how close is the resemblance:

"In mere feeling, or immediate presentation, we have the experience of a whole. This whole contains diversity, and, on the other hand, is not parted by relations. Such an experience, we must admit, is most imperfect and unstable, and its inconsistencies lead us at once to transcend it. Indeed, we hardly possess it as more than that which we are in the act of losing. But it serves to suggest to us the general idea of a total experience where will and thought and feeling may all once more be one. Further, this same unity, felt below distinctions, shows itself later in a kind of hostility against them. We find it in the efforts made by both theory and practice, each to complete itself and so pass into the other. And again, the relational form, as we saw, pointed everywhere to a unity. It implies a substantial totality beyond relations and above them, a whole endeavouring without success to realize itself in their detail. Further, the ideas of goodness, and of the beautiful, suggest in different ways the same result. They more or less involve the experience of a whole beyond relations though full of diversity. Now, if we gather (as we can) such considerations into one, they will assuredly supply us with a positive idea. We gain from them the knowledge of a unity which transcends and yet contains every manifold appearance. They supply not an

[1] Pp. 159–161.

experience but an abstract idea, an idea which we make by uniting given elements. And the mode of union, once more in the abstract, is actually given. Thus we know what is meant by an experience, which embraces all divisions, and yet somehow possesses the direct nature of feeling. We can form the general idea of an absolute experience in which phenomenal distinctions are merged, a whole become immediate at a higher stage without losing any richness. Our complete inability to understand this concrete unity in detail is no good ground for our declining to entertain it. Such a ground would be irrational, and its principle could hardly anywhere be adhered to. But if we can realize at all the general features of the Absolute, if we can see that somehow they come together in a way known vaguely and in the abstract, our result is certain."

The similarity of this conception to that which we have just been considering is obvious. There is also, however, a dissimilarity which, at first glance, appears equally significant. The God of Aquinas is, as we know, a transcendent being. The Absolute of Bradley includes all existence within itself. The one philosophy is theistic, the other pantheistic.

On closer examination we find, however, that the position of Aquinas is nearer to that of Bradley than would at first sight be supposed. It is true that for Aquinas a great gulf is set between the eternal and the temporal worlds, nevertheless this gulf is not so deep as the language of Aquinas might lead one to expect. We have already had occasion to remark that it is a characteristic of Scholastic philosophy, as well as of Roman Catholic theology, to draw sharp distinctions which are asserted to be inviolable, and then to introduce so great a number of qualifications that the dividing line tends to become blurred, and here and there to be erased altogether. One such distinction we have already examined and pronounced to be invalid—the distinction between the knowledge *that* God is, and the knowledge of *what* he is. A second distinction which we viewed with some suspicion was that between the eternal and temporal realms, or, in other words, between God and the universe. It is this which now confronts us once more.

It will be remembered that in the fourth proof of the existence of God Aquinas introduced a doctrine of degrees of truth and existence. In so doing he appealed to the authority of Aristotle.

The passage referred to is to be found at the end of the first chapter of the second book of the *Metaphysics* (993*b*).

" *Διὸ τὰς τῶν ἀεὶ ὄντων ἀρχὰς ἀναγκαῖον ἀεὶ εἶναι ἀληθεστάτας (οὐ γάρ ποτε ἀληθεῖς, οὐδ' ἐκείναις ἀίτιόν τί ἐστι τοῦ εἶναι, ἀλλ' ἐκεῖναι τοῖς ἄλλοις), ὥσθ' ἕκαστον ὡς ἔχει τοῦ εἶναι, οὕτω καὶ τῆς ἀληθείας.*"

"The principles of eternal things must therefore be always most true; for they are not merely sometimes true, nor is there any cause of their being, but they themselves are the cause of the being of other things, so that as each thing is in respect of being, so is it in respect of truth" (Smith's and Ross's translation).

There is an obvious kinship between such a doctrine and the theory of degrees and reality advanced by Bradley. For Aquinas also God enjoys existence in the highest degree—a degree that no other being can share. The implications of this doctrine are, in general, insufficiently stressed by Neoscholastic writers. An exception must be made to this statement in the case of Professor Gilson who, in his recent Gifford Lectures, has dwelt upon it most emphatically. God, he points out, on this view alone really is. Every other entity belongs to the realm of becoming, and is infected to some degree with unreality.[1]

In spite of the resemblance between the two theories, how-

---

[1] "Si ce que nous avons dit est exact, la révélation chrétienne exerça une influence décisive sur le développement de la métaphysique, en y introduisant l'identification de Dieu et de l'Être. Or cette première décision impliquait une modification corrélative de notre conception de l'Univers. Si Dieu est l'Être, il n'est pas seulement l'être total : *totum esse*, comme on vient de le voir, il est encore l'être véritable : *verum esse*, ce qui signifie que le reste n'est que de l'être partiel et ne mérite même pas véritablement le nom d'être. Voilà donc tout ce qui nous semble au premier abord constituer la réalité par excellence : le monde de l'étendue et du mouvement qui nous entoure, rejeté dans la pénombre de l'apparence et relégué dans la zone inférieure d'une quasi-irréalité. On ne saurait assez insister sur l'importance de ce corollaire et je voudrais aujourd'hui en marquer au moins la signification essentielle" (*L'esprit de la philosophie médiévale*, p. 67). Cf. also the following : "A partir du moment où l'on dit que Dieu est l'Être, il est clair qu'en un certain sens Dieu seul est. Admettre le contraire, c'est s'engager à sentenir que tout est Dieu, ce que la pensée chrétienne ne saurait faire, non seulement pour des raisons religieuses, mais aussi pour des raisons philosophiques, dont la principale est que, si tout est Dieu, il n'y a pas de Dieu. En effet, rien de ce qui nous est directement connu ne possède les caractères de l'être. D'abord, les corps ne sont pas infinis, puisque chacun d'eux est déterminé par une essence qui le limite en le définissant. Ce que nous connaissons est toujours tel

ever, one must not try to push the comparison too far. The God of St. Thomas, unlike the Absolute of Bradley, is not identical with the totality of existence. The universe is other than he. Moreover, for the Catholic philosopher, the higher the level of being, the greater is the degree of unity which it possesses. Thus in an angel, as we have seen, there is a lesser degree of composition than in a man. And in God, the supreme Reality, there is no composition at all, no plurality of any kind, but complete simplicity and unity.[1]

Again, the universe of Aquinas, being other than God, is not an appearance in the same sense as Bradley's.

The conception of the transcendence of God has, of course, its philosophical roots in Aristotle. It was also a fundamental feature of Neoplatonic philosophy, which, as has been shown, exercised a profound influence upon Aquinas through Dionysius the Areopagite. For the Neoplatonist the universe owed its existence to an overflowing of being from the One.[2] For Aquinas, the Christian, it was due, on the contrary, to an act of the divine will. Nor could he, like the Neoplatonist, regard its existence as unending. The problem of creation was thus, for him, a vital one. The comparison which we have just drawn between his philosophy and that of Bradley helps us to realize how vital it was. Unless it could be solved successfully, his theistic system was in danger of collapsing into the abyss of pantheism. We are not yet in a position to examine his treatment of the problem, but we are already able to realize how greatly his philosophy depends upon that treatment for its vindication.

ou tel être, jamais l'Être, et même en supposant effectué le total du réel et du possible, aucune sommation d'êtres particuliers ne pourrait reconstituer l'unité de ce qui est, purement et simplement. Mais il y a plus. A *l'Ego sum qui sum* de l'Exode correspond exactement cette autre parole de la Bible: *Ego Dominus et non mutor* (*Malach.* iii. 6). Et, en effet, tous les êtres connus de nous sont soumis au devenir, c'est-à-dire au changement; ce ne sont donc pas des êtres parfaits et immuables comme l'est nécessairement l'Être même. En ce sens, il n'y a pas de fait ni de problème plus important pour la pensée chrétienne que celui du mouvement, et c'est parce que la philosophie d'Aristote est essentiellement une analyse du devenir et de ses conditions métaphysiques, qu'elle est elle-même devenue et restera toujours partie intégrante de la métaphysique chrétienne" (*L'esprit de la philosophie médiévale*, pp. 68–69).

[1] Cf. Plotinus, *Enn.* VI. ix. 1.   [2] Cf. Plotinus, *Enn.* III. viii. 9 and 10.

The second argument has been shown to depend upon the absence in God of potentiality and of composition, which have been already discussed. The third argument also rests upon the absence of potentiality in God, and may here for a like reason be passed over.

To the fourth argument the interesting objection is raised in the *Commentary* of Francis Sylvester that it only succeeds in proving that there are in God no accidents which inhere "accidentally" (*accidentaliter*), and not that there are in God no *propria per se*. By *propria per se* are doubtless meant the *accidentia per se* or essential accidents referred to in the seventh argument, of which the example given in the *Summa Theologica* is that of the accident laughter in the substance man.[1] Clearly, it is not of the nature of such an accident sometimes to inhere and sometimes not to inhere in its subject. On the contrary, it is its nature to inhere continuously from the time of the generation of the substance until the time of its decomposition. Consequently, the argument from motion and change does not avail to show that such accidents cannot exist in God, since it is possible for God to possess them without changing.

The fifth argument rests upon the principle of causality as understood by Aquinas, a principle which is fundamental to his philosophy and which we have had occasion to discuss elsewhere.

In the *Commentary* of Sylvester the objection is raised in regard to the sixth argument that one thing may be dependent upon another and may yet naturally follow from it, so that the first thing will never be found without the second. The author remarks, however, that this is not true of accidents, since by definition they do not follow from the essence of a thing, and accordingly he holds that the argument is sound. On Aquinas's principles both the reason and the conclusion appear to be correct.

The seventh argument also depends upon the principle of causality and follows from it logically.

The eighth argument is slightly reminiscent of the ontological argument, especially of the Cartesian form of it, since it connects perfection with existence. No attempt is made, however, to deduce one from the other. The argument itself

[1] I.a. q. 3: a. 6. c.

depends upon the perfection of God, the proofs of which we have not yet discussed.

A formidable objection was brought by Aquinas against the doctrine of divine simplicity which these eight arguments support. According to Aristotle, he tells us, the same cause produces always the same effect.[1] But from the unity of God proceeds multiplicity. How is this possible if God be wholly simple? His answer deserves to be given *in extenso*.[2]

"In regard to the first objection, it is, therefore, to be said that Aristotle's meaning is not that it is not possible for a multiplicity to proceed from one. For when an agent acts so as to produce something like itself, and the effects are not equal to representing their cause, of necessity what is unified in the cause is multiplied in the effects; just as in the power of the sun all the forms of the bodies that may be generated are as one, and are yet separated in the effects. Thus it happens that through its single power a thing can produce diverse effects; just as fire through its heat liquefies and causes to coagulate, softens and hardens, burns and blackens. And man by the power of reason acquires diverse forms of knowledge and masters the performance of divers arts. So in a much greater degree is it possible for God to create many through his single and simple power. But the Philosopher means that the same thing, remaining the same, cannot produce diverse effects at diverse times, if it act by the necessity of nature, unless perchance this should occur accidentally through

---

[1] Cf. *De Generatione et Corruptione*, lib. II. cap. iv.

[2] "Ad primum ergo dicendum quod intentio Aristotelis non est quod ab uno non possit procedere multitudo. Cum enim agens agat sibi simile, et effectus deficiant a repraesentatione suae causae, oportet quod illud quod in causa est unitum, in effectibus multipliceter; sicut in virtute solis sunt quasi unum omnes formae generabilium corporum, et tamen in effectibus distinguuntur. Et exinde contingit quod per unam suam virtutem res aliqua potest inducere diversos effectus; sicut ignis per suum calorem liquefacit et coagulat, et mollificat et indurat, et comburit et denigrat. Et homo per virtutem rationis acquirit diversas scientas, et operatur diversum artium opera; unde et multo amplius Deus per unam suam simplicem virtutem potest multa creare. Sed Philosophus intendit, quod aliquid manens idem non facit diversa in diversis temporibus, si sit agens per necessitatem naturae; nisi forte per accidens hoc contingat ex diversitate materiae, vel alicuius alterius accidentis. Hoc tamen non est ad propositum" (*De Pot.* q. 7: a. 1. ad 1m).

the diversity of matter, or of some other accident. But this is
not germane to the proposition." With this reply we may dismiss the question for a time, and proceed to inspect the proofs
next in order which are intended to demonstrate that God cannot be designated or specified by the addition of any substantial
differences.

(j) DIFFERENTIA

This step is the logical consequence of the establishment of
absolute simplicity of God. Further application of the negative
method requires that it be shown that he is not the member of
any species and thus that another of the fundamental conceptions whereby we are wont to classify finite objects is
incapable of giving us any knowledge of God.

1. It is impossible for anything to exist actually (*esse in actu*)
unless all those characteristics which specify its substantial
being exist also. (For this reason, Aquinas informs us, the
Platonists did not posit the ideas of genera as existing, but
merely those of species, for the genera are distinguished by
essential differences.) Since this is the case, it is impossible for
the divine essence to exist unless all its essential differentiae
also exist. In other words, the existence of the essence is
dependent upon that of its differentiae. But this is impossible,
for the divine essence is its own existence, and consequently
cannot depend for its actuality on anything that is added
to it. Hence God cannot be specified by substantial differences.[1]

2. Whatever requires something else to be added to it in
order that it may exist is in potentiality with regard to that
other thing. But there is no potentiality in God. On the
contrary God's existence is his being. Hence God's essence
cannot be specified by anything added to it.[2]

3. That which is intrinsic to a thing and through which the
thing is made actually to exist is either the whole of its essence
or a part of it. Moreover, whatever specifies anything by an
essential specification makes it actual and is intrinsic to it;

---

[1] *Con. Gen.* lib. I. cap. 24; cf. *Com. Theol.* cap. xi.
[2] *Con. Gen.* loc. cit.; cf. *Com. Theol.* Pars Prima, cap. xi.

otherwise the thing would not be specified substantially. It must therefore be the essence itself, or a part of it. But if anything be added to the divine existence, it cannot be the whole essence that is added, for the existence of God is not other than his essence. On the other hand, if it be a part of the essence that is added, then God will be essentially composed of parts. This also is impossible, for there is no composition in God. It is impossible, therefore, for God to be specified by substantial differences.[1]

This argument is not very easy to follow at first glance, but if we try to separate the underlying idea from the somewhat awkward language in which it is expressed, its meaning seems to be quite definite and clear. It is impossible, for instance, that a dog should exist without possessing those characteristics common to all dogs, which distinguish them from cats and birds and sheep and elephants and all other kinds of animals. If it did not possess these characteristics or differentiae it would not be a dog. They are not something separate from its nature which can in reality (*secundum rem*) be added to it or subtracted from it. They are the manifestation of that nature. Yet, while the differentiae of the dog are not separable from its essence, nevertheless the essence of the dog is separable from its existence; as we know from the fact that the dog comes into existence and passes out of it again. As it is with the dog, so it is with all other finite beings, including man. With God, however, it is otherwise, since God's existence is not separable from or other than his essence. Now if God possess differentiae, these differentiae must be identical either with the divine essence or with some part of it. But they cannot be identical with the essence itself, for the essence is identical with the divine existence, and to existence, which is absolutely simple, no qualities or characteristics can be attached. Nor can they be identical with a part of the essence, for in God there are no parts, since God is simple and without composition. Therefore God possesses no substantial differences.

4. Essential specifications, when added to anything, do not constitute the conception of that thing. They merely cause it actually to exist. Thus *rational* added to *animal* constitutes the

---

[1] *Con. Gen.* loc. cit.; cf. *Com. Theol.* Pars Prima, cap. xiii.

existence of an actual animal, but does not constitute the conception of animal as animal; for the differentiae do not enter into the definition of the species. Yet, since in God essence and existence are one, essential specifications, if they be added to God's existence, must be added also to his essence. But this is contrary to the definition of essential specifications or differentiae. Therefore, it is impossible that they should exist in God.[1]

This argument, like its predecessor, is somewhat involved. Once more, however, the central thought is quite clear. All species which belong to any one genus, belong to it equally. A dog is just as much an animal as a cat. The fact that it is a different sort of animal does not make it more or less an animal. So it is also with man. The fact that man is a rational being does not in any way affect the fact that he is an animal. He is just as much an animal as any other member of the genus, no more and no less. But the fact that he belongs to a particular species of animal is all-important in determining his status in relation to the members of other species. While dog and cat and man are equally members of the same genus, they are unequal in so far as they are members of different species. Man, because he is possessed of reason, is vastly superior in the scale of being. Yet this superiority is due to the differentiae which characterize man's particular species. He is superior as *man*, not *as animal*. This superiority is an actual fact, but it has no relevance to the definition of the genus to which he belongs. He is endowed with a higher degree of being, with more being, but not with more animality.

With God it is otherwise. God is not being, or animal, or man plus something else. For, were any further or higher degree of being added to the being of God, it must be added also to God's essence, since in God essence and being or existence are identical. Moreover, since existence is altogether simple, so also is the divine essence simple. To it, therefore, nothing can be added; and so there can be no differentiae in God.[2]

The four arguments which we have just referred to are all based upon the conception of God as simple and pure actuality (*actus purus*) in whom essence and existence are one, which

---

[1] *Con. Gen.* loc. cit.   [2] Cf. *Com. Theol.* Pars Prima, cap. xiii.

has been gradually built up by the application of the negative method. They are the logical corollaries of this conception, and stand or fall with it. That God is not the member of a species[1] is clearly the conclusion to which the preceding discussion has been leading. It is involved in the very severance of eternity from time, and in the insistence upon the absolute transcendence of God, which formed the first link in the chain of argument. To admit that divinity could be predicated of more than one individual would be utterly false to the fundamental contentions of the Thomist philosophy. Monotheism, if it could be established at all, would then be in the nature of arbitrary fact. The untruth of the contrary hypothesis of polytheism would be equally arbitrary. It would be in no sense self-contradictory and absurd, as from the point of view of Aquinas it certainly was.

There is one point, however, which must be raised in connection with the last two arguments, and that is the nature of the difference between them. Both are based upon the identity of the divine essence and existence. But the former approaches the problem from the point of view of the species which is composed of genus and differentiae. Since the divine essence is identical with simple existence, it cannot be identical with the plurality of the differentiae; and since it has no parts, no portion of it can be identical therewith.

The latter argument takes as its point of departure the conception of genus. The essence of a genus remains unaffected by the dissimilarities of the differentiae of the various species subsumed under it. They are further degrees of being with which it has no concern. Yet in God, since essence and existence are one, added fullness of being would mean additional change of essence. But to simple existence, and to essence identical therewith, no addition can be made.

Thus the former argument emphasizes the fact that the member of a species must reconcile the simplicity of existence with an essence wherein plurality is involved, through its inclusion of the differentiae. It lays down that, since in God essence is existence, such plurality is impossible. The latter argument is concerned with the essence of the genus to which a species belongs and which does not participate in the differ-

---

[1] Cf. *Com. Theol.* Pars Prima, cap. xi.

entiae that characterize the species. It is maintained that this cannot be true of God, since the identity of essence and existence in God would confound genus with species, and absorb both into a unity which would resemble neither.

(k) GENUS

It has now to be shown that God is not in a genus.

1. This follows directly from the preceding argument, for, whatever is in a genus must be a member of some species which that genus includes. Therefore, since God is not in a species he cannot be in a genus.[1]

2. Furthermore, if God be in a genus, he must belong either to the genus *accident* or the genus *substance*. But God cannot belong to the genus *accident* since he is the primal being and the first cause. Nor can God be in the genus *substance*, because the genus substance is not existence itself; otherwise each individual substance would be its own existence, since the concept of the genus applies to each of its members. Were this the case no substance could be the effect of any cause. We know, however, that this is not the case, and that there are substances that are caused. Consequently God does not belong to the genus *substance*.[2]

It is to be noted that this argument divided itself into two others. That God cannot be in the genus *accident* is proved by deduction from the proposition that he is the primal being and the first cause. That he cannot be in the genus *substance* is proved by showing that it is incompatible with the identity of the divine essence and existence.

3. Whatever is in a genus differs according to its existence from other members of the genus,[3] otherwise the genus would not be predicated of a plurality of things. All the members must agree, however, in the quiddity or essence of the genus, because the genus is predicated of all of them in regard to what they are.[4] Thus the existence of any member of a genus is not included in its quiddity. But this cannot be true of God, as was shown in the preceding discussion (cf. the fourth

---

[1] *Con. Gen.* lib. I. cap. 25. [2] *Con. Gen.* loc. cit.

[3] "Secundum esse differt ab aliis quae in eodem genere sunt."

[4] "Quia de omnibus genus *in quod quid est* predicatur."

argument) concerning substantial differences; therefore God is not in a genus.[1]

4. A thing is classified under a certain genus according to its quiddity. But God's quiddity is his existence. Now nothing is classified under a genus according to its being, because being is not a genus. Therefore it is impossible that God should be in a genus.[2]

The proof that being cannot be a genus is derived from Aristotle. It is stated by Aquinas as follows:[3] "If being were a genus, it would be necessary to find some difference in order to arrive at the species. But no difference participates in the genus in such a way that the genus is in the concept of the species; for in that case the genus would be involved twice in the definition of the species; on the contrary the difference must be other than what is contained in the concept of the genus. Yet nothing can be other than what is contained in the concept of being, and at the same time be predicated of those things which are understood to have being. And so no difference can be found whereby the species may be determined. Therefore it must be admitted that being is not a genus; whence of necessity we must conclude that God is not in a genus."[4]

5. In the *Summa Theologica* the following argument is also to be found. A species is constituted of genus and differentia. Moreover, that from which the differentiae are derived is related to that from which the genus is derived as actuality to potentiality. Thus *animal* is derived from sensuous nature by the method of concretion (*per modum concretionis*); it is called animal because it has a sensuous nature. So *rational* is derived

---

[1] *Con. Gen.* loc. cit.; cf. *Sum. Theol.* I.a. q. 3: a. 5. c.; *Com. Theol.* Pars Prima, cap. xii; *De Pot.* q. 7: a. 3. c.

[2] *Con. Gen.* loc. cit.; cf. *Sum. Theol.* I.a. q. 3: a. 5. c.; *Com. Theol.* Pars Prima, cap. xii; *De Pot.* q. 7: a. 3. c.

[3] "Si ens esset genus, oportet differentiam aliquam inveniri per quam traheretur ad speciem. Nulla autem differentia participat genus, ita scilicet quod genus sit in ratione differentiae, quia sic genus poneretur bis in definitione speciei: sed oportet differentiam esse praeter id quod intelligitur in ratione generis. Nihil autem potest esse quod sit praeter id quod intelligitur per ens, si ens sit de intellectu eorum de quibus praedicatur. Et sic per nullam differentiam contrahi potest. Relinquitur igitur quod ens non sit genus. Unde ex hoc de necessitate concluditur quod Deus non sit in genere" (*Con. Gen.* loc. cit.).

[4] Cf. *Metaph.* lib. III. cap. iii.

from an intellectual nature, for it is rational because it has an intellectual nature. Thus we have *animal* as the genus and *rational* as the species. The intellectual nature, however, is to be compared to the sensuous as actuality to potentiality. But in God there is no potentiality. Consequently, God cannot, as a species, be a member of any genus.

It should be added that this argument was not intended to be absolutely conclusive, since the opening sentence of the corpus dealing with the subject[1] informs us that it must be said that a thing may be in a genus in one of two ways—in one way absolutely and properly as a species contained in a genus; in another way as principles and privations, just as point and unity are reduced to the genus *quantity* as its principles, and as blindness and every privation are reduced to the genus *habit* (habitus, ἕξις).[2]

The argument from the absence of potentiality in God is also to be found in the *De Potentia*,[3] although there it is presented in conjunction with another based upon the absence of composition in God.[4] "Although matter is not a genus nor form a differentia, yet the conception of genus is derived from matter and the conception of differentia from form; as is evident from the fact that in man the sensible nature, from which is derived the conception of animal, stands in the relation of matter to reason from which is derived the rational differentia. For *animal* is that which has a sensuous nature; and *rational* that which has reason. Whence it is necessary that in everything that is in a genus there should be a composition of matter

---

[1] *Sum. Theol.* I.a. q. 3: a. 5. c.

[2] "RESPONDEO DICENDUM quod aliquid est in genere dupliciter. Uno modo, simpliciter et proprie; sicut species, quae sub genere continentur. Alio modo, per reductionem, sicut principia et privationes: sicut punctus et unitas reducuntur ad genus quantitatis, sicut principia; caecitas autem, et omnis privatio, reducitur ad genus sui habitus."

[3] q. 7: a. 3. c.

[4] "Quamvis materia non sit genus, nec forma sit differentia, tamen ratio generis sumitur ex materia, et ratio differentiae sumitur ex forma; sicut patet quod in homine natura sensibilis ex qua sumitur ratio animalis est materialis respectu rationis, ex qua sumitur differentia rationalis. Nam animal est quod habet naturam sensitivam; rationale autem quod rationem habet. Unde in omni eo quod est in genere, oportet esse compositionem materiae et formae, vel actus et potentiae; quod quidem in Deo esse non potest, qui est actus purus."

and form, or of act and potentiality; which indeed cannot be existent in God who is pure act."

6. Two other arguments are to be found in the *De Potentia*.[1] One, which is elaborated in considerable detail, takes as its point of departure the perfection of God; a subject which we, who have been following the train of reasoning set forth in the *Contra Gentiles*, have not yet considered. God, we are told, since he is absolutely perfect, includes in himself the perfections of all genera. Whatever is in a genus is subject to and determined by the limits imposed by the conception of that genus. God, however, is infinite in essence, and absolutely perfect. Consequently, God can be subject to no limitations. The conclusions which follow are momentous.[2] "From this, furthermore, it appears that God is neither species nor *individuum*, nor has he differentia nor definition; for all definition is from genus and species; whence it is impossible that a demonstration (of his existence) should be given otherwise than from his effects, for the middle term of a demonstration *propter quid* should be the definition."

It is to be noted that the impossibility of defining God is deduced in this paragraph from the fact that God is not in a genus. Nevertheless, in the paragraph immediately preceding that from which this sentence has been quoted the procedure is reversed, and from the impossibility of defining God it is deduced that God cannot be in a genus. This is the other argument found only in the *De Potentia*.[3]

Here we have a clear case of arguing in a circle. We are told that God cannot be in a genus since it is impossible to define him, and that it is impossible to define God because he is not in a genus. None the less it would be a mistake to make too much of this fact especially in the case of an argument which is found

---

[1] q. 7: a. 3. c.

[2] "Ex hoc ulterius patet quod Deus non est species nec individuum, nec habet differentiam nec definitionem; nam omnis definitio est ex genere et specie; unde nec de ipso demonstratio fieri potest nisi per effectum, cum demonstrationis 'propter quid' medium sit definitio."

[3] "Omne quod est in genere potest definiri, vel sub aliquo definito comprehendi. Sed Deus cum sit infinitus, non est huismodi. Ergo non est in genere." "Everything which is in a genus can be defined, or comprehended under some definition. But with God it is not so, since he is infinite. Therefore God is not in a genus" (q. 7: a. 3. *sed contra*).

in the *sed contra* of an article. It is doubtless due to the desire, so characteristic of Aquinas, to state all possible arguments in support of every contention. Nor does it follow that we must reject one of the arguments as invalid. The sixth proof, as we have already seen, is based upon the perfection of God, and the impossibility of defining him is legitimately deduced from the conclusion thus established. On the other hand, the procedure of the seventh argument, in taking the impossibility of defining God as its premise, could easily be vindicated from the point of view of Aquinas by the *Via Remotionis*. If it be impossible to predicate any attributes of God, it is, of course, impossible to define him. If, however, we are prepared to contest the validity of the *Via Remotionis*, the foundation of this argument will be undermined.

With the exception of the sixth, these various proofs are based upon premises familiar to us from the previous discussion. It remains to consider certain objections which Aquinas advanced against his own position in order to refute them. In the first place it might be urged that, while the term *substance* cannot be applied to God with absolute accuracy—since he does not underlie or sustain any accidents—nevertheless it connotes being in itself (*ens per se*), and that it has been proved that God is such a being inasmuch as it has been shown that there are no accidents in him. To this Aquinas replied that substance is not to be defined as being in itself, since it had been proved that being is not a genus. Furthermore he argued the phrase "being in itself" is in reality a pure negation, for a thing is said to have its being in itself only because it does not have its being in some other thing. He then points out that the concept of a genus cannot consist in a negation, for in that case the genus would not indicate what a thing is, but only what it is not. On the contrary the term *substance* signifies "a thing to which it pertains not to exist in a subject" ("res cui conveniat esse non in subiecto"). The term *thing* (*res*) designates the quiddity; the term *being* (*ens*) the existence (*esse*); so that by substance we are to understand that which has a quiddity to which it does not pertain to exist in another. But God is not this sort of being, for his quiddity is identical with his existence. Therefore God is not in the genus *substance*.[1]

[1] *Con. Gen.* loc. cit.

The meaning of this reply seems to be that while an accident, from its very conception and definition, of necessity inheres in some entity which serves as its substratum—as whiteness, for instance, is to be found only as a quality of some white thing—substance, on the contrary, is conceived of as a self-contained and autonomous unity logically capable of existing by itself. Actually to exist it requires, of course, that existence be imparted to it from without by the fiat of God. But considered abstractedly in its essence it must be a harmonious and coherent whole, for existence cannot be imparted to that which is essentially incoherent and self-contradictory. Now it is obvious that God, the cause of all things, cannot be in the genus accident. And it is also clear that God cannot be in the genus substance, inasmuch as he is not possessed of an essence or quiddity which can be considered by itself and in abstraction from his existence. Since essence and existence in God are identical, neither can be comprehended apart from the other. Consequently, God is not a substance in the sense in which any other entity is a substance.[1]

Another weighty objection is stated in the *De Potentia*.[2] Things which exist and which do not differ in any respect are completely the same. But God is not the same as other things. He differs, therefore, from them in some respect. Moreover, everything which differs from something else does so by some difference. There is, therefore, some difference in God by which he differs from other things. Nor can it be an accidental difference, for in God there are no accidents. Furthermore, any substantial difference indicates a difference of genus. Therefore God is in a different genus from other things.

The reply is made upon lines already familiar to us from Aquinas's defence of the immateriality of God against David of Dinant, and rests upon the distinction between difference and diversity. A man differs from an ass by his rationality, but rationality does not differ from the ass by some further difference, for, were this the case, we should be confronted by an endless series of differences which would form what is known to modern philosophers as a vicious infinite. Rationality and the

[1] Cf. *Sum. Theol.* Ia. q. 3: a. 5. ob. 1. and reply; also *De Pot.* q. 7: a. 3: ob. 4. and reply.　　　　　　　　　　[2] q. 7: a. 3. ob. 2.

ass are simply diverse.[1] Hence the statement that things which
exist and which do not differ in some respect are completely
the same,[2] is not true if the word "differ" be taken in the
strict sense, for some things do not differ, they are simply
diverse. So it is with God and created things. God does not
differ from his creatures, but creator and created are diverse.[3]

The same difficulty which arose when this theory was
advanced in defence of the immateriality of God now confronts us again. In this instance, however, it is more acute.
Before we were concerned with primary matter which was
defined as pure potentiality, and which consequently is to be
conceived as totally destitute of all positive qualities. Now we
are concerned with the entire created universe in all its variety
.and multiplicity. If God be wholly diverse from everything
else that exists, it follows that existence itself is all that he can
have in common with his creatures. Since being is not a genus,
the admission that God and the creatures have so much in
common may be made safely. But beyond this point we cannot
go. No degree of similarity can be conceded. From this it
follows that absolutely nothing can be predicated of God, for
every predicate that we can conceive is derived from our
knowledge of creatures. In other words, we must accept the
principle of the *Via Remotionis* in its extreme form and without
qualification. We can know of God only that he exists, all
positive knowledge of his nature is denied us. It may be urged
that this is precisely the principle upon which Aquinas did
proceed through all the long course of reasoning which we
have been reviewing. Did he not assert that all the propositions
which he would demonstrate in regard to God would be purely
negative? We need not consider for the moment whether he
has kept his word, or whether each negation does not involve a
counter-affirmation. It need only be pointed out that Aquinas
himself taught that a real, if imperfect, knowledge of God can
be obtained by the method of analogy which we shall have to
deal with later, and that he explicitly repudiated the view of
Maimonides that no positive predicate when applied to God

[1] "Rationale autem ulterius non differt ab asino aliqua differentia (quia
sic esset, abire in infinitum), sed se ipso."
[2] "Quaecumque sunt et nullo modo differunt, sunt penitus eadem."
[3] Cf. *Dist.* 8. q. 1: a. 2. ad 3^{m}.

is truer of him than another.[1] Clearly, however, he cannot
have it both ways. If God be wholly diverse from everything
else, then no predication of any sort can be made respecting
God. On the other hand, if one predicate can be applied to
God more truly than another, then God is not wholly dissimilar to his creatures, since in one aspect at least he resembles
them more than in others. Finally it may be remarked that
the likeness to which attention has been called between the
Absolute of Bradley and the God of Aquinas is now more
marked than before. Aquinas's God is here distinctly stated to
be above the category of substance, as he had already been
stated to be above that of accident.

We are now approaching the end of the Negative Way, but
we have not yet reached it. The next proposition which is to
be demonstrated is that God is not the formal being of all
things.

(l) FORMAL BEING OF ALL THINGS

On more occasions than one we have had to ask ourselves
whether the theism of Aquinas is not in imminent danger of
collapsing into pantheism. It is a question which Aquinas
must have frequently put to himself, and we have now reached
the point where he thought it worth while to enter upon a
detailed refutation of such a charge. In doing so he was doubtless actuated not merely by philosophical but also by theological
and ecclesiastical considerations. The influence of the great
Neoplatonist, John Scotus Eriugena, was by no means dead.
Moreover, in Thomas's own century, David of Dinant and
Amalric of Bene had each put forward a theory which, in some
sense or other, identified God with the world, and which was
therefore regarded as inimical to the orthodox faith. The
heresy of David is already familiar to us—the identification of
God with primary matter. It is that of Amalric with which
we are now concerned—the assertion, namely, that God is
the formal being of all things (*esse formale uniuscuiusque rei*).

1. The first argument in refutation of this theory is as
follows. There are two modes of being or existence (*esse*) in all
created things, substantial and accidental. But it has already

---

[1] *Sum. Theol.* I.a. q. 13 : a. 2. c.

been proved that God is neither substance nor accident. Therefore God cannot be that being by which everything formally exists.[1]

If we admit that the categories of substance and accident are inapplicable to God, it follows that any being to which they are applicable must be other than God. So much is evident. Aquinas was, of course, prepared to assert that they were applicable to all beings other than God.[2] But what if someone should assert that there is no being other than God? In other words, is such an argument of any avail against a mode of thought such as that of Bradley, according to which the categories of substance and accident are fundamentally inadequate and self-contradictory, and the finite entities to which they are held to apply have no real existence in their own right, but are merely appearances of an underlying unity? Clearly it is not sufficient to show that the categories of substance and accident do not apply to God. In addition it must be shown that they do apply to anything else. It is not, of course, to be expected that Aquinas should have anticipated the objections which, seven centuries later, were to be urged against the validity of these categories; nor is it possible to speculate as to how he would have replied to them if he had known of them. We can but seek to discover whether his system contains any principle upon which a justification of the categories in question could be founded.

Such a principle appears to present itself in the doctrine of the identity of the divine essence and the divine existence, to which we have already referred. It is the identity of essence with existence that raises God above the categories of substance and accident. And, conversely, it is the otherness of essence and existence in all created things that renders these categories applicable to them.[3] That is to say, while substance and accident, and indeed all the other categories, are at home in the world of contingency and becoming, they are out of place and meaningless in the world of necessity and eternity.[4] Thus, we are once more face to face with the dualism between the two worlds upon which the entire Thomist system depends.

[1] Con. Gen. lib. I. cap. 26.   [2] Cf. Quodlib. vii. q. 3: a. 7.
[3] Cf. Quodlib. vii. q. 3: a. 7.   [4] Cf. Boethius, De Trinitate, cap. iv.

2. The second proof is differently worded, but is in reality another statement of the same principle. Things do not differ from one another so far as their existence is concerned, for in existence they all alike share. In order that they should differ, it is necessary either that certain specific differences be added to their being, or else that being itself pertain to natures specifically different. The first of these alternatives is inadmissible, for no addition can be made which does not itself exist, and so fall under the category of being. In other words, being, as we have already seen, is not a genus. Consequently, it must be admitted that things differ because existence pertains to dissimilar natures or essences. It is impossible, however, that the divine nature should pertain to anything other than itself, since God is his own existence.[1] Therefore, if it were true that God is the being of all things, it would be true also that all things are absolutely one.[2]

It is easy to see that the idea underlying this argument is the same as that which inspired its predecessor. There is the same contrast between the fleeting world of plurality in which essence and *suppositum* are separate and distinct, and the world of eternity in which there is neither essence nor *suppositum* but only unity. And again, we may make the same criticism as before. If the world of plurality be a real world apart from God and in its own right, then certainly it cannot be identical with God. Such a statement is tautologous. But it is possible to assert that this plurality is a plurality only of appearance, real only as an illusion is real, a manifoldness composed of partial and inadequate glimpses of a single individual. Aquinas of course accepts the conceptions of substance and accident, of essence and *suppositum*, of time and change, as adequately expressive of the universe of experience. It is, however, significant that he does not regard them as applicable to God. It is also noteworthy that God, in his terminology, has more "being" and is more "true"[3] than the realm of finitude and plurality. Furthermore, according to his conception of causality, all that is in the effect must have antecedently existed in the cause, and therefore an effect must in some degree resemble its

<hr />

[1] *Con. Gen.* loc. cit.; cf. *Com. Theol.* Pars Prima, cap. xiii.
[2] "Oporteret omnia simpliciter esse unum."
[3] Cf. *Con. Gen.* lib. I. cap. 13; *Sum. Theol.* I.a. q. 2 : a. 3. c.

cause, though it may fall short of the degree of being possessed by its source. All these considerations seem to render the position of Aquinas especially susceptible to an attack from the standpoint of the idealist or the mystic who is prepared to deny the existence of a temporal universe. Against the crude pantheism which would equate God with physical nature, against all forms of materialism or naturalism, it is indeed much more strongly fortified. But in spite of this it does seem open to an attack from the singularist or the acosmist. This is a criticism which we have had occasion to urge with almost wearisome frequency. We cannot deal with it satisfactorily until we have examined Aquinas's view of the relation of God to the world; but it is instructive to notice how often the doubt arises. Clearly it is one of the most crucial points in connection with the Thomist system, if it be not the most crucial of all.

3. The third proof is an application of the argument from causality. We know that in the universe there are beings which are caused, inasmuch as form is a principle of being, and the agent which causes anything to be actual. Therefore if God be identical with the being of all things, it follows that God will himself be caused. But God is the primal being, and therefore is caused by nothing. Hence God is not identical with the being of all things.[1]

It does not appear that this argument is capable of refuting a metaphysic according to which the temporal universe is merely a series of stages in the evolving life of God. Some such theory may have been held by the disciples of Amalric of Bene, whose beliefs seem to have been somewhat similar to those of the followers of Joachim of Floris, "who identified the succession of the great periods of history with the generation of the three Divine persons."[2] In such a world, finite realities would not, indeed, be caused in the sense that they were produced *ex nihilo*, but every event would be caused by antecedent events in the same sense that each state in a man's conscious life is the outcome of preceding states, and the entire series of temporal events would be caused in the same sense that the entire series of conscious states are involved in and sustained by an

---

[1] *Con. Gen.* loc. cit.
[2] De Wulf, *History of Mediaeval Philosophy*, vol. I. p. 192.

underlying unity. If any events at all take place in the life of
God they must be caused in some such fashion. Against a
cosmology which would identify the universe with a series of
such states the argument that Aquinas has advanced appears,
as it stands, to be powerless. To be made effective it would
require to be supplemented by a reference to what we may
well term the foundation-stone of the Thomist system, namely,
the immobility of God, from which his eternity and his freedom from potentiality have been deduced. Arguing from
these premises, Aquinas might urge legitimately enough that
since no sequence of events can take place in the life of God,
and since both time and causality are fundamental features in
the universe of our experience, therefore the being of this
universe must be distinct from the being of God. Such an
argument, it is needless to say, would presuppose the reality of
time. In a universe in which time was unreal, causality in so
far as it implies succession would be meaningless, and the
argument which we have been examining would lose its force.

4. The fourth proof is founded upon the theory of the nature
of universals which Aquinas inherited from Aristotle. A
universal, when abstracted from the multitude of particulars
in which it inheres, exists only for the mind which contemplates
it. It has no autonomous and separate existence of its own *in
rerum natura*. "Thus animal is not something other than Socrates
and Plato and all other animals, except for the intellect, which
apprehends the form of animal stripped of all individualizing
and specifying particulars; for man is what is truly animal;
otherwise it would follow that in Socrates and in Plato there
were many animals, animal in general, man in general, and
Plato himself. Much less, therefore, is being in general
itself something beyond all existent things, except for the
intellect alone."[1] Consequently, if God were being in general
he would have no existence except for the mind. But it has been

[1] "Sicut *animal* non est aliud praeter Socratem et Platonem et alia animalia
nisi intellectu, qui apprehendit formam animalis exspoliatam ab omnibus
individuantibus et specificantibus; homo enim est quod vere est animal;
alias sequeretur quod in Socrate et Platone essent plura animalia, scilicet
ipsum animal commune, et homo communis, et ipse Plato. Multo igitur
minus et ipsum esse commune est aliquid praeter omnes res existentes
nisi in intellectu solum" (*Con. Gen.* lib. I. cap. 26).

proved that God exists *in rerum natura*. Therefore God is not the universal being of all things.

The argument requires us to assume the validity of two presuppositions. In the first place, we must accept the Thomist theory of universals as opposed to an extreme realism of the Platonic type. In the second place, we must admit the existence of a plurality of real entities in the universe. If both these assumptions be granted, the argument is conclusive. If either be questioned, it loses its cogency.

5. The fifth proof is as follows. Generation is passage into being (*via in esse*), and corruption is passage into non-being (*via in non esse*): "for the term of generation is not form, nor that of corruption privation, unless it be true that form produces being and privation non-being."[1] Accordingly, were God the formal being of all things, he must also be the term of generation. But such is not the case, for God is eternal.[2]

This argument is evidently inspired by the same idea as that which lies at the root of the third argument. In the present instance, the defect which we noted in the previous statement is, however, remedied, and reference is made to the doctrine of the eternity of God. A much firmer foundation is thus given to the argument. Certainly, if God be a changeless being, he cannot be identical with the world of generation and corruption. Nor, if generation and corruption be realities and not mere illusory appearances, can the universe in which they are elements be identical with the static eternity of the divine nature.

6. The sixth argument is practically the same in substance as the fifth, although the wording is different. Its point of departure is the same—the eternity of God. Were it true that God is the being of all things, then everything must have existed from eternity. In such a case there could be neither generation nor corruption. In a world of that description generation would be the fresh acquisition of a being already existing.[3] Moreover, that which made the acquisition must itself either be pre-existent—in which case generation would consist, not in the

---

[1] "Non enim generationis terminus est forma, et corruptionis privatio, nisi quia forma facit esse et privatio non esse."

[2] *Con. Gen.* loc. cit.

[3] "Si enim sit, oportet quod esse praeexistens alicui rei de novo acquiratur."

acquisition of new being, but only of a new mode of being, and so would merely be equivalent to alteration—or else it must have been created out of nothing which is contrary to the idea of generation. Therefore, since it is impossible to reconcile the facts of generation and corruption with the theory that God is the being of all things, that theory must be rejected.[1]

For the understanding of the argument it is necessary to realize how generation differs from creation, and corruption from annihilation, and how both differ from alteration. Creation is the production of an entire being *de novo* and *ex nihilo*. To say that it is made out of nothing is not equivalent to asserting that nothing is the substance out of which it is made. On the contrary, the statement is meant to affirm that it is made out of no other substance at all, that its own substance with its proper accidents was, at some definite moment, brought into being, and that before this particular moment neither substance nor accidents had any existence.[2] In a corresponding sense, annihilation signifies complete cessation of being, an eventuality which has nothing in common with dissolution into minute particles or transformation into another substance. An object which has been annihilated no longer exists in any form whatsoever. Whereas once it was, now it is not.

Generation, on the other hand, is a very different process. In order to take place it requires the assistance of primary matter which is the necessary recipient of form. What is generated is composite, a union of matter and form, and this is also that which is corrupted. In corruption the composite structure dissolves, and the substratum relapses into primary matter, which, though devoid of all actuality, is yet something and not absolutely nothing. It is true that primary matter cannot exist when separated from form, and true also that form has no existence apart from matter except in the divine intellect. Nevertheless, primary matter, as pure potentiality, is not utter

[1] *Con. Gen.* loc. cit.

[2] Cf. the *De Aeternitate Mundi*, where Aquinas quotes with approval the statement of Anselm in the *Monologium*: "Tertia interpretatio, qua dicitur aliquid esse factum ex nihilo, est cum intelligimus esse quidem factum, sed non esse aliquid unde sit factum." "The third interpretation by which it is said that something is made out of nothing, is when we understand that something is made but that there is not any other thing out of which it is made."

nothingness, but possesses a kind of being whereby it is able to become receptive of the activity of form. This doctrine is, undoubtedly, one of the most obscure and difficult in Aquinas's philosophy. Evidently it is an attempt to state the relation between permanence and change, the union of which is—to all appearance at least—the basic fact in the world of our experience. Generation and corruption represent the rising and falling waves of change, and primary matter represents the underlying ocean of being.

The difference between generation and alteration can best be brought out by quoting Aquinas's own definition of each. "Alteration occurs when the same sensible subject remains, that is when, no transmutation having been made in its substance, a transmutation is made in its affections, that is in its qualities."[1] Generation occurs "when there is a transmutation not only as regards affections, but also as regards the whole substance of the thing, so that matter acquires a new substantial form, and so that there remains nothing sensible which is the same in number and actual being as the previous subject."[2]

The thought underlying the argument is that, while in the eternal nature of God nothing can ever come into being or pass out of being, yet generation and corruption are actualities in the physical world, and that consequently this world cannot be identical with the being of God.

These are, then, the six arguments advanced by St. Thomas in proof of his contention. It is clear that all of them require us to assume the reality of a physical world to which the categories of substance and accident truly apply. It may be urged that, in view of our everyday experience, this is not at all an unreasonable assumption. Nevertheless, the reality of multiplicity and time and change had been called in question long before the age of Aquinas. Yet it is by virtue of their presence

---

[1] "Alteratio est, quando manet idem subiectum sensibile: scilicet quando nulla transmutatione in eius substantia facta, fit transmutatio in passionibus eius, scilicet in qualitatibus ipsius" (*De Generatione et Corruptione*, cap. iv. lect. 10).

[2] "Quando est transmutatio non solum secundum passiones, sed etiam secundum totam rei substantiam: inquantum scilicet materia accipit aliam formam substantialem, ita scilicet quod non maneat aliquod sensibile: quasi sit idem subiectum numero ens actu."

in experience that the realm of physical nature is distinct from and other than the eternal nature of God. It is therefore legitimate to urge that none of these arguments can lay claim to consideration until some proof has been given that these features of the world of sense-experience are in some sense real and not illusory.

In the opinion of Aquinas there were three mistakes in reasoning, the commission of which led men to adopt a pantheistic philosophy.[1] The first is as follows. Since what is common is specified and individualized by addition, men tend to think that God, to whom nothing can be added, is common to all beings. The tendency is due to the fact that they do not realize that what is common or universal cannot exist without any addition, although it may be considered without any addition. Thus animal *cannot* exist apart from either a rational or irrational differentia—that is it must be either what we term a "lower" animal, or else a human being; but it may be considered by reason in abstraction and without such differentiae. Furthermore, although the universal can be thought apart from all addition, it cannot be thought apart from its receptivity of addition; for if it were impossible to add any differentia to *animal*, then *animal* would not be a genus. The divine being, on the contrary, is without addition, not only in intellect, but also *in rerum natura*; and not only without addition, but is without all receptivity of addition. Accordingly God is not a universal but an individual being.[2]

The second error consists in supposing that, since God is infinitely simple, that which is discovered in us in ultimate analysis (*in ultimo resolutionis*), and is therefore most simple, is God. The cause of this error is the failure to realize that what is discovered in us is most simple, not as a complete thing is simple, but as part of another thing; while the simplicity of God is that of a thing which has a perfect subsistence of its own.

The third mistake springs from the mode of speech according to which we say that God is in all things. But God is not to be thought of as an element in existing things. On the contrary, God is in them only as their ground or cause.

[1] *Con. Gen.* lib. I. cap. 26.
[2] "Non sit esse commune, sed proprium."

(m) CORPOREAL FORM

It remains to prove that God is not the form of a body.

1. The first proof is based upon the identity of the divine essence and existence. The wording, however, is obscure.[1] "The divine being cannot be the being of any quiddity which is not its own being, as has been shown. Moreover, that which is the divine being itself is not other than God. Therefore it is impossible that God should be the form of any other being."

The unexpected reference at the outset to the divine *being* or *existence* rather than to *form* is perplexing, and is reminiscent of the preceding discussion as to the being of all things. The intention seems to be, however, to remind us that in God essence and existence are one. But if God were the form of any body, his essence must unavoidably be distinct from his *suppositum*. Therefore it is impossible that he should be the form of a body.

2. The second argument is stated as follows:[2] "The form of a body is not being itself, but the principle of being. God, however, is being itself. Therefore God is not the form of a body." This argument is clearly little else than a restatement of its predecessor.

3. The third argument points out that any union of form and matter results in something which is composite. This composite being is a whole of which form and matter are parts. As parts they stand to the whole in a relation of potentiality to actuality. But in God there is no potentiality. Therefore it is impossible that he should be a composite of matter and form.[3]

We have here a logical development of the preceding train of reasoning. It may, however, be noted that Aquinas did not base it, as he might have done, upon the absence of composition in God. Instead he founded it upon the absence of potentiality in God, thus linking it directly with the doctrine of the eternity of God which forms the basis of his entire metaphysical structure.

[1] "Divinum esse non potest esse alicuius quidditatis quae non sit ipsum esse, ut ostensum est. Quod autem est ipsum esse divinum, non est aliud quam Deus. Impossibile est igitur Deum esse alicuius alterius formam" (*Con. Gen.* lib. I. cap. 27).

[2] "Forma corporis non est ipsum esse, sed essendi principium. Deus autem est ipsum esse. Non ergo est Deus forma corporis" (*Con. Gen.* loc. cit.).

[3] *Con. Gen.* loc. cit.

4. The fourth argument begins with the assertion that that which has being *per se* is nobler than that which has its being in another (*in alio*); or, in other words, that a self-existent being stands higher in the scale of existence than a being which is dependent upon another for its existence. It is then pointed out that the form of any body whatsoever has its being *in alio*. God, however, who is the primal cause of existence, is the noblest of all beings. Consequently it is impossible that God's existence should be *in alio*, and therefore it is impossible that God should be the form of a body.[1]

This argument appears to be based upon the fourth proof of the existence of God, wherein the attempt was made to show that there must be a supreme source and cause of all the grades of goodness and of being which are to be found in the universe of finite existents. The initial statement—that what has being *per se* is nobler than what has being *in alio*—is obviously in harmony with, and derived from, the theory that in God essence and existence are one. If the validity of these two propositions be admitted, the argument is sound.

5. If the eternity of motion be assumed, it is possible to set forth yet another argument in support of the same contention. God is, of course, the prime mover. Hence, were God the form of a body, it would be necessary that this composite entity should be its own mover; for were it dependent upon another being for its motion, God would not be the prime mover. But that which moves itself is capable both of being moved and of not being moved—in other words, it can choose between being in motion and remaining at rest. Clearly, then, such a being cannot be the source of perpetual motion. Consequently we must posit beyond and above it another prime mover which imparts to it perpetual motion; and thus God, who is the prime mover, is not the form of a self-moving body.[2]

It is evident that the opening assertion here needs supplementation and support. Why, we may ask, should it be assumed that God is the form of a moving body, or, rather, of a body which is capable of being either in motion or at rest? The answer is that we have no choice. It will be remembered that in the third proof of the incorporeality of God the statement was made that "every natural body is movable" (*omne autem*

---

[1] *Con. Gen.* loc. cit.　　　　　　　　[2] *Con. Gen.* loc. cit.

corpus naturale mobile est). The term "natural" is doubtless here intended to denote a physical body in contradistinction to a mathematical body, such as a circle or a square, which exists only for the intellect. The statement itself is made upon the authority of Aristotle.[1]

The whole argument is apt to impress one as clumsy and unnecessarily elaborate. What need is there, we may ask, to repeat at this point the proof that God is incapable of self-movement, and that, consequently, he must be completely immobile, an "unmoved mover"? All this has been said before in connection with the first proof of the existence of God. There, indeed, it was germane, but why repeat it here?

If with this question in mind we turn to the *Compendium Theologiae*, we shall find the argument stated with much greater clarity, brevity, and directness. "Neither is it possible for God to be the form of a body, nor any power in a body. For, as every body is movable, if a body be moved, of necessity those entities in that body will be moved also, if only *per accidens*. The prime mover, however, cannot be moved either *per se* or *per accidens*; for it is needful that it should be wholly immobile, as has been shown. Therefore it is impossible that it should be the form of a body or a power in a body."[2]

This formulation of the argument appears far more satisfactory than the other which we have been discussing. There is no need to introduce the hypothesis of the eternity of motion. To do so is not only useless, it actually provides an obstacle which has later on to be removed; for the eternity of motion could never be anything more for Aquinas than a purely provisional assumption, since it is contrary to the Catholic faith. Accordingly, he proceeded to adapt the argument to

---

[1] Cf. *Phys.* lib. II. cap. i. 1. "Τὰ μὲν γὰρ φύσει ὄντα πάντα φαίνεται ἔχοντα ἐν ἑαυτοῖς ἀρχὴν κινήσεως καὶ στάσεως, τὰ μὲν κατὰ τόπον, τὰ δὲ κατ' αὔξησιν καὶ φθίσιν, τὰ δὲ κατ' ἀλλοίωσιν." "For all natural things seem to have in themselves the principle of motion and rest, whether as regards local movement, augmentation and diminution, or alteration."

[2] "Neque etiam est possibile ipsum esse formam corporis, aut aliquam virtutem in corpore. Cum enim omne corpus mobile inveniatur, opportet corpore moto, ea quae sunt in corpore, moveri, saltem per accidens. Primum autem movens non potest nec per se, nec per accidens, moveri; cum oporteat ipsum omnino esse immobile, ut ostensum est. Impossibile est igitur quod sit forma, vel virtus in corpore" (Pars Prima, cap. xvi).

his own use by pointing out that the same conclusion could be reached by taking as the point of departure, not the eternity of motion, but the regularity of the movement of the heavens. For just as that which moves itself is capable of being either in motion or at rest, so also it is capable of moving with varying degrees of rapidity. Therefore the uniform rate of heavenly movement must owe its necessary character to some higher and immobile principle, which is not itself a part—as, were it the form, it must be a part—of a self-moving body.[1]

6. There is yet another argument to be found in the same chapter of the *Compendium Theologiae*, and it is also stated so lucidly and succinctly that it is better to quote it entire than to attempt to summarize it.[2] "It is necessary that every mover, in order that it may cause motion, should have control over that which it moves: for we see that according to the extent to which the mover exceeds the moved in power, so much more rapid is the motion. That which is the prime mover of all moving things must therefore, most of all, have control over the things moved. This, however, it cannot have if it be attached in any way to a movable thing; which it must be if it be the form of that thing or a power in it. Therefore the prime mover cannot be a body, nor a power in a body, nor the form of a body. Hence Anaxagoras posited a pure intellect as ruling and moving all things."

It is evident, from the words just quoted, that Aquinas was of the opinion that a pure form, separate from matter, would possess a greater degree of control over a material body than the form which was united to that body and gave it being. This is, perhaps, not unnatural, since a form which is united to a body must, to some extent at least, be involved in its fortunes and its fate. Yet it is not so clear that a form which

---

[1] *Con. Gen.* loc. cit.

[2] "Oportet omne movens, ad hoc quod moveat, dominium super rem quae movetur, habere: videmus enim quod quanto magis virtus movens excedit virtutem mobilis, tanto velocior est motus. Illud igitur quod est omnium moventium primum, oportet maxime dominari super res motas. Hoc autem esse non posset, si esset mobile aliquo modo alligatum; quod esse oporteret, si esset forma eius, vel virtus. Oportet igitur primum movens neque corpus esse, neque virtutem in corpore, neque formam in corpore. Hinc est quod Anaxagoras posuit intellectum immixtum, ad hoc quod imperet, et omnia moveat."

is not united to a body would have any control over that body at all. There are, according to Aquinas, a multitude of such forms—the angels, the demons, the souls of the dead, whether saved, damned, or in purgatory. Clearly it is impossible that each and all of these forms should have more control over our bodies than do our own souls which are united to them. It appears, then, that this step in the argument requires further justification.

If we turn to the *Summa Theologica*[1] we find there a discussion headed, "Whether God enters into the composition of other things."[2] This article deals in a very brief fashion not only with the question as to whether God is the form of a body, but also with the pantheistic theory of the Almaricians that he is the being of all things, as well as with the heresy of David of Dinant, which as we know consisted in identifying God with primary matter. Apparently St. Thomas regarded the three arguments which he advanced in this connection as equally destructive of all these three theories. They are as follows:

1. God is the first efficient cause. An efficient cause is not the same in number as the form of a thing made by it, but only in species. Thus man begets man. As for matter, it is the same as the efficient cause neither in number nor species, since it is in potentiality while the cause is in act.

2. Since God is the first efficient cause, action pertains to God primarily and *per se*. But that which enters into composition with anything does not act primarily and *per se*, for it is the composite being which acts. Thus the hand does not act, but a man acts by means of his hand; and so a fire warms by its heat. Accordingly God cannot be a part of a composite thing.

3. No part of a composite thing can be absolutely (*simpliciter*) primal among beings. This is true even of matter and form which are the primal parts of composite things. For matter is in potentiality, and potentiality is absolutely posterior to actuality. Moreover, the form which is part of a composite thing is a participated form. Now, just as that which participates is posterior to that which is essential (*per essentiam*), so is that which is participated in; just as fire in ignited things is posterior

---

[1] I.a. q. 3: a. 8.   [2] "Utrum Deus in compositionem aliorum veniat."

to essential fire. But God is absolutely primal being. Therefore
God cannot be part of a composite thing.

These three arguments are all thoroughly in accord with
the fundamental principles of Thomism. There is no need to
comment upon any but the last, where we find a departure
from strict Aristotelianism. "Just as that which participates is
posterior to that which is essential, so is that which is participated in."[1]

In other words, to use scholastic terminology, that which is
in re is posterior to that which is *ante rem*. Such a departure
from Aristotle was necessitated by the doctrine of creation.
Accordingly the pure form is conceived in Neoplatonic
fashion as existing in the divine intellect. The form which
is actually found in a material thing is a participated
form (*forma participata*). It is a copy, posterior to the divine
original.[2]

Here we come upon an important point in the development
of Aquinas's thought. The hypothesis of a world-soul has at
last been dealt with and rejected as untenable. For nothing
less than this is involved. And it is this which Aquinas had
fixedly before his mind. A world-soul, if there be one, must
unavoidably be united to the physical universe in a mode
more or less similar to that in which the human soul is united
to its body; otherwise, indeed, it would not deserve to be
called a world-soul. Consequently to prove that God cannot
be the form of any body is to refute completely this "idolatrous
error," as Aquinas describes the theory of his opponents.[3]

---

[1] "Sicut autem participans est posterius eo quod est per essentiam, ita et
ipsum participatum."

[2] Cf. Boethius, *De Trinitate*, cap. ii. "Forma uero quae est sine materia
non poterit esse subiectum nec uero inesse materiae, neque enim esset
forma sed imago. Ex his enim formis quae praeter materiam sunt, istae
formae uenerunt quae sunt in materia et corpus efficiunt. Nam ceteras
quae in corporibus sunt abutimur formas uocantes, dum imagines sint.
Adsimulantur enim formis his quae non sunt in materia constitutae."
"Form which is without matter cannot be a substrate, and cannot have
its essence in matter, else it would not be a form but a reflection. For
from those forms which are outside matter come the forms which are in
matter and produce bodies. We misname the entities that reside in bodies
when we call them forms; they are images; they only resemble those
forms which are not incorporate in matter" (Stewart's and Rand's translation).   [3] *Con. Gen.* lib. I. cap. 27.

The severity of this denunciation, a severity seldom found in the writings of Aquinas, reveals the importance which he attached to the doctrine of the complete transcendence of God, and the fear and detestation he felt for any theory which militated against it.

(n) PERFECTION

We have now reached the last stage of the negative way, and only one further step remains to be taken. We have yet to demonstrate that God is perfect. To modern ears the term *perfection* has a positive sound; and consequently it seems incongruous that it should be ascribed to God as a purely negative attribute. We shall see, however, that the notion of perfection is reached by a direct application of the method which we have been following, and that it is deduced from results already established by that method.

1. The first argument depends upon two premises. One of them is the proposition that a thing is more "noble" according as it has more being,[1] and the other is the doctrine which has already played so important a part in the development of Aquinas's thought, that in God essence and existence are identical.

Underlying the argument is the idea that a particular entity may possess certain modes of being, and at the same time be destitute of others, and that consequently one entity is of greater worth and excellence than another according as it possesses a greater number of modes of being. Thus a wise man is wise through his possession of the quality of wisdom which is a mode of being inhering in him. Similarly, the brave man is brave through his possession of courage which is another mode of being inhering in him. Now, the man who possesses both modes of being is superior to the man who possesses only one of them. But God, in whom there is no distinction of essence from existence, is being itself. Therefore God possesses every variety of excellence.

To illustrate his meaning in this context, Aquinas refers to the instance of a universal, such as whiteness. In a particular

[1] "Secundum modum quo res habet esse, est suus modus in nobilitate" (*Con. Gen.* lib. I. cap. 28).

existent object it is quite possible that whiteness should exist in an imperfect state, as the result of some deficiency in the recipient. But were it possible—as it is not—for the universal *whiteness* to exist by itself apart from all particulars, it would of necessity exist in its perfection, since it would be unaffected and unlimited by anything outside itself. Similarly, it would be contradictory to suppose that God, who is pure being, is deficient in any perfection.[1]

2. The second argument is founded on the principle, already familiar to us, that, in the last analysis, the perfect is prior to the imperfect. God is the first cause of all things. Therefore God is supremely perfect.[2]

3. The third argument rests upon the absence of potentiality in God. A thing is perfect in so far as it is actual, and imperfect in so far as it is in potentiality. Therefore, since God is wholly actual, he is wholly perfect.[3]

4. The fourth argument takes as its point of departure the doctrine that God is the first efficient cause. Nothing can act unless it itself is already actual, and all action is dependent upon the mode of actuality possessed by the agent. Consequently it is impossible that the effect produced by any action should be nobler than the cause. On the contrary, it is quite possible that it should be inferior to the cause, since the efficacy of the action may be diminished by the nature of the object upon which it acts. And since God is the first cause of all things, it follows that all perfections in created things must exist in a more eminent degree in him. Therefore God is perfect.[4]

5. The fifth argument is based upon the principle that in every genus there is some member which is the most perfect instance of that genus, and which serves as the normal standard in relation to which other members may be classified. Nearness to it constitutes approximation to perfection—so far as the genus itself is concerned—and remoteness from it constitutes

[1] *Con. Gen.* loc. cit.; cf. *Com. Theol.* Pars Prima, cap. xx; *Sum. Theol.* I.a. q. 4: a. 2. c. The argument in the *Compendium Theologiae* stresses the infinity of the divine essence, which, in the *Contra Gentiles,* has not been demonstrated.

[2] *Con. Gen.* loc. cit.; cf. *Com. Theol.* Pars Prima, cap. xix.

[3] *Con. Gen.* loc. cit.; cf. *Com. Theol.* Pars Prima, cap. xix; *Sum. Theol.* I.a. q. 4: a. 1. c.

[4] *Con. Gen.* loc. cit.; *Sum. Theol.* I.a. q. 4: a. 1. c. and a. 2. c.

imperfection. In the language of Aquinas, it is their "measure" (*mensura*). "Thus white is said to be the measure of all colours, and the virtuous man of all men."[1] Now, that by which all beings are measured must itself be being in the highest degree. Consequently it must be being itself, which is God. No perfection can therefore be lacking to that by which all things are measured, for did it lack perfection it would not be their measure. Therefore God is perfect.[2]

It is clear that here the analogy is being drawn between being and genus. As there is a member in each genus by which all members are measured, so, it is urged, there must be a being by which all beings are measured. But being is not a genus. The analogy would then appear to be illegitimate. Doubtless a defence could be made by falling back upon the fourth proof of the existence of God, by which St. Thomas believed himself to have demonstrated that there must exist some entity which is being in the highest degree.

6. In the *Compendium Theologiae* an additional argument is set forth which is of special interest, because it refers us to the conception of God as the unmoved mover which forms the starting-point of the entire train of reasoning we have just been following. It is stated thus.[3] Everything which moves something toward perfection has beforehand in itself the perfection which it confers upon others; just as a master has beforehand in himself the doctrine which he imparts. So, therefore, in order that God, the prime mover, should move all things toward his perfections, it is necessary that all the perfections of things should pre-exist superabundantly in him.

This argument is, indeed, to be found, not in the chapter[4] formally devoted to proving that God is perfect—the arguments contained in which we have already referred to—but in that[5] which is concerned to show "that all perfections which

---

[1] "Sicut album dicitur esse mensura in omnibus coloribus, et virtuosus inter omnes homines."

[2] *Con. Gen.* loc. cit.

[3] "Omne quod movet aliquid ad perfectionem, praehabet in se perfectionem quam aliis confert; sicut doctor praehabet in se doctrinam quam aliis tradit. Si igitur Deus, cum sit primum movens, omnia alia moveat in suas perfectiones, necesse est omnes perfectiones rerum in ipso praeexistere superabundantur" (Pars Prima, cap. xx).

[4] Pars Prima, cap. xix.   [5] Pars Prima, cap. xx.

are in things are originally and eminently in God."[1] Since
this theory has already been invoked in connection with the
fourth argument, it appears desirable to introduce the consideration of the proof in the present connection. The two
propositions are, indeed, inextricably united. In criticism of
this proof, it need only be said that the motion here referred
to is obviously not local movement but motion toward perfection. That, however, is thoroughly in accord with the conception of the prime mover as the object of the desire that
imparts motion by inspiring love.

It is evident that these six arguments are merely a further
application of principles whereof constant use has been made
throughout the entire negative way. To enter upon a further
discussion of them would be but to repeat what has been said
before. We have, then, now reached the end of the *Via Remotionis* as set forth in *Contra Gentiles*. In the *Compendium Theologiae*,
however, under the general topic of the divine perfection,
there is introduced a third chapter, which is entitled,[2] "That
in God all perfections are one identity." Nothing is to be
found in this chapter which is not at least implied in what
has been said already. Yet we find given here, with brevity
and clarity, a statement which is evidently intended to constitute a short résumé of the ground covered by the negative
way, and to emphasize the final result at which we have arrived.
The passage is worth quoting *in extenso*:[3]

[1] "Quod omnes perfectiones quae sunt in rebus originalitur et eminenter
sunt in Deo."
[2] "Quod in Deo omnes perfectiones sunt unum secundum rem" (Pars
Prima, cap. xxi).
[3] "Si autem colligamus ea quae superius dicta sunt, manifestum est quod
omnes perfectiones in Deo sunt unum secundum rem. Ostensum est enim
supra, Deum simplicem esse. Ubi autem est simplicitas, diversitas eorum
quae insunt, esse non potest. Si ergo in Deo sunt omnium perfectiones,
impossibile est quod sint diversae in ipso: relinquitur ergo quod omnes
sint unum in eo.
"Hoc autem manifestum fit consideranti in virtutibus cognoscitivis.
Nam superior vis secundum unum et idem est cognoscitiva omnium quae
ab inferioribus viribus secundum diversa cognoscuntur: omnia enim quae
visus, auditus, et ceteri sensus percipiunt, intellectus una et simplici virtute
diiudicat. Simile etiam apparet in scientiis: nam cum inferiores scientiae
secundum diversa genera rerum circa quae versatur eorum intentio, multi-
plicentur; una tamen scientia est in eis superior, ad omnia se habens

"If, moreover, we co-ordinate the things which have been said above, it is manifest that all perfections are one identity in God. It has been shown that God is simple. Now where there is simplicity there cannot be a diversity of contents. Therefore, if the perfections of all things exist in God, they cannot be diverse in him; hence it must be admitted that they are all one.

"This, moreover, will be manifest to one who considers the cognitive powers. For a superior power is aware of that as one and identical of which inferior powers are aware as a diversity; thus all those things which sight, hearing, and the other senses perceive, the intellect discriminates by one simple power. The case is similar as regards the sciences; for while the inferior sciences are multiplied according to the diverse genera of the things toward which their attention is directed, yet there is one science superior to them which is directed towards all of them, which is called first Philosophy. The same thing appears in regard to governmental powers; for in the royal power, which is one, are included all the powers which are distributed through diverse offices under the lordship of the king. And so, therefore, perfections which in inferior things are multiplied according to the diversity of those things must be unified from above in that which is being itself and in the highest degree."

There remains, however, yet a further question. When Aquinas ascribes being or existence (*esse*) to God, is this assertion also to be interpreted according to the principle of analogy? It seems clear that the answer must be in the affirmative. It has been shown that existence—in the case of any finite entity—is accidental in the sense that it is not included in its essence. But God is identical with his essence, hence the divine existence cannot be accidental. Again, in the *Divine Names*[1] we find the Pseudo-Dionysius refusing to affirm existence of God in the same sense in which it can be ascribed to anything else. Upon this passage Aquinas comments as follows: "Thereafter when he says, 'Truly God is not existent

quae Philosophia prima dicitur. Apparet etiam idem in potestatibus: nam in regia potestate, cum sit una, includuntur omnes potestates quae per diversa officia sub domino regni distribuuntur. Sic igitur et perfectiones, quae in inferioribus rebus secundum diversitatem rerum multiplicantur, oportet quod in ipso rerum vertice uniantur."   [1] Cap. v. 4.

in any mode but *simpliciter*,' he shows that all things unite in God in a certain mode. As evidence of this it is to be considered that since every form is received in something else, it is limited and bounded by the capacity of the recipient; whence *this* white body cannot possess the whole of whiteness according to the whole virtue of whiteness. But if whiteness were a separate form, nothing would be lacking whereby it could fall short of the whole virtue of whiteness. Moreover, all other things, as has been said above, possess a received and participated existence; and therefore they do not possess existence according to the whole virtue of existence; but God alone, who is himself subsistent being, possesses existence according to the virtue of existence; and this is why he says that, therefore, he is able to be the cause of the existence of all things, because he himself is not existent 'in any mode,' that is, according to some finite and limited mode, but himself universally and infinitely received and pre-received in himself the whole of existence, since in him it pre-exists as in its cause, and from him is imparted to others."[1]

In the *Commentary on the Sentences*[2] St. Thomas reverts to the same topic and insists that there are four reasons which justify us in ascribing existence to God:

(1) That is perfect no element in which is exterior to itself. ("*Illud enim est perfectum cuius nihil est extra ipsum*"). Our existence, however, has something exterior to itself, since it does not include its own past and future. But in the divine existence there is no past or future; on the contrary, it forms a perfect whole, hence the term *existence* pertains to it of right.

---

[1] "Deinde cum dicit: 'Etenim Deus non quodammodo est existens, sed simplicitur,' ostendit quod omnia conveniunt Deo quodam modo. Ad cuius evidentiam considerandum est quod omnis forma recepta in aliquo, limitatur et finitur secundum capacitatem recipientis; unde hoc corpus album non habet totam albedinem secundum totum posse albedinis. Sed si esset albedo separata, nihil deesset ei quod ad virtutem albedinis pertineret. Omnia autem alia, sicut superius dictum est, habent esse receptum et participatum; et ideo non habent esse secundum totam virtutem essendi, sed solus Deus, qui est ipsum esse subsistens, secundum totam virtutem essendi esse habet; et hoc est quod dicit quod ideo potest esse causa essendi omnibus, quia ipse 'non est existens quodam modo,' id est secundum aliquem modum finitum et limitatum, sed ipse universaliter et infinite accepit in seipso totum esse et praeaccepit, quia in eo praeexistit sicut in causa, et ab eo ad alia derivatur" (lect. 1). [2] 1 *Dist*. 8. q. 1: a. 1. sol.

(2) The phrase *qui est* signifies indeterminate being and not the *quid est*. Hence, since in this life we know *that* God is but not *what* God is—except by way of negation—most properly may we say that God exists.

(3) Dionysius has said that among all the modes of participation in the divine goodness the noblest is existence, because it includes all others as in some mode united in itself.

(4) According to Avicenna the term *res* has reference to the quiddity of a thing, whereas the phrase *qui est*, or the term *ens*, designates the existence whereby it is made actual. But since in God *quidditas* and *esse* are identical, the term which has reference to the divine existence properly designates the Deity.

To the objection that that which is the *proprium* of anything belongs to it alone, and that existence pertains not only to God but to the creatures, and therefore does not belong to God properly (*proprie*), Aquinas replied that the term *proprium* may be used in two senses; it may signify that which excludes everything extraneous to the nature of the subject, and in this sense laughter is a *proprium* of man, since it pertains to nothing extraneous to man's nature—in which sense existence is not a *proprium* of the Deity since it pertains also to the creatures— and it may also be used to exclude everything extraneous to the nature of the predicate, as a thing is said to be golden *proprie* if it has no admixture of any other metal—and in this sense existence is a *proprium* of God, for the divine existence is without any admixture of privation or potentiality, whereas this is not true of the existence of the creatures.[1]

If at this point one glances back over the path just traversed, it will be observed that among the consecutive steps whereby the argument advances two of the most important are the establishment of the absence of potentiality and of the absence of composition in the Deity. They are the base upon which rests the greater part of the superstructure. I have already urged that St. Thomas's treatment of composition is vitiated by the fact that he did not envisage the possibility of the presence in the primal being of an ultimate and underived complexity, and that he assumed, without any attempt at justification, that the only alternative to absolute simplicity is the combination of pre-existing elements by some external

[1] 1 *Dist.* 8. q. 1 : a. 1. ob. 1. and ad 1ᵐ.

agency. In his treatment of genus and difference and of
subject and accident he has not departed from this extraordinarily *naïf* point of view. Let us grant that Aquinas has
demolished the theory of a world soul. Has he also shown that
in God there is not a complexity of the sort that obtains in the
mental life of every self-conscious personality? It does not
appear so.

Can we regard Aquinas as having satisfactorily demonstrated the absence of all potentiality in God? How are we to
reconcile such a view with his insistence that motion in the
form of intellection is to be attributed to God? It will, of course,
be claimed that the divine intellection is not a process, that it
involves no change, and that it is to be conceived as a timeless
act of self-contemplation. But is not the notion of a timeless act
self-contradictory? And if it be not self-contradictory, does
it follow from what has gone before? The divine eternity is
deduced from the divine immobility, from the necessary
character of the divine existence, and from the impossibility
of the primal cause coming into existence or passing out of it.
But do these arguments establish more than duration in time?
What St. Thomas clearly requires is the existence of a Deity
who is not in time at all. But this is a very different conception.
By what justification does he pass from the one to the other?
Where there is no change, it will be said, there is no time; and
God is immovable, therefore God is changeless. Yet there is
change in the universe, hence the universe is in time; and
God has created and sustains, must not God, then, be involved
in the temporal process? Aquinas would undoubtedly reply
that, while the world is really related to God, God is not really
related to the world, and that accordingly changes in the
universe evoke no corresponding changes in the divine cognition and volition. To these questions we shall later return
when we discuss St. Thomas's theory of God's knowledge and
will, and the doctrines of creation and conservation. But I
wish now to stress the point that if St. Thomas failed successfully to defend his position in regard to the nature and reality
of relations, his doctrine of the eternity of God will be hopelessly
shattered, and the very foundation of his whole system will be
destroyed.

PART THREE

POSITIVE KNOWLEDGE OF GOD

CHAPTER VII

THE METHOD OF ANALOGY

HAVING reached the end of the negative way, we now stand face to face with one of the most fundamental of all the problems with which St. Thomas had to deal. That he himself felt it to be such we may reasonably infer from the frequency with which he reverted to it, and the thoroughness with which he discussed it.[1] The position which he was concerned to maintain was both in complete harmony with Christian Neoplatonic tradition as represented by such thinkers as Boethius, the Pseudo-Dionysius, and Eriugena, and at the same time diametrically opposed to that of the famous Jewish philosopher, Maimonides, whose powerful influence was widely felt, and whom Aquinas evidently regarded as his chief opponent.[2]

The negative method professed to yield veritable knowledge of God. Aquinas has applied it by taking as his starting-point the conception of an unmoved mover, and endeavouring to show that such notions as those of change, potentiality, composition, materiality, substance and accident, genus and species, etc., are inapplicable to it. Beyond this point, however, the negative method is unable to carry him. Yet it is essential that he should be able to advance farther into the region of metaphysics if a genuine theism is to be established at all. For the God of religion, not of Christianity only, but of every other theistic faith, is a living, conscious, intelligent being with whom his worshippers are able to enter into personal relations, and in whom they can confide and trust. The existence of such a being remains yet undemonstrated, and must continue

[1] *Con. Gen.* lib. I. cc. 29–36; *Sum. Theol.* I.a. q. 13; *Com. Theol.* Pars Prima, cc. xxiii–xxiv; *De Pot.* q. 7: aa. 4–7; *De Verit.* q. 2: a. 3. ad 4ᵐ, a. 11. c.; cf. q. 8: a. 1. ad 6; q. 23: a. 7. ad 9ᵐ; 1 *Dist.* 2. q. 1: aa. 2–3; *Dist.* 8. q. 1: a. 1; *Dist.* 22. q. 1: aa. 1–3; 3 *Dist.* 1. q. 1: a. 1. ad 3ᵐ; 4 *Dist.* 49. q. 2: a. 1. ad 6ᵐ; *Quodlib.* 10. q. 8: a. 17. ad 1ᵐ; *De Trin.* q. 1: a. 2. ad 3ᵐ; cf. *Dieu, son existence et sa nature*, pp. 513–588; also *S. Thomas d'Aquin*, tome. I. pp. 183–190.

[2] *Sum. Theol.* I.a. q. 13: a. 2. c.; *De Pot.* q. 7: a. 4. and a 7. c.; 1 *Dist.* 2. q. 1: a. 3. ad 3.

to remain undemonstrated unless the possibility of further predication be conceded. How is this possibility to be established?

It will be recalled that in a previous chapter upon the negative way, we have seen that while for Dionysius no quality could be ascribed to God in the same sense in which it can be attributed to any finite being, nevertheless he took pains to assert that some attributes may more truthfully be predicated of God than others.[1] In other words, while no concept which the human mind can frame is able adequately to express the divine nature, there are yet degrees of adequacy and inadequacy, of approximation to and remoteness from, the unrealizable goal. It is to this position that Aquinas reverts in order to build upon it his method of analogy, and it is at this point that he is compelled to join issue with Maimonides.

The Jewish philosopher was no less staunch a partisan of the *Via Negativa* than Aquinas, but, unlike Aquinas, he made no attempt to escape from what appear—at first sight at least— to be its logical consequences. On the contrary, he stated them with uncompromising clearness. "We do not know anything of him except that he is, that none of the beings which he has produced resembles him, that he has absolutely nothing in common with these last, that there is in him neither multiplicity nor lack of power to produce what is other than himself, and that his relation to this world is that of a captain to his vessel; not that this is really the relation, nor that the comparison is just, but it serves to lead the mind to comprehend that God governs all beings, that is to say, that he perpetuates and conserves them in order as is necessary."[2]

Nor did he hesitate to affirm that such notions as existence,

---

[1] Cf. *Mystical Theology*, cap. iii.

[2] "Nous ne saisissons de lui autre chose, si ce n'est *qu'il est*, qu'il y a un être auquel ne ressemble aucun des êtres qu'il a produits, qu'il n'y a absolument rien de commun avec ces derniers, qu'il n'y a en lui ni multiplicité, ni impuissance de produire ce qui est en dehors de lui, et que son rapport au monde est celui du capitaine au vaisseau; non pas que ce soit là le rapport véritable, ni que la comparaison soit juste, mais il sert de guide à l'esprit (pour comprendre) que Dieu gouverne les êtres, c'est-à-dire qu'il les perpétue et les maintient en ordre, comme il le faut" (*Le Guide des Égarés*, Première Partie, ch. lviii).

knowledge, power, will, and life, when applied to both God and Man, have nothing in common but the name.[1]

It is, of course, true that Maimonides was a Jew, not only by race but by religion, even as Aquinas was a Christian, and that he regarded his own teaching as in all respects thoroughly compatible with theism. It may therefore legitimately be asked upon what grounds the statement has just been made that St. Thomas found it needful to refute Maimonides in the interests of theism. Would it not have been wiser, as well as more consistent, for him to have taken up the same position? Such an attitude would have in no way embarrassed him in accepting the doctrine of the Trinity, since that dogma, according to Aquinas, is not demonstrable by philosophy, but must be accepted upon the authority of revelation.

The answer appears to be twofold. In the first place, St. Thomas's own position was in harmony with the tradition of Christian philosophy, and although he was not the man to shrink from espousing an unpopular doctrine when he believed it to be true—as he showed in his championship of the dreaded Aristotelian philosophy, in his rejection of the popular doctrine that angels and human souls are composed of matter and form,[2] and in his insistence upon the impossibility of demonstrating that the world had a beginning in time—yet he was far from turning a deaf ear to the voice of precedent, and was ever desirous of rendering it its due. Moreover, in the present instance, he believed it to be supported by the witness of the Scriptures.[3]

In the second place, it is evident that St. Thomas had a real and sympathetic interest in the "plain man."[4] Now, while it is true that the intense devotion of the mystics tends to disdain all intellectual concepts as unfit to express the fullness of the soul's experience, and to reject all possible predicates with the assertion, "God is not this," it is also true that most men are not mystics, and consequently, if they are to think of God

---

[1] *Le Guide des Égarés*, Première Partie, ch. lvi.
[2] Cf. *Le "De Ente et Essentia" de S. Thomas d'Aquin*, by M. D. Roland-Gosselin, O.P., p. xvii.
[3] *De Pot.* q. 7 : a. 5. c. ; *Con. Gen.* lib. I. cap. 29 ; *Sum. Theol.* I.a. q. 4 : a. 3.
[4] *Con. Gen.* lib. I. cap. 4 ; *Sum. Theol.* I.a. q. 1 : a. 1. c.

at all, they must make use of the ideas which ordinary human life has made familiar to them and has filled with meaning for them. In other words, they must be able to conceive of God as possessing positive qualities. With the mystics, St. Thomas, as we shall discover in due time, had only a very qualified sympathy; but to the needs of the "plain man" he was fully awake.

It would be wrong to suggest that Aquinas would have set out to refute Maimonides for the reasons just given, had he not honestly believed the latter's position to be unsound, but it is only just to emphasize the fact that the task was for him an extremely important one. The issue involved was more than a mere theoretical difference; its practical consequences were far-reaching.

In the *De Potentia*[1] we find considerable space devoted to a refutation of Maimonides, which is worth quoting in full. "I answer that some have supposed that names applied to God do not signify the divine essence, as is very expressly stated by the Rabbi (i.e. Maimonides), who further states that there are two ways in which names of this sort may be understood in reference to God. The one way is by resemblance to effect, so that God is called wise, not because wisdom is anything in him, but because he operates in his effects according to the mode of wisdom by manifestly ordering each to its proper end; and likewise he is said to be living, inasmuch as he operates after the mode of a living thing, that is, by acting of himself. The other way is by the mode of negation; according to which, though we say that God is living, we do not signify that life exists in him, but we remove from God that mode of being which pertains to inanimate things. Likewise, when we say that God is wise, we do not conceive ourselves to signify that intellect exists in him, but we remove from God that mode of being which pertains to brutes; and so as regards other predicates. Each way, however, seems to be insufficient and unsuitable; the first for two reasons, the former of which is that on this ground there would be no difference between the propositions God is wise, God is angry, and God is fire. For he is said to be angry because he operates in the mode of an angry man when he punishes; for this is what

[1] q. 7 : a. 5. c.

angry men are accustomed to do. And he is called fire, because he operates in the mode of fire when he purges, which fire does in its mode. But this is contrary to the position of the saints and prophets when they speak of God, for they consider some qualities to pertain to God, and others they remove from him; for they consider him to be living, wise, and possessed of other qualities of this sort and not to be a body, or to be subject to passions. Moreover, according to the aforesaid opinion, all qualities may with equal reason be ascribed to or removed from God, not this more than that. The second reason is that since, according to our faith, we believe that the creature did not always exist—which he (i.e. Maimonides) also concedes—it follows that we are not able to say that he was wise or good before there were creatures. For it is evident that before there were creatures he could perform no operations upon his effects, either in the mode of goodness or in that of wisdom. This, however, is altogether repugnant to sound faith, unless possibly the meaning is that before there were creatures he could be called wise, not because he operated as if wise, but because he was able to operate as if wise. And so it follows that something must be here signified as existing in God, and this must be his substance, for whatever is in God is his substance.

"Furthermore, the second mode is seen to be unsuitable for the same reason. For there is not any name of any species which is not in some mode unfit to apply to God. For in the name of any species is included the concept of the differentia by which is excluded another species which is divided from it; thus in the name *lion* is included the differentia of being a quadruped, by which the lion differs from the bird. If, therefore, predicates are not to be ascribed to God, except in a purely negative sense—just as we say that he is living because he has not the mode of being which pertains to inanimate things, as he himself (i.e. Maimonides) says—then we can say that God is a lion because he has not the mode of being which pertains to a bird.

Moreover, furthermore, the conception of negation is always founded upon some affirmation; as is evident from the fact that every negation is proved by an affirmation; whence it follows that unless the human intellect knew something affirmatively concerning God, it could deny nothing of God. For it could know nothing if nothing which it said of him could be verified affirmatively."[1]

[1] "Respondeo dicendum quod quidam posuerunt quod ista nomina dicta de Deo, non significant divinam substantiam, quod maxime expresse dicit Rabbi, dicit autem huiusmodi nomina de Deo dupliciter esse intelligenda. Uno modo per similitudinem effectus, ut dicatur Deus sapiens non quia sapientia aliquid sit in ipso, sed quia ad modum sapientis in suis effectibus operatur, ordinando scilicet unumquodque ad debitum finem; et similiter dicitur vivens inquantum ad modum viventis operatur, quasi ex seipso agens. Alio modo per modum negationis; ut per hoc quod dicimus Deum esse viventem, non significemus vitam in eo aliquid esse; sed removeamus a Deo illum modum essendi quo res inanimatae existunt. Similiter cum dicimus Deum intelligentem, non intelligimus significare intellectum aliquid in ipso esse; sed removemus a Deo illum modum essendi quo bruta existunt: et sic de aliis. Uterque autem modus videtur esse insufficiens et inconveniens; primo quidem duplici ratione: quarum prima est, quia secundum expositionem nulla differentia esset inter hoc quod dicitur, Deus est sapiens, et Deus est iratus, vel Deus ignis est. Dicitur enim iratus quia operatur ad modum irati dum punit: hoc enim homines irati facere consueverunt. Dicitur etiam ignis, quia operatur ad modum ignis dum purgat, quod ignis suo modo facit. Hoc autem est contra positionem sanctorum et prophetarum loquentium de Deo, qui quaedam de Deo probant, et quaedam ab eo removent; probant enim eum esse vivum, sapientem et huiusmodi, et non esse corpus, neque passionibus subiectum. Secundum autem praedictam opinionem omnia de Deo pari ratione possent dici et removeri, non magis haec quam illa. Secunda ratio, quia cum secundum fidem nostram ponamus creaturam non semper fuisse, quod et ipse concedit, sequeretur quod non possemus dicere fuisse sapientem vel bonum antequam creaturae essent. Constat enim quod antequam creaturae essent, nihil in effectibus operabatur, nec ad modum boni nec ad modum sapientis. Hoc autem omnino sanae fidei repugnat: nisi forte dicere velit quod ante creaturas sapiens dici poterat, non quia operaretur ut sapiens, sed quia poterat ut sapiens operari. Et sic sequeretur quod aliquid existens in Deo, per hoc significetur, et sit per consequens substania, cum quidquid est in Deo sit sua substantia. Secundus autem modus eadem ratione videtur esse inconveniens. Non enim est aliquod nomen alicuius speciei per quod non removeatur aliquis modus qui Deo non competit. In nomine enim cuiuslibet speciei includitur significatio differentiae, per quam excluditur alia species quae contra eam dividitur: sicut in nomine leonis includitur haec differentia quae est quadrupes, per quam leo difert ab ave. Si ergo praedicationes de Deo non essent introductae nisi ad removendum, sicut dicimus Deum esse viventem, quia non habet esse modum inanimatorum, ut ipse dicit; ita possemus dicere Deum esse leonem, quia non habet esse ad modum avis. Et praeterea intellectus negationis semper fundatur in aliqua affirmatione: quod ex hoc patet quia omnis negativa per affirmativam probatur; unde, nisi intellectus

The exposition of Maimonides's views given in the footnote is quite correct,[1] but the refutation which follows cannot be pronounced satisfactory. To the objection that Maimonides was unable, without contradicting himself, to affirm that God was good or wise before the creation, the latter would doubtless have answered that, strictly speaking, God was neither good nor wise, either before the creation or after it, but that Aquinas was right in supposing that just as God could be called good after the creation, inasmuch as he is the cause of good effects, so he could be called good before the creation, inasmuch as he was then equally able to produce good effects.

In the *Summa Theologica*[2] the same objection is raised in a slightly different form. Here it is contended that, since God is the cause of bodies, we should be justified, according to Maimonides, in calling God a body. Obviously what we have here is an *argumentum ad hominem*. Maimonides, had he been alive to reply, might well have urged that, if it once be admitted that in applying predicates to God we wish to be understood to mean only that God is the cause of entities which are characterized by these predicates, we can without inconsistency affirm not only that God is spiritual, but that God is material, and even that God is evil. Nevertheless Aquinas probably felt convinced that Maimonides in his heart of hearts would much prefer habitually to refer to God as spirit rather than as body, and that the existence of such a preference was inconsistent with his philosophy.

The second argument is of a similar character. Obviously Maimonides might have rejoined that if he were permitted to define *lion* as *not bird*, he would have no objection to calling God a lion; but evidently the purpose of Aquinas in raising these objections was to drive home his point that, on Maimonides's theory, "all qualities may with equal reason be ascribed to or removed from God," with the result that we are left with no knowledge of God at all. Clearly it was with this in mind that he brought forward his three propositions,

humanus aliquid de Deo affirmative cognosceret, nihil de Deo posset negare. Non autem cognosceret, si nihil quod de ipso dicit de eo verificaretur affirmative."

[1] For "the first way" *per similitudinem effectus*, see *Le Guide des Égarés*, Première Partie, ch. liv.   [2] I.a. q. 13: a. 2. c.

"God is wise," "God is angry," and "God is a fire," between which, upon such a view, there can be no difference. For Aquinas himself each was representative of a different class. The last proposition, he would have urged, is purely metaphorical; the second—and the second alone—is to be interpreted in accordance with the teaching of Maimonides; while the third illustrates his own method of analogy, and does yield us veritable knowledge of God's nature.

Neither of these arguments, however, has shown that Maimonides has committed any error in reasoning. The third argument, on the contrary, is very much to the point. In calling attention to the truth that every negation implies an affirmation, and that unless we knew something of God we could deny nothing of him, St. Thomas has laid bare the fundamental inconsistency of Maimonides's position. In a later article of the same question,[1] the same thought is carried further. It would follow, he argues, from the position we are considering, that "all demonstrations concerning God given by philosophers are sophistical: for instance, if it be asserted that everything which is in potentiality is brought to actuality through the agency of some actual being, and if from this the conclusion be drawn that God is actual Being since through his agency all things are brought into being, the fallacy of equivocation[2] will here have been committed; and so it will be in the case of all similar demonstrations. And therefore it must be the case that what is caused is in some way like its cause; hence it cannot be that anything is predicated purely equivocally of the caused and of the cause, as health, for instance, is predicated both of medicine and of an animal."[3]

---

[1] a. 7. c.; cf. *Con. Gen.* lib. I. cap. 33; *Sum. Theol.* I.a. q. 13: a. 5. c.

[2] When an attribute is ascribed to two or more different entities, in different senses, so that they can be said to have nothing in common but the name, such attribution is equivocal. See Aristotle's *Categories*, cap. i.

[3] "Sequeretur etiam quod omnes demonstrationes a philosophis datae de Deo, essent sophisticae; verbi gratia, si dicatur, quod omne quod est in potentia, reducitur ad actum per ens actu, et ex hoc concluderetur quod Deus esset ens actu, cum per ipsum omnia in esse educantur; erit fallacia aequivocationis; et sic de omnibus aliis. Et praeterea oportet causatum esse aliqualiter simile causae; unde oportet de causato et causa nihil pure aequivoce predicari, sicut sanum de medecina et animali" (*De Pot.* q. 7: a. 7. c.).

This argument is in reality twofold. In the first place, it assumes that the existence of God has been proved by arguments which take as their point of departure the world of finite and contingent beings; furthermore—and this is the point at issue—that it is possible to demonstrate that certain attributes are to be ascribed to God. It then proceeds to show how such demonstration is possible. Here we enter upon what is actually a second argument, based upon the principle of causality as understood by Aquinas. The sufficient reason for the existence of the world is to be found in God. Consequently there must be a relation of similarity between the multitude of beings which compose it and their common and sole cause. It is more correct, however, to say that the creatures are like God than to say that God is like the creatures, even as we say that a man's portrait resembles him, not that he resembles his portrait. For the relation of similarity is a real relation upon the part of the creature, inasmuch as the creature is produced by God and possesses its qualities by participation; upon the part of God, on the contrary, the relation exists only for the mind, since the Creator, who is perfect and self-sufficing, is in no way dependent upon the creature.[1]

In the thirty-third chapter of the first book of the *Contra Gentiles* we find five arguments which profess to prove that it is impossible that all predication with respect both to God and the creature should be *purely* equivocal. Of these, the last three are practically identical with the first of two arguments which we have just examined, while the first two are based upon the second, and differ from one another and from it only in method of presentation and point of view. The last three arguments are the following:

1. When some quality is predicated equivocally of several entities, it is impossible to argue from one to the other, since knowledge depends, not on mere words, but on the meaning of terms. It is possible, however, to argue from creature to Creator. Not all attributes, then, which are predicated of both God and the creatures are purely equivocal.[2]

---

[1] *Con. Gen.* lib. I. cap. 29; cf. *De Pot.* q. 7: aa. 8. 9. and 10.

[2] "Quando unum de pluribus secundum puram aequivocationem predicatur, ex uno eorum non possumus duci in cognitionem alterius: nam cognitio rerum non dependet ex vocibus, sed ex nominum ratione. Ex his

2. The introduction of equivocal predication arrests the progress of argumentation. Accordingly, if nothing could be predicated of God and the creatures except by equivocation, it would be impossible for an argument to proceed from the creatures to God. But it is possible to argue from the creatures to God; hence the predication involved in such arguments cannot be equivocal.[1]

3. It is useless to apply any term to anything unless we know the meaning of that term. If all terms applied both to God and the creatures were equivocal, we should have no notion of what they meant when applied to God, since we should know their meaning only when applied to creatures. Consequently it would be useless, even were it possible, to demonstrate that being, goodness, and terms of this sort are applicable to God.[2]

Clearly these arguments differ from one another only in words. Together they assume that it is possible to argue from the creatures to God, and to ascribe predicates to the Deity which have meaning for us, and they are designed to show that if this be the case, not all predication with respect to God and the creatures can be purely equivocal.[3]

The first two arguments are intended to make clear that the relation of cause and effect which holds between God and the world involves the possibility of predication which is not purely equivocal.

1. Between those things which chance to participate in an equivocal term there is neither order nor reference of one to another, but on the contrary it is wholly accidentally that the

autem quae in rebus aliis inveniuntur in divinorum cognitionem pervenimus, ut ex dictis patet. Non igitur secundum puram aequivocationem dicuntur huiusmodi de Deo et aliis rebus."

[1] "Aequivocatio nominis processum argumentationis impedit. Si igitur nihil diceretur de Deo et creaturis nisi pure aequivoce, nulla argumentatio fieri posset procedendo de creaturis ad Deum. Cuius contrarium patet ex omnibus loquentibus de divinis."

[2] "Frustra aliquod nomen de aliquo predicatur nisi per illud nomen aliquid de eo intelligamus. Sed si nomina dicuntur de Deo et creaturis omnino aequivoce, nihil per illa nomina de Deo intelligimus: cum significationes illorum nominum notae sunt nobis solum secundum quod de creaturis dicuntur. Frustra igitur diceretur aut probaretur de Deo quod Deus est ens, bonus, vel si quid aliud huiusmodi est."

[3] Cf. I *Dist.* 8. q. 1 : a. 2. sol.

same name is applied to these diverse things, for the imposition of the name does not imply that there is any order among them. But this is not the case with the names applied both to God and the creatures. For these names belong to them in common according to the relations which unite cause and caused, as is clear from what has been said; wherefore the predication with respect to God and these other entities is not purely equivocal.[1]

2. When there is pure equivocation, there is no similarity between the things concerned, but only the unity of a name. Between created things and God, however, there is a certain mode of similarity, as appears from what has already been said.[2] It must be admitted, therefore, that not all affirmations concerning God are purely equivocal.[3]

This last argument states clearly and succinctly the substance of the whole matter. Likeness between cause and effect, it is maintained, involves the possibility of a valid predication.

In the concluding paragraph of the thirty-ninth chapter Aquinas clinched his attack upon Maimonides with the contention that if it be asserted that every quality ascribed to God must be interpreted in a negative sense, so that God may be said to be living only to indicate that he does not belong to the genus of inanimate things, we may legitimately argue that the term *living*, as applied to God and to creatures, implies in each instance the negation of inanimate existence, and that, consequently, it is not, as so used, a purely equivocal term.

It is evident that Maimonides's doctrine of God is involved in the same predicament as the Kantian doctrine of the *thing-in-itself*. That of which we know nothing, we cannot know to

---

[1] "Nam in his quae sunt a casu aequivoca, nullus ordo aut respectus attenditur unius ad alterium, sed omnino per accidens est quod unum nomen diversis rebus attribuitur : non enim nomen impositum uni significat ipsum habere ordinem ad aliud. Sic autem non est de nominibus quae de Deo dicuntur et creaturis. Consideratur enim in huiusmodi nominum communitate ordo causae et causati, ut ex dictis patet. Non igitur secundum puram aequivocationem aliquid de Deo et rebus aliis predicatur" (*Con. Gen.* loc. cit.; cf. *Com. Theol.* cap. xxvi).

[2] Cf. *Con. Gen.* lib. I. cap. 29.

[3] "Ubi est pura aequivocatio, nulla similitudo in rebus attenditur, sed solum unitas nominis. Rerum autem ad Deum est aliquis modus similitudinis, ut ex supra dictis patet. Relinquitur igitur quod non dicuntur de Deo secundum puram aequivocationem" (*Con. Gen.* loc. cit.).

exist, or have any reason for believing to exist. Whether St. Thomas himself fully realized that the possibility of proving that the divine existence is bound up with the possibility of ascribing attributes to the Deity—although it is a direct consequence of his teaching—is a question in regard to which one cannot be dogmatic. Certainly it escaped the discerning eye of his illustrious commentator, Cardinal Cajetan.[1] However this may be, Aquinas's criticism is indeed a shattering one. But it at once gives rise to the question whether, in refuting Maimonides, he has not refuted himself. For the *Via Remotionis* has been, as we know, explicitly defended by him on the ground that we cannot know *what* God is, but only *what he is not*.[2] Our attention has already been drawn to this inconsistency in Aquinas's teaching. It remains for us to consider his attempt to escape from it.

The first point to be noticed, then, is the contention that nothing can be predicated of God and the creature univocally.[3] The following arguments are advanced in support of this view:

1. When cause and effect are univocal the form of the effect is of the same species as the form of the cause; consequently the same name can be used in the same sense to signify either. But this is not the case with respect to God and the creatures, for what exists in the creatures in division and particularity exists in God in simplicity and unity. Hence the same attribute cannot be applied univocally to both.[4]

2. Not only must the form of the effect be the same as that of the cause, but it must have the same mode of being if there is to be univocal predication. Thus, though the form of a house as it exists in the mind of an artist is the same as the form of the house as it exists materially, yet the mode of being

---

[1] *Sum. Theol.* I.a. q. 13: a. 5. Comment. 12. "*Secundum* est: ly *nihil* in consequente positum, non supponit pro nihilo simpliciter. Quoniam, dato quod omnia huiusmodi nomina aequivoca essent, adhuc possemus cognoscere quod Deus est Creator, et supra omnia, et quod non est corpus, etc. Sed supponit pro *nihilo formaliter communi Deo et creatoris*, puta esse ens, actum, bonum, sapientem, etc.: nihil enim horum posset sciri de Deo, sed semper incideret fallacia Aequivocationis, ut patet."

[2] *Con. Gen.* lib. I. cap. 14; *Sum. Theol.* I.a. q. 3: prolog.

[3] That is predicated univocally of two objects which is predicated of both of them in the same sense. See the *Categories*, loc. cit.

[4] *Con. Gen.* lib. I. cap. 32; *Sum. Theol.* I.a. q. 13: a. 5. c.; *De Pot.* q. 7: a. 7. c.

is different, and consequently the name *house* cannot be predicated univocally of them both. So, even were it possible that the same form should exist in God and in the creature, it would yet be impossible that they should have the same mode of being, for God is pure being itself, and there is nothing in him which is not his being, whereas this is not the case with any other being.[1]

3. That which is predicated univocally of many things is genus, or species, or differentia, or accident, or property. But neither genus nor differentiae can be predicated of God, and consequently neither species nor definition. Nor are there any accidents or properties in God. Hence nothing can be predicated univocally of God and of other beings.[2]

4. A quality which is predicated univocally of two or more substances is more simple than either of them, since every substance is compound. In other words, the more simple is predicated of the less simple. But nothing is more simple than God, either in fact or in conception. Nothing, therefore, can be predicated of God and of anything else univocally.[3]

5. An attribute which is predicated of various substances belongs to them by participation. But God, who is pure being, participates in nothing. Hence no attribute can be predicated of God in the same sense in which it may be predicated of anything else.[4]

6. That which is predicated according to priority and posteriority is not predicated univocally, for the prior is included in the definition of the posterior. Thus substance is included in the definition of accident; whence it follows that, if we predicate being univocally of substance and accident, substance will itself be included in the definition of being as predicated of it, which is clearly inadmissible. Now God is prior to the creatures, and they are posterior to him, since they possess their qualities through participation, whereas in God essence and being are identical. Hence there can be no univocal predication with respect to God and the creatures.[5]

It will be noticed that this last proof is practically identical

---

[1] *Con. Gen.* lib. I. cap. 32; *De Pot.* q. 7: a. 7. c.
[2] *Con. Gen.* loc. cit.; cf. *Com. Theol.* Pars Prima, cap. xxvi. Cf. *De Verit.* q. 2: a. 11. c.   [3] *Con. Gen.* loc. cit.
[4] *Con. Gen.* loc. cit.   [5] *Con. Gen.* loc. cit.; cf. *De. Pot.* q. 7: a. 7. c.

with its predecessor, the notion of priority and posteriority which is introduced in the later argument being implied in the earlier. It is also to be observed, as Francis Sylvester has pointed out,[1] that what St. Thomas has here in mind is an ontological order of priority and posteriority, and that another order of priority and posteriority can be found in which univocal predication is possible. The case which he cites is that of numbers. None the less it would be a mistake to suppose that this fact had escaped the eye of St. Thomas.[2]

We are now face to face with an apparent dilemma. On the one hand, univocal predication with respect to God and the creatures has been pronounced impossible, and on the other hand, the contention of Maimonides that all such predications are equivocal has been refuted. It seems that we have entered a *cul de sac*. We are assured, however, by St. Thomas that a way out can be found by applying the principle of analogy. He has repeatedly insisted that not all predication with respect to God and the creatures is *purely* equivocal (*non pure aequivocum*). This emphasis upon the qualifying word suggests that there is a mode of predication which is only partially equivocal, and such is in fact the position which St. Thomas was concerned to maintain: "This mode of community (of attributes) is midway between purely equivocal and completely univocal predication."[3]

There are two modes of analogous predication. "According to the first, something is predicated of two entities with reference to their relation to a third entity. Being is thus predicated of both quality and quantity with reference to substance. The other mode is that according to which something is predicated of two entities inasmuch as one of them has reference to the other; being is thus predicated of both substance and quantity. Furthermore, the first mode of predication requires some entity prior to the two other entities to which they both refer, as substance is prior to quantity and quality; but the second mode does not require this. It does require, however, that one of the two entities be prior to the other."[4]

---

[1] *Con. Gen.* cap. 32; *Comment.* 8. 2.

[2] Cf. *De Verit.* q. 2: a. 11. c.

[3] "Iste modus communitatis medius est inter puram aequivocationem et simplicem univocationem" (*Sum. Theol.* I.a. q. 13: a. 5. c.).

[4] "Unus quo aliquid praedicatur de duobus per respectum ad aliquod

It is evident that the first mode of analogous predication is not applicable in the case of God and the creatures, for there is nothing prior to or more simple than the Deity. Moreover, the only terms which we can apply to God are those which we have learned to use in connection with the creatures. Consequently it is the second mode of analogy which we must employ, that is, the analogy of one to another—"analogia quae est unius ad alterum."[1]

But is it possible to compare the finite to the infinite? The answer is that there are two modes of resemblance. "One is that which obtains between different genera. This is the mode of proportion or proportionality, according to which one thing stands in the same relation to a second thing as a third does to a fourth. * * * The other mode is that which holds between members of the same genus which participate in a common quality. Likeness, however, does not involve comparison according to the first mode, but only according to the second. Accordingly there is no reason why the first mode should not hold good between God and the creatures."[2]

It will be observed that, in the passage just quoted, the terms *proportion* and *proportionality* are used synonymously. Elsewhere, however, a distinction is drawn. Thus we read in the *De Veritate*[3] that "conformity according to proportion is of two

tertium, sicut ens de qualitate et quantitate per respectum ad substantiam. Alius modus est quo aliquid praedicatur de duobus per respectum unius ad alterum, sicut ens de substantia et quantitate. In primo autem modo praedicationis oportet esse aliquid prius duobus, ad quod ambo respectum habent, sicut substantia ad quantitatem et qualitatem; in secundo autem non, sed necesse est unum esse prius altero." *De Pot.* q. 7: a. 7. c.; cf. I. *Sent.* Prolog. a. 2. ad 2^m; *Con. Gen.* lib. I. cap. 34; *Sum. Theol.* I.a. q. 13: a. 5. c. For the notion of analogy, see the *Posterior Analytics*, lib. I. cap. 10, lib. II. cc. 14 and 17.

[1] For a detailed discussion of the two modes of analogy, cf. Francis Sylvester, *Con. Gen.* lib. I. cap. 34; *Comment.* 7–9.

[2] "Unum quod invenitur in diversis generibus; et hic attenditur secundum proportionem vel proportionalitatem, ut quando alterum se habet ad alterum sicut aliud ad aliud. * * * Alium modum in his quae sunt eiusdem generis, ut quando idem diversis inest. Similitudo autem non requirit comparationem secundum determinatam habitudinem quae primo modo dicitur, sed solum quae secundo modo; unde non oportet quod primus modus similitudinis a Deo removeatur respectu creaturae" (*De Verit.* q. 2: a. 11. ad 2^m). [3] q. 2: a. 11. c.

kinds, and consequently there is a twofold community of
analogy. Thus there is a conformity of those things between
which there is a mutual relationship of proportion, from the
fact that they are separated by a determinate distance, or that
they are in some other mutual relationship, such a relationship
as that which duality has to unity, inasmuch as it is its double;
and again there is a conformity of two things to each other
when there is between them no relation of proportion, but
only a relation of similarity of proportions, as the number six
conforms to the number four in this, that as six is the double
of three, so four is the double of two. The first conformity is
that of proportion, the second that of proportionality. According to the first mode of conformity, we find some quality
predicated analogously of two things, one of which has a
relationship to the other; just as being is predicated of substance and accident from the relationship which they bear to
each other, and as health is predicated both of urine and of
an animal, since the urine has a certain likeness to the health
of the animal. But at times analogous predication follows the
second mode of conformity; thus the name *vision* is applied
both to corporeal and to intellectual vision, since the intellect
is to the soul as vision is to the eye. Consequently analogous
predications made according to the first mode require a determinate relation between the entities of which the common
quality is predicated. Hence it is impossible that any quality
should be predicated both of God and the creature after this
mode, for no creature stands in such a relation to God that
from that relation it would be possible to determine the nature
of the divine perfection. But the other mode of analogy requires
no determinate relationship between the entities of which the
common quality is predicated; and so there is no reason why
a term should not be applied analogously to God and the
creature according to this mode.[1]

[1] "Convenientia enim secundum proportionem potest esse duplex; et
secundum hoc duplex attenditur analogiae communitas. Est enim quaedam
convenientia inter ipsa quorum est ad invicem proportio, eo quod habent
determinatum distantiam, vel aliam habitudinem ad invicem, sicut
binarius cum unitate, eo quod est eius duplum; convenientia etiam
quandoque attenditur duorum ad invicem inter quae non sit proportio,
sed similitudo duarum ad invicem proportionum; sicut senarius convenit
cum quaternario ex hoc quod sicut senarius est duplum ternarii, ita

It appears, then, that we are not justified in attempting to make any direct comparison between the goodness of man and the goodness of God, since the two are incommensurable, inasmuch as the former is finite, while the latter is infinite. But we are justified in asserting that as the goodness of man is to the man, so the goodness of God is to God, for in so doing we only affirm that as the finite is to the finite, so the infinite is to the infinite. It was by appealing to this principle that St. Thomas undertook to refute the objection that, since entities which do not resemble one another are farther removed from each other than entities which do resemble each other, and since God is infinitely distant from the creature, it is impossible that there should be any similarity between them. To this objection St. Thomas returned the following reply: "Likeness which arises from the fact that two entities partici- pate in the same quality, or from the fact that one entity has to the other a determinate relationship of such a sort that by means of the first the mind is able to comprehend the second entity, does diminish the distance between them; but not so the likeness which arises from the conformity of proportions; for such likeness is found in the same degree between great and small distances; for the likeness of proportionality between two and one and six and three is not greater than that between two and one and a hundred and fifty. And so the infinite

quaternarius binarii. Prima ergo convenientia est proportionis, secunda autem proportionalitatis; unde et secundum modum primae convenientiae invenimus aliquid analogice dictum de duobus quorum unum ad alterum habitudinem habet; sicut ens dicitur de substantia et accidente ex habi- tudine quam substantia et accidens habent; et sanum dicitur de urina et animali, ex eo quod urina habet aliquam similitudinem ad sanitatem animalis. Quandoque vero dicitur aliquid analogice secundo modo con- venientiae; sicut nomen visus dicitur de visu corporali et intellectu, eo quod sicut visus est in oculo, ita intellectus est in mente. Quia ergo in his quae primo modo analogice dicuntur, oportet esse aliquam determinatam habitudinem inter ea quibus est aliquid per analogiam commune, im- possibile est aliquid per hunc modum analogiae dici de Deo et creatura; quia nulla creatura habet talem habitudinem ad Deum per quam possit divina perfectio determinari. Sed in alio modo analogiae nulla determinata habitudo attenditur inter ea quibus est aliquid per analogiam commune; et ideo secundum illum modum nihil prohibet aliquod nomen analogice dici de Deo et creatura" (cf. *De Verit.* q. 2: a. 3. ad 4^m. and q. 23: a. 7. ad 9^m).

distance between the creature and God does not destroy the likeness predicated."[1]

Ingenious as this theory is, it nevertheless creates serious difficulties of its own. It relies upon the possibility of establishing a ratio between two mutually incommensurable orders, the temporal and the eternal, which shall justify us in asserting: as the finite is to the finite, so the infinite is to the infinite. But according to Aquinas's own teaching, this would seem to be impossible. A finite substance, such as a man, does indeed stand in relation to its own attributes, so that we can speak of a man *possessing* the quality of goodness. But Aquinas himself has claimed to demonstrate that God is not a substance in the sense which anything else is a substance, and that in him there are no accidents. God does not *possess* goodness, God *is* goodness. Goodness and being in him are identical. We have assumed that there is a differentiation in the infinite corresponding to the relation of substance to quality of which we are aware in the finite; but our assumption is false, for such differentiation is incompatible with the divine simplicity.

It might, of course, be contended that, while the relation of substance to attribute is to be found *in re* only in the finite, a corresponding relation of the divine to itself exists *in mente*. The distinction between "real" relations and relations existing only "for the mind" is one which we have already encountered, and which was fully recognized by Aquinas. But the reply might be made that we are not concerned with relations imposed by the mind, but with the mind's divine object as it exists in itself. Our ideas are many and relations hold between them, but that object is one and simple. The ratio we have sought to establish is therefore an impossible one.[2]

Nevertheless we cannot imagine that Aquinas was not

---

[1] "Similitudo quae attenditur ex eo quod aliqua duo participant unum, vel ex eo quod unum habet aptitudinem determinatam ad aliud, ex qua scilicet ex uno alterum comprehendi possit per intellectum, diminuit distantiam; non autem similitudo quae est secundum convenientiam proportionum: talis enim similitudo similiter invenitur in multum vel parum distantibus; non enim est maior similitudo proportionalitatis inter duo et unum, et sex et tria, quam inter duo et unum, et centum et quinquaginta. Et ideo infinita distantia creaturae ad Deum similitudinem praedictam non tollit" (*De Verit.* q. 2: a. 11. ad 4ᵐ).

[2] Cf. P. Pedro Descogs's *Institutiones Metaphysicae Generalis*, p. 266, obj. 2. a. and pp. 270, 275, and 294, sec. 4, para. 2. ff.

aware of the difficulty before us. And in truth his answer is to be found in the thirty-sixth chapter of the first book of the *Contra Gentiles*, where it is stated that "although our intellect arrives at the knowledge of God through divers conceptions, as has been said, yet it knows that that which corresponds to all these conceptions is wholly one: for the intellect does not attribute the mode in which it knows to the things known. Accordingly it does not attribute immateriality to a stone, although it knows it immaterially. Hence it expresses unity by verbal composition indicating identity, when it says *God is good*, or *goodness*; so that, if there be any diversity in such composition, it may be referred to the intellect, while unity is referred to the thing known."[1]

Why, then, since there is in God no differentiation corresponding to the relation of substance to attribute, did St. Thomas think it worth while to develop his elaborate theory of proportionality? It is clear that he was concerned to emphasize the incommensurability of the finite and the infinite, while insisting at the same time upon the legitimacy of analogous predication. But surely, we may urge, this might have been done more briefly, clearly, and consistently. And as a matter of fact it was done by Aquinas on a number of occasions in the course of his writing. Thus in the *Summa Theologica*[2] we find the following succinct statement: "Proportion is used in two senses. As used in one sense, it signifies a fixed relation of one quantity to another; and in this sense double, triple, and equal are species of proportion. In the other sense, proportion signifies any relation of one thing to another. And in this sense there can be a proportion of the creature to God, inasmuch as it related to him as effect to cause, and as potentiality to actuality."[3]

[1] "Quamvis namque intellectus noster in Dei cognitionem per diversas conceptiones deveniat, ut dictum est, intelligit tamen id quod omnibus eis respondet, omnino unum esse: non enim intellectus modum quo intelligit rebus attribuit intellectis; sicut nec lapidi immaterialitatem, quamvis eum immaterialiter cognoscat. Et ideo rei unitatem proponit per compositionem verbalem, quae est identitatis nota, cum dicit, *Deus est bonus* vel *bonitas*: ita quod, si qua est diversitas in compositione, ad intellectum referatur, unitas vero ad rem intellectam" (cf. *Sum. Theol.* I.a. q. 13: a. 12).   [2] I.a. q. 12: a. 1. ad 4m.
[3] "Proportio dicitur dupliciter. Uno modo, certa habitudo unius quantitatis ad alteram; secundum quod duplum, triplum et aequale sunt species

That the two passages just cited, contradictory as they appear at first sight, do not represent a conscious inconsistency or change of viewpoint on the part of Aquinas is evident from the fact that in the *Commentary on the Sentences* we find the alternative explanations given side by side with the obvious intent of providing us with two equivalent statements of the same position. "Although there can be no proportion of the finite to the infinite, since the excess of the infinite above the finite is not determinate, yet it is possible that between them there should be proportionality, which is likeness of proportions; so that even as the finite is equated to something finite, the infinite is equated to something infinite. Moreover, in order that anything should be wholly known, it is necessary that there should be a proportion between the knower and the known, for the virtue of the knower must be adequate to the knowability of the thing known; and equality is a certain proportion. But sometimes the knowability of a thing exceeds the virtue of the knower, as when we know God, and conversely when he knows the creatures; and then it is not necessary that there should be a proportion between the knower and the known, but only proportionality, so that as the knower stands to that which is to be known, so the knowable stands to that which is known; and such proportionality suffices for the infinite to be known by the finite, and conversely. Or it may be said that proportion, according to the first meaning of the term, signifies the relation of quantity to quantity according to some determinate excess or equality; but that afterward the meaning is altered to signify every relation of one thing to another. And in this sense we may say that matter must be proportionate to form. So nothing forbids that in this sense our intellect, although it is finite, should be said to be proportionate to the perception of the infinite essence."[1]

proportionis. Alio modo, quaelibet habitudo unius ad alterum proportio dicitur. Et sic potest esse proportio creaturae ad Deum, inquantum se habet ad ipsum ut effectus ad causam, et ut potentia ad actum." Cf. *De Trin.* q. 1: a. 2. ad 3[m]; 3 *Dist.* 1. q. 1: a. 1. ad 3[m]; *Quodlib.* 10. q. 8: a. 17. ad 1[m]; *De Pot.* q. 7: a. 10. ad 9[m].

[1] "Quamvis finiti ad infinitum non possit esse proportio, quia excessus infiniti supra finitum non est determinatus; potest tamen esse inter ea proportionalitas quae est similitudo proportionum; sicut enim finitum aequatur alicui finito, ita infinito infinitum. Ad hoc autem quod aliquid

This passage appears to be the interpretation of Aquinas's teaching which we have already suggested. Undoubtedly he was anxious to make it clear that the infinite can in no sense be measured by the finite, and yet in the same breath to insist that genuine inference from the finite to the infinite is possible, and that real, though fragmentary and imperfect, knowledge of the latter is attainable.[1]

Among the Neoscholastic writers Garrigou-Lagrange, Balthazar, Sertillanges, and Valensin have championed the method of proportionality, which, they contend, is capable of yielding us genuine knowledge of God. Descoqs, on the other hand, maintains that it presupposes the validity of the analogy of proportion, and consequently that it is metaphysically valueless. "From the point of view which we occupy," he writes, "it must be said that proportionality is of no metaphysical interest, and that the analogy of similitude (i.e. of proportion) is alone of importance."[2] This he does both for

totaliter cognoscatur, quandoque oportet esse proportionum inter cognoscens et cognitum; quia oportet virtutem cognoscentis adaequari cognoscibilitati rei cognitae; aequalitas autem proportio quaedam est. Sed quandoque cognoscibilitas rei excedit virtutem cognoscentis; sicut cum nos cognoscimus Deum, aut e converso, sicut cum ipse cognoscit creaturas; et tunc non oportet esse proportionem inter cognoscentem et cognitum, sed proportionalitatem tantum; ut scilicet sicut se habet cognoscens ad cognoscendum, ita se habeat cognoscibile ad hoc quod cognoscatur; et talis proportionalitas sufficit ad hoc quod infinitum cognoscatur a finito, et e converso. Vel dicendum, quod proportio secundum primam nominis institutionem significat habitudinem quantitatis ad quantitatem secundum aliquem determinatum excessum vel adaequationem; sed ulterius est translatum ad significandum omnem habitudinem cuiuscumque ad aliud; et per hunc modum dicimus, quod materia debet esse proportionata ad formam; et hoc modo nihil prohibet intellectum nostrum, quamvis sit finitus, dici proportionatum ad videndum essentiam infinitum" (4 *Dist.* 49. q. 2: a. 1. ad 6m).

[1] For an elaborate discussion of the theory of proportionality, cf. Garrigou-Lagrange, *Dieu, son existence et sa nature*, pp. 527–545; also Sertillanges, *S. Thomas d'Aquin*, tome I. pp. 183–190.

[2] "Du point de vue qui nous occupe, il faudra donc dire que la proportionnalité n'a plus aucun intérêt métaphysique et que seule importe l'analogie de similitude" (*Institutiones Metaphysicae Generalis*, p. 272). For his critique of his opponents' views, see the same work, pp. 271–293. In reading modern Roman Catholic writers, it is necessary to remember that Aquinas's analogy of proportion is generally termed by them the analogy of attribution, and that his analogy of proportionality is called by them the analogy of proportion.

the reason that I have already suggested—namely, that in God there can be no real relation between subject and attribute—and also on the ground that without making use of the analogy of proportion it would be impossible for us to formulate the propositions between which the relation of proportionality is said to hold. Thus we cannot say that the divine knowledge is related to the Deity as human knowledge is related to man, unless we first know in some degree what the divine knowledge is.[1] Furthermore, he insists that the passage quoted above from the *De Veritate*,[2] in which it is declared that the analogy of proportion does not hold between God and the creatures, does not represent the final opinion of St. Thomas as set forth in his later works, the *De Potentia*, the *Contra Gentiles*, and the *Summa Theologica*.[3] This may well be the case. I venture, however, again to call attention to the passage from the *Commentary on the Sentences* which I have already quoted at length, where the theory of proportionality is once more stated, and is declared to be identical with the second of the two possible interpretations of the theory of

---

[1] "Mais si l'être et l'intelligence de Dieu sont 'simplement différent' de l'être et de l'intelligence de la créature, qu'est-ce qui m'autorisera à construire cette équation, à les rapprocher l'un de l'autre? Assurément, pour que cette mise en équation soit légitime, il faudra bien supposer que par ailleurs nous possédons déjà la similitude de l'être de Dieu et de celui de la créature, que nous sommes par ailleurs déjà autorisés à les rapprocher. Comment, en effet, serait-on autorisé à parler de *similitude de rapports* si les termes de ce rapport n'étaient déjà semblables, et si l'on n'était en mesure d'assigner à cette similitude de rapport un fondement? Or, ce fondement sera-t-il une autre similitude de rapports? Ce serait reculer la question à l'infini et donc ne rien expliquer du tout. Sera-ce une relation des sujets en cause à un terme strictement un, *ratione sui*,— c'est à savoir dans le cas de Dieu et de la créature, la relation à l'*esse* considéré comme UN *ratione sui*? Mais alors on se heurte à l'univocité,—et c'est logiquement le panthéisme. Ces hypothèses étant exclues, il ne reste plus pour fonder la proportion, qu'une relation à un même terme analogue par lui-même; la question revient alors à expliquer l'unité de ce terme analogue et à montrer comment cette similitude de rapports n'est que l'application d'une analogie antérieure à elle et fondement de toute la construction. D'où suit nécessairement que la proportionnalité n'est pas première, fondamentale, que, tout au contraire, elle est dérivée et suppose une analogie de similitude antérieure" (*Institutiones Metaphysicae Generalis*, pp. 271–272).

[2] q. 2 : a. 11. c.   [3] Cf. Joyce's *Principles of Natural Theology*, p. 249 n.

proportion. It will be noticed that both here and in the *De Veritate*, the notion of proportion which Aquinas rejects is the same which the word conveys to us to-day—namely, that of definite arithmetical ratio. Thus the example given in the latter instance in the relation of duality to unity. It is obvious that proportion, in this sense, could not obtain between the creature and God. As Aquinas says, "the excess of the infinite above the finite is not determinate."[1] It also seems clear that it was in order to avoid falling, or appearing to fall, into this very error that he elaborated his theory of proportionality. But proportion, in the sense in which we have been using it, is by no means necessarily involved in the attribution of the same quality to God and to the creature in accordance with the doctrine of degrees of being. All that is necessary is that the creature resemble God. And Descoqs is clearly right in asserting that such "analogy of similitude" is presupposed by the theory of proportionality. In the *Commentary on the Sentences* Aquinas seems aware of this fact, else he could scarcely have equated proportion in the second sense with proportionality. Does the passage in question, then, record the change from an earlier to a later view, or does the fact that the equation is drawn at all signify, not a change of view, but only the fuller statement of an opinion previously held? The fact that the two meanings of proportion are stated in the second response to the same article in the *De Veritate* in which the theory of proportionality is expounded certainly points to the second possibility. On the other hand, the later use of St. Thomas in the two *Summae* of the analogy of proportion without reference to proportionality points to the first. It seems, therefore, that we lack evidence sufficient to enable us to embrace either opinion.

The whole doctrine of analogy rests upon and presupposes the theory of degrees of reality, which we have already had occasion to review in connection with the fourth argument for the existence of God. It will be remembered that the transcendentals—being, unity, goodness, and truth—are not genera. Generic terms are of necessity univocal. It is the peculiar characteristic of an analogous term that it is capable of application to different genera and to various levels of reality, to all

[1] *Commentary on the Sentences*, loc. cit.

of which it may legitimately be ascribed though not in the same mode.

It must also be emphasized that these various levels of reality must not be confused with the different degrees of intensity of a quality—such a quality, for instance, as brightness. All such degrees of intensity are strictly univocal.[1] What is involved in the doctrine of degrees of reality we can best realize from the contemplation of being as it is found in an accident—the nature of which is to inhere in something other than itself—in a substance—the nature of which is not to inhere in anything other than itself, but which is yet a contingent being inasmuch as its essence is distinct from its existence—and in God in whom essence and existence are one. To these three entities being pertains, but not in the same mode.[2]

What, then, is to be our guiding principle in predicating the qualities of God? The initial distinction is between those terms which apply to God literally and those which do so only metaphorically. The grounds upon which this distinction is based are briefly stated by St. Thomas in the *Summa Theologica*.[3] "Those names which are literally applied to God imply corporeal conditions, not in that which is signified by each name, but in the mode of signification. Those names which are metaphorically applied to God imply a corporeal condition in that which is signified."[4]

In other words, all names which imply any defect—that is, any falling short of the highest level of being—can be applied to God only metaphorically. It is thus permissible to call God a stone in order to suggest to the imagination the idea of strength, but inasmuch as the concept of a stone implies materiality, and as matter is a lower level of being than spirit, such a term is not applicable to God in its literal sense. On the

[1] Cf. Garrigou-Lagrange, *Dieu, son existence et sa nature*, p. 534, n. 1. "Il est une *analogie tout à fait improprement dite*, dont ne parle jamais S. Thomas, car elle est en réalité une univocité. C'est celle qui existe entre deux perfections univoques de degrés divers : deux murs inégalement blancs."

[2] *Dieu, son existence et sa nature*, p. 201, n. 2; cf. *De Verit.* q. 2 : a. 11. ad 2^m.

[3] I.a. q. 13: a. 3. ad 3^m.

[4] "Ista nomina quae proprie dicuntur de Deo, important conditiones corporales, non in ipso significato nominis, sed quantum ad modum significandi. Ea vero quae metaphorice de Deo dicuntur, important conditionem corporalem in ipso suo significato" (cf. *Con. Gen.* lib. I. cap. 30).

other hand, there are many terms which do not in themselves imply imperfection, although in the mode in which they apply to creatures they do of course imply it.[1] Such terms—according to St. Thomas—whose teaching is here based upon that of the Pseudo-Dionysius[2]—may either be ascribed to God or denied of him. They may be ascribed to God so far as their signification is concerned, they may be denied of God so far as their mode of signification is concerned, for they are known to us only as applied to creatures, whereas in the Deity they subsist "in a more eminent mode" (*per modum eminentiorem*). It is also to be observed that names applied metaphorically to God are to be ascribed to him only in a secondary sense, by reason of the fact that they apply primarily to creatures. On the other hand, those terms which may be ascribed to God literally, apply to him primarily, since the creatures possess them only by participation while in God they are identical with being.

The theory of degrees of reality is one which divides philosophers at the present day, and our attitude toward the problem it presents will doubtless affect our estimate of the inherent plausibility of Aquinas's doctrine of analogy. Nevertheless there is one question which we may raise at this point without fear of straying far afield, for it rises naturally before our eyes as we recall the position taken up by St. Thomas in his refutation of David of Dinant. In opposition to the latter's insistence that the identity of God and primary matter could be validly inferred from the absence of all differences between them, St. Thomas contended that, while things that are *different* do indeed differ from one another by differences, things which are *diverse* do not differ by differences but are simply and irreducibly dissimilar. It is evident that the goodness of God and the goodness of man cannot be diverse, for were they so the same name could be applied to both of them only by equivocation. On the contrary, the very conception of analogy appears at least to imply at once likeness and unlikeness. The goodness of man is said to resemble the goodness of God, yet it is also said to differ from it in the mode of its existence. Are we not then justified in affirming that the goodness of God and the goodness of man are different, that accordingly they differ

[1] *Con. Gen.* lib. I. cap. 30; *Sum. Theol.* I.a. q. 13: a. 3. c.
[2] *Coel. Hier.* 2. 3.

from each other by differences, and that the possession of differences implies the possession of similarities? If so, we may then argue that the term *goodness* is here applied to a compound or composite whole, to a group of qualities, or to a simple quality which is itself qualified by other qualities; and thus we shall be able to maintain that the similarity arises from the presence of the same quality or qualities in God and man, and that the dissimilarity is due to the presence in one or in each of these entities of some quality or qualities absent in the other. Our so-called analogue will thus have been dissected into a number of distinct and simple qualities, some similar, some dissimilar, but all strictly univocal. It is indeed difficult to see how a simple quality could manifest itself at more than one level of reality. Let us symbolize it for the moment by the letter x. How is x at level a to be recognized as distinct from and yet one with x at level b? Different in some respect it must be, or we should not be able to discriminate between the two. Similar in some respect they must also be, otherwise we should mistake our two x's for two distinct qualities. How is our analogue to be kept from lapsing into univocal identity on the one hand, or into differentiation and multiplicity on the other? Could we have propounded these questions to St. Thomas he would doubtless have replied that to treat being as a univocal concept is to turn it into a genus, with the consequence that all determinate forms of existence must be treated as something added to, and in themselves other than, being. He would probably also have asserted—as Neoscholastics do to-day—that while the concept of being has a certain unity so that we can think of it without thinking explicitly of all the degrees of reality, yet its unity is not absolute, since it contains and implies all of them *implicitly*.[1]

There is, however, another factor in the problem which

[1] "Le concept d'être a bien une certaine unité, c'est ainsi que nous pouvons penser à l'être sans penser *explicitement* à ses analogués: Dieu et la créature, la substance et l'accident; c'est ainsi encore que la métaphysique, qui a pour objet l'être en tant qu'être, peut être une science une. Mais l'unité de ce concept n'est pas absolue, car il contient actuellement et implicitement une multiplicité. Il est impossible en effet de concevoir *positivement l'être actuel dont l'actualité est essentiellement variée*, sans penser *confusément* ou *implicitement* à l'être qui existe par soi et à l'être qui n'existe pas par soi" (Garrigou-Lagrange, *Dieu, son existence et sa nature*, p. 538).

must not be forgotten, namely, the doctrine of the identity of the divine essence and existence. In man, goodness is a quality distinct from other qualities. A man may be good but not wise, or wise but not good. In God, on the contrary, goodness and wisdom are identical.

This consideration introduces us to a problem which confronted Aquinas as the result of his acceptance of the theory of analogy. Are the various terms which upon that theory we are justified in applying to God synonyms (*synonyma*)? To this question Aquinas responded, no. They are not synonyms, for they do not have the same meaning; but they refer to the same thing, that is, to the divine essence.[1]

Yet we are compelled to ask, if goodness and wisdom be two distinct and separate qualities in man, how can they be identical in God? Must we not conclude that their apparent diversity in man is, after all, illusory? But, then, whence arises the plurality of concepts in the mind, if no plurality correspond thereto in fact? We seem to have entered upon an infinite regress. But once more the doctrine of analogy comes to our aid. Goodness, wisdom, and the other "perfections" are, according to St. Thomas, really and truly distinct in finite beings; but at the highest level of reality They are, as it were, transmuted into the simplicity of the divine essence. It is this simplicity which corresponds to the multiplicity of our mental concepts, and which makes them true.

It is not easy to grasp Aquinas's thought upon this matter, for his language at times seems contradictory. Thus we read: "Certain names are applied literally to God which, in their primary sense, signify the creator rather than the creatures—such names as goodness, wisdom, and others of this sort—and their diversity does not arise through any relation to creatures, but rather the reverse; for it is because the concept of wisdom and the concept of goodness differ in God, that goodness and wisdom are differentiated in creatures, not only in conception, but in fact.[2]

---

[1] *Con. Gen.* lib. I. cap. 35; *Sum. Theol.* I.a. q. 13: a. 4; *Com. Theol.* Pars Prima, cap. xxiv; 1 *Dist.* 2. q. 1: a. 3. sol.

[2] "Quaedam nomina dicuntur proprie de Deo, quae quantum ad significata per prius sunt in Deo quam in creaturis, ut bonitas, sapientia, et huiusmodi; et horum diversitas non sumitur per respectum ad creaturas,

The contradiction, however, is only apparent, for we are
told in the *solutio* of the same article that these various qualities
in God are "one in fact but distinct as concepts."[1] In the
second distinction of the same book[2] the matter is put more
clearly. "So therefore it is plain that the plurality of names
arises from the fact that God himself exceeds our intellect.
Moreover, inasmuch as God exceeds our intellect, it arises on
his side because of the fullness of his perfection, and on our side
because of our intellect which is unable to comprehend that
perfection; whence it appears that the plurality of these concepts is not only due to our intellect, but also to God himself,
inasmuch as his perfection exceeds every conception of our
intellect."[3]

In concluding this discussion of Aquinas's theory of analogy,
it seems fitting to emphasize once more the unsatisfactory
nature of its relation to the *Via Remotionis*. In spite of all pro-
testations the two are forced to assume an attitude of flat
contradiction where no contradiction is necessary. If, as we
suggested in the preliminary discussion of the subject, the *Via
Remotionis* first came into being in order to give practical
assistance to the needs of the devout soul, it can hardly be
regarded as other than regrettable that it was ever elevated to
the rank of a metaphysical dogma. Having once committed
himself to the theory that the only possible knowledge of God
is to be obtained by negation, he was under the necessity of
making a covert retreat from a position which had become
untenable. The method of analogy offered a way of escape,
and we have seen how he availed himself of it. But in reality
there was no reason why the two methods should not openly

---

immo potius e converso. Quia ex hoc quod ratio sapientiae et bonitatis
differt in Deo, diversificatur in creaturis bonitas et sapentia non tantum
ratione, sed etiam re" (1 *Dist.* 22. q. 1 : a. 3. ad 3^m).

[1] "Omnia sunt unum re, et differunt ratione."   [2] q. 1 : a. 3. sol.
[3] "Sic ergo patet quod pluralitas nominum venit ex hoc quod ipse Deus
nostrum intellectum excedit. Quod autem Deus excedat intellectum nostrum est ex parte ipsius Dei, propter plenitudinem perfectionis eius, et ex
parte intellectus nostri, qui deficienter se habet ad eam comprehendendam.
Unde patet quod pluralitas istarum rationum non tantum est ex parte
intellectus nostri, sed etiam ex parte ipsius Dei, inquantum sua perfectio
superat unamquamque conceptionem nostri intellectus" (cf. *De Pot.* q. 7 :
a. 6. c).

have been used to supplement each other. As it is, the dogmatic assertion that no positive knowledge of God is possible leads to the inference that the results of the application of the method of analogy are in some sense not "knowledge." Possibly this is in part the consequence of a confusion of thought. It does not follow if we are unable, for instance, to appreciate the goodness of God, to know *how* good God is, that we cannot know the proposition, *God is Good*, to be true. But such a supposition has been entertained more than once, and it may be that even the acute mind of St. Thomas inadvertently harboured it.

We must notice, however, a recent attempt to vindicate his attitude in this matter by G. H. Joyce, S.J., in his *Principles of Natural Theology*.[1] "From a very different point of view it has been objected that in contending for a real, though analogical, knowledge of God, Scholasticism is inconsistent with itself. St. Thomas is express in asserting that while we can know God's existence, we cannot know *what* He is. We can know *quia est* (ὅτι ἔστι) but not *quid est* (τί ἐστι). And the same teaching is common to the Schoolmen generally. How, then, can it be maintained consistently that we are able by analogy to acquire a very considerable measure of knowledge regarding God's nature? This difficulty has been recently urged by some modernist writers in defence of their own position. Yet the inconsistency is only apparent. In the terminology of St. Thomas, on the one hand, knowledge of the essence of a thing (*quid res sit*) requires far more than the analogical knowledge which we have described, and, on the other, knowledge *quid est* may include a good deal besides the bare fact of existence. We know *quid res sit* when our mind can form a concept accurately representing its constitutive principle, the form which makes a thing what it is. Such is the knowledge we have, e.g., of a mathematical figure, when we are able to give its definition. This, manifestly, is impossible in regard of God. We cannot form a concept expressing His essential nature as it is in itself. We represent Him by a series of concepts, which either remove from Him some limitation proper to creatures, e.g., infinite, immutable, or else signify some perfection, which we know as found in finite creatures, and which, inasmuch as it is analogous and not confined to its

[1] Pp. 256–257.

finite mode of realization, is attributable to God. These, how-ever, give us only an imperfect and confused knowledge of Him. But when our knowledge of anything, though real as far as it goes, is thus obscure, and falls short of an apprehension of that essential nature which makes it what it is, it is still classed by the Schoolmen, following the Aristotelian terminology, as knowledge *quia est*."

If we accept this as a fair statement of Aquinas's position, it follows that the knowledge of God *quia est* includes, not only a "good-deal" but a very great-deal beside the knowledge that God exists. As a matter of fact we know, according to the Angelic Doctor, not only that God is infinite and immutable, but that God is good, that God is wise, that God is one, that God is intelligent, that God is possessed of will, and that God loves. What more, we may well ask, could we possibly know if we knew *quia est*? We are the more justified in pressing this question in that, it having been shown that there are no acci-dents in God, any knowledge that we have of God at all must, so it would seem, be knowledge of the divine essence.

We should, doubtless, receive the reply that to raise such a question is to betray an ignorance of the doctrines of degrees of being and of the simplicity of the Deity, an ignorance that good-ness, wisdom, will, etc., are not the same in God as they are in us, and, furthermore, that they are not distinct from one another *secundum rem*. By a multiplicity of concepts, we should be told, the human mind endeavours to render in some degree intel-ligible to itself, the simplicity of the divine nature. The multi-plicity is all in us; hence, although it is true to say that God is good and that God is wise, in the sense that the qualities which we know as goodness and wisdom are realized in God in a higher mode, yet it is not true in the sense that God possesses two distinct attributes which inhere in him as human goodness and wisdom inhere in a particular man who is a concrete substance. On the contrary, the divine essence contains un-differentiated in its utter simplicity those perfections which at a lower level of being exist as distinct and separate qualities.

But what if we cannot accept the doctrine of degrees of being, nor yet conceive how simplicity can contain within itself a multiplicity which is yet not a multiplicity? Certainly the position of St. Thomas will seem to us most unsatisfactory.

But the point which I wish to lay stress on is that it is also unsatisfactory even if the truth of these doctrines be admitted. For we have seen that St. Thomas, in opposition to Maimonides, insisted that the principle of analogy does justify us in predicating qualities of God. Now a statement can be justified only if it be true, that is, if it correspond to the facts. And if it be true, and we know that it is true, we have knowledge. Consequently, when St. Thomas asserts, in contradiction to Maimonides, that we are justified in affirming that God is good because goodness exists in God in some higher mode than it does in us, and then refuses to admit, upon precisely the same ground, that our knowledge that this statement is true constitutes knowledge of the divine essence, it is clear that he is trying to occupy two diametrical opposite positions at the same time. Had he maintained that our knowledge of the divine essence, though genuine, is imperfect, because while we can understand what is meant by the proposition, *God is good*, we cannot realize how good God is, for the reason that we have no direct perception of God, his position would not have been self-contradictory. But self-contradictory it is. The doctrine of degrees of being does not save him, on the contrary it condemns him; for it was formulated in order to sustain the view that goodness in God and goodness in man have something in common beside the name, that there really is a resemblance between the creature and the Creator in this particular respect that, in so far as the creature is what we call good, it is like God; from which the corollary inevitably follows that we know that God is good.

CHAPTER VIII

THE GOODNESS OF GOD

It is the virtue (*virtus*) of anything that makes it good.[1] And virtue is a perfection, for we call a thing perfect when it attains the virtue proper to it.[2] Hence the goodness of God follows from his perfection.[3]

It follows also from the theory that the primal unmoved mover causes motion inasmuch as it is the object of desire. For a thing is desired only because it is, or appears to be, good. The apparent good, however, does not cause motion of itself, but only in so far as it possess the species of the good. But the genuine good does cause motion of itself. Accordingly God, the *primum desideratum*, must be truly good.[4]

Again, the good is that which all things desire.[5] What everything desires, however, is to be actual in its own way, as is shown by the fact that every thing, according to its nature, strives against corruption. The concept of the good is, therefore, identical with that of actual being. Similarly, the privation of actuality constitutes evil. But God is wholly actual and without potentiality, therefore God is good.[6]

Lastly, the actuality and perfection of anything is its good. But everything acts according as it is actual. And the sign of the perfection of anything is that it is able to produce its like.[7] Accordingly it is from goodness that the communication of being and goodness proceeds. Moreover, the good is to be conceived as something appetible. And the appetible is an end which moves the agent to action. Hence the good is said to be diffusive of itself and of being.[8] Such diffusion, however, proceeds from God, the cause of all things; therefore God is good.[9] In the *Summa Theologica*,[10] the last two proofs are com-

---

[1] See *Nic. Eth.* lib. II. cap. v. lect. 6.
[2] See *Phys.* lib. VII. cap. iii. lect. 6.   [3] *Con. Gen.* lib. I. cap. 37.
[4] *Con. Gen.* loc., cit.   [5] See *Nic. Eth.* lib. I. cap. i. lect. 1.
[6] *Con. Gen.* loc. cit.
[7] See *Meteors*, lib. IV. cap. ii.
[8] See *Div. Nom.* cap. iv. lect. 1; also *Sum. Theol.* I.a. q. 5: a. 4. ob 2.
[9] *Con. Gen.* loc. cit.   [10] I.a. q. 6: a. 1. c.

bined in a single brief statement. A thing is good according as it is appetible. That which everything desires, however, is its own perfection, and this it attains in so far as it acquires the likeness of the agent that produced it. The agent then falls under the concept of the good. Hence to God, the effective cause of all things (*causa effectiva omnium*), the concepts of the good and of the appetible, are applicable.

The second of the above arguments appears to be incompatible with the third and fourth, inasmuch as the second includes the proposition that a thing is desired because it is good, whereas the third and fourth assume that the good is that which all things desire.

If these statements be intended as definitions of the good, it is clear that they cannot both be true. If the good be that which all things desire, it is impossible that all things should desire it because it is good. As regards Aquinas's own thought, however, there can be no doubt. What all things desire is fullness of being, and being and goodness are identical.[1]

In accordance with the teaching of Boethius,[2] St. Thomas goes on to affirm that God is not merely good but is goodness itself (*ipsa bonitas*). For the good of every entity is its own actual being; and God is not only actual being but is identical with his being.[3]

Furthermore, it has been made clear that the perfection of any entity is its goodness. The perfection of the divine existence does not result, however, from something additional to it, but is due to the fact that it is perfect in itself. Hence the goodness of God is not something additional to the divine substance, but is identical with it.[4]

Again, every particular good, which is not identical with goodness itself, is good by participation; and consequently presupposes something prior to itself whence it derives the characteristic of goodness. The concept of goodness, moreover, is subsumed under that of the end. But when we have to do with final causes, it is impossible to proceed to infinity.[5] Accordingly we must ultimately arrive at a primal good,

---

[1] See *Sum. Theol.* I.a. q. 5: a. 1. c.; cf. *De Verit.* q. 21: a. 1. c.
[2] *De Trinitate*, cap. iv. [3] *Con. Gen.* lib. I. cap. 38.
[4] *Con. Gen.* loc. cit. [5] See *Metaph.* lib. II. cap. ii. lect. 4.

which is good essentially and not by participation. And this is God, who is therefore identical with goodness itself.[1]

It is evident, furthermore, that while a particular entity is able to participate in some quality, being itself can participate in nothing; for that which participates is in potentiality, whereas being is actual. Hence God, who is his own being, cannot be good by participation but must be so essentially.[2] Also the being and the *id quod est* of every simple entity are one. And God is wholly simple; his being good is therefore identical with himself.[3] Accordingly God is identical with goodness itself.

Perfection is threefold. First a thing is perfect in the constitution of its being; secondly, it is perfect in so far as the accidents necessary for its perfect operation are added to it; and thirdly, in so far as it attains something else as its end. St. Thomas gives an illustration of his meaning by referring us to fire. The first perfection of fire is in the being which it has according to its substantial form; the second in such accidents as heat, lightness, and dryness; the third in its quiescence in its place. Now this threefold perfection pertains to God alone essentially, since in him there are no accidents—so that such qualities as wisdom and power, which are predicated of other intelligences accidentally, must be predicated of God essentially—and since he is not ordered with respect to anything else as his end, but is himself the end of all things.[4]

The *suppositum* of one perfection can be also the *suppositum* of another; thus the same body can be both white and sweet. But being, goodness, and all other qualities predicated of the essence are mingled with nothing other than themselves, for the nature of each is confined within the bounds of its concept. Accordingly a particular good thing can be mingled with something other than goodness, but in God, who is goodness itself, there is nothing beside goodness. Consequently there can be no evil in God.[5]

Again, that which is opposed to the essence of anything can have no place within it while it remains the same. Evil, therefore, which is opposed to the good, can have no place

---

[1] *Con. Gen.* loc. cit.   [2] *Con. Gen.* loc. cit.
[3] "Igitur ipsum esse bonum non est aliud quam ipse" (*Con. Gen.* loc. cit.).
[4] *Sum. Theol.* I.a. q. 6: a. 3. c.   [5] *Con. Gen.* lib. I. cap. 39.

within the divine essence unless it cease to be, which is impossible.[1]

It is obvious, furthermore, that evil cannot be predicated of God by participation. But it is also impossible that it should be predicated of the divine essence; for if evil be an essential predicate, like goodness and being, it can be mingled with nothing extraneous to itself. But evil is negation—essential evil, therefore, would not even be existent. Accordingly evil cannot be predicated of God.[2]

It is also the case that evil is the opposite of the good. The concept of good, however, has the same content as that of perfection; that of evil as imperfection. Since God, then, is perfect, no evil can be predicated of him.[3]

An entity is perfect, moreover, according as it is actual. Accordingly it will be evil in so far as it is deficient in actuality. Evil, therefore, is either identical with, or inclusive of, privation. And the subject of privation is a potentiality. But potentiality cannot be predicated of God.[4]

Finally, if the good be that which is desired by all things, evil must be that which all things flee. But if we find in anything something contrary to the motion of its natural appetite, that something is forced and alien to its nature (*praeter naturam*). Evil, therefore, as evil, is always forced and *praeter naturam*, although in a composite substance it may be natural to some element contained therein. God, however, is not composite, nor can there be in God anything forced or *praeter naturam*.[5]

It is also true that God is the good of every good,[6] and that all things are good by the divine goodness.[7] Sylvester

[1] *Con. Gen.* loc. cit. It is clear that this argument merely restates the idea expressed also in the first.
[2] *Con. Gen.* loc. cit.   [3] *Con. Gen.* loc. cit.   [4] *Con. Gen.* loc. cit.
[5] *Con. Gen.* loc. cit. Sylvester points out that this last argument seems to be self-contradictory, for if evil be natural to an element in any composite substance, it follows that it will always be found in conjunction with it. Hence it is not something forced or *praeter naturam*. His solution is that what is unnatural as regards a universal nature can be natural to a particular instance thereof, as blindness, which is unnatural in itself, is natural to a particular defective eye.
[6] "Omnis boni bonum" (*Con. Gen.* lib. I. cap. 40).
[7] "Bona bonitate divina" (*Sum. Theol.* I.a. q. 6: a. 4. c.).

warns us that we are not to suppose that God is the good of every good intrinsically, as though he inhered in finite entities as a form inheres in a body, but extrinsically, inasmuch as he is their effective, exemplar, and final cause. And Cajetan in turn points out that the question at issue is not whether all things derive their goodness from the divine goodness, but whether they are called good because of it, as white things are called white because of whiteness.

In the *Summa Theologica* Aquinas indulges in an historical résumé. Plato, he observes, taught the existence of separate forms through participation in which all things were nominated. Not only did he posit the ideas of man and horse, but also those of being and unity: through participation in which each thing is called being and one. Moreover, he held that what is in itself being (*per se ens*) and in itself one (*per se unum*) is the *summum bonum*; and because goodness and unity are convertible with being, he maintains that the good in itself (*per se bonum*) is God, because of whom all things are called good *per modum participationis*. Aristotle, while repudiating the doctrine of forms, concurred in the view that God is essentially being and goodness. Hence being and unity can be predicated of everything in so far as it participates through some mode of assimilation in the divine goodness which is the effective, efficient, and final cause of all goodness. None the less, since the likeness of the divine goodness inheres in each thing, it is also formally nominated good because of its own goodness. Thus there is one goodness of all things, and also there are many goodnesses (*multae bonitates*).

In the *Contra Gentiles* the approach is more direct. Since the goodness of anything is its perfection, and since God is perfect *simpliciter*, and comprehends in his perfection the perfections of all things, the divine goodness includes all goodnesses. Furthermore, a thing is said to be good by participation only because it bears some likeness to God who is good essentially. Again, a thing is appetible because of some end. And the good is to be conceived of as that which is appetible. Hence everything is said to be good either because it is an end or because it is ordered with respect to an end. The ultimate end, therefore, is that from which all things derive the characteristic of goodness—which end is God. Hence God is the good of every good.[1]

Inasmuch as the universal good is superior to the particular good, as the goodness and perfection of the whole are superior to the goodness and perfection of the part, and inasmuch as

---

[1] For the proof that God is the end with respect to which all things are ordered we are referred to the third book of the *Contra Gentiles* (cap. 17), where a number of arguments are to be found, which may briefly be summarized as follows:

1. Since nothing tends toward anything as toward an end except according as it is good, the good, as good, is an end. Hence God, the *summum bonum*, is the end of all things.

2. The maximum in any genus is the cause of all the members thereof. God, the *summum bonum*, is the cause of goodness in all good things. Accordingly, since whatever is an end is so in so far as it is good, God is the cause whereby every end is an end. But that because of which anything is what it is, is so itself to a greater degree. God therefore is the supreme end of all things.

3. The first cause is more a cause than the second, for that the second is a cause is due to the first. The first cause in the order of final causes must, then, be more a cause than the proximate final cause. And God is the primal final cause, being the first in the order of good things.

4. In all ordered ends, the ultimate end is the end of the preceding ends. A potion is prepared to be given to the sick, it is given that the sick may be purged, and so on. But all things are ordered in divers grades of goodness with respect to the *summum bonum*, the cause of all goodness. Hence, since the good falls under the concept of the end, God is the ultimate end of all ends. (It is difficult to see where this argument differs from its predecessor.)

5. The particular good is ordered with respect to the common good, and God is the common good of all things.

6. The hierarchy of ends is determined by that of agents, for as the supreme agent moves all secondary agents, so the ends of all secondary agents are ordered with respect to the end of the supreme agents. But God, the primal agent, has no end but his own goodness which is himself.

7. The ultimate end of every maker, in so far as he is a maker, is himself; for we use the things we make on our own behalf. But God is the cause of all things that are made, of some immediately, of others mediately, through intermediate causes. Hence God is the end of all things.

8. The final cause holds the primary place among causes, since from it all other causes derive their actuality. Hence the final cause of all things is the ultimate end.

It will be noted that the second and fifth arguments resemble the first and second of those employed to prove that God is the *summum bonum*.

the divine goodness is comparable to every other as the universal to the particular, it follows that God is the *summum bonum*.[1]

Again, that which is predicated essentially is predicated more truly than that which is predicated by participation. And God alone is good essentially, while all other things are good by participation. God, therefore, is the *summum bonum*.[2]

Moreover, that which is the maximum in any genus is the cause of all the other members of that genus, since the cause is more powerful than the effect. But all things derive the characteristic of goodness from God. Hence God is the *summum bonum*.[3]

As that is whiter which is less mingled with black, so that is better which is less mingled with evil. But God is wholly unmingled with evil, since it can be present in him neither actually nor potentially, and is, accordingly the *summum bonum*.[4]

The long and complicated process of reasoning in regard to the goodness of God, which I have just summarized, appears far more intricate than profound. With what seems unnecessary prolixity it expresses a fairly simple idea, namely, that God alone is good essentially and that all finite entities are good only by participation and through the resemblance which they bear—according to their rank in the scale of being —to that primal goodness.

---

[1] *Con. Gen.* lib. I. cap. 41.   [2] *Con. Gen.* loc. cit.
[3] *Con. Gen.* loc. cit. In the *Summa Theologica* (I.a. q. 6: a. 2) the same idea is expressed somewhat more elaborately. It is pointed out that God is the *summum bonum simpliciter*, and not in any genus, and that the effects which God brings into being are not good in the same sense in which God is good, not univocally but only analogously. The same point is made by Sylvester in his *Commentary on the Contra Gentiles*.   [4] *Con. Gen.* loc. cit.

CHAPTER IX

THE UNITY OF GOD

FROM the divine goodness we turn to the consideration of the divine unity. It is noteworthy that only at this stage of his argument did Aquinas take the step—so essential to the establishment of the theistic position—of attempting to show that such attributes as goodness and unity may justifiably be predicated of God. It is in the light of this fact that we must estimate the importance which he attached to his theory of analogy, and its vital significance for his system. The proofs of the divine unity advanced by Aquinas in the *Contra Gentiles* are sixteen in number.

1. The unity of God may be directly deduced from the proposition already established that God is the *summum bonum*. Whatever is highest or "superabundant" pertains to one entity alone. Hence God, who is the *summum bonum*, is also one.[1]

2. The same goal may be reached by arguing from the divine perfection. The assumption that there are more gods than one is self-contradictory, since it involves the existence of two or more perfect beings, which, by reason of the very fact that they were perfect, would be indistinguishable from each other, inasmuch as the possession by either of any distinctive quality could be due only to the presence of some "perfection" or the absence of some imperfection.[2]

3. That which can be accomplished by a single agent is better done so than if accomplished by a plurality of agents.[3] Now the order of the universe is the best possible.[4] For the power of the primal agent is sufficient to bring all things to

---

[1] *Con. Gen.* lib. I. cap. 42.

[2] *Con. Gen.* lib. I. cap. 42; *Sum. Theol.* I.a. q. 11: a. 3. c. For a similar argument with reference not to the divine perfection, but to the divine goodness, cf. 1 *Dist.* 2. q. 1: a. 1. contra, second argument.

[3] "Quod sufficienter fit uno posito, melius est per unum fieri quam per multa."

[4] For certain qualifications attached to this statement, see *Sum. Theol.* I.a. q. 25: a. 6. ad 3ᵐ; and 1 *Dist.* 44. q. 1: a. 2. sol.

1*

their potential perfection. Accordingly there is no need to posit any other first principle.[1]

4. The same conclusion can be reached if we take as our point of departure the analysis of motion given by Aristotle in the eighth book of the *Physics*. The primal motion is there shown to be one and continuous. That such motion should proceed from several movers is impossible. For if it be assumed that they all function together in the place of a single prime mover, it follows that none of them can be perfect, inasmuch as they are mutually interdependent. But the prime mover is perfect, inasmuch as the perfect is prior to the imperfect. On the other hand, if it be supposed that they function successively, we are faced with the fact that a mover which is not always functioning causes an irregular motion. This is evident in the case of inferior movers, in which motion begins with force only to lessen afterward, whereas natural motion is of the opposite character. Hence the primal motion, being one and continuous, must proceed from a single mover.[2]

5. Since spiritual substance ranks higher in the scale of being and goodness than corporeal substance, it follows that corporeal substance tends to resemble spiritual substance in obedience to the law that everything desires to attain the greatest good possible to it. Now of the three kinds of motion proper to corporeal substances, augmentation and diminution, alteration, and local motion, the latter is logically prior, and its presence is requisite for the occurrence of the other two.[3] To it, therefore, these other kinds of motion may be reduced. Consequently, beside the spiritual substance which is the end—the τέλος—of local motion, there is no other spiritual substance which cannot be reduced to it.[4]

As Francis Sylvester has justly observed, this proof is unsatisfactory, since it might be maintained that there are spiritual substances of the first order which do not function as "ends" of motion at all, either proximately or ultimately. The argument, he contends, presupposes that the number of "separate substances"—i.e. purely spiritual beings—can be determined on Aristotelian principles by the number of

[1] *Con. Gen.* lib. I. cap. 42.   [2] *Con. Gen.* lib. I. cap. 42.
[3] *Phys.* lib. VIII. cap. vii.   [4] *Con. Gen.* lib. I. cap. 42.

heavenly bodies in motion. This hypothesis in turn pre-supposes Aristotle's conception of the universe as an ordered whole, all the parts of which are related to a single ultimate principle.[1] Consequently, to quote the words of Sylvester, the proof "is not conclusive *simpliciter*, but is *ad hominem Peripateticum*."

6. In this proof the conception just referred to is explicitly stated and developed in detail. The order which obtains among the component parts of the universe is due to the fact that they are all related to a single principle productive of order, somewhat after the fashion in which the individual members of an army are related to the commander. Such order cannot spring from the natures of the various component parts of the universe, in so far as they are distinct from one another, for such distinction would tend rather to produce further distinction. Nor, for the same reason, can it be the work of a plurality of agents, since these also, like the component parts, would be diverse one from another. Hence, the order in the universe is either accidental or the result of the activity of a primal ordering power. "Furthermore, all parts of this world are found to be mutually so ordered that some are aided by others: thus, the inferior bodies are moved by the superior bodies, and these by incorporeal substances, as is clear from what has been said. Nor is this *per accidens*, since it occurs always, or in the majority of instances. All this world has, therefore, but one ordering and governing power. But beyond this world there is no other; wherefore there is but one governor of all things whom we call God."[2]

The sentences just quoted are obviously a mere restatement of the teleological argument. But such a restatement is here unnecessary. On the supposition that it has already been proved that the order which obtains in the universe involves

---

[1] Cf. *Metaph*. lib. XII. cap. x. lect. 9.

[2] "Omnes autem partes huius mundi invenientur ordinatae ad invicem, secundum quod quaedam a quibusdam iuvantur: sicut corpora inferiora moventur per superiora, et haec per substantias incorporeas, ut ex supra dictis patet. Nec hoc est per accidens: cum sit semper vel in maiore parte. Igitur totus hic mundus non habet nisi unum ordinatorem et gubernatorem. Sed praeter hunc mundum non est alius. Non est igitur nisi unus omnium rerum gubernator, quem Deum dicimus" (*Con. Gen.* lib. I. cap. 42; cf. I *Dist*. 2. q. 1: a. 1. sol.).

the presence of a controlling purpose, the question which now faces us is this: must we attribute this purpose to a single mind or may we with equal probability regard it as the joint purpose of a plurality of minds? St. Thomas's assertion that order cannot be caused by a plurality of agents is not in accordance with observed facts, since nothing is more familiar than the sight of united activity in pursuit of a common purpose. In the *Summa Theologica*, however, the same point is stated more at length.

"For a multitude is reduced into an ordered unity better by one cause than by many; for unity is the cause *per se* of unity, whereas many things are the cause of unity only *per accidens*, in so far as they are one in some mode. Accordingly, since that which is first is most perfect, and *per se* not *per accidens*, it must be that the primal entity which reduces all things into an ordered unity is only one."[1]

In our examination of the teleological argument we saw that a question had been raised as to the dependence of that argument upon the principle of induction. In the present connection we see Aquinas explicitly appealing to it to prove that the order prevailing among the component parts of the universe is not *per accidens*. The co-operation of various parts "in the majority of instances," *in maiore parte*, is advanced as a reason for rejecting the suggestion. Hence the present proof is in no sense *a priori*.

Moreover, the possibility of a plurality of divine agents cannot be dismissed in this way. Induction is of no avail here. Such an hypothesis may be inconsistent and untenable in itself, but if we assume that it is tenable, the presence of order in the universe is just what we should expect. Consequently it cannot be pointed to in disproof of the theory. Certain modern theologians have elaborated the theory of a Social Trinity of self-conscious Persons united in a relation of love. It is possible to conceive of a group of deities similarly related. Such a unity, says St. Thomas, would be accidental. Be it so. No

[1] "Melius enim multa reducuntur in unum ordinem per unum, quam per multa: quia per se unius unum est causa, et multa non sunt causa unius nisi per accidens, inquantum scilicet sunt aliquo modo unum. Cum igitur illud quod est primum, sit perfectissimum et per se, non per accidens, oportet quod primum reducens omnia in unum ordinem, sit unum tantum" (I.a. q. 11 : a. 3. c.).

appeal to empirical considerations will remove it from the bounds of possibility. He is on surer ground when, in the *Summa Theologica*, he affirms that the first principle is *per se* and not *per accidens*. Since in the Deity there are no accidents, the supposition can be rejected on *a priori* grounds as self-contradictory. This line of thought is resumed in the next argument.

7. God is a necessary being. Hence, if there be two gods, they are both necessary beings. Yet they must be differentiated from one another. But inasmuch as they are both necessary beings, they cannot be differentiated by necessity of being. Accordingly they must be differentiated by some other characteristic. One or both of them, therefore, will be composite. But this is impossible since in God there is no composition.

8. Furthermore, if we assume that it is possible for two necessary beings to be differentiated, that characteristic in respect to which they differ is either requisite as a complement to necessary being, or it is not. If not, it is not essential but accidental to the being to which it pertains. As an accident it has a cause. That cause is either the essence of that being or something external. If it be the essence, then, since in a necessary being essence is identical with existence, necessary being, *necessitas essendi*, is the cause of the accident. Consequently, inasmuch as both beings are necessary, they will both possess the accident which was supposed to be the ground of mutual differentiation.

To escape from this contradiction let us then assume that the cause of the accident is something external to the essence of the necessary being to which it pertains. But this hypothesis is also contradictory. For did not that cause exist, the accident would not exist either, and so the two necessary beings would no longer be differentiated. Manifestly, however, it is impossible that two necessary beings should depend for their differentiation upon a third entity, for by so doing they would cease to be necessary.

Accordingly we are driven to the alternative supposition that the differentiating characteristic is a necessary complement to necessary being—*necessarium ad necessitatem essendi complimendam*. This we can do either by conceiving it to be included in the notion of necessity, as *animate* is included in the notion of *animal*, or by regarding it as a specific difference whereby the notion of necessary being is completed, even as *animal* is completed by *rational*. The former mode of procedure cannot, however, be followed, since if the characteristic be included in the notion of necessity it will belong to both beings and so fail to differentiate them. There remains, then, the latter. But the difference which specifies a genus does not complete the notion of the genus. Thus the notion of animal is complete before the notion of rational is added to it. Yet an animal cannot exist without being rational or irrational. A concrete entity must be a member of a species as well as of a genus. Now a necessary being cannot owe its existence to anything complementary to necessary existence; the very suggestion involves us in self-contradiction. It is also unmindful of the identity of existence and essence in a necessary being. Accordingly, the hypothesis of the existence of a plurality of necessary beings is untenable.

9. If the word *God* be applied to more than one being, such application is either equivocal or univocal. If equivocal, it is purely arbitrary and without metaphysical significance. If univocal, it involves agreement in genus and species. But God is not in any genus or species. Moreover, the two entities to which deity is ascribed are, of necessity, numerically distinct. Numerical distinction is incompatible, however, with identity of essence and existence in both of them. But if they be not numerically distinct they are the same entity.[1]

10. From the nature of the case nothing pertaining to any particular thing in its singularity can pertain to anything else. So to a necessary being, necessity of being pertains in so far as it is this particular *signate* thing. For in so far as any thing is actual, it is distinct from all other things—and this is what we mean when we say that it is a *signate* thing. Obviously, then, it is impossible that a necessary being should depend upon anything else for its actual existence. Consequently necessity of being must pertain to it in its singularity. Hence there can be but one necessary being.[2]

This argument clearly presupposes that the attributes of

---

[1] *Con. Gen.* lib. I. cap. 42; *Com. Theol.* cap. xiv.
[2] *Con. Gen.* lib. I. cap. 42.

any substance are as truly particulars as the substance itself. Aquinas's Conceptualism is here in evidence.[1]

11. The divine essence is individuated either of itself, in *this* God, or by something other than itself. If by something other than itself, it follows that there is composition in the Deity, since essence and existence will in that case be distinct from one another. It must, therefore, be individuated of itself. But the principle of individuation cannot be common to more than one. Hence there cannot be more than one God.[2]

12. If there be many gods, the same divine nature must be present in each; yet the various deities must be distinct from one another. But it is impossible that they should be so distinct, for the divine nature has been shown to be incapable of receiving any addition either by way of essential or accidental differences, nor can it be differentiated, as the forms of corporeal substances are by matter; wherefore it cannot pertain to more than one being.[3]

13. This proof is stated with great brevity in the *Contra Gentiles*. "The existence proper to each individual is one alone.[4] But God is his own existence, as has been said. It is impossible, therefore, that there should be more than one God." In the *Compendium Theologiae*,[5] however, we find a fuller presentation of what appears to be the same argument. We are told that there are two ways in which a form can be "multiplied"; firstly, by specific differences, as the *genus* colour, for instance, is equally present in every shade of colour; secondly, by inhering in a plurality of individual substances. Consequently a form which cannot be rendered multiple by specific differences, and which does not inhere in any substance, is utterly unique. Thus whiteness, if it had being without inhering in any subject, would be absolutely one and devoid of all multiplicity. Now these conditions are fulfilled by the divine essence which is incapable of receiving differences, and

---

[1] "Una et eadem natura quae singularis erat et individuatur per materiam in singularibus hominibus, efficitur postea universalis per actionem intellectus depurantis ipsam a conditionibus quae sunt hic et nunc" (*De Universalibus*, tractatus primus).

[2] *Con. Gen.* lib. I. cap. 42; *Com. Theol.* cap. xiv.

[3] *Con. Gen.* lib. I. cap. 42; 1 *Dist.* 2. q. 1 : a. 1. contra, second argument.

[4] "Esse proprium uniuscuiusque rei est tantum unum."   [5] Cap. xiv.

which is *per se subsistens*; whence it cannot pertain to a plurality of entities, and so there can be only one God.[1]

14. According to the degree of being which a thing possesses it also possesses unity. Hence God, the supreme being, is absolutely One.[2]

15. The fifteenth proof is clearly nothing else than a restatement of its predecessor at somewhat greater length. In every genus multiplicity is observed to proceed from unity: accordingly in every genus there is some primal being by which all other members of that genus are "measured." Hence, in so far as entities have any characteristic in common, they depend upon some one principle. But all things exist. Consequently they must all depend upon one primal existent, which is God.[3]

It is obvious that this argument assumes that existence or being, *esse*, is a genus. But this is the position of David of Dinant. Once again, then, we find St. Thomas conceding by implication what he has elsewhere explicitly and vehemently denied.

If we admit the theory of degrees of being, obviously we must either posit an ultimate—a maximum—level of being, or else assume that the number of degrees is infinite. The latter alternative would scarcely be defended by any philosopher. But even if we embrace the former, there seems to be no reason why we should suppose that the unity which obtains at the highest level of being is numerical rather than generic. Aquinas's proof fails at this point.

16. In every government the ruler desires unity, wherefore monarchy is the highest form of government. Moreover, the members of the human body have but one head. Thus unity pertains to supremacy. Hence the primal cause of all things must be one.[4]

This "proof" is an analogy rather than an argument. It is also very similar to the first proof—so much so, in fact, that the distinction between them seems to be purely verbal.

---

[1] *Con. Gen.* lib. I. cap. 24; cf. *Sum. Theol.* I.a. q. 11 : a. 3. c.
[2] *Con. Gen.* lib. I. cap. 24. The same argument is stated at greater length in the *Commentary on the Sentences,* 1 *Dist.* 44. q. 1 : a. 2. sol.
[3] *Con. Gen.* lib. I. cap. 42; 1 *Dist.* 2. q. 1 : a. 1. contra, first argument.
[4] *Con. Gen.* loc. cit.

It is important to observe that the second, the seventh, the eighth, the ninth, the tenth, the eleventh, the twelfth, and the thirteenth proofs are all inspired by the same idea, and are, in fact, reducible to a single argument which takes as its starting-point the perfection and the necessary existence of the Deity, and thence reasons to the divine unity. The various other arguments advanced, whether they be based upon the order of the universe, the motion of corporeal objects, or the theory of degrees of being, are plainly inconclusive in that they fail to demonstrate that the ultimate principle of the universe is a single and individual entity. For their completion they require the support of that argument to which we have just referred, and which remains sufficient in itself.

It is because the Deity is both pure Being and necessarily existent that we are entitled to affirm his unity. Did these two characteristics not mutually imply each other there would be no contradiction in conceiving of two necessarily existent entities. But the opening sections of both the *Contra Gentiles* and the *Summa Theologica* are devoted, as we have seen, to the very task of showing that God, the necessarily existent being, is pure Being, is wholly actual, wholly simple, and, therefore, absolutely perfect. Hence, since perfection is nothing more or less than perfection, there is no conceivable way in which two perfect beings could differ from one another. In essence they must be identical; since neither possesses accidents, no differentiation can arise from that source; and since each is wholly simple a mere numerical difference is impossible. The same form can, indeed, inhere in a plurality of material of substances without losing its identity; but only because matter is itself the principle of differentiation. Among immaterial substances, however, differentiation requires dissimilarity of form. Every angel, therefore, as we already know, is a species of its own. But such differentiation is possible in the case of the angels only because they are not perfect. Perfection cannot differ from perfection, nor God from God. And since the divine perfection *is* the divine essence, which in turn *is* the divine existence, there is no room left even for numerical differentiation. God is absolutely unique and alone.

Thus we see that the principle for which Aquinas was contending is not identical with Leibniz's Identity of Indiscernibles. It is because essence and existence are the same in the case of the Perfect Being that numerical differentiation is inconceivable.[1]

In the *Summa Theologica*[2] and also in the *Quodlibeta*[3] Aquinas raises the question whether unity, when predicated of the Deity, has any positive significance, or is merely equivalent to a negation of division. He decides in favour of the latter hypothesis. We must distinguish, he tells us, between unity which is convertible with being and unity which is the principle of number. The former concept signifies only that the entity of which it is predicated is undivided. Through confusing this notion with that of the unity of number which is attributable only to extended and corporeal objects, Pythagoras and Plato committed the error of supposing that numbers were the substances of things, while Avicenna was led into the opposite mistake. "Considering that unity which is the principle of number contributes something additional to the substance of being (since otherwise a number composed of units would not be species of quantity), he believed that unity which is con-

---

[1] This is stated very clearly in the *Commentary on the Sentences*, 1 *Dist.* 2. q. 1 : a. 1. contra, third argument.

In the second book of the *Commentary on the Sentences* (*Dist.* 1. q. 1) the first article is entitled *Utrum sint plura principia prima.* Three proofs are there given of the existence of a single first principle :

(*a*) The order of the universe implies a single ultimate good, *unum summum bonum ultimum*, which is the object of universal desire.

(*b*) All things participate in being in various degrees, for the concept of being, though analogous, is yet one. Being itself, however, is identical with the essence of none of these things. Hence they must all receive their being from some source which is identical with Being itself, otherwise we should be involved in an infinite regress. Because of the unity of the concept of being, and because unity in the effect implies unity in the cause, this source must be one. (The authority here cited is that of Avicenna's *Metaphysics*, lib. VIII. Cf., however, Anselm's *Monologium*, cc. 1–7.)

(*c*) Aristotle has proved (*Phys.* lib. VIII) that the cause of the movement of the heaven is an immaterial being. But no diversity among immaterial beings is possible except with respect to completeness and actuality. Hence there must be one cause wholly actual, whence proceeds every thing in any way infected with potentiality, since actuality is logically prior to potentiality and completeness to imperfection, as Aristotle has proved in the ninth book of *Metaphysics*. The kinship of these proofs to certain of those discussed above is evident at a glance.

[2] I.a. q. 11 : a. 1.　　　　　　　　　　　　　　　　　　[3] *Quodlib.* x. a. 1.

vertible with being contributes something additional to the
substance of being, as *white* to *man*. But this is manifestly false:
because anything is one through its substance. If, indeed, anything were one through something else, then, since that other
would again be one, it would again be one only through some
other thing, which would lead us to infinity."[1]

Cardinal Cajetan, in his commentary on the *Summa Theologica*, suggests that it is because of this negative significance of
the concept of unity that the subject of the divine unity is
there discussed only after the "quidditative" predicates of
simplicity, perfection, infinity, and immutability have already
been discussed, and the "complementary" questions of the
divine goodness, of the divine existence *in rebus*, and of the
divine eternity have also been raised and answered. The
hypothesis does not seem plausible. We are distinctly warned
by Aquinas that the various attributes grouped by him under
the common heading *De Dei Simplicitate* and constituting the
third question of the first division of the *Summa* are all to be
interpreted in a negative sense. Are we not then justified in
assuming that the other qualities of goodness, immutability,
eternity, etc., are similarly and in accordance with example
set by the *Contra Gentiles*, to be interpreted negatively as successive stages of the *Via Remotionis*? It is only when we come to
the thirteenth question, entitled *De Nominibus Dei*, that we
find the method of analogy introduced. We should naturally
expect, therefore, that all positive qualities would be treated
in subsequent questions. If this be the case it is interesting that
we should find the divine unity classified among the negative
attributes; for in the *Contra Gentiles* the opposite order is followed. When, however, we turn to the *Compendium Theologiae*
we discover that it agrees in its arrangement with the *Summa
Theologica*. Do these facts indicate, as they appear to, an actual
change of viewpoint on the part of St. Thomas? If we may

[1] "Considerans quod unum quod est principium numeri, addit aliquam
rem supra substantiam entis (alias numerus ex unitatibus compositus non
esset species quantitatis), credidit quod unum quod convertitur cum ente
addat rem aliquam supra substantiam entis, sicut album supra hominem.—
Sed hoc manifeste falsum est: quia quaelibet res est una per suam substantiam. Si enim per aliquid aliud esset una quaelibet res, cum illud iterum
sit unum, si esset iterum unum per aliquid aliud, esset abire in infinitum"
(*Sum. Theol.* I.a. q. 11: a. 1. ad 1m.).

rely upon the chronologies of his works compiled by Gilson[1] and Grabmann[2] we may believe that both the *Contra Gentiles* and the *Compendium Theologiae* were written shortly after 1260. If we could be sure that the *Compendium Theologiae* was the later of the two, the inference would be obvious; but this is a point which we must leave to textual critics.

[1] *The Philosophy of St. Thomas Aquinas*, p. 4.
[2] *Thomas Aquinas*, pp. 21, 22, and 24.

CHAPTER X

THE INFINITY OF GOD

BEFORE attempting to prove that God is infinite, Aquinas thought it needful to distinguish between two kinds of infinity which he terms respectively *privative* and *negative*,[1] a course which appears to have been suggested to him by Aristotle's discussion of the concepts of "the complete" and of "limit" in the sixteenth and seventeenth chapters of book Δ of the *Metaphysics*. Privative infinity is found only in conjunction with the possible existence of a limit, which limit is yet non-existent in fact; negative infinity, on the other hand, implies the absence even of the possibility of limit. Privative infinity is quantitative infinity and pertains to bodies; negative infinity to the immaterial.[2] A point is the limit of a line, a surface that of a body. Of such a nature are the limits of all quantitative entities. Moreover form, once embodied in matter, shares to the full the finitude of its substance. Apart from matter it is, however, in a sense infinite—but only in a sense. "Every form," we are told, "abstractly considered as a pure concept, is infinite. Such is whiteness when abstractly conceived, for the concept of whiteness is not finite with respect to some other thing; yet the concept of colour and the concept of being are determinate therein, and so it is limited to a determinate species."[3] In other words, even an unembodied form, through its possession of certain qualities and its lack of certain other qualities—and also by reason of the fact that it is not identical with its

---

[1] *Con. Gen.* lib. I. cap. 43; 1 *Dist.* 43. q. 1: a. 1. sol.; *Com. Theol.* cap. xvii; *De Pot.* q. 1: a. 2. c.

[2] "Respondeo dicendum, quod infinitum dicitur dupliciter. Uno modo privative, et sic dicitur infinitum quod natum est habere finem et non habet; tale autem infinitum non invenitur nisi in quantitatibus. Alio modo dicitur infinitum negative, id est quod non habet finem" (*De Pot.* q. 1: a. 2. c.; cf. *Com. Theol.* cap. xvii).

[3] "Omnis enim forma in propria ratione, si abstracte consideretur, infinitatem habet; sicut in albedine abstracte intellecta, ratio albedinis non est finita ad aliquid; sed tamen ratio coloris et ratio essendi determinatur in ea, et contrahitur ad determinatum speciem" (1 *Dist.* 43. q. 1: a. 1. sol.).

own being—is a determinate, limited, and, therefore, finite entity, even though its limitations are only those inherent in itself and in no sense due to any connection with matter.

In the *De Potentia*[1] we are assured that God is infinite in essence, in wisdom, in power, and in goodness. It is further stated, however, that the divine power is infinite in a mode in which the essence is not. Similarly, in the *Contra Gentiles*[2] it is said that spiritual magnitude has a twofold significance— with respect to power, and with respect to the goodness or completion of a thing's proper nature. The article in the *De Potentia* to which we have referred is thus entitled *Utrum potentia Dei sit infinita*, and a corresponding article with an identical title is to be found in the *Commentary on the Sentences*. In the *Compendium Theologiae* the seventeenth chapter bears the heading *Quod Deus est infinitus*, and the eighteenth *Quod Deus est infinitae virtutis*. In the *Summa Theologica* the infinity of God is discussed in the seventh question (Part I) and the infinity of God's power in the twenty-fifth question. In the *Contra Gentiles* both topics are dealt with in a single chapter.[3]

The arguments advanced in proof of the divine infinity are the following:

1. Every being of a finite nature is a member of some genus. But God is no genus, although the divine perfection contains the perfections of all genera. God is therefore infinite.[4]

2. Everything actual which inheres in some other thing receives from that thing its limitations. Thus, form receives its limitations from matter, and matter from form. What does not exist in something else is, however, limited by nothing external to itself. If whiteness could exist *per se*, it would be perfect whiteness, whereas actually it qualifies physical objects and is dependent for its degree of purity upon the capacity of those objects to receive it. Yet pure form, as has just been pointed out, while free from all limitations imposed by external things, is subject to the determinations of its own nature; its being, moreover, is not identical with its essence. But in God all the conditions requisite for the presence of infinity are fulfilled, for the Deity is not the form of a body, neither does he inhere in anything other than himself; the divine essence, while

---

[1] q. 1 : a. 2. c.   [2] Lib. I. cap. 43.
[3] Lib. I. cap. 43.   [4] Lib. I. cap. 43.

containing in itself the perfections of all things, is absolutely
simple, and is identical with its own being. Hence, God alone
is infinite *simpliciter*.[1]

3. In the universe we find pure potentiality in primary
matter, pure actuality in God, and a mingling of actuality and
potentiality in everything else. And since potentiality is
relative to actuality, it is impossible that there should be an
excess of actuality, either in any particular thing, or *simpliciter*.
Yet primary matter is infinite in its potentiality; consequently,
God must be infinite in his actuality.[2]

4. The less actuality is mingled with potentiality, the more
nearly it approaches perfection, since in so far as it is mingled
with potentiality its perfection is limited, whereas pure actuality
is unlimited. Thus, since God is wholly actual, he is unlimited,
and therefore infinite.[3]

5. If we consider being in itself absolutely, it is infinite, since
it can be participated in by an infinite number of things in an
infinite number of ways. If, however, the being of any particular
thing is finite, it must be limited by something else which is
somehow its cause. But God, whose being is necessary, has no
cause. Hence, the being of God is infinite, and so God himself
is infinite.[4]

6. Anything which possesses a certain perfection does so by
participating in that perfection to a certain degree, and the
more fully it participates the greater the degree of perfection
to which it attains. God, however, we know to be essentially
perfect, so that it is impossible to conceive of anything more
perfect than he. And perfection implies infinity. Hence, God is
infinite.[5]

7. The human intellect is capable of attaining the infinite, as
is shown by the fact that, if any finite quantity be given, it is
always possible to conceive of a greater. It would, however,
be to no purpose for the intellect to conceive of an infinite
being, if, in point of fact, no such being existed. Consequently,
an infinite being must actually exist.[6]

1 *Dist.* 43. q. 1: a. 1. sol.; *Con. Gen.* lib. I. cap. 43; *Sum. Theol.* I.a. q. 7:
a. 1. c.; *De Pot.* q. 1: a. 2. c.   2 *Con. Gen.* loc. cit.
3 *Con. Gen.* loc. cit.; *De Pot.* q. 1: a. 2. c.; *Com. Theol.* Pars Prima,
cap. xvii.   4 *Con. Gen.* lib. I. cap. 43.
5 *Con. Gen.* lib. I. cap. 43.   6 *Con. Gen.* lib. I. cap. 43.

This argument is open to several objections. In the first place, it may be urged that it fails to show that the human intellect can conceive of an infinite being. It is, doubtless, true that, if any finite quantity be given, we can always think of a greater. But that greater quantity will itself be finite, and the process is one which can be continued indefinitely. In the second place, since the infinity of God is not quantitative, it is not clear that such reasoning is relevant, even if sound. And, in the third place, it may be questioned whether St. Thomas is justified in arguing from our ability to conceive of the infinite to the existence of an infinite being. There is, of course, no analogy between the present line of reasoning and the onto-logical argument, since the existence of God is here taken as proved. But it may be contended that our ability to conceive of the infinite is of use both in mathematics and in metaphysical speculation even if no infinite being exist. And, even if we waive this point, is it obvious that such a capacity on the part of the intellect must have some ulterior end or justification? A reference here to the character and veracity of God, after the manner of Descartes, would seem to be in order. The language of St. Thomas, however, indicates that he was thinking rather of his doctrine that everything in the universe is "ordered" in relation to God, the final cause.[1]

8. The human intellect is from God, the universal cause. Inasmuch as it is impossible for an effect to surpass its cause, it is impossible that the intellect should think of anything greater than God. But the intellect can conceive of something greater than any object presented to it. Consequently, God, than whom nothing greater can be conceived, is infinite.

9. Since the notion of power implies a principle of activity, and since everything acts by its form, which is its essence, or part of its essence,[2] it is impossible that infinite power should pertain to a finite essence. Now God is the source of motion

---

[1] "Frustra autem esset haec ordinatio intellectus ad infinitum nisi esset aliqua res intelligibilis infinita." *Con. Gen.* loc. cit.

[2] The form of a corporeal substance is part of its essence, since the essence includes both matter and form. In finite substances substantial form is the first but not the proximate principle of operation. This distinction, however, does not hold good with respect to the Deity (cf. the *Comment.* of Francis Sylvester; also *Sum. Theol.* I.a. q. 77: a. 1.).

through infinite time, inasmuch as the first motion is eternal;
(the Aristotelian theory of the eternity of the world and of
motion is here provisionally assumed to be true). Hence, the
divine essence is infinite.

This proof, Aquinas observed, should be sufficient even for
those who believe in the eternity of the world. For they admit
that an eternal God is the cause of the sempiternal world in
the sense in which a foot would be the cause of a footprint if it
were eternally pressed upon the dust. Moreover, active power
is proportionate to passive potentiality, since the greater the
passive potentiality which is pre-existent and pre-supposed, the
greater the distance from actuality, and the greater the power
which transmutes the one into the other. Now, the creative
power of God extends to the entire universe, even to the
pure potentiality of primary matter. Hence, that power is
infinite, and therefore the divine essence is also infinite.

For those who accept the Catholic doctrine of creation in
time, the argument, in the opinion of St. Thomas, is even
more conclusive. For what does not exist at all is infinitely
distant from actuality, and is not even in potentiality in any
way. Consequently, if the world were created in time its Maker's
power must have been infinite.

In the *Commentary on the Sentences* the infinity of the divine
power is deduced from that of the divine essence which, as we
have seen, is proved by the second argument. The same
inference is drawn in the *Summa Theologica*.[1] The *Compendium
Theologiae* takes the same course, but supports its position by
advancing another proof closely resembling the one now before
us, and also very similar to the third proof of the infinity of
the divine essence. Its premise is that, according to the degree
in which anything is in potentiality, it has a passive power;
and that, according to the degree in which a thing is actual,
it has an active power. From this it follows that, even as primary
matter, which is wholly potential, has an infinite receptive
passive power, so God, who is wholly actual, must possess an
infinite active power.

In the *De Potentia* the infinity of the divine power is also
inferred from that of the divine essence. "But it must be
understood that although this power derives its infinity from

---

[1] I.a. q. 25: a. 2. c.

the essence, yet, in so far as it is compared to those things of which it is the principle, it receives a certain mode of infinity which the essence does not possess. For in the objects upon which this power is directed there is found a certain multiplicity, and in its activity an intensity relative to the efficacy of the agent; and so it is possible to attribute to the divine power a certain infinity according to its conformity to the infinity of quantity, both continuous and discrete—discrete according as the quantity of power is considered with reference to many or few objects, and this is called extensive quantity—continuous according as the quantity of power is found in an agent which acts with less or more intensity, and this is called intensive quantity. The former quantity belongs to power as relative to its objects, the latter as relative to the agent. Active power is the principle of both. In each mode the divine power is infinite. For never does it produce so many objects that it could not produce more, and never does it operate with such intensity that it could not do so more intensely. Moreover, in the case of divine operation, intensity is not to be considered with respect to the operator, since it is infinite inasmuch as it is the divine essence, but with regard to its effects; even as objects are moved by God with greater or with less efficacy."[1]

10. The duration of anything depends upon the efficacy of

[1] "Sed sciendum, quod quamvis potentia habeat infinitatem ex essentia, tamen ex hoc ipso quod comparatur ad ea quorum est principium, recipit quemdam modum infinitatis quem essentia non habet. Nam in obiectis potentiae, quaedam multitudo invenitur; in actione etiam invenitur quaedam intensio secundum efficaciam agendi, et sic potest potentiae activae attribui quaedam infinitas secundum conformitatem ad infinitatem quantitatis et continuae et discretae. Discretae quidem, secundum quod quantitas potentiae attenditur secundum multa vel pauca obiecta; et haec vocatur quantitas extensiva; continuae vero secundum quod quantitas potentiae attenditur in hoc quod remisse vel intense agit; et haec vocatur quantitas intensiva. Prima autem quantitas convenit potentiae respectu obiectorum, secunda vero respectu actionis. Istorum enim duorum activa potentia est principium. Utroque autem modo divina potentia est infinita. Nam nunquam tot effectus facit quin plures facere possit, nec unquam ita intense operatur quin intensius operari possit. Intensio autem in operatione divina non est attendenda secundum quod operatio est in operante, quia sic semper est infinita, cum operatio sit divina essentia; sed attendenda est secundum quod attingit effectum; sic enim a deo moventur quaedam efficacius, quaedam minus efficaciter" (*De Pot.* q. 1 : a. 2. c.).

its cause. Thus, if anything endure for ever it must have a cause of infinite efficacy. But God not only endures for ever, but has no cause external to himself. Hence, God must be infinite.

To say that God endures for ever clearly implies that God is in time. We are, however, aware that, for Aquinas, God was eternal. The present argument plainly requires us to conceive of eternity as mere endless duration. But this, as we shall see when we examine his views as to the character of the divine knowledge,[1] is incompatible with Aquinas's own position. It appears, then, that this proof must be pronounced invalid.

These arguments, taken together, bring into bold relief the close connection between the concepts of perfection and of infinity. God is infinite because he is unlimited, and he is unlimited because he lacks nothing, because he is pure Being, because he is wholly actual and because all the positive qualities or "perfections" of his creatures are to be found in him *secundum modum alteriorem*, no longer multiple and divided, but identical in the absolute simplicity of the divine essence.

[1] Cf. *Con. Gen.* lib. I. cap. 66.

CHAPTER XI

THE DIVINE INTELLIGENCE

To demonstrate the truth of the proposition that God is an intelligent being was an undertaking which, in the eyes of St. Thomas, must have possessed an importance which it is impossible to over-estimate. It is one of the perennially crucial problems which confront every philosopher who attempts to do justice to the facts and claims of religious experience. Unless it can be satisfactorily solved, a theistic interpretation of the universe is impossible. Moreover, in the case of St. Thomas, the rigid requirements of Christian orthodoxy permitted of no alternative to an affirmative answer to the vital question before him. But to give this answer it was needful to enter upon a detailed discussion, not only of the immediate problem, but also of a host of closely related and scarcely less important questions which the original inquiry brought crowding in its train.

Hence it is not surprising that we find a vast amount of space in Aquinas's various works devoted to these topics. Twenty-eight chapters of the *Contra Gentiles*, a question of sixteen articles in the *Summa Theologica*, a question of fifteen articles in the *De Veritate*, three questions comprising thirteen articles in the *Commentary on the Sentences*, as well as four chapters in the comparatively brief *Compendium Theologiae*, are entirely occupied by discussions of the possibility and character of divine knowledge. In addition, the treatment of the theory of Ideas fills a question of three articles in the *Summa Theologica*, another question—also of three articles—in the *Commentary on the Sentences*, and a question of eight articles in the *De Veritate*. I shall endeavour to indicate as succinctly as possible the nature of the various arguments employed, and we shall concentrate our attention upon what appear to be the most important steps in the progress of Aquinas's thought.

The proposition that God is an intelligent being is demonstrated, in the first place, by reverting to the argument from motion. It will be recalled that, in his presentation of this argument, Aquinas, following Aristotle, recognized a twofold possibility. On the one hand it is possible that all things are moved by an immovable prime mover. On the other hand it may be that there exists a prime mover which moves itself. On the latter hypothesis, however, we must proceed to posit another mover which is itself separate and unmoved since, if the prime mover move itself, it must do so because of its appetite for some desired object. This appetite we cannot regard as sensuous, for a sensuous appetite is concerned only with the here and now, whereas that which is good and appetible *simpliciter* is logically prior to that which is good and appetible here and now. Consequently this appetite must pertain to an intelligence. Hence its object must also be an intelligible and intelligent being.

The same conclusion follows from the first hypothesis. The unmoved mover evokes movement in all things inasmuch as it is itself the universal object of desire. Accordingly the form whereby it causes movement must be universal form and universal good. But it is only in the intellect that universal form can be found. The unmoved mover must, therefore, be an intelligent being.[1]

Again, never in our experience do we find that an entity which causes motion by means of its intellect is the instrument of that which causes motion without the aid of intellect, but rather the reverse. All finite entities which cause motion are, however, mere instruments when compared to the prime mover. Yet many of these are endowed with intellects. Hence the prime mover must also possess an intellect.[2]

Moreover, the intellect, as distinct from sense, is concerned with universals, not with particulars, since the principle of individuation is matter. Knowledge, indeed, consists in the capacity of the knower to possess the species of the thing known.[3] Thus material entities are limited to their own forms while intelligent beings can possess the forms of other things, which forms then become one with the knowing intellect; for it is matter which contracts and limits, whereas intelligence confers amplitude and extension. Hence it is the immateriality of a substance which renders it intelligent. Consequently God,

---

[1] *Con. Gen.* lib. I. cap. 44.
[2] *Con. Gen.* loc. cit.; *Com. Theol.* cap. xxvii.
[3] Cf. *De Anima*, lib. III. cap. v. 1.

who is of all things farthest removed from matter, must be intelligent.[1]

Furthermore, it is impossible that God, the simple unity of whose essence includes, *secundum modum altiorem*, all the perfections to be found among his creatures, should not possess the highest perfection of all—that of knowledge, which is, in a sense, all things, and has in itself the perfections of all.[2]

The teleological argument, also, if valid at all, obviously justifies us in ascribing intelligence to God, inasmuch as the notion of purpose is introduced into the argument itself, and with it that of intelligence, so that we do not have to advance a single step beyond our immediate conclusion to reach the desired result. However, since Aquinas's theory of Analogy compels him to insist that it is not permissible to predicate any attribute, in the same sense, of God and of his creatures, it suited his purpose to ignore this feature of the teleological argument until he had completed the exposition of his doctrine of analogy, and to reintroduce it at this point.[3]

In a somewhat similar fashion it is possible to reintroduce the cosmological argument. Since matter, as has just been said, contracts and limits forms united to it, it follows that such forms as exist in particular things are imperfect, and attain their universality only when contemplated in abstraction by the intellect. Applying now the principle that the perfect is logically prior to the imperfect, we may infer that the imperfect forms existing in particulars owe their existence to perfect forms which have their being in the mind of God, who is the first subsistent actuality, *actus primus subsistens*, from whom all things are derived.[4]

Not only is God intelligent, however, but the act of his intelligence is identical with his essence; for knowledge is the act of an intelligent subject and exists within that subject,[5]

---

[1] *Con. Gen.* lib. I. cap. 44; *Sum. Theol.* I.a. q. 14: a. 1. c.; I *Dist.* 35. q. 1 : a. 1. sol.; *Com. Theol.* cap. xxvii.

[2] "Nam per hoc ipsum est quodammodo omnia, habens in se omnium perfectionem" (*Con. Gen.* lib. I. cap. 44; I *Dist.* 35. q. 1 : a. 1. sol.; *Com. Theol* cap. xxvii; *De Verit.* q. 2: a. 1. c.).

[3] *Con. Gen.* lib. I. cap. 44; I *Dist.* 35. q. 1 : a. 1. sol.

[4] *Con. Gen.* lib. I. cap. 44.

[5] "Intelligere enim est actus intelligentis in ipso existens" (*Con. Gen.* lib I. cap. 44).

being incapable of passing thence into another substance as heat passes into an object heated. On the contrary the act of knowledge makes no difference to the object known, but the intelligence which knows is by that act perfected. Since whatever is in God is identical with the divine essence, it follows that the divine knowledge is identical therewith.[1]

Approaching the subject from another point of view, we observe that the act of knowledge, from the very fact that it is not transeunt, but immanent within the knowing subject, can be compared to the intelligence as existence to essence. And since in God essence and existence are one, the divine intelligence is one with the act of knowledge; and since the divine essence and intelligence are one, the essence and the act of knowledge are one also.[2]

Indeed, were we to assume that the contrary is the case, we should be driven to the conclusion that there is something more perfect than God. For *actus secundus* is more perfect than *actus primus*. The term *actus primus* is used to designate a special power, the capacity for a definite form of activity; while the term *actus secundus* signifies the activity itself. In the present instance *actus primus* refers to the power or ability to know, which St. Thomas calls *scientia*; by *actus secundus*, on the other hand, is meant the act of knowledge, which he terms *consideratio*. The act of knowledge, then, is more perfect than the capacity to know. Consequently, if the act of knowledge be not identical with the divine essence, the latter will be inferior to it in perfection and goodness, which is impossible.[3]

It is also impossible that God should be related to anything else as potentiality to actuality. Yet to know is the act of an intelligent subject. Consequently if the divine intelligence be not identical with the act of knowledge, it will be related to it as potentiality to actuality.[4]

Lastly, every substance has its characteristic operation, for which, indeed, it exists.[5] But if the divine operation be other than the divine essence, the end, the τέλος, of that operation

---

[1] *Con. Gen.* lib. I. cap. 45; *Sum. Theol.* I.a. q. 14: a. 4. c.
[2] *Con. Gen.* lib. I. cap. 45; *Com. Theol.* Pars Prima, cap. xxx.
[3] *Con. Gen.* lib. I. cap. 45; *Com. Theol.* Pars Prima, cap. xxx.
[4] *Con. Gen.* lib. I. cap. 44; *Sum. Theol.* I.a. q. 14: a. 4. c.
[5] "Omnis substantia est propter suam operationem."

will also be other than the essence. In that case God will not be his own goodness, for the good of anything is its end. We have seen, however, that God is his own goodness. Accordingly the divine essence and the act of divine intelligence are one.[1]

The form of each agent is the principle of its operation. In human cognition this form is the intelligible species. It is evident, however, that there can be no intelligible species in God, since the divine essence being identical with the divine intelligence, the species would be the principle and cause of the divine essence itself.[2] Moreover, inasmuch as it is the intelligible species which renders the intellect intelligent *in actu*, the divine intellect would, upon this assumption, be related to the species as the potential to the actual.[3] And the species itself would enjoy a merely accidental being in the divine intellect, as does the intelligible species in the human intellect. But in God there are no accidents. The assumption is, therefore, inadmissible.[4]

Furthermore an intelligent species is the likeness of an object known. But in the case of God what can this object be? It cannot be the divine essence itself, for the function of an intelligible species is to transform the sensible into the intelligible, while the divine essence is intelligible already in its own proper being. Nor yet can it be anything external to the essence, for how is the species of such an object to be implanted in the essence? The operation cannot be performed by the essence itself, which would then be both agent and patient.[5] The very supposition is in conflict with the maxim that every agent impresses its own likeness upon the patient and not another's. And it is impossible that an external agent should, by its own activity, impress its likeness upon the essence of God, since to do so it must be prior to the essence.[6] Finally, since the divine intelligence and existence are one, did God under-

---

[1] *Con. Gen.* lib. I. cap. 45.   [2] *Con. Gen.* lib. I. cap. 46.
[3] *Con. Gen.* lib. I. cap. 46; *Com. Theol.* Pars Prima, cap. xxix.
[4] *Con. Gen.* lib. I. cap. 46.
[5] An interesting comment upon this statement is made by Francis Sylvester. The human intellect, he observes, produces not only the species, but the concept and the act of understanding, and in such an intellect these three are distinct. In the Deity, however, essence, concept, and act of understanding are one. Hence, were the divine intellect to produce intelligible species within itself, it would be at the same moment and in the same respect both agent and patient.   [6] *Con. Gen.* lib. I. cap. 46

stand by means of an intelligible species other than his essence his existence would be other than his essence, for the species is one with the knowing intellect. But the identity of the divine essence and existence renders this assumption untenable.[1]

God understands then by means of no intelligible species, but by his essence alone. From this an important consequence follows. To the perfection of the act of cognition two conditions are essential: first, that the intelligible species be perfectly conformed to the thing known, and, second, that it be perfectly conjoined to the knowing intellect. Now, since the divine essence functions in lieu of an intelligible species, and since it is identical with God himself, it follows that God knows himself perfectly.[2]

This conclusion is reinforced by these further considerations. A thing becomes intelligible by being abstracted from matter and made one *in actu* with the knowing intellect. Now God is absolutely immaterial and is identical with his own intelligence.[3] This union *in actu* of knower and known also follows from the doctrine that there is no potentiality in God, since the divine intelligence must therefore be wholly actual.[4] Again, whatever is in the intellect in an intelligible mode is understood by it. And the divine essence is in the divine intellect in an intelligible mode, since it is identical with it. Hence God knows his own essence perfectly. But God's essence is identical with his being; wherefore God knows himself perfectly.[5]

Furthermore, acts of the intellect are distinguished by their objects. The more perfect the object, the more perfect the intellectual operation. But the divine essence is the most perfect intelligible object; God's knowledge of it, therefore, is perfect also.[6] Moreover, the highest perfection to be found among created things is the knowledge of God. But in God are to be found in the highest degree the perfections of all things. Hence God must have perfect knowledge of himself.[7]

It is also true that God knows himself *primo et per se*. For that

---

[1] *Con. Gen.* lib. I. cap. 46; *Sum. Theol.* I.a. q. 14: a. 4. c.
[2] *Con. Gen.* lib. I. cap. 47.
[3] *Con. Gen.* lib. I. cap. 47; *De Verit.* q. 2: a. 2. c.; *Sum. Theol.* I.a. q. 14: a. 3. c.
[4] *Con. Gen.* lib. I. cap. 47; *Sum. Theol.* I.a. q. 14: a. 2. c.
[5] *Con. Gen.* lib. I. cap. 47; *Com. Theol.* Pars Prima, cap. xxix.
[6] *Con. Gen.* lib. I. cap. 47.   [7] *Con. Gen.* lib. I. cap. 47.

is known first and in itself the species of which is in the intellect in the act of cognition. Consequently, there being no species in God other than the divine essence, that which is *primo et per se* the object of divine knowledge can be nothing else than the essence itself. Indeed, since a plurality of objects implies a plurality of intellectual operations, the supposition that God knows *primo et per se* something other than himself compels us to posit a plurality of intellectual operations in the Deity. Not only so, but we are driven to assume successive acts of cognition, for, owing to the absence from it of intelligible species, the divine intellect cannot be aware simultaneously both of itself and of some other entity. Accordingly a change will take place in the divine intellect according as it contemplates, first itself, and secondly some other entity; a change, moreover, which will be for the worse, *in peius*, since this other, whatever it be, is less than God. But no change can take place in God, least of all a change for the worse.

In addition, a plurality of intellectual operations would involve the presence of plurality in the essence, a conclusion which could only be escaped on the hypothesis that God knows by means of something other than his essence. Also the divine intellect would be in potentiality with respect to this other entity, and in the act of knowledge would be perfected by it. And if there be many such entities, the divine knowledge would be composite, which would imply either that the essence is composite also, or that God's knowledge is accidental. But all these consequences and assumptions have been shown to be untenable.[1]

Having thus briefly summarized Aquinas's argument, we may now glance at two obvious and pertinent objections to his theory which he himself raised in order to refute. The first is that the relation of self-knowledge implies that there are two terms to be related and so involves otherness. In answer Aquinas invoked the distinction, so fundamental for his philosophy, between "real" and "rational" relations. The relation of self-knowledge is a rational one, and does not imply the existence of two distinct entities.[2] The second is that knowledge is concerned with universals, whereas God is not a uni-

[1] *Con. Gen.* lib. I. cap. 48; cf. *Metaph.* lib. XII. cap. ix.
[2] *De Verit.* q. 2: a. 2. ob. 1 and ad 1ᵐ; *Metaph.* lib. XII. cap. ix. lect. 8.

versal. Aquinas replied that a universal is intelligible because
it is abstracted from matter, and that God, while not a universal, is completely immaterial, and therefore in the highest
degree intelligible.[1]

We have now arrived at one of the most crucial transitions in
the philosophy of St. Thomas. Up to this point he has trodden
in the footprints of Aristotle. Gradually, step by step, he has
elaborated the notion of a changeless and transcendent God
who is engaged in perpetual self-contemplation. Differences,
of course, there are, both in emphasis and in content, between
the thought of Aquinas and that of his master. Thus, for the
former, God is not merely the source of motion and change,
but also of being. The Deity of St. Thomas resembles not only
that of Aristotle, but also the One of Plotinus and the Pseudo-
Dionysius. Yet such differences as we discern seem small, indeed,
in the light of the fundamental agreement. Now, however, a
difficulty arises, formidable if not insuperable. The unmoved
prime mover, the God who ceaselessly contemplates his own
essence in solitary and transcendent majesty, must be shown
to be identical with the Heavenly Father of the Christian
religion, who knows the thoughts of men and who numbers
the hairs of their heads.

At first sight such a reconciliation seems absolutely impossible.
The same problem, however, had already confronted the
philosophers of Islam, and while the solution which they
advanced did not satisfy St. Thomas, it seems, nevertheless, to
have suggested to him the method of procedure which he
actually adopted.[2] In fact his own position differs from theirs
only in so far as it is the result of a more radical and extensive
application of the same principle which they had employed.

Aquinas's solution will be found in germ in his *Commentary on
the Metaphysics*.[3] It does not follow, he urges, from Aristotle's
teaching that all things other than God are unknown to him,
"for in knowing himself he knows all things."[4] "Moreover,

---

[1] *De Verit.* q. 2: a. 2. ob. 4. and ad 4^m.
[2] For a concise statement of the view of Avicenna, cf. *Avicennae Metaphysices
Compendium*, libri primi secunda pars, tractatus IV. This work is a Latin
translation by Nematallah Carame of the third part of the Nadjat.
[3] Lib. XII. cap. ix. lect. 8.
[4] "Nam intelligendo se, intelligit omnia alia."

according as a cause is the more perfectly known, so is its effec the more known in the cause, for the effects are contained is the power of their cause. Since, therefore, upon the first cause which is God, depend the heaven and all nature, as has beer said, it appears that God, in knowing himself, knows all things."

Once more, in the *De Veritate*,[2] St. Thomas attempts to refute the charge that such an interpretation of Aristotle is precluded by the latter's assertion that God knows *only* himself, *quod Deu. tantum se ipsum cognoscit.* A thing is known, he replies, in two ways: firstly, in itself, and, secondly, in some other thing, which being known, it is known. "Hence God knows only himself in himself, other things, in truth, he knows in themselves, but in knowing his own essence; and in this sense the Philosophe said that God knows only himself."[3]

We may leave the student of Aristotle to pass judgment upor the soundness of this interpretation[4] and turn to Aquinas's owr exposition. This I shall first briefly outline, and then examine with a view to estimating the degree of success achieved in the difficult task of reconciliation.

As will be evident from the previous quotations, the know ledge which God has of other entities may be said to result from introspection. Since he has a perfect knowledge of his owr essence, he knows that it is the cause of all things other thar itself, and, since these things are its effects, they are known in the knowing of their cause, for the likeness of every effect pre-exists in its cause.[5] A material cause contains its effect in a material mode; an immaterial cause in an immaterial mode for everything which exists in something else exists therein according to the mode of being of the thing which receives it Hence immaterial effects are present in their cause in the sense

---

[1] "Quanto autem aliquod principium perfectius intelligitur, tanto magi intelligitur in eo effectus eius: nam principiata continentur in virtute principii. Cum igitur a primo principio, quod est Deus, dependeat coelum et tota natura, ut dictum est, patet quod Deus cognoscendo seipsum omnia cognoscit."

[2] q. 2: a. 3. ad 5^m.

[3] "Deus ergo se ipsum tantum cognoscit in se ipso, alia vero in se ipsi cognoscit, sed cognoscendo suam essentiam; et secundum hoc Philosophu. dixit, quod Deus tantum se ipsum cognoscit" (cf. 1 *Dist.* 35. q. 1 : a. 2. sol.)

[4] Cf. W. D. Ross's *Aristotle*, pp. 183–184.

[5] *Con. Gen.* lib. I. cap. 49; *Sum. Theol.* q. 14: a. 5. c.

that they are there knowable,[1] and thus an immaterial cause knows its effects.[2]

Again, we have seen that the order which obtains in the universe points to the activity of a controlling intelligence; wherefore that intelligence must be aware of the things which it controls.[3]

Since the likenesses of created things pre-exist in the divine essence, they are not the effects of those things; hence there is no question of the essence being perfected by something external to itself. There is, however, an extremely interesting objection to his theory which was raised by Aquinas, the answer to which brings into startling clearness the proximity of his position to that of complete Pantheism, or, rather, Acosmism. "Nothing," urges the hypothetical opponent, "is known except through the nature of being. But the creature is more not-being than being, as appears from many words of the Saints. The creature, therefore, is more unknown to God than known."[4] "Being," Aquinas responds, "when used *simpliciter* and absolutely, is understood to refer to the divine being alone; the reason for which is stated in Luke xviii. 19: *None is good but God alone*. Hence, according as the creature approaches God, so it has being; and according as it departs from God, so it has not being; and since it approaches God only as it participates in being to a finite degree, it is infinitely distant. For this reason it is said to be more not-being; and yet such being as it has, since this is from God, is known to God."[5]

The question must now be faced whether God has a proper knowledge of all things, *properiam cognitionem de omnibus rebus*.

[1] "In principiis activis immaterialibus effectus sunt secundum quod cognoscibiles sunt."

[2] *De Verit*. q. 2 : a. 3. c.   [3] *De Verit*. q. 2 : a. 3. c.

[4] "Nihil cognoscitur nisi per naturam entis. Sed creatura magis habet de non esse quam de esse, ut patet per multa Sanctorum dicta. Ergo creatura magis Deo est incognita quam nota" (*De Verit*. q. 2 : a. 3. ob. 16).

[5] " 'Esse' simpliciter et absolute dictum, de solo divino esse intelligitur, sicut et bonum; ratione cuius dicitur Luc xviii. 19: *Nemo bonus nisi solus Deus*. Unde quantum creatura accedit ad Deum, tantum habet de esse; quantum vero ab eo recedit, tantum habet de non esse; et quia non accedit ad Deum nisi secundum quod esse finitum participat, distat autem in infinitum; ideo dicitur quod plus habet de non esse; et tamen illud esse quod habet, cum a Deo sit, a Deo cognoscitur" (*De Verit*. q. 2 : a. 3. ad 16m).

This was a problem of extreme importance in view of the contrary opinion of the Averroists who formed an influential body among contemporary thinkers. "Some will have erred," wrote Aquinas, "in saying that God does not know things other than himself except with a general knowledge (*in communi*), that is, in so far as they are beings. Thus, just as fire, if it were able to know itself as the principle of heat, would know the nature of heat and would know all other things in so far as they are hot, so God, in so far as he knows himself as the principle of being, knows the nature of being, and knows all things in so far as they are beings."[1]

St. Thomas's contention is that, in knowing himself, God knows himself as the cause of all other things. For he *is* the cause of all other things either directly or indirectly. Consequently, all effects immediately caused by God pre-exist in the divine essence and are known by him in the knowing of that essence. The effects of those effects in like manner pre-exist in them as in their immediate causes, so that God, in knowing his immediate effects, knows also the secondary effects which issue from them; and thus the knowledge of God includes, as it were in a single glance, the entire hierarchy of causes and effects down to the most remote and ultimate effect of all.[2]

We are led to the same conclusion, St. Thomas insists, by reflecting upon the identity of the divine knowing and the divine existence. From this it follows as a corollary that it is by his intellect that God is the cause of all things. Consequently, God must know all things.[3] This position is strengthened when we reflect that the order in nature and the distinction among things cannot result from any cause that acts through necessity of nature, for a natural cause can produce only a single and determinate effect. Moreover, any secondary cause would itself be a part of the ordered whole which is the universe; and could not, therefore, by any possibility, account

---

[1] "Quidam erraverunt, dicentes quod Deus alia a se non cognoscit nisi in communi, scilicet inquantum sunt entia. Sicut enim ignis, si cognosceret seipsum ut est principium caloris, cognosceret naturam caloris, et omnia alia inquantum sunt calida; ita Deus, inquantum cognoscit se ut principium essendi, cognoscit naturam entis, et omnia alia inquantum sunt entia" (*Sum. Theol.* I.a. q. 14: a. 6. c.; cf. 1 *Dist.* 35. q. 1: a. 3. sol.).

[2] *Con. Gen.* lib. I. cap. 50; 1 *Dist.* 35. q. 1: a. 3. sol.

[3] *Con. Gen.* lib. I. cap. 50.

for the origin of that order. Accordingly, we must look for a cause above nature. Such a cause, however, cannot be productive only of general effects, for the universe contains particulars, and the order which obtains in the universe consists of the relations of these particulars to one another; whence it is necessary that the ultimate cause be productive of both general and particular effects, and this cause is the divine intelligence.[1]

Again, perfect knowledge includes not only a general but also a proper knowledge of things.[2] And God's knowledge is perfect. Furthermore, in knowing himself, God knows the universal nature of being. Consequently he knows that the *per se* accidents of being are *one* and *many*. But to know multitude he must know the distinctions, without which multitude cannot exist. Also he must be aware of the various modes of being and the various grades and levels of being constituted by them.[3] And, finally, self-knowledge must acquaint God with his own active power. He must know himself as the cause of all beings; and he must know that his nature is communicable in the sense that all other entities resemble it in so far as they have being at all.[4] All these various considerations lead us to the same conclusion, that God has a proper knowledge of all things.

Such, in brief, is Aquinas's solution of his difficult problem; such is his effort to escape from a seeming paradox. But is it a successful escape? Ingenious his argument is beyond a doubt. Indeed, it is scarcely possible not to feel that he has made out as good a case for the orthodox view as any philosopher could do. None the less, there arise very pressing and pertinent questions which it will be as well to bring at once into the light.

In the first place, then, is there not a contradiction between St. Thomas's assertion that it is only as he knows his own essence that God is aware of finite entities, and his statement that God is the cause of these entities "by his intellect"—*per intellectum*? If it be only in the act of divine introspection that God is cognizant of created things, it would appear necessarily to follow that the world is related to the divine essence either as consequent to ground, somewhat in the same

[1] *Con. Gen.* lib. I. cap. 50; 1 *Dist.* 35. q. 1 : a. 3. sol.; *De Verit.* q. 2 : a. 4. c.
[2] *Con. Gen.* lib. I. cap. 50; *Sum. Theol.* I.a. q. 14 : a. 6. c.
[3] *Con. Gen.* lib. I. cap. 50.   [4] *Con. Gen.* lib. I. cap. 50.

manner as conceived by Spinoza, or that it is the product of an unconscious "overflowing" of the fullness of divine Being, as was maintained by Plotinus. It would seem, in other words, that the causation of the world by the divine essence is logically, although not temporally, prior to God's awareness of the fact of such causation; and that it is due, therefore, to some necessity of the divine nature which functions, or has functioned, without the conjunction either of the divine intelligence or of the divine volition.

It might, doubtless, be urged in reply that the plausibility of this objection results from the error of taking the relation of divine self-knowledge as a "real" relation requiring two distinct entities to serve as its terms, whereas it has been explicitly stated to be a "rational" relation which has no subsistence *in re* apart from the conceiving mind. It must be admitted that there is much truth in this contention. The distinction between "real" and "rational" relations is a fundamental one in the philosophy of St. Thomas. If we are entitled to reject it, our objection will hold good. In the interest of further criticism, however, we shall provisionally accept it, in order to discover if we can whether the argument proceeds smoothly from this point.

We are required, then, to conceive of the divine intellect as a simple unity, a bare identity undifferentiated into subject and object, yet, withal, transparently intelligible to itself. But where, now, are we to find place for the plurality which forms the content of the divine knowledge? Obviously, it cannot be admitted within the essence without destroying the divine simplicity; nor yet can it be accidental thereto, for in God there are no accidents. Nevertheless, we have been assured that a perfect knowledge of the divine essence involves, not only a general but also a proper knowledge of all other things. But how can this be true if God be but a simple and absolute unity, a totally undifferentiated monad?

Aquinas's answer is that the plurality is to be found in the objects of the divine knowledge themselves and in the relations in which they stand to the divine essence; relations which, so far as the objects are concerned, are "real"—since they involve the dependence of these objects upon the essence—but which, when predicated of the Deity, are wholly "rational," inasmuch as the perfection of his nature is independent of and unaffected by them. Everything, in so far as it has being, resembles God; and in so far as it is finite and falls short of the fullness of Being fails to resemble him. The intellect, however, possesses the faculty of abstraction, and can consider separately elements or characteristics which, *in re*, are found in conjunction. Thus God is able to know in what respect a thing resembles him, and in what respect it falls short of his perfection. He is aware that it is possible for an entity to imitate his essence by possessing the characteristic of being alive, and at the same time to fail to imitate it by possessing the characteristic of knowledge; and thus God is aware of the proper form of a plant. In like manner he is aware that his essence can be imitated in respect of knowledge without being also imitated in respect of intellect; and so he is aware of the proper form of an animal. A certain plurality is involved in this, in so far as it is possible for different entities to imitate the divine essence in different respects; but the plurality is found only in the creatures and in their relations to the essence, and does not infect the essence itself. Thus life, knowledge, and intellect are not three distinct characteristics in God; because he is an intellect, he possesses knowledge and he is alive, but his knowledge and his life are not extraneous to his intellect, and are not added thereto, but are identical with it.[1]

But how, we may still ask, is it possible that the divine essence, which is absolutely one and absolutely simple, should be capable of being imitated in a multitude of modes? It is all very well to assert that life, knowledge, and intellect, so far as they are ascribed to the Deity, are identical *in re* and distinct only *in intellectu*. But this only raises the question: "Is it possible that the mind should distinguish what is not distinct?" And the answer must surely be in the negative. Any such activity on the part of mind could result in nothing else than a falsification of reality. A process of this character could not be called knowledge at all and would possess absolutely no validity whatever. To state the case with the aid of more modern terminology, "life is one concept," "awareness" is another, and "reason" is another. To say that these concepts are closely related to one another is to affirm what is obviously true; but

[1] *Con. Gen.* lib. I. cap. 54.

K*

to say that they are, or can be, identical is to speak without meaning. If the divine essence be indeed imitable in a plurality of modes, it cannot but possess a plurality of characteristics. If, on the other hand, it be a bare monad, then nothing except another bare monad can resemble it. Simplicity can be imitated only by simplicity, unity by unity.

It is clear that Aquinas's theory would be destitute of even a moderate degree of plausibility were it not for its connection with the doctrine of degrees of being. He has contended, as we are already aware, that perfect self-knowledge on the part of God involves perfect knowledge of the nature of being, by reason of the fact that God and pure Being are identical, and that perfect knowledge of the nature of being involves a knowledge of all possible modes and levels of being.[1] But what is meant by perfect knowledge? God's knowledge, as we shall see, is intuitive. Is it conceivable, however, that the intuition or perception of pure Being would involve an intuition or perception of each of the various possible grades of being? The question is a difficult one to attempt to answer unless we are first able to accept the notion of degrees of being as itself intelligible and defensible. The illustration used by St. Thomas is drawn from our experience of colour.[2] Whoever knows whiteness, he urges, knows that it is capable of *more* and *less*. But this is an illustration, not an exact analogy. The doctrine of degrees of being, as we have already had occasion to remark, is not to be confused with the notion of degrees of intensity. The most extreme Scotist never thought of maintaining that there are no degrees of brightness, of heat, of sweetness, etc. Such degrees of intensity, however, are not analogous but univocal. An intense degree of heat is no more really heat than a degree of less intensity; it is only hotter. But in the case of being we are dealing with an analogous conception. An accident, which exists in a substance, is less real than the substance, which does not exist in something other than itself. A material substance, which is composed both of matter and form and of essence and existence, is less real than an angel, which is composed only of essence and existence. And an angel is less real than God, in whom there is no composition at all.

[1] Cf. *Con. Gen.* lib. I. cap. 50.   [2] Cf. *Con. Gen.* lib. I. cap. 50.

Without attempting to anticipate the subsequent stages of St. Thomas's discussion of the character of divine knowledge, we may nevertheless advance the contention that knowledge of pure Being could never entail knowledge of lesser degrees of being unless these lesser degrees were somehow contained within pure Being itself. And a wholly undifferentiated monad, a mere ontological point, can neither contain anything nor imply anything. Yet, since the world has come into being as the product of the divine intelligence, God must have been aware of the various possible degrees of being before they actually existed. Before the creation, however, there was nothing for God to know but the divine essence itself. Thus the plurality which formed the content of divine knowledge could have subsisted neither in the divine essence nor in any reality external to it. We have arrived, therefore, at a flat contradiction.

A second difficulty arises from the fact that finite entities have, or appear to have, positive qualities of their own. Let us take, for example, an apple. The apple enjoys a certain degree of being, and, in so far as it does so, imitates God. But the apple is round and coloured, while God is neither round nor coloured. To say, therefore, that the apple imitates God in these respects appears absurd. It seems clear, on the contrary, that it is by its possession of these very characteristics of roundness and colour that the apple differs from God, and that these characteristics are positive qualities, quite as much so, in fact, as the qualities of immateriality and intellectuality which we are permitted to ascribe to God. Yet, according to St. Thomas, in so far as the apple fails to imitate God it falls short of true being. It would appear, then, that roundness and colour are not positive qualities at all, that they are illusory and unreal. And the same fate will befall every predicate which experience leads us to attribute to the apple, every characteristic which could serve to distinguish it from pure non-being. What, then, is the real apple? Is it mere being? If so, how does it differ from God, who is pure being?

We are here faced with the same problem which we have previously discussed in connection with the method of analogy. The notion that the fullness of divine Being contains in its simplicity *unum secundum rem* the perfections of all created things is familiar to us. The universe manifests, according to St.

Thomas, "in the multiple and various modes of creatures that which in the divine goodness pre-exists in simplicity and without distinction."[1] But is it conceivable that qualities which, at a lower level of being, are distinct and separate, should fuse, at a higher level, into an absolute identity? Does not such an assertion involve a direct denial of the validity of the laws of thought? A contemporary Neoscholastic writer has affirmed that the notion of degrees of being is "seized by an *experience* or intellectual intuition."[2] When intuition is appealed to, argument is out of place. We may, however, not unfittingly terminate our discussion, as Aquinas was sometimes wont to do, with a text from the Scriptures: "He that is able to receive it, let him receive it."

It appears, then, that St. Thomas's attempt to reconcile the Aristotelian and the Christian conceptions of God is beset with difficulties. We shall proceed, however, to outline the remaining portion of his argument.

It is possible for the same subject to be informed by species of different genera, but not by species of the same genus. Thus an object may be at once both round and red or square and blue, but it cannot be at once both round and square, or both red and blue. Now, intelligible species as such are all of the same genus, regardless of the genera of the objects from which they are derived. Accordingly, the mind cannot understand at one moment by the aid of more than one intelligible species; furthermore, all the entities which are known by means of a single intelligible species are known simultaneously. What the mind knows it knows as a whole continuum; not part after part. It does not, for instance, grasp first the subject of a proposition and afterward the predicate; on the contrary, it seizes the proposition by the aid of a single species of the whole.[3] Consequently, God, who employs no intelligible species besides his essence, understands all things simultaneously.

Moreover, the presence of an intelligible species in the

[1] "Per multiplices et varios modos creaturarum quod in divina bonitate simpliciter et indistincte praeexistit" (*De Pot.* q. 3: a. 16 c.; cf. *Div. Nom.* cap. v. lect. 1; *De Verit.* q. 8: a. 4. c.).

[2] "D'une *expérience* ou intuition intellectuelle" (Blaise Romeyer, *Saint Thomas et notre connaissance de l'esprit humain*, p. 10).

[3] "Secundum unam totius speciem omnes partes cognoscit" (*Con. Gen.* lib. I. cap. 55).

intellect does not suffice of itself to produce an act of cognition. The mind must also form an intention (*intentio*) or concept which is "a likeness of the exterior thing."[1] In the case of human cognition many *phantasmata* are simultaneously conserved in the sense-organ which are, nevertheless, not actually imagined by the mind because the intention is not turned upon them. God, however, having no intelligible species but his essence, has also but one intention which is directed upon his essence, which is the likeness of all things. Hence God is simultaneously aware of all things.

Again, the fact that intellectual operations are differentiated by their objects points to the same conclusion; for God, who has but one intellectual operation, cannot comprehend a plurality of objects successively. Any temporal sequence in the divine knowledge is also rendered impossible by the absence of motion and of potentiality in God, and by the identity of the act of divine knowledge with the divine being in which there is neither priority nor posteriority.[2]

The point is an extremely important one. To say that God's knowledge of all things is simultaneous is equivalent to saying that it is not in time at all, for by simultaneous is clearly meant *non-successive*, and where there is no succession there is no change. In discussing the argument from motion, as well as the doctrine of the eternity of God, I have pointed out that Aquinas's doctrine of an unmoved mover, changeless and eternal and therefore wholly actual, can be reconciled with his conception of God as an intelligent being only on the theory that the divine intellection is a timeless act. That theory is now before us. In so far as the proofs which support it are based upon propositions previously established in the course of Aquinas's argument, it is clear that there is danger of their being circular. For the base of his entire system is the doctrine of the eternal, unmoved mover, which, as I have said, presupposes the truth of the theory in question. But although the doctrine of the unmoved mover is the base of the Thomist system, it is not the point of departure of all the various proofs advanced in support of the successive steps in the development of his thought. Accordingly, it is possible to discover a chain of proofs which

---

[1] "Similitudo rei exterioris" (*Con. Gen.* lib. I. cap. 53).

[2] *Con. Gen.* lib. I. cap. 55; *Com. Theol.* cap. xxviii.

do not presuppose the theory which they profess to establish. This I will now indicate.

God's knowledge is said to be simultaneous because God makes use of no intelligible species, but only of his essence. And it was argued that God makes use of no intelligible species on the ground that it is the function of an intelligible species to transform the sensible into the intelligible, whereas the divine essence, which is the object of God's knowledge, is intelligible in itself. That the divine essence is intelligible follows from the immateriality of God, and the third proof of the immateriality of God is an adaptation of the teleological argument; and that God is able to be aware of his own essence follows from the proposition that God is an intelligent being, and that God is intelligent likewise follows from the teleological argument. Thus the theory of the timeless act is sustained by a series of proofs extending directly to the teleological argument itself, none of which presupposes the argument from motion. The fact that a single such chain of proofs can be pieced together suffices to acquit St. Thomas of the charge of arguing in a circle. But whether the concept of an eternal and intelligent unmoved mover be valid is another question. To be so, it must be consistent with the doctrine that the Deity is aware of the world, and of the particulars composing it; and that it is not so consistent I shall argue in due course.

Furthermore, the divine knowledge is not a *habitus*. The term *habitus* was defined by Aquinas in this connection as follows: "Habitus is either a certain capacity of the intellect to receive intelligible species by which it is made actually intelligent; or else it is an ordered aggregation of the species themselves existing in the intellect, not in a state of complete actuality, but in a mode which is midway between potentiality and actuality."[1] It is clear that in habitual knowledge all things are not known simultaneously. Hence God's knowledge is not habitual. It is also obvious that habitual knowledge is infected with potentiality, and that the possession of it involves a distinction between essence and intellectual

---

[1] "Habitus vel est habilitatio quaedam intellectus ad recipiendum species intelligibiles quibus actu fiat intelligens; vel est ordinata agreggatio ipsarum specierum existentium in intellectu non secundum completum actum, sed medio modo inter potentiam et actum" (*Con. Gen.* lib. I. cap. 56).

operation. Moreover, the intellect whose knowledge is habitual is not in a state of perfection, which is incompatible with aught but complete actuality. In addition, the very definition of *habitus* quoted above makes it clear that the presence of intelligible species in the mind is essential to it, whereas in God there are no intelligible species. And lastly, *habitus* is a quality, and in God, strictly speaking, there are no qualities.[1]

Since God knows all things simultaneously, it follows that the divine knowledge is not discursive, for discursive knowledge involves temporal sequence, inasmuch as it requires us to begin with the premises and to proceed thence to the conclusion.[2] Moreover, the premises are intuited by one *consideratio* and the conclusion by another; hence, the process includes a plurality of intellectual operations, whereas in God there is but one intellectual operation.[3] Also the conclusion is potentially in the premises and is caused by them; the divine knowledge, on the other hand, is free from all potentiality and is caused by nothing external to itself.[4] Again, the divine knowledge is natural (*naturalis*). Now the objects of natural knowledge, such as first principles, are known without any process of ratiocination. Furthermore, any such process involves a passage on the part of the intellect from *this* to *that*. But in God, the unmoved mover, there is no motion of any kind. Also it is clear that the highest form of human cognition is inferior to the divine cognition. The highest form of human cognition, however, is not reason, *ratio*, but intellect, *intellectus*. Hence there is no possibility of ratiocination in the divine intelligence. Such a process involves the knowing of one thing through another, whereas that is known most perfectly which is known in itself; and God's knowledge is, of course, perfect. Moreover, that which is known through the presence of its species in the knower is known by perception, and without the aid of discursive reasoning (*absque rationis discursu*). Consequently, since the divine essence is the likeness of all things, all things are known by God intuitively and not by discourse.[5]

---

[1] *Con. Gen.* lib. I. cap. 56; *Com. Theol.* cap. xxviii; 1 *Dist.* 35. q. 1 : a. 5. sol.
[2] *Con. Gen.* lib. I. cap. 57; *Sum. Theol.* I.a. q. 14: a. 7. c.
[3] *Con. Gen.* lib. I. cap. 57.
[4] *Con. Gen.* lib. I. cap. 57; *Sum. Theol.* I.a. q. 14: a. 7. c.; *Com. Theol.* Pars Prima, cap. xxviii.   [5] *Con. Gen.* lib. I. cap. 57.

By a single intuitive act (*uno intuito*), therefore, the Deity is aware of his own essence, and of all other things as contained its simplicity. Accordingly, in the divine cognition there is neither composition nor division. To use a more modern phraseology, there is no activity either of analysis or synthesis; and this for reasons very similar to those first given. The essence apprehended and the intuitive act of apprehension are wholly simple. Composition and division, analysis and synthesis involve, not only the presence of plurality in the apprehending mind and the content apprehended, but also temporal succession, for the mind turns to them only subsequently to its consideration of the given essence, the *quod quid est*, in which act of consideration they originate. Moreover, in its knowledge of its proper object, the *quod quid est*, the mind cannot be deceived except *per accidens*. It can be deceived, however, in the work of composition and division. Such knowledge, therefore, is accidental. Hence, it is foreign to God in whom there are no accidents. Again, the comprehension of each individual proposition requires a corresponding individual act on the part of the cognizing intellect. Knowledge of this sort involves, then, a plurality of intellectual operations, whereas God's knowledge of the entire universe involves but one intellectual operation, which is identical with the divine essence.[1]

We are not to infer from this that God is ignorant of the truth which is contained in propositions, *enuntiabilia*. On the contrary, inasmuch as the divine intuition extends simultaneously to all the entities in the universe and knows them all as reflected in the unity of the divine essence, God is aware of the truth contained in all true propositions.[2] The human mind, in so far as it apprehends only the simple (*incomplexa*), has not attained its ultimate perfection. This it arrives at only as the result of composition and division. Now, no perfection of the creature can be lacking in God. Accordingly, the divine essence must possess knowledge both of the simple and the complex, yet in such a manner that its simplicity remains unimpaired.

Truth, according to St. Thomas, is found first (*per prius*) in

---

[1] *Con. Gen.* lib. I. cap. 58.

[2] *Con. Gen.* lib. I. cap. 59; *Sum. Theol.* I.a. q. 14: a. 14. c.; 1 *Dist.* 38. q. 1: a. 3. sol.; *De Verit.* q. 2: a. 7. c.

the mind, and secondly (*per posterius*) in things.[1] Truth of the intellect is defined by him in the present connection as "an equation of the intellect and of the thing in accordance with which the intellect attributes being to that which is, or non-being to that which is not."[2] Accordingly, strange though it sounds to modern ears, the intellect, in becoming aware of the existent, itself becomes true. Now truth is "the good of the intellect" (*bonitas intellectus*).[3] And God is good, therefore God is true.

This assertion must not, however, be understood to imply that truth is a quality inhering in God. On the contrary, since the divine intelligence and the divine substance are one and the same, it implies that God is truth itself.[4] Moreover, it has already been proved that God is goodness itself (*ipsa bonitas*). Hence, since truth is a good, it follows that God is truth.[5] Again, a thing is said to be true in so far as it attains the actuality proper to its nature, whereby it imitates the idea of itself existing in the divine essence, and becomes capable of causing an estimate (*aestimatio*) of itself—which is to say that it becomes conformable to the intellect. But there can be no question of God lacking the actuality proper to his nature or essence, since he is identical with it, nor any doubt as to whether his being conforms to his intellect, for these are also identical.[6] Furthermore, were God not identical with truth, we should have to say that he was true by participation. But God, the ultimate Reality, can participate in nothing.[7]

Since the divine knowledge is not discursive but intuitive, and is also the highest grade of knowledge, it is all-comprehensive. Hence God knows all things *per se*, and not accidentally. In this connection it is to be remembered that while human knowledge is the effect of external objects and is measured by them, the divine knowledge is itself the cause of external objects. Hence the latter is absolutely free from error.[8] Indeed,

---

[1] *De Verit.* q. 1 : a. 2. c.

[2] "Adaequatio intellectus et rei, secundum quod intellectus dicit esse quod est vel non esse quod non est" (*Con. Gen.* lib. I. cap. 59).

[3] *Con. Gen.* lib. I. cap. 60; *Nic. Eth.* lib. VI. cap. ii. lect. 2.

[4] *Con. Gen.* lib. I. cap. 60; *Sum. Theol.* I.a. q. 16: a. 5. c.

[5] *Con. Gen.* lib. I. cap. 60.

[6] *Con. Gen.* lib. I. cap. 60; *Sum. Theol.* I. a. q.16: a. 5. c.

[7] *Con. Gen.* loc. cit.   [8] *Con. Gen.* lib. I. cap. 61.

the presence of error would mean the presence of imperfection in God, which is impossible.

As we have seen, not only are there degrees of being but also of truth. Consequently, the higher the degree of being possessed by an entity the greater its degree of truth. The origin of this doctrine is to be found in the second book of the *Metaphysics*.[1] Accordingly, God, the primal being, is also the primal truth.[2]

This primacy may also be inferred from the identity of the divine essence and truth. Moreover, the definition of truth as an equation between the mind and its object points to the same conclusion, for it is only in the divine intellect that subject and object are absolutely one.[3] And lastly, St. Thomas appeals to the familiar principle that the members of any genus are to be measured by the most perfect of their number. Thus the truth of every intellect is to be measured by the truth of God.[4] The logical implication of this last argument is that God is a member of the genus *true*. St. Thomas, however, would doubtless insist, as we have found him insisting before, that while God, strictly speaking, is in no genus, he is yet, in a sense, in every genus, inasmuch as he is its cause. But in arguing as though truth were a genus, is not Aquinas guilty of a further inconsistency? For truth and being are convertible terms,[5] yet being is not a genus. We may conjecture that he would have replied that while truth and being do not differ *in things* (*in re*), yet the term *truth* signifies an equation between the thing known and the knowing intellect.[6] It does not appear, however, that this constitutes a satisfactory way of escape. Possibly one would be safer in inferring that the reference to genus is intended to be a mere illustration or analogy. This is an assumption which we have already had occasion to make in connection with Aquinas's treatment of being.

The divine knowledge, in itself, is neither a universal nor a

---

[1] "῞Εκαστον ὡς ἔχει τοῦ εἶναι, οὕτω καὶ τῆς ἀληθείας," (sec. 993*b*; cf. also Aquinas's interesting comment: "Et hoc ideo, quia esse rei est causa verae existimationis quam mens habet de re. Verum enim et falsum non est in rebus, sed in mente, ut dicitur sexto huius." Lect. 2).

[2] *Con. Gen.* lib. I. cap. 62.   [3] *Con. Gen.* lib. I. cap. 62.

[4] *Con. Gen.* lib. I. cap. 62.; *Sum. Theol.* I.a. q. 16: a. 6. c.; *De Verit.* q. 1: a. 4. c.

[5] Cf. *Sum. Theol.* I.a. 2. 16: a. 3. c.   [6] Cf. *De Verit.* q. 1: a. 1.

particular. For "every universal receives an addition with respect to the entities by which it is determined";[1] in other words, it subsists only in the particulars which it qualifies. But the divine essence, which is the only medium whereby God knows, can receive no addition, neither can it be participated in by any creature. Moreover, the principle of particularity is matter, and there is no matter in God.

Is the divine knowledge the cause of finite beings? In his earlier work, the *Commentary on the Sentences*, St. Thomas appears to answer this question in the negative, although with important qualifications. In the *Contra Gentiles*[2], the *Summa Theologica*, and the *De Veritate*, he replies in the affirmative; again, however, with qualifications. A comparison of these various passages dissipates the first impression of a marked inconsistency between his earlier and later teaching, although a difference of emphasis there undoubtedly is. In the *Commentary* he is concerned to make it clear that the divine knowledge cannot function as a cause except in conjunction with the divine will.[3] This is, of course, obvious when we recall that in the divine essence there is no distinction between knowledge and will. We find the same point brought out in the *Summa Theologica*,[4] and the *De Veritate*.[5] It is only the native defect of human knowledge which compels us to seek, by ascribing a plurality of attributes to the essence, to express the fullness of its perfection. In the *Commentary*, however, St. Thomas is at pains to insist that, having ascribed volition and knowledge to God, we must regard causality—in the full sense of the word—as pertaining to the divine will alone.[6] Nevertheless, knowledge functions together with will, since it points out the desired end; to this extent, therefore, its activity is causal. Evil, which is a "deviation from form and end," is not, however, caused by the divine knowledge. It is, in other words, a failure on the part of the effect to imitate its cause.

In the *De Veritate* the argument for the causal activity of the divine knowledge receives its fullest statement. Since the effect cannot be more simple than the cause, all things which possess

---

[1] "Omne universale additionem recepit alicuius per quod determinatur" (1 Dist. 35. q. 1: a. 5. sol.).   [2] Lib. II. cap. 24.
[3] 1 *Dist.* 38. q. 1: a. 2. c.   [4] I.a. q. 14: a. 8. c.   [5] q. 2: a. 14. c.
[6] "Voluntas habet completam rationem causae, inquantum obiectum eius est finis secundum rationem boni, qui est causa causarum."

a common nature are dependent upon a single cause which possesses that nature in the highest degree. Thus, all hot things have their common cause in fire. Consequently, whenever we find two things of the same nature we know that they are either the effects of a common cause or that one of them is the cause of the other. Now, in the act of knowledge there is an assimilation of knower to known. Hence, either the act of knowledge is the cause of the thing known, or the thing known is the cause of the act of knowledge, or both are effects of a third cause. But the divine knowledge can be caused neither by its objects nor by anything else. Accordingly, it must itself be the cause of the things which it knows. The conjunction of the divine will is, of course, essential; nor must the activity of secondary causes be forgotten.

In the *Contra Gentiles* the whole topic is treated after the divine volition has already been discussed, and in connection with the problem of creation. There, and also in the *Summa Theologica*, it is said that the Divine knowledge functions somewhat after the manner of human knowledge in the case of an architect who designs a house. The order observable in the works of God is due to his knowledge; the fact that *these* effects and no others are produced is due to his will, for knowledge includes opposites, and cannot of itself determine upon this effect rather than that.

We have now to inquire whether or not the Deity is aware of particulars (*singularia*). It may seem that St. Thomas has already settled this question in deciding that God has a proper knowledge of all things. Such, however, was not his own opinion. The difference between the two problems is brought out most clearly in the *Commentary on the Sentences*.[1]

"The Commentator (i.e. Averroes), indeed, seems expressly to deny that God has knowledge of particulars, except in so far as he knows his essence, which is the principle of all being. But since God is not only the cause of the existence of things, but of all the characteristics of things, he must have knowledge of things, not only with respect to their existence, but also with respect to their characteristics."[2]

---

[1] 1 *Dist.* 36. q. 1 : a. 1. sol.
[2] "Commentator enim, in XI *Metaph.*, text. com. 51, videtur expresse negare Deo particularium cognitionem, nisi inquantum cognoscit essentiam

The position here stated and refuted is that of those who deny that God has a proper knowledge of all things.

"And therefore others, such as Avicenna and Algazel (i.e. Al Ghazzali)—according to Averroes—and their followers, have said that God knows particulars in a universal mode; which they explain by the following example: If anyone knew all the distances between the orbs and the planets and the time occupied by their motions, he would foresee every eclipse which could possibly take place, yet he would not know this eclipse in so far as it is *this* eclipse, unless he knew it by sense-perception; but he would know the eclipse which will take place to-morrow in a universal mode; that is, through its universal causes."[1]

Such is the view which Aquinas is now anxious to refute. He informs us that there are seven principal arguments advanced by the opponents of his own doctrine.[2]

In the first place, the principle of individuality, as St. Thomas himself has contended, is signate matter. Moreover, the act of knowledge involves the assimilation of knower to known. Thus the human intellect, by reason of its immateriality, cannot know particulars. These we become aware of through the powers of imagination and sense, which make use of material organs. But the divine intellect is at the farthest remove from matter. Consequently it cannot know particulars.[3]

In the second place, particulars do not exist for ever. It is, however, impossible that God should have knowledge of them

---

suam, quae est principium omnis esse. Sed cum Deus non tantum sit causa esse rerum, sed omnium quae in rebus sunt, oportet ut cognitionem rerum non tantum in eo quod sunt habeat, sed etiam in eo quod sunt talia vel talia."

[1] "Et ideo alii dixerunt, scilicet Avicenna, tract. VIII. *Metaph.* cap. vii, et Algazel apud Aver., lib. Destructionum, disput vi, et sequaces eorum, quod Deus cognoscit singularia universaliter; quod sic exponunt per exemplum. Si aliquis sciret omnes distantias orbium et planetarum, et tempus motuum ipsorum, ipse praevideret omnem eclipsim quae posset contingere; non tamen sciret hanc eclipsim inquantum est haec eclipsis, nisi per aliquid a sensu acceptum; sed sciret eclipsim quae cras contingeret, universaliter, scilicet secundum suas causas universales" (cf. *Sum. Theol.* I.a. q. 14: a. 11. c.; 1 *Dist.* 38. q. 1: a. 3. sol.; *De Verit.* q. 2: a. 5. c. For the example of the eclipse in Avicenna, see *Metaphysices Compendium*, libri primi, secunda pars, tract. 4. cap. ii).

[2] *Con. Gen.* lib. I. cap. 63.

[3] Cf. *Sum. Theol.* I.a. q. 14: a. 11. obiecta; 1 *Dist.* 36. q. 1: a. 1. ob. 1; *De Verit.* q. 2: a. 5. ob. 1, ob. 2, ob. 3; *Com. Theol.* cap. cxxxiii.

when they do not exist, for knowledge is of the true. Hence, if God know them at all, he must know them at some times and not at other times. In other words, awareness of particulars would infect the divine knowledge with change. But this is impossible, since it is identical with the divine essence.[1]

In the third place, some particulars are contingent, and about them there can be no knowledge except when they exist. Of future contingent particulars, then, no certain knowledge can be had, for if it were possible to have knowledge of them they would not be contingent. Accordingly, since the divine knowledge is certain, God cannot be aware of future contingent particulars.[2]

Fourthly, certain contingent particulars are willed by finite minds. Now an effect, before it actually exists, can be known only in its cause. When the cause, however, is a finite will there is only one being who can know it, namely, the being whose will it is.

Fifthly, the infinite as such is unknown,[3] for everything that is known is measured by the comprehension of the knower. But particulars are infinite in number, at least potentially. Consequently God cannot know them.[4]

Sixthly, the excellence of knowledge is measured by the excellence of its object, and the worthlessness of knowledge by the worthlessness of its object. The divine knowledge is, of course, most excellent. It is, therefore, impossible that God should know worthless things.[5]

Seventhly, since the known is in some mode in the knower, it is impossible that God should know evil things.

Aquinas now proceeds to answer these arguments one by one. In reply to the first, he stresses the dissimilarity between divine and human knowledge. The latter is derived from and caused by physical objects which affect the mind through the senses. Matter, being pure potentiality, is incapable of activity. Consequently, the external object acts upon the mind through its form alone.[6] It is impossible, however, that a form of lower

---

[1] Cf. *De Verit.* q. 2: a. 5. ob. 11; *Com. Theol.* Pars Prima, cap. cxxxiii.
[2] Cf. *Com. Theol.* cap. cxxxiii; *De Verit.* q. 2: a. 5. ob. 5.
[3] Cf. *Phys.* lib. I. cap. iv. lect. 9.
[4] Cf. *Com. Theol.* Pars Prima, cap. cxxxiii.
[5] Cf. *De Verit.* q. 2: a. 5. ob. 4.   [6] *De Verit.* q. 2: a. 5. c.

grade should produce its likeness in a higher grade.[1] Accordingly a form which is individuated by its materiality cannot produce a mental image of itself in its particularity. Its immediate effect, on the contrary, is the *phantasma*, or, as we should say, the sense-datum. From the *phantasma* the intelligible species is abstracted by the *intellectus agens* which strips the form apprehended "of all material conditions which are the principles of individuation,"[2] and transmutes it into a pure universal. Thus the human intellect cannot know particulars directly, but only as it reflects upon its own act.[3] It is permissible, however, to say that the *man* knows particulars, since he is aware of them through imagination and sense.[4]

The divine intellect, on the other hand, employs no intelligible species other than its essence, which is not abstracted from matter but exists *per seipsam*. Hence the essence contains the likeness of matter as well as that of form, and the likenesses of particulars as well as those of universals. In knowing himself, therefore, God knows all the particulars in the universe. His single act of apprehension includes all that a man might know through his various faculties—i.e. intellect, imagination, and sense. The divine knowledge is, as we have seen, causative. If anything, therefore, is unknown by God, it is also non-existent.[5]

Furthermore, knowledge of the constituent principles of anything involves knowledge of that thing. But matter, form, and individualizing accidents are all known by God. Universals, again, do not exist apart from the particulars in which they inhere, and cannot be known apart from them. Moreover, knowledge of any genus involves knowledge of its "primal differences and proper passions."[6] Thus we cannot know number unless without knowing odd and even. But the differences or passions of being are universal and parti-

---

[1] "Forma igitur quae est inferioris gradus non potest gendo perducere suam similitudinem in gradum altiorem" (*Con. Gen.* lib. I. cap. 65).

[2] "Ab omnibus materialibus conditionibus quae sunt individuationis principia" (*De Verit.* q. 2: a. 6. c.).

[3] *De Verit.* q. 2. a. 6. c.   [4] *De Verit.* q. 2: a. 6. ad 3m.

[5] *Con. Gen.* lib. I. cap. 65; cf. also *Sum. Theol.* I.a. q. 14: a. 11. c.; 1 *Dist.* 36. q. 1: a. 1. sol. and ad 1m; *De Verit.* q. 2: a. 5. c.; *Com. Theol.* cap. cxxxiv.

[6] "Differentiae primae et passiones propriae" (*Con. Gen.* loc. cit.).

cular.[1] For all these reasons, therefore, we must ascribe to God knowledge of particulars.[2]

Again, reverting to the argument from motion, as Aquinas loved to do, we recall that the *primum mobile* is moved by a mover which causes motion by the agency of intellect and appetite. This it could not do unless it knew the thing moved to be capable of local motion, and to exist here and now, which is to say that it knows it as a particular. Accordingly, if the mover in question be identical with God, God is aware of particulars. Should it, however, be an inferior power, it will none the less possess in the knowledge of particulars a perfection which the Deity cannot lack.[3] Indeed, since knowledge is a perfection, the fact that any finite being knows particulars is sufficient ground for attributing the same knowledge to God without reference to the argument from motion.[4]

In replying to the second argument St. Thomas makes use of the same distinction between divine and human knowledge. As we know, the divine knowledge stands in a causal relation to physical objects, and physical objects stand in a causal relation to human knowledge. But physical objects can exist even though unknown by us. Similarly, the divine knowledge can exist even if its objects be non-existent.[5] Finite beings exist, as we have seen, not merely because God knows them, but also because he wills them. When the divine will does not function the objects of divine knowledge are purely potential, yet as such they are known by God.[6] For the divine essence contains in itself the likenesses of all creatures. It is impossible, however, that the sum-total of finite entities, each with its limited being and perfection, should equal the unlimited perfection of the essence of God. Accordingly, the capacity for

---

[1] Here, once again, we find St. Thomas arguing as if being were a genus. Upon this passage Sylvester comments as follows: "Nam, ut superius est ostensum, ens differentias habere non potest: sed dicuntur differentiae entis, quia explicant aliquos modos essendi oppositos, qui nomine *entis* non exprimuntur. Non curat autem Sanctus Thomas an dicuntur isto modo *differentiae*, vel magis *passiones*, quia ad propositum nihil refert."

[2] *Con. Gen.* lib. I. cap. 65.

[3] *Con. Gen.* lib. I. cap. 65.

[4] *Con. Gen.* lib. I. cap. 65; *Sum. Theol.* I.a. q. 14: a. 11. c.

[5] *Con. Gen.* lib. I. cap. 66; *De Verit.* q. 2: a. 5. c.

[6] *Sum. Theol.* I.a. 2. 14: a. 9. ad 3m.

representation (*vis suae representationis*) possessed by the essence extends to non-existent realities.[1]

God's knowledge, indeed, is related to the universe somewhat as an artisan's knowledge is related to the articles which he makes. He knows them before he has made them, otherwise he could not make them. In addition, he knows things which he could make, but never has made and never will make.[2] That the human mind is capable of knowing the essences of non-existent things is obvious when we reflect that were all the horses and lions in the universe slain we should still know what the words *horse* and *lion* mean. And again, we all foresee things before they come to pass, through our knowledge of their causes, as an astronomer, for instance, foresees an eclipse.[3]

The divine knowledge, moreover, is non-temporal and without succession. It is a *totum simul semper manens*. Accordingly, it is related to time as an indivisible to a continuum. None the less, it co-exists with each instant of time. As each point in the circumference of a circle is directly opposite the centre, so every moment of time, although past or future in relation to every other moment of time, is present to the Eternal. Hence anything which exists at any instant is present to God, and is contemplated by him. The knowledge of such entities is called knowledge of vision,[4] or *practical cognition*.[5] Of those things which are merely possible which never actually exist at any moment, God is said to have *knowledge of simple intelligence*,[6] or *speculative cognition*.[7]

Since the divine knowledge is eternal it follows that God is aware of future contingent particulars. They are future for us but not for him. We, being in time, cannot perceive them directly and are compelled to resort to inference. The divine cognition, however, is related to its objects as "present to present."[8] The vision of the Deity is likened to that of a man standing upon an eminence who surveys the road beneath

---

[1] *Con. Gen.* lib. I. cap. 66.

[2] *Con. Gen.* lib. I. cap. 66; *Sum. Theol.* I.a. q. 14: a. 9. c.; *De Verit.* q. 2: a. 8. c.   [3] *Con. Gen.* loc. cit.

[4] *Con. Gen.* loc. cit.; *Sum. Theol.* I.a. q. 14: a. 9. c.; 1 *Dist.* 38. q. 1: a. 4. sol.   [5] *De Verit.* q. 2: a. 8. c.

[6] *Con. Gen.* lib. I. cap. 66; *Sum. Theol.* I.a. q. 14: a. 9. c.; 1 *Dist.* 38. q. 1: a. 4. sol.

[7] *De Verit.* q. 2: a. 8. c.   [8] *De Verit.* q. 2: a. 12. c.

with the stream of wayfarers passing along it, thus taking in the entire situation at a single glance.[1] Another illustration used by St. Thomas is strikingly similar to modern arguments in connection with the "time-span," and the "specious present." "Let there be five men who in five successive hours perceive five contingent particulars. I can then say that these five men perceive these successive contingent particulars as present. If, however, we suppose that these five acts of knowing subjects are one act, it can then be said that one act of cognition perceives as present all these successive objects. Since God, therefore, perceives all temporal things in one eternal and non-successive act of intuition, he will in his eternity perceive all contingent particulars in diverse times as present, and not merely as existing in his own cognition. For God has not merely from eternity known himself as the knower of these things—in which case they would exist only in his knowledge—but from eternity he sees in one intuition, and will see temporal particulars, and each thing as existing at *this* time and vanishing at *that*."

It is true that a contingent effect is so contained in its cause that it may result from it or may not, whereas a necessary effect follows inevitably upon its cause. Nevertheless a contingent effect, once it has come into being, exists just as truly as a necessary effect. Now, the divine cognition extends to all causes and effects so that God knows contingent effects not only in relation to their causes, but in themselves. Consequently God's knowledge of a contingent effect is not problematical but certain. Thus it is contingent and not necessary that

---

[1] *Sum. Theol.* I.a. q. 14: a. 13. ad 3^m; *Com. Theol.* cap. cxxxiv; *De Verit.* q. 2: a. 12. c.

[2] "Sint quinque homines qui successive in quinque horis quinque contingentia facta videant. Possum ergo dicere, quod isti quinque vident haec contingentia succedentia praesentialiter. Si autem poneretur quod isti quinque actus cognoscentium essent actus unus, posset dici quod una cognitio esset praesentialiter de omnibus illis cognitis successivis. Cum ergo Deus uno aeterno intuitu, non successivo, omnia tempora videat, omnia contingentia in temporibus diversis ab aeterno praesentialiter videt non tantum ut habentia esse in cognitione sua. Non enim Deus ab aeterno cognovit in rebus tantum se cognoscere ea, quod est esse in cognitione sua; sed etiam ab aeterno vidit uno intuitu et videbit singula tempora, et rem talem esse in hoc tempore, et in hoc deficere" (1 *Dist.* 38. q. 1: a. 5. sol.).

Socrates should be seated, but once he has seated himself it is necessary that he should be perceived as seated.[1]

It is, of course, true that, as a necessary effect follows certainly upon its cause, so a contingent effect will follow certainly from a complete contingent cause, unless it be impeded. So it might be supposed that since God's knowledge is both necessary and causative, the existence of its objects is, in all instances, necessary and not contingent. This is to forget, however, the existence of secondary causes, and the fact that the activity of certain of them may impede and frustrate that of others. The occurrence or non-occurrence of such interaction and impediment is evident to the Deity, and also the existence or non-existence of all contingent effects.[2] The third objection may, therefore, be dismissed.

Inasmuch as God is the cause of all finite beings, the divine causality extends to operations of intellect and will; for since everything acts by its form, the fount of all being, from which all form is derived, must be the principle of all operation. Even as the being of God is primal, and therefore the cause of all being, so the divine intellection is primal, and therefore the cause of all intellectual operations.[3] Accordingly, in knowing his essence God knows the thoughts of all minds and the volitions of all hearts. (*Cogitationes mentium et voluntates cordium.*)

As regards the nature of human consciousness itself, Aquinas urges that our actions are in our own minds as purposes before they pass into externality, and that minds themselves, by reason of their possessing a higher degree of reality (*puta magis in actu existentes*) than material objects, are inherently more knowable, and that, consequently, we can understand how inevitable it is that they should be fully known by the divine intelligence which is aware of effects, not only as they exist in themselves, but as contained in their causes.[4]

Since the divine knowledge extends to all particulars, if there be an infinite number of particulars or particulars which are infinite in any dimension, they must be known to God. As a matter of fact, it is impossible that an infinite should actually

---

[1] *Con. Gen.* lib. I. cap. 67; *Sum. Theol.* I.a. q. 14: a. 13. c.; 1 *Dist.* 38. q. 1: a. 5. ad 3^m; *De Verit.* q. 2: a. 12. ad 7^m.

[2] *Con. Gen.* lib. I. cap. 67.

[3] Cf. 1 *Dist.* 38. q. 1: a. 1. sol. [4] *Con. Gen.* lib. I. cap. 68.

exist.[1] It may exist potentially, nevertheless, in the form of a
process which is never completed but which may continue
indefinitely. Thus, if the process of generation and corruption
were without beginning or end, it would entail the existence
of an infinite number of beings, yet at any particular instant
the number of entities which had come into existence would
necessarily be finite, inasmuch as the succeeding instant would
bring with it an addition to it. Now the divine knowledge
has been proved to extend not merely to all past, present, or
future, but also to all potentially existent entities. And the
divine essence, being infinite, is susceptible of imitation in an
infinite number of modes, since it is impossible that any
creature, or any number of creatures, should imitate it perfectly. Consequently, God must know an infinite number of
entities of which the potential existence is contained in his own
power and goodness. Yet he does not know them by enumeration as a finite mind would do, but by a single act of intuition
directed upon his own essence which contains the likenesses
of all things.[2]

The perfection of the divine knowledge is incompatible with
any other theory than this. For the human intellect is potentially
capable of knowing the infinite in the sense that it can continue
indefinitely to contemplate the various species of numbers or
geometrical figures one after another. Hence the knowledge
of God, in whom there is no potentiality, must also extend to
the infinite. Moreover, the higher the degree of intellectuality,
the greater is the range of its knowledge. Hence an infinite
mind must be capable of knowing the infinite.[3]

In so far as the divine awareness is directed upon substances,
it is clear that it cannot know an infinite number of them by
knowledge of vision, for vision is directed upon the existent,
and the number of existent substances is always finite at any
instant. Moreover, the world began in time and will end in
time, hence the total number of substances that are destined

---

[1] *Con. Gen.* lib. I. cap. 69; *Sum. Theol.* I.a. q. 7: aa. 2, 3, 4; 1 *Dist.*
39. q. 1: a. 3. sol.; *Quodlib*, ix. q. 1: a. 1. Cf., however, *De Verit.* q. 2:
a. 9, a. 10, where the question appears to be left undecided.
[2] *Con. Gen.* lib. I. cap. 69; *Sum. Theol.* I.a. q. 14: a. 12. c.; *De Verit.* q. 2:
a. 9. c.; 1 *Dist.* 39. q. 1: a. 3. sol.; *Com. Theol.* cap. cxxxiv.
[3] *Con. Gen.* lib. I. cap. 69.

to exist is finite. And potential substances can be known only by "knowledge of simple intelligence" (*scientia simplicis intelligentiae*).[1] Since, however, the thoughts and affections of finite minds will continue to multiply for ever, it follows that the divine knowledge of such accidental existence is knowledge of vision.[2]

The divine knowledge being all-inclusive, it follows that the unimportance or triviality of any fact is no barrier to its being known by God. For everything that exists has, *ipso facto*, a certain degree of "nobility" (*ex hoc nobilitatem habet*). It can be pronounced worthless or mean (*vile*) only in comparison with something nobler than itself. The gap which separates the noblest of finite beings from God is, however, far greater than that which sunders these in turn from the meanest of creatures. Accordingly, since the former is no obstacle to God's knowledge, neither is the latter. Moreover, the order of the universe is nobler than any particular part of the universe, since it is the end with respect to which the parts are ordered. Hence, if God knows anything other than himself, it will be this that he will know. But the order of the universe is a hierarchy, the constituent elements of which are noble or mean as compared to one another. Accordingly, knowledge of such an order involves knowledge of its parts, both noble and mean.[3]

Again, the meanness of that which is known does not infect the knower, for although knowledge involves the passage of the species of the object into the apprehending mind, yet it exists there "according to the mode" of the knower, as the representation of an external object, and not in the mode in which the object itself exists.[4] It may, indeed, affect the knower *accidentally*, in so far as it draws him aside from nobler thoughts, or inspires him with unworthy emotions, but this is impossible in the case of God who knows all things at once.[5]

Knowledge of all things of necessity includes knowledge of evil things. It may be contended, however, that God can have no knowledge of evil; for the divine knowledge is the cause of

[1] *Con. Gen.* lib. I. cap. 69; 1 *Dist.* 39. q. 1: a. 3. sol.; *De Verit.* q. 2: a. 9. c.
[2] *Sum. Theol.* I.a. q. 14: a. 12. c.
[3] *Con. Gen.* lib. I. cap. 70.   [4] *Con. Gen.* lib. I. cap. 70.
[5] *Con. Gen.* lib. I. cap. 70; *Metaph.* lib. XII. lect. 8.

its objects, and so, were it true that God knew evil, it would also be true that he caused it.[1] In answer to this objection Aquinas urged that since evil is wholly negative, a mere privation, it is incorrect to speak of it as being caused by God. The entity which suffers a privation has, indeed, been created; but in so far as it has being it is good, wherefore there is no difficulty in admitting that God is its cause.

In a similar strain he replied to the following objections:

(1) Knowledge involves the assimilation of knower to known. But God is wholly devoid of evil, and cannot be assimilated to it.[2]

(2) Whatever is known is known through its likeness or through its contrary. But there is no likeness of evil in the divine essence; nor is evil the contrary of God, for God has no contrary. Hence it is impossible that in knowing his own essence God should know evil.[3]

Aquinas responded that evil can be known *per similitudinem boni*. Knowledge of the divine essence involves knowledge of all particulars and of all their properties, including their defects and privations. And evil is a defect, and a privation of due perfection. Thus, while not the contrary of God, it is opposed to his effects and is known in the knowing of them. For it is impossible that God should know both universals and particulars as mutually distinct from one another, and not know the meaning of negation and privation. Moreover, it is as true that evil is evil as that good is good; hence the perfection of the divine intellect requires a knowledge of evil.[4]

Since God is immutable and eternal, it follows that the divine knowledge does not vary.[5] This is also implied by the conclusions which we have just reached, namely, that God knows all things at once with a knowledge which is not discursive, but intuitive, and that he perceives all things as present. Thus an entity which comes into existence in time and later passes out of existence is eternally perceived by God as existent during a certain period of time and as non-existent

---

[1] *Sum. Theol.* I.a. q. 14: a. 10. ob. 2; 1 *Dist.* 36. q. 1: a. 2. ob. 2; *De Verit.* q. 2: a. 15. ob. 1.
[2] 1 *Dist.* 36. q. 1: a. 2. ob. 3.
[3] *Sum. Theol.* I.a. q. 14: a. 10. ob. 3; *De Verit.* q. 2: a. 15. ob. 4.
[4] *Con. Gen.* lib. I. cap. 71.   [5] *Sum. Theol.* I.a. q. 14: a. 15. c.

at all other periods. Consequently awareness of time and change involves no change on the part of the Deity.[1]

Speculative knowledge has as its end the consideration of truth, while the end of practical knowledge is operation. Of himself, then, God has a purely speculative knowledge; of all other things, however, his knowledge is both speculative and practical, since he both thoroughly comprehends all things and is also able to create them.[2]

[1] *Sum. Theol.* I.a. q. 14: a. 15. ad 2ᵐ; cf. *De Verit.* q. 2: a. 13. c.
[2] *Sum. Theol.* I.a. q. 14: a. 16. c.

CHAPTER XII

THE THEORY OF IDEAS

As we should expect, the theory of Ideas survives in the Thomist system only in an extremely mutilated form. The significance of the term was expounded by Aquinas as follows: "Formas rerum in Deo existentes ideas dicimus, quae sunt sicut formae operativae."[1] That is to say, Ideas are identical with forms as they exist *ante rem* in the divine consciousness, which uses them as archetypes in the process of creation.[2] In addition, they provide the Deity with a speculative knowledge of those potential entities which have not yet passed into actuality.[3] The theory of St. Thomas is thus of the nature of a compromise between pure Neoplatonism and Christian theism.

Is it possible, however, to reconcile a plurality of Ideas with the divine simplicity, or must we assume that there is only one Idea? Aquinas replies that there are many Ideas. "Since the term *Idea* signifies the divine essence in so far as it is the exemplar imitated by some creature, the divine essence will be the proper Idea of that thing according to a determinate mode of imitation. And because other creatures imitate it in other modes it must be said that the Idea or *ratio* by which a man is created is other than that by which a horse is created; and from this it follows that according to the relations of the divine essence to the many things which imitate it in different modes there is a plurality of Ideas, although the essence imitated is one."[4]

[1] 1 *Dist.* 36. q. 2: a. 1. sol.; cf. *Sum. Theol.* I.a. q. 15: a. 1. c.; also *De Verit.* q. 3: a. 1. c.

[2] 1 *Dist.* 36. q. 2: a. 1. sol.; cf. *Sum. Theol.* I. a. q. 15: a.1. c.; also *De Verit.* q. 3: a. 1. c.

[3] 1 Dist. 36. q. 2: a. 1. sol.

[4] "Unde cum hoc nomen 'idea' nominet essentiam divinam secundum quod est exemplar imitatum a creatura, divina essentia erit propria idea istius rei secundum determinatum imitationis modum. Et quia alio modo imitantur eam diversae creaturae, ideo dicitur quod est alia idea vel ratio qua creatur homo et equus; et exinde sequitur quod secundum respectum ad plures res quae divinam essentiam diversimode imitantur, sit pluralitas in ideis, quamvis essentia imitata sit una" (1 *Dist.* 36. q. 2: a. 2. sol.; cf. ad 1^m; cf. *Sum. Theol.* I.a. q. 15: a. 2. ad 1^m).

To the objection that it is impossible that Ideas should be eternally differentiated from one another by the relations of the divine essence to entities which exist in time, it is answered that the plurality of modes in which the essence is susceptible of imitation is eternally known by God, and that this suffices for the differentiation of the Ideas.[1] Nevertheless, it may still be urged that, since God is not really related to the creatures—although the creatures are really related to God—there can be no ground for distinction in the divine essence. To this St. Thomas replies, as we might expect, that, while a relation between God and the creature is not in God *secundum rem*, it is in God *secundum intellectum suum.* In other words, such relations are purely "rational" so far as the Deity is concerned, and not "real"; none the less, the fact that they are known as such by him is all that is requisite for differentiating one Idea from another.[2]

It is clear that this discussion adds nothing to what had already been written by Aquinas in his previous attempt to explain how the undifferentiated unity of the divine essence can be susceptible of imitation in a plurality of modes. His concern at this point was to vindicate his right to make use of the term *Idea.* And now the further question arose, are there ideas of all the things which God knows? Upon examination it appears that the answer to this query involves the raising of six subordinate questions:

1. Has God Ideas of evil things?
2. Has God an Idea of primary matter?
3. Has God Ideas of things which never exist at any time?
4. Has God Ideas of genera?
5. Has God Ideas of all accidents?
6. Has God Ideas of particulars?

Before considering Aquinas's answers to these questions, it will be well to notice the distinction which he saw fit to institute, in this context, between the terms *exemplar* and *ratio.* An Idea,

[1] *Sum. Theol.* I.a. q. 15: a. 2. ad 3ᵐ; 1 *Dist.* 36. q. 2: a. 2. ad 2ᵐ; *De Verit.* q. 3: a. 2. ad 7ᵐ.
[2] *De Verit.* q. 3: a. 2. ad 8ᵐ; *Sum. Theol.* I.a. q. 15: a. 2. ad 4ᵐ; 1 *Dist.* 36. q. 2: a. 2. ad 4ᵐ.

in so far as it serves as "the principle for the making of things" (*secundum quod est principium factionis rerum*) is termed an *exemplar*, and as such it belongs to the domain of practical knowledge. On the other hand, in so far as it is simply a principle of cognition, it is termed a *ratio*, and as such it is included in the sphere of speculative knowledge.[1] Accordingly St. Thomas urges in reply to the first question that, inasmuch as evil is mere privation, it cannot possess in the divine essence either *exemplar* or *ratio*. On the contrary, it is known by God through the opposing idea of the good.[2]

As regards primary matter we are compelled to assume, since it has been created by God, that there is some sort of Idea of it in the divine essence. Nevertheless, it is only in conjunction with form that matter can be said to possess "perfect being," *esse perfectum*; in itself it has only "imperfect being," consequently its mode of representation in the divine essence will be imperfect also.[3] For this reason we must conclude that the essence contains an *exemplar* neither of the matter nor of the form of a composite substance, but only of the substance itself as a whole, for it is the substance, and not its matter or its form, which is the term of the creative act. But since it is possible to consider separately entities which cannot exist apart, the Deity will certainly possess a *ratio* of primary matter.[4]

With respect to things which do not exist, which have never existed, and which never will exist, the divine knowledge is

---

[1] *Sum. Theol.* I.a. q. 15: a. 3. c. For the same distinction expressed in other terms, cf. *De Verit.* q. 3: a. 3. c.; 1 *Dist.* 36. q. 2: a. 1. c.

[2] *Sum. Theol.* I.a. q. 15: a. 3. ad 1ᵐ; *De Verit.* q. 3: a. 4; q. 5: a. 1. ad 1ᵐ; 1 *Dist.* 36. q. 2 :a. 3. ad 1ᵐ.

[3] 1 *Dist.* 36. q. 2: a. 3. ad 2ᵐ. The use of the phrase *esse perfectum* to designate the mode of being which pertains to matter in conjunction with form as contrasted with that which matter possesses in its own right indicates that the doctrine of degrees of being is not here directly referred to. For St. Thomas no material substance could occupy other than a very humble level in the *gradus essendi*. None the less, such a substance does actually exist, whereas primary matter, being pure potentiality, can neither be said to exist, nor yet be assigned with "privation" (*privatio*) to the region of non-existence, but must be left to hover in a mysterious half-real realm of its own.

[4] *De Verit.* q. 3: a. 5. c.; cf. *Sum. Theol.* I.a. q. 15: a. 3. ad 3ᵐ.

only virtually practical. Hence the Deity possesses no *exemplares* of such entities, but only *rationes*.[1] Since genus cannot exist apart from species any more than matter apart from form, and since any object of God's creative activity inevitably partakes of both, it is clear that the divine essence contains no *exemplar* of any genus as such; but it would seem that it must contain *rationes* of all genera.[2]

In the case of accidents the situation is more complicated. The term *proprium* signifies an accident which invariably accompanies the subject in which it inheres, its presence being implied by the very nature or essence of that subject. Because of this inevitable association, the Deity possesses no *exemplar*[3] of the *proprium* as such, but only of the subject *in toto*. He does, however, possess a *ratio* or *similitudo* of it. Accidents which are not inseparably united to their subjects, but which may or may not qualify them, are each represented by a corresponding *exemplar*.[4]

Since the divine providence extends to particulars, it follows that there are Ideas of all particulars in the divine essence.[5] But the question may be raised: Is the Idea of a particular other than the Idea of its species? If we answer in the affirmative, we admit that there can be two Ideas of the same thing. If we reply in the negative, must we not conclude that all the particulars which fall under a single species are represented by a single Idea? Aquinas replies that to particular species and genus there corresponds but one *idea propria* (i.e. one *exemplar*), but that to each there may correspond a *ratio* or *similitudo*.[6] When we reflect that Ideas are said to be dis-

---

[1] *Sum. Theol.* I.a. q. 15: a. 3. ad 2ᵐ. In the *De Verit.* (q. 3: a. 6), where a different terminology is employed, the phrase *indeterminatas ideas* is used instead of *rationes*.

[2] *Sum. Theol.* I.a. q. 15: a. 3. ad 4ᵐ; cf. *Quodlib.* viii. q. 1: a. 2.

[3] *Sum. Theol.* I.a. q. 15: a. 3. ad 4ᵐ; cf. *De Verit.* q. 3: a. 7. c., where the phrase *idea distincta* is used instead of *exemplar*.

[4] Cf., however, 1 *Dist.* 36. q. 2: a. 3. ad 4ᵐ, where it is asserted that accidents, inasmuch as they do not possess "perfect being," "fall short of the perfection of the idea," yet "in so far as they have being through their imitation of the divine essence, to that extent the divine essence is the idea of them."

[5] *Sum. Theol.* I.a. q. 15: a. 3. ad 4ᵐ; *De Verit.* q. 3: a. 8. c.

[6] *De Verit.* q. 3: a. 8. ad 2ᵐ; cf. *Quodlib.* viii. q. 1: a. 2.

tinguished from one another merely by "rational relations," and that their plurality is due only to the diversity of their objects and in no way taints the simplicity of the divine essence, the highly artificial character of this question becomes almost painfully evident.

CHAPTER XIII

THE WILL OF GOD

THE discussion of the character of divine knowledge leads naturally to the question as to whether there is will in God. So close, indeed, is the connection between cognition and volition that an affirmative answer appears not only plausible but practically inevitable. The arguments advanced by St. Thomas are, however, eight in number.

1. The good as known, the *bonum intellectum*, is the proper object of the will. But knowledge implied a knower. Everyone, therefore, who knows the good must will it. And God, who is perfect intelligence, has knowledge of being and at the same time of the concept of the good. Hence there is will in God.[1]

This reference to God's knowledge of being, which appears uncalled for, is thus explained by Sylvester. The intellect can apprehend an object either materially or formally. When a thing which in itself is good is actually apprehended, although apprehended not by means of the concept of goodness but by some other concept, such as that of truth, it is apprehended materially. When, however, it is apprehended by means of the concept of goodness, it is apprehended formally. For this reason, then, St. Thomas desired to emphasize that God apprehends being as good, or, in other words, that he apprehends goodness both materially and formally.[2]

2. The possession of a form by any entity establishes relations between that entity and other entities. Thus white wood,

---

[1] *Con. Gen.* lib. I. cap. 72.

[2] In addition, Sylvester raises the objection that to say that the good is willed because it is the proper object of the will is equivalent to saying that the good is willed because it is willed. The two expressions, he contends, are tautologous. Plausible as this criticism appears, we may yet conjecture that what Aquinas had here in mind was merely the familiar scholastic theory that the intellect necessarily wills the good. This seems to be clearly the case in the *Compendium Theologiae* (cap. xxxi), where we find a succinct and lucid statement of the same proof. "Ipse enim se ipsum intelligit, qui est bonum perfectum, ut ex dictis patet. Bonum autem intellectum ex necessitate diligitur. Hoc autem fit per voluntatem. Necesse est igitur Deum volentem esse."

through its possession of the quality of whiteness, stands in a relation of similarity to all other white things, and in a relation of dissimilarity to everything which is not white. Now every intelligent or sentient subject possesses, as the result of a process of abstraction, the form of the object known or sensed. Such abstraction does not, however, establish a relation between the subject and the object, but rather between the object and the subject, inasmuch as things are known or sensed as they are in the intellect or sense.[1] Consequently we must look for some other relation which subsists between the subject and the object as it exists *in rerum natura*, and such a relation we observe to spring from appetite and will which are characteristics of sentient and intelligent beings, and are by them directed toward external objects. Hence all sentient and intelligent beings must possess appetite and will; the Deity, who is an intelligent being, must therefore also possess a will.

This argument appears to be extraordinarily faulty. It sets out from the presupposition that anything which possesses the quality X must be similar to every other entity which possesses the same quality and dissimilar to every entity which does not; or, in other words, that everything in the universe is related to everything else. We are then informed that, in the case of abstraction of forms, the subject is not related to the object, although the object is related to the subject. Our attention is thus diverted from relations of similarity and dissimilarity, and is directed upon the relation of *abstracting* and *being abstracted from*. We are next told that, since the subject must in some manner be related to the object—apparently because of the presupposition with which we began—we must seek in appetite and will the ground of that relation. This is strange reasoning. And it is all the stranger when we reflect that, if the exercise of will establishes a relation between the subject and its object, and if God be possessed of will, then God must be related to the universe the existence of which he wills, a conclusion which is directly contrary to Aquinas's teaching.[2]

[1] We may ask whether this is consistent with what Aquinas asserts elsewhere. Cf. *Sum. Theol.* I.a. q. 13: a. 7. c.

[2] In the *Quaestiones Disputatae* (*De Verit.* q. 23: a. 1. c.) essentially the same argument is to be found. It seems there to be assumed that everything in the universe is related to everything else. The relations obtaining

3. That which is found in all beings pertains to being as such; hence it must be present in the primal being. And we find that every thing desires the perfection and conservation of its own being. In intellectual substances, this desire springs from the will, in animals from the sensuous appetite, and in beings devoid of sense from the natural appetite. Those which have not what they desire struggle to attain it, and those which have it rest in it. This also must be true of the Deity, because he is intelligent. There must, then, be will in God whereby he is pleased with his being and his goodness.[1]

4. The more perfect our knowing, the greater pleasure it yields. But the divine knowing is most perfect; it is therefore most pleasant. And the pleasure of an intelligent being is of the will; wherefore there is will in God.[2] The thought expressed in this argument is obviously the same as that which inspired the third proof, namely, that all intelligent beings seek satisfaction and find it through the will.

5. A form which is contemplated by the intellect does not cause motion of itself, but only through the mediation of the will. But the form of the divine intellect is the cause of the motion and the being of all other things, for God moves all things through his intellect, as is hereafter to be proved. Consequently there must be will in God.[3]

6. In all intellectual substances the will is the primal motive power, because we think and imagine only in so far as we will, although the intellect in turn moves the will by providing it with an object and final cause. Hence in God, the prime mover, there must be will.[4]

The fifth and sixth arguments are so similar that it is difficult to discover any difference between them, except in phraseology.

among material things are, however, imposed *ab extra*. Immaterial and intellectual substances, on the other hand, are free to order themselves. Hence, while material substances possess only natural appetite, intellectual substances are endowed with will. Yet their exercise of will appears to be conditioned by relations already subsisting between themselves and the external world. The argument is not very clear, and it seems unnecessary to examine it in detail.

[1] *Con. Gen.* lib. I. cap. 72; cf. *Sum. Theol.* I.a. q. 19: a. 1. c.; 1 *Dist.* 45. q. 1: a. 1. sol.   [2] *Con. Gen.* lib. I. cap. 72.
[3] *Con. Gen.* lib. I. cap. 72; cf. *Com. Theol.* Pars Prima, cap. xxxi.
[4] *Con. Gen.* lib. I. cap. 72.

It will be noted, however, that the sixth argument is circular, whereas the fifth is not. The fifth proof asserts that the intellect does not act of itself but by the aid of the will. The sixth proof asserts that the exercise of the intellect is itself dependent upon the will, and at the same time affirms that it is the intellect which moves the will to function by providing it with an object. The two statements are obviously in conflict. If the will cannot act until the intellect has provided it with an object, and the intellect cannot function until the will has acted, no mental processes will be possible at all.

7. The free is that which is *causa sui*; accordingly it is that which exists *per se*.[1] Consequently the initial freedom in action rests in the will, since whoever acts voluntarily is said to act freely. And so the primal agent, who acts *per se*, must act voluntarily.

8. Agent and end belong always to the same order of being, hence the proximate end, which is proportionate to the agent, falls in the same species as the agent. Nothing, however, is of the same grade of being as God. He is therefore both agent and end, both *appetens* and *finis appetibilis*. And since God is intelligent his striving must be intellectual, which is to say that it is will.[2]

The frequency with which St. Thomas, in stating the above arguments, refers to activity in connection with the divine will, leads us naturally to question his right to do so. Is not God the unmoved mover, and does not activity imply motion and change? St. Thomas has himself foreseen the inevitability of this query, and has replied to it in anticipation.[3] The divine will is, indeed, moved by the divine goodness as its final cause; yet, since God's will and goodness are identical with his essence, it is true to say that the essence moves itself. But the term motion, when used in this connection, can signify only intellection and volition. And this was what Plato meant when he said that the prime mover moves itself.

It will be recalled that, in his presentation of the argument from motion, Aquinas endeavoured to reconcile the teaching

---

[1] "*Liberum est quod sui causa est*: et sic liberum habet rationem eius quod est per se" (*Con. Gen.* lib. I. cap. 72).   [2] *Con. Gen.* lib. I. cap. 72.
[3] *Sum. Theol.* I.a. q. 19: a. 1. ad 3[m]; 1 *Dist.* 45. q. 1: a. 1. ad 3[m]; *De Verit.* q. 23: a. 1. ad 7[m].

of Plato with that of Aristotle by asserting that the latter, in
calling God the unmoved mover, had reference to local motion,
whereas Plato applied the term motion to mental activity.[1]
We have, however, already seen reason to hold, in company
with certain Neoscholastics, that Aquinas's own use of the term
clearly shows that, at least at certain stages of his thought, he
regarded the argument from motion as resting upon the fact
of change as such, irrespective of the occurrence of local
motion. The contradiction therefore remains. Nor is it removed
by St. Thomas's statement that motion cannot, strictly speaking,
be predicated of God, since "whatever is moved is other than
its mover."[2] For this last assertion is not a definition of
motion, but merely a statement in regard to its nature, which
the instance of divine motion would merely disprove.

Yet there is a genuine distinction between divine and human
activity, even if we take the term motion in the widest sense.
For the activity of God is conceived of as ceaseless, unvarying,
unwaxing, having neither origin nor end external to itself.
Moreover, whether consistently or not, Aquinas asserts it to be
timeless. In all these respects it differs from the activity of any
creature. Possibly, then, it was this distinction which St. Thomas
had in mind. For a timeless and changeless act, whatever it
may be, is certainly very different from any sort of activity,
physical or mental, which is ever encountered in human
experience.[3]

Aquinas's discussion of the character of the divine will
conforms, in its main outlines, to that already accorded to the
divine knowledge. Our examination will likewise resemble our
treatment of the former topic; we shall follow his various steps,
note the types of argument employed, and concentrate our
attention upon what seem to be the most crucial points.

---

[1] Cf. *Con. Gen.* lib. I. cap. 13.   [2] I *Dist.* 45. q. 1: a. 1. ad 3^m.
[3] In support of this suggestion I may quote Aquinas's reply to the above
question contained in the *De Veritate* (loc. cit.). "Dicendum quod quando
volitum est aliud a voluntate, volitum movet voluntatem realiter: sed
quando volitum est idem voluntati, tunc non movet nisi secundum modum
significandi: et quantum ad hunc modum loquendi, secundum Com-
mentatorem, in viii *Phys.*, com. lx, verificatur dictum Platonis, qui
dicebat quod primum movens movet se ipsum. Nec tamen quia vult
creaturas, sequitur quod a creaturis movetur; quia creaturis non vult
nisi ratione suae bonitatis."

L*

In the first place, St. Thomas affirms that God's will is identical with his essence. So evident, indeed, in the light of the previous discussion, is this identity that in the *Summa Theologica*[1] he is actually content to state it as a corollary. In the *Contra Gentiles*, however, he follows his usual practice of justifying every step, no matter how unmistakably obvious, with a numerous array of arguments.[2]

It is, of course, clear from what has been said that it is through his intelligence that God possesses will. Accordingly, inasmuch as his intelligence is identical with his essence, his will must be identical with that essence also. Moreover, the first of the arguments used to demonstrate the identity of the divine intelligence and the divine essence is also applicable in the case of the divine volition. Even as knowing is the perfection of an intelligent being, so willing is the perfection of a being endowed with will. But knowing and willing are both actions existing in an agent and not passing thence into the object known or willed, as heat passes into the object heated. Since, however, the divine essence in its perfection will admit of no addition, it follows that both knowledge and will are identical with it. Again, the activity of any agent is proportionate to its actuality. Hence God, who is pure actuality, must act by his essence. Consequently, his essence is one with his will. And, lastly, if the divine will be related to the divine essence as accident to subject, it would, *ipso facto*, stand to it as actuality to potentiality; whence it would follow that there is composition in God. But in God there is neither composition nor potentiality.[3]

In the *Compendium Theologiae*[4] two additional proofs are given. The will, it is pointed out, is moved by the *bonum intellectum*. But in God mover and moved are one. Accordingly the divine will is identical with the *intellectum*, and therefore with the divine essence. Furthermore, both intellect and will rank as the highest perfections of created things. And we know that the divine essence contains "in a higher mode" all the perfections of the creatures, no longer distinct but fused into a simple unity. Hence in God will and intellect are one with essence.

[1] I.a. q. 18: a. 1. c., ad 2^m.   [2] *Con. Gen.* lib. I. cap. 73.
[3] *Con. Gen.* lib. I. cap. 73.   [4] Pars Prima, cap. xxxii.

It may now be asked, what is the principal object of the divine will? The answer is, the divine essence. The truth of this proposition is proved by five arguments.[1]

1. The object of every will is always the *bonum intellectum*. But, as we have seen, the primal object of God's knowledge is his essence. The essence is therefore the primal object of God's will.

2. The object of the will is the source of its motion. Hence, if the essence be not the principal object of God's will, there must exist something superior (*superius*) to it, which is impossible.

3. The object of the will is the cause of its activity. If, then, God were principally to will anything other than his essence, that other thing would be the cause of God's act of willing. But the divine volition is identical with the divine existence. The supposition is therefore absurd.

4. What is willed as a means is willed with reference to an ultimate end. But God himself is the ultimate end, inasmuch as he is the *summum bonum*. Hence God must will himself.

5. Every capacity is proportionate to its principal object in the matter of equality.[2] But nothing is equal to the divine will except the divine essence. The essence is therefore the principal object of God's will.[3]

Even as God has, in the knowledge of his own essence, a knowledge of all things, so, in willing his own essence, God likewise wills all things. For, since he is both the efficient and the final cause of all beings, in willing himself God wills all

---

[1] *Con. Gen.* lib. I. cap. 74.

[2] "Unaquaeque virtus ad suum objectum principale secundum aequalitatem proportionatur" (cf. *De Caelo et Mundo*, lib. I. cap. xi. lect. 25).

[3] If the second, third, and fifth arguments be compared, it will be observed that, while the third and the fifth are genuinely distinct, the second appears to be a muddle of the other two. Sylvester insists that it must not be confused with the third, inasmuch as the latter is founded on the notion of cause and effect, whereas the former is based upon "a comparison of object to faculty" (in illa comparabatur obiectum ad potentiam). So, indeed, the use of the word *superius* would suggest. Nevertheless this is the theme of the fifth argument. Where then is the distinction between it and the second? If, however, we try to find another meaning in the second, we must take in earnest the relation between mover and moved. But this is only a particular instance of causal connection. How then are we to avoid identifying the second proof with the third?

created things both as his effects and also as directed toward himself as their ultimate end.[1]

Furthermore, God loves himself, as in due course is to be proved. All of us, however, desire the perfection of that which we love; in other words, we wish it to be improved and multiplied. But the divine essence cannot be improved and multiplied in itself. Yet its perfection can be imitated by the creatures in manifold ways; hence their existence is willed by the Deity.[2] Moreover, anyone who loves something for itself loves all things in which it is found. Consequently, since God wills and loves his being for itself, and since everything that exists is a participation in his being through likeness (*est quaedam sui esse secundum similitudinem participatio*), God loves and wills all things that exist.[3] Again, the more powerful a thing

[1] *Con. Gen.* lib. I. cap. 75; cf. 1 *Dist.* 45. q. 1: a. 2. sol. By pointing out that God is both the efficient and the ultimate cause, Aquinas lays the foundations of two distinct arguments. Not content with this, however, he advances an additional proof, which professes to be based upon the act of divine knowledge. "Will follows upon intellect. But God, by his intellect, knows himself first of all, and in himself he knows all other things. Accordingly he likewise wills himself first of all, and in willing himself wills all other things." ("Voluntas consequitur intellectum. Sed Deus intellectu suo intelligit se principaliter et in se intelligit alia. Igitur similiter principaliter vult se, et, volendo se, vult omnia alia.") It is clear that this proof embraces in itself the other two arguments. Since willing is subsequent to knowing, God cannot will himself as the efficient cause and the ultimate end of all things, without first knowing himself to be such. Aquinas has first emphasized the distinction between final and efficient causes in order to found upon it two separate arguments, and then blurred the distinction to obtain thereby a third argument.

[2] *Con. Gen.* lib. I. cap. 75; cf. 1 *Dist.* 45. q. 1: a. 2. sol.; *Sum. Theol.* I.a. q. 19: a. 2. c. Sylvester remarks that from the conclusion of this argument one might draw the inference that God wills the creation of as many creatures as possible. Nevertheless he insists that such an inference would be mistaken, and that the Deity does not desire quantity, but rather that his essence be imitated by precisely the number of creatures and in precisely the number of modes prescribed by the divine wisdom. Sylvester also points out the danger of the argument being interpreted in a pantheistic sense, as though the existence of the creatures were necessary to God's perfection. We must distinguish, he contends, between intrinsic and extrinsic perfection. In himself, intrinsically, God is perfect. The imitation of his essence by the creatures, however, constitutes God's extrinsic perfection. It is the nature of goodness to impart itself; and therefore such impartation is especially characteristic of God, the supreme good.

[3] *Con. Gen.* lib. I. cap. 75.

is, the greater is the range of its causal activity. When the cause in question is a final cause, this means that the more perfect it is and the more it is willed, the greater is the number of things which the willer wills for its sake. But the divine essence is perfect, and is the final cause of all things. In willing it, therefore, God also wills all the creatures.

Since God knows both his essence and all other entities by a single act of knowledge, it follows that he wills his essence and all other entities by a single act of will. Moreover, God's act of will is identical with his being, and the divine being is one and simple; hence there can be in God but one act of will.[1]

The conclusion thus so easily reached can likewise be approached by more circuitous paths. Every power or capacity arrives by a single operation or act at its object, and also at the *ratio formalis* of that object. Thus by one act of vision we see both light and colour. But when we will something merely as a means to an ulterior end, the thing willed acquires the *ratio formalis* of the end.[2] In such a case the end will stand to the thing willed as *ratio formalis* to object, or as light to colour. Accordingly, since God wills all things because of himself inasmuch as he is their ultimate end, he must will himself and all other entities by one act of will.[3]

Furthermore, it had already been shown that the divine knowledge is not discursive. But as the premises are related to the conclusions in processes of ratiocination, so the end stands to the means in affairs of operation and striving. Consequently, were the Deity to will end and means by successive acts of will, he would be involved in motion. Nor is it possible that the two acts should be simultaneous, for there cannot at one time be two operations of a single power or capacity. Moreover, were God to will the means—i.e. created things—by an act of will distinct from that whereby he wills his essence, it would follow that in this act he is moved by something external to himself, which has been shown to be impossible.[4]

---

[1] *Con. Gen.* lib. I. cap. 76.
[2] To use the example given by Sylvester, we may desire a sweet medicine, not because it is sweet but because it is health-giving, and the end which we have in view is health.
[3] *Con. Gen.* lib. I. cap. 76.   [4] *Con. Gen.* lib. I. cap. 76.

It is clear, then, that the will of God is unchangeable.[1] None the less, it is permissible to speak of an antecedent and consequent in connection therewith, not as implying temporal succession in the Deity, which would be incompatible with his eternity, but as indicating dissimilar relations to the things willed.[2]

In elucidating this statement Aquinas insists in quite modern fashion upon the necessity, in inquiring into the character of any event, of taking into account, not only the nature of the agent, but also that of the patient or, as he terms it, that of the recipient. For the agent is limited, in the exercise of his activity, by the capacity of the material with which he works. "Accordingly the end, as it is in itself, to which God ordained the creature is said to be willed by him, as of first intention, or by antecedent volition; but when the creature, through his own defect, falls short of this end, God nevertheless causes him to realize the degree of goodness of which he is capable, and this is by his second intention and is called consequent volition. Thus, since God made all men for the sake of beatitude, God is said to will the salvation of all by antecedent volition; but because some are opposed to his salvation, whom the decree of his wisdom does not permit to attain salvation because of their defect, he fulfils in them in another mode that which pertains to his goodness, by condemning them for the sake of his justice; and so while they are found wanting in the first grade of will, they fall under the second; and while they do not carry out the will of God, God's will is fulfilled in them. The defect of sin, in virtue of which anyone is rendered worthy of punishment in the present or in the future, is not itself willed by God, either antecedently or consequently; but is merely permitted by him."[3]

---

[1] Cf. *Sum. Theol.* I.a. q. 19: a. 7. c.; *Com. Theol.* Pars Prima, cap. xcvi.

[2] "Dicendum quod in voluntate Dei non ponuntur antecedens et consequens ad importandum ordinem successionis, qui repugnat aeternitati; sed ad denotandum diversam comparationem eius ad volita" (*De Verit.* q. 23: a. 2. ad 8m).

[3] "Illud ergo ad quod Deus creaturam ordinavit quantum est de se, dicitur esse volitum ab eo quasi prima intentione, sive voluntate antecedente; sed quando creatura impeditur propter sui defectum ab hoc fine, nihilominus tamen Deus implet in ea id bonitatis cuius est capax; et hoc est quasi de secunda intentione eius, et dicitur voluntas consequens. Quia

It is further clear that, according to St. Thomas, the multiplicity of things willed is not inconsistent with the divine simplicity. For, in the first place, they are all willed by a single act of the divine volition, as has just been shown. And, in the second place, the object of the divine will is the divine goodness, in which all created things are contained, *materialia immaterialiter et multa unite*.[1] In the third place, the divine intellect and the divine will are of equal simplicity, since each is identical with the divine essence. Consequently, since the knowing of the multitude of created entities does not taint the simplicity of the divine essence, neither does the willing of them. And, lastly, there is this difference between knowledge and appetite, that in the case of the former the thing known must in some mode be in the knower, whereas with the latter the situation is reversed, for the appetite seeks an external object, and, having attained it, rests therein. Hence it is no more inconsistent with the divine simplicity that the Deity should will the multitude of creatures than it is inconsistent with unity that it should be the principle of the multiplicity of numbers.[2]

In my criticism of St. Thomas's treatment of the problem of divine knowledge I have noticed certain objections which appeared to be fatal to his theory, and which it is needless to restate here. It suffices to point out that if it be true, as he has affirmed, that the exercise of the will follows upon that of the intellect,[3] these objections will be equally fatal to his teaching with respect to the divine volition. We cannot, however, disregard the view outlined in the previous paragraph regarding the dissimilar relations which obtain between knowledge and

ergo Deus omnes homines propter beatitudinem fecit, dicitur voluntate antecedente omnium salutem velle: sed quia quidam suae saluti adversantur, quos ordo suae sapientiae ad salutem venire non patitur propter eorum defectum, implet in eis alio modo id quod ad suam bonitatem pertinet, scilicet eos per iustitiam damnans; ut sic dum a primo ordine voluntatis deficiunt, in secundum labantur; et dum Dei voluntatem non faciunt, impleatur in eis voluntas Dei. Ipse autem defectus peccati, quo aliquis redditur dignus poena in presenti vel in futuro, non est volitus a Deo neque voluntate antedente neque consequente; sed est ab eo solummodo permissus" (*De Verit*. q. 23 : a. 2. c.).

[1] It will be recalled that the divine goodness is identical with the divine being, from the simple unity of which all things proceed.

[2] *Con. Gen*. lib. I. cap. 77.

[3] "Voluntas consequitur intellectum" (*Con. Gen*. lib. I. cap. 75).

appetite, on the one hand, and their respective objects on the other. It would seem that Aquinas is here maintaining that, even if his theory in the matter of the divine cognition be erroneous, yet his doctrine concerning the divine volition is capable of standing by itself. If this be, in truth, his contention, it is inadmissible upon two counts. In the first place, it is obviously impossible that appetite or will should be directed upon a definite object, or group of objects, unless that object, or group of objects, has already been distinguished by the cognizing mind; hence, if the very act of cognition implies the entry of multiplicity into the divine essence, the simplicity thereof will be destroyed before the act of volition can occur; and, secondly, it must be remembered that one of the principal difficulties which we encountered in St. Thomas's teaching with regard to the divine knowledge is the fact that he insists upon the proposition that the divine simplicity is imitated by creatures in a plurality of modes. This difficulty is equally acute in the case of the divine volition. Even if his claim that the willing of a plurality of objects does not involve the presence of plurality in the willing subject be granted, the obstacle remains. How, we are compelled to ask, can utterly un-differentiated unity, how can absolute simplicity, devoid alike of accidents and of essential qualities, be imitated in any mode whatsoever, let alone in a plurality of modes? Yet, unless such imitation be possible, the universe cannot exist, and so can neither be known nor willed. As this point has been already discussed at length in an earlier connection,[1] I need not dwell upon it further, but may at once proceed to scrutinize St. Thomas's attempt to demonstrate that the will of God extends to particular goods.

The proposition that the simplicity of the willing subject is compatible with the plurality of the objects willed, upon the truth of which Aquinas has just insisted, serves as the basis of his various proofs. From this it follows that God may be compared to particulars; and so we may say that God is the best and the first. But if God can be compared to particulars, God can also will them. Moreover, the divine will can be compared to finite entities in so far as they participate in the divine goodness. But all finite entities participate in the

---

[1] Pp. 297–300.

divine goodness inasmuch as they exist, for existence is a good. Accordingly the divine will extends to particular goods.[1]

It is difficult to understand how any "comparison" between the Deity and his creatures can hold good unless God is as truly related to the world as the world is to God; yet this, it is clear, was not Aquinas's contention. I shall return to this point. I am concerned now with a brief argument which states in adequate and clear phraseology what appears to be the obvious line of reasoning to follow. "The good, when known as such, is always willed. But God knows particular goods, as has been proved; therefore he also wills particular goods."[2]

Another argument appears to have been suggested to Aquinas by Aristotle's observation that the nature of the whole contains the good both as something separate and by itself, and also as abiding in the order of the parts.[3] The separate good is, of course, the prime mover, who exists *extra universum*, with respect to whom the universe is ordered much as an army is ordered with respect to its commander. There is also, however, the order in which the various parts of the universe stand to one another, which resembles that obtaining between the different units of an army. But this second order exists only for the sake of the first. Nevertheless, since God wills the first, he must will the second, which is needful to the first. But the goodness of this second order has its origin in particular goods. Accordingly these also must be willed by God.[4]

In conclusion, Aquinas contends that the harmonious arrangement of particular goods cannot be due to any one part of the universe; therefore, since order exists, its source must be found in the will of God.[5]

The question must now be raised as to whether God wills those things which do not exist as yet. St. Thomas concedes that there are several considerations which could be advanced in support of the view that he does not. Thus it might be urged that entities which are relative to one another can only exist

[1] *Con. Gen.* lib. I. cap. 78.
[2] "Bonum intellectum, inquantum huismodi, est volitum. Sed Deus intelligit etiam particularia bona, ut supra probatum est. Vult igitur etiam particularia bona."
[3] *Metaph.* lib. XII. cap. x. lect. 9.
[4] *Con. Gen.* lib. I. cap. 78.   [5] *Con. Gen.* lib. I. cap. 78.

simultaneously, and therefore that the act of will, involving as it does a comparison of the willer to the object willed, cannot occur when that object is non-existent. Again, the will stands to its objects in the relation of cause and creator; if, then, God cannot be called the creator of non-existent things, can he be said to will them? And, thirdly, it might be maintained that, inasmuch as the divine will is changeless, God can will only those things which exist always.

Nor does it avail to assert that entities which do not exist as yet are willed by the Deity as existing in the divine intellect. For a thing exists in the mode in which it is willed to exist, or, in the language of Aquinas, as the will is referred to it.[1] Accordingly, if God will anything to exist in his intellect, it will exist there and not *in rerum natura*. Moreover, the formal object of the will is the *bonum intellectum*. It is by means of this *bonum intellectum* that the will is "compared" to the material object, and it is in the identity of the two that it finds its satisfaction. But the will is "compared" to the *bonum intellectum* not merely as it exists in the knower but as it exists in itself.[2] Hence the suggested solution must be rejected.

Aquinas's statement of his own view is so complicated by his epistemology that it seems best to give it in his own words. "We say therefore that, since the apprehended good moves the will, it is necessary that the act of willing should follow the condition of apprehension, even as the motions of all other movable things follow the conditions of the mover which is the cause of that motion. Moreover, the relation of the apprehending subject to the object apprehended follows upon the act of apprehension itself: for the apprehending mind is referred to the thing apprehended by the fact that it apprehends it. But the apprehending subject does not apprehend the thing only as it is in the mind, but also as it is in its proper nature; for not only are we aware that something is known by us, which constitutes its being in the intellect, but we know that it is or was or will be in its proper nature. Hence, although that thing does not now exist except in the knower, yet the relation following upon the act of apprehension has reference

---

[1] "Nam secundum hoc dicitur quilibet volens aliquid velle, quod voluntas sua refertur ad volitum" (*Con. Gen.* lib. I. cap. 79).

[2] Cf. the *Comment.* of Francis Sylvester.

to it not as it is in the knower, but as it exists according to its own nature which the apprehending subject apprehends."[1]

What is this relation which is said to follow upon the act of apprehension? Is it one of cognition? How, then, does cognition differ from apprehension? Or are we to think of a *relation* of apprehension as following from and established by an *act* of apprehension? Or, again, can we take the act of apprehension as equivalent to the stimulation of the sense organs, and the ensuing relation as that of a direct awareness of an external object? The language of St. Thomas vaguely suggests a process of "projection," to use the phraseology of certain contemporary philosophers. However this may be, the external reality somehow becomes the object of knowledge, and the will in turn is focussed upon it. "The relation of the divine will is therefore to a thing as yet non-existent, as it is in its proper nature and with respect to a certain time, not merely as it is in the divine knowledge. God wills that a thing which is now non-existent shall exist at a certain time: he does not merely will to know it."[2] None the less, "the relation of willer to thing willed is not like that of creator to creature, or of maker to thing made, nor yet of Lord to subject creature. For willing is an activity immanent in the willer, hence it does not require us to conceive that something exists externally. But *to make* or *to create* or *to*

---

[1] "Dicamus igitur quod, cum bonum apprehensum moveat voluntatem, oportet quod ipsum velle sequatur conditionem apprehensionis: sicut et motus aliorum mobilium sequuntur conditiones moventis quod est causa motus. Relatio autem apprehendentis ad apprehensum est consequens ad apprehensionem ipsam: per hoc enim refertur apprehendens ad apprehensum quod apprehendit ipsum. Non autem solum apprehendens apprehendit rem secundum quod est in ipso, sed secundum quod est in propria natura: quia non solum cognoscimus rem intelligi a nobis, quod est eam esse in intellectu, sed eam esse vel fuisse vel futuram esse in propria natura. Licet igitur tunc res illa non sit nisi in cognoscente, relatio tamen consequens apprehensionem est ad eam non prout est in cognoscente, sed prout est secondum propriam naturam, quam apprehendit apprehendens" (*Con. Gen.* lib. I. cap. 79).

[2] "Voluntatis igitur divinae relatio est ad rem non existentem secundum quod est in propria natura secundum aliquod tempus, et non solum secundum quod est in Deo cognoscente. Vult igitur Deus rem quae non est nunc, esse secundum aliquod tempus: et non solum vult quod ipse eam intelligit" (*Con. Gen.* lib. I. cap. 79).

govern are expressions that signify an activity terminating in an external effect, without the existence of which such activity is inconceivable."[1]

Although the wording of these passages is somewhat confused, so that it seems to imply that the will both requires and does not require the existence of an external object, the underlying thought appears to be self-consistent. The relation of creator to creature, or that of cause to effect, can hold only between two simultaneously existing terms. The will can, however, be directed upon an object which does not exist as yet and is not willed to exist as yet. If that object be continuously willed to exist at a particular time, its coming into existence does not involve any change in the willing subject. Eternally known, the object is also eternally willed, and thus the divine nature remains immutable.

It may, however, well be asked what St. Thomas meant by his assertion that the act of will involves a comparison of the willer to the thing willed.[2] What is the precise significance of *comparatio*? Clearly, it is intended to connote a relation of some sort existing between subject and object. In the case of God, however, this can be only a "rational" relation. "A real relation," writes Sylvester, "requires a real and existent ground; it is therefore impossible that real relations should have being apart from actual entities which are relative to one another and which serve as grounds for these relations. A rational relation, on the other hand, does not require a real ground existing in the realm of nature, but it suffices if it exist in the apprehending mind."[3] Since all points in time are equally present to the divine knowledge, and events which to

---

[1] "Neo est simile de relatione volentis ad volitum, et creantis ad creatum, et facientis ad factum aut Domini ad subiectam creaturam. Nam velle est actio in volente manens: unde non cogit intelligi aliquid extra existens. Sed facere et creare et gubernare significant actionem terminatam ad exteriorem effectum, sine cuius existentia huiusmodi actio non potest intelligi" (*Con. Gen.* lib. I. cap. 79).

[2] "Velle est per comparationem volentis ad volitum" (*Con. Gen.* lib. I. cap. 79).

[3] "Relatio realis exigit fundamentum reale et existens: ideo non possunt simul esse relationes reales quin etiam sint in actu res relativae et fundamenta relationum. Relatio autem rationis non exigit fundamentum reale et in natura existens, sed sufficit quod sit in apprehensione."

us are future are perceived by God with the same immediacy as those that are present, it is obvious that these same future events can as easily be willed by God as known by him. As to the distinction between "real" and "rational" relations, we need not concern ourselves at this juncture. We shall have occasion to examine it at length hereafter.

Since the divine volition is identical with the divine being which is wholly actual and eternally active, it cannot cease to function. Does it, however, choose its objects freely or of necessity? We have seen that its principal object is the divine essence, for the sake of which all other things are willed. Clearly, then, the essence itself is willed of necessity.[1]

This conclusion Aquinas attempted to reinforce by the following argument: Whoever wills of necessity wills his own ultimate end. Thus man of necessity wills his own happiness. But God wills himself as his own ultimate end; God therefore wills himself of necessity.[2]

This proof is obviously defective, inasmuch as it does not demonstrate the impossibility of the ultimate end being freely willed. The third proof, however, makes good this deficiency. The mind, Aquinas holds, can no more refrain from willing its ultimate end than it can refuse to assent to the self-evident principles of logical demonstration. Accordingly, since God is his own ultimate end, he cannot do otherwise than will his own being and goodness.[3] This argument is thoroughly consistent with the principles of Thomist psychology, but it is also obviously identical in substance with the first proof.

Two more arguments were advanced by St. Thomas in support of this same conclusion. The first of these is based upon the likeness which, according to the doctrine of degrees of being, all things bear to God in so far as they exist (*inquantum sunt*). All things, we are told, in so far as they exist, naturally love their own being. In a far greater degree, therefore, does God love his own being; and, loving it, necessarily will it.[4] The last argument is based upon the closely related doctrine that every perfection of the creature belongs to God essentially.

[1] *Con. Gen.* lib. I. cap. 80; cf. *De Verit.* q. 23: a. 4. c.
[2] *Con. Gen.* lib. I. cap. 80.
[3] *Con. Gen.* lib. I. cap. 80.; cf. *De Verit.* q. 23: a. 4. c.
[4] *Con. Gen.* lib. I. cap. 80.

Since the highest perfection of the rational creature is to love God, God must love himself, and so must will himself.[1]

The statement that God wills himself must not, of course, be interpreted to mean that God brings himself into existence by an act of his will. No such absurdity is intended. We should probably not be far wrong if we understood *will*, as used in this connection, in the sense of *acquiescence*. But it must not be forgotten that the doctrine of analogy forbids us to attribute will, or any other quality, to God and man in a univocal sense.

It might well seem that the divine volition must be subject to necessity, not only in willing the divine essence, but also in willing finite entities. It might be contended that, were the divine will undetermined, it would be indifferent (*ad utrumlibet*) with respect to two or more possible existents, and so would be in potentiality, which is impossible. Moreover, being in potentiality, it would be susceptible to change, which is also impossible. Again, if the divine will be indifferent with respect to two or more possibilities, its choice can be determined only by something external to itself. But this something would thus be prior to God, which supposition is absurd. Furthermore, if it be natural to God to direct his will upon finite entities, it must be necessary; and it has been shown that in God there is nothing unnatural.

To these four arguments Aquinas replied as follows. The divine will is indifferent in regard to two or more possible existents, not because it is in potentiality with respect to them, but because it transcends their limitations, inasmuch as none of them is necessary to it, whereas the existence of any one of them is compatible with its activity.[2]

Being ever wholly actual, it can never pass from potentiality to actuality, hence it never becomes involved in change and time.[3] Nor is its choice determined by anything external to itself, since it is the divine intellect that provides it with an end to be willed, and in the Deity, as we are aware, intellect and will are not really distinct from one another. Moreover, the finite entities which are willed are perceived by the divine intellect as likenesses of the divine goodness, not as its principles,

---

[1] *Con. Gen.* lib. I. cap. 80.
[2] *Con. Gen.* lib. I. cap. 82.   [3] *Con. Gen.* lib. I. cap. 82.

and hence as compatible with it, but not as necessary to it.[1] Accordingly, while the divine essence is the necessary and natural object of the divine volition, finite entities are willed neither necessarily nor naturally, not yet violently nor unnaturally, but voluntarily.[2]

Means are necessary to an end only when that end is unattainable without them. Often, however, this is not the case. Thus a horse is not necessary for a journey which we can make on foot. Now the divine essence is perfect and self-sufficing. Hence whatever is willed with the divine essence as an end is not necessary, but is willed freely.[3] Furthermore, although the existence of anything is as such a good, yet its non-existence can be willed in order to secure the existence of a greater good. Consequently there is only one entity which cannot be willed not to exist, and that is the divine essence itself. If it were true that the creatures proceeded from God of necessity, then indeed they would necessarily be willed by him. But this opinion is erroneous. On the contrary, the creatures are related to God as artifacts to their maker. And, since the infinity of the divine goodness is imitable in an infinite number of modes, were it the case that the Deity could not will his goodness without also willing all things capable of participating in it, the number of the creatures would be infinite. We know, however, that such is not the case. Accordingly the finite number of the creatures testifies to the freedom of their creator.[4]

It may appear at first glance that this argument is invalidated by the fact that, as we have seen, Aquinas maintained—at least at a certain stage in the development of his thought— that the actual existence of a quantitative infinite is impossible. From this it might be argued that the non-existence of such an infinite is no evidence of the freedom of the Creator. But it must not be forgotten that St. Thomas saw no contradiction in the potential existence of a quantitative infinite in the form of an unending creative process. It is only by revelation that we know that this process will in fact cease at the end of a

---

[1] "Ut suae bonitati convenientia, non ut ad suam bonitatem necessaria" (*Con. Gen.* lib. I. cap. 82).
[2] *Con. Gen.* lib. I. cap. 82; cf. *Sum. Theol.* I.a. q. 19: a. 3. ad 3m.
[3] *Con. Gen.* lib. I. cap. 81; cf. *Sum. Theol.* I.a. q. 19: a. 3. c.; *De Verit.* q. 23: a. 4. c.; *Com. Theol.* Pars Prima, cap. xcv.   [4] *Con. Gen.* lib. I. cap. 81.

finite period. Nevertheless, since we have this knowledge, we may legitimately reason from it to the freedom of the creator who has limited that process by an arbitrary act of will.

In the *Compendium Theologiae*[1] the problem is presented in a slightly different guise. There the contrast is not between free and necessitated volition, but between will on the one hand and external necessity on the other. An intelligent and willing agent, St. Thomas maintains, is logically and ontologically prior to a "natural"—i.e. an inanimate—agent. Moreover, a natural agent, inasmuch as it possesses but a single form, is capable of producing immediately but one type of effect, whereas the intellect, being receptive of a multitude of forms, is capable of producing immediately a variety of effects. The diversified character of the effects of the divine activity bears witness, therefore, that they are the offspring of will, not of necessity.[2]

To admit that God is constrained by necessity to will the universe would be for Aquinas a fatal concession, for it would open the door to the entry of pantheism; hence his insistence upon the self-sufficiency of the divine nature. This very insistence involves him, however, in one of the age-old difficulties which have always beset the advocates of extreme transcendence. If the universe contributes nothing to the divine perfection, for what conceivable purpose can the Deity be supposed to will its existence? It is not even a means to an end; it fulfils no function; it is merely the product of an inexplicable display of divine activity. To say, as St. Thomas said, that God's love of his own perfection leads him to will that it be imitated by the creatures in a plurality of modes, involves the implicit admission that the universe contributes something to the divine perfection after all. Whatever motive be attributed to the Deity, bounty, a desire to communicate his goodness to other beings, etc., the logical outcome is the same. The universe must serve some purpose, it must fill some need in the divine nature. It cannot be said that Aquinas has discovered any way of avoiding this unpalatable but unescapable conclusion.

We must now take cognizance of the distinction drawn by our author between "absolute necessity" and "necessity of supposition." "A proposition is judged to be absolutely neces-

[1] Pars Prima, cap. xcv.   [2] Cf. *De Verit.* q. 23: a. 4. c.

sary from the relation of its terms, either because the predicate is included in the definition of the subject, as, for instance, it is necessary that a man should be an animal; or because the subject is included in the concept of the predicate, and thus it is necessary for any number to be either equal or unequal. So it is not necessary for Socrates to be seated; that is it is not necessary absolutely, but it can be said to be necessary from supposition; for, on the supposition that he sits, it is necessary for him to sit while he sits."[1]

This notion, with which we have already been made familiar in Aquinas's discussion of the possibility of divine knowledge of future contingent particulars, is practically equivalent to what we are accustomed to call the law of non-contradiction. Since the divine volition is unchanging and eternal, it is impossible that God should not will what he wills, or should will what he does not will; nor can God will now what he has not willed in the past, nor yet cease to will that which he has willed.[2] Moreover, the will of God cannot fail through ignorance or defect. Informed by perfect knowledge, it extends to all the essential characteristics of its object. Thus if God will the existence of a man, he also wills perforce the existence of a rational soul.[3] And it is impossible that God should will anything incompatible with these characteristics. He cannot, for example, will that a man should be an ass, for this would involve that a rational soul should be also irrational. Thus he cannot will anything self-contradictory, for the self-contradictory is incompatible with the conception of being, and whatever is willed by God, is willed as imitating in some mode the divine essence, which is pure being. Moreover, the object willed must first be apprehended as good by the intellect, but that which is inherently impossible and self-contradictory is unacceptable to the intellect in so far as it is free from error. Also the impos-

---

[1] "Necessarium absolute iudicatur aliquid ex habitudine terminorum: utpote quia praedicatum est in definitione subiecti, sicut necessarium est hominem esse animal; vel quia subiectum est de ratione praedicati, sicut hoc est necessarium, numerum esse parem vel imparem. Sic autem non est necessarium Socratem sedere. Unde non est necessarium absolute, sed potest dici necessarium ex suppositione: supposito enim quod sedeat, necesse est eum sedere dum sedet" (*Sum. Theol.* I.a. q. 19: a. 3. c.; cf. *Con. Gen.* lib. I. cap. 83; *De Verit.* q. 23: a. 4. ad 1ᵐ).

[2] *Con. Gen.* lib. I. cap. 83.   [3] *Con. Gen.* lib. I. cap. 83.

sible cannot exist, and what cannot exist is not good, since being and goodness are identical. And God can will only what is good. For all these reasons, therefore, God cannot will that which is inherently impossible.[1]

St. Thomas was also emphatic in his assertion that the activity of the divine will is perfectly compatible with the presence of contingency in the universe. Even among created things the effect of a sufficiently powerful cause will resemble that cause not only as regards its species, but also accidentally. God is, however, the cause of all being, both substantial and accidental; consequently his effects not only exist, but they exist in that mode in which he wills them to exist. Accordingly, whatever God has willed to exist of necessity necessarily exists, and whatever he has willed to exist contingently exists contingently.[2]

Furthermore, the completeness of the universe requires the realization therein of all degrees of being, and hence the presence of both necessary and contingent beings. Or, to state the same contention in another form, it requires the existence of physical objects. But physical objects are subject to change, since they cause motion only when they themselves are moved. And from mutable causes only contingent effects can follow.[3] It is true that whatever God wills to exist, exists of necessity of supposition; but from necessity of supposition in the cause we cannot infer absolute necessity in the effect.[4]

Every created thing is, of course, contingent in comparison with God, in whom alone essence and existence are one; and it is upon this contingent character of all finite beings that the third argument for the divine existence is founded. Accordingly it would seem that in the present instance the terms *necessary* and *contingent* have been employed by Aquinas in a purely relative sense to indicate the relations of finite existents to one another. This conclusion appears to be confirmed by his assertion[5] that the statement, "God is able to predestinate one not predestinated, or not to predestinate one predestinated," if understood in a composite sense (*in sensu composita*) is false,

---

[1] *Con. Gen.* lib. I. cap. 84.
[2] *Con. Gen.* lib. I. cap. 85; *Sum. Theol.* I.a. q. 19: a. 8. c.; *De Verit.* q. 23: a. 5. c.
[3] *Con. Gen.* lib. I. cap. 85.
[4] *Con. Gen.* lib. I. cap. 85.
[5] *De Verit.* q. 6: a. 4. ad 8.

if in a divided sense (*in diviso*) true. In other words, there is
nothing in the nature of any particular man which is incompatible with his being predestinated either to heaven or hell,
but as a matter of fact each man is predestinated or repro-
bated by a changeless act of the divine will, and thus he is
predestinated, not of absolute necessity, but of necessity of
supposition.

The matter becomes more complicated, however, when we
reflect that the universe contains human wills which act as
secondary causes. Without entering into a discussion of Aquinas's
attitude toward the problem of free will—a topic which falls
outside the purpose of this essay—it may be said at once that
he professed to vindicate, within somewhat narrow limits
indeed, man's freedom of choice and action.[1] Yet how is such
freedom compatible with his present position? In the *De
Veritate*,[2] for instance, we are told that "although the non-
existence of an effect of the divine will is not compatible with
the divine will, yet the potential absence of the effect is compatible with the divine will."[3] That God should will a man to
be saved, and that the same man should be damned, are
two assumptions which, we are assured, are "incompossible";
but the assumption that God wills a man to be saved and the
assumption that it is possible for him to be damned are not
"incompossible."[4] At first sight these assertions appear to be
utterly self-contradictory.

They cease to be so, however, if we suppose that the freedom
which Aquinas is anxious to save is merely a temporal freedom,
a freedom which is relative to other finite substances, other
events, and other acts of volition. If this conjecture be correct,
the theory of St. Thomas is directly opposed to that of Kant.
Not noumenal freedom and phenomenal determinism, but
noumenal determinism and phenomenal freedom seem to be
implied by his words.[5] We may doubt whether he himself

---

[1] *Sum. Theol.* I.a.–II.ae. q. 10; *Con. Gen.* lib. III. cap. 72, and cc. 147–153;
cf. Garrigou-Lagrange, *Dieu, son existence et sa nature*, IIme Partie, ch. iv.

[2] q. 23: a. 5. ob. 3.

[3] "Quamvis non esse effectus divinae voluntatis non possit simul stare
cum divina voluntate; tamen potentia deficiendi effectum, simul stat cum
divina voluntate."

[4] *De Verit.* q. 23: a. 5. ob. 3.

[5] Cf. *Sum. Theol.* I.a.–II.ae. q. 10: a. 4. ad 3^{m}. "Si Deus movet volun-

would have assented to this interpretation, but it is difficult to see any way of escape from this conclusion that does not lead to the pitfall of self-contradiction.

In the *Summa Theologica*[1] we find St. Thomas taking pains to emphasize a point which, in the *Contra Gentiles*, he had passed over in silence. Some, he tells us, have contended that contingency is due to the interaction of secondary causes. It is not so much the assertion itself to which he objects—as we have just seen, he has made it himself in the *Contra Gentiles*— but to the unwarranted inferences which might be drawn from it. A secondary cause is rendered contingent through its own deficiency which impedes the activity of the primary cause. But the divine activity cannot be impeded, hence this explanation is insufficient in the case of God. Furthermore, if the distinction between necessity and contingency has reference only to secondary causes, it is something which has arisen apart from the intention of the Deity, which is inadmissible. Accordingly we must hold that contingent effects follow upon contingent causes, not merely because these causes are contingent, but because God has willed the contingent effects and has provided contingent causes for them.

From what has been said it follows that the divine will does not function arbitrarily, but that there is always a reason for its activity. The ultimate reason is, of course, the divine goodness. The chief subordinate reason is the good of the universe as a whole. And the willing of any particular good is a reason for willing whatever is necessary for the realization of that good. Thus "God wills that man shall have reason in order that man may exist; he wills the existence of man that the universe may be complete; and he wills the good of the universe because it is in keeping with his goodness."[2] "Thus the reason for the activity of the divine will is sometimes only seemliness, sometimes utility, sometimes even necessity of supposi-

tatem ad aliquid, incompossibile est huic positioni quod voluntas non moveatur. Non tamen est impossible simpliciter. Unde non sequitur quod voluntas a Deo ex necessitate moveatur."

[1] I.a. q. 19: a. 8. c.

[2] "Deus vult hominem habere rationem ad hoc quod homo sit; vult autem hominum esse ad hoc quod completio universi sit; vult autem bonum universi esse quia decet bonitatem ipsius" (*Con. Gen.* lib. I. cap. 86).

tion; but absolute necessity only when God wills himself."[1]

The point is an important one, for St. Thomas was anxious to refute those who held that God's will is purely arbitrary, and that it is useless to seek any reason for its dispositions. How strongly he felt on the subject becomes evident in the *De Veritate*,[2] where we find him opposing the view that "justice in created things depends simply upon the divine will." "To say that justice depends simply upon the will is," he writes, "to say that the divine will does not proceed according to the ordination of wisdom, which is blasphemy."[3] The divine will and the divine wisdom are, of course, identical, but since will is other than wisdom in us, and since the terms which we are forced to use in speaking of God are drawn from human experience, we can best express the truth by saying that "the will is directed by intellect and wisdom, not only in us, but in God."[4]

It is false, however, to say that there is any cause of the divine will. For the cause of any act of will is the end toward which it is directed, which in the case of God is the divine goodness; and, since God's goodness is identical with his essence and so with his act of will, it cannot be the cause of that act. Moreover, although one created thing may be the proximate end for which another created thing exists, yet the act of willing the latter is not caused by the act of willing the former, since all things are willed by a single divine act.[5] To the objection that, if the divine will, which is the cause of all things, be itself uncaused, it is vain to seek any scientific explanation of natural phenomena, Aquinas replied that science is concerned only with secondary causes, and that its activity will therefore be unaffected by the acceptance of this view.[6]

[1] "Aliquando igitur ratio divinae voluntatis continet solum decentiam; aliquando utilitatem; aliquando autem necessitatem quae est ex suppositione; necessitatem vero absolutam, solum cum vult seipsum" (*Con. Gen.* lib. I. cap. 86). [2] q. 23: a. 6.

[3] "Dicere autem quod ex simplici voluntate dependeat iustitia, est dicere quod divina voluntas non procedat secundum ordinem sapientiae, quod est blasphemum."

[4] "Voluntas . . . dirigitur enim per rationem et intellectum, non solum in nobis, sed in Deo" (*De Verit.* q. 23: a. 6).

[5] *Con. Gen.* lib. I. cap. 87; *Sum. Theol.* I.a. q. 19: a. 5. c.

[6] *Sum. Theol.* I.a. q. 19: a. 5. ob. 2. and ad 2[m]; 1 *Dist.* 45. q. 1: a. 3. ob. 5. and ad 5[m].

Since God does not necessarily will anything other than himself, the divine will is free.[1] This conclusion also follows from the theory that God's will functions under the direction of his intellect, and thus acts in accordance with reason and not in obedience to mere appetite. Moreover, Aristotle has affirmed[2] that the will is directed to the end, whereas choice is concerned with the means. According to this view, then, since God is the end and all created things are means, God's will must be directed entirely upon himself, while all finite beings will be the objects of his choice. But choice is always the offspring of free will. And, finally, we call a man free who is master of his actions; consequently God, the primal agent, is supremely free.[3]

In his discussion of the character of the divine knowledge, Aquinas insisted, as we have seen, that the creative activity of God proceeds from his intellect through the mediation of his will.[4] In the *Summa Theologica*,[5] further emphasis is laid upon the causal activity of the will, and the following arguments are advanced to prove it. In the first place, the existence of every natural cause involves that of a superior cause which is able to determine it to a definite end, and such a cause must be possessed of intellect and will. This is practically the contention of the teleological argument. Secondly, every natural agent, through the limitations of its nature, is productive of a definite effect. But God, in his perfection, is wholly undetermined; hence he cannot act through necessity of nature; the divine effects must therefore be produced through intelligence and will. Thirdly, effects proceeding from an agent pre-exist in that agent according to the mode and degree of being which that agent enjoys. Since God is an intelligent agent, his effects pre-exist in the divine intellect. Accordingly their procession from him must occur in an intellectual mode, and this can be only through the will which brings into actuality what the mind has conceived.[6]

In the *Summa Theologica*[7] it is asserted that although particular causes may fail to produce their effects because of the activity

---

[1] *Con. Gen.* lib. I. cap. 88; *Sum. Theol.* I.a. q. 19: a. 10. c.
[2] *Nic. Eth.* lib. III. cap. ii. lect. 5; cap. v. lect. 11.
[3] *Con. Gen.* lib. I. cap. 88.   [4] *De Verit.* q. 2: a. 14. c.
[5] I.a. q. 19: a. 4. c.   [6] Cf. 1 *Dist.* 45. q. 1: a. 3.   [7] I.a. q. 19: a. 6. c.

of other particular causes, yet it is impossible that the universal cause, within the sphere of whose activity all these particular causes fall, should likewise fail; and that therefore the divine will, which is the universal cause, must always be fulfilled. In the *Commentary on the Sentences*[1] and the *De Veritate*[2] the matter is discussed at greater length. As we have seen, a distinction is to be drawn between antecedent and consequent will in the Deity. That which God wills antecedently, he wills by *first intention* and *secundum quid*; that which he wills consequently, he wills by *second intention* or *simpliciter*. Thus antecedently God wills that all men be saved, but consequently he wills that the wicked be damned. Obviously then God's antecedent will is not necessarily fulfilled. St. Thomas was, of course, careful to insist that this distinction is based solely upon the character of the divine effects and is not to be taken as implying the presence of multiplicity in God.[3]

Returning now to the *Contra Gentiles*,[4] we find that at this point Aquinas has digressed into a lengthy discussion of

[1] 1 *Dist.* 47. q. 1 : a. 1.   [2] q. 23 : a. 2.

[3] "In voluntate divina nec ordo nec distinctio est ex parte actus voluntatis, sed solummodo ex parte volitorum" (*De Verit.* q. 23 : a. 2. ad 1ᵐ).

Being identical with the divine essence, and operating, as it does, by a single timeless act, the will of God is, of course, absolutely one; and as such it is termed *voluntas beneplaciti*. To it the distinction between antecedent and consequent will applies. Speaking metaphorically, however, we may refer to some specific action, command, or event as "The Will of God." When will is ascribed to God in this sense, it is called *voluntas signi*. (Cf. *Sum. Theol.* I.a. q. 19 : a. 11; 1 *Dist.* 45. q. 1 : a. 2; *De Verit.* q. 23 : a. 3.) The five *signa* of the divine will are *prohibitio, praeceptum, consilium, operatio,* and *permissio*. Thus we say that an evil action is *prohibited*, or *permitted* by God, that a good action is *commanded*, and that an action which is useful but not essential for the attainment of a good end is *counselled*. And since every action is carried out only in conjunction with the causal activity of God, we speak of the divine *operation* as appearing in the passage of events. (For an elaborate classification of the *signa* see *Comm. on Sentences*, loc. cit., and *De Verit.* loc. cit.) *Praeceptum, consilium* and *prohibitio* correspond to the antecedent will of God, *beyond* or *contrary* to which acts can be committed (cf. 1. *Dist.* 47. q. 1: a. 4. sol.); *permissio* and *operatio* to the consequent will of God, *contrary* to which nothing can be done. Actions can, however, be performed *beyond* although not *contrary* to the divine *operatio*. But no action can be performed *beyond* the divine *permissio*. (Cf. 1 *Dist.* 47. q. 1: a. 2. c.) Thus every deed committed contrary to the antecedent will is nevertheless obedient to the consequent will. (Cf. 1 *Dist.* 47. q. 1 : a. 3. c.)   [4] Lib. I. cap. 89.

passions (*passiones*) and virtues (*virtutes*), and the question as to whether or not they can be attributed to God. Inasmuch as the interest attaching to these sections is primarily theological rather than philosophical, I shall restrict myself to summarizing his arguments as succinctly as possible.

In God, St. Thomas maintains, there are no *passiones affectum*. By this phrase he means to indicate that passions pertain to the sphere of the appetite rather than to that of awareness.[1] Such appetite is, however, purely sensuous, and the exercise of any passion involves physical changes; furthermore, the subject of that passion must be in a state of potentiality. None of these conditions is, of course, realized in the case of God. Again, the subject of any passion "is drawn out of his normal, even, or natural disposition,"[2] whereas God is immutable. And lastly, every emotion which accompanies a passion is determined with respect to a single, definite end; while God, on the contrary, is not determined with respect to any creature, except by his own wisdom. For all these reasons, therefore, the very concept of the genus under which all passions fall renders them unworthy to be ascribed to God.

Certain passions, moreover, are unworthy for additional reasons. In the first place, the species of every passion is determined by its object, and the objects of some passions, such as sorrow and pain, are evil. In the second place, the mode in which the subject is related to it must also be taken into account, for some modes imply imperfection in the subject, and are therefore inapplicable to God. For this reason neither hope nor desire can be ascribed to the Deity. The notion of fear, too, is inapplicable, both because it implies potentiality in its subject and because its object is always an evil. Repentance, again, implies change. And finally, since there can be no error in the divine cognition, it is impossible that God should ever apprehend good as evil or evil as good. But envy consists in regarding another's good as an evil, and

---

[1] "Ratio passionis magis invenitur in parte appetitiva quam in parte apprehensiva" (*Sum. Theol.* I.a.–II.ae. q. 22: a. 2. c.). Cf. the relevant section of Cardinal Cajetan's comm. on the *Summa*; also Sylvester's comm. on the *Contra Gentiles*.

[2] "Trahitur extra suam communem, aequalem, vel connaturalem dispositionem" (*Con. Gen.* lib. I. cap. 89).

anger in regarding another's evil as a good. Hence envy and anger cannot pertain to God.

None the less there are certain passions which, in spite of the fact that they fall under the same genus as the others, yet, so far as their species are concerned, are not incompatible with the divine perfection. Such passions are delectation (*delectatio*) and joy (*gaudium*). For the object of joy is a present good; accordingly, neither in respect to its object, nor its mode of relation to that object, is it unworthy of God. Furthermore, delectation and joy pertain to the intellect as well as to the senses, and also they involve the quiescence of the will in its possession of the object willed. Again, delectation is a perfection of operation, as Aristotle has shown,[1] and the act of the divine intelligence, as we have seen, is the most perfect of operations. Furthermore, everything rejoices in its like. But every good resembles the divine goodness; wherefore God rejoices in every good. Yet there is this difference between delectation and joy, that delectation rejoices in a good which is united to the subject which feels the emotion, while joy extends to external goods. Hence God experiences delectation only in himself, but joy both in himself and in all other things.[2]

Moreover, there is love in God; for to love is to will the good of the beloved, and God wills both his own good and that of other things. In addition, love requires that the good of the beloved be willed not merely as conducive to the good of another, but as his own (*ut eius*); and this condition is also fulfilled.[3] Again, love is the source of all the emotions, for joy and desire are directed only upon a good that is loved, and fear and sorrow upon an evil that is the contrary of such a good. Accordingly, since joy and delectation are in God, love must also be experienced by him.[4] We may reach the same conclusion by considering that it is the nature of love to seek union with its beloved, and that God, who bestows upon the creatures their perfections, also moves them toward union with himself. Furthermore, inasmuch as the object of love is the good, and as that object is loved the more according as it is the more closely united with the subject, there is nothing either in the

---

[1] *Nic. Eth.* lib. X. lect. 6. [2] *Con. Gen.* lib. I. cap. 90.
[3] *Con. Gen.* lib. I. cap. 91; 3 *Dist.* 32. q. 1: a. 1. sol.
[4] *Con. Gen.* lib I. cap. 91; *Sum. Theol.* I.a. q. 20: a. 1. c.

object of love or the relation which it involves to that object, which is unworthy of God. Since the intensity of love depends upon the closeness of the union of lover and beloved, the more firmly the cause of that union is rooted in the nature of the lover the stronger will be the love. Now, the cause of God's love is the divine goodness which all creatures imitate; and this is identical with God's very essence and being.[1] The divine love is, therefore, of all loves most perfect. Inasmuch as every creature is good in so far as it exists, and inasmuch as God is the cause of its goodness and existence, it follows that God wills the good of everything that exists, which is equivalent to saying that God loves every creature.[2] The question may be raised, however, as to whether God loves all creatures equally. Aquinas answers that we may love one person more than another in two different ways. We may will a greater good to one person than to another, or we may will an equal good to one person more frequently and efficaciously than to another. But it is impossible that God should will more intensely in one instance than another, for the strength of every activity is measured by the power whence it proceeds, which, in the case of God, is immutable. Yet God can and does will a greater good to one creature than another.[3] Thus since God's will is the cause of one creature being better than another, it is clear that the better any creature is the more God loves it,[4] and since the divine nature is changeless it is evident that God has loved the creatures from eternity.[5]

We have now to inquire how the various virtues can be ascribed to God.[6] Since the divine goodness contains in some mode the perfection of all the creatures, it must contain all the virtues, yet not in the same mode in which they are possessed by human beings. For virtue in us is a *habitus*. Now a *habitus* is a mean between potentiality and actuality ("quasi medius inter potentiam et actum"), it is something extraneous to the

---

[1] *Con. Gen.* lib. I. cap. 91.
[2] *Sum. Theol.* I.a. q. 20: a. 2. c.; 3 *Dist.* 32. q. 1: a. 2. sol. Regarding the divine love of irrational beings, see *Sum. Theol.* I.a. q. 20: a. 2. ad 3^m; 3 *Dist.* 32. q. 1: a. 2. ad. 1^m, 2^m. With respect to the non-elect, see *Sum. Theol.* I.a. q. 20: a. 1. ad 4^m; 3 *Dist.* 32. q. 1: a. 2. sol., and ad 3^m.
[3] *Con. Gen.* lib. I. cap. 91; *Sum. Theol.* I.a. q. 20: a. 3; 3 *Dist.* 32. q. 1: a. 4. sol., and ad 4^m.   [4] *Sum. Theol.* I.a. q. 20: a. 4.
[5] 3 *Dist.* 32. q. 1: a. 3.   [6] *Con. Gen.* lib. I. cap. 92.

essence of a substance, in fact it belongs to the genus *accident*, and its function is to perfect an antecedent potentiality. Hence, as such, virtue cannot be attributed to the Deity. Human life is, however, twofold, active and contemplative. The former has to do with corporeal goods and their possession and with political life. Obviously, then, the virtues which pertain to it cannot be predicated of God. Nor can those be virtues which control the passions, for in God there are no passions. Such virtues, furthermore, belong to the sensuous and not to the intellectual part of the soul. Some of the passions which these virtues control spring from physical appetite; but even those which are engendered by appetite for a spiritual good, such as honour, victory, etc., are none the less passions, and cannot be ascribed to God except metaphorically; and the same is true of virtues like bravery, magnanimity, and mildness which bear upon our hopes and ventures.

Certain virtues, moreover, have to do, not with passions, but with actions. The examples given are truth, justice, mercy, liberality, high-mindedness, prudence, and art. In the objects of these virtues there is nothing unworthy of God. Also they are perfections of the will and intellect, which are immaterial realities operating without conjunction with the passions. Hence all these virtues are to be ascribed to God.[1]

The contemplative virtues are, however, more worthy than any others to be predicated of the Deity. They are wisdom (*sapientia*), knowledge (*scientia*), and understanding (*intellectus*). "Wisdom consists in the cognition of the highest causes,"[2] and it has been shown that God, who is the primal cause, knows himself first and *per se*. "Knowledge is the cognition of a thing through its proper cause,"[3] and God, who knows the order of causes and effects, knows through this order the causes of particulars. Lastly, "understanding is the immaterial and non-discursive cognition of certain things,"[4] and it has been shown that this is the kind of knowledge which God has of all things.

[1] *Con. Gen.* lib. I. cap. 93; cf. *Sum. Theol.* I.a. q. 21; 4 *Dist.* 46.
[2] "Sapientia in *cognitione altissimarum causarum* consistit" (*Con. Gen.* lib. I. cap. 94).
[3] "Scientia est *rei cognitio per propriam causam*" (loc. cit.).
[4] "Immaterialis cognito aliquarum rerum absque discursu intellectus est" (loc. cit.).

From what has been said it is clear that in attributing virtues to God we are not merely speaking metaphorically. Yet the doctrine of analogy forbids us to suppose that a plurality of virtues inhere in the divine essence as accidents in a substance. On the contrary, the essence is virtue itself, simple and un-differentiated; the plurality subsists only in the human intellect which endeavours by a multiplicity of concepts to express the fullness of the divine nature.

Inasmuch, however, as the divine essence is identical with virtue, it is impossible that God should will evil.[1] This impossi-bility can also be inferred from Aquinas's theory that the object of the will is always the good, for if this be true one can will evil only when it is mistaken for the good, and the occur-rence of a mistake is out of the question in the case of the divine cognition.[2] Such at least is the teaching of the *Contra Gentiles*. In the *Summa Theologica*[3] we are told that while it is impossible to desire evil *per se* it is possible to desire it *per accidens* in so far as it accompanies some good. Accordingly, while God cannot will the evil of sin, he can and does will the evil of defect and the evil of punishment when the willing of either is involved in the willing of some good.[4] In the *Contra Gentiles*[5] Aquinas also points out that the supposition that God might will evil is incompatible with the view that the Deity is the *summum bonum*, since the highest good can no more be mingled with evil than the intensest heat with cold. And, as a final argument, he urges that the will is directed to the good as its proper end, so that in choosing the evil it must depart from that end, and that such departure is impossible in the case of God, who, it has been shown, can will all things only in willing himself.[6]

Since God cannot will evil, and since he does will good to all

---

[1] *Con. Gen.* lib. I. cap. 95.   [2] Loc. cit.
[3] I.a. q. 19: a. 9. c.   [4] Cf. 1 *Dist.* 46. q. 1: a. 4. sol.
[5] Loc. cit.
[6] It is evident that the last of these arguments presupposes its predecessor, since, were God not the *summum bonum* he might will evil in willing himself. In regard to the apparent discrepancy between the *Contra Gentiles*, on the one hand, and the *Summa Theologica* and the *Commentary on the Sentences*, on the other, all conflict disappears if we assume—and the assumption seems plausible—that, in the former work, St. Thomas, in asserting that God can never will evil, had in mind moral evil only (cf. *Con. Gen.* cap. 96, *in fine*).

things, God can hate nothing. Indeed, it is the nature of all agents to love their effects in their own way (*suo modo*). Thus parents love their children, poets their poems, artificers their handiwork. What is true of all active causes[1] must also be true of God, the cause of all things. Moreover, were God to hate anything, he must will that it should not exist, for existence is a good. But this would necessitate his willing that his own creative act which brings it into being should not take place, and this is impossible. Hatred can then be ascribed to the Deity only metaphorically.[2]

It has been proved that God possesses intelligence and will, therefore God is a living being.[3] This conclusion can also be demonstrated if we take as our point of departure the proposition that the power of self-movement is the criterion by which we may determine the presence of life. As we pass from the lower to the higher orders of living beings we find a corresponding increase in the ability of creatures to move themselves. Yet even the human intellect is moved to some extent by external causes. It cannot refuse to assent to first principles, nor can it abstain from willing what it takes to be the good. But the Deity is wholly self-moved, wherefore he is preeminently alive.[4] And, lastly, we may argue that life is a perfection, and that therefore it must be found in God who contains in himself all perfections.[5]

The second of these arguments is of interest to us in that it requires us to conceive of God as a self-mover. We are familiar with the controversy as to whether the argument from motion is based merely upon the occurrence of local motion or simply upon change as such, and it is clear that one of two alternatives must be accepted. Either motion is to be interpreted to mean local motion alone—and then it will be nonsense to say that the unmoved mover moves himself when he thinks or wills; or else motion is to be regarded as including every form of change—and then the theory of the unmoved mover

---

[1] "Causis activis"—a peculiar expression probably intended to designate efficient causes in distinction from material, formal, and final causes. The illustrations employed all have reference to conscious agents.

[2] *Con. Gen.* lib. I. cap. 96.

[3] *Con. Gen.* lib. I. cap. 97; cf. *Metaph.* lib. XII. lect. 5.

[4] *Con. Gen.* loc. cit.; *Sum. Theol.* I.a. q. 18: a. 3. c.

[5] *Con. Gen.* loc. cit.

can be saved—if saved at all—only by assuming that the divine intellection is unvarying in its character, that the Deity is engaged in a process of perpetual self-contemplation. In the present instance Aquinas seems to be arguing on both sides of the case at once. Self-movement is the common characteristic of all living beings; therefore, to show that God is a living being, we must admit that he moves himself, and accordingly knowledge and will must be declared forms of motion—not merely knowledge and will as they are found in human minds, but *divine* knowledge and will! What now of the unmoved mover? We can only answer, He has disappeared. In the *Summa Theologica*[1] St. Thomas tries to meet the difficulty, but his solution is merely once more to distinguish between local motion and intellection, and to affirm that "in the sense in which knowledge is motion, that which knows itself, is said to move itself."[2] But this is precisely the point at issue, in what sense are knowledge and will motion at all? If he once admit that they are not really motion, then he has cut the thread of his own argument from the character of living beings to a living God.

Life is identical with the act of living, and the act of living on the part of any being is identical with its existence. (The concept of existence, it will be remembered, is an analogous one.) But God is identical with his own existence, God is therefore also identical with his own life. Again, intelligence is a form of life, and God is identical with his own intelligence, and thus, for this reason also, with his life. Were it not so, God would be alive by participation in life; hence there would necessarily exist some reality prior to God, which is impossible. Moreover, if we say that there is life in God but that God is not identical with that life, we imply that there is composition in God, whom we know to be wholly simple.[3]

Aquinas next proceeds to show that the divine life is eternal (*sempiterna*). It is difficult to understand why he should think it worth while to do so, in view of the fact that he has already tried to prove that God is eternal; nevertheless such is his procedure. The arguments advanced are four in number. The

[1] I.a. q. 18: a. 3. ob. 1., and ad 1ᵐ.
[2] "Hoc igitur modo quo intelligere est motus, id quod se intelligit, dicitur se movere."   [3] *Con. Gen.* lib. I. cap. 98; cf. *Metaph.* loc. cit.

most obvious is based upon the divine immutability. Since God is changeless, he is eternal, therefore his life is eternal. Another proof reverts to the familiar principle of sufficient reason. Whatever exists at one time and not at another must have a cause. But the divine life has no cause; therefore it exists always. A third is founded upon the identity of God with his own life which has just been proved. Nothing can cease to live except by separation from life. Yet nothing can be separated from itself, for separation is the division of one thing from another. Accordingly it is impossible that God should cease to live. The remaining argument is more complicated. In every ordinary operation there is a subject which abides while the successive states of the operation pass. God, however, does not fall under the genus *substance*, nor does he possess accidents. Accordingly the divine operation is itself the subject; it must therefore exist as a whole without succession, *tota simul*. And since in God knowledge and life are identical with existence, the divine life itself must be *tota simul*, which is to say that it is eternal.[1]

It is noteworthy that the second and third of these arguments —in the order in which we have placed them—do not prove what they profess to prove. If valid, they demonstrate that the divine life is everlasting, not that it is eternal. The first proof is thoroughly in accord with Thomist principles and demands no special notice. The fourth argument is interesting because it reveals with unusual clearness the difficulties inherent in the conception of a timeless act. An activity in which there is no succession would be removed, not merely from the sphere of change, but even from that of duration. We seem to be dealing here with a notion which does not even deserve the lighter sentence of being pronounced unintelligible; rather it appears to stand condemned in the blazing light of self-contradiction.

In the *Summa Theologica*[2] Aquinas raises the extraordinary question "whether all things are life in God."[3] He answers that "in God intellect and the act of knowing and that which is known are identical. Hence, whatever is in God as known by him is also his act of living or his life. Hence, since all things which are made by God are in him as objects of

---

[1] *Con. Gen.* lib. I. cap. 99; cf. *Metaph.* loc. cit.
[2] I.a. q. 18: a. 4.   [3] "Utrum omnia sint vita in Deo."

knowledge, it follows that all things in him are the divine life itself."[1]

This language has, indeed, a startlingly pantheistic sound, yet when we reflect that it is not the things themselves, but only the ideas of them, that are in God, we realize that the impression which it creates is largely a mistaken one. Nevertheless it is worthy of remark that Aquinas takes pains to emphasize a second time his doctrine that there are no ideas of evil things in God, as though their presence in the divine intelligence would be a pollution.[2]

St. Thomas's next step is to attempt to prove that God is blessed (*beatus*). Beatitude is the good proper to an intellectual nature. God is an intelligent being, beatitude is therefore God's good. Moreover, a good which is not yet possessed pertains to a nature that is both changeable and in potentiality. But God is neither; he must therefore not only desire blessedness, but also enjoy the possession of it.[3]

Furthermore, an intellectual nature desires and wills what is most perfect in itself, and this is its beatitude. But that which is most perfect in any being is operation (*operatio*): for it is through operation that potentiality and *habitus* are perfected. And the perfection of operation depends upon:

(*a*) Genus—the operation must be immanent in the operator, for a transeunt operation perfects, not the operator, but that which it produces. Moreover, it must monopolize the activity of the operator to the exclusion of all else, such as seeing or hearing.

(*b*) The principle of operation—it must be of the highest power. Hence our felicity is found, not in any operation of the senses, but in that of the intellect.

(*c*) The object of operation. Our ultimate felicity lies in knowing the *altissimum intelligible*.

(*d*) The form of operation—its perfection, ease, strength, and delectation.

---

[1] "In Deo autem est idem intellectus, et quod intelligitur, et ipsum intelligere eius. Unde quidquid est in Deo ut intellectum, est ipsum vivere vel vita eius. Unde, cum omnia quae facta sunt a Deo, sint in ipso ut intellecta, sequitur quod omnia in ipso sunt ipsa vita divina."

[2] *Sum. Theol.* I.a. q. 18: a. 4. ad 4m.

[3] *Con. Gen.* lib. I. cap. 100; cf. *Sum. Theol.* I.a. q. 26: a. 1.

All these conditions are realized in the divine operation. God is intelligent, his intelligence is the highest power, it does not require the perfection of any *habitus*, but is perfect in itself; its object is God himself, the highest of intelligible beings; it operates perfectly—since without difficulty—and delectably.[1]

Again, beatitude involves the quiescence of all desire in the attainment of an ultimate end. Whoever therefore is perfect in all things that can be desired is blessed; and such is the divine perfection which includes all perfections within itself.

Whoever lacks anything is not blessed. But God has been shown to lack nothing, inasmuch as he is dependent on no exterior perfection, nor does he will the creatures because he needs them, but rather because it comports with his goodness; God is therefore blessed.[2]

Finally, God cannot will the impossible. But it is impossible that God should possess anything which he does not possess, since he is in no way in potentiality. Accordingly God cannot will to have anything which he does not have. Neither can he will evil. Hence God is blessed.[3]

The divine beatitude is, of course, identical with God himself; for it has just been shown that it consists in intellectual operation, and we know that God's intellectual operation is identical with the divine essence. Beatitude, moreover, since it is the ultimate end, is that which all things principally desire. But that which God principally desires is his own essence, hence the divine essence is identical with the divine beatitude. Again, the process of desiring one thing for the sake of another cannot continue *ad infinitum*, but there must be something which is desired for itself, and this is beatitude. With respect to this everyone orders everything that he wills. Yet that because of which God wills all things is his essence, which must therefore be his beatitude. Furthermore, there cannot be two *summa bona*, for one would lack what the other possessed and neither would be perfect. Beatitude is, however, the *summum bonum* because it is the ultimate end. Hence it must be identical with God.[4]

[1] *Con. Gen.* loc. cit.; cf. *Sum. Theol.* I.a. q. 26: a. 2. c.
[2] *Con. Gen.* loc. cit. Clearly this proof merely expresses in different language the contention set forth in the preceding paragraph.
[3] *Con. Gen.* loc. cit.   [4] *Con. Gen.* loc. cit.

M*

In conclusion, seven arguments are advanced by St. Thomas to prove that the divine beatitude is perfect and singular, exceeding all other beatitude.[1]

1. The nearer a thing is to beatitude, the more is it blessed. But God is identical with his beatitude; God is therefore singularly and perfectly blessed.

2. Delectation is caused by love, and the stronger the love the greater the delectation in possessing the thing loved. *Ceteris paribus*, everything loves itself more than anything else, as is shown by the fact that the nearer anything is to us the more we love it. Hence God has more delectation in his beatitude which is identical with himself than any other being can feel in a beatitude which is not identical with itself.

3. That which is *per essentiam* is superior to that which is *per participationem*. And God is blessed *per essentiam*, whereas all other beings that are blessed are so *per participationem*. Accordingly the divine blessedness must exceed all other blessedness.

4. Beatitude has been shown to consist in intellectual operation, and no intellectual operation is comparable to that of the Deity, not only because his is a subsistent operation, whereas that of any other being is the act of a subsistent subject, but also because by this single operation God knows perfectly both himself and all other things, whether existent or non-existent, whether good or evil. Hence God's beatitude is immeasurably superior to that of any creature.

5. The more united anything is, the greater is its power and its goodness. Now, a successive operation is divided according to different parts of time. Accordingly its perfection is no way comparable to that of an operation which is *tota simul*, especially if, instead of being instantaneous, it abides for ever. "Thus the divine beatitude infinitely exceeds the human, even as the duration of eternity exceeds the flowing *now* of time."[2]

6. The contemplation wherein human happiness principally consists is interrupted by fatigue, occupations, errors, doubts, and the various mishaps of this life, whereby it is rendered wholly unworthy to be compared to the divine felicity.

[1] *Con. Gen.* lib. I. cap. 102.
[2] "Divina igitur beatitudo in infinitum excedit humanam: sicut duratio aeternitatis excedit nunc temporis fluens." Notice the phrase "the *duration* of eternity."

7. The perfection of the divine beatitude includes in itself in the most perfect mode all beatitudes whether contemplative —since God enjoys the perpetual consideration both of himself and of all other things—and active—inasmuch as God governs the entire universe. Hence it is superior to all other beatitude which is only a shadow of its felicity.

We have here reached a most important stage in the development of Aquinas's thought. To use his own words: "What has been said suffices as regards that which pertains to the unity of the divine essence."[1] He has now demonstrated to his own satisfaction that the Deity is not only a being eternal, immutable, wholly actual, engaged in perpetual self-contemplation, but also that he possesses intelligence, will, love, and the other attributes essential to the theistic conception of God. We are now in a position to appreciate the truth of M. Sertillanges's observation—perhaps the most pregnant comment ever made upon the philosophy of St. Thomas—that "the proof of God is the task of the entire theodicy."[2]

None of the famous five proofs suffices of itself to demonstrate the existence of a God in the sense in which that word is used of the object of religious devotion.[3] The teleological argument does indeed, if valid, establish the existence of a controlling intelligence, but, as Kant pointed out, it is powerless to conduct us farther. Similarly the argument from possibility and necessity may compel us to admit the existence of a necessary being, but it cannot certify the identity of that being with the *ens realissimum*, nor that of either with the God of Christian Theology. On the contrary, eighty-nine chapters of the *Contra Gentiles* and twenty-four questions of the *Summa Theologica* are devoted

[1] "Et haec dicta sufficiant de his quae pertinent ad divinae essentiae unitatem" (*Sum. Theol.* I.a. q. 26: a. 4. ad 2ᵐ). It should be added that the arrangement of the *Summa Theologica* differs from that of the *Contra Gentiles*, which we have elected to follow, in that it treats of the divine power, *potentia*, and of providence in connection with the divine essence, whereas the latter discusses them under the general topic of the relation between God and the world. It does not appear, however, that this dissimilarity of procedure is due to any change of view. We may with more probability conjecture that it was dictated merely by convenience and method of approach.

[2] "La preuve de Dieu est l'œuvre de toute la théodicée" (*S. Thomas d'Aquin*, tome I. p. 157; cf. p. 161).

[3] Cf. McTaggart's *Some Dogmas of Religion*, secs. 152–153.

to precisely this endeavour, with what success we have tried to estimate. And not even yet has the task been completed, for it still remains to be shown that the Deity whose essential attributes have now been determined is also the creator of the world. Accordingly we shall now proceed to follow Aquinas in his effort to prove that such is in fact the case.

PART FOUR

GOD AND THE WORLD

CHAPTER XIV

CREATION

As we have seen, there are two possible modes of operation, of which one is immanent in and involves the perfection of the subject, and the other is transeunt and involves the perfection of the effect. Examples of the former are sensing, knowing, and willing; of the latter, heating, cutting, and building. Since the agent is naturally prior to the effect of which it is the cause, so the former type of operation is the reason of the second and is naturally prior thereto. It is therefore termed *operation* or *action*; whereas the second is called *making*,[1] whence the products of an artificer are said to be *manufactured*. *Operation* has been show to belong to God, inasmuch as he knows, wills, rejoices, and loves; we are now to see that he engages also in *making*, since he brings the creatures into existence, conserves them therein, and governs them.[2]

At this point, before taking up the consideration of the problem of creation, Aquinas saw fit to introduce a brief discussion of the differences between the method employed by philosophers and that of the theologians.[3] The former, he tells us, deal with finite entities as they are in themselves and are interested in them for their own sake, whereas the latter consider them as they represent and are related to the divine essence. Moreover, the philosopher bases his arguments upon the causes of such entities; but the theologian upon the primal cause. Consequently theology can justly be called the highest wisdom, and it is the function of "human philosophy" to be of service to it. Nevertheless it is true that divine wisdom sometimes proceeds according to the principles of human philosophy, even as the first philosophy makes use of the teachings of the sciences. Even in such cases, however, the methods employed are different, for philosophy begins with the creatures, and from these ascends to the knowledge of God; whereas theology, on the other hand, considers God first and the creatures afterwards, in so far as they are related to God. It is this

---

[1] "*Factionis* nomen assumit."
[2] *Con. Gen.* lib. II. cap. 1.   [3] *Con. Gen.* lib. II. cap. 4.

characteristic of theology, in fact, which renders it the most perfect form of knowledge, for it thereby most nearly resembles the divine cognition, inasmuch as the Deity, as has been shown, is aware of all things only through his knowledge of himself.

In the *Summa Theologica* and the *Commentary on the Sentences* the method proper to theology is treated at greater length, although its relation to that of philosophy is discussed briefly and as it were incidentally. Theology, we are informed, is based upon principles communicated to it by revelation and which it accepts by faith. The necessity for such communication is due to the fact that, while the end for which man is made is the contemplation of the divine essence, the Deity himself is utterly beyond the grasp of human reason which can know him only *ex rationibus creaturarum*. Yet man cannot order his actions with respect to his own ultimate end unless he knows what that end is. Hence it is needful that certain truths to which he could never attain by the exercise of his reason be imparted to him by revelation. In addition, there are other truths of which a few men by long endeavour might acquire a knowledge, yet always with the risk of accompanying errors, while the majority would for ever remain in ignorance of them. Consequently it was necessary that such truths be certified to men by revelation.[1]

There are two kinds of sciences, those which are founded upon principles known by the natural light of human reason—such as arithmetic and geometry—and those which derive their principles from a superior science, as the science of perspective owes its principles to geometry and music its principles to arithmetic. Theology belongs in the latter class,[2] and the science from which it derives its principles is that "of God and of the blessed."[3]

To its exclusive preoccupation with that which is divinely revealed, theology owes its unity as a science.[4] The higher

[1] *Sum. Theol.* I.a. q. 1 : a. 1. c.; cf. 1 *Prolog.* q. 1 : a. 1. sol.
[2] *Sum. Theol.* I.a. q. 1 : a. 2; cf. 1 *Prolog.* q. 1 : a. 3. sol. 2.
[3] "Scientia Dei et beatorum" (*Sum. Theol.* loc. cit.). This is an excellent illustration of the difficulty of translating into English a word like *scientia*, which is habitually used as the equivalent both of *science* and of *knowledge*.
[4] *Sum. Theol.* I.a. q. 1 : a. 3.

the mode of knowledge, the greater the unity which it possesses; thus the divine intellect, while remaining one, yet takes cognizance of all things. Accordingly theology, which most nearly approximates to the divine knowledge, by the light of heavenly inspiration considers a diversity of objects and yet remains one.[1] The object of this science is God, and whatever other topics are treated of are discussed only in so far as they are related to God.[2] Theology is therefore primarily speculative; yet, inasmuch as it concerns Man's salvation, it has also an extremely practical aspect.[3]

The worth or dignity of a speculative science is dependent upon the certitude attaching to it, or upon the dignity of its subject-matter. In the case of the practical sciences, on the other hand, one is ranked more highly than another according as it is related to a more ultimate end; thus politics is superior to military science because the good of an army is a means to the good of the State. Theology is, however, pre-eminent both as a speculative and as a practical science, for its certitude is superior to that of any other—since its principles are communicated to it by God—and its subject-matter transcends human reason; moreover, the end which it has in view is man's ultimate goal—eternal beatitude.[4] Consequently it deserves to be regarded as wisdom *par excellence*.[5]

It is not the business of any science to argue in defence of its fundamental principles. This is true even of the philosophical sciences, with the exception of metaphysics. Each of them leaves to a superior science the task of vindicating the principles which it presupposes. Metaphysics, however, inasmuch as it is the supreme philosophical science, is unable to refer us to any authority above itself. The principles upon which it is founded are self-evident propositions. With him who denies one or more of these propositions, but admits the truth of the remainder, it is possible to dispute, founding one's arguments upon the principles which he accepts. But against the thorough sceptic who denies the truth of all self-evident propositions it

[1] I *Prolog.* q. 1 : a. 2.
[2] *Sum. Theol.* I.a. q. 1 : a. 7; cf. I *Prolog.* q. 1 : a. 4.
[3] *Sum. Theol.* I.a. q. 1 : a. 4; cf. I *Prolog.* q. 1 : a. 3. sol. 1.
[4] *Sum. Theol.* I.a. q. 1 : a. 5; cf. I *Prolog.* q. 1 : a. 3. sol. 2.
[5] *Sum. Theol.* I.a. q. 1 : a. 6; cf. I *Prolog.* q. 1 : a. 3. sol. 3.

is impossible to argue, although it is possible to refute any arguments which the sceptic himself may advance.

In the case of theology the situation is similar. It is possible to dispute with a heretic who denies that any particular article of faith has been revealed by basing one's arguments upon the articles which he does admit to have been revealed. But against one who denies the existence of any revelation at all it is impossible to argue, although it is possible to dispose of any considerations which he in turn may urge against the faith. For, since faith rests upon infallible truth, and what is contrary to the truth can never be proved, it is certain that all such arguments will be fallacious.[1]

In the light of these statements it is possible for us to appreciate the extent to which the philosopher in St. Thomas was absorbed in the theologian. Nowhere among his works does there exist a systematic formulation of his philosophy. We are forced to extract it piecemeal from his theological treatises, his commentaries upon Aristotle, and from his various brief philosophical *opuscula*. In the *Summa contra Gentiles* we are fortunate enough to possess a work from his pen, written to assist Christian disputants in their discussions with Moslems and Jews, and in which, therefore, purely rational argumentation occupies a prominent place; and yet, as Gilson points out, "The *Contra Gentiles*, which is constantly called a *Summa Philosophica*, in contrast to the *Summa Theologica*, in no sense deserves that name as far as the order of demonstration is concerned."[2]

It is no doubt also true, as Gilson elsewhere maintains,[3] that St. Thomas, in conjunction with his teacher, Albertus Magnus, succeeded in establishing a hard-and-fast distinction between the provinces of philosophy and theology, and that they did furthermore insist that within her own field philosophy must be allowed to pursue her own methods without interference upon the part of theology. We may even admit that in doing so they liberated philosophy to a very great extent from the dominion of theology, and that St. Thomas, for the courageous thoroughness with which he carried out this

---

[1] *Sum. Theol.* I.a. q. 1: a. 8. c.
[2] *The Philosophy of St. Thomas Aquinas*, p. 35, n. 22.
[3] See *La signification historique du thomisme* in his *Études de Philosophie Médiévale*.

reform, deserves to be called "the first of the moderns." Never-theless, the right of veto accorded theology, whereby any conclusion resulting from philosophical speculation which was not in harmony with the faith might be condemned, constituted a permanent shackle upon the reason. Nor is it justifiable to describe the influence thus exercised by theology as purely limiting and negative. From the nature of the case it must be impossible for a thinker who knows beforehand the prescribed conclusions at which he must arrive, or with which the results of his own deliberations must at least be capable of being harmonized, not to be continually influenced through-out the development of his thought by the desire to conform to the dictates of an external authority, in spite of the fact that his duty as a philosopher is "to follow the argument wherever it may lead."

In taking up the problem of creation, Aquinas first proceeds to show that it is consistent with the idea of God at which we have already arrived that he should be the cause of the existence of other beings, a contention which is supported by six arguments.[1]

1. The second proof of the divine existence establishes the fact that God is the primal efficient cause. And an efficient cause brings its effects into being; whence it follows that God will be productive of effects.

2. The prime mover in any order of movements is the cause of all the other movements in that order. Now, the movement of the heaven brings many things into existence. But God, the ultimate prime mover, causes the movement of the heaven, therefore he also causes the existence of these things.

3. Whatever pertains to any nature *per se* is found in every instance of it. And it pertains to actual being to be productive of effects, since everything acts in so far as it is actual.[2] But God is wholly actual; he will therefore be productive of effects.

4. It is a token of perfection in inferior beings that they can produce their like,[3] hence this power cannot be lacking in the perfect being, God.

---

[1] *Con. Gen.* lib. II. cap. 6.
[2] "*Unumquodque agens secundum hoc agit quod in actu est*" (cf. *Phys.* lib. III. cap. ii. lect. 4).   [3] *Meteors*, lib. IV. cap. iii.

5. God, as we have seen, wills to communicate his being to other entities *per modum similitudinis*. But the perfection of the will requires that it be the principle of motion and action.[1] And the divine will is perfect; wherefore it cannot lack the power of communicating its being to other things.

6. The more perfect the principle of activity in any substance, the greater will be the range of that activity. The principle of activity is, moreover, actuality, and God is wholly actual. Consequently, since we, in whom actuality is mingled with potentiality, are capable of engaging in transeunt activity, it is evident that the Deity possesses the same capacity in a far higher degree.

It would seem then that power is to be ascribed to God. It is to be remarked, however, that the Latin *potentia* is used both in the sense of *power* and also in that of *potentiality*. Accordingly the adjectives *activa* and *passiva* are habitually employed to make clear which meaning is intended. Moreover, the correlative term *actus* is similarly ambiguous. It may, indeed, connote *actuality*, *activity*, or *act*. But in the present connection[2] Aquinas draws a distinction between *actus secundus*, which is *operatio*, and *actus primus*, which is form, the principle of *operatio*. The correlative of *operatio* is *potentia activa*; that of form *potentia passiva*, for every agent possesses *potentia activa*, and every patient possesses *potentia passiva*. Now, God is *actus purus et primus*, hence *potentia activa* belongs to him preeminently.[3]

This position can also be reached from the conclusion previously demonstrated that God is the cause of other entities. For *potentia activa* is nothing else than "the principle of acting upon another according as it is another."[4] In other

---

[1] *De Anima*, lib. III. cap. x. lect. 15.

[2] Cf. *De Pot.* q. 1 : a. 1. c.

[3] *De Pot.* q. 1 : a. 1. c. In the *Contra Gentiles* (lib. II. cap. 7) the argument is stated more briefly as follows: "Sicut potentia passive sequitur ens in potentia, ita potentia activa sequitur ens in actu: *unumquodque enim ex hoc agit quod est actu, patitur vero ex hoc quod est potentia.* Sed Deo convenit esse actu. Igitur convenit sibi potentia activa." Cf. also *Sum. Theol.* I.a. q. 25: a. 1. c.; 1 *Dist.* 42. q. 1 : a. 1. sol. See *Phys.* lib. III. cap. iii. lect. 4.

[4] "*Principium agendi in aliud secundum quod est aliud*" (*Con. Gen.* loc. cit.; cf. *Metaph.* lib. V. lect. 17, and lib. IX. lect. 2).

words, when we have proved that God is an efficient cause, we have also proved that he has power.[1]

Again, power accompanies perfection, so that the more perfect anything is, the more does it possess *virtus activa*. Thus, since the divine essence contains in itself the perfections of all beings, there must be active power in God.[2]

Furthermore, nothing acts unless it is able to do so. But the first and second proofs of the divine existence make it evident that God both acts and is the source of motion; wherefore active and not passive *potentia* must be attributed to him.[3]

Potentia activa pertains to anything according as it is actual and according as it is perfect. And the Deity is wholly actual and wholly perfect; in him, therefore, substance and power are identical. Were it not so, God would possess power only by participation, which is impossible, since God, who is identical with his own existence, participates in nothing. Moreover, power would then inhere in God as an accident, which is also impossible. And, lastly, everything that exists through another can be reduced to that which exists of itself. Thus, as all agents can be reduced to God, the primal agent, consequently God is *agens per se*. But that which acts *per se* acts by its essence, and that whereby a thing acts is its *potentia activa*; in God, therefore, essence and active power are identical.[4] Accordingly, since there is no distinction between essence and existence in the Deity, the divine power is identical with the divine substance.

It has already been proved, however, that the divine activity, which is intellection, is identical with the divine substance;

---

[1] Cf. *Sum. Theol.* loc. cit.

[2] *Con. Gen.* loc. cit.; *Sum. Theol.* loc. cit. In the *Commentary on the Sentences* (I *Dist.* 42. q. I: a. I. sol.) we find a similar argument based upon the same principle of the divine perfection, but expressed in very different phraseology. *Potentia*, we are told, is a word which first acquired meaning from being applied to human beings. Hence we call that powerful which cannot be acted upon—for example something hard, which lacks potentiality with respect to being cut. The Deity, however, cannot possibly be acted upon, since in him there is no matter. On the contrary, being *actus purus et perfectus*, God can do anything that it is befitting that he should do; we are therefore justified in calling him powerful.

[3] *Con. Gen.* loc. cit.　　　　　　　　　　[4] *Con. Gen.* lib. II. cap. 8.

power and activity are therefore identical in God. In a finite being, indeed, activity is the complement of *potentia*, inasmuch as it is related to it as *actus secundus* to *actus primus*. But the divine *potentia* is completed by nothing, since it is identical with the divine essence; therefore it must be identical also with the divine activity.[1]

In addition the following very complicated proof is brought forward to sustain this conclusion: As the divine power is something in action, so its essence is something in existence.[2] Now, we know that the divine power is identical with the divine essence, the divine activity must therefore be identical with the divine existence. But God's existence is his substance; accordingly his activity also is identical therewith. And the substance, again, is identical with the essence; hence the divine power and activity are identical.[3]

This proof is an application of the principle that "things identical with one and the same thing are identical with each other,"[4] which is the basis of the first argument. The method of approach is, however, far less direct. The presupposition that power is related to activity as essence to existence is in accordance with the Thomist view that existence is that which

---

[1] *Con. Gen.* lib. II. cap. 9.

A third proof advanced by St. Thomas is as follows: Were the divine activity other than the divine substance it must be an accident. But there are no accidents in God, hence activity and substance are identical. And it has just been shown that the divine substance and power are identical, whence it follows that the divine activity is identical with the divine power (*Con. Gen.* loc. cit.).

There is a strange confusion of thought in this argument. It undertakes to prove what the other arguments have taken as proven—the identity of the divine activity and the divine substance. They were justified in so doing, for as the divine activity consists in intellection and volition, the identity of intellection and volition with the divine essence—which is in turn identical with the divine substance—has already been demonstrated; moreover, the second argument advanced in the case of intellection, and the fourth advanced in that of volition, are founded upon this very impossibility of accidents inhering in God upon which the present argument is built.

[2] "Sicut potentia activa est aliquid agens, ita essentia eius est aliquid ens."
[3] *Con. Gen.* lib. II. cap. 9.
[4] "Quae enim uni et eidem sunt eadem, sibi invicem sunt eadem."

confers actuality upon essence.[1] Power in finite beings is a principle of operation. In the Deity operation and essence are, however, identical, and we know that the divine essence does not proceed from any principle more ultimate than itself.[2] Power, when predicated of God, does not therefore signify "the principle of activity, but the principle of the thing made,"[3] or of "the effect."[4]

It is true that, in the *Commentary on the Sentences*, power is said to be "the principle of operation."[5] But this is obviously intended to be interpreted in harmony with the statement in the same article that operation and power are *idem secundum rem*.[6] The position is clearly the same as that taken in the *Summa Theologica*. "Power is not posited in God as something other than knowledge and will *secundum rem*, but only *secundum rationem*; since the concept of power is that of a principle which executes that which the will commands and knowledge directs, which three are identical in God. Or, it may be said, that the divine knowledge or the divine will, in so far as it is a principle productive of effects, is subsumed under the concept of power. Hence the consideration of the divine knowledge and will logically precedes the consideration of the divine power, as cause precedes operation and effect."[7]

[1] Cf. Francis Sylvester's comment: "Sicut actus potentiae est agere, cum potentia sit agens quo, agens autem sit agens per ipsum agere; ita essentiae actus est esse, cum omne quod est ens sit ens per ipsum esse."

[2] *Sum. Theol.* I.a. q. 25: a. 1. c. ad 3ᵐ; *De Pot.* q. 1: a. 1. ad 1ᵐ.

[3] "Potentia non dicitur in Deo sicut principium actionis, sed sicut principium facti" (*Con. Gen.* lib. II. cap. 10).

[4] "Potentia in rebus creatis non solum est principium actionis sed etiam effectus. Sic igitur in Deo salvatur ratio potentiae quantum ad hoc, quod est principium effectus: non autem quantum ad hoc, quod est principium actionis, quae est divina essentia" (*Sum. Theol.* loc. cit.).

[5] "Suum esse est suum operari, et suum operari est sua essentia: nihilominus tamen essentia significatur ut principium essendi; et eadem ratione potest significari potentia ut principium operandi, et praeter hoc ut principium operati" (1 *Dist.* 42. q. 1: a. 1. ad 4ᵐ).

[6] Ad 5ᵐ.

[7] "Potentia non ponitur in Deo ut aliquid differens a scientia et voluntate secundum rem, sed solum secundum rationem; inquantum scilicet potentia importat rationem principii exequentis id quod voluntas imperat, et ad quod scientia dirigit; quae tria Deo secundum idem conveniunt.—Vel dicendum quod ipsa scientia vel voluntas divina, secundum quod est principium effectivum, habet rationem potentiae. Unde consideratio

In other words, the concepts of power, operation, and activity are distinct from one another in the human intellect; but in the divine Object to which they refer there is no corresponding differentiation. The doctrine of analogy has rendered us familiar with this point of view, so that we need not dwell upon it in the present connection. It follows as a corollary, however, that the term *power* can be applied to the immanent activity of God only as a concession to our understandings and not in strict correctness. "Intellect and will are not, therefore, in God as powers, but only as actions."[1] Nor are they really distinct even as actions, for, as we know, God is absolutely simple.[2] It is only with respect to created things that power can legitimately be predicated of the Deity.[3]

As we have already seen, Aquinas had explicitly stated that transeunt as well as immanent activity is to be attributed to God.[4] It is, however, maintained by Roman Catholic commentators that this statement is not to be taken at its face value, and that the divine activity is in reality immanent and only *virtually* transeunt.[5] The reason for this is that transeunt activity involves the passage of form from agent to patient. It is thus accidental in its character, and cannot therefore be predicated of God. This position appears to be sustained by Aquinas's statement in the twenty-third chapter of the second book of the *Contra Gentiles* that "action is twofold. One variety of it is that which remains in the agent and is its

scientiae et voluntatis praecedit in Deo considerationem potentiae, sicut causa praecedit operationem et effectum" (I.a. q. 25: a. 1. ad 4ᵐ; cf. *Con. Gen.* loc. cit.; *De Pot.* q. 1: a. 1. ad 1ᵐ, 6ᵐ).

[1] "Intellectus igitur et voluntas in Deo non sunt ut potentiae, sed solum ut actiones" (*Con. Gen.* loc. cit.).

[2] "Patet etiam ex praedictis quod multitudo actionum quae Deo attribuitur, ut intelligere, velle, producere res, et similia, non sunt diversae res: cum quaelibet harum actionum in Deo sit ipsum eius esse, quod est unum et idem" (*Con. Gen.* loc. cit.).

[3] "Manifestum est quod potentia dicitur in Deo per respectum ad facta, secundum rei veritatem; non per respectum ad actionem nisi secundum modum intelligendi, prout intellectus noster diversis conceptionibus utrumque considerat, divinam scilicet potentiam et eius actionem" (*Con. Gen.* loc. cit.).

[4] *Con. Gen.* lib. II. cap. 1; cf. *De Pot.* q. 10: a. 1. c.; see above, p. 367.

[5] Cf. Joyce's *Principles of Natural Theology*, pp. 412–413.

perfection, such as sight; the other kind passes into external objects and is the perfection of the thing made, as burning in the case of fire. The divine action cannot, however, belong in the genus of those actions which are not in the agent, since his action is his substance."[1]

The solution of the difficulty is, of course, suggested by the method of analogy. God's activity is not transitive in the same sense as that of human beings; yet it is permissible to call it so, since it is the cause of all finite beings. To quote the explanation of Sylvester: "If our will were in itself productive of things, so that the act of willing were itself the act of production, the production of things would actually be an immanent activity, since it would be wholly identical with willing; yet it could be described as transitive activity passing into something other than itself. So the divine activity by which things are brought into being, since it is not other than the divine will itself, and is itself the substance of God, which is wholly separated from the genus *motion*, is not in fact transitive activity but immanent, inasmuch as it is will and intellection; and so according as God knows and wills so things come into being without any mediate action and motion."[2]

I must now take cognizance of a formidable objection which may be urged against Aquinas's view. Either the divine power is always actual, or sometimes actual and sometimes not. But any power which is not actual is imperfect, and is perfected by being brought into actuality. On the other hand,

---

[1] "Duplex est actio: una quae manet in agente et est perfectio ipsius, ut videre; alia quae transit in exteriora et est perfectio facti, sicut comburere in igne. Divina autem actio non potest esse de genere illarum actionum quae non sunt in agente: cum sua actio sit sua substantia."

[2] "Sic enim, si velle nostrum esset secundum se rerum productivum, ut ipsum velle esset ipsum producere, producere res esset secundum rei veritatem actio immanens, quia esset idem omnino quod velle, tamen significaretur per modum in alterum transeuntis. Actio ergo divina qua res in esse producuntur, cum non sit aliud quam ipsum velle divinum et ipsa Dei substantia, quae a genere motus est omnino separata, non est actio transiens secundum rei veritatem, sed actio immanens quae est velle et intelligere: secundum enim quod Deus intelligit et vult, ita res in esse procedunt, absque alia media actione et motu" (*Con. Gen.* lib. II. cap. 16; *Comment.* 6). The entire passage from which this quotation is taken is of considerable interest.

if it be always actual, the process of creation will be without beginning or end, which is contrary to the faith.[1] St. Thomas replies that the divine power is always "wholly actual";[2] but that the effect does not always follow from it, but only when commanded by the divine will in accordance with the divine wisdom. The reply may seem of doubtful cogency; consideration of it may, however, be postponed until we come to examine the relation doctrine of creation to time.

We have now to consider the problem of the relation between God and the created universe. And, in the first place, we may well ask, what is St. Thomas's idea of a relation? Is it a concept ultimate and indefinable, or is its meaning capable of being stated in terms of which the significance is logically prior to its own? For answer we may turn to the *De Potentia*,[3] where our doubts are resolved by the following clear statement: "It is therefore necessary that among things themselves there should be a certain order; this order, moreover, is a certain relation. Hence it is necessary that among things themselves there should be certain relations according to which one is ordered with respect to another. Moreover, one thing is ordered with respect to another either according to quantity or according to active or passive power."[4]

From this it would seem that relation, at least in the case of finite beings,[5] involves, or is identical with, dependence.[6] Here we find the root of that distinction between "real"

---

[1] 1 *Dist.* 42. q. 1 : a. 1. ob. 5; *De Pot.* q. 1 : a. 1. ob. 8.

[2] Aquinas's phrase is "coniuncta actui," and thus might be rendered "wholly active." Possibly, however, the adjective *active* is to our ears somewhat more suggestive of transitive, as distinct from immanent, action than was the word *actus* to those of St. Thomas.

[3] q. 7 : a. 9. c.

[4] "Oportet ergo in ipsis rebus ordinem quemdam esse; hic autem ordo relatio quaedam est. Unde oportet in rebus ipsis relationes quasdam esse, secundum quas unum ad alterum ordinatur. Ordinatur autem una res ad aliam vel secundum quantitatem, vel secundum virtutem activam seu passivam."

[5] We are not here concerned with the problems arising from the presence of relations within the divine nature. Cf., however, *Con. Gen.* lib. IV. cap. 14.

[6] "Ibi enim est relatio ubi realiter aliquid dependet ab altero, vel simpliciter vel secundum quid" (*De Pot.* q. 7 : a. 1. ad 9[m]; *Con. Gen.* lib. II. cap. 12; *De Verit.* q. 21 : a. 1. c.).

relations and relations "of reason" which we have so often encountered in the pages of Aquinas. "Yet it must be known that, since a relation requires two extremes,[1] there is a three-fold possibility with regard to its being a relation of nature or of reason. Sometimes on either part it is only a relation of reason, when the order or habitude between certain entities has its being only in the apprehension of reason, as when we say that something is the same as itself. For reason, apprehending some one thing twice, considers it as two; and so it apprehends a certain habitude of the thing to itself. Similarly all the relations between being and non-being are formed by the reason, inasmuch as it apprehends non-being as one extreme. And the same holds true of all relations which follow from the activity of the reason, as genus and species, and others of the same sort. Certain relations do truly belong to nature in each of their extremes, when there is a habitude between two entities in respect of something really pertaining to both; as is evident in all relations which follow from quantity, such as great and small, double and half, and others of the same sort, since quantity is in each of their extremes. In a similar case are those relations which follow from action and passion, such as those of mover and moved, father and son, and the like.

Sometimes a relation belongs, in truth, to nature in one of its extremes and in the other only to reason. And this happens when the two extremes are not of the same order. Thus sense and knowledge are referred to the sensible and the knowable, which, in so far as they are things existing in nature, are outside the order of sensible and intelligible being; wherefore in knowledge and in sense there is a real relation according to which they are ordered with respect to things to be known or sensed; but these things considered in themselves are outside this order. Hence, in them, there is no real relation to knowledge and sense, but only according to reason, inasmuch as the intellect apprehends them as terms of the relations of knowledge and sense. Thus the Philosopher says, in the fifth book of the *Metaphysics*, that they are not called relative because they are referred to other things, but because other things are referred to them. And likewise *right* is not predicated

[1] *Extrema*—i.e., terms.

of a column except in so far as it is placed to the right of an animal; whence a relation of this kind is not really in the column but in the animal."[1]

St. Thomas was familiar with the view advanced by the Porretani—i.e. by the disciples of Gilbert de la Porrée—that all relations are relations of reason and not of nature.[2] This objection he dismissed with the answer that things themselves are mutually interconnected by a natural order and habitude.[3] Relation is one of the ten *praedicamenta* which are found in the actually existing world—whence the mind has derived the notion of it—and not as such a mental fiction, although the mind is capable of introducing it where it has does not exist *in rerum natura*.[4]

It is now clear that the problem before us is susceptible of a threefold division, whereby it can be resolved into the following questions: (1) Are there any relations between God and the creatures? (2) If there be such, are they real in the creatures? (3) Are they also real in God? Any other questions which we may raise in this connection are obviously subordinate to these three.

Aquinas answered the first question in the affirmative. He also took occasion to criticize Maimonides for holding the opposite view on the ground that God is not a body, and stands, therefore, in no relation to time or place.[5] The Jewish thinker's error lay in considering relation only with respect to quantity, and not with respect to action and passion. Since God is not included in the ordered system of the universe but exists outside it, whereas the creatures are all ordered with respect to God, it is evident they are related to him, although he is not related to them.

Such is the concise statement which we find in the *Summa*

[1] For a discussion of the nature of relations very similar to that just quoted, cf. *De Pot*. q. 7: a. 10. c.; 1 *Dist*. 26. q. 2: a. 1. sol.; 1 *Dist*. 30. q. 1: a. 1. sol. and ad 3m; *Phys*. lib. V. cap. ii. lect. 3.

[2] *Sum. Theol*. I.a. q. 13: a. 7. c.; q. 28: a. 2. c.; 1 *Dist*. 26. q. 2: a. 1. sol.; *Dist*. 33. q. 1: a. 5. sol.; *De Pot*. q. 7: a. 8. c.; a. 9. c.; *Com. Theol*. Pars Prima, cap. lxvi.

[3] "Quod quidem apparet esse falsum, ex hoc quod ipsae res naturalem ordinem et habitudinem habent ad invicem" (*Sum. Theol*. I.a. q. 13: a. 7. c.). Cf. *De Pot*. q. 7: a. 9. c.; *Metaph*. lib. V. lect. 20.

[4] See *De Pot*. loc. cit.

[5] See *Le Guide des Égarés*, vol. I. pp. 199–204. Cf. Isaac Husiks's *A History of Jewish Medieval Philosophy*, p. 263.

Theologica.[1] In the *Contra Gentiles*, on the contrary, the matter is dealt with in greater detail. The concept of *principium* is, St. Thomas urges, relative to that of *principiatum*. And power, which, as we have just seen, may legitimately be predicated of God, can be subsumed under the concept of *principium*.[2] Again, the concepts of mover and agent are relative to those of thing moved and thing made. Hence it is evident that it must be possible to say something of God with respect to his effects. Furthermore, "it is impossible for one thing to be relative to another unless that other is relative to it."[3] But other entities are relative to God—in regard to their existence, for instance. God must therefore be relative to them. Likeness is, moreover, a relation, and God, like other agents, produces effects resembling himself, and which are, accordingly, relative to him. Again, knowledge is relative to the object known; and it has proved that God knows, not only himself, but other beings. Lastly, the concepts of the *first* and the *highest* are relative concepts, and it has been shown that they are applicable to God. Consequently the conclusion that there are relations between God and the creatures is inescapable. From what has been said it is equally clear that these relations must be real in the creatures, inasmuch as these are ordered with respect to God and are dependent upon him.[4] Among the various objections to this view which are mentioned by Aquinas there are two of considerable importance. One of these sounds indeed strangely anticipatory of Bradley. If, it is contended, there be in the creature any relation to God, this relation itself, if it be anything real, must also be a creature; hence a second relation will be required to relate it to God, and so we may proceed to infinity. To this objection Aquinas answers that relations are not related to their terms by other relations, but directly, *per seipsas*, "because essentially they are relations."[5]

[1] I.a. q. 13 : a. 7. c.
[2] *Con. Gen.* lib. II. cap. 11 ; cf. *De Pot.* q. 7 : a. 8. c. ; 1 *Dist.* 30. q. 1 : a. 1. sol.
[3] "Non potest intelligi aliquid relative dici ad alterum nisi e converso illud relative diceretur ad ipsum" (*Con. Gen.* lib. II. cap. 11). Cf. the following statement in the *De Potentia*: "Intellectus non potest intelligere relationem huius ad illud, nisi e converso intelligat relationem illius ad hoc" (q. 7 : a. 1. ad 9^m).
[4] *De Pot.* q. 7 : a. 9. c. ; *Sum. Theol.* I.a. q. 13 : a. 7. c.
[5] "Quia essentialiter relationes sunt" (*De Pot.* q. 7 : a. 9. ad 2^m).

In the second place, it had been maintained that relations have no metaphysical standing. They are not substances, they should therefore be accidents. But it is the nature of an accident to inhere in a subject from which it cannot be removed without involving that subject in change. To this St. Thomas replies: "Relation itself, which is nothing else than the order in which one creature stands to another, can be regarded either as accident or as relation or order. In so far as it is an accident it inheres in a subject, but not in so far as it is relation or order; for as such it is only, as it were, a transition to something else, and thus somehow conjoined to the related object. And so a relation is something inherent, although not inasmuch as it is a relation; just as action, in so far as it is action, is considered as proceeding from an agent, but in so far as it is an accident, it is considered as inhering in a subject. Thus there is no reason why such an accident should not cease to be without any change on the part of its subject; for the concept of it is not completed according as it inheres in the subject itself, but according as it makes a transition to something else, which being removed, the concept of this accident is also removed as regards action, but remains as regards cause; just as, if the matter which is being warmed be taken away, the process of warming is also removed, although the cause of the warming remains."[1]

Inasmuch as God is neither included in nor dependent upon the ordered structure of the universe, it is clear that he is not

[1] "Ipsa relatio quae nihil est aliud quam ordo unius creaturae ad aliam aliud habet inquantum est accidens, et aliud inquantum est relatio vel ordo. Inquantum enim accidens est, habet quod sit in subiecto, non autem inquantum est relatio vel ordo; sed solum quod ad aliud sit quasi in aliud transiens, et quodammodo rei relatae assistens. Et ita relatio est aliquid inhaerens, licet non ex hoc ipso quod est relatio; sicut et actio ex hoc quod est actio, consideratur ut ab agente; inquantum vero est accidens, consideratur ut in subiecto agente. Et ideo nihil prohibet quod esse desinat huiusmodi accidens sine mutatione eius in quo est: quia sua ratio non perficitur prout est in ipso subiecto, sed prout transit in aliud; quo sublato, ratio huius accidentis tollitur quidem quantum ad actum, sed manet quantum ad causam; sicut et subtracta materia, tollitur calefactio, licet maneat calefactionis causa" (*De Pot.* q. 7: a. 9. ad 7ᵐ; cf. q. 7: a. 8. c.; ob, 5 and ad 5ᵐ; also *Sum. Theol.* I.a. q. 13: a. 7. ob. 2 and ad 2ᵐ; q. 28: a. 2. c.).

really related to it.[1] Relations cannot, of course, inhere in
God as accidents in a subject; neither can they be identical
with the divine essence, for relative terms are relative only
in so far as they refer to something else, and to suppose that the
divine essence is essentially relative to something else would
be ridiculous. Furthermore, God is the primal measure of all
beings, whereas our knowledge is measured by the things
which it knows, since its truth depends upon its correspondence
with facts. Consequently God is to be compared to all things
as knowable things are to be compared to our knowledge.
But knowledge is really related to its object, while the object,
on the contrary, is related to knowledge only by reason. And
so all creatures are really related to God, but God is not really
related to them.[2]

Furthermore, relations are predicated of God, not only with
respect to entities which are actual but also with respect to
those which are potential, inasmuch as God knows them, and
with respect to them is called the primal being and the highest
good. Real relations hold, however, only between actualities;
otherwise, a single subject would be involved in an infinite
number of real relations. Thus the series of cardinal numbers
greater than two is potentially infinite, and were the relations
between two and these numbers real, they also would be
infinite in number. Now, since God by his creative activity
is not involved in change, it is clear that he is not related to
things actually existent in any other way than to things potentially existent. Accordingly, these relations cannot be real.[3]

It is interesting to observe the manner in which Aquinas
brushed aside the possibility that a finite substance might be
involved in an infinite number of relations.[4] His motive could
scarcely have been theological, for his treatment of infinity

---

[1] *Sum. Theol.* I.a. q. 13: a. 7. c.; cf. 1 *Dist.* 30. q. 1: a. 3. sol.
[2] *Con. Gen.* lib. II. cap. 12.   [3] *Con. Gon.* lib. II. cap. 12.
[4] Cf. the following passage from the *Physics* (lib. V. cap. ii. lect. 3): "Sunt
enim quaedam relationes quae non sunt aliquid realiter in eo de quo
praedicantur. Quod quidem quandoque contingit ex parte utriusque
extremi, sicut cum dicitur idem eidem idem: haec enim identitatis relatio
in infinitum multiplicaretur, si quaelibet res esset sibi eadem per relationem additam: manifestum est enim quod quodlibet sibi ipsi est idem.
Est ergo haec relatio secundum rationem tantum, inquantum scilicet unam
et eandem rem ratio accipit ut duo extrema relationis."

shows that he was fully aware of the fact that infinity in one
dimension is compatible with finitude in other dimensions.
None the less he rejects the suggestion as though it were self-
evidently absurd.

The next argument presents in another form the same idea
as that which is set forth in the proof which we have just
examined. That to which something is imparted *de novo* must
undergo change. Relations are, however, predicated of God
de novo. Thus God is called lord and governor of an entity
which comes into existence. Were such relations, then, real in
God, the Deity would be involved in change, either *per se*
or *per accidens*. Hence they can be only relations of reason.[1]

Again, the divine activity, which is the divine substance, is
not in the same genus as its effects, neither does any good
accrue to God from the production of the creature. Hence
God is not really related to his effects.[2]

We must not, however, think of the relations between God
and the creatures as though they were realities external to
God—*quasi res aliquae extra Deum*—for, as we have already
seen, we should then be compelled to seek yet other relations
whereby these were related to God, and so we should become
involved in a vicious regress. Furthermore, a thing can be
denominated from something external to it—from time and
place, for instance—or from something within it, such as
whiteness; but it cannot be nominated from a relation existing
externally, but only from one inherent within it, as a man is
called father only from the relation of fatherhood inhering in
him. Consequently the relations by which God is referred to
the creatures cannot exist externally to him.[3]

From this it follows that relations are to be attributed to God
only according to the mode of the intelligence—*secundum
intelligentiae modum*. Thus they differ from qualities, such as
wisdom, will, etc., which are predicated of the essence.[4] At
first sight this may seem a false contrast, since we know that,
according to the doctrine of analogy, neither wisdom nor
will nor any other quality exists in God in the same sense that

[1] *Con. Gen.* lib. II. cap. 12.   [2] *De Pot.* q. 7: a. 10. c.
[3] *Con. Gen.* lib. II. cc. 13 and 14.
[4] *Con. Gen.* lib. II. cc. 13 and 14; cf., however, the somewhat confused
statements in *Sum. Theol.* I.a. q. 13: a. 7. ad 1ᵐ; 1 *Dist.* 30. q. 1: aa. 1 and 2.

it exists in the creatures. Yet it does exist in the Deity *secundum modum altiorem*. In the case of relations there is, however, no question of degrees of being. Relations of reason simply do not exist at all in the external world. Yet the mind in framing them does not err. It merely submits to what it knows to be the limitations of its own nature which compel it to work by the aid of certain formulae. Genus and species are, for example, products of the mind. In external nature there exists but a multitude of individuals. Yet in comparing one species with another the mind is not reasoning falsely.[1] In this fashion a multitude of relations can be attributed to the divine essence without impairing its simplicity, to which in fact they bear testimony. For the simpler a thing is, the fewer are its limitations, the greater is its power, and the farther extends its causal efficacy. Thus the point is the principle of more things than the line, and the line than the surface.[2]

Relations of reason imply only the habitude of one entity to another. This can happen in four ways:

1. When there is nothing *in rei natura* upon which the relation is founded. This is sometimes the case with one term and not with the other, as in all relations between God and the world.

2. When there is no real diversity between the terms, as in the relation of identity.

3. When the relation is one of being to non-being, as of present to future.

4. When the relation is between a relation and its subject.[3]

It may be objected that qualities are attributes of God which arise from his relations to his effects, and that, consequently, if these relations be unreal in God, the qualities in question are illegitimately ascribed to the Deity. Thus God is called lord because he stands to the creatures in the relation of controller and governor. If the relation be unreal, the quality is unreal also. To this Aquinas replies that the creature is really subject to God, wherefore God is really the creature's lord, and that this suffices to justify the ascription to God of the quality of lordship.[4]

---

[1] *Con. Gen.* loc. cit. Cf. *Comment.* of Sylvester, iv; 1 *Dist.* 30. q. 1 : a. 3. ad 1ᵐ.
[2] *Con. Gen.* loc. cit.; *De Pot.* q. 7 : a. 8. c.
[3] 1 *Dist.* 26. q. 2 : a. 1. sol.; cf. *De Pot.* q. 7 : a. 11. c.
[4] *Sum. Theol.* I.a. q. 13 : a. 7. ob. 5 and ad 5ᵐ.

Again, it may be objected that relation involves comparison, and that God cannot be compared to the creatures, inasmuch as he is not in the same genus as the creature. To this St. Thomas rejoins that, while strictly speaking God is in no genus, yet he is in all genera as the principle and cause of every genus.[1]

Having now scrutinized Aquinas's defence of his position, we may ask ourselves the question, Is it valid? The foregoing discussion has at least made it clear that his theory is founded upon the notion that it is possible for the intellect to introduce between objects relations which have no being *in rerum natura*. To make use of his own illustration in a passage already quoted, the relation of identity subsists only for the apprehending mind, and is apprehended only by means of two distinct mental acts whereby the same object is twice considered. Strange as this view may appear, his subsequent assertion that a relation can be real in one term and not in the other is even more difficult to grasp. The statement that the relation *to the right of*, in which a particular column stands to a certain animal "non est realiter in columna sed in animali," is indeed a hard saying. From this it would appear to follow that the animal is really to the left of the column, but that the column is not really to the right of the animal. Are we to infer from these utterances that a thing is identical with itself only when it is perceived to be so, and that, while the animal is to the left of the column, even when no intelligence is aware of its position, the column, at the same instant, is not to the right of the animal? These are precisely the conclusions which logic compels us to draw. But what would Aquinas have said? He would probably have insisted that the whole process whereby reason establishes relations which do not subsist in the external world is due to the mind's native limitations which compel it to represent reality to itself as best it can instead of directly apprehending it exactly as it is.

The difficulty which faces us is obviously similar to that which we encountered in trying to solve the problem as to how reason can justifiably ascribe a plurality of attributes to the absolute simplicity of the divine essence. But, though similar, the difficulties are not identical. In the former instance the situa-

[1] *De Pot.* q. 7: a. 8. ob. 2 and ad 2^m.

tion was relieved or complicated, according to the point of view, by the doctrine of degrees of being. Thus goodness and wisdom are really separate and distinct qualities in man. We know the meaning of the terms from actual experience, and though goodness and wisdom are identical in God, yet our minds, incapable as they are of understanding *how* this can be true, can most accurately represent the fact to themselves by formulating the judgments, God is good, and God is wise. In the case now before us, however, the theory of degrees of being cannot be invoked. A thing is either identical with itself, or it is not; a column is either to the right of an animal or it is not. The sole task of the intellect is to make its judgments correspond to the facts. By picturing to itself relations which are not to be found in the actual world, the mind neither mirrors nor interprets nor comprehends reality—it falsifies it.[1] This is the fundamental objection to Aquinas's view, and having stated it we may leave the matter there.

It is evident that a real relation requires two extremes together with a real accident which serves as its foundation. Is it, however, in itself a real relative entity independent of every apprehending mind, or is it, on the other hand, apart from its extremes and its foundation, a mere construct of reason? To this question the scholastic interpreters of St. Thomas return opposing answers. If we are to believe those who reply in the negative, his position, despite his terminology, is practically identical with that of those philosophers who, admitting the reality of qualities, would explain away relations altogether.

[1] For a statement of the opposing view, see P. Coffey's *Ontology*, p. 339: "Furthermore, we are forced by the imperfection of the thought-processes whereby we apprehend reality—conception of *abstract* ideas, *limitation* of conception in extension and intension, *affirmation* and *negation*, etc.—to apprehend *conceptual* limitations, negations, comparisons, etc., in a word, all *logical entities*, as if they were *realities*, or after the manner of realities, i.e. to conceive what is really 'nothing' as if it were really 'something,' to conceive the *non-ens* as if it were an *ens*, to conceive it *per modum entis*. And when we compare these logical entities with one another, or with real entities, the relations thus established by our thought are all *logical relations*. Finally, it follows from this same imperfection in our human modes of thought that we sometimes understand things only by attributing to these certain logical relations, i.e. relations which affect not the reality of these things, their *esse reale*, but only the mode of their presence in our minds, their *esse ideale*."

It is, of course, clear that this view is wholly in line with the conceptualist treatment of universals as mental constructs having *fundamenta in re*.[1] Nevertheless, it is not easy to reconcile with Aquinas's insistence that there is a real order among actually existing entities in the external world, and that it is just this order itself which constitutes relation.[2] Both parties are able to appeal to the actual words of St. Thomas in support of their interpretations.[3] Fortunately there is no need for us to become involved in this dispute, since it has no bearing upon our subject, which is man's knowledge of God. There is, however, a further matter which must be cleared up.

We have seen that Aquinas defines a real relation both as order and as dependence. In what sense are we to take this latter term? The world is said to be related to God because it is dependent upon him, whereas God is not related to the world, since he is independent of it. What then are we to say of the case of a child and his parents? A son is begotten by his father and born of his mother; he is, therefore, dependent upon them, and is, *ipso facto*, related to them. His parents, on the contrary, are not dependent upon him for their existence. Are they related to him?

The answer is that they are related to him, and that such mutual relationship is to be found in all cases of univocal causation. The son perpetuates his parents' species, and may thus be said to *perfect* them.[4] In a passage already quoted St. Thomas informs us that relation is "a habitude between two entities in respect of something really pertaining to both," such as quantity, or action and passion, and as an example of the latter type of relation we are referred to that of father and son.[5] Under the same head fall the relations of mover to thing moved, of that which heats to that which is heated, etc.[6]

---

[1] Thus a relation also is said to have a *fundamentum in re*; see 1 *Dist*. 26. q. 2: a. 1. sol., and ad 3ᵐ.

[2] *De Pot*. q. 7: a. 9. c.; *Sum. Theol*. I.a. q. 13: a. 7. c.; *Metaph*. lib. V. lect. 20.

[3] For a discussion of the point at issue, see P. Coffey's *Ontology*, pp. 349–356. Cf. Sertillanges's *S. Thomas d'Aquin*, tome I. pp. 112–117; Mercier's *Ontologie*, pp. 367–372; and Rickaby's *General Metaphysics*, pp. 357–362.

[4] Cf. Colley's *Ontology*, pp. 347–348; also Mercier's *Ontologie*, p. 374.

[5] *Sum. Theol*. I.a. q. 13: a. 7. c.; cf. *De Pot*. q. 7: a. 10. ob. 3 and ad 3ᵐ; 3 *Dist*. 5. q. 1: a. 1. sol. 1. [6] *Sum. Theol*. loc. cit.; *Metaph*. lib. V. lect. 20.

But what of the relation of equivocal causation? Here also, whenever such causation involves change on the part of the cause as well as upon that of the effect, it would seem to be rightly regarded as real in both terms. Thus the builder is related to the house which he builds.[1]

It is clear, then, that *dependence* and *order* are practically identical concepts. We have noticed, however, that there are, for St. Thomas, non-mutual relations in which one entity is dependent upon and ordered with respect to another entity which is itself independent of, and is not ordered with respect to, the former. The example given was that of knowledge. The knowing mind is ordered with respect to, and is dependent upon, its object for its knowledge, but the relation is not mutual. Somewhat in this fashion every created being is ordered with respect to, and is dependent upon, God. For the process of creation involves no change, whether quantitative, qualitative, temporal, or any other, upon the part of the Deity. God is wholly self-sufficient; the divine perfection is not augmented by the world's coming into being; and the production thereof is accomplished without any new or fresh activity on the part of the Creator. How this can be we must now consider.

Since every contingent being is caused, directly or indirectly, by a necessary being, and since it is impossible that more than one being should be necessary *per se*, it follows that God is the source of all existence.[2] So obvious, indeed, is this inference that one might have supposed that even St. Thomas would have been content to state it and pass on. Actually, however, the *Contra Gentiles*[3] contains six additional proofs supporting this conclusion.

1. Any characteristic which does not belong to its subject essentially, *secundum quod ipsum esse*, belongs to it as the effect of some cause. Now, if the same characteristic pertain to two entities, it cannot be uncaused in both, but must either be present in one as the effect of the other, as heat is present in a body as the effect of fire, or else be due in each instance to the activity of a common cause, as the burning of two candles is caused by fire. But being pertains to all things. Accordingly

---

[1] See Coffey's *Ontology*, p. 348.
[2] *Con. Gen.* lib. II. cap. 15; *De Pot.* q. 3: a. 5. c.; cf. a. 6.   [3] Loc. cit.

there cannot be two things of which the existence is uncaused; but, on the contrary, all things must owe their existence to the one uncaused Being, God.[1]

2. That which is present in any substance essentially is present therein in the highest degree, and is capable neither of augmentation nor diminution. That which is present in an inferior degree does not pertain to the essence, but is the result of causal activity from without. The cause of all the instances of a genus is that to which the attribute in question pertains in the maximum degree. Thus fire, for instance, is the cause of heat in all things. But God is supremely being, *maxime ens*; he is therefore the cause of all things that have being.[2]

3. Not only are there particular causes productive of particular effects, but also universal or common causes the activity of which extends to a multitude of effects. Accordingly, what is common to two or more substances must be due to a common and not to a particular cause. Being is, however, common to all things; there must therefore be a cause common to all existents.[3]

4. As fire is the cause of all conflagration, so that which is essentially this or that is the cause of whatever is this or that by participation. But God is essentially being, whereas all other things have being by participation, whence God is the cause of all things.[4]

5. We have seen that God is wholly active even as he is wholly actual, and that he contains in himself the perfections of all things, and is virtually all things. All things must therefore be created by God, which would not be the case were there anything which did not owe its existence to him.

6. The imperfect can originate only from the perfect. But God is the perfect being. Hence God is the cause of all things,

---

[1] Cf. *De Pot.* q. 3: a. 5. c.

[2] Cf. *De Pot.* loc. cit. For St. Thomas, of course, being is not a genus, neither are the degrees of being degrees of greater or less intensity, as are the degrees of heat. Nevertheless here once more, be it noted, we find him treating being precisely *as if* it were a genus.

[3] Cf. *De Pot.* q. 3: a. 5. c.

[4] Cf. *Sum. Theol.* I.a. q. 44: a. 1. c.; cf. *Com. Theol.* Pars Prima, cap. lxvii; *De Pot.* q. 3: a. 5. c.

especially since it has been shown that there are no gods but one.[1]

It is evident that the third of these arguments is really identical with the first, since, if we ask why the presence of the same characteristic in two or more entities must be due to a single cause, the answer is that there is only one being or type of being in which it can be essential. Moreover, it is clear that all these arguments, whether they employ the notions of common cause, of degrees of intensity (or of being), of participation, or of perfection, alike fail to conduct us to a cause which is numerically rather than generically one. Hence they are valueless. For it is only because the necessarily existent being is numerically one that we are justified in asserting the derived and contingent nature of all entities other than God. And the numerical unity of God has already been demonstrated. Hence all that is necessary and all that is possible is for us to make the immediate and inevitable inference that God is the cause of all things. And since God brings all things into being, he is their efficient cause. Moreover, he is their primal exemplar cause, for universals do not exist *ante rem*, except in the divine mind which contains the archetypes of all things. And since God has no other end in creation than the communication of his own goodness to the creatures, he is also their final cause.

It is an article of faith that creation is *ex nihilo*. This, of course, is not to be taken as meaning that nothing is the material out of which things are made. On the contrary, we are intended to understand that they are not created out of anything, that there is nothing pre-existent out of which they are made.[2] This is a proposition which is not merely to be accepted on authority, but which is also susceptible of proof.

1. It is plain that any effect of the divine power must either follow upon something pre-existent or else be created out of nothing. If we accept the former hypothesis, the same question will arise with respect to this pre-existent reality. To escape from the doctrine of creation, we must assume either that it also is made out of something pre-existent or that it presupposes nothing prior to itself. Clearly the former assumption will

---

[1] Cf. *Sum. Theol.* I.a. q. 44: a. 1. c.; cf. *Com. Theol.* Pars Prima, cap. lxvii; *De Pot.* q. 3: a. 5. c.

[2] *Sum. Theol.* I.a. q. 45: a. 1. ad 3ᵐ; *De Pot.* q. 3: a. 1. ad 7ᵐ; see p. 207, n. 2.

involve us in an infinite regress, which has already been shown to be vicious; nor is the latter open to us, since we know that God is the only being whose existence is underived. Thus we are driven to accept the notion of creation.[1]

The infinite regress I have referred to is obviously ontological and not temporal, for we have seen that Aquinas held that there is no contradiction in the idea of an infinite series of beings succeeding one another in time. But the successive members of such an endless process of generation and corruption would be formed out of a common matter, and the point which St. Thomas is anxious to press is that it is impossible for us either to regard this matter as self-existent or to account for its existence by the supposition that it is created out of something else.

2. Again, every cause which requires an already existing matter for its activity is a particular cause. For it operates by imposing upon matter the determinate and limiting form of a particular species, and since causes are proportionate to their effects,[2] such a cause must itself be particular. God is, however, a universal cause; pre-existent matter is therefore not requisite to the divine activity.[3]

3. It is an established principle that the higher the onto-

[1] *Con. Gen.* lib. II. cap. 16.

[2] The reference here is to the *Physics*, lib. II. cap. iii: "῎Ετι τὰ μὲν γένη τῶν γένων, τὰ δὲ καθ᾽ ἕκαστον τῶν καθ᾽ ἕκαστον, οἷον ἀνδριαντοποιὸς μὲν ἀνδριάντος, ὁδὶ δὲ πουδὶ· καὶ τὰς μὲν δυνάμεις τῶν δυνατῶν, τὰ δ᾽ ἐνεργοῦντα πρὸς τὰ ἐνεργούμενα," Upon which passage Aquinas comments as follows: "Et est, quod causis debent proportionaliter respondere effectus, ita quod generalibus causis generales effectus reddantur, et singularibus singulares; puta, si dicatur quod statuae causa est statuam faciens, et huius statuae hic statuam faciens. Et similiter causis in potentia respondent effectus in potentia, et causis in actu effectus in actu" (lect. 6).

[3] *Con. Gen.* loc. cit. Cf. the following passage from the *Compendium Theologiae* (Pars Prima, cap. lxviii): "Quanto aliqua causa est magis universalis, tanto effectus eius est universalior. Nam causae particulares, effectus universalium causarum ad aliquid determinatum appropriant: quae quidem determinatio ad effectum universalem comparatur sicut actus ad potentiam. Omnis igitur causa quae facit aliquid esse in actu, praesupposito eo quod est in potentia ad actum illum, est causa particularis respectu alicuius universalioris causae. Hoc autem Deo non competit, cum ipse sit causa prima, ut supra ostensum est. Non igitur praeexigit materiam ad suam actionem."

logical status of any cause, the wider will be the range of its activity. Hence the more universal the effect, the higher will be the status of its cause. Now, being is more universal than motion, for, as we know, there are things such as stones and metals which do not possess the power of movement. Accordingly, above the cause of motion and change, there must be a higher cause, the cause of being, which is God. God does not therefore act *only* by causing motion and change. But any cause which produces things out of pre-existing matter must act by causing motion and change. Consequently God has not created things out of pre-existing matter.[1]

There is some danger of this argument proving too much. Logically we should infer that the first cause is not the cause of motion and change, but this conclusion would be in direct conflict with all that St. Thomas has already determined with regard to God. Hence his insistence that God does not act only (*tantum*) by causing motion and change. He does not so act, in other words, from necessity but from choice, and the reality in which he causes motion and change to occur is a reality the existence of which he has already caused.[2]

4. It is impossible that the universal cause should act only through motion and change, for by motion and change being is never made from non-being *simpliciter*, but only *this* being from this non-being. But God is the universal cause of being. He does not therefore act only through motion and change, and consequently he does not need pre-existent matter upon which to act.[3]

This argument may be compared with the following proof from the *Summa Theologica*:[4]

5. That which proceeds by a particular emanation is not presupposed by that emanation; thus a man does not exist before he is generated, on the contrary, man is made from not-man, and white from not-white. Accordingly, in the case of the emanation of the entire universe from the first principle, it is impossible that the existence of any being should be presupposed.

Are these two apparently contradictory arguments capable of being reconciled? At the start, it may be observed that it

[1] *Con. Gen.* loc. cit.   [2] Cf. Sylvester's *Comment.*
[3] *Con. Gen.* loc. cit.   [4] I.a. q. 45 : a. 1. c.

N*

was evidently Aquinas's intention to insist, in the former proof, upon the continuity which accompanies change. A particular effect has its particular cause; thus the body of an individual man is produced by his parents, it does not simply come into being without antecedents in the physical world. In other words, change involves an ordered sequence, it is not chaos. But the entire universe can have no antecedent reality; it is a universal effect, and can follow only from the universal cause, God. Hence it must have been created out of nothing.

In the latter argument he is, however, concerned to point out that emanation involves the appearance of something new. Although a man's parents are the cause of his existence, the man himself is yet a new creature. Now, the entire universe has emanated from God; it is therefore all *de novo*. Consequently it must have been created out of nothing. Thus it appears that the two arguments, far from being contradictory, are supplementary.

6. Everything acts according as it is actual. A particular thing is therefore actual in a particular way, and this both as regards itself and as regards other things. As regards itself, it is composed of matter and form, and so it is not wholly actual, since matter is pure potentiality and is actualized by form. Consequently it does not act with its whole being (*secundum se totam*) but by its form. As regards other things, it does not possess all their perfections but only its own determinate perfection. Accordingly a natural agent acts through motion, and so requires matter to serve as the subject of motion and change; wherefore it cannot create out of nothing. But God is wholly actual, and possesses in himself the perfections of all things. Hence the divine activity is capable of producing an entire substance, and needs no material upon which to act.[1]

7. When one physical object acts upon another, it is matter which receives the action of the agent, for the action of the agent, received in the patient, is the patient's actuality and form, or some beginning of form in it.[2] Without matter, there-

---

[1] *De Pot.* q. 3: a. 1. c. For other formulations of what is essentially the same argument, see *Con. Gen.* loc. cit. and *Com. Theol.* Pars Prima, loc. cit.
[2] "Igitur requiritur materia ab aliquo agente ut recipiat actionem ipsius: ipsa enim actio agentis in patiente recepta est actus patientis et forma, aut aliqua inchoatio formae, in ipso."

fore, such an agent cannot act. But the divine activity, since it is identical with the divine substance, is not received in matter, and so requires no pre-existent matter upon which to act.[1]

8. The potentiality of the matter upon which an agent acts must be proportionate to the action of the agent, otherwise it cannot receive it. But between God and matter there is no proportion, for the God's power is infinite. It is evident, then, that God will not need pre-existent matter in order to act.[2]

9. That there is no proportion between God and matter is also evident from the fact that there are different kinds of matter in different classes of substances. For the property of matter is receptivity. Now receptivity, in spiritual substances, is intelligible, since in them the intellect receives an intelligible species. The heavenly bodies, on the other hand, receive newness of situation; and terrestrial bodies receive, not only newness of situation, but newness of being. Clearly, then, there is no one matter which is in potentiality to universal being. But the divine activity extends universally to all being, hence there is no matter proportional to it. Matter cannot therefore be requisite to the divine activity.[3]

This was an extraordinary argument for Aquinas to advance. It assumes without question the correctness of the view that in every finite substance there is matter as well as form—in spiritual substances, indeed, an incorporeal and spiritual matter, but still a matter of some kind—a view which identifies matter and potentiality. But it was precisely upon this point that Aquinas differed from the majority of contemporary, as well as of earlier, theologians.[4] As we have seen, he maintained that in all spiritual substances—except God—there is potentiality, but no matter. Why then did he frame such an argument as the one before us? Sylvester suggests that, in the present instance, the term *matter* is to be interpreted "largely," in the sense of "everything receptive."[5] If this be true, we can

---

[1] *Con. Gen.* loc. cit.   [2] Loc. cit.   [3] Loc. cit.

[4] Cf. M.-D. Roland-Gosselin's edition of the *De Ente et Essentia*, Preface, pp. xvii–xviii.

[5] "Advertendum quod nomine *materiae* non accipitur hic materia prima, quae est pars essentialis rerum materialium, sed accipitur omne receptivum. Quia enim proprium materiae primae est esse receptivum formae substantialis, ideo omne alterius formae receptivum, ut sic, habet rationem materiae, largo modo accipiendo materiam. Et quia susceptiva sunt

state the same contention in St. Thomas's usual terminology as follows: Primary matter pertains only to corporeal substances. In spiritual substances there is potentiality, but no matter. Primary matter is, indeed, pure potentiality, but it is not the same *kind* of potentiality as that which belongs to spiritual substances. Accordingly it is not in potentiality to universal being.[1]

We have not thereby answered the question, however, as to why Aquinas chose to express himself in so strange a fashion. Was he striving to present an *argumentum ad hominem* to those who admitted the reality of a spiritual matter? The question is perhaps worth asking, but it would be foolish to give a categorical answer.

10. Even if it be admitted that there is matter proportional to the divine action, it can none the less be demonstrated that this matter owes its existence to God. In the first argument advanced to prove that God is the cause of all being it was shown that, in the case of any two entities, one of these entities will be the cause of the other, or else both entities will depend upon a third. We may apply the same principle here. It is clearly impossible that God should depend for his existence either upon our hypothetical matter or upon a third entity; matter must therefore owe its existence to God.[2]

11. It has already been proven that the primal being is the cause of all other beings and of the order obtaining among them. But potentiality and actuality are so ordered with respect to each other that, while in the case of any particular being potentiality may precede actuality in point of time, nevertheless this potentiality can be transformed into actuality only through the agency of some being already actual. Now, matter is being in potentiality (*ens in potentia*). And so God, who is pure actuality, must be prior to matter and, consequently, its cause.[3]

12. Primary matter is some sort of being, since it is being in

diversarum rationum, sicut et recipere diversificatur secundum rationem, eo quod aliud sit recipere formae immaterialis et aliud formae substantialis, et corpora caelestia recipiunt innovationem situs non autem innovationem essendi; ideo dicuntur diversarum rerum diversae esse materiae." (*Comment.* 8).

[1] "Ad esse universale"—i.e. to every mode of being.
[2] *Con. Gen.* loc. cit.
                                         [3] *Con. Gen.* loc. cit.

potentiality.[1] And God is the cause of all that is. God is therefore the cause of primary matter.[2]

The last proof is at once the briefest and most direct. If, as
has already been shown, God is the cause of all that exists, it is
immediately evident that creation must be *ex nihilo*, and that
primary matter, like everything else, must be the product of
the divine activity. The first and the eleventh proofs, which are
only more elaborate statements of the same contention, are
therefore unnecessary. The tenth proof, again, needlessly
retraverses steps already taken at an earlier stage in the process
of argumentation. The second, sixth, seventh, and eighth
proofs are unmistakably akin, inasmuch as they are all based
upon the composite nature of a particular cause and its need of
pre-existent matter upon which to act. To these the ninth
proof must be regarded as supplementary.[3]

Inasmuch as God is the cause of all that exists, he is the
cause, not only of accidental and substantial forms, but also of
primary matter.[4] To suppose, however, that this last, which is
in itself pure potentiality, can exist apart from conjunction

[1] "Materia prima aliquo modo est: quia est ens in potentia."

[2] *Con. Gen.* loc. cit. Cf. *Com. Theol.* Pars Prima, cap. lxviii; *Sum. Theol.*
I.a. q. 45: a. 2. c.

[3] Among the various objections to the doctrine of creation *ex nihilo* which
were stated and replied to by St. Thomas, the following is of especial
interest. It was contended that it is a corollary of the theory in question
that at a certain definite instant non-being must have come to an end,
and that likewise there must have been a certain definite instant which
was the beginning of being. Now, these two instants cannot be identical,
for the law of non-contradiction forbids us to assume that the universe
should both exist and not exist at the same time; nor yet can they be
diverse, since in that case we must posit between them a *tempus medium*
in which there would be something midway between affirmation and
negation ("*aliquid esse medium inter affirmationem et negationem*") (*De Pot.* q. 13:
a. 1. ob. 10).

To this St. Thomas replied that non-being cannot have occupied any
instant of real time, since before the universe existed there was no real
time, although it is possible for us to imagine a time before creation.
Moreover, since real time and imaginary time are not continuous, the
suggested positing of a *tempus medium* is illegitimate (*De Pot.* q. 3: a. 1.
ad 10[m]). Cf. also the following statement: "Deus praecedit mundum non
tantum natura, sed etiam duratione: non tamen duratione temporis, sed
aeternitatis: quia ante mundum non fuit tempus in rerum natura existens,
sed imaginatione tantum" (2 *Dist.* 1. q. 1: a. 5. ad 7[m]).

[4] *Sum. Theol.* I.a. q. 44: a. 2. c.

with form, is equivalent to assuming that it can be actual before it is actual.[1] That which is created is a concrete thing, a *res subsistens*; whence, not only of matter, but also of form and accident, it must be said that, in the strict sense of the word, they are not created, but rather that they are con-created.[2]

Since this is the case, it is clear that creation, strictly speaking (*proprie loquendo*), is neither motion nor change,[3] for motion or change is the act of that which is already in potentiality.[4] The truth that it is only the permanent that can change was thoroughly grasped by Aquinas. "In order that there should be change," he wrote, "there must be something which remains the same and yet is different now from what it was before."[5] A more thorough analysis lays bare the following three factors necessarily involved in every occurrence of change: (*a*) two terms, or extremes (*extrema*), the *terminus a quo*, and the *terminus ad quem*; (*b*) a subject which remains throughout identical with itself; and (*c*) a process of transition in which the subject ceases to be conditioned by the first term and begins to be conditioned by the second.[6] In creation, however, none of these requisites is present. There is neither a *terminus a quo* nor a pre-existent subject, and since no process can take place without a subject there can be no transition. Creation is, then, the instantaneous production of the entire substance of the thing created, for where there can be no change there can be no succession.[7]

The absence of succession from creation can also be proved by a method of argumentation similar to that just employed. In every movement of succession there is a mean between two extremes. In creation, as we have seen, there are not two

---

[1] *Sum. Theol.* I.a. q. 66: a. 1. c.; cf. I.a. q. 44: a. 2. ad 3ᵐ; I.a. q. 84: a. 3. ad 2ᵐ; *De Pot.* q. 4: a. 1. c.; 2 *Dist.* 12. q. 1: a. 4. sol.

[2] *De Pot.* q. 3: a. 1. ad 12ᵐ.

[3] "Quod creatio non est motus nec mutatio."

[4] *Con. Gen.* lib. II. cap. 17.

[5] "Oportet autem ad hoc quod sit mutatio, quod sit aliquid idem dissimiliter se habens nunc et prius" (*De Pot.* q. 3: a. 2. ad 4ᵐ). Cf. the body of the same article, wherein this contention is set forth at length. See also *Con. Gen.* loc. cit.

[6] *Con. Gen.* loc. cit.; *De Pot.* q. 3: a. 2. c.

[7] *Con. Gen.* lib. II. cap. 19; cf. *Com. Theol.* Pars Prima, cap. xcviii.

extremes; yet we may agree, for purposes of argument, to treat non-being and being as if they were its extremes. Now, it is evident that between non-being and being there can be no mean. Hence there can be no succession.[1]

Again, if there were succession in creation, the process of making would necessarily precede the state of being made, and such a process would require a subject. But before creation God alone existed. Yet it is impossible that God should have been the subject of the creative process, for motion is the act of that which is moved, not of the mover.[2]

In addition, two novel arguments are advanced to prove the same conclusion.[3] In the first place, we are reminded that succession occupies time, and that time, motion, and that which moves in time are alike divisible. This is evident in local motion, but is also true of alteration. In this case the division of forms which corresponds to the division of time consists of greater and lesser degrees of intensity (*intensio* and *remissio*). Thus, in the process of heating, degrees of intensity correspond to moments of time. Furthermore, there are divisions in the disposition of matter to the reception of the new form which also correspond to the moments of time. But in creation there are no degrees of intensity, for it is substances that are created, and substance does not admit of more or less.[4] And, since there is no pre-existent matter, there can be no divisions in the dispositions thereof; there can therefore be no succession.

In the second place, succession in the making of things is the result of matter not being properly disposed to the reception of form. Where matter is so disposed, form is received instantaneously, as in the case of the illumination of a transparent body. Here no local motion is required of the body illuminated, but only of the illuminator. In the process of creation, of course, there can be no local motion on the part of a matter which does not yet exist, nor yet on the part of God, the unmoved mover. Consequently creation is instantaneous. The world is, at one and the same instant, both created and being created, even as the same object is at once in a state of illumina-

[1] *Con. Gen.* lib. II. cap. 19.   [2] *Con. Gen.* lib. II. cap. 19.
[3] *Con. Gen.* lib. II. cap. 19.
[4] It will be recalled that degrees of intensity are not to be identified with degrees of being.

tion and being illumined.[1] Thus the objection that the doctrine of creation *ex nihilo* involves the occurrence of process and succession without a subject falls to the ground.[2]

Creation is a relation between the creature and God. In the Deity, of course, it is not a real relation, but is identical with the divine activity, and so with the divine essence.[3] In the creature it is a real relation.[4] As such it is an accident, and so the creature, as its subject, is logically prior to it. On the other hand, inasmuch as it is the beginning of the creature, it is in a certain mode (*quodammodo*) prior to the creature.[5]

Creativity, in St. Thomas's view, pertains to God alone. In the first place, he holds that it is impossible that any body should create. For no body acts unless it be moved; moreover, in accordance with the axiom that every agent produces its like, it must in turn cause motion in that upon which it acts. And movement implies succession, which is incompatible with creation.[6] Again, Aristotle has shown[7] that the mover and the entity moved must be together (*simul*), and in the case of bodies this involves contact. But before creation only the creator exists; it would be impossible, therefore, for a creating body to establish contact with anything.[8] Furthermore, since

[1] Cf. *De Pot.* q. 3: a. 1. ob. 11 and ad 11m.

[2] Cf. *Sum. Theol.* I.a. q. 45: a. 2. ob. 3 and ad 3m. Since primary matter cannot exist apart from form, it is clear that it, like everything else, is created instantaneously. Cf. *De Pot.* q. 4: a. 2. In the *Commentary on the Sentences* (2 *Dist.* 12. q. 1 : a. 4. sol.). Aquinas advocates the theory that the substances brought into being by the original act of creation were destitute of the active and passive powers (*virtutes activae et passivae*), which they later acquired through being perfected in "second being" (*esse secundo*). Cf. *De Pot.* q. 4: a. 1. c.

[3] *De Pot.* q. 3: a. 3. c. and ad 2m.

[4] But we must not make the mistake of supposing that, because it is a real entity apart from God, it is itself created; for this second creation would be also a real entity, and must likewise have been created, and so we should become involved in an infinite regress which is vicious (*Con. Gen.* lib. II. cap 18; *Sum. Theol.* I.a. q. 45: a. 3. ad 2m; *De Pot.* q. 3: a. 3. ad 2m). The point is one which has already been raised in connection with the general topics of relations between God and the creatures. It is the function of relations to relate, and they do not require to be connected with their terms by yet other relations.

[5] *De Pot.* q. 3: a. 3. ob. 3 and ad 3m; cf. *Sum. Theol.* I.a. q. 45: a. 3. ob. 3 and ad 3m.

[6] *Con. Gen.* lib. II. cap. 20.

[7] Cf. *Phys.* lib. VII. cap. ii.

[8] *Con. Gen.* loc. cit.; *Sum. Theol.* I.a. q. 45: a. 5. c.

agent and thing made are alike, a whole substance can be
produced only by another substance acting as a whole. But no
body can act as a whole substance, for it contains both matter
and form, whereas it acts by its form alone.[1] And, lastly, it is
clear that, the farther from actuality any potentiality may be,
the greater is the power of the agent which brings that potentiality into existence. Where there is no pre-existing potentiality, however, all determinate proportion disappears; consequently the power of an agent which brings something
into being *ex nihilo* is incomparably greater than that of any
agent which makes something out of matter. But no body is of
infinite power;[2] no body therefore can create.[3]

But what of spiritual beings other than God? These present
a more difficult problem. Here Aquinas's great adversary is
Avicenna. The Moslem philosopher had maintained that only
unity can proceed from unity. In accordance with this view,
he had taught that from the first principle there emanates
immediately only the first intelligence. This intelligence in
itself is not a necessary but only a possible or contingent being;
yet as relative to the first principle it is necessary. Furthermore,
it is able to contemplate both the first principle and itself. Its
contemplation of the first principle is productive of a second
intelligence, while, from its contemplation of itself, under its
two aspects of necessity and possibility, there proceed respectively the soul and the body of the first sphere, Saturn. From
the second intelligence, in like manner, there emanates a
similar triad, and thus descending we arrive at last at the
intellectus agens and the planet on which we live.[4]

The situation was further complicated by the fact that
certain Catholic theologians, among them Peter Lombard,[5]
had conceded that it was possible that the power to create

[1] *Con. Gen.* loc. cit.
[2] Cf. *Phys.* lib. VIII. cap. x; lib. III. cap. v.   [3] *Con. Gen.* loc. cit
[4] See *Metaphysices Compendium*, libri primi, quarta pars, tractatus II. cap. i.
Cf. Baron Carra de Vaux's *Avicenne*, ch. ix, also Djemil Saliba's *Étude sur
la Métaphysique d'Avicenne*, deuxième partie, ch. iv.
[5] "Ita etiam posset Deus per aliquem creare aliqua, non per eum tanquam
auctorem, sed ministrum, cum quo et in quo operaretur; sicut in bonis
operibus nostris ipse operatur et nos, nec ipse tantum nec nos tantum,
sed ipse nobiscum et in nobis: et tamen in illis agendis ministri eius sumus,
non auctores" (4 *Dist.* 5).

should be communicated by the Deity to a subordinate intelligence whose creative activity would nevertheless remain purely instrumental, since it would not operate by exercising its own inherent capacities but only in virtue of an ability imparted from without. It is not quite clear in what respect Aquinas conceived this position to differ from that of Avicenna. In the *De Potentia* he admits that "neither did the philosophers themselves"—presumably Avicenna and his followers—"hold that angels or intelligences create something except through a divine power existing in themselves, so that we are to understand that a second cause can have a twofold action, one pertaining to its proper nature, the other through the power of a prior cause."[1] Nevertheless, here, and in the *Commentary on the Sentences*,[2] he brands this opinion as heretical, and insists that it tends to idolatry. The heresy, however, apparently consisted in the belief that a creative power actually *had been* imparted to creatures. Peter Lombard's view that it *could have been* imparted[3] is merely "impossible."[4]

It is true that a first reading of Aquinas's preliminary discussion of Peter Lombard's position in the early work, the *Commentary on the Sentences*,[5] is apt to produce the impression that he is giving assent thereto.[6] Yet this is scarcely possible in view of his statement in the article immediately following that God alone is the immediate cause of all creatures,[7] as well as of his emphatic repudiation of the doctrine in the fourth book.[8] But, whether these apparent discrepancies are due to an actual change of opinion or not, there can be no doubt that in his later works he remained a steadfast opponent of the theory.

Avicenna's position was assailed by St. Thomas on the

[1] "Nec etiam ipsi philosophi posuerunt angelos vel intelligentias aliquid creare, nisi per virtutem divinam in ipsis existentem, ut intelligamus quod causa secunda duplicem actionem habere potest: unam ex propria natura, aliam ex virtute prioris causa" (q. 3 : a. 4. c.).   [2] 2 *Dist.* 1. q. 1 : a. 3. sol.
[3] "Communicari tamen potuisse" (*Comm.* loc. cit.).
[4] *De Pot.* loc. cit. Emphasis is here laid on the fact that for Peter the creative activity of the creatures could only have been instrumental—even if it had been real—and not *quasi auctoritate*, as apparently it was for "the philosophers."   [5] 2 *Dist.* 1. q. 1 : a. 3. sol.
[6] Cf. Carame's footnote to p. xxv of his Introduction to his edition of Avicenna's *Metaphysices Compendium*.
[7] "Ideo omnium illorum quae per creationem in esse exeunt, solus Deus immediate causa est."   [8] *Dist.* 5. q. 1 : a. 3. sol. 3.

following grounds. In the first place, it involves the limitation
of the divine power to a single effect. But this is impossible, for
before creation nothing existed which could impose any limitations upon the divine activity;[1] furthermore, the divine power
is infinite, and the divine goodness, which is the end of creation,
is not increased by the production of the creatures, and so is
independent of them. And, in the second place, it is a corollary
of the theory in question that the order obtaining in the universe is the result of chance, and not of intention,[2] which is
incredible.

The arguments advanced by Aquinas in defence of his own
view are the following:

1. The act of creation involves the production as a complete
substance of the thing created, and does not presuppose the
existence of anything whatsoever. Creativity pertains, therefore, to that which does not presuppose a prior and universal
cause, but is itself such a cause. Now, it has already been
proved that God is the cause of all things. It is clear, therefore, that no creature can create, inasmuch as no creature can
take the place of God.[3]

2. The more distant any potentiality is from actuality, the
greater is the power required to bring it into actuality. But the
distance between non-being and being is infinite. The creator
must therefore be possessed of infinite power which can be
found only in an infinite essence.[4]

---

[1] We are not here concerned with logical impossibilities, but with arbitrary
conditions imposed by some external reality, such as primary matter.

[2] *De Pot.* q. 3 : a. 16. c.; cf. *Sum. Theol.* I.a. q. 47 : a. 1. c.

[3] This argument is found in somewhat different forms in the *Contra Gentiles*
(lib. II. cap. 21), the *Summa Theologica* (I.a. q. 65 : a. 3. c.), the *Compendium
Theologiae* (Pars Prima, cap. lxix), the *Commentary on the Sentences* (2 *Dist.*
1. q. 1 : a. 3. sol.), and the *De Potentia* (q. 3 : a. 4. c.).

[4] *De Pot.* q. 3 : a. 4. sol.; 4 *Dist.* 5. q. 1 : a. 3. sol. 3; *Com. Theol.* Pars
Prima, cap. lxix. In the *De Potentia* four additional proofs are given of
the infinity of the creator's power. "Secunda ratio est, quia hoc modo
factum agitur quo faciens est. Agens autem agit secundum quod actu est;
unde id solum se toto agit quod totum actu est, quod non est nisi actus
infiniti, qui est actus primus; unde et rem agere secundum totam eius
substantiam solius infinitae virtutis est. Tertia ratio est, quia cum omne
accidens oporteat esse in subiecto, subiectum autem actionis sit recipiens
actionem; illud solum faciendo aliquid recipientem materiam non
requirit, cuius actio non est accidens, sed ipsa substantia sua, quod solius

3. The nobler (*nobilior*) the agent, the nobler is its action, for the order of actions corresponds to the order of causes. But the first[1] action is creation; it can therefore be due only to the primal agent, God.[2]

4. The higher the rank of a cause, the wider is the range of its activity. There is, therefore, a universal cause of all things, and the activity of any other cause presupposes as its subject an effect of this primal cause. Accordingly, since creation is the production of something *ex nihilo*, only the primal cause can create.[3]

5. The more universal the effect, the more universal and the prior is its cause. But the most universal effect is being; hence being is the effect of the universal cause, God.[4]

6. Nothing which is caused according to a certain nature (*secundum aliquam naturam*) can itself be the primal cause of that nature. Thus the humanity of Socrates is caused. Socrates cannot, therefore, be the primal cause of Humanity. Every universal agent is instrumental with respect to the primal cause of the whole species according to which it generates. But the being of everything other than God is caused. Hence it is

Dei est; et ideo solius eius est creare. Quarto ratio est, quia cum omnes secundae causae agentes a primo agente habeant hoc ipsam quod agant, ut in lib. *De Causis*, prop. xix et xx probatur: oportet quod a primo agente, omnibus secundis agentibus modus et ordo imponatur; ei autem non imponitur modus vel ordo ab aliquo. Cum autem modus actionis ex materia dependeat quae recipit actionem agentis, solius primi agentis erit absque materia praesupposita ab alio agente agere, et aliis omnibus secundis agentibus materiam ministrare. Quinta ratio est ducens ad impossibile. Nam secundum elongationem potentiae ab actu est proportio potentiarum de potentia in actum reducentium: quanto enim plus distat potentia ab actu, tanto maiori potentia indigetur. Si ergo sit aliqua potentia finita quae de nulla potentia praesupposita aliquid operetur, oportet eius esse aliquam proportionem ad illam potentiam activam quae educit aliquid de potentia in actum; et sic est aliqua proportio nullius potentiae ad aliquam potentiam, quod est impossibile. Nihili enim ad ens nulla est proportio, ut habetur IV Physic. Relinquitur ergo quod nulla potentia creaturae potest aliquid creare neque propria virtute, neque sicut alterius instrumentum."

[1] "First" in this instance is to be taken as equivalent to "highest" or "noblest"; cf. the *Comment.* of Francis Sylvester, 1.

[2] *Con. Gen.* lib. II. cap. 21.

[3] *Quodlib.* 3: a. 6. c. In the *Summa Theologica* (I.a. q. 65: a. 3. c.) this proof is found combined with the following.

[4] *Con. Gen.* loc. cit.; *Sum. Theol.* I.a. q. 45: a. 5. c.; *De Pot.* q. 3: a. 4. c.

clear that nothing except God can be the cause of being, unless instrumentally. Yet even this last is impossible, for the concept of an instrument is that of a moved mover, and there is no motion in creation.[1]

7. But although that which is caused according to a certain nature cannot be the cause of that nature *simpliciter*—since it would then be its own cause—yet it can be the cause of a concrete instance of it. So Plato can be the cause of the humanity of Socrates, although not *simpliciter*, for he would then have caused himself also. A univocal cause then acts by communicating a common nature to something by which it is specified or individuated. But in creation there is nothing previously existent which could be the cause of individuation. Consequently it is impossible that any created thing should itself create.[2]

8. Everything acts according as it is actual; the mode of action must therefore follow the mode of actuality. Thus the hotter a thing is, the more it heats. The action of each thing is accordingly determined with regard to genus, species, and accidents. But no determinate being can resemble another of the same genus or species except in genus or species, for in so far as anything is particular it is distinct from every other. No finite agent then can be the cause of anything in so far as it is distinct from others, but only of its genus or species. So that the activity of every such agent presupposes that whereby its effect individually subsists. Hence it does not create. Creativity pertains to an infinite being which contains in itself the likenesses of all things.[3]

9. Again, an instrument is a medium between a primal cause and its effect, whereby the influence of the primal cause is transmitted to the effect. Hence there must be something in that which is caused by the instrument which receives the influence of the primal cause. But this involves that the thing in question exists before it is created. It is evident, therefore, that nothing can function as an instrumental cause in creation.[4]

---

[1] *Con. Gen.* loc. cit.   [2] *Con. Gen.* loc. cit.
[3] *Con. Gen.* loc. cit. It will be observed that this argument states in different language the same idea as its predecessor, also that both arguments are concerned only with univocal causation. But the emanation of one intelligence from another is not an instance of univocal causation.
[4] *Con. Gen.* loc. cit.

10. Every instrumental agent accomplishes the end of the principal agent by acting in a manner that is in accordance with its own nature, consequently its effect will be prior in the order of generation to the effect of the principal agent. Thus the cutting of wood by a saw precedes the form of the bench which the carpenter is fashioning from that wood. Hence, if the Deity employ an instrument in creation, that instrument will produce an effect of its own which will be prior to being. But this is impossible, for that which is more universal is prior in the way of generation. Thus *animal* is prior to *man*.[1] And that which is most universal is being.[2]

11. A thing can be made either *per se* or *per accidens*. If, before it is made, it was not, it is made *per se*; if, before it is made, it was, it is made *per accidens*. Thus, if a white thing be made black, it is made both black and coloured, but black *per se*, since it is made so from non-black; seeing, however, that it was just as truly coloured when white as it is now that it is black, it is made coloured only *per accidens*. And so if anything, a man, for instance, or a stone, be made to exist, it is made man or stone *per se*, but being only *per accidens*, inasmuch as it is not made from non-being *simpliciter*, but only from *this* non-being.[3] Whatever, therefore, is made wholly from non-being is wholly made *per se*. But effects are proportionate to their causes; consequently its cause must be *per se* the cause of being, which cause is God.[4]

Thus the view which we sometimes hear advanced to-day that the noblest exercise of the creative power would be "the creation of creators" is at the opposite pole from the position of St. Thomas. To his mind it is the utter inability of even the most exalted finite being to create that reveals unmistakably the divine character of the act.

We now turn to the question of divine omnipotence. Since the creative activity of God produces its effects immediately, it is clear that this activity cannot be limited to any single effect. Did the Deity employ any instrument in creation, the resultant diversity might be attributed to the agency of this

[1] This illustration makes it clear that the priority referred to is ontological, not temporal. Cf. the *Comment.* of Sylvester, 9. 2.

[2] *Con. Gen.* loc. cit.; *Sum. Theol.* I.a. q. 45 : a. 5. c.

[3] The question as to whether the human soul is or is not created is not now within our purview.   [4] *Con. Gen.* loc. cit.

intermediary. Or, did he produce his effects from matter, a similar suggestion might be made, for we know that the same cause acting upon the diversity of matter will cause diverse effects. Thus fire, for example, will harden clay and melt wax. In creation, however, no cause can be found for the variety and diversity in the universe other than God himself, so that the range of the divine power must be unbounded.[1]

Moreover, to every perfect power there corresponds a class of its own *per se* and proper effects[2] to which it is able to extend. So the power of building, if perfect, extends to everything that can have the form of a house. But the divine power is the cause *per se* of being, and being is its proper effect; consequently it extends to all things which are not incompatible with being. The opposite of being is, of course, non-being. God can therefore do anything which does not include the concept of non-being—in other words, what does not involve a contradiction.[3]

Again, every agent acts according as it is actual; according to the mode in which anything is actual is, therefore, the mode of its power of acting. Thus man generates man, and fire fire. God is, however, the perfect actuality, containing in himself the perfections of all things. The divine power is, therefore, also perfect; accordingly, it must extend to all things which are not incompatible with the concept of actuality.[4] But only those things are so incompatible which involve a contradiction.[5]

Furthermore, since it is impossible for that which is potential to become actual except through the agency of an already existent actuality, did no such actuality exist, the potentiality would be otiose. But in nature there is nothing otiose. On the contrary, potentiality is for the sake of actuality (*propter actum*), and so to every potentiality there corresponds an active power.[6] Thus all things which are included within the potentiality of matter are brought into actuality by the active power in the

[1] *Con. Gen.* lib. II. cap. 22.   [2] "Per se et proprius effectus."
[3] *Con. Gen.* loc. cit.; cf. *Sum. Theol.* I.a. q. 25: a. 3. c.; also *De Pot.* q. 1: a. 7.
[4] "Est igitur sua virtus activa perfecta, ad omnia se habens quaecumque non repugnant rationi eius quod est esse in actu."
[5] *Con. Gen.* loc. cit.
[6] The contrast in the Latin is between *potentia passiva* and *potentia activa*.

heavenly body which is the primal active force in nature. But
God is the primal agent with respect to all created being. It is
possible, therefore, for God to produce whatever is included
within the potentiality of created being—in other words, whatever is not incompatible with the concept of created being.[1]

There are three ways in which an effect may be beyond the
power of a particular agent. In the first place, it may not
resemble it, and so cannot be caused by it; for every agent, as
we know, produces what is like itself in some respect. In the
second place, the excellence of the effect may surpass the
capacity of the agent. And, in the third place, the agent may
be unable to act upon a particular matter which is requisite
for the effect. Thus a carpenter cannot make a saw, because
he cannot make the iron of which the saw is made. But in
none of these ways can an effect be beyond the power of God
—not in the first, for everything, in so far as it has being,
resembles God; nor yet in the second, since God excels all
things in goodness and perfection; nor again because of any
defect of matter, for God does not require an already existing
matter upon which to act, but is himself the cause of matter,
which can be produced only by creation.[2]

At this point St. Thomas raises the question as to whether
God acts *ex necessitate naturae*. By "necessity of nature" he
appears to mean such necessity as constrains the forces of the
physical world to their habitual activities, the necessity which
makes stones sink in water and causes thunder to follow
lightning. That God does not act in this manner is, of course,
obvious from what has already been determined with respect
to the divine intelligence and will. Nevertheless, the point is
an important one for Aquinas, since, as Professor Gilson has
pointed out,[3] it was Avicenna's insistence that the divine
creativity is limited to a single effect which led him to main-

[1] The potentiality of created being, as Sylvester points out, is a logical
and not a passive potentiality. "Dicitur quod, licet potentia entis creati
non sit potentia passiva existens in natura, habet tamen quandam similitudinem cum potentia passiva: inquantum, sicut existens in potentia
passiva potest ab aliquo in actum produci, et sic esse in tali potentia est
posse de tali potentia produci; ita quod est in potentia entis creati, potest
creari" (*Con. Gen.* loc. cit.; *Comment.* 4. 3).

[2] *Con. Gen.* loc. cit.; cf. *De Pot.* q. 1: a. 3. c.

[3] *The Philosophy of St. Thomas Aquinas*, pp. 108–109.

tain that the power to create could be communicated to creatures, on the ground that otherwise there would be no more than a single finite existent. Accordingly, the following nine arguments are proffered us in support of his position.

1. In the discussion of divine omnipotence it has just been demonstrated that the divine power is not limited to one effect. But the power of any agent which acts from natural necessity is so limited. Hence God does not act from natural necessity.[1]

2. We have also seen that God can create anything the existence of which does not involve a contradiction. Yet there are many things which do not involve a contradiction that do not exist. The size of the various stars, for instance, as well as the distances separating them, might well be other than they are. But a power which brings into existence only a portion of the things which it is capable of causing does not act from natural necessity.[2]

3. Furthermore, God, the universal cause, contains within himself the likenesses of all his effects. And God is an intelligent being. Consequently, the likenesses of all things are in God in an intelligible mode. Accordingly, God acts by his intellect. But it has already been shown that the intellect acts only through the mediation of the will; the divine activity is, therefore, voluntary.[3]

4. Again, we are familiar with the distinction between immanent activity, which remains in the agent and perfects it, and transeunt activity, which passes into externality and perfects the thing made. The divine activity is of the former type, since it is identical with the divine substance. But actions of this kind proceed from knowledge and appetite, not from natural necessity.[4]

5. Since the universe is not the product of chance, but is ordered with respect to some good, it is clear that God acts with a definite end in view. Among agents that act toward the

[1] *Con. Gen.* lib. II. cap. 23; cf. *De Pot.* q. 3: a. 15. c.; *Com. Theol.* Pars Prima, cap. xcv.
[2] *Con. Gen.* lib. II. cap. 23. Cf. *Com. Theol.* Pars Prima, cap. xcv, where it is argued that infinite power cannot be determined with respect to this or that effect, and that consequently, since God is of infinite power, God must act freely. Clearly this proof adds nothing to the first.
[3] *Con. Gen.* lib. II. cap. 23; cf. *De Pot.* q. 3: a. 15. c.
[4] *Con. Gen.* lib. II. cap. 23; cf. *De Pot.* loc. cit.

accomplishment of some end, the first must be an agent which acts through its intellect and will, for those things which lack intellect act toward an end only as directed by something else. Accordingly, God acts intelligently and, therefore, voluntarily.[1]

6. Moreover, that which acts of itself is ontologically prior to that which acts because of another, otherwise we should be lost in an infinite regress. But that which does not control its own actions does not act of itself. Yet the primal agent must control its own actions. It must, therefore, act of itself, and this it can do only by its will.[2]

7. Again, the activity of the will is naturally and logically prior to the action of nature; for that which is more perfect is naturally (*naturaliter*) prior although temporally it may be posterior; and that which acts by its will is more perfect than that which acts from natural necessity. Accordingly, the activity of the primal agent must be voluntary.[3]

8. Furthermore, wherever there is joint action of will and nature, the power which acts by its will is superior. Thus, in man, the intellect which acts by its will is superior to the vegetable soul which acts from natural necessity. Hence, the divine power, which is superior to all, must act through the will.[4]

9. The object of the will is the good conceived as good. But a natural cause, since it is incapable of conceiving the good, acts only as directed to *this* particular good. Hence the former stands to the latter as a universal to a particular agent. But the particular agent is ontologically posterior to the universal agent, and acts as its instrument. Consequently, the primal agent must act voluntarily and not from natural necessity.[5]

The will, as we know, is moved to action only through some

---

[1] *Con. Gen*, lib. II. cap. 23. In the *Commentary on the Sentences* the argument is somewhat differently presented. "That which is ordered with respect to an end must," we are told, "be so ordered by something which is either separate from or conjoined to itself. But God cannot be ordered by anything external to himself. The divine activity must, therefore, be directed by some element in the nature of the Deity, and that element is his wisdom." See 1 *Dist.* 43. q. 2 : a. 1. sol.; also *De Pot.* q. 1 : a. 5. c.; q. 3 : a. 15. c.

[2] *Con. Gen.* loc. cit.

[3] *Con. Gen.* loc. cit.; cf. *Com. Theol.* Pars Prima, cap. xcv.

[4] *Con. Gen.* loc. cit. We have here in reality nothing more than an illustration annexed to the previous argument. Yet it is stated by St. Thomas as if it were an independent proof. 　　　　　[5] *Con. Gen.* loc. cit.

form of apprehension, whether sensuous or intellectual.[1]
Accordingly, since in God there is only intellectual apprehension, and since God knows other beings only through his
knowledge of himself, and since to know God is wisdom, it is
clear that God acts in accordance with his wisdom.[2] Again,
we have just seen that the likenesses of his effects subsist in God
in an intelligible mode, and that thus God is able freely to
produce a variety of objects, whereas the activity of a natural
agent is limited to one effect. Now, every voluntary agent
produces its effect in accordance with an intellectual concept.
Hence God, who is a voluntary agent, also produces his effects
through the wisdom of his intellect.[3] Moreover, the process of
ordering involves a twofold knowledge—a knowledge of the
relations and proportions in which they stand to one another,
and also a knowledge of those in which they stand to something higher which is their end. But God has ordered the
universe with respect to himself as its end. And to judge of
things by the highest cause is wisdom. God has, therefore,
brought things into being through his wisdom.[4] And we are
led to the same conclusion when we remember that the creatures are to be compared to God as artifacts to their maker,
for an artificer produces his effects by his wisdom and intellect.[5]

Although it has been made plain that God cannot do anything which involves a contradiction, Aquinas is not content
to dismiss the matter so, but proceeds to investigate the various
kinds of acts which would fall under this head. We know that
in God there is active power but no potentiality. It is plain,
therefore, that God cannot perform any action involving the
presence of potentiality in its subject. Active power is directed
to doing (*agere*), potentiality to being (*esse*); God cannot,
therefore, perform any action which would affect his being.
He cannot become a body, or be moved, or change. Nor can
he fail, for failure is a form of corruption. Furthermore, failure
implies privation, and so involves the presence of potentiality.

[1] Cf. *Con. Gen.* lib. I. cap. 72.   [2] *Con. Gen.* lib. II. cap. 24.
[3] *Con. Gen.* lib. II. cap. 24.   [4] *Con. Gen.* lib. II. cap. 24.
[5] *Con. Gen.* lib. II. cap. 24. The various considerations here presented have
already been set forth in the earlier discussions of the divine intelligence
and will. It is difficult to understand why Aquinas should have reverted
to these topics at this point, or what advance is made beyond the conclusions previously reached.

For the same reason it is impossible for God to be fatigued, to forget, to be conquered, to suffer violence, to repent, to be angry, to sorrow, or to sin.[1]

Moreover, the object and effect of active power is *made being* (*ens factum*). But no power can operate, except where the concept of its object has place. Sight, for example, is impossible where there is nothing actually visible. Consequently, God can do nothing contrary to the concept of *being* as being, or of *made being* as made. But the opposite of being is non-being. Hence, God cannot cause contraries to exist simultaneously.[2] He cannot cause the same thing to be and not to be at the same time, nor to possess at once incompatible qualities, nor yet to continue to exist when deprived of one of its essential characteristics. Hence the principles of such sciences as logic, geometry, and arithmetic, which are derived solely from the formal principles of things (*ex solis principiis formalibus rerum*), and upon which the essence of a thing depends, cannot be altered by God.[3] To make the past not to have been would also involve a contradiction, so this too is impossible *per se*.[4]

Similarly, there are certain actions which are incompatible with the concept of *being made*, as made. Thus, God cannot make another God, for the concept of being made includes the notion of dependence upon a cause; neither can he make another being equal to himself, for that which depends upon nothing is greater than that which depends upon another.[5] Again, God cannot cause anything to be conserved apart from himself,[6] for the conservation of anything is due to its cause.[7] Moreover, it has just been proved that God does not act from natural necessity, but is a voluntary agent; accordingly, he

---

[1] *Con. Gen.* lib. II. cap. 25; cf. 1 *Dist.* 42. q. 2 : a. 2. sol.; also *Sum. Theol.* I.a. q. 25 : a. 3. ad 2^m.

[2] *Con. Gen.* loc. cit.; cf. *Quodlib.* xii. q. 2. 1 : a. 2.

[3] *Con. Gen.* loc. cit.; 1 *Dist.* 42. q. 2 : a. 2. sol.

[4] *Con. Gen.* loc. cit.; *Sum. Theol.* I.a. q. 25 : a. 4. Cf. the following succinct statement in the *Commentary on the Sentences* (loc. cit.) : "Necesse est esse dum est, et impossibile est non esse tunc dum est, et cum ista necessitate et impossibilitate in praeteritum transit." See also *De Pot.* q. 1 : a. 3. ad 9^m.

[5] *Con. Gen.* loc. cit.

[6] The reference here is to the doctrine of divine conservation, which we shall later examine.   [7] *Con. Gen.* loc. cit.; cf. *De Pot.* q. 5 : a. 2.

cannot do what he cannot will. Now, it has been shown that God necessarily wills his own being and goodness and blessedness; he cannot, therefore, will the contrary of any of these.[1] And since God cannot will evil[2] he cannot sin.[3] It has also been shown[4] that the divine will is unchangeable; God cannot, therefore, prevent that which he wills from being fulfilled. His inability in this instance proceeds, however, from a necessity of supposition,[5] not from a necessity of his own nature. The divine will is not constrained with respect to the creatures[6]— on the contrary it acts freely, as has been proved; but that which it is presupposed to will it cannot also prevent from coming to pass.[7] And since God acts, not only by his will, but also by his wisdom and knowledge,[8] it follows that God cannot do what he has not foreseen that he will do, nor fail to do what he has foreseen that he will do.[9]

The doctrine of degrees of being also forbids us to assume that God can do whatever can be done by any creature. What there is of perfection in the creature is caused by God, but, in so far as the creature falls short of the divine likeness, it falls short of perfection. Thus, a stone, in so far as it has being, is like God; yet God is not a stone. Similarly, God is the cause whereby a man possesses the power of walking, yet God cannot walk for God is not a body.[10]

Such are the limitations which, in the opinion of St. Thomas, the law of non-contradiction places upon the divine activity. Since our interest is in the nature of God and not in the created universe, it is needless for us to follow our author in his efforts to determine whether certain specific actions do or do not fall

[1] The necessity which constrains God to will his own being, etc., is not a necessity of "nature" in the sense in which that word is here used—i.e. physical nature—but it is a necessity of the divine nature, which is identical with the divine essence. Cf. *Con. Gen.* lib. I. cap. 80.

[2] *Con. Gen.* lib. I. cap. 95.

[3] *Con. Gen.* lib. II. cap. 25; cf. 1 *Dist.* 42. q. 2 : a. 2. sol.; *De Pot.* q. 1 : a. 6.

[4] *Con. Gen.* lib. I. cap. 82.

[5] *Con. Gen.* lib. I. cap. 83.

[6] *Con. Gen.* lib. I. cap. 81–82; cf. *De Pot.* q. 1 : a. 5.

[7] *Con. Gen.* lib. II. cap. 25; *De Pot.* loc. cit.

[8] The divine will, wisdom, and knowledge are, it will be recalled, identical with the divine essence, and so, in reality, with one another, being distinguished only by the reason.

[9] *Con. Gen.* loc. cit.   [10] 1 *Dist.* 42. q. 2 : a. 1. sol.; *De Pot.* q. 1 : a. 6.

within the scope of the divine power—whether, for instance, God is able to make any creature better than he has made it,[1] to make a better universe,[2] or to cause the same body to be in two places at once;[3] for the principles determining the answers to these questions are already before us.

We may, therefore, pass on to the next problem confronting us. Can we be sure that the divine knowledge is not limited to a certain definite number of possible effects, in which case God would act, not indeed from a necessity of "nature," but yet from a necessity of knowledge? The point is an important one, since a negative answer would certainly have been returned by the followers of Avicenna, in accordance with their view that the universe emanates of necessity from the eternal act of divine self-knowledge, and that God is ignorant of particulars. To emphasize his complete disagreement with them Aquinas thought it worth while to raise the question at this point. The answer is, of course, obvious. It has been shown, in the discussion of the character of the divine knowledge, that God contains in himself the likenesses of all the effects which he is capable of producing, and, in intuiting his own essence, is aware of them all. The divine knowledge is, therefore, not limited to certain determinate effects. Again, the divine essence is infinite; whereas everything else that exists is essentially finite; and is, by the very concept of its essence, included in a definite genus and species. Consequently, even were the creatures infinite in number, they could not be equated with, nor could they exhaust, the divine essence which, in its limitless fecundity, would always contain the likenesses of yet other possible effects. And, in knowing his own essence, God is aware of this infinite richness. It follows that God, as has already been proved, knows an infinite number of things. And it is by his knowledge that he brings his effects into existence. Clearly, then, God's knowledge cannot be confined to any determinate number of effects. It could be so confined if it were true that God was aware only of those effects which he does actually bring into being, and was ignorant of those which are merely possible. But it has been demonstrated that God knows even those things which do not exist, which never

---

[1] 1 *Dist.* 44. q. 1 : a. 1 ; *Sum. Theol.* I.a. q. 25 : a. 6.
[2] 1 *Dist.* 44. q. 1 : a. 2.   [3] *Quodlib.* III. q. 1 : a. 2.

did exist, and which never will exist. Hence, God does not act from necessity of intellect or of knowledge.[1]

These arguments are, indeed, mere restatements of what has already been said, in effect at least, in treating of the divine knowledge. There is yet a further proof, however, which, while closely resembling the second argument advanced in the twenty-sixth chapter of the first book of the *Contra Gentiles*, yet differs from it slightly in method of approach, and is interesting from the manner in which it is stated. The divine knowledge, as we have frequently been told, is related to its effects as the knowledge of an artificer to his artifacts. Every art includes, however, within its sphere all things included in the genus subject to that art. So the art of building includes within its sphere all houses. But the genus subject to the divine art is being,[2] for God through his intellect is the universal principle of being. The causality of the divine intellect extends, therefore, to everything not incompatible with the concept of being, and is able to create at pleasure without being limited to any definite effects.[3]

It will be recalled that, upon several occasions, we have found St. Thomas treating being *as if* it were a genus, but never before have we discovered him admitting in so many words that it is a genus. What now of the ferocious condemnations passed upon David of Dinant for saying precisely the same thing? Are we to assume, in defence of St. Thomas's consistency, that he is here using the term *genus* in a purely analogical sense? But might not the same apology be made for the heretical David? And is it not, to say the least, strange that the requirements of his own philosophy should lead Aquinas so often to imply, and at last directly to assert—in whatever sense that assertion be understood—what he has elsewhere so explicitly and so vehemently denied?

Since the object of the will is the *bonum intellectum*, everything which the intellect can apprehend under the concept of *good* falls within the scope of the will. Consequently, inasmuch as the divine intellect is not limited to certain determinate effects, neither is the divine will. Moreover, it has previously been demonstrated that God does not of necessity will anything

[1] *Con. Gen.* lib. II. cap. 26.
[2] "Genus autem subiectum divinae arti est ens."   [3] *Con. Gen.* loc. cit.

other than himself. Accordingly, no effects of the divine will proceed from necessity, but, on the contrary, all effects proceed from its free disposition.[1]

Nevertheless, it might be contended that God can do only that which he ought to do, that the divine creativity operates in response to "a debt of justice" (*ex debito justitiae*), to use the language of Aquinas. That such is not the case is, however, clear for the following reasons:

1. Before the creation nothing existed; there was, therefore, no one to whom justice was due.

2. Justice is the rendering to each one of that which is his own. Accordingly, the act of justice is subsequent to another act whereby the subject acquires that which is his own. But it is through creation that a creature begins to have that which is his own. Consequently, creation is not an act of justice.

3. No one owes anything to another upon whom he is not in some way dependent, or from whom he has not directly or indirectly received something which he owes. But God is dependent upon nothing, neither does he lack anything which he could receive from another. The same conclusion, therefore, follows.

4. In any genus that which exists for its own sake (*propter se*) is prior to that which exists for the sake of another (*propter aliud*). But that which is first among all causes acts as a cause for its own sake alone; whereas that which acts because of a debt of justice acts, not for its own sake, but for the sake of that to which it is in debt. God did not, therefore, create, because of a debt of justice.[2]

Is it possible, however, that creation was due to the divine goodness itself which is its end? There are two ways in which a thing may be due—in return for benefactions, or as requisite to the perfection of some subject, as hands, for instance, are requisite to the perfection of a man. But before creation nothing existed which could owe aught to the divine goodness; while God, on the other hand, is perfect in himself. Moreover, it has been proved that God does not of necessity will anything other than himself. And it has just been shown that God does

---

[1] *Con. Gen.* lib. II. cap. 27.

[2] *Con. Gen.* lib. II. cc. 28 and 29. The importance of the first argument obviously far transcends that of the three other proofs, which are little more than amplifications of it.

not create from necessity of nature, or from necessity of knowledge, or from necessity of will, or from necessity of justice.
Accordingly, the act of creation is not due to the divine
goodness in any mode of necessity.[1]

If, indeed, the term *justice* be interpreted largely, we may
say that there is justice in the creation of things, inasmuch as
it becomes the divine goodness to create. Yet, strictly speaking,
we cannot say that God owed it to himself to create, for the
relation of justice can hold only between two or more persons.[2]

But when we turn our attention from creation as a whole to
the production of a particular thing, we find that a relation of
justice can hold between a creature naturally (i.e. ontologically)
prior and another naturally posterior. If the entity naturally
prior be prior also in order of existence, the entity posterior
will become due because of its predecessor; if the entity
naturally prior be posterior in order of existence, the entity
which is earlier in time becomes due because of the later.
Thus medicine is due to precede that health may follow. But,
in each case, the "debt or necessity" (*debitum sive necessitas*) is
owed by that which is naturally posterior to that which is
naturally prior. And in each case the necessity is not absolute
but conditional. If *that* is to be made, *this* must first exist. In
the production of the creatures, there is a threefold conditional
necessity. First, what is conditionally owed may be owed by
the universe as a whole to each of its parts which is necessary
for the perfection of the whole. Thus, if God willed to create
this particular universe, it was necessary that he should make
the sun and moon, without which the universe could not exist.
Secondly, what is conditionally due may be owed by one
creature to another. Thus, if God willed that plants and
animals should exist, it was necessary that he should make the
heavenly bodies by which that existence is conserved. Thirdly,
what is conditionally due in each creature is in regard to its
parts, properties, and accidents, which are requisite to its
existence or to one of its perfections. Thus, if God willed to
make man, it was necessary that he should give him will, body,
and sense. In all this God is not said to be a debtor with
respect to the creature, but with respect to the completion of
his own dispositions.[3]

[1] *Con. Gen.* loc. cit.   [2] *Con. Gen.* loc. cit.   [3] *Con. Gen.* loc. cit.

Absolute necessity is to be found in connection with essential principles and efficient causes. In creation the only efficient cause is God, but between an efficient created cause and its effect absolute necessity also obtains. The relation between a created material or formal cause and its effect is likewise absolutely necessary. A body made up of the elements must be either hot or cold. The angles of a triangular surface must be equal to two right angles.[1] But, according to this, God cannot be called a debtor, rather the debt of necessity lies in the creature.[2]

It might be supposed that the fact that all things are contingent upon the divine will, which acts from no other necessity than that of supposition,[3] is incompatible with the presence of absolute necessity among them in any form. Yet there are entities which possess no possibility of non-existence, either because they exist apart from matter—i.e. the spiritual substances—or because their matter is incapable of receiving any other forms—i.e. the heavenly bodies; and such entities exist of simple and absolute necessity. The objection may, of course, be raised that all things, inasmuch as they come from nothing, tend to return to nothing, and that so there must be in them a potentiality to non-being. But to this it may be replied that they tend to return to nothing even as they came from nothing, by the power of the divine agent; and that accordingly, while there is in them no potentiality (*potentia*) of non-being, there is in the Creator power (*potentia*) either to give them being or to stop the inflow of being into them.[4] Moreover, it has been proved that created things exist in the mode in which God wills them to exist, and that God wills some of them to exist necessarily and others contingently.[5] It has also been shown that it comports with the divine perfection that God should impart his likeness to the creatures in so far as it is compatible with created being. To exist necessarily is,

---

[1] *Con. Gen.* loc. cit.

[2] "Secundum hanc Deus debitor dici non potest, sed magis in creaturam necessitatis debitum cadit."   [3] See pp. 344–345.

[4] "Sed Creatori inest potentia ut eis det esse vel eis desinat esse influere" (*Con. Gen.* lib. II. cap. 30). The phraseology is here reminiscent of the Neoplatonic doctrine of emanation by "overflowing."

[5] "Uterque enim modus habet aliquam similitudinem cum Deo" (Sylvester, 2. 2).

however, not incompatible with created being, for nothing
prevents that that which is necessary should have a cause of
its necessity, even as the conclusions of a proposition follow
from its premises. Again, the farther anything is from being in
itself[1]—which is God—the nearer it is to non-being, and *vice
versa*. But the things which already exist are near to non-being
because they have a potentiality to non-being.[2] The completeness of the order of the universe requires, therefore, that the
entities nearest to God be devoid of all potentiality to
non-being; consequently, they will be absolutely necessary.

Thus it will be seen that the fact that all things are contingent
with respect to God does not prevent particular effects following
of necessity upon their proximate causes. It is not necessary
that an animal be composed of contraries, but since it is so
composed, its death is inevitable. The natures of created beings
are what they are because of the free will of God, but since
they are what they are, their effects are absolutely necessary.[3]

Since matter and form are the essential principles of a thing,
whatever pertains to anything by reason of its matter or form
belongs to it of absolute necessity. This is true in a threefold
sense. Firstly, with respect to the being of a substance. Matter
is being in potentiality, and what is capable of being is also
capable of not being; every body in the matter of which there
is potentiality to another form is, therefore, necessarily corruptible. Form, on the other hand, is actuality, and through it
things actually exist. Hence spiritual substances have, as we
have seen, no potentiality to non-being, and so necessarily
exist. In the case of the heavenly bodies again, perfection of
form is equal to the entire potentiality of matter, with the
result that there remains no potentiality to any other form,
hence the absolute necessity of their existence. Secondly, there
is absolute necessity in the relation to the parts of their matter
and form where these principles are not simple. Thus the
matter proper to man is composite and necessarily contains

---

[1] "Ab eo quod per seipsum est ens."
[2] "Quae autem iam sunt, propinqua sunt ad non esse per hoc quod habent
potentiam ad non esse"—a curious statement in view of what has just
been said concerning the nature of the heavenly bodies. Evidently Aquinas
had in mind sublunary objects (*Con. Gen.* loc. cit.).
[3] *Con. Gen.* loc. cit.

elements, humours, and principal organs. Also, the form of man is that of a rational animal; man must, therefore, needs be both rational and animal. Thirdly, there is absolute necessity in the relation of the essential principles to the properties following upon matter and form. A saw, because it is of iron, must needs be hard; a man must be susceptible to instruction.

The necessity pertaining to an agent can be considered from the point of view of the action or from the point of view of the ensuing effect. The former is like the necessity which an accident draws from its essential principles. As the accident follows from these principles, so does the action from the form whereby the agent is rendered actual. If the action be of the immanent variety, such as sensing or knowing, its necessity is dependent upon nothing external. Transeunt action may, on the other hand, be frustrated by the absence of potentiality in the object to receive its action. Thus wool cannot be made into a saw. For an effect to follow it is requisite that there be receptive potentiality in the patient, and in the agent victory over the patient, so that it is able to transmute it to a contrary disposition.[1] This may take place through violence if the effect be contrary to the nature of the patient, as when a stone is thrown into the air. If, however, the action be in accordance with the nature of the patient, then the necessity will not be of violence but of the natural order. If the disposition whereby the effect necessary follows be absolutely necessary both in agent and patient, we have a case of absolutely necessary causation such as occurs in those entities which act of necessity and always. If the necessity be not absolute, then there will be no necessary causation, unless we suppose that both agent and patient happen to be disposed to such an action. This holds true of these causes which can fail through defect of power or be thwarted by the violence of some contrary nature, and which, accordingly, do not act uniformly or necessarily, but only in most instances.

Lastly, a twofold necessity follows from a final cause. Whether the cause be voluntary or necessary, it intends its end, and in so far as it intends it, acts. If voluntary, it acts through the will;

---

[1] "Oportet igitur, ad hoc quod sequatur effectus, quod in passo sit potentia ad recipiendum, et in agente sit victoria supra passum, ut possit ipsum transmutare ad contrariam dispositionem."

if natural, its action follows from its form. Hence, necessity is in the end in the same mode that it is in the agent. Furthermore, necessity is the end inasmuch as it is later in the order of existence. Thus we say that a saw must be of iron if it is to do the work of a saw. But such necessity is conditional.

This lengthy inquiry into the nature and modes of causality was prefixed[1] by St. Thomas to his discussion of the various arguments for and against the eternity of the world, and its findings were accordingly presupposed by him throughout his treatment of this problem, a problem so vitally related to his view of the nature of God that it is imperative that we examine it in detail.

Aquinas's first step was to attempt to show that the universe does not necessarily exist perpetually. If we assume that it does, we are compelled, as he pointed out, to assume that this necessity either pertains to the universe in itself, or else is imparted to it from without. But the former alternative is impossible, for it has been proved that every finite entity owes its being to the primal cause. Yet, if the necessity be due to an external cause, that cause must be either efficient or final. The effect of an efficient cause is, however, necessary only when the agent acts of necessity; and we know that God, the efficient cause of the universe, does not act of necessity. In the case of a final cause, that is necessary without which the end cannot exist—as life cannot exist without food—or without which it cannot so well exist, as a journey cannot so well take place without a horse. But the end of the divine will is the divine goodness which does not depend upon the creatures either for its being, which is necessary *per se*, or for its well-being, since it is perfect *simpliciter*.[2] Hence the perpetual existence of the creatures is not necessary. Moreover, the result of the activity of the will is not necessary unless the will must will it, and we have seen that God does not will of necessity but freely.[3] Again, we are aware that the divine activity is immanent and not transeunt, being identical with the divine will; hence things exist in the mode in which God wills them

[1] *Con. Gen.* lib. II. cap. 30.   [2] *Con. Gen.* lib. II. cap. 31.
[3] *Con. Gen.* loc. cit. This argument obviously differs from the latter portion of the previous proof only in that it stresses the freedom with which the divine will acts.

to exist. And it is not necessary that God will the creatures to exist perpetually, since it is not even necessary that God will them to exist at all.[1] Furthermore, a voluntary agent does not will of necessity unless because of something "due." But it has been shown that God does not produce the creation as a whole because of any debt.[2]

It has also been made clear that absolute necessity is not found in the relation of the creatures to the primal principle, the existence of which is necessary *per se*, but in the relations of particular effects to created causes the existence of which is not necessary *per se*. But the necessity which springs from a relation to something the existence of which is not necessary *per se* cannot require anything to have existed always. Thus, if something runs, it follows that it is moved, but not that it should always be moved, for running is not necessary *per se*. It is not necessary, therefore, that the existence of creatures should be perpetual.[3]

Arguments have, however, been advanced to prove that the world must be eternal. These can be divided into three classes according as they proceed *ex parte Dei, ex parte creaturae*, or *mundi ex parte factionis*. The proofs comprised in the first class are the following:

1. Every agent which is not perpetually active, when moved, is moved either *per se* or *per accidens*. But God, the unmoved mover, is moved neither *per se* nor *per accidens*. Yet the creatures are products of the divine activity; they must, therefore, have always existed.[4]

2. The divine action is eternal. Were it not so, the Deity would require to be transformed from a potential into an actual agent, which in turn would require the existence of a prior actuality, which is impossible. Moreover, the divine action is identical with the divine substance. Accordingly,

---

[1] *Con. Gen.* loc. cit.   [2] *Con. Gen.* loc. cit.   [3] *Con. Gen.* loc. cit.
[4] *Con. Gen.* lib. II. cap. 32. The difference between being moved *per se* and *per accidens* is thus illustrated by St. Thomas. The action of fire, which has not always been burning, but which begins to burn, either because it is newly kindled, or because it is moved into contact with something combustible, is an example of the former. A mover which moves an animal anew, either from within—as when it wakens after digesting and begins to move—or from without—as when fresh actions lead to the beginning of another action—is an example of the latter.

since the divine action is eternal, its effects must also be eternal.[1]

3. If we posit a sufficient cause, we must also posit its effect, for if the effect do not necessarily follow, the cause is not a sufficient cause. But God is the sufficient cause of the universe, since he is at once its final, exemplar, and efficient cause, neither does he lack any power which might be found in another cause. Consequently, since God is eternal, the divine effects must also be eternal.[2]

4. A voluntary agent does not postpone the execution of his intent except because of something anticipated which is not yet present. This may be something in the agent himself such as the perfection of a capacity to act or the removal of some impediment; or it may be something external, the presence of the person before whom it is to be done or the opportune time to do it. But there is no imperfection in or impediment to the divine activity. Furthermore, it is eternal, for the divine will is unchangeable; and, even were it not so, no external stimulus could have existed before the creation which could move it to fresh activity. Hence the effects of the divine will must be eternal.[3]

5. Every agent which wills to act at one time and not at another can do so only with reference to an imagined time-series. But to imagine a time-series involves change in the imagination or in that which is imagined, since temporal succession is caused by sequence of movements. It is, therefore, impossible that the will should initiate a new motion which is not preceded by a prior motion; and so the sequence of movements and things moved can have had no beginning.[4]

6. An intelligent agent selects one alternative rather than another only because the one enjoys a certain pre-eminence over the other. Where there is no difference there can be no choice. An agent which is utterly indifferent to two alternatives is in a state of potentiality akin to that of matter, and from it

[1] *Con. Gen.* loc. cit.; *De Pot.* q. 3: a. 17. ob. 12, 26; cf. *Sum. Theol.* I.a. q. 46: a. 1. ob. 10.
[2] *Con. Gen.* loc. cit.; *De Pot.* q. 3: a. 17. ob. 4; *Sum. Theol.* I.a. q. 46: a. 1. ob. 9. Cf. also the third argument in the *De Aeternitate Mundi.*
[3] *Con. Gen.* loc. cit.; *De Pot.* q. 3: a. 17. ob. 9, 13; 2 *Dist.* 1. q. 1: a. 5. ob. 12, 14; *Com. Theol.* Pars Prima, cap. xcvii.
[4] 2 *Dist.* 1. q. 1: a. 5. ob. 13; cf. *De Pot.* q. 3: a. 17. c.

no action can issue. Now between non-being and non-being there can be no difference. Had the universe, then, been ever non-existent, nothing could ever have come into existence. For beside God nothing would have existed, and in nothingness there is no difference of moment from moment whereby one might be preferred to the other as the moment suitable for creation. Nor could any ground of preference be found in the eternity of God which is uniform and simple. Consequently, God must will either that nothing should ever exist or that creatures should always exist. But creatures do exist; they have, therefore, always existed.[1]

7. We have seen that things which are willed with respect to an end derive their necessity from that end. So long, then, as the end remains the same that necessity continues, unless the relation of the entities in question to that end be altered. Now, the divine goodness is the end of the universe, and it always remains the same in itself and in its relation to the divine will. Accordingly, through all eternity creatures must have been produced in the same way by the divine will.[2]

8. It has been made clear that the purpose of God in creation is not the increase of the divine goodness, which is impossible, but the communication of it to others as far as possible. Consequently, since all things participate in the divine goodness in so far as they have being, the longer they exist the more they will participate therein. But the divine goodness is infinite, hence it pertains to it to communicate itself in an infinite mode and not in a determinate time. Thus, the divine goodness requires the perpetual existence of the universe.[3]

9. God necessarily wills his own goodness and all that pertains to it. But the production of creatures does pertain to the divine goodness; God, therefore, necessarily wills to produce creatures throughout eternity.[4]

To these various arguments Aquinas replied as follows:

1. Newness of an effect is indicative of a change in the cause in the case of a cause which requires to be moved from quiescence to activity, but not in the case of God whose action is identical with his essence. Hence the divine effects can come

---

[1] *Con. Gen.* loc. cit.   [2] *Con. Gen.* loc. cit.; *De Pot.* q. 3: a. 17. ob. 14.
[3] *Con. Gen.* loc. cit.; *De Pot.* q. 3: a. 17. ob. 1.
[4] *De Pot.* q. 3: a. 17. ob. 7.

into being *de novo* without the Deity being moved either *per se* or *per accidens*.[1]

2. Although the divine action is eternal, it is not necessary that its effect be eternal; for God is a voluntary agent, neither is there any intermediary between the act of his will and its effect similar to the action of the motive power in us. God's will being identical with his intelligence, the effect follows as determined by his intellect and as ordered by his will. And as the intellect determines every other condition of the thing made, so it determines its place in time. Hence, no new volition is requisite to bring the effect into existence, for the effect follows from the changeless and eternal volition of God at the time when it is eternally willed to follow. For, the action being presupposed, the effect follows according to the requirements of the form which is the principle of action; and in voluntary agents the form is that which is conceived.[2]

3. From the sufficiency of the cause the eternity of the effect cannot be deduced. The effect of a natural cause must, indeed, follow upon its cause, for the action of nature is according to what the nature is. But the proper effect of will is what the will wills, otherwise it would not be a proper effect but alien. And as the will wills its effect to be of such a nature, so it wills it to exist at such a time. Consequently, if the will be a sufficient cause, its effect will exist, not when the will exists, but when it wills the effect to exist.[3]

4. The effect of the divine will is not delayed, for it exists at the time when it is willed to exist by an agent which does not act in time but which has willed it from eternity.[4]

5. It has been proved that the divine intellect knows all things at once, and knows them as present; whence the fact that God wills a creature to exist at a certain moment of

---

[1] *Con. Gen.* lib. II. cap. 35.

[2] *Con. Gen.* loc. cit.; cf. *Sum. Theol.* I.a. q. 46: a. 1. c. ad 10^m; *De Pot.* q. 3: a. 17. ad 12, 26. It is to be remarked that, as Sylvester points out (*Comment.* 2. 3), it is only an immanent activity which could be eternal and yet produce an effect which is not eternal.

[3] *Con. Gen.* loc. cit.; cf. *De Pot.* q. 3: a. 17. ad 4^m; *Sum. Theol.* I.a. q. 46: a. 1. ad 9^m.

[4] *Con. Gen.* loc. cit.; cf. *De Pot.* q. 3: a. 17. ad 9^m, 13^m; 2 *Dist.* 1. q. 1: a. 5. ad 12^m, 14^m; *Com. Theol.* Pars Prima, cap. xcvii.

time, before which it has not existed, involves no change in himself.[1]

6. This argument refutes itself. Before creation not only were there no differences because of which one moment of time could be preferred to another, there were no moments of time at all. God is not an agent who acts in time, but who produced time together with the creatures. Consequently, it is meaningless to ask why God created the universe now and not before, although it is not meaningless to ask why God was not always bringing it into existence. There is an analogy in this respect between time and space, for particular objects are in space, yet the heaven which encloses them all is not in space, so that it would be meaningless to ask why the heaven was created in this portion of space and not in that.[2]

7. The end of the divine activity is, indeed, the divine goodness, yet God does not act in order to bring that goodness into existence, nor to make it better—for it is already perfect—nor even to possess it, for he is identical with it. On the contrary, God acts, as we know, in order to produce effects which will participate in that goodness. The reason for the divine activity is, then, not the uniform relation of end to agent, but the relation of end to effect. Hence, the eternity of the effect does not follow from the uniform relation of end to agent. The divine action is not necessitated by the divine goodness, but proceeds *ex simplici voluntate*.[3]

8. Every agent which produces an effect that participates in its form intends to impress on it its own likèness. But, in the case of God, such representation cannot be in the way of equality, for cause and effect are not univocal. If they were, the divine effects would of necessity be eternal. But actually, God is represented by his effects as the transcendent is represented by that which it transcends, and this transcendence is made evident most of all by the fact that the created universe has not always existed; for by this we are led to realize that all things have God as their author, and that his power is not constrained to produce its effects after the manner of a natural cause, and, consequently, that he is a voluntary and intelligent agent.[4]

---

[1] 2 *Dist*. 1. q. 1 : a. 5. ad 13^{m}; *De Pot*. q. 3 : a. 17. c.
[2] *Con. Gen*. loc. cit.   [3] *Con. Gen*. loc. cit.; *De Pot*. q. 3 : a. 17. ad 14^{m}.
[4] *Con. Gen*. loc. cit.; *De Pot*. q. 3 : a. 17. ad 1^{m}.

, 9. God necessarily wills his own goodness, as has been proved, but he does not necessarily will the existence of anything external to himself, as has also been proved.[1]

I turn now to the arguments of the second class:

1. Things which have no potentiality to non-being must be. And such things there are. For we have seen that only creatures in which there is matter susceptible to contrary forms (*materiam contrarieti subiectam*) have a potentiality to non-being, whereas intellectual substances and composite substances, like the heavenly bodies, of which the matter is not subject to contrary forms, and which are, therefore, incorruptible, necessarily exist, and, consequently, have existed always.[2]

2. The duration of anything is according to the power of being which it possesses—unless, indeed, it be corrupted *per accidens*, as by violence. But the power of being of spiritual substances and the heavenly bodies is not determined to a limited time but to being always.[3]

3. Whenever anything begins to be moved *de novo*, either the mover or the moved must be other now that the movement is taking place from what it was before, or else this must be true of both of them; for a new relation does not come into being without a change of one or both of its extremes. Consequently, before any movement which begins *de novo*, there must have been another movement either in the mover or the thing moved. So either we must proceed to infinity in a series of movements, or else posit an eternal motion. On either alternative, there will always have been motion and things that were moved. Hence there have always been creatures in existence.[4]

4. Every agent which generates its like intends to conserve in the species that perpetual being which it cannot conserve in the individual. But it is impossible that a natural yearning should be deceptive (*vanus*). The species must, therefore, be perpetual.[5]

---

[1] *De Pot.* q. 3: a. 17. ad 7ᵐ.
[2] *Con. Gen.* lib. II. cap. 33; *Sum. Theol.* I.a. q. 46: a. 1. ob. 2; *De Pot.* q. 3: a. 17. ob. 2.
[3] *Con. Gen.* loc. cit.
[4] *Con. Gen.* loc. cit.; *Sum. Theol.* I.a. q. 46: a. 1. ob. 5; cf. 2 *Dist.* 1. q. 1: a. 5. ob. 8.　　　　　　　　　　　[5] *Con. Gen.* loc. cit.

5. If time be perpetual, motion must be perpetual; for time is the "number of motion."[1] Accordingly, there will always be movable entities, for motion is the act of the movable. But time must be perpetual, since we can no more conceive it to be without a *now* than we can conceive a line to be without a point; and a *now* is always the end of a past and the beginning of a future,[2] for the *now* of time differs from the now of eternity in that it is to be conceived of as flowing. No *now* can, therefore, be the first or last *now*. Hence, there must always have been motion and movable things.[3]

6. If one cannot deny without, in the very act of denial, affirming the being of some thing, then that thing must be. So it is with time. For if time be not perpetual, then, before it began to be, it was not. And if it shall not always be, its nonbeing will follow after its being. But time is nothing else than "the number of before and after."[4] Consequently, time was before it began to be, and after it shall cease to be, it will be. But these statements are contradictory, hence time must be "eternal."[5] Moreover, time is an accident which cannot exist without a subject. And God cannot be that subject, since God is supra-temporal. Some created substance must, therefore, be eternal.[6]

7. Similarly, there are many propositions the truth of which cannot be denied without being implicitly asserted at the same time. Such, for instance, are the propositions, *there is truth*, and *contradictories cannot be simultaneous*. Such propositions are, therefore, eternal. Hence there are some entities beside God that are eternal.[7]

---

[1] "Numerus motus." Cf. *Phys.* lib. IV. cap. xi. " '*Αριθμὸς κινήσεως κατὰ τὸ πρότερον καὶ ὕσστερον.*"

[2] "*Finis praeteriti et principium futuri.*" Cf. *Phys.* lib. IV. cap. xiii.; "*Συνέχει γὰρ τὸν χρόνον τὸν παρελθόντα καὶ ἐσόμενον, καὶ ὅλως πέρας χρόνου ἐστίν.*"

[3] *Con. Gen.* loc. cit.; *Sum. Theol.* I.a. q. 46: a. 1. ob. 7; *De Pot.* q. 3: a. 17. ob. 15, 16; 2 *Dist.* 1. q. 1: a. 5. ob. 5, 6.

[4] "Numerus prioris et posterioris tempus est" (cf. *Phys.* loc. cit.).

[5] *Aeternum* is evidently used here in the sense of *everlasting*, otherwise the affirmation would be self-contradictory. It is unfortunate that, in Latin as in English, the same word can signify either temporal succession without beginning or end, or a mode of being which is not in time at all.

[6] *Con. Gen.* loc. cit. Cf. *Sum. Theol.* I.a. q. 46: a. 1. ob. 8; *De Pot.* q. 3: a. 17. ob. 20; 2 *Dist.* 1. q. 1: a. 5. ob. 7. So far as Aquinas's argument is concerned, it is a matter of indifference whether any particular creature or creatures be everlasting or merely the temporal process in which various creatures succeed one another.   [7] *Con. Gen.* loc. cit.

Aquinas's rejoinders to the foregoing arguments, given in a corresponding order, are:

1. Necessity of being, as it is found in creatures, is a necessity of order; consequently, it does not involve the perpetual existence of the things to which it pertains. Although the substance of the heaven, because of its lack of potentiality to non-being, exists of necessity, yet this necessity qualifies the substance only when it already exists. There is no question of existence being involved in the essence of the heaven as the author of the ontological argument conceived it to be involved in the essence of God. But, once existing, the matter of the heaven is not receptive of any other than its proper form. Incapable of being transformed into anything else, it is, therefore, incorruptible. Yet it can cease to be in the same fashion as it began to be, as a consequence of the divine will.[1]

2. The power of always existing likewise presupposes the existence of the substance to which it pertains.[2]

3. The refutation of the first of the arguments *ex parte Dei* has made it clear that God, while remaining himself unchanged, can produce a new effect. In the same way, it is possible for something to be moved by God *de novo*, for the new motion follows from the decree of God's eternal will that motion shall not be perpetual. Creation is, moreover, not change or succession; hence it involves no alteration of already subsisting relations.[3]

4. The intention of natural agents to perpetuate their species presupposes the natural agents themselves to have been already produced. Accordingly, this argument does not apply to the bringing of things into being, but only to those natural agents which already exist. It can, therefore, prove nothing in regard to the divine activity.[4]

5. This argument is circular in that it attempts to deduce the eternity of motion from that of time. But, in point of fact, the same instant is the beginning of the future and the end of the past only because there is something definite (*signatum*) in motion which is the beginning and the end of actual parts of motion. There is no reason why there should not be a first or

---

[1] *Con. Gen.* lib. II. cap. 36.　　　　[2] *Con. Gen.* loc. cit.
[3] *Con. Gen.* loc. cit.; *Sum. Theol.* I.a. q. 46: a. 1. ad 5m; cf. 2 *Dist.* 1. q. 1: a. 5. ad 8m.　　　　[4] *Con. Gen.* loc. cit.

a last instant of time, unless we suppose motion to be perpetual. The objection may, indeed, be raised that the *now* of time is not like a point in a line, inasmuch as the latter is stationary whereas the former is flowing, and that there can, therefore, be no first *now*. But the unsoundness of this argument is apparent when we turn to particular movements, for in these there is something definite which we can distinguish as the beginning and not the end, otherwise every movement would be everlasting.[1]

6. When we say that there is nothing above the heaven we do not mean that there is a place which can be called above with respect to the heaven. So when we say that *before* time began to be it was not, the word *before* does not refer to any portion of time *in re* but only in the imagination. What we mean is that there was no portion of time before this particular *now*.[2]

7. The necessity which pertains to such propositions is the necessity which relates predicate to subject, whence it does not require anything to exist always except in the divine intellect, wherein is the root of all truth.[3]

There remain the arguments *mundi ex parte factionis:*

1. An opinion common to all must be true. For a false opinion is an infirmity of the intellect, even as a false judgment is due to an infirmity of the senses. A defect of this sort is *per accidens* since it is beyond the intention of nature (*praeter naturae intentionem*). But what is *per accidens* is not to be found always in everyone. It is impossible, for instance, that all those who taste a particular flavour should be mistaken in their judgments about it. Now, it is the common opinion of all philosophers that nothing can come from nothing; and this opinion must be true. Accordingly, whatever is made must be made out of something else. But we cannot go on to infinity; we must, therefore, postulate something which is not made, and which, consequently, is eternal. This cannot be God, for it is impossible that he should be the matter of anything. It must, then, be primary matter. Matter cannot, however, exist

---

[1] *Con. Gen.* loc. cit.; *Sum. Theol.* I.a. q. 46: a. 1. ad 7^m; *De Pot.* q. 3: a. 17. ad 15^m, 16^m; 2 *Dist.* 1. q. 1: a. 5. ad 5^m, 6^m.

[2] *Con. Gen.* loc. cit.; *Sum. Theol.* I.a. q. 46: a. 1. ad 8^m; *De Pot.* q. 3: a. 17. ad 20^m; 2 *Dist.* 1. q. 1: a. 5. ad 7^m.   [3] *Con. Gen.* loc. cit.

apart from form. Accordingly, it must have existed in conjunction with the forms of the various species. The universe
must, therefore, be eternal.[1]

2. The second argument is very closely related to the third
of the arguments *ex parte creaturae*. Our point of departure is,
again, the occurrence of movement and change; and, again, it
is urged that every instance thereof must itself be preceded
by another movement or change.[2] On the present occasion,
however, we pursue, not the temporal, but the ontological
regress. Every movement is the act of a movable subject. If
this subject be itself the product of movement, it cannot be
eternal; moreover, the movement which produced it will in
turn be the act of another movable subject. To avoid becoming
involved in an infinite regress we must, therefore, suppose that
there is some primal subject which does not come into being
de novo, but is eternal.[3]

3. That which begins to be *de novo* must be possible before
it is actual; otherwise it would be impossible for it to come
into existence, and necessary for it not to exist. Consequently,
everything which comes into being must have pre-existed as a
potential being; in other words, it must have pre-existed as
subject or matter, for potentiality is to be found only in some
subject. Hence, since we cannot proceed to infinity, we must
assume that there is a primal subject which does not begin to
be *de novo*.[4]

4. No permanent substance exists while it is being made, for
it is made in order that it may exist, and if it did exist it would
not be making. But while it is making, there must be some
entity which is the subject of the making, since making is an
accident, and cannot have being apart from a subject.

[1] *Con. Gen.* lib. II. cap. 24; 2 *Dist.* 1. q. 1: a. 5. ob. 1.
[2] The similarity of this reasoning to Bradley's contention that every
relation will require yet other relations to connect it with its terms is, of
course, obvious.
[3] *Con. Gen.* loc. cit. ; *Com. Theol.* Pars Prima, cap. xcviii.
[4] *Con. Gen.* loc. cit.; *De Pot.* q. 3: a. 17. ob. 11. In the preceding objection
in the *De Potentia* a different turn is given to the argument. If the subject
potentially existent be matter, it cannot be devoid of form, for without
form matter cannot exist. But, if it be joined to form, we are face to face
once more with the actual universe, which must, therefore, be eternal.
Cf. *Com. Theol.* Pars Prima, cap. xcviii.

Accordingly, everything which is making has a pre-existent subject. To escape a vicious infinite we must, therefore, postulate a primal subject which is unmade and eternal. Accordingly, there must be something other than God which is eternal, since God cannot be the subject of making or of motion.[1]

1. To the first of these arguments Aquinas replied with an historical résumé. Since human knowledge begins with sense, which has to do with particulars, it proceeds from particular considerations to universals. Accordingly, the problem which confronted the earliest thinkers was the making of *this fire* or *this stone*. As a result, they were led to think of making as simply alteration of accidental dispositions; nor did they conceive that something could be made out of anything but actual being. Gradually, however, philosophers envisaged the making of substance, and so realized that it is not necessary for a thing to be made from actual being, except *per accidens*, but that it is made *per se* from potential being. Still, however, they were concerned with the particular, with the making of *this man*, or *this fire*. But, at last, they arrived at the notion of the procession of the totality of being from the first cause, wherein there is no making of anything from anything else pre-existing. Now, the first Naturalists were agreed that nothing is made from nothing, but they had not attained to the concept of creation, or, if they had, they did not call it *making*, which term, indeed, since it implies motion or change, is applicable to creation only metaphorically.[2]

2. Since creation can be called change only metaphorically—on the ground that the existence of that which is created is posterior to its non-existence—the second argument is unsound. The introduction of the concept of motion does not avail to prove that what begins to exist is different now from what it was before, since what is non-existent does not exist in any mode.[3]

3. In the case of entities which have their origin in motion it is necessary that they should first be possible through some potentiality, and afterwards actual, since motion is the act of that which exists in potentiality (*potentia passiva*). A created thing, however, before it began to exist, was possible in two

[1] *Con. Gen.* loc. cit.　　　　　　　　[2] *Con. Gen.* lib. II. cap. 37.
[3] *Con. Gen.* loc. cit ; *Com. Theol.* Pars. Prima. cap. xcviii.

ways, neither of which involves potentiality. It was possible through the power (*potentia*) of the agent, and it was possible in the sense that its existence involved no logical contradiction. Thus, the predicate *existence* is not incompatible with the subject *world* or the subject *man* as the predicate *commensurable* is incompatible with the subject *diameter*: these are, then, said to be possible, but possible according to no potentiality.[1] Hence it is not only possible for such entities to exist; it was also possible for them to exist before they did exist, although there was no existing potentiality. For before creation there was nothing which could be the subject of potentiality, not even the pure potentiality of primary matter.[2]

4. In those things which originate in motion, existence and the process of being made are not simultaneous, for making involves succession. But in the case of those entities which are not brought into being through motion, the process of being made is not prior to existence.[3]

We have now to consider the position of those who professed to demonstrate that the world cannot be eternal. The truth of the proposition Aquinas, of course, did not contest. It forms part of the Catholic faith, and is made known to us by revelation. But he did maintain, in opposition to the general opinion of both his predecessors and contemporaries, that it cannot be proved by philosophy. The following arguments were ascribed by him to his opponents:

1. God is the cause of all things, and the cause must be prior in duration to its effects.[4]

2. Since the totality of being is created by God, it cannot have been made out of something else. It must, therefore, have been made from nothing, hence its existence must be subsequent to its non-existence.[5]

3. The infinite cannot be traversed. But, if the world have always existed, an infinite number of days is already past, and, therefore, an infinite will have already been traversed.[6]

---

[1] "*Secundam nullam potentiam.*" The reference is to the *Metaphysics*, lib. V. cap. xii.

[2] *Con. Gen.* loc. cit.; *De Pot.* q. 3: a. 17 ad 10^m, 11^m; *Com. Theol.* Pars Prima, cap. xcviii.

[3] *Con. Gen.* loc. cit.   [4] *Con. Gen.* lib. II. cap. 38.

[5] *Con. Gen.* loc. cit.; cf. *Sum. Theol.* I.a. q. 46: a. 2. ob. 2.

[6] *Con. Gen.* loc. cit.; *Sum. Theol.* I.a. q. 46: a. 2. ob. 6.

4. Since the passage of time continually adds days to the days that are past, if the world have always existed and the past days be infinite in number, an addition will be constantly made to the infinite, which is impossible.[1]

5. If the process of generation have no beginning, the series of efficient causes will be infinite. Thus, a father will be the cause of his son, and will in turn be caused by another man, and so *in infinitum*. But this is impossible.[2]

6. Furthermore, there will exist actual infinities. Thus, the immortal souls of the men who have already lived and died will be infinite in number. But actual infinities cannot exist.[3]

These six arguments were in turn refuted by Aquinas:

1. It is true that an agent which produces its effect through motion must be prior in time to that effect, for the cause must exist when the motion begins, whereas the effect does not exist until the motion terminates. But it is not necessary that causes which act instantaneously should precede their effects, as we know from experience; for as soon as the sun rises in the east (*simul dum sol est in puncto orientis*) it illumines all our hemisphere.[4] But it can also be proved by reason. For, at whatever instant anything be postulated as existing, the beginning of its action can be postulated also, as appears in the case of all things that are generated. Thus, fire begins to heat at the same instant that it begins to burn. But in an instantaneous operation the beginning and the end are identical, as in all indivisible things. Accordingly, in whatever instant the agent be postulated to produce its effect instantaneously, at that instant also the term of its action can be postulated to exist. But the term of the action is simultaneous with the thing made. Hence it is not repugnant to the intellect that a cause which produces its effect instantaneously should not precede that effect.[5]

---

[1] *Con. Gen.* loc. cit.

[2] *Con. Gen.* loc. cit.; *Sum. Theol.* I.a. q. 46: a. 2. ob. 7.

[3] *Con. Gen.* loc. cit.; *Sum. Theol.* I.a. q. 46: a. 2. ob. 8; *De Aeternitate Mundi*, ad finem.

[4] *Con. Gen.* loc. cit.; *De Aeternitate Mundi*.

[5] *De Aeternitate Mundi*. Three other arguments are stated in the same work in support of the same conclusion: (*a*) The cause which produces the whole substance of its effect is not less powerful in its way than the cause which produces only the form. In fact, it is more powerful, for the latter cause merely educes the form from the potentiality of matter. But such a

2. The contradictory of the proposition, *Something is made out of something else*, is *Something is not made out of something else*, not *Something is made out of nothing*. Hence, we cannot infer that what is made is posterior to non-being in duration, although it is so imagined by us.[1]

3. Even if an actual infinity cannot exist simultaneously, yet it can exist successively, because at any particular stage in the process the number of entities which have already existed is finite. Thus, any particular day can be passed through, for it is finite. Moreover, if the world always existed, there is no first term in the temporal series, and so the infinite will not have been traversed, since this involves a passage from one extreme to another.[2]

4. On the supposition which we are now considering, the time-series extends from the present an infinite distance into the past. The obvious analogy would be a line with only one end. Time, in other words, is infinite *ex parte ante*, but finite *ex parte post*. But it is this finite dimension of time which perpetually receives additions. There is, therefore, no contradiction.[3]

5. We are already familiar with the answer to this argument. In causes acting simultaneously it is impossible to proceed to infinity, since the effect would then depend upon an infinite number of simultaneous actions. Moreover, causes of this kind are infinite *per se*, inasmuch as the entire infinite series of them is requisite to the effect. But an infinite series of non-

cause can keep its effect in being whenever it itself is in being, as in the case of the illuminating sun. Much more, then, is God able to ensure that what is caused by him exists while he exists. (*b*) If it be possible to posit the existence of any cause at a particular instant without also positing the existence of its effect, this can only be because the cause is incomplete. A complete cause is simultaneous with its effect. And God is a complete cause, since he is in no respect deficient. (*c*) If it be said that the same cause will always produce the same effect except in the case of a voluntary agent, and that God is a voluntary agent, and that, therefore, his effects need not be co-existent with himself, it can be said in reply that it does not follow that a voluntary agent cannot bring it to pass that its effects shall be incapable of being ever non-existent.

[1] *Con. Gen.* loc. cit. See *Comment.* of Francis Sylvester, sec. **2**. **1**; cf. *Sum. Theol.* I.a. q. 46: a. 2. ad 2ᵐ.

[2] *Con. Gen.* loc. cit.; *Sum. Theol.* I.a. q. 46: a. 2. ad 6ᵐ.

[3] *Con. Gen.* loc. cit.

simultaneous causes is not impossible, and such a series is infinite only *per accidens*. For it is accidental to the father of Socrates that he is himself the son of another man; but it is not accidental to a stick, in so far as it moves a stone, that it is itself moved by the hand, for it moves in so far as it is moved.[1]

6. The issue here is, according to St. Thomas, more difficult; he adds, however, that the argument is not of much use (*non est multum utilis*) since it involves too many presuppositions. For some of those who have affirmed the eternity of the world have denied the immortality of the soul; others have held that the individual soul is not immortal, and that an intelligence separated from matter[2] alone abides; while yet others have espoused the theory of reincarnation.[3] Furthermore, it has been maintained that it is not impossible that there should exist an infinite number of things which are not mutually ordered with respect to one another.[4] And, again, it has been maintained that Aristotle has, indeed, proved that an infinite number of bodies cannot exist, but that he has not proved that an infinite number of immaterial substances cannot do so. Or we might deny that humanity has always existed, and yet assert that the world, or at least some creature such as an angel, has always been in existence.[5]

It appears, then, that philosophy is helpless to prove either of the alternative opinions before us, although it is able to show that neither is self-contradictory nor impossible. One reason for this, according to Aquinas, is that a thing in its perfection differs from the same thing in the making. One cannot argue from the nature of a grown man to the nature which he had before birth.[6] Again, one can argue with respect to a particular creature that it is what it is because of some other creature, or because of the order of the universe. But, in the case of the universe itself as a whole, there is nothing which can serve as the ground for such reasoning. The principle of demonstration

---

[1] *Con. Gen.* loc. cit.; cf. *Sum. Theol.* I.a. q. 46: a. 2. ad 7ᵐ.

[2] The *intellectus agens* or the *intellectus possibilis*.

[3] None of these possible solutions can, of course, be defended by a Catholic philosopher.

[4] *Con. Gen.* loc. cit.; cf. lib. II. cc. 80 and 81; also *Sum. Theol.* I.a. q. 46: a. 2. ad 8ᵐ; *De Aeternitate Mundi*, ad finem.

[5] *Sum. Theol.* loc. cit.   [6] 2 *Dist.* 1. q. 1: a. 5. sol.

is the essence, the *quid quod est*. But this is reached by abstracting from the here and now; wherefore universals are everywhere and always. Hence, it cannot be demonstrated that man, or heaven, or a stone, did not always exist. Nor can we find in the divine nature a basis for demonstration, for the divine power is infinite, and the divine goodness does not require that the universe should exist; whereas we can hope to attain to demonstration only in regard to that which God wills of necessity.[1]

It is clear that Aquinas's theory of creation is intimately related to his conception of God.[2] We cannot avoid asking whether God is the Creator as well as the Governor of the world; whether the divine power is limited or unlimited, and, if limited, in what respects; and how the realm of change and becoming is related to the immutable eternity of God. Accordingly, we have followed St. Thomas in his laborious attempt to answer these questions fairly and fully. It is impossible not to respect the ability with which he has done so, and the thoroughness with which he has thought out the implications of his own doctrines. His treatment of this topic has been so elaborately expounded and defended by modern Neoscholastic writers[3] that I shall confine myself to laying stress on a few salient points and to indicating certain apparent difficulties.

In the first place, then, it is to be remarked that creation, as St. Thomas conceived it, is something utterly foreign to and

---

[1] *De Pot.* q. 3 : a. 17. c.; *Sum. Theol.* I.a. q. 46 : a. 2. c.

[2] "Le problème de la création n'est pas moins délicat et difficile que le problème de Dieu. Au fond, c'est le même. La création se conçoit comme le terme frontière que rencontre la pensée en s'élevant de la créature à Dieu, en redescendant de Dieu à la créature. Demander ce que c'est que la création, c'est demander comment le monde dépend, comment Dieu le pose, et dans les deux cas la nature de Dieu telle que nous la pouvons connaître, en fonction de ce monde, est incluse. Nous ne pouvons pas savoir ce que c'est qu'un commencement ou un non-commencement, ce que c'est que le temps et l'éternité; or l'éternité est un des attributs de Dieu, et la question de la valeur objective de ces attributs va donc faire retour" (Sertillanges's *Les grandes thèses de la philosophie thomiste*, ch. iv. p. 81).

[3] Cf. Sertillanges's *S. Thomas d'Aquin*, tome I. lib. III. ch. i; *Les grandes thèses de la philosophie thomiste*, ch. iv; Garrigou-Lagrange's *Dieu, son existence et sa nature*, deuxième partie, ch. ii. a. ii. pp. 465–473; D. Nys, *La notion de temps*, ch. ii. a. 5; Joyce's *Principles of Natural Theology*, part III. ch. xiv.

remote from human experience. As a contemporary upholder of the doctrine has said: "Theism must frankly confess that the kernel of positive meaning in the notion of creation, viz. positing, is inexplicable. Indeed, if it were explicable it would not be creation. The various analogies that have been employed for its elucidation, such as man's 'creative' art, throw no light on the ultimate mystery. Just as the gradations between the infinite One and the finite many, devised by Philo, Plotinus, Spinoza, etc., conduct nearer to the abyss but do not bridge it, so these comparisons break down at the crucial point— origination of something out of no pre-existent material such as is forthcoming and utilized in the case of causation within the course of Nature, and in all 'creative' imagination or ideation within the minds of men of genius. The *modus operandi* of divine creativity is wholly unimaginable and inconceivable. And this inexplicability is inevitable. For explanation, in all its forms, establishes some connection, similarity, or continuity with what is experienced or lies within Experience; whereas creation is the activity through which experients and what is experienced by them come to be. The notion of creation, consequently, is not derivable from experience, and analogies valid within experience cannot reach beyond its bounds."[1]

In the light of what has already been argued, the truth of these observations cannot fail to be apparent. A typical instance of the analogies drawn from human "imagination or ideation," to which Dr. Tennant adverts, is that which refers us to the activity of Shakspeare's mind in the composition of *Hamlet*. Could we have presented this analogy to the consideration of Aquinas, he would probably have observed that Hamlet himself, as well as every other character in this great drama, is non-existent, and that what does not exist is not created. Shakspeare's thoughts, transmitted to us by the printed page, do indeed awaken corresponding thoughts in ourselves; but this is not creation, it is generation. Whether or not creation is a valid concept, it is certainly something to which the utmost reach of our imagination fails to attain.

In his discussion of the divine omnipotence Aquinas reveals a keen appreciation of the problems involved, and a resolute effort to save the doctrine from being interpreted in a sense

[1] Dr. F. R. Tennant, *Philosophical Theology*, vol. II. p. 125.

either paradoxical or ridiculous. Nevertheless, he makes an
extremely significant admission,[1] namely, that God could have
created a better universe than that which actually exists. This
is, indeed, a momentous assertion. Evil has been declared by
St. Thomas to be a mere negation, a defect of being, and God
has, therefore, been freed from all responsibility for it. But it
is now apparent that many, if not all, of the evils which infect
the actual universe would have been absent from a better
universe which the Deity might have created in its stead had
he chosen. Hence the presence of these evils in the actual
world is the result of his arbitrary will. It is clear that St.
Thomas does not conceive God to be under any obligation in
the matter. His goodness does not require him to create anything; what he has created is, therefore, the fruit of his mere
good pleasure, and neither his justice nor his goodness can be
impugned because he has not created something better. In
other words, Aquinas's God is quite as much an ontological
tyrant as the Allah of the Koran. To any pleas which humanity
or pity might utter against his arbitrary decrees, he might well
be represented as replying in the words of Marlowe's Tambur-
laine, "This is my mind, and I will have it so."[2]

It is in St. Thomas's treatment of the relation of time to
eternity, however, that our chief interest lies. Has he succeeded in saving both the reality of time and the eternity of
God? This is the crucial question. Has he reconciled these two
doctrines one with the other? or is his attempt a failure? and
must we, consequently, abandon one in favour of the other?
and if this be the case, which dogma is vindicated and which
stands condemned?

It is obvious that our approach to this problem is greatly
aided by the clearness and emphasis with which Aquinas has
stated his view that the universe was created not *in* time but
with time. We are thereby delivered from a number of natural
misconceptions. Thus, when we read that God from eternity
willed the creation of the world, we are prone to think of the
divine mind as persisting in this resolution through a vast
number of successive moments of time, and then, suddenly,

---

[1] 1 *Dist.* 44. q.1: a. 2. sol.; *Sum. Theol.* I.a. q. 25: a. 6.; *De Pot.* q. 3: a. 16. c.
[2] Cf. Sertillanges's *Les grandes thèses de la philosophie thomiste*, ch. iv. p. 113;
M. C. D'Arcy's *Thomas Aquinas*, p. 185.

realizing it through external activity at a certain definite instant; and we are apt to wonder why God chose this instant rather than another before it or after it. The Angelic Doctor has anticipated such misunderstandings. We have seen that God, in his eternity, is supra-temporal. The being of the time-series is not willed by him in time; it is willed by a timeless, immutable act which is identical with the divine essence, that is, with God himself. The extent of the series depends entirely upon this act. It might be longer, it might be shorter, it might even be without beginning and without end; but it is what God wills it to be. We can imagine a time before the creation of the world just as we can imagine the non-existence of the world that now is; but the fact remains that there is a world, and that before that world there was no time.[1]

Not only the beginning of the world, but also the entire sequence of events which fills the time series, is willed by the same single and supra-temporal act. Creation is thus separable from conservation only in thought; actually the two are identical. The relation of the world to God is one of dependence. When we refer to the beginning of that dependence we speak of creation; when we have in mind its continuance we use the term *conservation*.[2]

Against the view that a timeless being can be the cause of events in time the following criticism was levelled by Dr. McTaggart. "An event happens, and makes the state of the universe different from what it had been before. The cause is said to be God's timeless nature. That nature is the same, however, before and after the event. (In itself, of course, there is no question of before or after. I mean that a human being who was judging of God's nature before the event, and one who was judging of it after the event, would be right if they made the same judgment.) Then there is nothing in that nature which accounts for the change; and it cannot be the cause. If, while the so-called cause remains the same, the effect varies, it is clear that the variation of the effect—that is, the event—is uncaused."[3]

Fatal as this objection may be to other forms of the theory

---

[1] Cf. *Les grandes thèses de la philosophie thomiste*, pp. 99–100.
[2] Cf. *Les grandes thèses de la philosophie thomiste*, pp. 89–90; *S. Thomas d'Aquin*, tome I. pp. 296 ff.   [3] *Some Dogmas of Religion*, sec. 159.

in question, it seems clear that it does not apply—and doubtless was not intended to apply—to the position of Aquinas.
For, according to him, particular events in time are not
caused by particular volitions on the part of God; on the
contrary, all the events which have happened, which are
happening, or which will ever happen, are caused by the same
timeless act.

There is another difficulty confronting us, however, which
appears more formidable. It will be recalled[1] that, in treating
of the divine knowledge of future contingent particulars
Aquinas has asserted that things which are future to us God is
aware of as present. By this phraseology he did not, of course,
intend to convey the idea that the divine consciousness is in
time; indeed, his purpose was the exact opposite. Since all
things, present, past, or future, are perceived by God by a
single act of awareness, it is evident that he neither anticipates
nor remembers anything. All things are present to him in the
sense that he directly perceives them. This does not mean, however, that God is not aware of the temporal relations in which
they stand to one another, as the following quotation will show.

"If anyone were to see many people travelling in succession
by the same road, and this through a certain period of time,
he would see in particular parts of time certain ones passing
by, so that at the end of his gazing he would have seen all those
passing by as present; yet he would not have seen them all as
present at once, because the time in which he saw them was
not a *totum simul*. If, however, his seeing could be a *visio tota
simul*, he would see them all present at once, although they
would not all be present at once as passing by; whence, since
the vision of the divine knowledge is measured by eternity,
which is *tota simul*, and yet includes the whole of time, nor is
absent from any part of time, it follows that it sees whatever
happens in any part of time, not as future, but as present. For
that which is seen by God is future with respect to some other
thing which it follows in time, but, to the divine vision itself,
which is not in time, but is above time, it is not future but
present. We, therefore, see the future as future, because to our
vision, which is measured by time, it is future; but to the
divine vision, which is above time, it is not future. For he who

[1] See pp. 313-314.

is in the same class as those passing by, and who sees only those who are before him, sees them differently from him who is above the class of those passing by, and who sees them all at once. Accordingly, just as our sight never errs in seeing contingent things that are present, and yet this is not incompatible with the fact that they are contingent, so God infallibly sees all contingent things, whether to us they be present, past, or future, because they are not future to him, and yet he sees them as existing whenever they do exist, whence this is not incompatible with the fact that they are contingent."[1]

In other words, God perceives certain events as present, and yet as being future to us. In like manner certain other events are perceived by God as present, and yet as past to us. And a third class of events are perceived by God as present both to himself and to us. But when we say that a thing is perceived as present by God, we mean that it is perceived by him as existing, since in the Deity there is no transition from past to present and future.[2] From this it follows that entities which

[1] "Si aliquis videret multos transeuntes per unam viam successive, et hoc per aliquod tempus; in singulis partibus temporis videret praesentialiter aliquos transeuntes, ita quod in toto tempore suae visionis omnes transeuntes praesentialiter videret; nec tamen simul omnes praesentialiter, quia tempus suae visiones non est totum simul. Si autem sua visio tota simul potest existere, simul praesentialiter omnes videret, quamvis non omnes simul praesentialiter transirent; unde, cum visio divinae scientiae aeternitate mensuretur, quae est tota simul, et tamen totum tempus includit, nec alicui parti temporis deest; sequitur ut quidquid in tempore geritur, non ut futurum, sed ut praesens videat; hoc enim quod a Deo visum est, futurum est rei alteri, cui succedit in tempore; sed ipsi divinae visioni, quae non in tempore, sed extra tempus est, non est futurum, sed praesens. Ita ergo nos videmus futurum ut futurum, quia visioni nostrae futurum est, cum ipsa tempore mensuretur; sed divinae visioni, quae est extra tempus, futurum non est: sicut et aliter videt transeuntes ille qui est in ordine transeuntium, qui non videt nisi illos qui ante ipsum sunt; et aliter ille qui extra ordinem transeuntium esset, qui omnes transeuntes simul inspiceret. Sicut ergo noster visus non fallitur unquam videns contingentia ut sint praesentia, et tamen ex hoc non removetur quin illa contingenter eveniant; ita Deus infallibiliter videt omnia contingentia, sive quae nobis sunt praesentia, sive praeterita, sive quae futura, quia sibi non sunt futura, sed ea inspiceret esse tunc quando sunt; unde ex hoc non removetur quin contingenter eveniant" (De Verit. q. 2: a. 12. c.).

[2] "Rursus, cum, dictur, Deus scit, vel scivit, hoc futurum, medium quoddam accipitur inter divinam scientiam et rem scitam, scilicet tempus in quo est locutio, respectu cuius illud quod a Deo scitum dicitur est futurum.

are not perceived by us because they are future are perceived by God as existing. Can a thing, then, both exist and not exist? Not at the same time, we answer. For us, who are in time, the future does not exist; for God, there is no time. So it may seem that Aquinas's theory escapes violation of the law of non-contradiction. But does it? God is, indeed, eternal, but that which he perceives is not eternal: it is in time. That which is in future time is, however, as yet non-existent. But God perceives that which is future, and that which God perceives must exist. It thus appears that we are confronted after all by an unescapable contradiction.

It would seem that from this only one conclusion can follow, namely, that the future is real and that time is unreal. But now, as always when we read Aquinas, we must be careful not to lose sight of the doctrine of degrees of being. Nothing is in the highest sense real but God. Indeed, since the gap between Creator and creature is infinite, the creatures can be said to be infinitely less real than God; yet they are not wholly unreal, they are not nothing. Time, then, it may be urged, is partially real but not wholly so, and in ultimate Reality there is no time. Such, as we know, was the conclusion of Mr. Bradley. Possibly we should be right in attributing the same view to Aquinas.

Among the various arguments directed to proving that the world must have had a beginning, which we have previously reviewed, there is one that claims our attention by reason of the fact that the refutation of it proffered by St. Thomas appears extraordinarily inadequate. The argument in question points out that, if the world has always existed, an infinite number of

Non autem est futurum respectu divinae scientiae, quae, in momento aeternitatis existens, ad omnia praesentialiter se habet. Respectu cuius, si tempus locutionis de medio subtrahatur, non est dicere hoc esse cognitum quasi non existens, ut locum habeat quaestio qua quaeritur an possit non esse: sed sic cognitum dicetur a Deo ut iam in sua existentia visum. Quo posito, non remanet praedictae quaestioni locus: quia quod iam est, non potest, quantum ad allud instans, non esse. Deceptio igitur accidit ex hoc quod tempus in quo loquimur, coexistit aeternitati, vel etiam tempus praeteritum (quod designatur cum dicimus, *Deus scivit*): unde habitudo temporis praeteriti vel praesentis ad futurum aeternitati attribuitur, quae omnino ei non competit. Et ex hoc accidit *secundum accidens* falli" (*Con. Gen.* lib. I. cap. 67).

days will have already passed by. This, it asserts, is impossible, for the infinite cannot be traversed. St. Thomas responds that any particular day can be passed through, inasmuch as it is finite, but that such passage or transition requires two extremes, and that, if the world has always existed, there will have been no first day, and so no first extreme.[1]

This reply fails completely to meet the issue. The objection is based upon the proposition that the past has been traversed —*quod praeteritum est, pertransitum est*—and its point is that, if an infinite cannot be traversed, the number of days past must be finite. To reply, as St. Thomas has done, that there can be no question of traversing because there is no first day, is simply to state this objection in other words. It is upon him, and not upon his opponents, that the responsibility rests for asserting that there is no first day. Yet, if each individual day has been passed through, and the number of days be infinite, it is clear that an infinite number of days must have been passed through. On the other hand, if the infinite cannot be traversed, not all of these days will have been passed through. If the past be infinite and have been passed through, then an infinite past has been passed through. From this conclusion there is no escape.

Professor Jolivet, while admitting that the doctrine of creation nowhere enters into the purview of Aristotle, a fact which he considers strange,[2] nevertheless maintains that, not only is it compatible with the fundamental principles of his philosophy, but that its introduction by Aquinas into the body of his system merely carried these principles to their logical conclusion, and resulted in the establishment of a more coherent metaphysical structure. Thus he considers that, owing to his failure to envisage such a doctrine, Aristotle's treatment of necessity is involved in inconsistency. For him, the real, the intelligible, and the necessary are identical; hence the necessary is changeless. Accordingly, the world of becoming is not absolutely necessary. Logic demands that it should be referred to a Creator.[3] But instead Aristotle was

---

[1] Cf. *S. Thomas d'Aquin*, tome I. pp. 286–287; *Les grandes thèses de la philosophie thomiste*, pp. 98–99; *La notion de temps*, pp. 166–167.

[2] *Essai sur les rapports entre la pensée grecque et la pensée chrétienne*, p. 84.

[3] *Essai sur les rapports entre la pensée grecque et la pensée chrétienne*, p. 43.

content to elaborate another conception of the necessary, the eternally recurrent.[1] It is the contention of Professor Jolivet that the doctrines of the eternity of time and motion and of the impossibility of knowledge of the world on the part of God are not the cause but the result of the absence from the Aristotelian system of a doctrine of creation, a contention which he has defended in detail in the first two chapters of his book. It is impossible for us here to pursue the question further; but it is obvious that, apart from all questions of textual criticism, our agreement or disagreement with his judgment that St. Thomas's system is the logical completion of the work of Aristotle will principally depend upon whether we consider the notion of creation to be itself tenable.

In conclusion, I wish to call attention to the fact that there is nothing in Aquinas's treatment of the problem of creation which tends in any way to relieve his conception of matter from the difficulties with which we have already found it to be burdened. Primary matter is still pure potentiality, whatever that may be, and nothing further has been said to make such a notion intelligible.

[1] "Mais pourquoi ce brusque recul d'Aristote, après sa première définition du nécessaire? C'est apparemment que cette notion entraînait logiquement la contingence radicale du Cosmos. Or, il ne pouvait s'élever à l'idée de commencement absolu, car il ne concevait, comme on l'a vu, de commencement que par voie de nature, c'est-à-dire par mouvement et génération. Aussi chercha-t-il dans la notion de périodicité et de retour éternel un équivalent de cette immutabilité absolue dont il avait d'abord reconnu qu'elle était le privilège essentiel du Nécessaire. . . . Assurément l'acte créateur est l'acte d'une volonté libre, et il n'y a pas, en ce sens, de lien nécessaire entre le monde et Dieu: tout essai de déduction de l'univers à partir de Dieu est panthéisme pur. Il y a donc là une rupture de l'intelligibilité conçue comme identique à la nécessité. Mais aussi bien, lorsqu'il s'agit d'un être intelligent et libre, l'intelligible ne peut plus être le logique, c'est-à-dire l'analytiquement nécessaire, mais le déterminisme rationnel, le nécessaire hypothétique, en d'autres termes: ce qui a sa raison" (*Essai sur les rapports entre la pensée grecque et la pensée chrétienne*, p. 45).

CHAPTER XV

CONSERVATION

It has already been made clear that the terms *creation* and *conservation* refer to the same divine act viewed from two different standpoints. The world is not first brought into being and subsequently kept in being; on the contrary, the initial stage of the temporal process, and all succeeding stages, depend alike upon the changeless will of God. It is impossible, therefore, to consider the former doctrine apart from the latter, and it is natural for us to pass directly from the one to the other. We find, however, that, in the *Contra Gentiles*, Aquinas has adopted a different mode of procedure. There the doctrine of conservation is discussed in connection with that of providence, and is explicitly said to follow from it. Again, in the *Summa Theologica* it is treated immediately after the doctrine of divine government, a topic obviously closely related to the divine providence; and, in the *Compendium Theologiae*, governance and conservation are dealt with in the same chapter. None the less, when we come to examine the arguments advanced to prove the theory of divine conservation, we discover that the majority of them do not presuppose the establishment of any doctrine of providence or divine government. Accordingly, I shall proceed at once to scrutinize Aquinas's view of divine conservation, and then turn to the consideration of providence. Inasmuch as we have no interest in these questions apart from the light which St. Thomas's treatment of them throws upon his conception of God, we may concern ourselves only with the broad outlines of his theory.

1. The first proof of divine conservation which is given in the *Contra Gentiles*[1] does presuppose the reality of divine providence. Its point of departure is the proposition that all things which are necessary to the attainment by any subject of its end fall under the governance of that subject. Now, God directs all things toward their ultimate end—namely, his goodness—not only in so far as they are operative, but also in so far as they exist, since, inasmuch as they exist, they have

---

[1] Lib. III. cap. 65.

a similitude to the divine goodness. Hence the conservation of all things in being pertains to God's providence.

2. The cause of a thing and the cause of its conservation are identical, for the conservation of any thing is only the continuation of its being. Accordingly, since God produces all things through his intellect and will, in like manner also he conserves them.[1]

3. No particular agent can be the cause of its own species (for then it would be the cause of itself), but only of individual members of the species. The species itself, however, requires a cause, and this cause is God. Hence God stands to the species as the individual which generates another stands to the thing generated. But generation no longer takes place when the activity of the generating subject has ceased. Accordingly, were the divine operation to cease, all species would become non-existent.[2]

4. Motion is something extraneous to the being of a body, although it can pertain to it *per accidens*. Furthermore, no body is the cause of anything except in so far as it is moved, for it is through motion that a body acts. Accordingly, no body is the cause of anything in so far as it is being, but it is the cause whereby it is moved toward being, that is, of its being made. But the being of any finite entity is a participated being, because in it essence and being are not identical. In God, however, they are identical; hence the Deity is *primo et per se* the cause of all being. Consequently the divine operation stands to the being of all things as the motion of a bodily mover to the making and moving of the things made or moved. But such making or movement cannot continue when the motion of the bodily mover has ceased. Similarly, then, the existence of every finite entity must cease upon the cessation of the divine operation.[3]

5. Work of art presupposes work of nature, as work of nature presupposes the work of a creating God; for the matter with which art deals is derived from nature, while the matter

---

[1] Lib. III. cap. 65.
[2] Lib. III. cap. 65; cf. *Sum. Theol.* I.a. q. 104: a. 1. c.
[3] *Con. Gen.* lib. III. cap. 65; cf. *Com. Theol.* Pars Prima, cap. cxxxi. In the *Summa Theologica* (I.a. q. 104: a. 1) this argument is combined with the third.

of nature is derived from God. Now works of art are kept in being by nature; thus a house, for example, is conserved through the solidity of its stones. And, in like manner, all natural things are conserved by the power of God.[1]

6. The action of a cause does not persist after that action has ceased, unless it has passed into the nature of the effect. Thus the forms and properties of things generated remain in them after generation because they are made natural to them. For this reason habits are difficult to break because they have become natural. Dispositions and passions, however, whether corporeal or natural, persist for a while but not always, because they are only on the way to become natural. But what belongs to the nature of a superior genus does not remain in any mode after the agent's action has ceased. So light, for instance, does not remain in a diaphanous object after that which illumines it has been removed. Accordingly, since being pertains to the essence of God alone, no created thing could remain in existence, were the divine operation to cease.[2]

7. There are two possible explanations of the origin of finite beings—creation or emanation. On either theory, however, the doctrine of conservation must be true. For, if God brought things into existence which before did not exist, it follows that their existence and their non-existence both depend upon the divine will, and accordingly they exist so long as God wills. They are therefore kept in existence by God. If, on the other hand, they flow forth eternally from the Deity, they are nevertheless preserved by him as long as they exist.[3]

The doctrine of conservation, as St. Thomas takes pains to point out,[4] is thus directly opposed to the theory of the Loquentes,[5] according to which, as he informs us, all forms are accidental, and no accident is able to endure for more than a single instant, whence it follows that all things are continually in a process of formation. In his opinion, their motive in defending such a view was the desire to show that the world is continually dependent upon God for its existence. But it

---

[1] *Con. Gen.* loc. cit. ; *Com. Theol.* loc. cit.   [2] *Con. Gen.* loc. cit.
[3] *Con. Gen.* loc. cit.   [4] *Con. Gen.* loc. cit.
[5] By this term Scholastic writers were wont to translate the Arabic *Mutakallimun*. The Mutakallimun were the orthodox theologians of Islam.

entailed consequences which, in his eyes, were absurd. For certain of the Loquentes found themselves driven to assert that the indivisible atoms, of which all things, as they held, are composed, were capable of existing for a time even if the divine governance were withdrawn; while others went so far as to affirm that nothing could cease to exist unless God implanted in it the accident of ceasing to exist.

Conservation can be direct or indirect, *per se* or *per accidens*. A thing is conserved indirectly and accidentally when it is protected from whatever might cause corruption in it. Not everything is conserved after this manner by God, for certain substances—i.e. the heavenly bodies—are incorruptible. A thing is conserved directly and *per se* when it depends on something else as its cause. And in this manner all things are conserved by God. Yet it does not follow that God conserves all things immediately. It is obvious, of course, that it is often possible for one creature to protect another from corruption. It is less obvious, and yet it is true, that it is possible for one creature to be the intermediate cause of the being of another. Every agent acts so as to produce its own likeness. When it succeeds, it produces a form of the same species as itself, and of such an effect it is only the *causa in fieri* and not the *causa in esse*. When, however, the matter upon which it acts has not the aptitude to receive the form of the agent, the result is a form of an inferior species, and of such a form the agent is the *causa in esse*. Thus the light in the air which is produced by the sun ceases to exist when the sun has set. But in the case of fire and water we have an instance of another sort, for the heat persists in the water when the fire has been removed. Were the water capable of receiving perfectly the form of the fire, it would continue to possess it indefinitely, and thus we should have here a perfect instance of causation *in fieri*; but because it is not the heat will gradually fail. It is clear then that, even in direct conservation, God makes use frequently of intermediate causes.[1]

[1] *Sum. Theol.* I.a. q. 104: aa. 1. and 2.

CHAPTER XVI

PROVIDENCE

WE TURN now to the consideration of the notion of providence. The term knowledge, *scientia*, connotes pure cognition which is unconcerned with any process of operation. That form of cognition which is directed upon operation is called disposition, *dispositio*; while that which is concerned with things as they moved toward an end is called providence. Since God is aware of all things, he is possessed of knowledge; since he has imposed upon the universe a twofold order—that of the parts one to another, and that of the whole universe to himself—he is possessed of disposition; and since he assigns to the ordered entities the powers that keep them so ordered, and represses disorder, he is possessed of providence. Such is the statement of the matter in the *Commentary on the Sentences*.[1] In the *De Veritate*[2] we are told that knowledge involves cognition of the end, and, of those entities which are ordered with respect to the end; that through knowledge God is aware of himself and of the creatures; but that providence is concerned only with those things which are ordered with respect to the end, and only in so far as they are so ordered. Hence providence includes both knowledge and will, yet the essential element in it is cognition, not speculative but practical. The action of power presupposes that of providence, power is therefore not included in the definition of providence. In the *Summa Theologica*[3] we are informed that by disposition may be meant either the order of entities with respect to an end or the order of parts in the whole, whereas the term providence applies to the former alone.

The proofs of the reality of a divine providence given by St. Thomas are these:

1. Whenever certain things are ordered with respect to a certain end, they are subject to the entity to which the end principally pertains.[4] Now all things are ordered with respect

---

[1] 1 *Dist.* 39. q. 2: a. 1. sol.   [2] q. 5: a. 1. c.   [3] I.a. q. 22: a. 1. c.
[4] A curious illustration of his meaning is here given by Aquinas. All the parts of an army, and their various operations, are ordered—so he tells us—with respect to the good of the leader, which is victory. The additional

to the divine goodness. God is therefore the governor
of all.[1]

2. Whoever makes something with a certain end in view uses
this thing as a means to the end. But God has made all things
for an end, namely, his goodness. Accordingly, God uses all
things, directing them toward himself—in other words, God
governs all things.[2]

3. God is the primal unmoved mover. But the prime mover
is no less the cause of motion than secondary movers, rather
more, since without him no secondary mover could cause
motion. Moreover, all things moved are moved because of an
end. Accordingly, God moves all things because of an end,
and, as we have seen, he does so by his intellect and will. But
to move things by the intellect is nothing else than to govern
them by providence.[3]

4. God is the cause, not only of the activity of secondary
agents, but even of their being. Accordingly, God is present
in all things.[4]

5. Physical bodies are moved and operate with respect to
an end, although they do not know that end, as is evident
from the fact that what is best usually befalls them, and that
they would not have been made otherwise had they been made
by art. And this must be due, immediately or mediately, to the
divine intelligence.[5]

6. Things which are distinct according to nature do not
combine in one order unless they be brought together by some
ordering power. In the universe, however, there are entities
with distinct, and even contrary, natures, which nevertheless
do so combine; so that there must be a single power which
orders and governs the universe.[6]

7. In regard to the heavenly bodies no reason can be assigned

illustrations are more fortunate. An art which is directed toward an end
gives their rules to those arts which deal with the things which are ordered
with respect to that end. So civics stands to the military art, and this in
turn stands to the art of equitation; and so the art of steering stands to
that of ship-building.

[1] *Con. Gen.* lib. III. cap. 64; cf. *Sum. Theol.* I. a. q. 103: a. 5. c.

[2] *Con. Gen.* loc. cit.; cf. *Com. Theol.* Pars Prima, cap. cxxiii.

[3] *Con. Gen.* loc. cit.; cf. *Com. Theol.* Pars Prima, cap. cxxxi.

[4] *Com. Theol.* loc. cit.

[5] *Con. Gen.* loc. cit.; cf. *De Verit.* q. 5: a. 2. c.   [6] *Con. Gen.* loc. cit.

why some have more motions than others, and motions utterly different. Hence the ordering of all these motions, and of all the motions and operations which result from them here below, must be ascribed to providence.[1]

8. The nearer anything is to its cause the more it participates in the effect of that cause. Consequently, if something be more perfectly participated in by a number of entities according as some of them are nearer to it than others, this is a sign that it is the cause of that wherein they participate in different ways.[2] We find, however, that things are more perfectly ordered according as they are nearer to God. For inferior bodies, which are the most distant from the Deity in point of likeness, sometimes exhibit deflections from the normal course of nature, as in the occurrence of monstrosities; a thing that never happens in the case of the heavenly bodies—although these are yet in a certain mode changeable—nor yet in the case of unembodied intelligences. It is manifest, therefore, that God is the cause of the order of the universe.[3]

9. It has been shown that God brought all things into being by his intellect and will. But his intellect and will can have no other end than the communication of his goodness to the creatures. And the creatures imitate the divine goodness, in so far as they themselves are good. And the greatest good in created things is the good order of the universe, which is especially willed and intended by God. Accordingly, since government is the imposition of order, God governs the universe.[4]

---

[1] *Con. Gen.* loc. cit.

[2] Aquinas has worded his argument rather awkwardly: "Unde, si aliquid tanto participatur perfectius ab aliquibus quanto alicui rei magis appropinquant, signum est quod illa res sit causa illius quod diversimode participatur: sicut, si aliqua magis sunt calida secundum quod magis appropinquant igni, signum est quod ignis sit causa caloris." Taken literally, this would mean that the characteristic participated in is the cause of itself. But what Aquinas obviously had in mind was the passage of form from one subject to another, as is shown by the example of the fire which he has given us. The nearer a thing is to the fire, the more intense the degree in which it receives the form of heat; accordingly the fire must be the cause of the heat.

[3] *Con. Gen.* loc. cit.; cf. *Com. Theol.* Pars Prima, cap. cxxiii.

[4] *Con. Gen.* loc. cit.; cf. *Sum. Theol.* I.a. q. 22 : a. 1. c. The third argument in the one hundred and twenty-third chapter of the first part of the

10. Everyone who intends some end cares more for an end . which is nearer the ultimate end, the end of all other ends. Now, that which is nearest the ultimate end of the divine will— which is the divine goodness—is the good order of the whole universe, since every particular good of this or that thing is ordered with respect to it, as the less perfect to the more perfect. Hence every part exists for the good of the whole. What God cares for most in created things must, then, be the order of the universe, and therefore God is its governor.[1]

11. Every creature arrives at its ultimate perfection through the operation proper to it, for the ultimate end and perfection of a thing must be either an operation, or the terminus or effect of an operation. Moreover, the form by which anything exists is its primary perfection.[2] And since the order of the creatures, with its distinctions of nature and grade, proceeds from the divine wisdom, so must the order of operations through which the creatures attain their ultimate end. But to order the actions of entities with respect to an end is to govern them. Consequently, God by his providence governs the universe.[3]

It is clear that the fourth argument—that from the *Compendium Theologiae*—presupposes the truth of the doctrine of conservation. But we have already remarked that the first proof of the doctrine in question presupposes the reality of the divine providence. None the less it would be manifestly unjust to accuse St. Thomas of arguing in a circle. For in the *Contra Gentiles*, where the doctrine of providence is treated previously to that of conservation, none of the proofs whereby the former doctrine is established presupposes the truth of the latter. In

Compendium Theologiae states the same general idea in a slightly different form. Those things which exist by participation are to be referred to that which exists *per se* as their cause. Since God alone is good essentially, and all other things, in so far as they are good, are good by participation, these other things must have been produced by God. But then they are ruled and governed by God, for things are ruled and governed as they are arranged in the order of goodness.

[1] *Con. Gen.* loc. cit.
[2] "Forma vero, secundum quam res est, est perfectio prima." The reference is to the *De Anima*, lib. II. cap. i. "Διὸ ἡ ψυχή ἐστιν ἐντελέχεια ἡ πρώτη σώματος φυσικοῦ δυνάμει ζωὴν ἔχοντος."
[3] *Con. Gen.* loc. cit.; cf. *Sum. Theol.* I.a. q. 103: a. 5. c.

the *Compendium Theologiae*, on the other hand, the proof just referred to[1] is unmistakably designed to prove the doctrine of conservation, and is also intended—so it would seem—to prove that of providence as well.[2] Nor does any other argument in favour of a divine providence there given presuppose the truth of the doctrine of conservation.

According to Professor R. Jolivet, the proofs of the existence of a providence can be divided into two main classes—i.e. those which are *a priori*, and those which are *a posteriori*. The arguments comprised in the first class are two in number—that from the contingent nature of created beings which involves perpetual conservation on the part of God, and that from the attributes of wisdom, goodness, and power which pertain to the Deity. Those of the second-class are likewise two in number, that from the order obtaining in the physical universe, and that from the moral order in the spiritual world.[3] This classification has the advantage of clarity, and it would be possible to arrange St. Thomas's more numerous proofs as subdivisions under these various heads. It will be noticed, however, that Jolivet's fourth argument—that from the reality of a moral order—has no exact counterpart among the proofs of Aquinas. It is briefly stated by him as follows: "The moral order rules man's will by the moral law which his conscience reveals to him. It makes it manifest that a Providence presides over the free acts of reasonable creatures in order to carry them to their end."[4] Of St. Thomas's proofs the eleventh does indeed remotely resemble Jolivet's, yet the order with which it is concerned is not primarily moral, but rather ontological. On the other hand, the fifth and seventh proofs could easily be subsumed under Jolivet's third. But the eighth, like the eleventh, envisages an ontological order of degrees of being including both the spiritual and material worlds, and this would seem to be true

---

[1] The fourth in the order in which the arguments are arranged above and the second in cap. cxxxi. *Com. Theol.* Pars Prima.

[2] It would appear to be so understood by Professor R. Jolivet in his *Précis de Philosophie*, p. 119, 1. a.

[3] *Précis de Philosophie*, pp. 119–120.

[4] "*L'ordre moral* règle la volonté de l'homme par la loi morale que sa conscience lui révèle. Il manifeste qu'une Providence préside aux actes libres des créatures raisonnables pour les conduire à leur fin" (*Précis de Philosophie*, p. 120).

of the sixth also, and probably of the ninth and tenth. The ninth, however, invokes the divine intellect and will, and the tenth the divine goodness, and so might claim kinship with the second of Jolivet's *a priori* arguments. The first three proofs would fall under the same head, whereas the fourth is identical with Jolivet's first.

The division, however, of proofs into *a priori* and *a posteriori* appears indefensible. All Aquinas's arguments concerning the nature of God are *a priori* in the sense that they profess to give absolute demonstration in accordance with logical principles accepted as self-evident, and are in no way dependent upon a process of induction. On the other hand, all of them ultimately rest upon an empirical basis, since all knowledge—in his opinion—has its origin in the senses. We have followed the long course of argumentation by which he sought to justify the ascription of attributes to God, and we know that the presence of order in the universe is one of the foundations upon which it rests. How then are arguments based upon the nature of God or the contingency of created things more *a priori* than those which are built upon the order which reigns in the physical or spiritual world? I pointed out at the beginning of this essay the unsatisfactory character of the same distinction in the case of the proofs of God's existence. But here it is even more obnoxious. For the ontological argument, although no more *a priori* in the modern sense than the argument from motion, is none the less distinguished in this respect, that it takes as its point of departure no observed fact or facts, but an abstract idea for the validity of which it offers no empirical justification. Yet Jolivet's first two arguments, although their point of departure is also the nature of God, are not without empirical foundations, since it is only by arguing from observed facts that we are able to learn anything about the divine nature.

According to St. Thomas it is impossible that any inferior agent should be the cause of the being of anything except in so far as it acts by the power of God. At first glance it appears that this statement is a mere repetition of the conclusion previously reached that God alone is able to create; but this misapprehension is dispelled when we read that "being is the common effect of all agents, for every agent is productive of actual being."[1] Obviously, then, the assertion has reference to the process of generation and becoming. Nevertheless, the arguments by which it is supported have their analogues among those which were framed to sustain the former proposition.

1. Only actual being is capable of imparting being to others. But God, through his providence, keeps all things in being; whatever imparts being does so, therefore, through the divine power.

2. When divers agents are subordinate to a single agent, an effect which is common to them all must result from their participation in the movement and power of that agent, for many agents are not productive of unity except in so far as they are one.[2] But God is the primal agent, and being is the common effect of all agents. Accordingly, in so far as inferior agents are productive of being, in so far they are subordinate to God.

3. In any instance of the concerted action of superior and inferior agents, that effect which is last in the process of generation but first in intention is the effect proper to the primal agent. Thus, the form of a house, which is the effect proper to the architect, comes into being later than the preparation of cement, stones, and wood, which is carried out by his workmen. In every action, however, actual being is what is principally intended; for when that is gained the action of the agent and the moving of the effect alike cease. Hence, being is the effect proper to the primal agent, and all things which produce being act by its power.

4. Among the effects of a secondary agent the maximum in goodness and perfection cannot exceed the capacity of the primary agent. But being is the most perfect of all effects, for every nature and form is perfected by becoming actually existent, and is compared to actual being as potentiality to actuality; so that being is produced by secondary agents only through the power of the primal agent.

5. The order of effects follows the order of causes. And the

---

[1] "Cum igitur esse sit communis effectus omnium agentium, nam omne agens facit esse actu" (*Con. Gen.* lib. III. cap. 66).

[2] The illustration of the army and its leader is here once more made use of.

first effect of all is being, since all others are determinations thereof. Accordingly, being is the effect proper to the first agent, and is produced by secondary agents only through its power according as they particularize and determine its activity.

6. That which is what it is essentially is the cause of that which is what is by participation. God alone is essentially being, and all other things have being only by participation. Hence the being of every existent is an effect proper to God, and every agent which brings anything into existence does so by his power.

Furthermore God is the cause of every operation that takes place.[1] This is an important point, inasmuch as a somewhat similar view was held by the Loquentes, whose position we shall presently consider. According to St. Thomas, it is, however, a direct consequence of the proposition just established; for, since everything which operates is a cause of being in some mode—either substantial or accidental—and since nothing can cause being except in so far as it acts by the divine power, it is clear that God operates in every operation.[2] Moreover, God is the cause of all forms. Not only does he give each entity its form whereby it operates, he also conserves these forms, and so perpetually renews the operative virtues of all things.[3] Again, as we have seen, secondary causes always act through the power of the primary cause. And the entity through whose power an action is accomplished is more truly its cause than the entity which performs it, even as the principal agent can more truly be said to act than the instrument. Accordingly, God, the ultimate efficient cause, is the principal cause of every action performed by an inferior cause.[4] It will also be remembered that the final cause of every operation is a real or apparent good, and that nothing is good except in so far as it resembles the Deity; hence, God is the ultimate final cause of every operation.[5] Furthermore, since every operation is directed toward an ultimate end; and, since it has been shown that the divine providence directs all things toward their ultimate ends, it is clear that the divine activity is involved in every

[1] *Con. Gen.* lib. III. cap. 67; *Sum. Theol.* I.a. q. 105: a. 5; *De Pot.* q. 3: a. 7.
[2] *Con. Gen.* loc. cit.   [3] *Con. Gen.* loc. cit.; *Sum. Theol.* loc. cit.
[4] *Con. Gen.* loc. cit.; *Sum. Theol.* loc. cit.   [5] *Sum. Theol.* loc. cit.

operation.[1] And, lastly, all operative powers are applied to their proper objects by some motion either of body or soul. But God is the principle of both. For all physical changes are due to him, inasmuch as he is the unmoved mover, and all motions of the will are likewise to be referred to him as to "the first appetible and the first willer."[2]

It must not be supposed, however, that creative activity on the part of God is mingled with the operations of nature. This not unnatural error follows from the acceptance of the opinion of Avicenna that forms are created by the *intellectus agens*.[3] Aquinas, however, held the view that forms are educed from the potentiality of primary matter, "For what is made is not form, but a composite entity; which is made out of matter and not out of nothing. And it is made indeed out of matter, inasmuch as matter is in potentiality with respect to the composite entity itself, since it is in potentiality with respect to form. And so form cannot properly be said to be made in matter, but rather to be educed from the potentiality of matter."[4]

Since the divine activity is involved in every operation God can be said to be present in all things, not as an accident is present in its subject but as an agent is present in the thing upon which it acts. For mover and moved, agent and patient, operator and *operatum* must always be together.[5] In the case of corporeal entities which are essentially spatial, it is possible for mover and moved to be together only by contact, since two bodies cannot occupy the same place. A spiritual agent, on the other hand, which is essentially free from quantity and place,

---

[1] *Con. Gen.* loc. cit.

[2] "Similiter etiam omnis motus voluntatis quo applicantur aliquae virtutes ad operandum, reducitur in Deum sicut in primum appetibile et in primum volentem" (*Con. Gen.* loc. cit.). It is evident that this passage supports the contention of Garrigou-Lagrange that the point of departure of the argument from motion is not merely local motion, but any form of change, whether physical or mental.

[3] See *Metaphysices Compendium*, pp. 191–192, 199, n. 5.

[4] "Nam id quod fit, non est forma, sed compositum; quod ex materia fit, et non ex nihilo. Et fit quidem ex materia, inquantum materia est in potentia ad ipsum compositum, per hoc quod est in potentia ad formam. Et sic non proprie dicitur quod forma fiat in materia, sed magis quod de materiae potentia educatur" (*De Pot.* q. 3: a. 8. c.).

[5] See *Phys.* lib. VII. cap. ii. lect. 4.

is not separated by space from that which it moves, but wherever the entity moved is, there is the mover, as the soul is in the body.[1] Again the being of everything and every part of everything is immediately from God, the Creator, and for this reason also we are justified in saying that God is in all things.[2] Moreover, it has been shown that God, who is essentially being, conserves all things, and that without divine conservation they would cease to exist, from which the same conclusion follows.[3]

Since mover and moved, agent and patient, must be together, and since God creates, conserves, and moves all things, it is clear that God is everywhere.[4] Furthermore, everything which is in a place is in some way in contact with it. A corporeal entity makes contact through its quantity; a spiritual entity through its power. If any body were of infinite quantity it would be everywhere; and, similarly, if a spiritual being were of infinite power it would be everywhere. But God is of infinite power. God is, therefore, everywhere.[5] Were we to assume the contrary, and to suppose that God is present in only one of his effects, such as the *primum mobile*, we should be driven to assert an impossible conclusion. For every cause must be in contact with its immediate effect. And every creature—in regard to its being and to some, at least, of its qualities—is an immediate effect of God. Hence God must be present in all things.[6]

---

[1] I *Dist.* 37. q. 1 : a. 1. sol.; cf. *Sum. Theol.* I.a. q. 8: a. 1. c.

[2] I *Dist.* 37. loc. cit; *Sum. Theol.* loc. cit.

[3] I *Dist.* 37. loc. cit.; *Sum. Theol.* loc. cit.

[4] *Con. Gen.* lib. III. cap. 68; cf. *Com. Theol.* Pars Prima, cap. cxxxvi. In the *Contra Gentiles* we also find the following argument: As a particular cause stands to its effect, so must a universal cause stand to a universal effect. But a particular cause and its effect must be together, hence a universal cause and its effect must be together also. But God is the universal cause of all being, wherever being is, therefore, God must be. Consequently God is everywhere. This argument adds nothing to those given above. The God who creates and conserves all beings is, of course, the universal cause of all being, but it is a matter of indifference whether we reason from the dependence of all things upon God to the presence of God in all things, or formulate two arguments from the creation and conservation of all things. Since creation and conservation are in reality a single act, it is clear that the two arguments are only formally distinct.

[5] *Con. Gen.* lib. III. cap. 68; cf. *Quodlib.* XI. q. 1 : a. 1.

[6] *Con. Gen.* lib. III. cap. 68.

The assertion that God is everywhere is not, of course, to be understood to mean that God is extended, but rather that he is active in every place.[1]

Furthermore God is everywhere and in all things by essence, presence, and power; by essence since all things participate in the divine existence whence their own is derived, by power since all things are subject to and act by the divine power, and by presence since all things are known to and are immediately ordered by God.[2] Moreover, in rational creatures, which know and love him, God is present as the known in the knower and the desired in the desirer, and in this mode he is present by grace.[3]

---

[1] *Con. Gen.* lib. III. cap. 68. In the *Commentary on the Sentences* (1 *Dist.* 37. q. 2: a. 1) the contrast is emphasized between corporeal substance which is in something in the sense of being contained by it, and spiritual substance which is in something as containing and conserving it. In the former sense God can be said to be everywhere only metaphorically, inasmuch as he is causally active everywhere. In the second sense, however, God can properly be said to be in space inasmuch as he gives to it its nature, even as he can be said to be in man since he gives to man human nature. In the *Summa Theologica* (I.a q. 8: a. 2. c.) it is stated that there are two ways of being in space; first, according to the mode of other things, that is, as something is in something else in any mode whatever—and in this way the accidents of a place are in the place—and, secondly, according to the mode proper to place, which is that of things located in a place: "vel per modum aliarum rerum, idest sicut dicitur aliquid esse in aliis rebus quocumque modo, sicut accidentia loci sunt in loco; vel per modum proprium loci, sicut locata sunt in loco." In each way God can be said to be everywhere *secundum quid*; in the first, because he gives to everything its being, power, and operation; in the second, because he fills space in the sense that he is the cause of all extended things. The distinction is less clear than one could wish.

[2] *Sum. Theol.* I.a. q. 8: a. 3. c.; *Com. Theol.* Pars Prima, cap. cxxxvi.

[3] *Sum. Theol.* loc. cit. In the *Commentary on the Sentences* (1 *Dist.* 37. q. 1: a. 2. sol.) the matter is stated somewhat differently. There are three modes in which creatures can be joined to God. The first is by similitude, and this is common to all things, since every creature in so far as it exists, imitates God. Thus God is in all things by essence, presence, and power. It is to be remarked, however, that in this way no creature is joined to God by its substance. A creature that is joined to God in the second mode, i.e., by its substance, is joined by operation, as when someone adheres by faith to the primal truth and by charity to the highest good, and in this mode God is in the saints by grace. But this does not involve that the creature be joined to God in the third mode, according to being, as is the case of the hypostatic union in Christ. Thus modes are really

To be everywhere *per se* pertains to God alone. To be everywhere *per accidens* is, indeed, a quality which can be conceived to pertain to a creature—and this in two modes, *ex parte eius quod in loco est*, and *ex parte loci*. In the first mode, an infinite body would be everywhere *per accidens*, since it would be everywhere according to its parts, divers parts being in divers places. Yet it would not be everywhere *per se*, since it would not be everywhere as a whole. In the second mode, a minute body, such a grain of millet, would be everywhere if there were no other place except that which it occupied. But to be everywhere *per se* belongs to God alone, since he is wholly in every place and in the whole, for his power is efficacious not only in what is common to the universe, but in what is proper to every particular; and he is, therefore, in all things as in one place and as in many places, which is what we mean by being everywhere; and, moreover, he is in all things past, present, and to come.[1] Since the creatures exist only in time, and since the time series had its beginning, the relation of being in the creatures, like the relations of lordship and of creation, can be predicated of God only *de tempore*, for a relation of this sort, which is founded upon an operation, requires each of its terms to be actually existent.[2]

I pass now to Aquinas's refutation of the Loquentes.[3] These theologians denied, as we have seen, the reality of substantial forms. Furthermore, they maintained that form cannot be made out of matter, and that all forms must, therefore, be created *ex nihilo*.[4] In this opinion they had been supported, to some extent at least, by certain philosophers. Plato had taught that, since the forms of material entities do not exist distinct *ex parte creaturae*, but *ex parte Dei* they are distinct only for the reason. For the divine essence is unconditioned by any creature; but according as God operates in anything he is said to be in it by presence, and because his operation is immanent and does not flow out from the divine power, God is said to be in that thing by power, and since the divine power is identical with the divine essence, God is said to be in it by essence.

[1] *Sum. Theol.* I.a. q. 8: a. 4. c.; 1 *Dist.* 37. q. 2: a. 2. sol.; *Quodlib.* XI. q. 1 : a. 1. c.
[2] 1 *Dist.* 37. q. 2: a. 3. sol.
[3] This topic has been treated at length by Professor Gilson in an article entitled "Pourquoi saint Thomas a critiqué saint Augustin," in the *Archives d'Histoire Doctrinale et Littéraire du Moyen Age* for 1926–27, pp. 8–35.
[4] *Con. Gen.* lib. III. cap. 69.

per se, they must be caused by forms existing *per se* apart from matter, and so he posited separate forms of every species.[1] Avicenna had referred substantial forms to the *intellectus agens*, and had regarded accidental forms as dispositions of matter due to the action of inferior causes.[2] In proof of this view it could be pointed out that no active powers which are not accidental can be found in any body, and it could be urged that accidental forms are not equal to causing substantial forms. Moreover, among inferior bodies there are some—such as the bodies of those animals which are generated from putrefaction—which are not generated from their own kind, so that it would seem that their forms must be due to principles of a higher order.[3]

In addition there are three arguments to be considered which were formulated by Avicebron (Solomon ibn Gabirol). The first is based upon the proposition that quantity impedes action and motion, in proof of which it is urged that the larger a body is the heavier it is and the slower is its motion; and the inference is drawn that body is wholly passive and that spirit alone is active.[4] The second affirms that every patient is subject to its agent, and that every agent, with the exception of the Creator, requires a subject inferior to itself, and that, therefore, matter, to which nothing is inferior, is necessarily incapable of action.[5] The third stresses the distance which sunders corporeal substance from the primal agent, and the consequent difficulty of supposing that capacity for action can descend to such a low level. As God is wholly agent, so corporeal substance, the lowest of beings, must, we are told, be wholly passive.[6] And, lastly, there is yet another argument of the Loquentes, that accidents do not pass from one subject to another, and that, therefore, they are not produced by the action of bodies, and, accordingly, must have been created by God.[7]

To these various objections Aquinas returned the following replies:

[1] *Con. Gen.* loc. cit.; *Sum. Theol.* I.a. q. 115: a. 1. c.
[2] *Con. Gen.* loc. cit.; cf. *Sum. Theol.* loc. cit.   [3] *Con. Gen.* loc. cit.
[4] *Con. Gen.* loc. cit.; *Sum. Theol.* I.a. q. 115: a. 1. c.; *De Pot.* q. 3: a. 7. c.; cf. Baeumker's edition of the *Fons Vitae*, pp. 40–42.
[5] *Con. Gen.* loc. cit.; *De Pot.* loc. cit.; cf. *Fons Vitae*, p. 40.
[6] *Con. Gen.* loc. cit.; *De Pot.* loc. cit.; *Fons Vitae*, II. 10. pp. 41 and 42.
[7] *Con. Gen.* loc. cit.

In response to the first it is to be said that form does not in itself possess being, but that through it some composite substance exists, and that accordingly it is not *made* at all—in the proper sense of the word—but that it begins to be by reason of the passage of the composite substance from potentiality to actuality.[1]

In answer to Plato it suffices to point out that it is not necessary that everything which has its form by participation should receive it immediately from that which is essentially form; it may receive it immediately from another entity which has by participation a form similar to its own, which yet acts by virtue of the separate form, if such there be.[2]

Against Avicenna it may be contended that, although interaction among inferior bodies takes place by means of active and passive qualities which are themselves accidents, yet it cannot be inferred that only accidents are produced thereby; for even as these accidental forms are caused by a substantial form—in conjunction with matter—so by virtue of this substantial form do they act, and that which acts by virtue of some other entity produces an effect which resembles that other more than itself. So the action of an instrument produces in the product of an art the likeness of the art,[3] and so accidental forms acting as the instruments of substantial forms produce other substantial forms.[4]

Again in the case of animals generated from putrefaction, the substantial form is caused by a corporeal agent, such as a heavenly body, which is the *primum alterans*, and which is capable, without the action of a univocal agent, of producing such imperfect forms as these.

As regards Avicebron's first argument, it does not prove that quantity deprives corporeal form of all agency, but only of universal agency. Were fire a separate form it would be the cause of all ignition, but *this* particular flaming body can be the cause only of *this* ignition.[5] In fact, increase of quantity tends to greater activity rather than less. Thus the greater the size of a body which burns with a certain intensity of heat, the greater

---

[1] *Con. Gen.* loc. cit.   [2] *Con. Gen.* loc. cit.
[3] "Sicut ex actione instrumenti fit in artificatio similitudo formae artis."
[4] *Con. Gen.* loc. cit.
[5] *Con. Gen.* loc. cit.; *Sum. Theol.* loc. cit.

amount of heat does it give forth.[1] Nor is it true that quantity is the cause of weight,[2] nor yet that weight implies motion, for only the quantitative is moved,[3] and the heavier anything is the more powerfully it is moved in the way that is proper to it.[4]

Avicebron's second contention was pronounced unsound on the ground that it treats corporeal substance as though it were numerically singular. If a plurality of substantial forms be admitted, it will follow that not every corporeal substance will be at the farthest remove from God, but one, according as it is more formal (*formalius*) and more active than another, will be superior to that other, and nearer the primal agent, and so will be able to act on that other.[5] But, as a matter of fact, none of them will be incapable of action. For every body is composed of matter and form, potentiality and actuality. And, since everything acts according as it is actual, a body acts by its form. The matter of the body acted upon is in potentiality with respect to the form of the agent. If the matter of the agent be itself in potentiality with respect to the form of the patient, interaction takes place.[6]

The third argument is unsound for the same reason. Primary matter is, indeed, at the ultimate distance from God, and it is wholly passive. But bodies, being composed of matter and form, by their forms tend to resemble the Deity, and in so far as they are forms each has matter subject to it. Hence, according as they have form they act, and according as they possess matter they are passive.[7]

In reply to the Loquentes, St. Thomas points out that while it is true that an accident cannot pass from one substance to another in the sense that it is numerically the same in both, yet it can cause in another subject a similar instance of its own species.[8]

Not content with thus responding to his opponents' arguments, Aquinas himself bought forward nine counter arguments :[9]

[1] *Con. Gen.* loc. cit.
[2] *Sum. Theol.* loc. cit.; *De Pot.* q. 3 : a. 7. c.; cf. *De Caelo et Mundo*, lib. III. cap. ii. 2.
[3] *De Pot.* loc. cit.   [4] *De. pot.* cit. loc.; *Sum. Theol.* I.a. q. 115 : a. 1. ad 3^m.
[5] *De Pot.* loc. cit.; *Con. Gen.* loc. cit.
[6] *Con. Gen.* loc. cit.; *De Pot.* loc. cit.
[7] *Con. Gen.* loc. cit.; cf. *De Pot.* loc. cit.
[8] *De Pot.* loc. cit.; *Con. Gen.* loc. cit.   [9] *Con. Gen.* loc. cit.

1. Since the activity of God is unvarying, if God alone operate in all things, no diverse effects will follow from the diversity of the things upon which he acts. But the senses testify that this is false, for the touch of a hot thing always produces a sensation of heat and not of cold.[1]

2. It is inconsistent with the notion of wisdom that there should be anything useless in the operations of a wise man. But if the creatures do not operate it will be useless for God to order them with respect to the production of certain effects. Such a supposition is, therefore, inconsistent with the notion of divine wisdom.[2]

3. To provide a principle is to provide all that follows from it, as the cause responsible for gravity is responsible also for downward motion. But from actual existence there follows the making of something else actual, as is evident in the case of God who is both pure actuality and the primal cause of all being. If, therefore, God have communicated to all things his likeness according to being he will have communicated to them also his likeness according to acting.[3]

4. Perfection of effect indicates perfection of cause, for the greater the power of the cause the more perfect the effect. And God is the most perfect agent. Hence, to detract from the perfection of the creatures is to detract from the divine perfection. But if no creature be able to act, much is taken away from the perfection of the creature; for it is from the abundance of its perfection that it is able to communicate the perfection which it has. Accordingly, the theory in question detracts from the divine power.[4]

5. As it pertains to the good to make what is good, so it pertains to the highest good to make what is best. And God is the highest good; it, therefore, pertains to God to make all things best. But it is better that the good conferred upon something should be common rather than proper to it alone, for common good is more divine than the good of one. But the good of one becomes common if it be capable of being trans-

---

[1] The illustration is one of uniformity and not of diversity. But what Aquinas had in mind was evidently the multifarious modes in which the law of cause and effect manifests itself in the world of nature. Cf. *De Pot.* q. 3 : a. 7. c.

[2] Cf. *Sum. Theol.* I.a. q. 105 : a. 1. c.; cf. *De Pot.* q. 3 : a. 7. c.

[3] *Con. Gen.* loc. cit.   [4] *Con. Gen.* loc. cit.; cf. *Sum. Theol.* loc. cit.

mitted to others, which can take place only through the action of one creature upon another. To deny the creatures their proper actions is to derogate from the divine goodness.[1]

6. To take away order from the creatures is to take away what is best, for while particulars are good in themselves, all things are best together, because of the order of the universe, for the whole is better than its parts. But if things be denied the power to act, the order of the universe is taken away, since things diverse in nature are bound in unity of order only by action and passion. Hence, the assumption that they do not act is inadmissible.[2]

7. If effects be not produced by the action of the creatures, the power of no created cause can be made manifest, for it is the effect which reveals the power of its cause and only so is it known. All knowledge of natural science will, therefore, be impossible.[3]

8. From induction it is apparent that like produces like. What is generated in the case of inferior creatures is not, however, form alone, but an entity composed of matter and form. That which generates must, therefore, be likewise composed of matter and form.[4]

9. If action follow upon being, the more perfect actuality cannot be without activity. Substantial form is more perfect actuality than accidental form. Accordingly, if accidental forms have actions proper to themselves, much more must this be true of substantial forms. But substantial forms do not act through the mere disposition of matter, for this is alteration for which accidental forms suffice. Hence, the form of the generating entity must be capable of introducing a substantial form into the thing generated.[5]

If the position of Aquinas's opponents were sound, generation and corruption would be impossible,[6] and the Aristotelian foundations of his system would be undermined; hence, the importance which he attached to disprove their contentions. But is his own view consistent? Can the same effect be produced

---

[1] *Con. Gen.* loc. cit. Since goodness and perfection are identical in God, this argument is only formally distinct from its predecessor.

[2] *Con. Gen.* loc. cit.

[3] *Con. Gen.* loc. cit. This is clearly not a conclusive proof, but an *argumentum ad hominem*.   [4] *Con. Gen.* loc. cit.

[5] *Con. Gen.* loc. cit.   [6] *De Pot.* q. 3: a. 7. c.

both by God and by a natural agent? Can it thus have two
causes? Must not one of these be superfluous? And if God
produce the whole effect, what will there be left for the natural
agent to produce?

These objections were taken up in their order by Aquinas
and replied to as follows:[1]

In the case of any agent there are two things to consider,
the thing itself which acts, and the power by which it
acts. The power of an inferior cause is derived from, and is
conserved and even directed to action by, a superior cause.
But this superior and proximate cause is likewise entirely
dependent upon its own superior, and so we ascend the
hierarchy of causes until we arrive at the supreme agent, whose
power is thus as immediately active in the production of the
ultimate effect as is that of the lowest agent.

Neither the divine nor the natural agent is superfluous—
not the divine, for the natural acts only by virtue of the divine;
and not the natural, since the Deity, in his goodness, wills to
communicate his likeness to the creatures not only as regards
their existence, but also regards their power of causation.

We are not to suppose that part of the effect is to be attributed to God, and part to the natural agent. The entire effect
is produced by each cause, each acting in its own mode, even
as the same effect is produced by an instrument and by the
principal agent.

"Thus," he wrote, "if any inquire as to the 'why' (*propter
quid*) of some natural effect, we can return a reason from some
proximate cause, while yet we refer all things to the divine
will as their primal cause. And so, if any ask why wood is
heated in the presence of fire, it can be said that heating is the
natural action of fire, and that this is so because heat is an
accident proper to fire, and that this follows from the form
proper to fire; and so on until we arrive at the divine will.
Hence, if someone reply to the question why wood is heated,
because God wills it, he replies correctly indeed if he intend to
refer the question to the primal cause, but incorrectly if he
intend to exclude other causes."[2]

[1] *Con. Gen.* lib. III. cap. 70.
[2] "Sic ergo, cum quaeritur *propter quid* de aliquo naturali effectu,
possumus reddere rationem ex aliqua proxima causa: dum tamen, sicut in

Is St. Thomas's position, however, as far removed from that of the Loquentes as he would have us believe? According to his own statements fire is dependent upon God, not only for its being, but also for its active power, and even for the actual putting forth of that power on any particular occasion. Did the Loquentes say more than this? They did, indeed, assert that no accident endures for more than one instant. But St. Thomas has insisted upon the necessity of the perpetual conservation of all things by God, and has also maintained that conservation and creation are in reality identical. Wherein, then, does his view essentially differ from theirs? It is evident, of course, that Aquinas was anxious to vindicate the reality of the laws of nature. But he had also emphasized the purely instrumental character of every secondary cause, and had affirmed that the primal cause is as immediately present in the effect of any inferior cause as is the inferior cause itself. Moreover, the analogy between inferior causes and the instruments of human activity fails in this, that all inferior causes are themselves created and conserved by God. In contending, then, that natural agents are endowed with modes of causation proper to themselves, did St. Thomas really mean any more than that God habitually acts in certain ways? If he did, it does not appear that he was justified. If not, the difference between himself and his opponents appears negligible.[1]

It is obvious that there is evil in the universe. Accordingly, it must be shown that this fact is not incompatible with the existence of a divine providence.[2] That it is not inconsistent is apparent, St. Thomas maintains, when we realize that God makes use of secondary causes; since from a defect in such a cause there may result a defect in the effect, while yet the

primam causam, reducamus omnia in voluntatem divinam. Sicut, si quaeritur *Quare lignum est calefactum ad praesentiam ignis?* dicitur *Quia calefactio est naturalis actio ignis.* Hoc autem, *quia calor est proprium accidens eius.* Hoc autem consequitur propriam formam eius. Et sic inde, quousque perveniatur ad divinam voluntatem. Unde, si quis respondet quaerenti quare lignum calefactum est, *Quia Deus voluit:* convenienter quidem respondet si intendit reducere quaestionem in primam causam; inconvenienter vero si intendit omnes alias excludere causas." (*Con. Gen.* lib. III. cap. 97).

[1] Cf. *Le Guide des Égarés*, Première Partie, pp. 393–4.
[2] *Con. Gen.* lib. III. cap. 71.

primal agent remains untainted by imperfection.[1] Moreover,
if perfect goodness is to obtain in the universe, all possible
grades of goodness must be fulfilled,[2] otherwise no creature
would resemble God in being better than another. Not only
would the greatest beauty of the universe be destroyed were
the inequalities of goodness removed, but also multiplicity
would disappear, since, in respect of the differences whereby
one creature differs from another, one creature is better than
another. As a result only one created good would be left.[3]
The superior grade of goodness is that which does not contain
within itself the possibility of non-existence, while the inferior
grade can cease to exist. Each is requisite to the perfection of
the universe.[4] Furthermore, justice requires that the creatures
be permitted to act in accordance with their natures; and that
where one acts inimically to another evil must result. Yet
nothing acts except in so far as it intends some good, and were
providence to prohibit such action the universe would lose
much good. It must also be considered that much good has its
origin in evil, the patience of the just, for instance, and vin-
dictive justice.[5] Again the beauty of the universe arises from the
ordered arrangement of good and evil.[6] And, finally, the good
is better known and more ardently desired when compared

[1] *Con. Gen.* lib. IV. cap. 71; cf. *Com. Theol.* Pars Prima, cap. cxlii.
[2] *Con. Gen.* lib. IV. cap. 71; cf. *Sum. Theol.* I.a. q. 22: a. 4. c.
[3] Aquinas's thought here is difficult to follow. At first sight it appears
that he assumes not only that there cannot be two substances exactly
similar to each other, but also that there cannot be two substances equally
good. This last would indeed be an amazing assumption. It seems probable,
however, that what Aquinas meant was that the removal of degrees of
goodness from the universe would involve the removal also of degrees of
being, with the result that the realm of possible existence would be cir-
cumscribed within very narrow limits. I cite the Latin in full.
  "Tolleretur etiam summus decor a rebus, si ab eis ordo distinctorum
et disparium tolleretur. Et quod est amplius, tolleretur multitudo a rebus,
inaequalitate bonitatis sublata: cum per differentias quibus res ad
invicem differunt, unum altero melius existat; sicut animatum inanimato,
et rationale irrationali. Et sic, si aequalitas omnimoda esset in rebus, non
esset nisi unum bonum creatum."
[4] This division seems to imply that there are only two grades of goodness
in the universe, which we know was not Aquinas's view. Doubtless the
various grades are to be taken as subsumed under this classification.
[5] *Con. Gen.* loc. cit.; cf. *Com. Theol.* Pars Prima, cap. cxliii.
[6] *Con. Gen.* loc. cit.; cf. *Com. Theol.* Pars Prima, cap. cxliii.

with the evil.[1] In fact St. Thomas goes so far as to say that the existence of evil is a proof of the existence of God, because, if the order of the good were annihilated, evil, which is the privation of that order, would be annihilated also.[2]

The willingness of St. Thomas to acquiesce in the sacrifice of individual good to the good of the whole is indeed striking. But what is the good of the whole, and for whom is it good? God undoubtedly is the being for whom the universe is good, and its goodness seems to be of an aesthetic character. The notion that evil is a necessary element in the harmony and beauty of the universe is a familiar one both in religion and philosophy, repugnant as it is sure to seem to the minds of many. Yet a God who could forgo creating a better universe to create a worse one—and, as we have seen, this is what Aquinas believed to have actually occurred—would doubtless be capable of finding pleasure in the contemplation of evil as well as of good.

We have already learned that the presence of contingency in the universe is in accordance with the divine will. Obviously, then, it will also be in accordance with the divine providence, which is nothing else than the ordering of all things by the divine intellect and will. None the less St. Thomas produces proofs that this is so.[3] In the first place, he argues that certain effects must be contingent because certain secondary causes are contingent.[4] But how do we know that any secondary causes are contingent? In itself this proof is evidently invalid. Passing, then, to the second argument—an argument which has already been used to prove that the presence of contingency in the universe is in accord with the divine will, and that the presence of evil is compatible with providence—it is argued that if all the possible grades of being are actually filled, there must be contingent as well as necessary entities in the universe. A third proof restates the contention in other words. The beings nearest to God are, like him, immovable.[5] These are

---

[1] *Con. Gen.* loc. cit; cf. *Com. Theol.* Pars Prima, cap. cxliii.

[2] "*Si malum est, Deus est.* Non enim esset malum sublato ordine boni, cuius privatio est malum. Hic autem ordo non esset, si Deus non esset."

[3] *Con. Gen.* lib. III. cap. 72.

[4] Cf. *Com. Theol.* Pars Prima, cap. cxl.

[5] Evidently it is local motion that Aquinas here has in mind.

purely spiritual substances. Lower than they are the heavenly bodies, which retain a certain immobility in that they move always in the same way, and herein the beauty of order appears. Yet with them contingency enters.[1] Again, without contingency there could be neither generation nor corruption—for the necessary is always existent—nor yet motion, for in everything moved something begins to be and something ceases to be, which is a kind of generation and corruption.[2]

Aquinas also contends that failure of power on the part of a secondary cause, or encounter with an opposing cause, will be productive of some change, and that such failures and such encounters, which cannot be avoided so long as providence does not immobilize its creatures, explain why the creatures do not always act in the same way.[3]

It is clear that, on this theory, while every substance is contingent in the sense that it depends upon God for its existence, no event is contingent in the sense that it might not have happened, or might have happened otherwise, since events are willed by God and happen as he wills them. Yet events can be contingent or necessary with respect to other events. "It must be admitted, then, that all things that are made here below, according as they are referred to the first cause, are found ordered and not existing *per accidens*; although when compared to other causes they are found to exist *per accidens*. . . . Moreover, as has been said, being as such has God himself for its cause; accordingly, as being itself is subject to the divine power, so are all accidents of being as such, among which are necessity and contingency. To the divine providence it pertains, therefore, not only to make *this* being, but to give it contingency or necessity. And so, according as it wishes to give to each one contingency or necessity, it prepares for it intermediate causes from which it follows of necessity or contingently."[4]

[1] Cf. *Sum. Theol.* I.a. q. 22 : a. 4. c.

[2] It is clear that these arguments add nothing to, and, indeed, presuppose the second.

[3] Cf. *Con. Gen.* lib. III. cap. 94. argument 5.

[4] "Relinquitur igitur quod omnia, quae hic fiunt, prout ad primam causam divinam referuntur, inveniuntur ordinata et non per accidens existere: licet par comparationem ad alias causas per accidens esse inveniantur. . . . Sicut autem dictum est, ens inquantum ens est habet causam ipsum Deum : unde sicut divinae providentiae subditur ipsum ens, ita etiam

There remains a last argument drawn from our experience. We know empirically that there are contingent causes, since we see that they can fail to produce their effects. And we observe that such failure can often be counteracted by human prudence.[1] Contingency must, then, be compatible with providence.

But what of free will? Is it compatible with providence? St. Thomas replies in the affirmative. In inanimate things contingency is an imperfection, but that the will is a contingent cause is due to its perfection. Moreover, providence makes use of anything according to the mode of its existence which follows from its form. But the form through which the will acts is not determinate, for it is moved to act by a form apprehended by the intellect, and the intellect comprehends not one form but a multiplicity of forms; hence the will can produce a multiplicity of effects. Again, God is man's ultimate end; and man attains to the divine likeness by acting freely. Also, were the will deprived of its freedom, the praise of virtue, the justice of punishment, and many other good things would disappear. For all these reasons, then, freedom of the will is sustained by providence.[2]

Things which happen infrequently (*in minori parte*) we attribute to chance (*casus*) or fortune (*fortuna*), nor is this incompatible with the existence of providence. For it has just been shown that it would be contrary to the notion of providence that all things should occur of necessity, and that no agent should ever fail to attain its intended end. And it has also been shown that the activity of subordinate causes must sometimes conflict. Now, such failures and conflicts are what we mean by chance. Again, it has been made plain that according to the order of the universe some things should exist *per se*[3] and others *per accidens*. Hence there must be *causae per accidens*.

omnia accidentia entis inquantum est ens, inter quae sunt necessarium et contingens. Ad divinam igitur providentiam pertinet non solum quod faciat hoc ens, sed quod det ei contingentiam vel necessitatem. Secundum enim quod unicuique dare voluit contingentiam vel necessitatem, praeparavit ei causas medias, ex quibus de necessitate sequatur, vel contingenter" (*Metaph.* lib. VI. cap. iii. lect. 3).

[1] Cf. *Com. Theol.* Pars Prima, cap. cxli.

[2] *Con. Gen.* lib. III. cap. 73; cf. *Sum. Theol.* I.a. q. 22: a. 3. ad 2ᵐ, 4ᵐ.

[3] It is strange that St. Thomas should use the phrase *entia per se*, when on his view there is only one *ens per se*.

And the effects of accidental causes are due to chance. Furthermore, the order of providence requires that there should be a
hierarchy of causes. The higher the cause, the further the
extent of its power. But the intention of no natural cause
extends further than its power, for such intention would be in
vain. It is impossible, however, that the intention of any particular cause should extend to all contingencies. Consequently
that which happens beyond the intention of the agent occurs
by chance.[1]

It is strange that Aquinas should have deemed it worth
while thus to discuss in detail a point which obviously involves
no new principle. His treatment of contingency has already
covered all the ground. None the less such repetition is characteristic of his method; in fact, we are straightway confronted
by another instance of it. Aquinas has already argued that the
divine intelligence and the divine will extend to particulars.
It therefore follows that the divine providence extends to
particulars. No less than ten proofs were, however, offered by
him in confirmation of this statement, which, briefly summarized, are as follows:

1. The only reason for denying that providence extends to contingent particulars is their contingency, and the fact that many of
them happen from chance. But it has already been shown that
contingency and chance are not incompatible with providence.[2]

2. If providence have no care for particulars, it can only
be because God does not know them, or because God cannot
or will not care for them. But it has been proved that God does
know them, and that his infinite power is able to care for them.
Furthermore, God universally wills the good, and the good of
things governed consists in their order.[3]

3. All secondary causes, in that they are causes, imitate the
divine simplicity.[4] But causes which produce something care
for it. Thus animals care for their young. And so God cares
for things which he has caused.[5]

4. God acts through will and intellect. But all things accomplished through will and intellect are subject to providence,

---

[1] *Con. Gen.* lib. III. cap. 74; cf. *Com. Theol.* Pars Prima, cap. cxxxviii.
[2] *Con. Gen.* lib. III. cap. 75; cf. 1 *Dist.* 39. q. 2: a. 2. ad 2ᵐ, 5ᵐ.
[3] *Con. Gen.* loc. cit.; cf. *Com. Theol.* Pars Prima, cap. cxxxiv; *Sum. Theol.*
I.a. q. 22: a. 2. c.; q. 103: a. 5. c.
[4] See *Con. Gen.* lib. III. cap. 21.   [5] *Con. Gen.* loc. cit.

which consists in arranging things by means of the intellect. All that God does is therefore subject to his providence. Now, God acts in all secondary causes; hence all particulars fall under the divine providence.[1]

5. Universals exist only in particulars, so that it is impossible that providence should not extend to the latter. Not only their conservation and corruption but all that befalls them must be subject to providence, since nothing can happen to a particular member of any species which does not in some way involve the principles of that species.[2]

6. Accidents exist on account of substance and matter on account of form, and so it is evident that the particular exists because of the universal. This is evident from the fact that where the universal nature of the species can be conserved in a single individual—as in the case of the sun or the moon—there is no more than one member of the species. Now, providence orders things with respect to their ends. It cares, therefore, both for the ends and the things ordered, both for universals, and particulars.[3]

7. Speculative cognition is perfected in the universal, but practical in the particular, for the end of the former is truth while that of the latter is operation. Now, providence pertains to practical cognition, since it orders things with respect to their ends; therefore it would be imperfect if it did not extend to particulars.[4]

8. Speculative knowledge is perfected in the universal rather than in the particular, because universals are better known than particulars. But he who is perfected in speculative knowledge is cognizant, not only of the universal, but also of the particulars. Hence he is more perfect in practical knowledge who has not only a general but a particular knowledge of the entities the activities of which he controls. And God's knowledge is perfect.[5]

9. God is the cause of being as such, and therefore his providence extends to all beings. But particulars are beings, and more so than universals, because the latter do not exist *per se*, but only in particulars.[6]

[1] *Con. Gen.* loc. cit.   [2] *Con. Gen.* loc. cit.   [3] *Con. Gen.* loc. cit.
[4] *Con. Gen.* loc. cit.   [5] *Con. Gen.* loc. cit.
[6] *Con. Gen.* loc. cit. This proof greatly resembles the sixth, the chief difference being that here the emphasis is upon the efficient causality of God, while in the former it was upon the final causality of the universal.

10. Creatures are subject to the divine providence according as it orders them with respect to an end, which is the divine goodness. Consequently, participation in the divine goodness is due to the divine providence. But contingent particulars participate in the divine goodness, so that the divine providence must extend to them.[1]

Furthermore, providence is concerned with particulars immediately.[2] For God has immediate knowledge of particulars.[3] It would therefore be absurd to suppose that God does not order all things by his will, since such order is their greatest good.[4] Again, arguing from the analogy of human government, we can see that if God governs the creatures through subordinate powers, these powers must learn from God the order which they are to impose upon the creatures. And this order must relate to particulars, for the particulars have to be governed. But it is impossible that this order should be more perfect for the subordinates than for God; particulars must therefore be immediately governed by God.[5] A human governor does, indeed, allow his subordinates to deal with particular matters, but this is due to his own limitations. Human subordinates, again, devote themselves to such tasks with a diligence which they do not owe to their superiors, whereas to God are due the wisdom and intellect of his agents. Moreover, the laws transmitted to the subordinate powers either apply to particulars or else they do not. If they do, particulars are the concern of providence; if not, the treatment of particular cases will require judgment and interpretation, which cannot be left to subordinates, but must be undertaken by the ultimate authority, and the ultimate authority will thus be compelled to concern itself with particulars. Moreover, the arrangements of inferiors are always subject to the approval of the superior, and

[1] *Con. Gen.* loc. cit.; cf. *Sum. Theol.* I.a. q. 22: a 2. c.; q. 103: a. 5 c.
[2] *Con. Gen.* lib. III. cap. 76.
[3] It has been shown that God knows only the divine essence *primo et per se*. By his statement that particulars are known immediately, Aquinas meant that they are not known mediately through any created thing.
[4] Cf. *Sum. Theol.* I.a. q. 22: a. 3. c.; q. 103: a. 6. c.
[5] It may be impossible that the subordinate powers should know the creatures more thoroughly than God, but it does not follow that God must therefore act directly upon all creatures. To reach this conclusion we must fall back upon the preceding argument.

such judgments demand a knowledge of the particulars which have to be put in order. The only reason which could be advanced in favour of the view that God does not care for particulars immediately would be that it is beneath his dignity; but, on the contrary, it is entirely in accordance with his dignity and his goodness that his providence should be concerned with even the least particulars.[1] And it is also in accordance with the divine wisdom. The wise man is he who regulates the output of his power by the end which he has in view, otherwise his power would not be subordinate to his wisdom, and thus he takes cognizance of even the humblest things.

Since God operates in all secondary causes it is clear that divine providence uses them as intermediaries in its activity.[2] This obvious inference is reinforced, however, by several other proofs. Two things are essential to providence, an ordered scheme and the carrying of it into execution. The first pertains to wisdom, and the second to operation; and in God each is found in its perfection. But order, if it is to be perfect, must embrace all things, even the most insignificant; whereas the execution of subordinate tasks pertains to the inferior power proportionate to the effect. Accordingly, God orders all things through his wisdom, but makes use of secondary causes to produce inferior effects.[3] Moreover, we are familiar with the proposition that the greater the power of the cause, the wider is the extent of its effects. Yet a cause which does not act through intermediary agents can effect only the entities in its immediate environment. The power of providence is, however, the weightiest of causes; it acts, therefore, through intermediaries.[4] Again, it befits the dignity of a ruler that he should have many subordinates to carry out his will, and especially the dignity of God who is above all.[5] Furthermore, the perfection of the divine providence requires that nothing be left

---

[1] Cf. *Sum. Theol.* I.a. q. 103: a. 6. c.

[2] *Con. Gen.* lib. III. cap. 77.

[3] *Con. Gen.* loc. cit. See also lib. III. cap. 94; *Sum. Theol.* I.a. q. 22: a. 3. c.; q. 103: a. 6. c.; *Com. Theol.* Pars Prima, cap. cxxxii.

[4] *Con. Gen.* loc. cit. This argument fails to take account of the fact that it has already been shown that God is immediately active in every operation, and also of Aquinas's contention that God can produce effects without their proximate causes. Cf. *Con. Gen.* lib. III. cap. 99.

[5] *Con. Gen.* lib. III. cap. 77.

untouched by its ordering activity, and that consequently the excess of some entities over others be reduced to order. From the superabundance of those who have more must come some good to those who have less. And this is brought about by those entities which participate more fully in the divine goodness functioning as subordinate agents in the administration of providence.[1] Moreover, the order of causes is nobler than the order of effects; hence, in the former, the perfection of providence is more fully manifest. Still, were there no intermediate causes, there would be no order of causes at all. The existence of such intermediate causes is, accordingly, requisite to the perfection of divine providence.[2]

Since the divine goodness is the ultimate end of all things, the reason for the dispositions of divine providence is the will to imprint the divine likeness upon the creatures so far as possible. And inasmuch as every created substance falls short of the perfection of the divine goodness, it is necessary that there should be a diversity of creatures, in order that that which cannot be perfectly represented by a single individual may by diverse individuals in diverse ways be more perfectly represented. Accordingly it is their end that furnishes the reason for the diversity of forms.

The diversity of forms provides, moreover, the reason for the order obtaining among the creatures; for it is the form which imparts existence to anything, and everything, according as it exists, tends to resemble God. But God is wholly simple; hence one entity can resemble him more than another

[1] *Con. Gen.* loc. cit. Cf. *Com. Theol.* Pars Prima, cap. cxxiv. In the same chapter two very similar arguments are to be found: (1) An entity which participates more in any perfection stands to that which participates less as actuality to potentiality, and as agent to patient. Hence the superior creatures in the order of divine providence stand to their inferiors in the relation of agent to patient. (2) It pertains to the divine goodness to communicate its perfection to the creatures. And it also pertains to the perfection of the divine goodness, not only that it should be good in itself, but that it should draw all other things to the good. Hence it communicates to creatures, not only the capacity for being good in themselves, but also for leading other creatures to the good. The creatures to whom this is communicated are superior creatures, since that which participates in the likeness both of the form and of the activity of an agent is superior to that which participates in the likeness of the form alone.

[2] *Con. Gen.* loc. cit.

only in so far as the likeness is nearer and less remote.[1] Consequently there are various degrees of perfection. From the diversity of forms follows also a diversity of operations, and likewise a diversity of ends proper to the various creatures, although the ultimate end common to all remains the same.

Again, the diversity of forms produces a diversity of habitudes on the part of matter with respect to things. For some forms, more perfect than others, require no material foundation, whereas others cannot exist apart from it; and, of the latter, some require simple matter and some composite. And from the diversity of the habitudes of matter there results a diversity of agents and patients; for everything acts by reason of its form and is a patient by reason of its matter, and entities of which the forms are more perfect and less material act upon others which are more material and of which the forms are more imperfect.

From the diversity of forms, matters, and agents follows the diversity of properties and accidents. Substance is the cause of accident, as the perfect of the imperfect, and so from diverse substantial principles diverse accidents result. And by diverse agents, diverse impressions are made in patients, and produce a diversity of accidents. "As the first reason for divine providence, therefore, is *simpliciter*, the divine goodness; so the first reason with respect to the creatures is their multiplicity, with regard to the establishment and conservation of which all other things seem to be ordered."[2] It is, accordingly, manifest that providence disposes of all things for a reason, or in conformity with some conception, which yet presupposes the action of the divine will, since God, whose creativity is not constrained by necessity, is free to choose what degrees of perfection and what number of participants therein he will produce.[3]

Among the effects of every cause a certain order obtains, and, as cause is subject to cause, so is order to order, every subordinate order being embraced within the universal order

[1] The degrees of being, it will be remembered, are also degrees of simplicity; the higher the ontological rank of any entity, the simpler it is, and the more closely does it approximate the absolute simplicity of God.

[2] "Sicut ergo prima ratio divinae providentiae simpliciter est divina bonitas, ita prima ratio in creaturis est earum numerositas, ad cuius institutionem et conservationem omnia alia ordinari videntur" (*Con. Gen.* lib. III. cap. 97). [3] *Con. Gen.* loc. cit.

which depends upon the primal cause. It is clear that God cannot do anything beyond (*praeter*) the universal order, since this proceeds from his own knowledge, will, and goodness, without which God cannot act; but it is also clear that God can act beyond any order depending upon a subordinate cause, inasmuch as he is not subject to such an order, but it, on the contrary, is subject to him.[1]

It is possible, then, for God to operate beyond the order of nature by producing effects without their proximate causes. This contention St. Thomas endeavoured to make good by seven arguments.[2]

1. According to the order instituted by God, inferior entities are moved by their superior. Now an agent which acts by necessity of nature must produce an effect proportionate to itself. It is true that the effect sometimes possesses less power than its cause, and so the ultimate effect of a chain of such subordinate causes may not be at all proportionate to the original cause; none the less, the proximate effect must be proportionate. But an agent acting by its will can produce without any intermediate cause any effect which does not exceed its power. Accordingly, God can produce minor effects, such as would ordinarily be produced by inferior causes, without employing these causes.

2. The divine power stands to all active powers as the universal to the particular. But an active universal power can be determined with respect to the production of a particular effect in one of two ways—by an intermediate particular cause, or by the intellect which apprehends a determinate form and produces it in an effect. Now, the divine intellect is not only aware of its own essence, which is like a universal active power, and in addition of universal and primary causes, but also of all particular causes; hence, it can produce any effect which a particular agent can produce.

---

[1] *Sum. Theol.* I.a. q. 105: a. 6. c. In the *Contra Gentiles* (lib. III. cap. 98) a second distinction is drawn in the case of the universal order. This can be regarded, we are told, from two points of view. We can consider it with respect to the entities which are subject to it, or with respect to the reason or concept thereof, which depends upon the principle of the order. The Deity is able to act beyond the former but not beyond the latter, for the reasons given above.   [2] *Con. Gen.* lib. III. cap. 99.

3. Inasmuch as accidents follow from the substantial principle of anything, the power which can produce the substance of a thing can produce also whatever follows from that substance. But God has produced all things immediately through creation, consequently God is able to produce any effect independently of intermediate causes.

4. The order obtaining among the creatures flows forth from God according as it is conceived in the divine intellect. But the divine intellect is not determined to this order by necessity, for even we are able to conceive of another order. Accordingly, God is able to produce effects proper to inferior causes without the aid of those causes themselves.[1]

5. Although the order impressed upon the creatures represents in its own way the divine goodness, yet it does not represent it perfectly, for the goodness of the creature cannot equal the goodness of God. But that which is not perfectly represented in a particular instance must be capable of being also represented in some other mode. The representation of the divine goodness in creatures is the end for which they are produced, but the divine will is not determined with respect to the production of *this* order of causes and effects, so that it could not produce some effect immediately independently of all other causes.[2]

6. Every creature is more subject to God than is the body to the soul, for the soul is proportionate to the body of which it is the form. Yet the soul, when powerfully stirred by the imagination, is capable of affecting the body in the matter of health or sickness. Accordingly, the Deity, whose power exceeds that of the creature beyond all proportion, can produce effects without the causes which naturally do produce them.

7. According to the order of nature, the active powers of the elements fall under the active powers of the heavenly bodies, and the effect proper to the power of the elements is sometimes produced by the power of the heavenly body without any action of the element, as when the sun warms without the aid of fire. Much more, then, can the divine power, without

---

[1] This argument is really identical with the second, although no mention is made in the earlier proof of the freedom of the divine activity.

[2] This proof, like the second and the fourth, is based upon the doctrine that the divine will functions freely and not of necessity of nature.

availing itself of the activities of created causes, produce effects proper to them.

It is easy to see that Aquinas was here concerned to refute opponents who appealed to the teaching of Avicenna according to which God knows only universals and not particulars.[1] As it is in the power of God to produce effects without their proper causes, so it is within his power to restrain causes from producing their proper effects.[2]

God does not, however, act contrary to nature (*contra naturam*). For God is *actus purus*, whereas all other beings are infected with potentiality. Accordingly, God stands to them as the mover to the moved, and as the actual to the potential. And it is not contrary to nature *simpliciter* that that which is in potentiality, according to order of nature, with respect to some agent, should be acted upon by it, although it may be contrary to the particular form that is corrupted through this action. In whatever way, therefore, God acts upon the creatures it is not contrary to the order of nature, although it may seem to be contrary to the order proper to some nature. Moreover, God is the primal agent, and all things are God's instruments. But it is not contrary to nature that an instrument should be moved by the principal agent, but very much in accord therewith; accordingly, it is not contrary to nature that created things should be moved in any way whatever by God. Again, in the case of corporeal agents, the motions imparted to inferior by superior bodies do not seem violent or contrary to nature, although they may not be in accord with the natural motion which the inferior body enjoys through its own form. Thus, the motion of the tide is not a violent motion, since it is caused by a heavenly body, although the natural motion of water is toward the centre. By so much the more, then, is any effect produced by God in the creature neither violent nor contrary to nature. Furthermore, God is the first measure of the essence or nature of anything, since he is the primal being, and the cause of all existence. And since a thing is judged by its measure, that is natural to it which conforms to its measure. Whatever, therefore, is imprinted upon the creature by God is natural to it, and were something else imprinted by God it would be equally natural. Lastly, all creatures stand to God

[1] Cf. *De Pot.* q. 6: a. 1. c.   [2] Cf. *De Pot.* q. 6: a. 1. c.

as artifacts to an artificer; indeed the whole of nature is a divine artifact. Yet it is not contrary to the concept of an artifact that the artificer—even after he has given it its first form—should alter it. Neither, then, is it contrary to nature that God should operate on natural objects in a manner different from accustomed course of nature.[1]

St. Thomas's doctrine of providence follows so logically from his theories of the divine cognition and volition that it clearly stands or falls with them. Consequently, I shall attempt no further criticism of it.

Our author's conception of the nature of God as he is in himself has now been set forth in detail, and his view of the relations subsisting between the world and God has been stated with especial reference to its fundamental principles. It might appear that the next step should be a discussion of the doctrine of the Trinity. Into this field, however, I do not propose to enter, for the reason that it does not lie within the province of philosophy. Unlike his predecessors, Anselm and Abelard, Aquinas maintained that the truth of this doctrine cannot be proved by philosophy, and is made known to us only by revelation. It is permissible, indeed, to seek to understand it, and one may avail oneself of philosophical terminology in the effort to state as accurately and clearly as possible what it is that is revealed; one can even argue in the philosophic manner concerning the interpretation thereof, but that is all. "When one step of your argument has helped you to get into effective touch with a dogmatic truth and the next step that seems inevitably to follow, contradicts another dogmatic truth, you are neither to refrain from going so far, nor to insist on going further. The intelligence is to put out its tentacles and feel its way everywhere, but we must only follow it where 'it finds a yielding element.' "[2] It is evident that here we have to do, not with philosophy, but with theology, and to the theologians, therefore, we may leave it.

---

[1] *Con. Gen.* lib. III. cap. 100.
[2] P. Wicksteed, *Reactions between Dogma and Philosophy*, p. 268.

CHAPTER XVII

MYSTICAL KNOWLEDGE OF GOD

A LAST topic remains, however, to be discussed. What was St. Thomas's attitude toward mysticism? Did he believe that a direct, intuitive knowledge of God is possible? The question is clearly an important one, in view of the perennial influence of mysticism upon philosophy.[1] To rise upon the wings of philosophic speculation to an immediate apprehension of the Deity, and even to systematize all one's knowledge in the light of that vision, has been a recurrent hope throughout the centuries since the days of Plotinus. Inevitably, then, in the case of every theistic or idealistic philosopher, we have to inquire whether his philosophy culminates in or issues out of such an experience. With regard to St. Thomas, however, the query is especially apropos. To the older Augustinian Scholasticism, with its fundamentally Neoplatonic outlook, the experience of super-sensible reality was a matter of course. But for the Aristotelianism of Aquinas the situation was reversed. If all knowledge be derived, directly or indirectly, from the senses, the perception of a purely spiritual being is obviously beyond the capacity of the human intellect.

None the less Aquinas vehemently insisted that man's ultimate beatitude consists in the vision of the divine essence.[2] In fact, the third book of the *Contra Gentiles*, from the sixteenth to the sixty-third chapters, is devoted to a closely reasoned argument intended to prove that all things tend to resemble God who is

---

[1] The subject has been treated at length by Dr. Philip H. Wicksteed in his Hibbert Lectures. See *Reactions between Dogma and Philosophy*, lect. V and excursus II. Cf. the Rev. A. B. Sharpe's essay, *The Ascetical and Mystical Teaching of St. Thomas*, in the volume of essays entitled *St. Thomas Aquinas*, edited by the Rev. C. Lattey, S.J.; also Fr. Vincent McNabb's article, "The Mysticism of St. Thomas," in the volume published by Basil Blackwell under the title *Saint Thomas Aquinas*; Dom Cuthbert Butlers's *Western Mysticism*, p. 84 ff.; Jean Rimaud's *Thomisme et Méthode*, Appendix II.

[2] *Con. Gen.* lib. III. cc. 48, 50 and 51; *Sum. Theol.* I.a. q. 12: a. 1. c.; 4 *Dist.* 49. q. 2: a. 1; *Com. Theol.* cc. clxv, clxvi; *Quodlib.* VII. q. 1: a. 1; q. 10: a. 17.

their end, and that the ultimate felicity of man is not to be found in the exercise of the will, nor in bodily pleasures, nor in honours, nor in glory, nor in wealth, nor in power, nor in the senses, nor in moral or prudent actions, nor in the operations of art, nor in anything other than God; and that the knowledge of God which satisfies the soul is not of faith, nor of demonstration, but of vision.[1] Inasmuch as a discussion of the Thomist psychology does not come within the scope of this essay, I shall make no attempt to summarise Aquinas's arguments, but shall merely call attention to the depth and width of the gap which, in his view, separates the human being in this life from his ultimate end. "To take our account of man's goal from the Neoplatonist, therefore, and our account of his constitution from Aristotle, leaves us with a huge gap in our theory. But this gap is exactly what Aquinas wants. For there was something else that he could not do without, in addition to the Platonic and Aristotelian elements we have examined. He had been nurtured in the bosom of the Christian church, he had been spiritually fed by the Christian scriptures, his deepest devotions had been taught to cling around mysteries of which Aristotle knew nothing, and of which the Neoplatonists, if they seemed to know anything, knew it wrong. In a word, he wanted the Christian revelation and its promise; and they fitted exactly into the gap he had made for them by his Platonic mysticism united with his Aristotelian ejection of the mystic sense."[2]

The justice of these observations can scarcely be questioned. Mysticism is very apt to breed either indifference to or impatience with a sacramental system. The mystic is often recalcitrant to ecclesiastical control, and is prone, like the Calvinist, to find his ultimate authority in the *testimonium Spiritus Sancti internum*. Jeanne d'Arc is an outstanding example of such invincible individualism, but there were many others both before her and after her. The Beghards and the Brethren of the Free Spirit were a constant source of danger to the established order. The Roman church, in spite of the claims of her adherents, has been, instead of a loving nurse, rather a

---

[1] Cf. *Sum. Theol.* I.a.–II.ae. questions 1–5; 5 *Dist.* 49. q. 1; also Wicksteed, *Reactions between Dogma and Philosophy*, lect. II.

[2] Wicksteed, op. cit. p. 159.

domineering stepmother, of the mystics. She has encouraged them within limits, she has pointed to them with pride as the product of her training, but she has excommunicated and burned them when they have professed to obey God rather than her. In this matter Aquinas's attitude was typical of the institution to which he belonged. A profound mystic himself, he was first of all a devoted son of the church. Consequently, in the inability of man to attain to the vision of God in this life, he must have seen a precious witness to the truth of her dogmas and the necessity for her sacraments.

I have said that Aquinas was himself a mystic, a statement which appears inconsistent with what I have just written. But it is not so in reality. The attainment of the vision of God was by no means deemed essential to the enjoyment of mystical states of consciousness. According to St. Thomas the *lumen naturale* in the soul may be strengthened by the infusion of the *lumen gratuitum*; and *phantasmata* in the imagination, or objects perceptible to the senses, expressive of divine truth, are sometimes formed by grace.[1] Thus the soul may be elevated by divine assistance far above the highest reaches of its native powers, and may perceive manifestations of the Deity which, although incapable of adequately representing the divine essence that is their cause, yet far surpass the loftiest conceptions of the unaided human mind.

But this is not all. St. Thomas was confronted by the fact that in the Old Testament[2] it is explicitly stated that Moses saw God, and this testimony he could not set aside. Although he felt it possible to explain the visions vouchsafed to Jacob,[3] to Job,[4] and to Isaiah;[5] and even another granted to Moses himself,[6] as well as the famous vision of St. Benedict,[7] as imaginary or corporeal appearances communicated to the soul through the ministry of angels,[8] yet, in the present instance, the words of scripture were too definite for him to reject, and he admits that Moses actually perceived the divine essence

[1] *Sum. Theol.* I.a. q. 12: a. 13. c.; *Con. Gen.* lib. III. cap. 47.
[2] Num. xii. 8.
[3] See *Sum. Theol.* I.a. q. 12: a. 11. ad 1ᵐ; II.a.–II.ae. q. 180: a. 5 ad 1ᵐ;
[4] *Dist.* 49. q. 2: a. 7. ad 2ᵐ.   [4] 4 *Dist.* 49. q. 2: a. 7. ad 3ᵐ.
[5] 5 *Dist.* 49. q. 2: a. 7. ad 1ᵐ.   [6] 4 *Dist.* 49. q. 2: a. 7. ad 4ᵐ.
[7] *Quodlib.* i. q. 1: a. 1; *Sum. Theol.* II.a.–II.ae. q. 180: a. 5. ad 3ᵐ.
[8] 4 *Dist.* 49. a. 2: a. 7. ad 1ᵐ.

while yet a *viator*.[1] Furthermore, he is driven to make the same admission in the case of St. Paul, who was "caught up into the third heaven."[2] From the amount of space which he devoted to the discussion of this topic,[3] it would appear that Aquinas deemed the language of scripture in his case less unequivocal, but the balance is finally turned in the Apostle's favour by the consideration that it would be strange indeed had the vision granted to the legislator of the Jews not been vouchsafed also to the doctor of the Gentiles.[4]

In the interest of his theology, St. Thomas was therefore compelled to confess that, after all, it is possible that the vision of God should be granted to man while yet in this life. One is apt to fancy—unjustifiably perhaps—that he makes the concession grudgingly, in spite of the protests of his Aristotelian conscience; but make it he does, hence he is forced to provide a theoretical vindication of it. This he accomplishes by an appeal to the miraculous. Although the vision of God is far above human attainment, yet it is not beyond the power of God to raise man thereto.

"As there is a certain operation natural to any thing inasmuch as it is *this* thing, such as fire or stone, so to man there belongs a certain operation, inasmuch as he is man. Among natural things there are, moreover, two ways in which a thing may be altered with regard to its natural operation—in one way because of the defect of its proper power, due to some cause extrinsic or intrinsic, as when a monster is generated because of the defect of the formative power of the semen—in another way because of the operation of the divine power to whose command all nature is obedient, as happens in the case of miracles, as when a virgin conceives, or a blind person receives sight. And, similarly, man can be altered with respect to his natural and proper operation. For the proper operation of man is to know through the mediation of imagination and sense, an operation which inheres in intellectual substances

---

[1] *Sum. Theol.* I.a. q. 12: a. 11. ad 2ᵐ; II.a.–II.ae. q. 175: a. 3. ad 1ᵐ; 4 *Dist.* 49. q. 2: a. 7. ad 4ᵐ; *De Verit.* q. 10: a. 11. ad 1ᵐ; q. 13: a. 2. c.
[2] 2 Cor. xii. 2.
[3] *Sum. Theol.* II.a.–II.ae. q. 175: a. 3; *De Verit.* q. 13: a. 2.
[4] *Sum. Theol.* I.a. q. 12: a. 11. ad 2ᵐ; II.a.–II.ae. q. 175: a. 3. ad 1ᵐ; 4 *Dist.* 49. q. 2: a. 7. ad 5ᵐ; *De Verit.* q. 10: a. 11. ad 1ᵐ; q. 13: a. 2. c.

alone, and which, denied to all inferior substances, is not his inasmuch as he is man, but inasmuch as in him there is something divine, as is said in the tenth book of the *Ethics*, chapter seven, about the middle. The operation in truth which inheres only in sensible substances which are without intellect and reason, is not his inasmuch as he is man, but according to the nature which he has in common with the brutes. From his natural mode of cognition he can, then, be changed when, in abstraction from the senses, he beholds things beyond sense. This transmutation is therefore sometimes due to a defect of his proper power, as happens in the case of madmen, and others deprived of mentality; and such abstraction from the senses is not an elevation of man, but rather a depression. Sometimes in truth such abstraction is due to divine power, and then it is properly an elevation; because when the agent assimilates the patient to itself, the abstraction made by divine power, which is beyond man, is with respect to something higher than is natural to man. So, therefore, in the description of the *raptus*, according to which it is defined as a certain motion, its genus is indicated in that it is called *elevation*, that of the efficient cause in that it is said to be due to a *power of superior nature*, and the two terms of motion—'*a quo*' and '*in quem*'—in that the motion is said to be from that which is according to nature into that which is contrary to nature."[1]

[1] "Respondeo dicendum quod sicut cuiuslibet alterius rei est quaedam operatio naturalis rei, inquantum est haec res, ut ignis aut lapidis; ita etiam hominis est quaedam operatio inquantum est homo, quae est ei naturalis. In rebus autem naturalibus dupliciter contingit transmutari rem aliquam a sua operatione naturali. Uno modo ex defectu propriae virtutis, undecumque talis defectus contingat, sive ex causa extrinseca, sive ex intrinseca; sicut est cum ex defectu virtutis formativae in semine generatur fetus monstruosus. Alio modo ex operatione divinae virtutis, cui omnis natura ad nutum obedit; sicut fit in miraculis; ut cum virgo concepit, vel caecus illuminatur. Et similiter etiam homo a sua naturali et propria operatione dupliciter immutari potest. Est autem hominis operatio propria intelligere mediante imaginatione et sensu: operatio enim eius qua solis intellectualibus inhaeret, omnibus inferioribus praetermissis, non est eius inquantum est homo, sed inquantum aliquid in eo divinum existit, ut dicitur X *Ethic.*, capit. vii. a med.; operatio vero qua solis sensibilibus inhaeret praeter intellectum et rationem, non est eius inquantum est homo, sed secundum naturam quam cum brutis habet communem.

In regard to the last phrase Aquinas adds the following explanation. The same thing may be *contra naturam* and *secundum naturam* according to diverse states, for the nature of a thing is not the same when it is *in fieri* as when it is *in perfecto esse*. To know God is natural in some way to the human intelligence in any state, but *in statu vitae* it is natural that it should know God through *creaturas sensibiles*. That it should arrive at the knowledge of God in himself, *in patria*, is also natural. But that *in statu vitae* it should know God *secundum statum patriae* is *contra naturam*, as it is *contra naturam* that a newborn child should have a beard.[1] To the objection that God, the author of nature, never acts in a manner contrary to nature, he replies that the *raptus* is said to be *contra naturam* because it is "contrary to the accustomed course of nature."[2]

To ordinary intellectual cognition three media are requisite,[3] first, the light of the *intellectus agens* which is the medium under which we perceive (the *medium sub quo*); secondly, the intelligible species which determines the *intellectus possibilis*, and so is the medium by which we perceive (the *medium quo*); and, thirdly, the medium in which we perceive (the *medium in quo*), by which is meant the relationship of one object to another which enables us to know the one indirectly through the other as in a mirror. It is clear that *in patria* the third medium will have no place, since God will be known directly in himself. Nor can

Tunc igitur a naturali modo suae cognitionis transmutatur, quando a sensibus abstractus aliqua praeter sensum inspicit. Haec igitur transmutatio quandoque fit ex defectu propriae virtutis, sicut accidit in phreneticis, et aliis mente captis; et haec quidem abstractio a sensibus non est elevatio hominis, sed potius depressio. Aliquando vere talis abstractio fit virtute divina: et tunc proprie elevatio quaedam est: quia cum agens assimilet sibi patiens, abstractio quae fit virtute divina, quae est supra hominem, est in aliquid altius quam sit naturale homini. Sic ergo in descriptione raptus, qua definitur ut quidam motus, tangitur eius genus in hoc quod dicitur 'elevatio,' causa efficiens in hoc quod dicitur 'vi superioris naturae'; et duo termini motus 'a quo,' et 'in quem,' cum dicitur 'ab eo quod est secundum naturam in id quod est contra naturam'" (*De Verit.* q. 13: a. 1. c.; cf. 4 *Dist.* 49. q. 2 : a. 7. sol.; *Sum. Theol.* I.a. q. 12 : a. 11; II.a.–II.ae. q. 180: a. 5; *Con. Gen.* lib. III. cap. 47; *De Verit.* q. 10: a. 11).

[1] *De Verit.* q. 12: a. 1. ad 1[m].

[2] "Contra solitum cursum naturae" (*De Verit.* q. 13: a. 1. ad 3[m]).

[3] See *Quodlib.* vii. q. 1: a. 1. c.; 4 *Dist.* 49. q. 2: a. 1. ad 15[m]; cf. Wicksteed, op. cit. pp. 622–626. In the *De Veritate* (q. 18: a. 1. c.) the medium in quo is termed the *medium a quo*.

the second medium be present, for no intelligible species is adequate to represent the divine essence.[1] Nor yet can the *intellectus agens*, which is a faculty of the human mind, of itself enable us to see God. Consequently, the soul will require the aid of the light of glory (the *lumen gloriae*), which will raise the mind above itself until it perceives its divine object. And that which it perceives is no intelligible species but the divine essence itself with which it is directly united, "so that the soul is wholly carried into God."[2] It is clear that the thought of St. Thomas at this point comes very close to pantheism. The union, however, stops short of complete absorption.[3]

In the case of the soul of the *viator* not yet *in patria*, who, nevertheless, is caught up in rapture, the situation is much the same. As Wicksteed has pointed out, St. Thomas was not consistent in his view with regard to the illumination of the soul of the *viator* by the *lumen gloriae*. In the *De Veritate*[4] he taught that the same results were miraculously attained without its aid. In his commentary on *Second Corinthians*,[5] and in the *Summa Theologica*,[6] as well as in the thirteenth question of the *De Veritate*,[7] he took the opposite position.

The soul *in raptu* is for the time being divorced from the senses, so that it can be said to be sundered from this mortal

---

[1] "The reason why there can be no true image of God is that such an image would be a self-contradiction; but God cannot contradict himself. For God essentially exists: His 'essence' and 'existence' are one. There is nothing else of which this is true: we can make a true (though not necessarily complete) mental image of anything else the nature of which we know, and the picture will be a real likeness of the thing, though not the thing itself. But any image of God must be unlike Him because it must leave out the essential element of His being, viz. His actual existence—as if instead of a picture of a man we were shown a list of his abstract qualities" (A. B. Sharpe's *The Ascetical and Mystical Teaching of St. Thomas*, in *St. Thomas Aquinas*, pp. 218–219).

[2] "Scilicet quod nihil intelligat aliud ex phastasmalibus sed totaliter feratur in Deum" (*Sum. Theol.* II.a.–II.ae. q. 175: a. 4. c.).

[3] In the following century Ruysbroeck and Tauler were at great pains to emphasize this feature of the orthodox faith.

[4] q. 10: a. 11. c. Possibly the same view is implied in 5 *Dist.* 49. q. 2: a. 7. sol.

[5] Cap. xii. lect. i.

[6] II.a.–II.ae. q. 175: a. 3. ad 2ᵐ. [7] a. 2. c.

life.[1] One can be in this life, not only actually, but also potentially, in which state the soul, being still united to the body as
its form, avails itself neither of the senses nor of the imagination,
and this is true of the enraptured spirit.[2]

Did St. Thomas believe that the *visio Dei* was in fact actually
granted to many devout souls, or did he feel himself compelled
to work out his theory merely to make room in his philosophy
for the reported experiences of Moses and St. Paul? It is impossible to answer this question with certitude. That the *raptus*
is miraculous in its nature does not imply that it is uncommon.
The mass also is miraculous. Yet even the Augustinian Scholastics held that the vision of God was vouchsafed to very few.
In regard to Aquinas's own teaching opinions differ. It has
been maintained that he meant to assert that the *raptus* had
been experienced by no others beside Moses and Paul. Dom
Cuthbert Butler has, however, cogently argued that[3] the
language of the *De Veritate*, and the use of the word *some*
(*aliqui*) in the *Summa Theologica*[4] make it impossible to accept
this view. Mr. A. B. Sharpe would apparently go farther than
this, and even suggests that St. Thomas himself had been so
favoured.[5] My own impression is that he meant to concede the
raptus to very few. In the *De Veritate* and the *Commentary on the
Sentences* his language seems open to a somewhat wider interpretation than in the *Contra Gentiles* or in question twelve in the
first part of the *Summa Theologica*, where the very possibility of
its occurrence is admitted with apparent reluctance. In his
discussion of the *raptus* and of the contemplative life, in the
second part of the last work, his attitude impresses me as
more liberal. Whether this is due to any inconsistency in his
thought, or is to be ascribed to the character of the topics
which he was discussing, who can say?

Two points, however, are worthy of emphasis. In the first
place, St. Thomas makes, as we have seen, no appeal to
religious experience as an evidence of the existence of God.
Even in the sixth chapter of the *Contra Gentiles*, when he argues

[1] *Con. Gen.* lib. III. cap. 47; *Sum. Theol.* II.a.–II.ae. q. 175: a. 4. c.;
Quodlib. I. q. 1: a. 1. c.; *Comment. on Second Corinthians*, loc. cit.
[2] *Sum. Theol.* II.a.–II.ae. q. 180: a. 5. c.
[3] *Western Mysticism*, pp. 84–85.
[4] I.a. q. 12: a. 11. ad 2ᵐ.   [5] *St. Thomas Aquinas*, pp. 225–226.

on behalf of the trustworthiness of the Christian revelation, it is to the miracles of Christ and to the virtues and constancy of the early martyrs that he looks for proof of its divine origin. The nearest he comes to it is his insistence that man's natural desire for beatitude cannot be in vain.[1] In the second place, the occurrence of the *visio Dei* provides him with no additional data with which to enlarge or correct his conception of God. The doctrine of the *raptus* is as remote from the rest of his system as the occurrence of the *raptus* is from the life of the average Christian.

It would be unjust to end this essay without a reference to the extraordinary experience which befell St. Thomas when celebrating mass in Naples two years before his death, an experience which caused him to discontinue the writing of his yet unfinished *Summa Theologica*. All that he had written seemed small, he is reported to have said, in comparison with that which he had seen. Small, yet not contradictory, may we surmise? It is scarcely conceivable that the Angelic Doctor would have allowed the last systematic formulation of his views to remain unaltered had he believed that it was erroneous in any important particular. Doubtless, like many of his fellow mystics, he had experienced that which he found it difficult, if not impossible, to set forth in words. And it is permissible to hope that he did believe himself to have been granted the vision which satisfies the souls of those *in patria*.

---

[1] *Inane, frustra.* See *Con. Gen.* lib. III. cap. 48.

BIBLIOGRAPHY

THE main contributions to this book have been made by the following works:

Dieu, son existence et sa nature, by R. Garrigou-Lagrange, O.P.

Principles of Natural Theology, by G. H. Joyce, S.J.

The Philosophy of St. Thomas, by E. Gilson.

S. Thomas d'Aquin, by A. D. Sertillanges.

Institutiones Metaphysicae Generalis, by Pedro Descoqs, S.J.

Reactions between Dogma and Philosophy, by P. H. Wicksteed.

David de Dinant, by G. Théry, O.P.

La Notion de temps, by D. Nys.

Essai sur les rapports entre la pensée grecque et la pensée chrétienne, by Régis Jolivet, D-és-L.

Les grandes thèses de la philosophie thomiste, by A. D. Sertillanges.

Le "De Ente et Essentia" de S. Thomas D'Aquin, by M.-D. Rowland-Gosselin, O.P.

INDEX

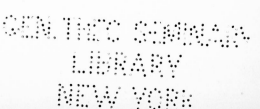

GEORGE ALLEN & UNWIN LTD
LONDON: 40 MUSEUM STREET, W.C.1
CAPE TOWN: 73 ST. GEORGE'S STREET
SYDNEY, N.S.W.: WYNYARD SQUARE
AUCKLAND, N.Z.: 41 ALBERT STREET
TORONTO: 91 WELLINGTON STREET, WEST

Kant's Conception of God

Demy 8vo. by F. E. ENGLAND, Ph.D. 10s. 6d.

"Dr. England's contribution is as timely as it is competent and lucid.
. . . Not only therefore as a valuable discussion of his problem on its
merits, but equally as an unusually clear and able analysis of Kant's
fundamental standpoint, his book deserves careful consideration from
all to whom philosophical theology appeals."—*Church Quarterly Review*

A Study in the Philosophy of Malebranche

Demy 8vo. by R. W. CHURCH, D.Phil. 10s. 6d.

"Masterly. . . . The author has done valuable and original work in
elucidating and criticizing the great Oratorian's theories."—*Baptist
Times*

Scepticism and Construction

Bradley's Sceptical Principle as the Basis of Constructive Philosophy
by CHARLES A. CAMPBELL

Demy 8vo. Lecturer in Moral Philosophy, University of Glasgow 12s. 6d.

The purpose of the book is twofold. In the first place it seeks to defend
and develop the Sceptical side of the philosophy of Bradley, urging that
Bradley's epistemological conclusions are decisively confirmed by
evidence from many aspects of experience other than the cognitive. In
the second place it endeavours, on the basis of metaphysical scepticism,
to establish the "final phenomenal truth"—the highest truth accessible
to man—of certain vital propositions in the domain of human values.

"This is an able and interesting book, especially to students of Ethics."
—*London Quarterly Review*

The Mystic Will

by HOWARD H. BRINTON, Ph.D.

Introduction by Rufus M. Jones, D.Litt.

La. Cr. 8vo. 8s. 6d.

This illuminating study of the philosophy of Protestant mysticism is
based upon the work of Jacob Boehme, the saintly shoemaker of Görlitz
who, though entirely unfavoured by circumstance, yet made a permanent contribution to the intellectual life and the spiritual progress of
the world. At the same time it presents a survey of the nature and
historical significance of positive ethical types of mysticism. Here at
last is a book which gives a lucid presentation of Boehme's teachings
and places him in his true historical perspective.

The Revelation of Deity

by J. E. TURNER, M.A., Ph.D.

Author of "Personality and Reality," "The Nature of Deity," etc.
(Reader in Philosophy in the University of Liverpool)

Demy 8vo. 8s. 6d.

This volume pursues the course of argument already developed in
Personality and Reality and *The Nature of Deity*. The various ways
whereby the Divine Nature can manifest itself so as to be comprehended
by the human mind are discussed, and it is shown that these form an
ascending series marked by fuller degrees of adequacy, culminating
in the Incarnation. In spite of its connection with the author's earlier
books, this work is new and independent.

"Dr. Turner has won the reputation of being one of the ablest apologists
for theism."—*Saturday Review*

The Life of Jesus
by MAURICE GOGUEL

Medium 8vo.   TRANSLATED BY OLIVE WYON   25s.

This important historical book by the Director of Studies in Primitive Christianity and the New Testament at the *École des Hautes Études* is a scholarly, reverent and critical work, based upon a long, detailed and profound study of the sources of the Gospel story, both Christian and non-Christian. Written in the full light of the most recent criticism, this new *Vie de Jésus* is an illuminating and timely work, admirably conceived and executed.

Jewish Views of Jesus
Cr. 8vo.   by THOMAS WALKER, D.D.   4s. 6d.

The author tries to serve both Jews and Christians by presenting to them genuinely representative Jewish views of Jesus. The Orthodox and Liberal Jews are each allowed two spokesmen, from which may be gathered the agreements and disagreements in their outlook. The reader is also introduced to two full-sized literary portraits of Jesus, after which Dr. Walker supplies his own comments on what has gone before.

The Hope of a World to Come
underlying Judaism and Christianity
by EDWYN BEVAN
Arthur Davis Memorial Lecture, 1930

Fcap. 8vo.   *Cloth 2s., Paper 1s.*

"This fine lecture, with its wide outlook upon history, its brave faith and its cheerful yet solemn hope, is at once an intellectual treat and a spiritual stimulus."—*Expository Times*
"This is a little book of rare charm and distinction, the work of a true scholar, and deeply suggestive on every page."—*Church Times*

The Holy and the Living God
Demy 8vo.   by M. D. R. WILLINK   10s.

Some years ago Professor Otto's book, *The Idea of the Holy*, brought into prominence the awful and daunting side of our apprehension of deity. The present writer has traced the idea in the Bible and Christian history, and shows that it plays an essential part in the working of spiritual forces, that it throws light on obscure passages of the Old Testament, and that the present weakness of our religious life may be partly due to our forgetfulness of this aspect of religious consciousness.

The Social Teaching of the Christian Churches
by ERNST TROELTSCH
TRANSLATED BY OLIVE WYON

Sm. Royal 8vo.   *Two Vols.   42s. the set*

Dean Inge, in the *Church of England Newspaper*, writes: "It is the standard work on the subject, immensely learned, judicially impartial, and full of interest to all who are occupied with modern social problems."